Praise for
An Asian Introduction to the New Testament

"We all read from a location. The contributors to this important volume demonstrate the significance of Asian approaches to interpreting the New Testament, and not only for Asian Christians. Of special consequence are the affinities between Asian values, life experiences, and texts and New Testament realities: honor and shame, family and community, persecution and perseverance, colonialism and resistance, poverty and pain. I highly recommend this unique, eye-opening, and helpful guide to the New Testament."

—Michael J. Gorman, Raymond E. Brown Professor of Biblical Studies and Theology, St. Mary's Seminary and University, Baltimore, Maryland, USA

"*An Asian Introduction to the New Testament* breaks new ground and creates a much-needed and long-awaited space for Asian voices in the study of the New Testament. It is an essential resource for those of us teaching New Testament texts, as it locates the growth of Christianity in both Jewish and Asian contexts and brings forth a unique perspective that is critical to the study of the New Testament."

—Sharon Jacob, assistant professor of New Testament, Pacific School of Religion, Berkeley, California, USA

"This ambitious volume featuring diverse Asian and Asian American voices breaks new ground and makes a significant contribution to the field of biblical studies. By placing New Testament texts and figures in conversation with disparate Asian religious traditions, contributors offer fresh and powerful insights that have deep implications for Asian realities. The volume will stimulate lively conversations about the New Testament and prove to be a valuable resource for students and scholars alike within and outside Asia."

—Raj Nadella, Samuel A. Cartledge Associate Professor of New Testament, Columbia Theological Seminary, Georgia, USA

"What this collection of essays has shown is that Asian interpreters are constantly challenged by several interpretative contexts and scriptural texts. The hermeneutical folly is to confine to one context and identify with one text. This compendium is a smart and substantial piece of scholarship and adds a significant new perspective to biblical hermeneutics, which mainstream biblical studies have thus far been reluctant to appreciate both as a new way of approaching the texts and as something of exceptional vision and vigor."

—R. S. Sugirtharajah, emeritus professor,
University of Birmingham, United Kingdom

"*An Asian Introduction to the New Testament* is an excellent and insightful contribution to the study of the Bible. The contributors are all qualified biblical scholars, interested in and attentive to the first-century context of each text. But they are also Asians who bring to the text their rich experiences that can shed fresh light on biblical interpretation. I hope this introduction will stimulate fresh conversations about non-Western contributions to New Testament studies."

—Nijay K. Gupta, professor of New Testament,
Northern Seminary, Lisle, Illinois, USA

AN Asian Introduction TO THE New Testament

AN

Asian Introduction

TO THE

New Testament

Editor

Johnson Thomaskutty

Consulting Editors

Brian C. Wintle,

Tatsiong Benny Liew,

K. K. Yeo

FORTRESS PRESS

Minneapolis

AN ASIAN INTRODUCTION TO THE NEW TESTAMENT

Cover image: iStock 2021; abstract textured colorful red orange background by wepix
Cover design: Alisha Lofgren

Print ISBN: 978-1-5064-6269-1
eBook ISBN: 978-1-5064-6270-7

Contents

Contributors

Autero, Esa, DTh, University of Helsinki, Finland, is dean of faculty and professor of biblical studies at South Florida Bible College and Theological Seminary, USA. He is the author of numerous peer-reviewed articles and books including *Reading the Bible across Contexts: Luke's Gospel, Socio-economic Marginality, and Latin American Biblical Hermeneutics* (Brill, 2016). His forthcoming writings include *Epistle of James: A Pentecostal-Charismatic Commentary* (PCNT Series; Wipf & Stock).

Benny Liew, Tatsiong, PhD, Vanderbilt University, USA, is class of 1956 professor in NT studies at the College of the Holy Cross, USA. He is the author of *Politics of Parousia* (Brill, 1999) and *What Is Asian American Biblical Hermeneutics?* (University of Hawaii Press, 2008). In addition, he is the editor of the *Semeia* volume on "The Bible in Asian America" (with Gale Yee; SBL, 2002), *Postcolonial Interventions* (Sheffield Phoenix, 2009), and others. Benny Liew is also the series editor of *T&T Clark's Study Guides to the NT* (Bloomsbury).

Cailing, Rolex M., PhD, Torch Trinity Graduate University, South Korea, teaches NT at Asia Graduate School of Theology, Quezon City, Philippines. He is author of several essays including "Vulnerability and a Vision of Hope: Engaging Creation's Groaning in Romans 8 and Disasters in the Philippines" (in *Tackling Trauma*, Langham, 2018) and "The Use of Isaiah in Qumran" (in *Scripture and Service*, BSOP, 2019). His current projects include *The Use of Isaiah in 1 Corinthians* (Langham Monograph Series).

Ceu Hnin, Thawng, PhD (NT) candidate, is a faculty of NT at Hindustan Bible Institute and College, Chennai, India. He has published several articles related to the NT. Currently, he is doing his research under the title "A Cognitive Grammatical Analysis of Greek Improper Prepositions and Their Theological Significance in the Selected Passages of the NT" under the supervision of Dr. Johnson Thomaskutty.

Chacko, Biju, DTh, Senate of Serampore University, teaches NT at New Theological College, Dehradun, India. He is the managing editor of *Doon Theological Journal* and coordinator of the publication department of New Theological College (NTC). He authored several academic articles related to the NT.

Cho, Jae Hyung, PhD, Claremont Graduate University, USA, is a lecturer at Korea Christian University, South Korea. He is author of *Early Christianity and Gnosticism* (Dongyeon, 2020, in Korean), *Greco-Roman Religion and the NT: The History of Ideas on Christian Origins* (Bookk, 2018, in Korean), and nineteen Korea Citation Index articles. His forthcoming books include *This Is My Flesh: John's Eucharist and the Dionysus Cult* and *The Power of Innocent Fiction: The Journey of the Soul in the NT and the Nag Hammadi Library*.

Eng, Daniel K., PhD, University of Cambridge, UK, was an affiliated lecturer at the University of Cambridge and adjunct professor at Moody Theological Seminary. He is author of *James, an Honor-Shame Paraphrase* (Timé, 2018). Currently, he serves as assistant professor of New Testament at Western Seminary, Portland, USA. He is also the author of the commentary on James in the forthcoming *New Testament in Colour* (IVP).

George, Roji Thomas, DTh, Senate of Serampore University, is professor of NT at South Asia Institute of Advanced Christian Studies, Bangalore, India. In addition to writing more than forty academic articles, he is author of *Paul's Identity in Galatians: A Postcolonial Appraisal* (CWI, 2016), *Philippians: A Pastoral and Contextual Commentary* (Asia Bible Commentary Series; Langham Global Library, 2019), and *Called into the Mission of God: A Missional Reading of Paul's Thessalonian Correspondence* (Fortress, 2020). His forthcoming writings include *An Indian Commentary on the Gospel of Matthew* (Primalogue) and *A Commentary on the Letter to Galatians* (Baker Academic). He serves as a series editor of India Commentary of the New Testament (ICNT) and is the theological editor (NT) of the *South Asia Study Bible* (SASB).

Jebaraj, Edwin, DTh, Senate of Serampore University, is associate professor and head of the department of NT at Gurukul Lutheran Theological College and Research Institute, Chennai, India. He has written the article "Justice and Renewal of Mission." Currently, he is working on a book, *Justice and Judgment in the Book of Revelation: An Indian Reading*, and an article, "Aging and Intergenerational Solidarity in the NT: Towards Age-Friendly Communities" (Gurukul).

Jones, J. Stanly, DTh, Senate of Serampore University, is assistant professor of NT at Union Biblical Seminary, Pune, India. He is the author of academic articles related to the NT in the Indian theological journals and monographs entitled *The Jesus Movement and Its Resistance to Oppressive Institutions: A Study of Healing Narratives in Mark's Gospel* (ISPCK, 2020) and *A Study of Pauline Interpretation of Jesus's Ethical Sayings in "Q" and Its Significance in Today's Indian Context* (ISPCK, 2007).

Kim, Yung Suk, PhD, Vanderbilt University, USA, is professor of NT and early Christianity at Virginia Union University, Richmond, USA. He is author of more than a dozen books, including *Christ's Body in Corinth: The Politics of a Metaphor* (Fortress, 2008) and *Toward Decentering the NT* (2018, coauthored with Mitzi J. Smith). He also edited *1–2 Corinthians: Texts at Contexts Series* (Fortress, 2013). His forthcoming book is *How to Read Paul: A Brief Introduction to His Theology, Writings, and World* (Fortress, 2021).

Koshy, Asish Thomas, DTh, Senate of Serampore University, is professor of NT at SAIACS, Bengaluru, India. He is the author of the book *Identity, Mission and Community: A Study of the Johannine Resurrection Narrative* (CWI, 2018). His forthcoming publications include *India Commentary on the Epistles of John* (Fortress) and *An Asian Commentary on the First Epistle of John* (Langham).

Lalitha, Jayachitra, DTh, Senate of Serampore University, is a professor of NT and currently the director of *Ekklesia* Centre for Biblical Research and Pastoral Accompaniment, Bengaluru, India. She is author of *Re-reading Household Relationships Christologically: Ephesians, Empire and Egalitarianism* (CWI, 2017) and coeditor of *Teaching All Nations: Interrogating Matthean Great Commission* (Fortress, 2014) and *Evangelical Postcolonial Conversations: Global Awakenings in Theology and Praxis* (IVP, 2014).

Lawrence, Arren Bennet, PhD, Asia Graduate School of Theology, Philippines, is assistant regional secretary of Asia Theological Association. He is author of *Legalistic Nomism: A Socio-rhetorical Reading of Paul's Letter to the Galatians* (ISPCK, 2015), *Comparative Characterization in the Sermon on the Mount: Characterization of the Ideal Disciple* (Wipf & Stock, 2017), and *Approaches to the NT* (SAIACS, 2018). His forthcoming writings include *One Gospel, Many Cultures* and *An Asian Commentary on the Epistles of Thessalonians* (Langham).

Lim, Kar Yong, PhD, University of Wales Lampeter, is dean of Kuala Lumpur Centre and lecturer in NT studies at Seminari Theoloji Malaysia. He is author of *The Sufferings of Christ Are Abundant in Us: A Narrative Dynamics Investigation of Paul's Sufferings in 2 Corinthians* (T&T Clark, 2009), *Jesus the Storyteller: Hearing the Parables Afresh Today* (Armour, 2015), *Metaphors and Social Identity Formation in Paul's Letters to the Corinthians* (Pickwick, 2017), and *Following Jesus: An Illustrated Guide to the Places of the Holy Land According to the Gospel of Mark* (Armour, 2019).

Philip, Finny, PhD, University of Durham, UK, is principal of Filadelfia Bible College, Udaipur, India. He authored the book *The Origins of Pauline Pneumatology* and served as a theological editor for the *South Asia Bible Commentary: A One-Volume Commentary on the Whole Bible* and as the publisher for the forthcoming *South Asia Study Bible* project. His other academic writings include "1 Corinthians" and "Galatians" in *South Asia Bible Commentary*, among others.

Seng Ja, Layang, DTh, Lutheran Theological Seminary, Hong Kong, is associate professor of NT and director of research and documentation at Kachin Theological College and Seminary, Myanmar. She is author of *Matthew's Intention in Portraying the Pharisees* (SMBS, Yangon, 2019), *Civil War, Refugees, Disability and Theology* (Edan-WCC, 2019), and *Compassion as an Imperative Tackle in Building Harmonious Empire for Myanmar Ethnicity* (MIT, 2019).

Shin, Sookgoo, PhD, University of Cambridge, USA, is assistant professor of NT at Torch Trinity Graduate University, South Korea. He is author of *Ethics in the Gospel of John: Discipleship as Moral Progress* (Brill, 2019), and his forthcoming work will be *How to Read the Gospel of John* (Scripture Union).

Soo Hoo, Gilbert, PhD, Catholic University of America, USA, is adjunct professor of NT at Singapore Bible College, Singapore. He is author of *1, 2, 3 John: A Pastoral and Contextual Commentary* (Langham, 2016). Currently, he is working on a book tentatively entitled *Voices from the Grassroots: A Sociological and Biblical Study of the Singaporean Marketplace.*

Spurgeon, Andrew B., PhD, Dallas Theological Seminary, USA, is professor of NT at Singapore Bible College and adjunct professor of world missions and intercultural studies at Dallas Theological Seminary. He is the general editor for the Asia

Biblical Commentary Series and the publications secretary for the Asia Theological Association. His recent publication is *Romans: A Pastoral and Contextual Commentary* (Langham, 2020).

Tar Gay, Naw Eh, PhD, University of Birmingham, UK, is professor of NT at Myanmar Institute of Theology, Myanmar. She is vice president of MIT and director of Gender Studies Centre, MIT. She is author of *A Feminist Commentary on the Letter to Romans* (Karen Baptist Convention, 2014) and *Research Methodology for Theological Students* (MIT, 2019; in Burmese).

Thomaskutty, Johnson, PhD, Radboud University Nijmegen, Holland, is professor of NT at the United Theological College, Bengaluru, India. He is author of more than fifty peer-reviewed academic articles related to the NT and the monographs entitled *The Gospel of John: A Universalistic Reading* (CWI, 2020), *Saint Thomas the Apostle: New Testament, Apocrypha, and Historical Traditions* (Bloomsbury T&T Clark, 2018), and *Dialogue in the Book of Signs: A Polyvalent Analysis of John 1:19–12:50* (Brill, 2015). His forthcoming writings include *Asia Commentary on the Gospel of John* (Langham) and *Reading the New Testament in India* (OUP).

Tupamahu, Ekaputra, PhD, Vanderbilt University, is assistant professor of NT at Portland Seminary in Oregon, USA. His other writings have appeared in, among others, *Journal for the Study of the NT*, *Pneuma: Journal of the Society for Pentecostal Studies*, *Indonesian Journal of Theology*, *Asian Journal of Pentecostal Studies*, *Encyclopaedia of Christianity in the Global South*, *Global Renewal Christianity*, and *T&T Clark Handbook to Asian American Biblical Hermeneutics*. His current book project on the politics of language in the early Christian movement is under contract with Oxford University Press.

Wintle, Brian C., PhD, University of Manchester, UK, formerly served in the Biblical Studies department of the Union Biblical Seminary, Yavatmal and Pune, India (1978–95) and as principal (1987–95). He subsequently served in the Asia Theological Association, first as the Asia dean, Asia Graduate School of Theology (1995–2000), and then as the regional secretary, India (2000–2014). He was the general editor of the one-volume *South Asia Bible Commentary* (Open Door, 2015).

Yang, Xiaoli, PhD, University of Divinity, is a research scholar of Charles Sturt University, Australia. She is an ordained minister, accredited spiritual director, and bilingual poet. She is author of *A Dialogue between Haizi's Poetry and the Gospel of Luke* (Brill, 2018) and has published book chapters, peer-reviewed articles, encyclopedia entries, and poetry widely for both academic and general readers. Her forthcoming books include *Towards a Chinese Theology of Displacement* and *Words of Love—Reading the Letters of John.*

Yeo, K. K., PhD, Northwestern University, Evanston, is Harry R. Kendall professor of NT at Garrett-Evangelical Theological Seminary and an affiliate professor in the Department of Asian Languages and Cultures, Northwestern University. He is a Lilly Scholar (1999) and Henry Luce III Scholar (2003) and has authored and edited more than forty books on critical engagement between Bible and cultures, including authoring *Musing with Confucius and Paul* (Cascades, 2008) and *Zhuangzi and James* (in Chinese, 2012), coediting (with Gene Green and Steve Pardue) the Majority World Theology Series (Eerdmans & Langham, 2014–19), and editing *The Oxford Handbook of the Bible in China* (Oxford: Oxford University Press, 2021).

Foreword

R. S. Sugirtharajah

Three decades ago when I approached a publisher with a view to producing a reader on Asian interpretations of the Bible, the response I received was, "Do you have enough material for a volume?" Though Asia has produced remarkable theologians, biblical scholars were unheard of and a rare species at that time. Johnson Thomaskutty's volume is a strikingly visible testimony to how things have moved on over the years. He has assembled an array of impressive essays that could be for most readers an entry into an enlarging and enriching world of Asian biblical interpretation—a remarkable encounter between the Bible and its Asian readers.

There is a long and hidden history of Asia's involvement with the Bible that has hardly received any serious attention in Western biblical studies. Asia has had a lengthy, productive, and compelling presence in the biblical world. Indian moral tales, proverbs, vocabularies, perfume products, and even gods have found their way into both the canonical books and the Scriptures that were left out. Contrary to popular perception, the Bible reached Asia before the advent of modern colonialism. It came with West Asian missionaries of the Churches of the East to India. The Bible that was introduced was not the Western canon but the Eastern canon in the form of the Peshitta. One of the earlier attempts at Asian biblical interpretation was in the seventh century when the same missionaries of the Church of the East tried to relate Matthew's Gospel to the Mahayana concepts in China. Since then, there have been other endeavors that have not been taken seriously. Mainstream biblical scholarship tends to dismiss them as part of mission history or to not accord them importance because some of these pioneering efforts were done before biblical studies moved to academics and became professionalized and a specialist enterprise.

There is a tendency among mainstream scholars to disregard anything east of Antioch as of no value and to treat the post-Nicene experience of the West as the universally accepted norm. Tied to this is the outdated understanding of what orthodoxy is and what heresy is. The victims of this narrow division are the apocryphal gospels that were set aside by ecclesiastical authorities due to political and theological reasons. There are plenty of hermeneutical insights to harvest from these left-out Scriptures. One such text is the Apocryphal Acts of Thomas, which had an intriguing relationship with the community of Thomas Christians of India. Admirable though this collection is, wistfully, it still works within the accepted canon.

Sadly, Asian appropriation of the Bible is peripheralized not only by the Western mainstream but also within the works of Asian theology and Christianity. Two conspicuous cases are the following: Felix Wilfred, ed., *The Oxford Handbook of Asian Christianity* (2014) and Sebastian C. H. Kim, ed., *Christian Theology in Asia* (2008)—both commit the unpardonable blunder of omitting the Bible's role in Asian thinking. This volume aptly rectifies this indefensible oversight and error.

It may be obvious to say that biblical scholarship has been hitherto historically and ideologically the preserve of the West. However, what Ashis Nandy said in a different context is equally true of biblical studies: "The West is everywhere." This is patently evident in the chapters here when historical questions of various NT books are discussed. In these discussions, the essayists draw predominately from the works of Western scholars.

For the most part, Asian scholars were uninterested in seeking the historical origins and reliability of the biblical texts, raising critical questions, and placing them in their social and cultural framework. Historical criticism emerged as a solution to Western problems—problems that Asians hardly faced. Since the introduction of historical criticism, just as the puranic Sita underwent *agni pariksha* (an ordeal of fire) to prove her chastity, non-Western biblical scholars are expected to pass the historical criticism test before they are accepted. There are four *W*s of traditional historical criticism: who wrote it, when it was composed, where it was written, and to whom it was addressed. To this, Asians have added another *W*—what next. Instead of confining biblical texts to the past and consigning them as texts of their time, these scholars have seen the contemporary relevance of them—a feature hardly seen in the mainstream introductory volumes on biblical books. Whereas mainstream Western biblical criticism is concerned with historical inquiry, this collection has shown that one could combine historical scrutiny with larger theological and contextual questions.

This volume not only stands in the long process of decolonization where minority voices exercise their agency but also shows how the minority reads the canonical text that was imposed upon them. These essays are an ample proof of the limitations of reading the biblical texts from the confines of a white, male, Eurocentric perspective.

Although these scholars approach the text from different life contexts and concerns which are often poles apart, the one concern apparent in their articulation is that the Bible cannot be read in a vacuum. Reading the Bible in Asia is not as natural as reading the *Gita* or *Analects* or the *Dhammapada*. It has to be read in conjunction with indigenous sources and insights of Asia. The essays in this volume embody and amplify this inclusive approach.

Biblical interpretation has gone through different phases. In its earlier phase, it was an intertextual exercise, studied across the testaments to drive at the meanings of the texts. Later it was the confessional interpretation that took over and read the Bible in the light of ecclesiastical creeds, church catechisms, and conciliar statements. Now the focus is on the contextual approach where meanings flow from indigenous impulses and insights.

What this collection of essays has shown is that Asian interpreters are constantly challenged by several interpretative contexts and Scriptural texts. The hermeneutical folly is to confine to one context and identify with one text. This compendium is a smart and substantial piece of scholarship and adds a significant new perspective to biblical hermeneutics, which thus far the mainstream biblical studies have been reluctant to appreciate both as a new way of approaching the texts and as something of exceptional vision and vigor.

Preface

When I was beginning my theological education in seminary, I took numerous courses on biblical interpretation. I studied Greek, biblical intertextuality, sentence diagramming and discourse analysis, ancient background and context, and basic literary criticism. I have benefited immensely from this knowledge and these tools in my scholarship on the NT. But back then, I hardly learned anything about what I bring to the text as a reader—my age, gender, ethnicity, social class, cultural heritage, geographic location, and economic privileges. These seemed marginally important at best. Actually, I think I left seminary with the impression that if some feature of the reader were beneficial, it would be a classic white American experience. You see, I grew up in Ohio (USA) as the son of immigrants from India, Mohinder and Sudesh Gupta. My parents were well educated in India, but in our American house, we didn't have a single Western classic novel. I never read Dante or Shakespeare, Tolkien or Steinbeck. I always felt this gave me a disadvantage in studying the Bible.

It didn't really occur to me that there was a great advantage in drawing from my Asian heritage and culture knowledge and experiences until I started to teach the Bible as a professor. Even though I didn't grow up in India, I grew up in a "little India," my immigrant household in Ashland, Ohio. I now teach students across the United States, and whenever my students struggle to grasp certain cultural dynamics in the Bible, often I have a similar concept from the Asian world that I can use to illustrate. Here is one example: The Bible is full of bowing not just before angels and God but also before high-status humans. In the handshake world of American life, this can seem bizarre: *Aren't we all equal as humans?* But in India there is a very common practice of touching the feet of one's elders as a sign of respect. Yes, "we are all equal" is a value, but paying someone respect reflects the values of our society.

This *Asian Introduction to the New Testament* is an excellent and insightful contribution to the study of the Bible. The contributors are all qualified biblical scholars, interested in and attentive to the first-century context of each text. But they are also Asians who bring to the text their rich experiences that can shed fresh light on biblical interpretation. I hope this introduction will stimulate fresh conversations about non-Western contributions to NT studies.

Nijay K. Gupta
Professor of New Testament
Northern Seminary
Lisle, IL, USA

Acknowledgments

This book is an editorial venture of twenty-three essays written by twenty-three scholars in the field of NT studies. Their introductory reflections on the NT writings take into consideration the unique realities of the Asian culture and human identity.

I owe my thanks to many people who have helped me to materialize this project. I thank Dr. Brian C. Wintle (former principal of UBS, Pune), Dr. Tatsiong Benny Liew (College of the Holy Cross, USA), and Dr. K. K. Yeo (Garrett-Evangelical Theological Seminary, USA) for serving as the consulting editors of the project and supporting me with needed suggestions and critical evaluations on multifarious occasions.

I would also like to acknowledge and express my sincere gratitude to many of those who provided sincere engagements with the content of the manuscript and insights into it at different occasions and places. I remain thankful to all of them.

I offer public thanks to the anonymous reviewers and the readers of the manuscript for clear and helpful criticisms. Thanks are also due to Mr. Will Bergkamp and Dr. Jesudas M. Athyal for accepting this project to be published by Fortress Press.

I am deeply indebted to my students, my colleagues, and the administration of the United Theological College, Bengaluru, for their moral and intellectual support. I thank my family members for their sacrifice and continuous support. This edited work is dedicated to all the Asian Christians around the world for their unique faith and identity.

Johnson Thomaskutty
The United Theological College
Bengaluru, India
September 1, 2021

Introduction

An Asian Introduction to the New Testament is the first book of its kind with a focus on the NT writings in relation to the wider Asian realities. The Asian realities such as the multireligious, multiethnic, multicultural, and pluralistic phenomena set some of the common aspects of Asian societies. As the Jesus Movement emerged out of the contextual realities of his time and the growth of Christianity was spearheaded in Jewish and Asian contexts, understanding the NT writings from the Asian context might provide a unique perspective in the interpretation of the Christian Scriptures.

Contemporary issues such as poverty, casteism, class structure, honor-shame aspects, colonial realities, discrimination against women, and others cannot be neglected when an interpreter engages in NT exegesis and its hermeneutical application. Perceiving the NT from the above-mentioned contextual perspective, from both the "there and then" and "here and now" aspects, enables the reader to throw light on those issues and relate the Jesus Movement with the contemporary situations. The beginnings of the Jesus Movement in the Asian context, the spread of the mission through the initiatives of Paul and other apostles across the globe, and the later canonization of the Christian Scriptures can be understood as progressive movements only if it is accepted that the kernels of Christianity sprouted out of the Asian contextual realities.

In the NT writings, Asian realities are reflected in the socioreligious and politico-cultural areas of human existence. An Asian who reads the NT writings in the twenty-first century CE can observe the realities of the current time reflected through the rural familial ties (Luke 1:27, 69; 2:4; 11:17; Acts 3:25; 10:2; 1 Cor 1:16; 1 Tim 3:5, 12; 2 Tim 1:6; Heb 11:7; Eph 3:15), the seasonal religious festivals (John 7:2; 10:22), the marriage contracts between families (Matt 24:38; Luke 17:27; 1 Cor 7:38), the wedding feasts (Matt 22:2; Luke 14:8), the rituals related to marriage (John 3:29), and the religious pilgrimages

(Luke 2:41).[1] Matthews says, "Religious obligations could be fulfilled while leaving enough time to shop, see family and old friends, and pass on to the young the importance of their cultural heritage" (Luke 2:22–24).[2] In the contemporary Asian context, all the mentioned aspects are significant factors in determining a person's social ties.

In this book, the authors of the twenty-three essays adopt an integrated approach to finding the meaning of the NT in contemporary contexts. As a focus on the world behind the text helps readers appreciate the historical and cultural background of the biblical authors, the authors of the essays attempt to understand the text in relation to the historical context. W. Randolph Tate states, "The content of the text and its message are clothed in the terms, ideas, symbols, concepts, and categories which are current in the author's world."[3] Looking at not only the history of the text but also the literary artistry is important in the process of interpreting a text.[4] In that process, the micro- and macro-genres, literary figures of speech, key terms and concepts, implied author and implied reader interactions, and structural master plan combined give an overall idea of the text.[5] The setting, character and characterization, point of view, style, intertextual dynamics, thematic development, and other features provide a broader outlook of the narrative artistry of the text.[6] An Asian reader can also see a world in front of the text through the social norms, literary allusions, existential strategies, universalistic linguistic pattern, constraints upon the reader, contextual and circumstantial selections, and other features embedded within the text.[7] The current reading is an attempt to see how these three methods can be integrated for an overarching understanding of the NT writings.[8]

1 Victor H. Matthews, *The Cultural World of the Bible: An Illustrated Guide to Manners and Customs*, 4th ed. (Grand Rapids, MI: Baker Academic, 2015), 236.
2 Matthews, 236.
3 W. Randolph Tate, *Biblical Interpretation: An Integrated Approach*, 3rd ed. (Peabody, MA: Hendrickson, 2008), 70–71.
4 Tate, 89–101.
5 Tate, 100–101.
6 Tate, 102–37.
7 Tate, 189–218.
8 Tate, 245–65.

NT monographs, commentaries, and introductory documents are usually written with a focus on the authors/narrators, the protagonists like Jesus, Paul, Peter, and John, by placing them against Jewish and Greco-Roman backgrounds. The current book shifts the emphasis from the traditional and Western framework in interpreting the NT documents. The ultimate aim of this project is not to add yet another *NT Introduction* to the pool of NT introductions that exist already. Rather, it is an attempt to analyze how NT writings can be understood, exegeted, and interpreted with a different idiom and with a different rhetorical punch. In that sense, the thought-world of the NT writings can be closely integrated with Asian realities. Moreover, Christianity's shift from the Western Hemisphere to the Eastern (especially Asian) contexts necessitates readings conducive to the new contexts.

Because Asian realities are family centered and community oriented, an emphasis on the integral relationship within the family, clan, and tribe can be explored within the framework of the NT thought-world. The household codes of the biblical narratives demand significant treatment in that regard. Frederick C. Tiffany and Sharon H. Ringe state, "The journey of biblical interpretation begins at home, with attention to the immediate contemporary environment in which the biblical text is encountered."[9] Because Asian realities are community oriented, individuals are well connected to other social institutions and systems.[10] This aspect of the Asian reality can be connected to the NT worldview through the oral and written reflections of Jesus, Paul, and other apostles. Thus it is possible to build bridges between the historical situations of the authors and the contemporary realities of the Asian readers.

Asia is the cradle of some of the major religions of the world, such as Judaism, Hinduism, Zoroastrianism, Buddhism, Jainism, Islam, Sikhism, Shintoism, Taoism, Confucianism, Shamanism, and others. Therefore, the NT writings should be interpreted in the light of the pluriform religious and ideological aspects. Moreover, the existence of multiple Christian denominations demands a doctrinally and conceptually balanced interpretation of the Scriptures. The present book shall demonstrate inclusive biblical claims within the multireligious and multidenominational contexts. With the understanding of

9 Frederick C. Tiffany and Sharon H. Ringe, *Biblical Interpretation: A Roadmap* (Nashville, TN: Abingdon, 1996), 25.

10 See Tiffany and Ringe, 28–29.

these diversities, the authors of the essays guide their readers toward the core biblical axioms, belief aspects, and anthropocentric and cosmic realities for a new way forward.

The influence of Eastern thought upon the biblical writings is yet to be thoroughly explored in scholarly circles. R. S. Sugirtharajah comments, "Judeo-Christian faith owed an intellectual debt to Zoroastrianism for such theological ideas as a universal god, notions of angels, Satan, heaven, hell, resurrection of the body, life after death, the final judgment, and the apocalyptic ending of the world."[11] He further states that there is a lack of enthusiasm on the part of mainstream biblical scholars to admit a reciprocal exchange between the Mediterranean world and India.[12] The conscientized masses called the Minjung in Korea, the Japanese Burakumins, the Indian tribal communities, the Aboriginals, the Dalits, and the dehumanized Asian women can see the relevance of the NT message in today's context.[13] Such a reading may provide us an avenue for interpreting the NT writings with a renewed interest in the contemporary Asian context. That may be done with an emphasis on both the ancient and contemporary realities of the Asian communities.

The traditional approaches to the NT from Western perspectives do not challenge us to look at the Christian Testament with new eyes. A new approach may help readers to understand the Asian backgrounds, sociocultural and religious ideologies, and contemporary missional and theological paradigms in a new light. A comprehensive study that focuses on NT writings and traditions from the Eastern and Asian contexts is a genuine need of the time. Therefore, this book begins with a proposition that NT writings should be treated differently. A study that bridges the first-century Christian and the contemporary Asian realities will throw more light on the NT Scriptures. This book attempts to explore that possibility.

Johnson Thomaskutty
Editor

---

11 R. S. Sugirtharajah, *The Bible and Asia: From the Pre-Christian Era to the Postcolonial Age* (Cambridge, MA: Harvard University Press, 2013), 44.

12 See Sugirtharajah, 45.

13 See Sugirtharajah, 190–223.

ONE

The New Testament and the Sociocultural and Religious Realities of the Asian Contexts

Kar Yong Lim
Seminari Theoloji Malaysia
Seremban, Malaysia

Deep in the rainforest of Malaysia is the small settlement of a native tribe with a population of a few hundred. Access to this remote village is by way of a two-hour motorized boat ride upstream on the river from the nearest town, followed by another two- to three-hour hike through the dense jungle. When foreign missionaries arrived and converted this village to Christianity, they built a church according to Western architecture, with a pulpit and pews. As a result, this community no longer sits cross-legged on the floor, which was their usual custom when they gathered. The traditional musical instruments of *sape'*, *gong*, and *sompoton* were replaced with guitars, drums, and keyboards. The people were told that many of their cultural beliefs, practices, and symbols were incompatible with the teaching of the Bible and needed to be abandoned.[1]

1 See Loh I-to, *In Search for Asian Sounds and Symbols in Worship*, CSCA Christianity in Southeast Asia Series 5 (Singapore: Trinity Theological College, 2012); Loh I-to, *Hymnal Companion to Sound the Bamboo: Asian Hymns in Their Cultural and Liturgical Contexts* (Chicago: GIA, 2011).

It is not uncommon for many Asians to encounter such an experience. This is not to downplay the enormous contribution by Western missionaries—far from it. I strongly believe that they did what they knew best and that there was no ill intention on their part to set aside Asian heritage and tradition in their pedagogical approaches to bringing the gospel to Asia. I highlighted this experience to showcase that in much of the history of interpretation of the NT, Christians have brought their Western cultural assumptions and biases to the reading of the Scripture, and this was spread to other parts of the non-Western world.[2] As a result, much of the life of the Asian church is reflective of the Western missionary movement's culture. This can be seen in the liturgy we observe, the architectural design of the churches we build, and the hymns we sing. Because the nature of the gospel as presented by some of these Western missionaries seemed alien to local culture, I, a Christian of Chinese descent living in a Muslim-majority Malaysia, grew up hearing many of my kinfolk describing Christianity as a *xi yang jiao* (Western religion). When someone of Chinese descent became a Christian, a common reaction was "One more Christian, one fewer Chinese."

It is not surprising that after two millennia, few people read the NT through an Asian lens. As the church's geographic center of gravity begins to shift from the West to the Majority World in the last two decades, the face of Christianity has also begun to change. In recent years, there has been greater emphasis on the need for constructing an authentic Asian theology.[3] This is certainly laudable, but much less work has been done in the field of NT studies from an Asian perspective. However, in recent years, there is a growing awareness leading to some encouraging efforts being carried out in reading Scriptures from an honor-shame perspective, which closely resembles Asian culture, and from an interdisciplinary approach, thereby offering fresh insights in reading the text.[4] While this is

2 E. Randolph Richards and Brandon J. O'Brien, *Misreading Scripture with Western Eyes: Removing Cultural Blinders to Better Understand the Bible* (Downers Grove, IL: IVP, 2012).

3 See Hwa Yung, *Mangoes or Bananas? The Quest of an Authentic Asian Theology*, 2nd ed. (Oxford: Regnum, 2014); Donald Leroy Stults, *Developing an Asian Evangelical Theology* (Denver: iAcademicBooks, 2001).

4 See David A. deSilva, *Honor, Patronage, Kinship and Purity: Unlocking New Testament Culture* (Downers Grove, IL: InterVarsity, 2000); Bruce J. Malina, *The New Testament World: Insight from Cultural Anthropology*, 3rd ed. (Louisville, KY: Westminster John Knox, 2001), 27–57.

certainly a welcome change, most of these works are written by Western scholars who have some exposure to Asian culture, with very few contributions by Asian scholars. In light of this, this volume attempts to fill the lacuna in current NT scholarship.

In this chapter, I aim to demonstrate how the NT can be profitably read with a broader lens by considering some of the Asian cultural norms, with examples primarily drawn from Malaysia, a context with which I am more familiar. In biblical interpretation, the first key to hear and understand the NT is to consider what its authors' intended meaning was and how its first audiences understood it. To do so, the historical, social, and cultural contexts of the NT era are explored. At the same time, it has also been widely acknowledged that ancient Mediterranean societies have similar cultural characteristics with Asian cultures. By embarking on an Asian reading of the NT, we are taking advantage of Asian cultures and traditions that we are broadly familiar with that resemble some of the ancient cultures of the biblical world. In so doing, I hope to discover key ideas and messages that are often overlooked by Western interpreters in the reading and teaching of the Scripture in our own context. I will also raise a number of questions for further reflection on how the message of the NT could possibly speak meaningfully and powerfully to our context.

THREE CULTURAL PARADIGMS AFFECTING OUR UNDERSTANDING OF THE BIBLE

In cultural anthropology, there is a tendency to categorize different cultures into three major paradigms: power-fear, honor-shame, and innocence-guilt worldviews. Each of these paradigms explains how behavior is governed with respect to the laws of the land, business and social etiquettes, and relationships in family and community with the aim of maintaining social order.

In a power-fear society, control is often kept by the fear of retribution and focuses on dominance by the person in authority. This can be seen in cultures or nations where power is concentrated on one figure of authority, such as an absolute monarch, a dictator, or a leader of a tribe. Those being ruled are expected to obey the directives of the leader without questioning, and failure to do so often leads to severe punishment not only of the individuals but also of their immediate and extended families. North Korea is an example of a country that is still ruled by a power-fear paradigm. The paradigm can also be seen in many animistic cultures, where the fear of the spirits and the supernatural world found in the habitat or natural surroundings often governs cultural practices and behaviors. According to this worldview, the universe is a place filled with gods, demons, and spirits of the ancestors. In this culture, the priests, witch doctors, or shamans wield control over the people by using fear. In order that all can live in peace with these unseen powers, the people are required to live quietly or appease these powers through some form of sacrifices or rituals.

In an honor-shame society, control is maintained by the inculcation of shame in the wrongful behavior of a person who does not conform to the norms of the society.[5] Most cultures that operate from this paradigm are collectivist in nature. In this respect, seeking the honor of the community and protecting or restoring the honor of the tribe, family, or clan is far more important than an individual's actions. If shame is caused to a community by outsiders and cannot be rectified, revenge may result in order to restore the honor of a family and tribe, and this may include killing. If any behavior of an individual brings shame to the tribe, the tribe may react by punishing the individual, including ostracizing or killing the offender and the immediate family, to restore the honor of the tribe. This is particularly true in an Islamic context, where apostasy is seen as a crime and is punishable. A Muslim who converts to another religion is often ostracized from the family and community, and some are killed. The first-century world operated on an honor-shame paradigm—not too different from many parts of Asia today.

In an innocence-guilt culture, the means of control is by creating or reinforcing the feeling of guilt and the expectation of punishment for wrongful behaviors based on a set of laws or regulations. In this culture, regulating an individual's conscience, maintaining justice, and upholding law and order are crucial in ensuring social order. The fundamental belief is in right versus wrong, justice versus injustice, and order versus crime. This yardstick is used to measure the cultural norms and behaviors. If one is guilty, one must pay for one's crime by receiving some form of punishment that is commensurate with the degree of wrongdoing. The Western world operates according to this paradigm.

5 See Roland Muller, *Honor and Shame: Unlocking the Door* (Bloomington, IN: Xlibris, 2000).

These three worldviews affect the way we understand theology and the way we read the Scripture. For example, this can be seen in how we present our understanding of sin. In the innocence-guilt paradigm, when people sin, their conscience kicks in, and they are now aware of their fallen nature. Therefore, they need redemption from their sin. This is how Western Christian theology presents the fall of humanity in the garden of Eden based on Genesis 3. When humanity broke God's law, they were in a position of guilt. Yet we also read that in Genesis 3, when Adam and Eve sinned, they immediately hid themselves from God. They were ashamed. They could no longer honor God with their shame. When humanity broke their relationship with God, they were in a position of shame. We can also see that Adam and Eve were afraid of God when they hid from him. When humanity broke God's trust, they were in a position of fear. In other words, we see how these three worldviews operate in Genesis 3, and yet the Western reading based on the innocence-guilt paradigm remains the dominant reading.

Furthermore, theological concepts of justice, righteousness, condemnation, sin, forgiveness, and heaven and hell are central in the thinking of the innocence-guilt worldview because this is the language that appeals to those who operate within this culture. Much of this language and understanding are rooted in legal or forensic language.

One way in which the Evangelicals present the gospel representative of this worldview is the popular use of "The Four Spiritual Laws" written by Bill Bright of Cru (formerly known as Campus Crusade for Christ).[6] The first spiritual law is that God loves us and offers a wonderful plan for us. Second, we are sinful and separated from God. We are sinners, we are guilty, and God's punishment for sin is death. Third, God loves us by sending his son, Jesus, to die for us. Finally, we must individually accept Jesus as Savior; only then can we escape God's wrath. This dominant perspective subsequently affects and governs the way we read and understand the NT and is typical of Western Christianity and even Asian Christianity at large.

While there is nothing inherently wrong with the innocence-guilt reading, the other readings, particularly the honor-shame perspective, have not been fully explored. The remainder of this chapter aims to draw insights from

6 See "4 Spiritual Laws," 4laws.com, accessed October 22, 2019, http://www.4laws.com.

the Asian honor-shame perspective and bring them into helpful conversation regarding how we could read and understand the NT.

SOCIOCULTURAL REALITIES OF ASIA AND THE NT

Asia is vast, and every country on this continent has its own distinctive cultures, traditions, and religious practices. For example, South Korea and Japan lean toward monoethnic and monocultural society, whereas Malaysia is religiously, culturally, and ethnically diverse with about one hundred different ethnic groups. In terms of religious beliefs, India is Hindu majority, Thailand is Buddhist majority, and Indonesia is Muslim majority. There is no single, well-defined Asian culture and tradition, but there are common traits. Asian culture particularly stresses past orientation, where tradition and beliefs are respected; social relationships, where collectivism is commonly practiced; and relational hierarchy, where respect for elders is accorded and harmony with others is highly valued. All these common traits shape the honor-shame culture that often governs the identity and behavior of communities and individuals. This Asian social environment of honor and shame is not too far removed from the world of the Bible; it has deep affinities with the biblical world. Because of this, Asian Christians are probably better positioned to appreciate the corporate and relational nature of the world of the NT.

A Collectivist Society

The Asian community is predominantly a collectivist or group-oriented culture that practices communal living, and this is not dissimilar from the ancient Mediterranean world.[7] In light of this, many of the metaphors used in the NT, particularly in the Pauline epistles, naturally appeal to Asians. These include, among others, church as a communal assembly, family, siblings, body, and temple metaphors.[8] These metaphors should be read as addressing not simply individuals but the entire community.

7 See Malina, *New Testament World*, 58–80; also see 76–78.

8 See Kar Yong Lim, *Metaphors and Social Identity Formation in Paul's Letters to the Corinthians* (Eugene, OR: Pickwick, 2017), 51–187, 191–202.

Within a collectivist community, maintaining harmony is important. Respect and honor accorded to the elders of the community are esteemed values. It is also common to see three to four generations living under the same roof in Asia, often subject to the authority of a patriarch or matriarch of the household. In light of this, the Household Codes in the NT (Eph 5:21–6:9; Col 3:18–4:1; 1 Pet 3:1–7) are read as primarily maintaining cohesiveness within the community and are less about gender roles or limiting the roles of women in the community or the church, a prevalent interpretation particularly among Evangelicals in the West.

With high honor accorded to parents, both living and dead, it is extremely shocking to read the words of Jesus in Matthew 10:34–39 regarding turning against and hating one's parents. This statement drives home the point that one should always consider the cost of making the decision to follow Jesus—more so if one is the eldest son of a Taoist or Chinese family and is expected to carry on the traditional rituals of ancestral veneration or worship in the family in keeping the virtue of filial piety, a core teaching of Taoism and Confucianism.[9] For many Asians, the decision to follow Jesus often comes at a great cost; they encounter suffering, persecution, and ostracization from the community. Discipleship, taken seriously, is not seen as an individual decision or one that is to be taken lightly. Chinese parents may object to their eldest son becoming a Christian because this would be seen as disrespectful and disobedient. This naturally affects the harmonious relationship within the family and the community.

As a collectivist community, many decisions affecting the community or family are often made by the chiefs or heads of the family. In matters of religious belief, these heads of communities or families wield considerable power and authority, and any conversion from one religion to another is often decided by the tribal chiefs. This can be seen in many tribal communities in Malaysia. For example, once the tribal chief decides to embrace Christianity, the entire village will follow it. In other words, salvation is hardly a private or individual decision; the notion of "accepting Jesus as *my* personal Lord and Savior," which is popular among Western Evangelicals, is an alien concept.

9 For further information, see Confucius, *Xiaojing: The Classic of Filial Piety*, Chinese-English edition (London: FV Editions, 2020); also see James Legge, *The Hsiao King, or Classic of Filial Piety* (Whitefish, MT: Kessinger, 2010).

Conversion in many parts of Asia is a communal matter; it is not different from the experience of the Philippian jailor when Paul declared that he and his household would be saved (Acts 16:31). Similarly, the conversion and subsequent baptism of Lydia and her household is another example of a typical response of a collectivist society in the NT (Acts 16:13–15).

Gathering together was important in early Christianity (see Acts 2:42–47) and in many communities in Asia. In Malaysia, it is not unusual to see an entire village or community coming together to share responsibility in organizing weddings, festival celebrations, and other activities for the common good. This concept of *gotong royong* (working together) is a common feature in the Malaysian communal life. Coming together as a community of Christ followers is an imperative frequently mentioned in the NT (see Eph 5:19; Col 3:16; Heb 10:24–25). By the second century, Christian meetings took place once a week on a Sunday, as attested by Justin (1 *Apol.* 67) and Ignatius (*Magn.* 9:1). What we know is that when the assembly gathered together, common activities included reciting psalms, singing hymns, teaching from the Scripture, practicing spiritual gifts such as speaking in tongues and interpreting tongues, and celebrating the Eucharist (see 1 Cor 11–14; Eph 5:19; Col 3:16).

The fundamental purpose of coming together as a community of believers was to build up the community; it was never intended primarily for personal gratification. It was meant to promote group cohesion and solidarity, common traits of collectivist communities, and not meant to worship with personal preferences over style, choice of songs and sermons, and length of service, which may be the trademarks of a Western individualistic society. In this respect, Asian culture, which is collectivist and communal, can better appreciate NT ecclesiology.

Finally, in any community, there are bound to be disciplinary issues. Any disciplinary measures taken as in the day of the NT (1 Cor 5:1–13; Acts 5:1–11) are for the sake of the community. It is noteworthy that in carrying out church discipline, Paul never addresses the guilty man in question who slept with his stepmother (1 Cor 5:1), but he reprimands the community for failing to exercise the necessary corrective disciplines. This approach taken by Paul is common among collectivist societies, where an individual's wrongdoing affects the whole community.

Honor-Shame in Practice

Honor-shame is a dominant sociocultural paradigm in many parts of Asia. Seen from a Western perspective, shame is often closely identified with a lack of self-esteem, a sense of being timid or intimidated, and an uncomfortable sense of humiliation when one has done something wrong.

When Paul declares that he is not ashamed of the gospel (Rom 1:16), this is often interpreted as him not feeling intimidated by the gospel even in the heart of the Roman Empire. Some suggest that Paul is not ashamed because he is bold, and he "emphatically stands by the message" because there are people in Rome who despise the simplicity of the message and look down on the Christians and their unusual gospel.[10] Paul declares that he is "mighty proud of the gospel,"[11] and "he glories in the gospel."[12] This reading is in line with Western culture, where the opposite of shame is glory, pride, or boldness.[13]

The word translated as "ashamed" (ἐπαισχύνομαι) in Romans 1:16 literally means "to experience a painful feeling or sense of loss of status because of some particular event or activity."[14] In other words, Paul is not talking about being intimidated or proud of the gospel in this context, although all these are true. Paul is talking about the loss of status and a deep sense of shame for degrading oneself within an honor-shame culture.

The gospel is shameful because Christ was crucified on the cross, an instrument of shame that publicly exposed naked prisoners where all sense of dignity was lost. The gospel is shameful because a man was subjected to torture where his masculinity was called into question, and he was subjected to degrading punishment.[15] Yet Paul does not sense any shame in proclaiming Christ crucified (see 1 Cor 2:1–5). On the contrary, by proclaiming the

10 Leon Morris, *The Epistle to the Romans*, PNTC (Grand Rapids, MI: Eerdmans, 1988), 66.

11 Brendan Byrne, *Romans*, Sacra Pagina 6 (Collegeville, MN: Liturgical, 1996), 51.

12 F. F. Bruce, *Romans*, rev. ed., TNTC (Leicester, UK: InterVarsity, 1985), 74.

13 See Robert Jewett, *Romans: A Commentary*, Hermeneia (Minneapolis: Fortress, 2007), 136–37.

14 Frederick William Danker et al., *A Greek-English Lexicon of the New Testament and Other Early Christian Literature* (Chicago, IL: University of Chicago Press, 2001).

15 See Maud W. Gleason, *Making Men: Sophists and Self-Presentation in Ancient Rome* (Princeton, NJ: Princeton University Press, 1995); Mikeal C. Parsons, *Body and Character in Luke and Acts: The Subversion of Physiognomy in Early Christianity* (Grand Rapids, MI: Baker Academic, 2006), esp. 17–38.

saving power of the gospel and the righteousness of God, Paul is honoring Christ and the gospel. Pursuing honor was a value deeply appreciated in the Greco-Roman world.[16] Cicero once said, "By nature we yearn and hunger for honor, and once we have glimpsed, as it were, some part of its radiance, there is nothing we are not prepared to bear and suffer in order to secure it" (*Tusc.* 2.24.58). Rightly understood, Paul's desire to honor God by proclaiming the gospel would certainly impact the way we understand Romans and how the gospel is proclaimed in Asia. As Chinese honor their parents through veneration,[17] how much more we must honor God and the gospel and not be ashamed of the gospel.

Patronage and the Language of Grace

Patronage is another common practice within an honor-shame community. In a collectivist society, patrons are expected to be generous and grant favors and assistance to those who are less fortunate or in lower strata of the society. In return, the recipients, or clients, respond by giving honor and gratitude and being loyal to patrons for all favors and assistance accorded. This complex system of reciprocal generosity is perceived as a moral obligation, and there are obvious consequences if this is not properly adhered to. When a wealthy or elite person fails to function as a patron, they can be described as uncaring, arrogant, and lacking virtue. For the recipients or clients, the failure to respond appropriately when receiving favor from the patron is morally wrong. This mutual reciprocity governs the unifying fabric of some parts of Asian society. In Malaysia, this is prominent within the Malay and Chinese customs.[18]

The Greco-Roman culture was also one of patronage.[19] Philosophers like Aristotle, Cicero, and Seneca frequently discussed patronage in ethical contexts where proper behavior should be governed in giving or reciprocating benefaction

16 See Joseph E. Hellerman, *Reconstructing Honor in Roman Philippi*, SNTSMS 132 (Cambridge: Cambridge University Press, 2005), 34–63.

17 Confucius, *Classic of Filial Piety*, para. 10.

18 See Harold Crouch, *Government and Society in Malaysia* (St. Leonards, Australia: Allen & Unwin, 1996), 152–76.

19 See John K. Chow, *Patronage and Power: A Study of Social Networks in Corinth*, JSNTSup 75 (Sheffield, UK: JSOT, 1992), 38–82.

in a virtuous manner. The language that was used to describe benefaction is the language of grace bestowed upon an individual.[20]

Seneca, in his opening words of his writing on benefaction, declares that "almost nothing . . . is more disgraceful than the fact that we do not know how either to give or to receive benefits."[21] This underscores the practice that "constitutes the chief bond of human society."[22] He further elaborates that the greater the favor is showered upon us, the more earnestly must we express ourselves, resorting to such compliments as "I shall never be able to repay you my gratitude, but, at any rate, I shall not cease from declaring everywhere that I am unable to repay it."[23] Clients must always express honor and loyalty to the patrons, as testified by Seneca: "Let us show how grateful we are for the blessing that has come to us by pouring forth our feelings, and let us bear witness to them, not merely in the hearing of the giver, but everywhere."[24] As a recipient of grace, one should not behave in such a way that would bring dishonor to the benefactor. If a client shows disrespect for the patron, the client would receive the wrath of the patron.[25] If a client does not return gratitude for the benefaction received, it is considered a "disgrace."[26]

This same language of grace is often used in the NT, particularly by Paul in describing what God has done for us.[27] Theologically, grace (χάρις) is understood as the unmerited favor of God showered upon humanity. Within Protestant circles, salvation is viewed as the grace of God, something humanity receives through faith rather than works.[28] This transactional understanding can be traced back to Luther and the Reformation. Sinful humanity stands condemned before a righteous God, and only a sinless Christ can fulfill the requirements of the Law in bringing reconciliation between God and

20 See James R. Harrison, *Paul's Language of Grace in Its Graeco-Roman Context*, WUNT 2/172 (Tübingen, Germany: Mohr Siebeck, 2003), 167–210.

21 Seneca, *Ben.* 1.1.1.

22 Seneca, 1.4.2.

23 Seneca, 2.24.4.

24 Seneca, 2.22.1.

25 Aristotle, *Rhet.* 2.2.8.

26 Seneca, *Ben.* 3.1.1.

27 See Rom 3:23–24; 4:16; 5:15–21; 6:14; 11:5; Eph 2:4–10.

28 See Eph 2:8–9. Oftentimes, Eph 2:10, which speaks of doing good works, is neglected in expounding on grace.

humanity. While this understanding of soteriology is theologically sound, it is truncated if viewed strictly from an innocence-guilt perspective, where grace is seen as a transactional relationship.

Within an honor-shame context, grace as a language of benefaction dictates that the recipients of this benefaction, although unworthy, are to respond with honor, faithfulness, and loyalty to the benefactor in all that they say and do. The recipients are always reminded that any dishonor they bring to their patron as a result of their behavior constitutes disgrace and is incompatible to the grace they receive. This is how first-century hearers would have understood as they reflected on their response to the grace of God in an honor-shame context.[29] Reciprocity to the patron, represented by God, is the commitment of faithfulness by offering honor, gratitude, and loyalty, and this governs their behaviors so that they do not bring dishonor and shame to the patron and the patron's reputation (see also 1 Pet 2:4–8).

In Asian culture, particularly in countries where the widening gap between the rich or elites and the poor can be clearly seen, the notion of benefaction is often practiced. Those holding senior positions in the civil service, wealthy individuals, and those from noble families often serve as benefactors for those who are poor by providing assistance or charitable services to them. In return, the poor offer honor, respect, and gratitude to the benefactors. This patron-client relationship can be further explored in expounding the meaning of grace in our relationship with God. We can use this notion to explain how we, as Christians saved by the grace of God, should always reciprocate by being faithful to God in our worship of him, honoring him through our words and deeds and not bringing shame to his name in our social relationships.

Ritual Purity

Another aspect that Asian readers readily identify with in the Jewish and Greco-Roman world of the NT is ritual purity, which is deeply rooted in Asian religions and folk beliefs.[30] Ritual washing is dominant in Hinduism and Islam. For the Chinese, there are certain days of the lunar calendar where eating meat is avoided. The seventh month of the lunar calendar is popularly known as the Hungry Ghost Festival, and this season is seen as inauspicious

29 See also Harrison, *Paul's Language of Grace*, 211–344.

30 See Malina, *New Testament World*, 161–97.

for weddings and other major events in one's life. Time, space, food, and how one lives one's life are filled with connotations of being clean or unclean.[31] The NT contains numerous references to the sacred, the holy, and the pure as well as the unclean, the profane, and the unholy. The command to be holy and clean that rings throughout Leviticus is repeated in the NT (e.g., 1 Pet 1:16; Eph 1:4). Pollution and purity are central themes of the Bible and universal concerns for humanity—even more so in Asia, where religious purification rites and festivals are common practices. Being unclean can be seen as shameful, and this underscores the need for ritual purity.[32]

The portrayal of Jesus in the Gospels frequently features his encounter with the ritually unclean, particularly in the Gospel of Mark. For example, Jesus delivers people from unclean spirits (Mark 1:21–28; 9:2–8); heals lepers, who are considered ritually unclean (Mark 1:40–44; 14:3–9); heals a gentile possessed by legions of spirits (Mark 1:1–20); and heals and restores a ritually unclean hemorrhaging woman (Mark 5:25–34). Apart from these events, Jesus also talks about defilement (Mark 7:14–15, 17–23). In these incidents, Jesus identifies with the ritually unclean so he might bring cleansing and healing to the people, delivering them from their shameful conditions. No one is too unclean to be touched by God. This can be a powerful message in reaching out to those who may be deemed as "untouchables," such as the Dalits in India, and those deemed ritually unclean in the eyes of the community in Asia. The marginalized, the poor, and the destitute are all welcome to the banquet of the Lord, as clearly expressed in the parable of the great banquet (Luke 14:16–24; see also Matt 22:1–14).

Suffering and Persecution

Another issue that deserves some attention is suffering as a result of religious persecution, economic injustice, and poverty in Asia. One of the issues related to religious persecution is the notion of shame a community feels when one of their own converts to Christianity, particularly among the Muslims. According

31 See James E. Morrison, "Sharing the Gospel with Tibetan Buddhists through the Cultural Paradigm of Pollution and Purity," in *Majority World Theologies: Theologizing from Africa, Asia, Latin America, and the Ends of the Earth*, Evangelical Missiological Society Series 26, ed. Allen Yeh and Tite Tiénou (Littleton, CO: William Carey, 2018), 116–30.

32 For example, see the Quran 5:6.

to the 2019 World Watch List published by Open Doors, trends suggest that Christians in Asia and the Middle East are the most vulnerable in terms of suffering. Now in its twenty-seventh year, this annual ranking tracks fifty countries where it is most dangerous to be a Christian. Out of those ranked, twenty-three countries are in Asia, while ten others are in the Middle East, and a large number of these countries are Muslim majority. The report highlights that suffering in Asia rose to unprecedented levels, and this resulted in Bangladesh, Laos, Bhutan, and Sri Lanka joining the list for the first time in 2017 and Nepal joining in 2018. In 2019, India entered the top ten, while China jumped sixteen spots, the highest thus far. The magnitude of persecution is clearly illustrated by the sobering statistic that 245 million Christians experience high levels of persecution. This means that one in nine Christians live in places where Christianity is illegal, forbidden, or persecuted. The 2019 Watch List also reports that 4,136 Christians were killed; 2,625 Christians were arrested and imprisoned without trial; and 1,266 churches were attacked during the reporting period.[33]

This sad reality in Asia allows a very robust and biblically rooted understanding of suffering and persecution to be developed based on the NT, especially on the meaning of taking up one's cross to follow Jesus. The theme of suffering in Acts and the letters of Paul (e.g., Acts 5:17–42; 7:54–60; 12:1–19; 16:16–40; 2 Cor 1:3–11; 4:7–12; 6:3–13; 11:22–12:10; Phil 1:12–26) can be a source of encouragement for Christians who suffer marginality in Islamic and Hindu contexts.[34]

Apart from religious persecution, there is also increasing persecution against women and those who are marginalized and living in poverty. The income disparity in Asia is wide, and some of the wealthiest and poorest nations and individuals can be found on the same continent and in the same country. Many passages in the NT dealing with poverty can be read with fresh insights. How would reading Luke's Gospel, where the poor and marginalized

33 See "World Watch List," Open Doors, accessed October 25, 2019, https://www.opendoorsusa.org/christian-persecution/world-watch-list/.

34 See Kar Yong Lim, *"The Sufferings of Christ Are Abundant in Us": A Narrative Dynamics Investigation of Paul's Sufferings in 2 Corinthians*, Library of New Testament Studies 399 (London: T&T Clark, 2009); Kar Yong Lim, "A Theology of Suffering and Mission for the Asian Church," in *Asian Christian Theology: Evangelical Perspective*, ed. T. D. Gener and S. T. Pardue (Carlisle, UK: Langham Global Library, 2019), 181–98.

are dominant, affect both rich and poor Asian readers? What about Paul's desire in Galatians 2:20 to remember the poor, resulting in his major collection project for the poor in Jerusalem?[35] What about the appointment of the seven deacons in ensuring that there is fair distribution of food for those who need it most? These passages have the potential to start meaningful conversations leading to appropriate actions among the Christian communities in Asia.

Reconciliation

On a continent where ethnic and religious conflicts are rife (such as the Rohingya refugee crises, the Israeli-Palestinian conflicts, and the Muslim-Hindu conflicts in India), how do we make sense of the theme of reconciliation in the NT? How do we grasp a meaning of ecclesiology where the church is to comprise a new community for all people?

The early Christian community had its fair share of ethnic and religious conflicts, as seen in Acts. The controversial distribution of food between the Palestinian and Hellenistic Jews leading to the appointment of seven deacons (Acts 6:1–7), the issue of circumcision of gentiles (Acts 15:1–29), and table fellowship with different ethnic groups (Gal 2:11–13) are just some examples that threatened the survival of the fledgling community. These controversial issues, if not resolved with care, could have changed the landscape of the Jew-gentile relationship and, subsequently, the history of the church. That the church is meant to be an inclusive community comprising both Jews and gentiles is clear from Christ's Great Commission (Matt 28:18–20); the coming of the Holy Spirit on Pentecost, where many people heard the gospel preached in their own mother tongues (Acts 2:1–47); the conversion of the Ethiopian eunuch (Acts 8:26–39); the call of Paul to be the apostle to the gentiles (Acts 9:1–22); and Peter's vision of the unclean animals with the command to eat them and the subsequent encounter with Cornelius's household (Acts 10:1–48). Yet the full acceptance of the gentiles, who were deemed unclean by the Jews, was not

35 For further discussion on Paul's Jerusalem collection, see Kar Yong Lim, "Generosity from Pauline Perspective: Insights from Paul's Letters to the Corinthians," Special Edition on Contagious Generosity, *Evangelical Review of Theology* 37 (2013): 20–30; Kar Yong Lim, "Paul the Economist? Economic Principles in Pauline Literature with the Jerusalem Collection as a Test Case," *Evangelical Review of Theology* 41 (2017): 19–31.

fully resolved until the Jerusalem council was convened in the late forties CE (Acts 15:1–29). If the ascension of Christ and Pentecost could be dated in the early thirties, this means that the complex issue of the Jew-gentile relationship was not settled for at least another fifteen years. How can this speak to conflicts in Asia? Can all parties move beyond deep-rooted religious, ethnic, and political differences to work toward reconciliation?

The issue of reconciliation is even more urgent in a nation like Malaysia, where there are more than one hundred different ethnic groups with diverse cultural practices and religious beliefs. Despite general peaceful ethnic relations and goodwill, each ethnic group tends to stick to itself when it comes to forming friendships and partnerships. Almost every aspect of life in Malaysia is defined by ethnic and religious boundaries. Political parties, educational frameworks, and economic policies are often racially based and defined. With a widening divide between ethnic groups, fostering unity for a nation like Malaysia can be a daunting task. This is where a firm understanding of reconciliation rooted in the gospel can be a linchpin for Christians to consider how the church can be the agent of reconciliation in a fragmented society and a true living example of how people from diverse backgrounds can be united in Christ.

RELIGIOUS REALITIES OF ASIA AND THE NT

When the apostle Paul was in Athens, he encountered a city where many idols and deities were worshipped (Acts 17:16–34). In the Greco-Roman religious practice, worship was nonexclusive.[36] Even the devotion to a particular patron deity of the family or clan did not preclude the worship of other gods. Therefore, the message of Paul proclaiming a God without image and representation stood in sharp contrast with the abundance of deities represented in the form of statues, shrines, and temples. As such, the Christian faith's demand to worship only one true God was unheard of in the Greco-Roman world. If there was a new God to be worshipped, he was merely added to the list of other deities. In addition, there were beliefs in magic, superstitions, demons,

36 See Everett Ferguson, *Backgrounds of Early Christianity*, 3rd ed. (Grand Rapids, MI: Eerdmans, 2003), 148–318.

and astrology. The modern concept of conversion from worshipping one God to another in our Christian faith was alien in the Greco-Roman world.

Religious Pluralism

In the Greco-Roman world, religious beliefs and practices typically centered around not how one ought to live but how one earned blessing from gods. For example, the worship of Asclepius as the god of physicians ensured that sickness of the various parts of the body was cured, and this led the devotees to make votive offerings of the parts of the body that were healed to Asclepius. Morality was not closely associated with religious beliefs, and rules and rituals were more ceremonial than ethical, although there were exceptions.[37]

The corporate nature of religious practices and civic religion was also a central feature of Greco-Roman religions. In the cities of the Greco-Roman world, different deities were worshipped as patron gods. For example, Athena was worshipped in Athens, Zeus and Hermes were worshipped in Lystra (Acts 14:13), and Artemis was worshipped in Ephesus (see Acts 19:1–41). In the Greco-Roman world, religion was closely interwoven into every strata of the society. This is very different in the Western society today, where there is a clear separation between religion and the state, where the former is considered a private matter. Every part of life in the ancient world was related to the worship of some form of deity, be it civic gods, domestic patron gods, imperial ruler cults, or personal religious practices. In every region of the Roman Empire, there were regional deities, heroes, and spirits that were worshipped. There were also festivals where worship was offered to different gods. For example, the worship of Zeus was closely related to the Olympic Games celebrated in Olympia. The height of civic religion in the Greco-Roman world was the worship of the imperial cult in the Roman Empire. Julius Caesar was venerated as God by his successor, Caesar Augustus, who then claimed the title "Son of God." Public funds were used to build temples. It is no wonder that temples and shrines filled the architectural landscape of the cities of the Greco-Roman world. This religious scenario is different from the West, where there is a state and church separation.

The religious context of the Greco-Roman world is no different in many parts of Asia today. Asia is the birthplace for the world's major religions—Buddhism, Jainism, Hinduism, Islam, Judaism, Christianity, and Sikhism,

37 Ferguson, 177.

as well as many other folk religious practices such as Shintoism, Shamanism, Taoism, Confucianism, and Animism, among others. In addition, beliefs in magic and divination are also common in Asia. In Malaysia, the belief in charms, *bomoh* (witch doctors), ancestral spirits, and *toyol* and *pontianak* (different forms of evil spirits and ghosts) that could possibly cause harm to people is common. For some Chinese folk religions, devotion to patron gods was nonexclusive. For some, religion is part of the national identity and civic religion. This can be seen in Malaysia, where Islam is declared as the official religion of the federation and constitutes part of the civic religion of the nation.[38] An ethnic Malay is also defined in the Federal Constitution of Malaysia as a person who professes the religion of Islam, habitually speaks the Malay language, and conforms to Malay custom.[39] Because of this, religious faith is part of the expression of daily life in both the public and private spheres as seen in the daily activities of the temples, shrines, and other places of worship, coupled with religious festivals or cultural celebrations rooted in religious practices. In this regard, apologetics, which is often taught from the Western perspective and typically begins with the defense of the existence of God, is of not much relevance in Asia. The issue in Asia is about not the existence of God but who is the true and living God amid religious pluralism.

How are we to read the NT from this perspective? How can we proclaim an invisible God who does not live in dwellings made by human hands or is represented by idols in Asia, not unlike Paul's encounter with the "unknown" God in Athens (Acts 17:23)? What were the challenges for Paul, as he preached an "unknown God" and an unseen God (see Rom 1:19–20), regarding a gentile world where deities were manifested through various forms of representation such as temples, shrines, statues, rituals, and even magic? Can some of the meaning and value of our religious background and experience serve as a possible entry point for our reading of the NT? For example, in India, the concern for holy living, release from bondage, and search for a guru could possibly be excellent entry points in reading the life and ministry of Jesus in the Gospels. In a traditional Chinese context, the fear of betrayal to the patron God of the family and the obligation of filial piety of the eldest son in carrying out ancestral worship involving the sacrifice of food within

38 Article 3, Federal Constitution of Malaysia.

39 Article 160, Federal Constitution of Malaysia.

the traditional family and clan when a family turns to Christ should also be adequately addressed. In this respect, Paul's instructions to the Corinthians on food sacrificed to idols in 1 Corinthians 8–10 should be sensitively dealt with. At the same time, those living in Islamic contexts where all meat sold in the market is halal (where animals are slaughtered according to Islamic rites with prayers recited) could find this passage relevant as well.

Folk Religions in Practice

In many parts of Asia, there is a strong belief in spiritual powers, spirits, magic, rituals, charms, and the forces of evil.[40] Scott Sunquist related an account of a Thai professor, deeply influenced by a Western theological framework, desiring to write the first book on systematic theology from the Thai perspective in Thai. When Sunquist asked about how this Thai professor intended to handle the issue of ancestors and spirits, he indicated that he had not thought much about this issue. Sunquist commented, "What good is a systematic theology if it does not answer questions presented by a local culture, and how could a Thai Christian think of writing a theology that does not mention what every Thai sees every day: spirit houses?"[41] This experience in Thailand is no different in other parts of Asia.

This reality of folk religions and strong belief in the supernatural and evil forces could be addressed through the careful reading of the NT. The power encounters in the Gospels and Acts are excellent places to begin exploring biblical teachings on demonic forces, exorcisms, and power encounters. This allows us to read the reality of the miracles of Jesus and the purpose and functions of the supernatural and miracles in the NT not merely as historical accounts but as power encounters with the forces of darkness. It is unfortunate that miracles and exorcisms have been downplayed in the West as a result of the Enlightenment, followed by the demythologizing of miracles as championed by Rudolf Bultmann, a German NT scholar.[42]

40 See Paul G. Hiebert, R. Daniel Shaw, and Tite Tiénou, *Understanding Folk Religion: A Christian Response to Popular Beliefs and Practices* (Grand Rapids, MI: Baker Academic, 2000).

41 Scott W. Sunquist, *Explorations in Asian Christianity: History, Theology, and Mission* (Downers Grove, IL: IVP Academic, 2017), 145.

42 Rudolf Bultmann, *New Testament and Mythology and Other Basic Writings*, trans. Schubert M. Ogden (Philadelphia: Fortress, 1984), 1–44.

In the Greco-Roman world, magic was a popular expression of human relations with the powers of the universe. Superstitions, sorcery, use of amulets, formulas for healing and cursing, and divination were some of the common expressions. In Samaria, Philip encountered Simon the magician, known as someone who had the power of God and was called great by the locals who were mesmerized by his power of magic (Acts 8:9–24). During their first missionary journey, Paul and Barnabas encountered magicians in Paphos, which was the seat of the worship of Aphrodite (Acts 13:4–12). In Ephesus, those who practiced magic burned their books worth fifty thousand pieces of silver (Acts 19:19). Magic and divination, exorcisms, and encountering the evil and unclean spirits are also a reality in Asia as well.[43] In this respect, Paul's exhortation on how to respond to spiritual warfare by putting on the whole armor of God (Eph 6:10–16) can also be applied. Finally, fortune telling and divination, especially in Chinese and East Asian culture, also affect our understanding of prophecy in the NT, especially in Paul's letter to the Corinthians (1 Cor 12–14).

These passages in the NT are examples of how our God is far more powerful than all the evil forces and power of magic. They can be used to prepare believers in Asia to encounter and confront the forces of evil in the proclamation of the gospel. We are comforted that the power of the gospel delivers all of us from all evil spirits and breaks all chains of bondage.

Religious Rites

As part of religious practices, rituals and rites are important in Asia. Chinese ancestral worship, lighting of joss sticks, and offering worship daily to honor the patron deities of the family are common scenes in many traditional homes and businesses in Malaysia. Initiation rites such as the *upanayana*, the sacred thread ceremony among the Hindu communities confirming that boys are now ready to take on religious responsibility, are significant. In this respect, Asian communities take seriously religious rituals and rites. This can be an excellent entry point to consider the importance of baptism and confirmation as initiation rites of admitting one into the Christian community. Reading the NT in light of the familiarity of an initiation rite could cast deep significance

43 A. Scott Moreau et al., eds., *Deliver Us from Evil: An Uneasy Frontier in Christian Mission* (Morovia: MARC, 2002).

as a turning point in a person's life, drawing rich meaning on turning from the old to the new and from death to life (1 Cor 6:11; Rom 6:4; Col 2:2; see also 2 Cor 5:17)—a symbolic death with Christ and rising with Christ.

As in all initiation rites in an Asian context, baptism or confirmation is a communal event in the Greco-Roman world, and Asian readers will appreciate the significance of this event as a decisive point of entry into a community where new identity formation as Christians takes place. James Dunn reinforces this when he suggests that baptism is an "initiation rite, a rite marking the baptisand's transfer into a new grouping, a new sect, a sect marked by a committed discipleship of Jesus."[44] The rite of baptism, according to Dunn, was also used in "group formation and boundary marking which was in due course to result in Christianity's distinct and separate identity among the religions of antiquity."[45] For many first-generation believers in Asia, baptism often marks a significant turning point in one's spiritual life where one has to abandon all deities previously worshipped and other associated religious acts practiced. It is not uncommon to see many first-generation Chinese believers in Malaysia removing and destroying all religious altars with statues representing different deities when they come to faith.

The celebration of Eucharist, properly understood, can hold deep significance for many of us in Asia. In early Pauline communities, Eucharist was celebrated as part of a love feast. According to 1 Corinthians 11:17–34, Paul advocates for unity in addressing the problems surrounding divisions in the assembly in Corinth. Paul insists that the Eucharist should be celebrated as a common meal where all needs are cared for—those who were hungry should eat in their homes first (addressing the rich and elite because they were the ones who had homes), and everyone should wait for all to be present before the meal was served. In this regard, the egalitarian treatment of one another is accepted.[46] Festive meals were a common feature not only of the life of voluntary associations in the Greco-Roman world but also among Asians, where food seems to unite and feature prominently in our communal life. As a rite of solidarity, the Eucharist is celebrated not merely as a symbol of remembrance as practiced in some of our tradition, particularly among the reformed and

44 James D. G. Dunn, *Beginning from Jerusalem*, Christianity in the Making 2 (Grand Rapids, MI: Eerdmans, 2009), 189.

45 Dunn, 189.

46 See Lim, *Metaphors and Social Identity Formation*, 179–87.

evangelical circles, but also as an expression of our unity in Christ and with one another as well. Social class distinctions that are common in Asia are obliterated when we come to the table of the Lord, and the two acts of breaking of bread and drinking of the cup to commemorate the death of Jesus are central in this ritual that unites the entire community and the eschatological expectation of the Lord's return.

CONCLUSION

Reading the NT from the sociocultural and religious realities of Asia is my initial and humble attempt to bring some awareness to how as Asians, we can appropriate our roots and heritage and weave them carefully into reading and understanding the text because there are many similarities between the Mediterranean world and our context. By doing so, we can explore how this reading brings us closer to the world of the NT and better understand how the first recipients would have heard and understood the text. In this essay, I have looked at some of the similar sociocultural and religious norms and practices, and I hope the result is a reflection of how this attempt can bring fresh insights to understanding and teaching the NT in the church today. At the same time, I also hope that an Asian reading of the NT will open up further discussion on how we can reflect on the message of Scripture and how we may learn from each other as followers of Jesus Christ.

FURTHER READING

Baily, K. E. 2008. *Jesus through Middle Eastern Eyes: Cultural Studies in the Gospels*. London: SPCK.

Chan, S. 2014. *Grassroots Asian Theology: Thinking the Faith from the Ground Up*. Downers Grove, IL: IVP Academic.

Gener, T. D., and S. T. Pardue, eds. 2019. *Asian Christian Theology: Evangelical Perspectives*. Carlisle, UK: Langham Global Library.

Georges, J., and M. D. Baker. 2016. *Ministering in Honor-Shame Cultures: Biblical Foundations and Practical Essentials*. Downers Grove, IL: IVP Academic.

Hiebert, P. G., R. D. Shaw, and T. Tiénou. 2000. *Understanding Folk Religion: A Christian Response to Popular Beliefs and Practices*. Grand Rapids, MI: Baker Academic.

Hwa, Y. 2014. *Mangoes or Bananas? The Quest of an Authentic Asian Theology*. 2nd ed. Oxford: Regnum.

Jesudason, P., and R. Rajkumar, eds. 2012. *Asian Theology on the Way: Christianity, Culture and Context*. London: SPCK.

Loh I-to. 2011. *Hymnal Companion to Sound the Bamboo: Asian Hymns in Their Cultural and Liturgical Contexts*. Chicago: GIA.

Low, T. H., ed. 2014. *What Young Asian Theologians Are Thinking*. Singapore: Trinity Theological College.

Yeh, A., and T. Tiénou, eds. 2018. *Majority World Theologies: Theologizing from Africa, Asia, Latin America, and the Ends of the Earth*. Evangelical Missiological Society Series 26. Littleton, CO: William Carey.

Yeo, K. K. 2018. *What Has Jerusalem to Do with Beijing? Biblical Interpretation from a Chinese Perspective*. 20th anniversary ed. Eugene, OR: Pickwick.

TWO

An Introduction to Asian Biblical Hermeneutics

Yung Suk Kim
Virginia Union University
Richmond, Virginia, USA

Today, about 60 percent of the total world population live in Asia, and some of the world religions that originated in this area include Buddhism, Taoism, Confucianism, Hinduism, Christianity, and Islam.[1] Asians have never been a homogenous group but have long maintained a rich tradition of culture and religion. However, into this vital area of religious and cultural diversity, Christianity was reintroduced by Western forces with their unique theological interpretation that dominated churches and Christian schools. Now this longtime dominance is dwindling, and a new paradigm of interpretation is gaining strength in Asia and in the world.[2] This new paradigm involves a critical and contextual reading of the Scriptures in the contexts of the readers. We may read familiar texts in a new way from our Asian context without mimicking Western interpretations.

1 See Daniel Patte, ed., *The Cambridge Dictionary of Christianity* (New York: Cambridge University Press, 2010).

2 In terms of theory about contextual biblical interpretation, see Cristina Grenholm and Daniel Patte, "Overture: Reception, Critical Interpretations, and Scriptural Criticism," in *Reading Israel in Romans: Legitimacy and Plausibility of Divergent Interpretations*, ed. Cristina Grenholm and Daniel Patte (Harrisburg, PA: Trinity International, 2000), 1:1–54.

WHAT DOES IT MEAN TO READ THE NT AS ASIANS?

There is no objective, value-free, neutral interpretation, and any biblical interpretation involves asking readers the following questions: first, why they read; second, how they read; and third, what they read.[3] Regarding why they read, the assumption is that every reader has a purpose in reading the text. While some may have an interest in devotional reading, others read the text to gain insights into matters of social justice or human liberation. The purpose of reading is decided by several factors concerning the reader: social location, personal experience, life agenda, and worldview.

Depending on the purpose of reading, methods of interpretation may be decided. This is the question of how they read—that is, how they treat the text. Indeed, in an academic context, there are myriad ways to approach the text. First, the text may be treated as a historical document through which we can reconstruct ancient social realities. For example, the Gospel of Matthew helps us understand the nature and struggle of the Matthean community in conflict with mainline Judaism or imperial power. But the caution is that even in this historical reading, any interpretation is framed by readers who make choices about their interpretation. Therefore, we have to determine with whose social realities we are dealing. Whereas some may focus on Matthew's salvation history from a traditional theological perspective, others may have more interest in the community's identity struggle under the Roman Empire. Still others may look into the community's conflict with the Jewish synagogue authorities.

In other words, even the historical-critical approach is perspectival. So we must recognize the inevitable partial reading of this approach and should not treat any one particular reading as absolute. Otherwise, a certain normative reading may lead to the exclusion of others. For example, the normative reading of the Pastoral Letters is that women are not allowed to be ordained (see 1 Tim 2:11–15). But because there are several competing voices in the text, the question arises, Which reading should the reader take? The pastor's position in these letters is to not allow women's ordination because a contemporary household

3 See Yung Suk Kim, *Biblical Interpretation: Theory, Process, and Criteria* (Eugene, OR: Pickwick, 2013), 1–44.

code was adopted in the church.[4] But women in the church had a different view—namely, that they were also equal recipients of the Spirit. In fact, in the early church, as reflected in 1 Corinthians 11:5, women actively participated in church, and some of them were ministers (e.g., Phoebe, in Rom 16:1). But as time went by, Paul's egalitarianism faded out. Therefore, any interpretation regarding women's ordination must consider the previously mentioned competing voices within the text.

Second, the text is more than referential language. It can be read as story, as in a narrative reading of the Scriptures. This dimension of a text cannot be ignored, but the problem is that a gap exists between the historical reality and the story world. In such a case, interpreters should know the difference between history and story. For example, there are discrepancies in relation to the day of Jesus's crucifixion in the gospel story. In the Gospel of John, Jesus does not eat the Passover meal because he is a paschal lamb and is crucified before the day of preparation. In the Synoptic Gospels, Jesus eats the last meal, which is the Passover meal, and dies after Passover. Which account is correct? Or are both of them incorrect? When we read the Gospels as story, what can we say about the historical Jesus? Asian readers need to distinguish the historical Jesus from the gospel traditions. Although the gospel account is not the same as the historical Jesus, readers can still appreciate the gospel story because it contains important information about the historical Jesus. At the same time, they may learn to appreciate each gospel's faith story in itself.[5]

Third, the text is more than story. It involves the reader's engagement. Here the dictum is that there is no meaning without the reader. Typically, reader-response criticism is included in this approach, but broadly speaking, all contextual readings, including feminist or postcolonial approaches, are examples of this approach to the text. From this perspective, readers are not merely meaning-takers but meaning-producers. They may bring to the text their hermeneutical lenses or life experiences. But this does not mean that they can

4 These codes are found in the deuteropauline and Pastoral letters, which are considered not written by Paul: Col 3:18–4:1; Eph 5:21–6:9; and 1 Tim 6:1–2. Household codes also appear in 1 Pet 2:18–3:7.

5 See Mark Allan Powell, *Fortress Introduction to the Gospels* (Minneapolis: Fortress, 2019), 57–217.

make any meaning out of the text or out of context. This approach empowers Asian readers to engage fully with the text in their contexts. For example, Asian readers may take the Lord's Supper seriously and expand its meaning to include and invite all the poor to the table. In other words, the Eucharist would be incomplete without a sense of solidarity with the marginalized in society.

Regarding what they read, we see the importance of hermeneutical choices in interpretation. Even the same text or topic in the NT can be interpreted another way because of the different hermeneutical choices made. For example, Jesus's crucifixion in Mark involves a few interpretive perspectives. Some people may focus on Jesus's love of God and humanity, but others take seriously injustice and the problem of evil in his tragic death. Still others may focus on his bold proclamation of God's reign and his righteousness. In this regard, his death is the result of his radical proclamation of God's rule, not Rome's rule. Obviously, the NT does not give us a single view of Jesus's death. Whereas Hebrews thinks of Jesus's death as sin-sacrifice (e.g., Heb 10:12), the Synoptic Gospels tell us that he was brought to death because of his seemingly dangerous words about and deeds for God's rule. Paul's undisputed letters also seem to emphasize Jesus's moral sacrifice, which is the result of his work of God—that is, revealing God's righteousness to the world (see Rom 3:21–26).

The bottom line is that biblical texts are not self-revealing, and we must interpret them carefully, faithfully, and diversely. Asian readers can make a difference in interpreting the NT because they can bring different theological concerns or choices to the text. For example, we may appreciate Paul's metaphor of the body of Christ to emphasize not so much unity (*homonoia*) but rather union or solidarity. According to the Western rhetorical reading, unity is emphasized. But we can see Paul emphasizing diversity or solidarity within the community. The point is not that all in the church are one but that all are united with Christ, following the way of Jesus. In the next sections, we will explore how Asians can read the NT differently and what they may read or emphasize in the text.

HOW CAN WE READ THE NT AS ASIANS?

In this section, we will seek to answer the question regarding what it means to read the NT as Asians. In what sense do Asians read the NT differently? Among other things, we can think of three distinctive approaches to the NT: reading intertextually, reading interculturally, and reading intercontextually.

Reading Intertextually

Reading intertextually means Asians may read the NT with Asian texts, whether classical or modern. For example, we can read the parables of Jesus with the Dao De Jing (The Book of the Way and Virtue), which is a classical wisdom book from ancient China. Jesus's parables may be understood clearer with the Dao De Jing, which deconstructs the conventional wisdom of the world. Just as Jesus deals with everyday life through parabolic, deconstructive language, the Dao De Jing does the same and raises critical questions about everyday life: What is an ideal life? What is the meaning of life here? What can we do as we seek an ideal life in the community? Key themes or perspectives of the Dao De Jing may be summarized as follows:[6]

Wisdom/Enlightenment

- Zì zhī zhě míng: "Those who know themselves are enlightened" (Dao De Jing 33). Those who know others are called clever, but those who know themselves are wise or enlightened.
- Jiàn xiǎo yuē míng: "To see small is enlightenment" (52). Often we do not see great potential in smallness. All beginnings are small. "The tallest tree begins as a tiny sprout. A nine-story tower begins with one shovel of dirt. A journey of a thousand miles starts with a single step" (64).
- Tóng qí chén: "Become one with the dust" (4, 56). Dust is a metaphor or metonymy that represents a small thing. People must know they are small.
- Fǎn zhě dào zhī dòng: "To return is the movement of the Way" (40). To what must people return? It is the sense of smallness or dust. Interestingly, the idea of returning echoes the Hebrew verb *shub* ("to turn back") and the Greek verb *metanoeō* ("to change a mind").

Strength

- Zì shèng zhě jiàng: "The wise conquer themselves and therefore they are strong" (33). Those who conquer others are forceful, but those who conquer

6 Yung Suk Kim, *Reading Jesus' Parables with Dao De Jing: Appendix: A New Translation of the Dao De Jing* (Eugene, OR: Resource, 2018), 2–3.

themselves are strong. These people are supposed to be weak or soft like water.

- Shǒu róu yuē jiàng: "To keep softness is strength" (52). In the Dao De Jing, the ideal way of life is to be like water, which is soft (chs. 3–4, 10, 36, 43, 52, 55–56, 58, 76, 78) and weak (chs. 29, 36, 55, 76, 78). A virtuous person is like a newborn infant whose bones are soft and whose muscles are weak, yet their grip is secure.
- Shǎng shàn ruò shuǐ: "Water is the best thing in the world" (8). Water does not compete with things in the world; rather, it flows to lower places such as rivers and seas. Simply, water is humble and serves all.
- Ruò zhě dào zhī yòng: "To be soft or weak is the function of the Way" (40). Water is soft or weak, and therefore, it is very useful. If water is hard, it is useless. This idea may apply to the human world.

Impartiality

- Tiān dì bù rén: "Heaven and earth are impartial" (5). Heaven is vast and empty; it does not seek its own will but does great works for all. Like a bellows, what is empty inside can produce more than what is filled.

Reversal

- Dà zhí ruò qū: "What is most straight seems devious" (45). Dao De Jing 77 has a similar saying: "The Way of heaven reduces what is excessive and supplements what is insufficient. The humanistic way is different. It reduces the insufficient and increases the excessive."

Comparing all the above themes with Jesus's parables is beyond the purview of this chapter. Instead, we will see the theme of impartiality, which is found in Dao De Jing 5 and 7:

> Heaven and earth are impartial. They treat all things as straw dogs. The wise are also impartial. They treat people as straw dogs. Heaven and earth are like a bellows. While empty, it is never exhausted. The more it is worked, the more it produces. Much talk counts little. Keep focused on the inside of you. (Dao De Jing 5)

> Heaven and earth are big, lasting long because they do not live for themselves. The wise put themselves behind; therefore, they

advance. Giving up themselves, they find themselves. Giving up selfish desire, they fulfill themselves. (Dao De Jing 7)

The central theme of Dao De Jing 5 is "Heaven and earth are impartial to all" (*tiān dì bù rén*). Heaven is impartial and treats all the same. Nobody can avoid natural disasters, and the sun shines upon all. The wind blows to all, big and small houses, plazas and streets. It favors nothing. Earth is also impartial. The conditions of the earth are the same for all people.

Jesus also talks about the impartiality of God's reign or rule. The most important feature of God's reign is that God is impartial toward humanity. Jesus says, "God makes his sun rise on the evil and on the good, and sends rain on the righteous and on the unrighteous" (Matt 5:45). Jesus infuses his parables with this theme of impartiality. For example, God's mercy and his opportunities are given to all, and this idea is widely seen in the following parables: Seed Growing Secretly (Mark 4:26–29), Mustard Seed (Mark 4:30–31), Wheat and Weed (Matt 13:24–30), Vineyard Laborers (Matt 20:1–16), and Father and Two Sons (Luke 15:11–32).[7] Among these parables, the parable of the Sower (Mark 4:3–8) stands out, as we may readily recognize the sower's impartial work. He scatters seeds profusely to a wider area he may find. He does not choose which lot to sow. He takes a risk of losing or wasting some seeds. In fact, some fall on the path, on the rocky ground, and among the thorns. But this is not the end of his work; he will plow the land after sowing. Therefore, the implication is that taking care of seeds and the ground is important. Sowing is not the end, and it is an important beginning that leads to plowing and eventual harvest. This sower resembles the character of God that Jesus emphasizes in Matthew 5:45.

Reading intertextually can be done with other classical texts of Asia, as K. K. Yeo reads 1 Corinthians through Zhuangzi in "Pauline Theological Counseling of Love in the Language of the *Zhuangzi*: A Reading of Love in 1 Corinthians in a Chinese Philosophical Context."[8] Yeo relates Paul's love in 1 Corinthians to the Chinese reading of love in Zhuangzi. His point is that Paul's love is well understood through the lens of Zhuangzi. Both Paul and

7 For more, see my *Jesus's Truth: Life in Parables* (Eugene, OR: Resource, 2018), 17–95.

8 K. K. Yeo, "Pauline Theological Counseling of Love in the Language of the *Zhuangzi*: A Reading of Love in 1 Corinthians in a Chinese Philosophical Context," in *1 and 2 Corinthians*, ed. Yung Suk Kim (Minneapolis: Fortress, 2013), 117–28.

Zhuangzi find the importance of selfless communal spirit rather than self-centered pride.

Reading Interculturally

Reading interculturally means Asian readers can bring to the text their cultural values or perspectives. In the Asian context, community is very important and can be used as a primary lens in reading the text. In Asian culture, the concept of human may be different from Western individualism.[9] For example, in Confucianism, the human is expressed with *ren*, which means "humaneness" or "relational love in community." No person can live apart from a community. With this communal perspective, along with other Asian values, we can read NT texts differently. For example, Matthew 6:25–34 can be well illuminated through this perspective.[10] If people strive for God's reign, there will be abundance in the community that all can share. In other words, the true blessing of God requires a community of people that seeks God's rule in their midst. Similarly, we may read the parable of the Vineyard Laborers (Matt 20:1–16) differently from the perspective of the community. Here the point is not that some laborers worked harder or longer than others but that they all need the usual daily wage. The landlord is concerned with the whole community and all the workers in his vineyard. This is a matter of economic justice.[11] We may read the parable of Father and Two Sons (Luke 15:11–32) too differently from the perspective of family and community. The point of the parable is not who is right or who is wrong. What is more important in the family is not to judge each other but to have reconciliation and peace. The father in the parable does not favor either son, and his wish is to restore the family from a potential dysfunction. He believes that justice can be established after love and mercy.

9 See Robert Bellah, *Habits of the Heart* (New York: Harper & Row, 1985), 37. He goes on to say, "Such folk owe no man anything and hardly expect anything from anybody. They form the habit of thinking of themselves in isolation and imagine that their whole destiny is in their hands."

10 Yung Suk Kim, "Rereading *Basileia* and *Dikaiosyne* from a Communal Perspective in a Korean and African-American Context (Matthew 6:25–34)," SBL Annual Meeting, November 18–21, 2017.

11 Yung Suk Kim, "Justice Matters, but Which Justice? In the Case of Jesus's Parables," *Currents in Theology and Mission* 46, no. 2 (2019): 41–43.

We can also think of another way of intercultural reading in view of honor-and-shame culture. Indeed, this culture is found everywhere throughout history and is not unique to Asia. The NT texts may be read through this lens, and we may better understand them because of that lens. In other words, in this culture of honor and shame, people live by honor and die with shame. Honor is a sense of worthiness in one's life; it may come from family tradition, one's social status, or one's achievements. In this culture, shame is the opposite of honor, and those who do not have a sense of honor according to the norms of society are ignored and considered nobodies. But the most honorable and perfect character in the Bible is God, who honors the most despised in the society. This is a reversal of the culture of honor and shame, as Paul makes clear when writing to the Corinthian *ekklesia* in 1 Corinthians 1:26–30, the most radical version of the Christian gospel:

> Consider your own call, brothers and sisters: not many of you were wise by human standards, not many were powerful, not many were of noble birth. But God chose what is foolish in the world to shame the wise; God chose what is weak in the world to shame the strong; God chose what is low and despised in the world, things that are not, to reduce to nothing that are, so that no one might boast in the presence of God. He is the source of your life in Christ Jesus, who became for us wisdom from God, and righteousness and sanctification and redemption.

Paul reverses a culture of honor and shame through the love of God. Jesus was shamed when he did God's work of righteousness for the poor and the weak. He was crucified because of that, but God made him live again and honored him (2 Cor 13:4; see Phil 2:6–11).

Reading Intercontextually

Reading intercontextually involves bringing Asian contexts to bear on the text. For example, Ma. Marilou Ibita interprets the Lord's Supper in 1 Corinthians from a Filipino Christian context in an essay titled "A Conversation with the Story of the Lord's Supper in 1 Corinthians 11:17–34: Engaging the Scripture

Text and the Filipino Christians' Context."[12] Ibita finds community divisions at the Lord's Supper in Corinth and critiques the lack of mutual care, growth, unity, and shared identity. Then she connects the story of the Lord's Supper at Corinth to that of meal culture in the lowland Filipino context. She argues that the Lord's Supper and meal culture should go hand in hand. Participants must find mutual care and support, extending this ritual and meal culture to the poor and hungry.

Menghun Goh also reads the text intercontextually in an essay titled "The Issue of *Eidōlothyta*: An Inter(con)textual Interpretation of 1 Corinthians 8:1–11:1 and Chinese Ancestor Veneration."[13] Goh examines the issue of food offered to idols in Corinth and argues that the issue is not food but the strong people's uncaring mind for the weak. As Paul embraces the spirit of mutual care in the Corinthian assembly, Chinese Christians find a symbolic space of unity and solidarity through the ritual of ancestor veneration.

Such examples of intercontextual reading abound in Asia, as Asian readers need to address various issues about justice, liberation, and human rights.[14] Dalit theology in India deals with the exploitation of the most vulnerable, and in the 1970s and 1980s, Minjung theology was developed in Korea and dealt with the liberation of the poor and weak in society. Asian readers must continue reading the text intercontextually, addressing not only the context of the NT but also their context today as they deal with so many issues in their communities and society.

WHAT CAN WE READ IN THE NT AS ASIANS?

By giving due importance to contextual concerns in the Asian context and looking at the text through an Asian hermeneutical lens, we can make a

12 Ma. Marilou Ibita, "A Conversation with the Story of the Lord's Supper in 1 Corinthians 11:17–34: Engaging the Scripture Text and the Filipino Christians' Context," in *1 and 2 Corinthians*, ed. Yung Suk Kim (Minneapolis: Fortress, 2013), 97–114.

13 Menghun Goh, "The Issue of *Eidōlothyta*: An Inter(con)textual Interpretation of 1 Corinthians 8:1–11:1 and Chinese Ancestor Veneration," in *1 and 2 Corinthians*, ed. Yung Suk Kim (Minneapolis: Fortress, 2013), 79–96.

14 R. S. Sugirtharajah, ed., *Voices from the Margin: Interpreting the Bible in the Third World* (Maryknoll, NY: Orbis, 2006).

difference in NT interpretation. To illustrate this point, we will examine the following texts: Matthew 6:25–34; 20:1–16; Luke 15:11–32; and John 14:6. These texts have been interpreted mainly either from a Western cultural perspective or from an individualistic pietistic perspective. Before we go into each of these texts, let me make some brief observations about them. Matthew 6:25–34 has been interpreted on the basis of individualistic faith or pietism, and the usual lesson is the priority of faith over other secular work. But if seen from a communal perspective, the meaning of this passage changes. What Jesus really comments on is not a person's pietistic faith but their communal faith that seeks God's rule and his righteousness. Matthew 20:1–16 ("The Vineyard Laborers") may also be reinterpreted from the perspective of community or justice.[15] Luke 15:11–34 ("Father and Two Sons") may also be read from the perspective of community or family.[16] John 14:6 has been read through the lens of high Christology and as an exclusive statement about salvation. But through the communal perspective of true love rooted in Jesus's work, this verse gives us a whole lot of new meaning. That is, we need to extend the rule of God to all in the world, as Jesus does.[17]

Matthew 6:25–34

Matthew 6:25–34 is often read through the eyes of individualistic pietism or eschatology.[18] In this reading, one is blessed with all things if one strives for God's kingdom or his righteousness (6:33).[19] Interestingly, some modern English translations reflect this tendency of individualism with subheadings such as "Care and Anxiety" (RSV) or "Do Not Worry" (NRSV and NIV). But if we read 6:25–34 from the perspective of the community, the point is not how one can be blessed but how one can live according to the rule of God

15 Kim, *Jesus's Truth*, 55–63.

16 Kim, 82–95.

17 Yung Suk Kim, *Truth, Testimony, and Transformation: A New Reading of the "I Am" Sayings of Jesus in the Fourth Gospel* (Eugene, OR: Cascade, 2014).

18 Bruce Chilton, ed., *The Kingdom of God in the Teaching of Jesus* (Philadelphia: Fortress, 1984); W. Willis, ed., *The Kingdom of God in 20th Century Interpretation* (Peabody, MA: Hendrickson, 1987); M. Eugene Boring, "Matthew," in *The New Interpreter's Bible*, ed. Leander Keck et al. (Nashville: Abingdon, 1995), 8:211.

19 See W. D. Davies and Dale C. Allison, *Matthew* (Edinburgh: T&T Clark, 1988), 1:659–63. For them, 6:33a is a condition of now, and 6:33b is the result in the future.

or God's righteousness. If there is God's rule in place in the community, all things will be available to all. With this community perspective, we can find a chiasm in 6:25–34:

A Do not worry about your life (v. 25)

- ***B*** Look at God's creation (v. 26–32)
  - *x* The birds of the air and the lilies of the field do not strive; they are taken care of by God (v. 26–31)
  - *x′* The gentiles strive for all these things: what to eat, what to drink, or what to wear (v. 32)
    - ***C*** But strive for God's kingdom and his righteousness (v. 33a)
- ***B′*** Look at God's reign in which "all these things will proceed to you" (v. 33b)

A′ Do not worry about tomorrow (v. 34)

In *A* (v. 25), Jesus asks his disciples not to worry about their lives. On the one hand, worrying about their lives seems natural or necessary because they have to survive in a harsh, competitive world. But on the other hand, worrying about their own lives may cause excessive competition with one another and ruin the well-being of the community. Then in *B* (v. 26–32), Jesus talks about God's creation, where there are two different ways of living. First, birds and lilies do not strive, and yet God takes care of them (v. 26–31, *x*). Second, the gentiles strive for all these things: "what to eat, what to drink, and what to wear," which means a greedy pursuit of wealth and power (v. 32, *x′*).

Then the solution is found in *C* (v. 33a): "But strive for God's kingdom and his righteousness." If people seek God's rule or God's way and righteousness, there will be justice and peace. Seeking God's rule means to change one's mind toward God and share what one has with others. Here *basileia tou theou* (often translated as "the kingdom of God") means not a territorial space or a future eschatological kingdom but God's reign or rule in the here and now. It is God's rule that humans must follow. Then we have "all these things will proceed to you" (*B′*, v. 33b). That is, people may live abundantly without fighting or striving for all these things. Therefore, worrying about tomorrow is not necessary (*A′*, v. 34). Each day, people have to live by the grace of God, taking care of others who do not have enough for the day. The problem is, they seek more than what they need. Jesus teaches about this: "Thy kingdom [or rule] come . . . give us this day our daily bread" (6:10–11). As we saw from the Dao De Jing, we Asians need to take this wisdom book seriously and cultivate the virtue of a simple mind so we may find peace within ourselves by caring for others. In Asian literature and culture, we may find resources and virtues about "simple, happy life" in community.

Matthew 20:1–16

The parable of the Vineyard Laborers can be understood well from the perspective of community or that of economic justice for all.[20] The landowner is very much concerned with full employment and stable income for all the workers. Because of these concerns, he goes out to hire workers not one time but five times, and he sends all of them to his vineyard. He promises to pay the usual daily wage or "what is just" to all of them because he knows that they all need their daily food. Those who are hired late are not lazy people; they are employed very late because no one hired them early enough. At pay time, the employer's manager pays all the workers the same amount, one denarius, which is the usual daily wage. Those who were hired early complain to the employer because they expected to receive more; they are not satisfied with the usual daily wage that was promised by the employer. They do not see the need of others—those who joined the vineyard late.

In our communal reading, the landowner did the right thing. Unlike the everyday employer in society, he takes care of all of them equally. To those who complain against him, he argues he is *agathos* (20:15), which is translated as "generous" in many of the English Bibles (NRSV, NIV, and NAS). But from the perspective of economic justice, a better translation would be "good" because his point is not simply about generosity but about justice for all.[21] The landowner insists that he is good because he cares about all who need work and the daily wage. He is good because he cares about distributive justice (or economic justice for all).[22] He is good because he cares about full employment and makes sure that all workers will get daily food. Otherwise, this parable

20 Kim, *Jesus's Truth*, 55–63.

21 In Mark 10:18, Jesus rebukes a person for calling him "good" (*agathos*) because God is the only one who is good.

22 Kim, "Justice Matters," 41–43.

is not about attributive justice, in which the logic is, "The more one works, the more one is paid." This view is held by those who argue that the landlord abused the early comers by not paying enough or more than the rest. But this is not the case. First, there is no guarantee that the early comers worked harder than the latecomers. Moreover, they agreed to work for the usual daily wage, which is not too much or too little. Their grumbling against the landlord does not stand ground. Finally, the vineyard owner says, "Am I not allowed to do what I choose with what belongs to me? Or are you envious because I am good [*agathos*; Matt 20:15]?" Unfortunately, the NRSV, NIV, and CEB, and most of the English Bibles, translate *agathos* as "generous," which connotes a sense of charity, defending the landlord's wealth or power. Generosity is not the same as justice. The landowner's perspective is very different from typical masters in society.[23] He has an impartial perspective toward all workers in his vineyard regardless of what time they joined his vineyard. He thinks all workers need equal pay to support their families. In other words, his simple perspective is justice for all. This kind of justice is called distributive justice.[24]

Luke 15:11–32

The parable is typically interpreted allegorically, relating the father to God, the older son to the Pharisees or Jews, and the younger son to gentile sinners who repent. But this parable is about a dysfunctional family that struggles and needs reconciliation.[25] In the family, the goal is not to judge who is right and who is wrong but to seek a loving family for all members. Because this parable is open-ended, readers have to wonder about the remaining process or time of reconciliation after the younger son returns home.

The main character is the father whose heart was broken and weak due to his younger son's immature behavior. He appears to be mother-like and has a weak image throughout the story. He waits for his son outside his house and hugs and kisses him upon his return. The father's response to his son may be seen as weak and soft. He behaves very unconventionally and risks his honor as a typical father in a village. All he wants is to restore the family;

23 See David Buttrick, *Speaking Parables: A Homiletic Guide* (Louisville: WJKP, 2000), 114.

24 The landowner's perspective may be understood better through "dà zhí ruò qū" in Dao De Jing 45: "What is most straight seems devious."

25 Kim, *Jesus's Truth*, 82–95.

justice can be done after that. The problem of the older brother is that he has a "hard" heart. He does not understand why his father has prepared a feast for his younger brother. The father responds to his older son, "For this *your brother* was dead, and is alive; he was lost, and is found" (Luke 15:32; emphasis mine). Certainly, the older brother's view is not wrong because justice for him is also important. If someone does wrong, they must be punished. He hardly understands his younger brother's immature action of betraying his family and wasting the family's property. So the older son serves as a prosecutor to his family. The only thing he lacks is a soft heart that welcomes his younger brother first, as the father does. The priority is not to punish but to welcome him and have reconciliation in the family. In other words, mercy or love go first, and justice can be done after that. The father welcomes his son not because he repented or did a good thing. Even before his son came back, the father was ready to accept him because he had unconditional love for him.

John 14:6

Often John 14:6 is read as an exclusive statement about Christianity.[26] Does Jesus really mean that Christianity is the only way of salvation? I grew up in a typical countryside in Korea and with a typical Protestant culture, so I was taught all other religions are not the way of salvation. But my critical rereading of John's Gospel in its historical context has led me to a new reading of the "I am" sayings of Jesus. That is, the Johannine community is not a triumphant community but a small, struggling community that deals with their separation from the Jewish synagogue. In this context, the Johannine Jesus comforts them by saying, "Do not let your hearts be troubled. Believe in God, believe also in me" (John 14:1).

From this historical context of the Johannine community, Jesus's saying "I am the way, the truth, and the life" (John 14:6) is a word of encouragement to the members of the community. He tells them to keep following the way he lived, testifying to the truth, and living abundantly in him. Otherwise, he does not mean to conquer other non-Christian people by the gospel. If we find Jesus's love and truth testimony from his word, what he really says is the command of love, as God loves the world so much (John 3:16). Therefore, in a multireligious context throughout Asia, what Christians have to do is not

26 Kim, *Truth, Testimony, and Transformation*, 47–55.

to separate themselves from others, judge them, or conquer them with the gospel but to love them without conditions. If we read John 14 this way, we actually hear "a voice of inclusivism rather than exclusivism, solidarity rather than marginalization, and liberation rather than oppression."[27]

CONCLUSION

Asian readers may read the NT differently because of their different contexts and different hermeneutical choices (reading lenses). Different contexts and different reading choices are important, but we also have to know that our interpretation is very limited and contextual. This means we need to be humble and keep alert through diligent study and self-examination. We must be aware of the diverse communities and cultures within Asia. So we need to ensure that no one context or perspective dominates our interpretation. In the end, good interpretation needs critical analysis of the self, the community, and the text. Often we forget why we read the Scriptures or who we are individually and communally. Good interpretation also needs a balance between the reader and the text. Even good reading should be tested by a group of readers or the community of readers. Asian readers also must engage in the global context where they can read along with other people in other cultures, standing in solidarity with them. In this way, we may strengthen our faith and deepen our relationships with them.

FURTHER READING

Buttrick, D. 2000. *Speaking Parables: A Homiletic Guide*. Louisville: WJKP.

Chilton B., ed. 1984. *The Kingdom of God in the Teaching of Jesus*. Philadelphia: Fortress.

Ibita, M. M. 2013. "A Conversation with the Story of the Lord's Supper in 1 Corinthians 11:17–34: Engaging the Scripture Text and the Filipino Christians' Context." In *1 and 2 Corinthians*, edited by Yung Suk Kim, 97–114. Minneapolis: Fortress.

27 Kim, ix.

Kim, Y. S. 2013. *Biblical Interpretation: Theory, Process, and Criteria*. Eugene, OR: Pickwick.

———. 2014. *Truth, Testimony, and Transformation: A New Reading of the "I Am" Sayings of Jesus in the Fourth Gospel*. Eugene, OR: Cascade.

———. 2018. *Reading Jesus' Parables with Dao De Jing: Appendix: A New Translation of the Dao De Jing*. Eugene, OR: Resource.

Segovia, F. 2000. *Reading from This Place*. Vol. 2, Social Location and Biblical Interpretation in Global Perspective. Minneapolis: Fortress.

Smith, M. J., and Y. S. Kim. 2018. *Toward Decentering the New Testament: A Reintroduction*. Eugene, OR: Cascade.

Sugirtharajah, R. S., ed. 2006. *Voices from the Margin: Interpreting the Bible in the Third World*. Maryknoll, NY: Orbis.

THREE

The Gospel of Matthew

Jae Hyung Cho
Korea Christian University
Seoul, South Korea

The Gospel of Matthew acquired prominence as the book of the Church in the early Christian period itself, and it was regarded as first in its significance. Although modern scholars have started studying the Gospels based on the priority of the Gospel of Mark, the rich heritage and content of Matthew constitute an important part of the Christian faith. Without Matthew, we cannot imagine four sexually immoral foreign women being included in Jesus's genealogy, the visit of the magi, the ongoing validity of the Mosaic laws, and the anonymous Christian who practices justice and love in the parable of the Sheep and the Goats (ch. 25). Matthew comprehensively reports the moving content of Jesus's Sermon on the Mount (Matt 5–7), which includes the ethics of nonviolence, love for enemies, the beatitudes, the Golden Rule, and the Lord's Prayer.[1] Thus, "to disparage Matthew is a great mistake," and "nobody should minimize the importance of the Gospel."[2] Keeping all the above aspects in mind, we shall approach Matthew from an Asian perspective.

1 Bart D. Ehrman, *The New Testament: A Historical Introduction to the Early Christian Writings*, 2nd ed. (New York: Oxford University Press, 2000), 84.

2 Leon Morris, *The Gospel According to Matthew* (Grand Rapids, MI: Eerdmans, 1992), 1.

CRITICAL INFORMATION ABOUT MATTHEW

Before we turn to a consideration of the teaching of Matthew, we shall look at critical issues relating to the Gospel, such as its authorship, date and place of writing, purpose, and related Asian realities.

Authorship

Apart from the seven letters of Paul that scholars regard as authentic, we do not know for certain the authors of other individual NT books.[3] The Gospel of Matthew makes no direct reference to its author, but the oldest testimony is the record of Papias, who reports, "Matthew compiled the reports in the Hebrew language, and each one interpreted them as best he could" (Eusebius, *EH* 3.39.16).[4] However, most scholars believe that Papias's report is "a completely groundless assumption."[5] There is no evidence to prove that the Gospel of Matthew existed in Hebrew, and the fact that there was a collection of sayings like Q. Eusebius's writing makes it clear Matthew had wide circulation that extended even to the South Asian context (*EH* 5.10). Guthrie states, "Pantaenus, according to Eusebius, found that the Gospel according to Matthew had preceded him to India and was preserved there in Hebrew letters, having been left there by Bartholomew. The veracity of this story must be doubted, but the fact remains that it bears testimony to a circulating tradition which is, at any rate, in harmony with the interpretation of Papias' *logia* as Matthew's Gospel."[6] From the tradition of the Church fathers as well as in the modern scholarship, it is argued that Matthew's Gospel was very popular and widely circulated.

The Gospel is written in Koine Greek and is dependent on Q and Mark.[7] Traditionally, in the church, the author of the Gospel is portrayed as a tax

3 See R. E. Brown, *An Introduction to the New Testament*, ABRL 9 (New York: Doubleday, 1997), 7–8.

4 Robert A. Spivey and D. Moody Smith, *Anatomy of the New Testament* (New York: Macmillan, 1969), 97.

5 W. G. Kümmel, *Introduction to the New Testament*, trans. Howard C. Kee (Nashville: Abingdon, 1975), 120.

6 Donald Guthrie, *NT Introduction*, rev. ed. (Leicester, UK: Apollos, 1990), 47. See Eusebius, *EH* 5.10.

7 Robert J. Miller, ed., *The Complete Gospels: Annotated Scholars Version* (San Francisco: Harper, 1994), 56.

collector and as one among the Twelve (Matt 9:9–10; 10:3). However, some of the modern biblical scholars reject the traditional understanding related to the Gospel's authorship. If the author himself was Matthew, "why, for example, would someone who had spent so much time with Jesus rely on another author (Mark) for nearly two-thirds of his stories, often repeating them word for word (including the story of his own call to discipleship; 9:9–13)?"[8] The author who apparently knew Greek, Aramaic, and Hebrew might be a second- or third-generation Christian of Jewish origin.[9] The author was living in the Greek-speaking area and was well accustomed to both Greek and Jewish cultures. As of now, we have information about the author limited to his being an unknown Christian scribe, "similar to the Jewish scribes of the law" (Matt 13:52).[10]

Place and Date of Writing

The origin of the Gospel could not have been Palestine or Alexandria. It is a generally accepted view that this Gospel was written in Antioch in Syria mainly because of the fact that Ignatius of Antioch knew this Gospel.[11] Matthew presents Peter as an ideal disciple and does not include Mark's negative references to him. After Peter's great confession that Jesus is the Messiah in both Mark (8:29) and Matthew (16:16), Matthew includes a reference to Peter's great role in that Jesus will build the church and give him the keys of the kingdom of heaven (Matt 16:18–19), a narration that does not appear in Mark. Geographically, Peter was more connected to the Syrian area. According to Acts 12:7, Peter might have departed from Jerusalem and gone to Antioch in Syria.[12] If Antioch was representative of "a variety of churches in Syria and even North Palestine,"[13] it would be the best fit for the place of the writing of Matthew. Because the author of Matthew was focusing more on the Syrian and the North Palestinian contexts, it is not difficult to connect this Gospel with Asian realities.

---

8 Ehrman, *New Testament*, 84.

9 Kümmel, *Introduction to the New Testament*, 119.

10 Spivey and Smith, *Anatomy of the New Testament*, 97.

11 Kümmel, *Introduction to the New Testament*, 119.

12 Eduard Schweizer, *The Good News According to Matthew*, trans. David E. Green (Atlanta: John Knox, 1975), 16.

13 David A. deSilva, *An Introduction to the New Testament: Contexts, Methods and Ministry Formation* (Downers Grove, IL: InterVarsity, 2004), 9:238.

The date of writing ought to be after 70 CE, when Mark was in its final form, because Matthew uses 80 percent of Mark's materials and references to the destruction of Jerusalem (Matt 22:7; 23:38). Harsh curses on the Pharisees (Matt 23:1–39) reflect "the competition and conflict with so-called formative Judaism,"[14] and this suggests the circumstances relating to the Jewish conference at Jamnia (around 85–90 CE). Thus the date of writing was probably around 85–90 CE.

Purpose of the Gospel

The use of Mosaic typology suggests that the purpose of Matthew is to present Jesus Christ as the Savior (Messiah), as prophesied in the OT.[15] Not long after his birth, Jesus escaped from the persecution of Herod, a vested political power (Matt 2:13–18), much like Moses escaped from Pharaoh (Exod 2:1–21). The important factors of Matthew's community and its development were "the competition and conflict with so-called formative Judaism."[16] After the destruction of the Jerusalem temple (70 CE), while the Matthean community and formative Judaism were reinterpreting the law,[17] the Matthean community "most actively ordered and defined their life and beliefs."[18] Because they regarded the temple and law as primary in their religious lives, they shared "the same cultural context, and, in short, inhabit[ed] the same world."[19] This ideology of the Matthean community is reminiscent of the widespread Christian communities in Asia who adopt the majoritarian cultural context and dwell in the same world. The implications of this inclusive framework of the Matthean mission are important in contemporary Asian contexts.

14 J. Andrew Overman, *Matthew's Gospel and Formative Judaism: The Social World of the Matthean Community* (Minneapolis: Fortress, 1990), 2; Bruce Chilton and Jacob Neusner, *Types of Authority in Formative Christianity and Judaism* (London: Routledge, 1999), 11.

15 R. C. H. Lenski, *The Interpretation of St. Matthew's Gospel* (Minneapolis: Augsburg, 1961), 20.

16 Overman, *Matthew's Gospel*, 2; Chilton and Neusner, *Types of Authority*, 11.

17 Overman, 69.

18 Overman, 69.

19 Overman, 4.

I use the historical, the literary, and the postcolonial approaches to the study of Matthew. The two-documentary hypothesis provides a starting point for looking at the Gospel of Matthew. It presumes that the author used Mark alongside a saying source (Q document) when he composed the Gospel. Later, by expanding it into a four-documentary hypothesis, the special material of Matthew (M) and of Luke (L) were incorporated into the discussion.[20] Form criticism avoids reading Matthew in the literal sense of the word because Matthew contains various literary forms, and each form reflects various religious settings of the early Christian church. In due course, form criticism led to redaction criticism and, further, to literary criticism. As the Hindu Dharma is composed of both the *Śruti* (lit. hearing) traditions and the *Śmṛti* (lit. remembrance) traditions, the Gospel traditions are developed from what was *heard* in the *Sitz im Leben Jesu* and what was remembered and handed down in the *Sitz im Leben Kirche.*[21] Just as the Asian religious scriptures developed out of various sources and were derived from various forms, the Matthean traditions in the final composition are derived from various sources and forms.

To investigate the theology of Matthew, redaction critics look at the Gospel on its own terms and investigate the differences in comparison/relation to other Gospels. This involves looking at the author of Matthew as a well-equipped editor who had special theological intentions and thought patterns for his community (or the Matthean church). From the perspective of redaction criticism, which foregrounds the theology of Matthew with adequate comparisons with other traditions, we can also incorporate ideals from the sociopolitical, postmodern, and postcolonial interpretations of the gospel. In particular, "opposing the heritage of western political, cultural and ideological dominance in Asian and African,"[22] the postcolonial interpretation of Matthew is significant to reckon with. It pursues "a hermeneutics that exposes

20 Kümmel, *Introduction to the New Testament*, 105–10.

21 Shlomo Biderman, "Authority and Action: An Indian Perspective," in *Scripture and Knowledge: An Essay on Religious Epistemology*, Studies in the History of Religions 69 (New York: Brill, 1995), 175.

22 Oh Wang Kwon, "A Postcolonial Reflection on Minjung Theologies," *Korean Journal of Christian Studies* 84, no. 1 (2012): 169. Kwon uses "anti-colonial" as "postcolonial."

the imperialist oppression effected by biblical interpretation, accompanying colonial rule as the twin pillars of imperial control"[23] from the Edict of Milan (314 CE) to the present day.[24]

In the 1960s, literary critics similarly studied the areas covered by modern form criticism and redaction criticism. Today, biblical literary critics take the literary unity of the biblical text by accepting some of the theories of secular literary criticism. I also look at the Gospel of Matthew from a literary perspective and use various methodologies of literary criticism. Although I have briefly described the purpose of Matthew, to understand its theme, contents, Christology, community dynamics, and purpose, the structure of Matthew is an important area to focus on. It demonstrates the core theology of Matthew's Gospel. By doing so, we can avoid a subjective approach to the study of the first Gospel, and it will give us an idea of how to read Matthew from an Asian perspective. A rereading of the Gospel of Matthew by reimagining the contemporary Asian settings, characters and characterization, themes and ideological constellations, point of view and plot development, and literary devices can help the readers create bridges between the Matthean realities of the first century CE and Asian realities of the twenty-first century context.

STRUCTURE OF MATTHEW

I will discuss the two primary perspectives regarding Matthew's structure: one is redaction critical, and the other is literary (narrative) critical. The difference between the two is that "whereas redaction critics have focused on the book's *compositional structure*, narrative critics have focused on its *plot structure*."[25] Redaction criticism, founded on B. W. Bacon's fivefold discourse, "typically understands structural analysis to mean discernment of the evangelist's strategy for organizing his source materials."[26] In contrast, narrative criticism looks

23 David Jasper, "Literature: Critical Theory and Religious Studies," in *Encyclopedia of Religion*, ed. Lindsay Jones (Detroit: Macmillan Reference, 2005), 5488.

24 Sam P. Mathew, "Indian Biblical Hermeneutics: Methods and Principles," *Neotestamentica* 38, no. 1 (2004): 108.

25 M. A. Powell, "Toward a Narrative-Critical Understanding of Matthew," *Union Seminary Review* 46, no. 4 (1992): 343.

26 Powell, 344.

into the structure of the Gospel "without reference to any particular source theory."[27] It focuses on how the story that Matthew tells unfolds for the reader. It also emphasizes the development of the plot or the flow of the narrative by describing features that preserve continuity between episodes.[28] Several of the narrative and structural dynamics of the Matthean Gospel have similarities with other religious scriptures in Asia. For example, as Matthew begins the Gospel with a genealogy (1:1–17), the *Mahabharata* begins with *Adi Parva*, which describes the families of Dhritarashtra and Pandu.[29] In a broader sense, scholars categorize the structure of Matthew as the geographical structure, topical structure, and literary structure in detail. These structures are familiar to readers of the other Asian scriptures.

The Geographical or Chronological Structure

Most of the earlier structural studies in the Matthean scholarship placed emphasis on the geographical or the chronological aspects. This approach follows the Markan outline in which the geographical order and the chronological order go together.[30] In addition, in this Gospel, the geographical and chronological order do not go together. Mark's chronological statements are often omitted in Matthew. Further, Matthew also radically alters Mark's order in the interests of a seemingly better topical arrangement.[31] Therefore, the geographical or chronological factors are not an essential part of Matthew's structure and are secondary. Most of the recent scholars have interpreted Matthew in favor of some sort of topical structures.[32]

When Asians read Matthew, the geographical information from first-century Palestine is not a familiar category for interpretation, but they are able to trace the chronological order in which topics and contents are organized. For instance, in Korea, the *Joseon wangjo sillok* (朝鮮王朝實錄, Veritable Records of the Joseon Dynasty) listed on the UNESCO World Heritage List as Memory

27 Powell, 344.
28 Richard Alan Edwards, *Matthew's Story of Jesus* (Philadelphia: Fortress, 1985), 9.
29 Roshen Dalal, *Hinduism: An Alphabetical Guide* (Gurgaon: Penguin, 2010), 230.
30 R. T. France, *Matthew*, ed. Canon Leon Morris, TNTC (Grand Rapids, MI: Eerdmans, 1985), 58; Ulrich Luz, *Matthew 1–7*, trans. Wilhelm C. Linss (Minneapolis: Fortress, 1992), 37.
31 Vincent Taylor, *The Gospels: A Short Introduction*, 8th ed. (London: Epworth, 1956), 76.
32 David R. Bauer, *The Structure of Matthew's Gospel: A Study in Literary Design*, The Library of New Testament Studies (London: Bloomsbury Academic, 2015), 136.

of the World include twenty-eight different sets of chronological records compiled immediately after the death of the king. It is a typical chronological history that covers "the reigns of 25 rulers, from King Taejo to King Cheoljong, and spans a period of 472 years."[33] As Asians attribute much significance to the aspects of time and space, the Matthean chronology enables a reader to understand the historical value of the text.

The Topical Structure

The topical structure depends on patterns that the author of Matthew has used to set in order certain material in his Gospel. In other words, this divides "the Gospel into sections according to perceived changes in subject matter [that] have come the closest to a concentration on plot."[34] There are three major topical structures: the fivefold alternating pattern, the chiastic pattern, and the threefold division. Without doubt, B. W. Bacon's fivefold outline of Matthew's Gospel has been widely accepted for much of the last century. Bacon proposed the following outline: "The first on filial righteousness (chaps. 5–7), the second on the duty of evangelists (chap. 10), the third on the mystery of the kingdom (chap. 13), the fourth on the duty of church administrators (chap. 18), the fifth on preparedness for the coming (chaps. 23–25)."[35] Describing Jesus as the new Moses, Bacon first presented the reason why Matthew had composed his Gospel along these lines. The fivefold discourse structure explains "the salvation-historical continuity between the Law of the OT and the Law Jesus promulgates to his church."[36] As Moses mounted Sinai, received the law, and discoursed to people, Jesus climbs the mountain (Matt 5:1) and teaches "the new law"[37] to people. Asians consider mountaintops as sacred spaces for divine-human interactions. The Matthean portrayal of Jesus is a significant narrative kernel for Asian readers to relate with. When one compares this with Luke's account that Jesus stood to teach on a level place (Luke 6:17), Matthew's

33 "Veritable Records of the Joseon Dynasty," National Institute of Korean History, accessed on June 25, 2020, http://sillok.history.go.kr/intro/english.do.

34 Janice Capel Anderson, *Matthew's Narrative Web: Over, and Over, and Over Again* (Sheffield, UK: JSOT, 1994), 134.

35 Benjamin W. Bacon, *Studies in Matthew* (New York: Henry Holt, 1930), 82.

36 Bauer, "Structure of Matthew's Gospel," 136.

37 Edwin D. Freed, *The New Testament: A Critical Introduction* (Belmont, CA: Wadsworth, 1986), 127.

emphasis is clear. Bacon's arguments are simple and attractive, but his most significant weakness is that he relegates "the infancy narratives of chaps. 1 and 2 and the passion and resurrection accounts of chaps. 26–28 to 'prologue' and 'epilogue' respectively, because they did not fit into his five-book format."[38]

Ellis's idea is developed from Matthew's use of the number seven.[39] There are, indeed, many uses of sevens in Matthew's text: Matthew's seven-multiple genealogy (1:1–17), seven petitions in the Lord's prayer (6:5–13), seven evil spirits (12:45), seven vices (15:19), seven loaves (15:34), seven brothers (22:25), seven "woes" (23:13ff.), seven references to the "thirty pieces of silver" (27:3–10), and forgiveness of seventy times seven (18:22). Ellis points out that Matthew added "the two minor discourses of 3:8–12 and 28:18–20" to complete "the teaching of Jesus."[40] This development of the Gospel of Matthew is reminiscent of the sevenfold *Kandas* or the books of *Rāmāyana* tell the story of Rama, his associates, and Sita. As Jesus, the protagonist, is Son of God, confronts oppositions, and undergoes trials, crucifixion, and death, Rama, a divine figure, experiences several troublesome situations in his earthly *avatāra*. These similarities enable the readers to develop a dialogical interpretation of the Gospel of Matthew in relation to the Asian scriptures and the socioreligious realities.

Ellis somewhat overcomes Bacon's weak points, which had omitted Matthew's crucial passages, while still acknowledging Bacon's clear merit—that is, the structure based on Moses typology. Senior says that Ellis agrees with Bacon in his chiastic patterns and improves Bacon's structure, even though Ellis considers Matthew 11–12 as a "narrative" despite a lot of discourse material in Matthew 11:7–30.[41]

The Threefold Principal Section

Some scholars have discovered problems with both Bacon's fivefold schema and outlines based on chiasm. They have refused formal patterns and have argued that another set of signals, superscriptions (Ἀπὸ τότε), can be found

38 Donald Senior, *What Are They Saying about Matthew?* (New York: Paulist, 1996), 27.

39 Peter F. Ellis, *Matthew: His Mind and His Message* (Collegeville, MN: Liturgical, 1974), 13. Also see Luz, *Matthew 1–7*, 38.

40 Ellis, *Matthew*, 13.

41 Senior, *What Are They Saying?*, 29–30.

in Matthew 4:17 and 16:21.[42] These superscriptions "mark the boundaries of the major divisions" of the Gospel.[43] The words Ἀπὸ τότε (from that time) show Matthew's special intention to "mark the beginning of a new phase in the life of Jesus."[44] Therefore, Matthew employs this phrase to arrange his Gospel according to topic. Jack Dean Kingsbury demonstrates this arrangement:

> First, the Person of Jesus the Messiah (1:1–4:16);
> Second, the Proclamation of Jesus the Messiah (4:17–16:20); and
> Third, the Suffering, Death, and Resurrection of Jesus the Messiah (16:21–28:20)[45]

Kingsbury's threefold structure is a pervasive understanding of the Christology in Matthew's concept of salvation history by which Matthew divides time into two parts: "the time of Israel" and "the time of Jesus."[46] Kingsbury's arguments are valuable in that his theory first opened the way to abandon the traditional fivefold structure of Bacon. His proposal sees the Gospel as a whole unit and emphasizes Matthew's special theology and Christology.[47] Although Kingsbury has turned to literary critical methods in his study of the Gospel, he had first proposed this structure in a series of redactional studies.[48]

As with Bacon, however, Kingsbury can be criticized for his choice and application of criteria. Janice Capel Anderson says, "Why should the phrase, 'From then Jesus began . . .' in 4:17 and 16:21 receive a greater weight than the transitional formulas at the end of the discourses?"[49] Another criticism against Kingsbury is that he disregards Ἀπὸ τότε in 26:16. Nevertheless, Kingsbury admits that the words Ἀπὸ τότε appear just four times in the NT (Luke 16:16; Matt 4:17; 16:21; 26:16); he disregards 26:16 because it does

42 Bauer, "Structure of Matthew's Gospel," 137; Senior, *What Are They Saying?*, 31.

43 See Jack Dean Kingsbury, "The Structure of Matthew's Gospel and His Concept of Salvation-History," *Catholic Biblical Quarterly* 35, no. 4 (1973): 453.

44 Jack Dean Kingsbury, *Matthew: Structure, Christology, Kingdom* (Philadelphia: Fortress, 1975), 8.

45 Kingsbury, "Structure of Matthew's Gospel," 454.

46 Kingsbury, 473–74.

47 Bauer, "Structure of Matthew's Gospel," 137.

48 Kingsbury, *Matthew*, 32.

49 Anderson, *Matthew's Narrative Web*, 137.

not "appear as part of a fixed formula"[50] and refers directly to Judas. Unlike Kingsbury's threefold structure, Jesus's public ministry "does not come to a close at 16:20."[51] Frans Neirynck suggests rather "a graphic presentation of Jesus' ministry in Matthew."[52]

The threefold development suggested here has several similarities with some of the Hindu scriptures. The Sanskrit text called *Brihaddharma Purana* has three sections that deal with teachings on *Dharma*, conversations between god/goddess and human beings, and stories related to worship. It also includes duties to gurus and parents and of the various castes.[53] Similarly, another Sanskrit text called *Brihadaranyaka Upanishad* has six chapters, normally divided into three *kandas* (sections) of two chapters each: first, *Madhu Kanda* deals with sacrifices, creation, and the knowledge of the self; second, *Yajnavalkya Kanda* describes the teachings of the rishi Yajnavalkya; and third, *Khila Kanda* deals with Brahman the Absolute.[54] Matthew follows a similar pattern, describing Jesus's birth, his teachings, and his victory over death. The threefold pattern of Matthew takes into account the person, the proclamation, and the practice of the Messiah.

The Literary Structure

As seen in this chapter, the literary structure is becoming the pervasive trend in studying Matthew's structure. Kingsbury's threefold division in redaction criticism has also turned to literary criticism to refine his threefold structure. According to Bauer, "The purpose of analyzing literary structure is to determine the major units and sub-units of any given book and to identify the structural relationships between and within these units."[55] The development of the story in Matthew's narrative plan is built from a combination of geographical, chronological, topical, and conceptual elements.[56] Bauer suggests that "the Gospel of Matthew is structured according to the

50 Kingsbury, "Structure of Matthew's Gospel," 453.

51 Frans Neirynck, "*Apo Tote Erkzato* and the Structure of Matthew," in *Evangelica Ii 1982–1991*, ed. F. Van Segbroeck (Leuven: Leuven University Press, 1991), 178.

52 Neirynck, 178.

53 See Dalal, *Hinduism*, 85.

54 See Dalal, 85.

55 Bauer, "Structure of Matthew's Gospel," 135.

56 Senior, *What Are They Saying?*, 35.

following compositional relationships: repetition of particularization and climax."[57] Keeping in mind the discussions of the literary characteristics above, Edwards uses the narrative method that follows the development of the plot or the flow of the narrative.[58] He presents the six divisions[59] as follows:

Matt 1:1–4:22	Establishing the Framework of the Story
Matt 4:23–7:29	The Demands of the Kingdom
Matt 8:1–11:1	The Power of the Kingdom
Matt 11:2–18:35	The Response to the Coming of the Kingdom
Matt 19:1–25:46	The Message of the Kingdom Presented in Judea
Matt 26:1–28:20	The Conflict Takes Place[60]

The *Brihadaranyaka Upanishad* has six chapters, and the *Bhagavad Gita* is divided into three parts with six chapters each. These studies demonstrate that the Gospel of Matthew has some structural dynamics similar to the Asian religious texts. Thus the literary structure has merit in that it helps to see the Gospel as a whole unit, as a complete literary structure.[61] However, France says, relevantly, "It is doubtful whether Matthew would have recognized in any of them a total structural pattern which he consciously designed."[62] In addition, the literary structure does not have specific evidence that one can discern, like the topical structure. Thus it would be premature to abandon a conception of Matthew's Gospel as built around five major discourses.[63] Based on the above discussion, it is claimed "the core of Matthew's gospel thus consists of five consecutive narrative-discourse pairs,"[64] which supports Jesus's liberative role as a new Moses.

57 Bauer, "Structure of Matthew's Gospel," 137.

58 Edwards, *Matthew's Story of Jesus*, 9.

59 Craig S. Keener, *A Commentary on the Gospel of Matthew* (Grand Rapids, MI: Eerdmans, 1999), 37.

60 Edwards, *Matthew's Story of Jesus*, 9.

61 France, *Matthew*, 153.

62 France, 153–54.

63 Christopher R. Smith, "Literary Evidences of a Fivefold Structure in the Gospel of Matthew," *New Testament Studies* 43, no. 4 (1997): 540.

64 Smith, 545.

A Brief Literary Outline of the Gospel[65]

Introduction	Genealogy (1:1–17)	
Foundations of the Kingdom	First Narrative (1:18–4:25)	First Discourse (5:1–7:29)
The Mission of the Kingdom	Second Narrative (8:1–9:38)	Second Discourse (10:1–42)
The Mystery of the Kingdom	Third Narrative (11:1–13:9)	Third Discourse (13:10–53)
The Family of the Kingdom	Fourth Narrative (13:54–17:27)	Fourth Discourse (18:1–35)
The Destiny of the Kingdom	Fifth Narrative (19:1–23:39)	Fifth Discourse (24:1–25:46)
Conclusion	Passion Narrative (26:1–28:20)	

The stated structural patterns of Matthew demonstrate the plot structure of other Asian religious scriptures. The Hindu epic *Rāmāyana* is divided into seven *kandas* (or books) as follows: *Bala Kanda*, *Ayodhya Kanda*, *Aranya Kanda*, *Kishkindha Kanda*, *Sundara Kanda*, *Yuddha Kanda*, and *Uttara Kanda*. Each kanda deals with a particular period of Rama's life in a chronological order. *Bala Kanda* depicts the origin of Rama and his siblings; in a similar way, Matthew begins with the birth narratives of Jesus. As *Rāmāyana* deals with a story of the victory of good over evil, there is a development in the life and characterization of the protagonist Rama. The same pattern is obvious in the Matthean narrative framework.[66] The structural patterns discerned within the framework of the Gospel are not alien to the narrative sequence and plot development of other Asian religious scriptures. As stated earlier, a dialogical reading of the Gospel of Matthew in relationship with an Asian socioreligious understanding can be facilitated for a wider contextualized biblical interpretation.[67]

65 Smith, 549.

66 "The 7 Kandas of Ramayana," Temple Purohit, accessed June 28, 2020, https://www.templepurohit.com/7-kandas-ramayana/.

67 See Johnson Thomaskutty and Mathew Chandrankunnel, eds., *Wider Contextualized Biblical Spirituality* (Bengaluru: Ecumenical Christian Center, 2021), xvii–xxiv.

A DISCUSSION RELATING TO CONTEMPORARY ASIAN REALITIES

The following discussion concerns the law in Matthew and its implications in the Asian context, postcolonial interpretation of Matthew's mission in 28:18–20, Confucian filial piety and the respect for the parents, and Moses typology of Jesus as a liberator.

Law in Mathew and in the Asian Context

Of the four Gospels, the Gospel of Matthew is the most Jewish because it tries to "defend Christianity in the eyes of Jewish-Christian readers, to make it acceptable to them, and to prove to them that Jesus was the Jewish Messiah."[68] From Matthew 1:1, Jesus appears as "the son of David, the son of Abraham," which represents "Matthew's theme,"[69] compared to Mark's simple designation of Jesus as "the Son of God" (Mark 1:1) and Luke's description of Jesus as Savior and Messiah (Luke 1:11). Although the Gospel of Mark does not value the law, the Gospel of Matthew claims the validity of Jewish law. Jesus's words in Matthew 5:17, "Do not think that I have come to abolish the law or the prophets; I have come not to abolish (καταλῦσαι) but to fulfill (πληρῶσαι)," are a good example of the attitude of the Matthean community toward Jewish traditions and laws.[70] And just as keeping the Jewish identity reinforced in the Matthean community, maintaining the Asian identity helps Asian Christians understand themselves.

Matthew 5:17 is especially important for understanding Matthew's view of the law. It has no parallel in Mark or Luke, but 5:18 has a parallel in Luke 16:17.[71] In addition, 5:17 contains a direct statement about the law being fulfilled. The phrase "to fulfill the Law and the Prophets" can have many connotations, and some of its possible meanings are ambiguous.[72] In particular, "to fulfill

68 Kümmel, *Introduction to the New Testament*, 114.
69 Lenski, *Interpretation of St. Matthew's Gospel*, 20.
70 Schweizer, *Good News*, 16.
71 Stephenson H. Brooks, *Matthew's Community: The Evidence of His Special Sayings Material*, JSNTSS (Sheffield, UK: JSOT, 1987), 25.
72 Daniel Patte, *The Gospel According to Matthew: A Structural Commentary on Matthew's Faith* (Philadelphia: Fortress, 1987), 71.

(πληρῶσαι)[73] the Law" has been problematic. Each scholar's understanding of πληρῶσαι directly influences the interpretation of this verse.[74] Just as the Jewish community was a law-oriented society and the Matthean community attempted to function within that framework, Asian communities value law and order in the sociopolitical and religiocultural frameworks. As in the case of the Jewish community, Hindu society emphasizes law. For example, *Manu Smiti*, or *Manava Dharma Shastra*, consists of various laws, customs, and ethics for the functioning of the Hindu community.[75] Similarly, religious and social laws are highly valued among several Asian religious communities.

Daniel Patte and K. Snodgrass analyze Matthew 5:17 from a different angle. Patte connects this verse with Matthew 4:4: "It is written: 'Man does not live on bread alone, but on every word that comes from the mouth of God.'"[76] He thinks that the expression "the Law and Prophets" refers to God's Scripture, stating, "Jesus fulfills the Prophets because of his vocation, because He is sent by God and has accepted this vocation by nourishing himself with the Law."[77] Here, the Law is God's words, a view that emphasizes the continuity of it. Similarly, Snodgrass understands the prophets as those who most forcefully stressed love, mercy, and justice, and if that is so, it means that Matthew's references to the prophets[78] relate to the law. All eight occurrences of "nomos" in Matthew are connected to the prophetic writings. In particular, four of the eight occur in the expression "the Law and the Prophets" (5:17; 7:12; 11:13; 22:40). In 5:17, therefore, the prophets must explain the law. As in Judaism, in Hinduism, the *Manu Smriti* is attributed to the *Manu Svayambhuva*, the spiritual son of the god Brahma.[79] Though regarded as a mythical figure, as in the prophetic traditions of Judaism, *Manu Svayambhuva* functions as an intermediary to explain the law.[80]

73 The verb πληρῶσαι is used sixteen times in Matthew, the majority of which deal with the fulfillment of prophecy (Matt 1:22; 2:15, 23; 4:14; 8:17; 12:17; 13:35, 48; 21:4; 26:54, 56).

74 William Foxwell Albright and C. S. Mann, *Matthew* (New York: Doubleday, 1971), 58. But *Manu Dharma Shastra* is criticised for the subjugation of women and support for the caste system in India.

75 Dalal, *Hinduism*, 242–43.

76 Patte, *Gospel According to Matthew*, 72.

77 Patte, 73.

78 Brooks, *Matthew's Community*, 27.

79 Dalal, *Hinduism*, 242.

80 Dalal, 242.

However, these ideas are insufficient to explain the historical background of Matthew's community; neither do they explain the contradiction posed by Matthew 11:13, where Jesus limits the duration of the law: "For all the Prophets and the Law prophesied until John." One must look at Matthew 5:17–18 as a part of the whole Sermon on the Mount, Matthew's Gospel, and the flow of redemptive history.[81] The law and the prophets are imperfect, but they are fulfilled in the coming of the kingdom.[82] In other words, Matthew introduces Jesus as the heir to David's throne (Matt 1:1) and as having come to establish a kingdom.[83] In *Manu Smriti*, there are customs and laws relating to inheritance, birth, marriage, and death; also, the four traditional stages are prescribed. Toward the end of *Manu Smriti*, there is a description of the mind, the *Jiva* or individual soul, and the means whereby it unites with the *Atman*.[84] Whereas Matthew emphasizes the inheritance of the kingdom of God, *Manu Smriti* gives significance to the union of *Jiva* with the *Atman*.[85]

The antitheses represent Matthew's own view of Jesus as the authoritative teacher, whose words sometimes intensify and sometimes replace the Old Law (see 7:12; 12:1–7; 15:1–20; 19:1–9). Here to fulfill the law in 5:17 means to obey the *halaka* of Jesus, set out in 5:21–48 and summarized in 7:12 and 22:4 as the command.[86] Matthew interprets the law using the two commands to love God and love one's neighbor. Therefore, the true understanding of the concept of law in Matthew 5:17 cannot be separated from the Matthean community's attitude toward the law. On this point, Matthew's community seems to consist of two groups, a Palestinian group and a Hellenistic group.[87] The teachings of Jesus and the teachings of the Matthean community are interspersed here. In the Indian context, Raja Ram Mohan Roy and Mahatma Gandhi respected and gave much significance to Jesus's teachings in the Sermon on the Mount.

81 Stewart E. Lauer, "Must We Obey the Law?," *Kerux* 8 (December 1993): 4.
82 Lauer, 7.
83 Lauer, 5.
84 Dalal, *Hinduism*, 243.
85 Dalal, 242–43.
86 Robert Hamerton-Kelly, *Attitudes toward the Law in Matthew's Gospel: A Discussion of Matthew 5:18* (Chicago: Chicago Society of Biblical Research, 1972), 31.
87 Gerhard Barth, "Matthew's Understanding of the Law," in *Tradition and Interpretation in Matthew*, ed. Günther Bornkamm, Gerhard Barth, and Heinz Joachim Held (Philadelphia: Westminster, 1963), 66.

Gandhi's movements called *Satyagraha* and *Ahimsa* owe their ideological substance to the teachings of Jesus with particular emphasis on the Sermon on the Mount.[88] Satyavrata considers "Christ as the fulfillment of Hindu religious experience" and Farquhar understands Christ as "crown of Hinduism." Whereas Panikkar postulated "the unknown Christ of Hinduism," M. M. Thomas foregrounded "the acknowledged Christ of Indian renaissance."[89] Similarly, Confucius as a teacher gave much significance to personal, familial, and communal morality and ethics. In that sense, Jesus's ethical and moral teachings about familial and communal living could have been a model for all other teachers in the Asian context.[90]

Matthew 5:17, in the context of chapters 5–7, stresses the order of the life of the community[91] and the Matthean community's distinctive interpretation and application of the law fulfilled by the love command (Matt 22:37–40).[92] This attitude is also reflected in the Sabbath law controversy between Matthew's community and formative Judaism (Matt 11:28–12:14; 24:20). In the contemporary Asian context, Christianity as a minority religion interprets the majority of cultural and forensic aspects in close relationship with both the political scenario and the religiocultural ethos of the Christian community. That is suggestive of how the Matthean community in the "there and then" context and the minority Christian community in the "here and now" context look similar.

As an Asian, when I read the text of Matthew, I am impressed that Matthew insisted on the validity of the law and did not forsake Jewish culture and identity. In Korean church history, wherever Western missionaries went, Korean traditional shrines and the totem pole (*Janseng*) standing at the village

88 See Pascal Alan Nazareth, "Gandhi, Christ, and Humanity," mkgandhi.org, accessed June 29, 2020, https://www.mkgandhi.org/articles/gandhi_christ.html.

89 See Ivan M. Satyavrata, *To Fulfill, not to Destroy: Christ as the Fulfillment of Hindu Religious Experience in Indian Christian Theology* (Minneapolis: 1517 Media, 2019); J. N. Farquhar, *Crown of Hinduism* (Wales: South Asia Books, 1971); Raimon Panikkar, *The Unknown Christ of Hinduism: Toward an Ecumenical Christophany* (New York: Orbis, 1981); M. M. Thomas, *Acknowledged Christ of the Indian Renaissance* (London: SCM Press, 1970).

90 See *Encyclopaedia Britannica Online*, s.v. "Confucius," accessed June 29, 2020, https://www.britannica.com/biography/Confucius.

91 Overman, *Matthew's Gospel*, 90–95.

92 Overman, 89.

entrance were destroyed.[93] The missionaries also thought that Korean traditional music, customs, and architecture were related to shamanism, Confucianism, and Buddhism, and therefore, they regarded Korean traditional dance as idolatrous. As a result, the Korean church has rejected their own cultural identity and accepted Western culture in their faith lives. In this respect, Matthew's presentation has implications for how Asian identity may be preserved when people come to faith in Christ in various religious contexts in Asia.

A Postcolonial Interpretation of Matthew's Mission in 28:18–20

Although the Great Commission has played an important role in Christian mission and evangelism, the imperialism and mission of Western countries are interwoven.[94] Because "in many colonial contexts, mission ceases to be an act of service or sacrifice and instead becomes a tool for exercising institutional survival, expansion, and power," the function of the Great Commission becomes "to evoke triumphal and imperial elements in mission fields."[95] Unusually, the imperialism of the West toward the East has been closely related to the mission policy of Western churches. Choan-Seng Song observes that Western foreign mission became, in effect, spiritual imperialism.[96]

After the Edict of Milan in 314 CE, Western Christianity was changed from being persecuted to ruling over the world. Thus Song points out that the West lost the cross, and "without the cross there is no resurrection."[97] Though they forgot the true meaning of the cross, they did understand Eastern cultures and religions. As Western countries colonized the East, the church in the West colonized the church in the East, according to Song's expression, with "formidable manpower and economic strength."[98]

93 Conservative Christians thought these structures were idols, so many traditional totem poles and big trees considered to be the village's guard gods have been cut down.

94 For a better understanding, refer to Jae Hyung Cho, "A Postcolonial Interpretation of Matthew 28:18–20," *Korean Journal of Christian Studies* 105 (2017): 9–25.

95 YongHan Chung, "A Postcolonial Reading of the Great Commission (Matt 28:16–20) with a Korean Myth," *Theology Today* 72, no. 3 (2015): 277.

96 Choan-Seng Song, *Christian Mission in Reconstruction: An Asian Analysis* (Maryknoll, NY: Orbis, 1977), 10.

97 Song, 13.

98 Song, 13.

Although the Great Commission has contributed to the spread of Christianity, Western missionary efforts have been often interpreted as imperialistic and as having disregarded the reality of the colonized. They have not been scrutinized in "their colonial entanglements."[99] In this respect, the Great Commission can be differently interpreted from the perspective of the colonized: "And Jesus came and said to them, 'All authority in heaven and on earth has been given to me. Go therefore and make disciples of all nations, baptizing them in the name of the Father and of the Son and of the Holy Spirit, and teaching them to obey everything that I have commanded you. And remember, I am with you always, to the end of the age'" (Matt 28:18–20 NRSV). These texts have long served as a "job description" for the church. Matthew describes that Jesus has authority like Moses, which explains Matthew's social situation. For this, Overman states that "Matthew's community was clearly sectarian."[100] Because Matthew's community had to struggle with the opposition of Pharisaic Judaism toward the Jewish mission, it needed to emphasize that Jesus had more authority than that of Moses after resurrection. In particular, the risen Jesus had the authority to interpret the law against Pharisaic Judaism. Although Matthew's community was a new sect, it did not forsake its Jewish heritage and culture as it tried to reach the Jewish people. The Matthean communitarian understanding can be significantly aligned with the communal atmosphere of Asian cultures.

Finally, Matthew says that Jesus has all authority in heaven and on earth. Jesus's authority is to demonstrate the mercy of God (healing), to proclaim (preach) the goodness of God the Father, and to teach the kingdom of God.[101] It is different from that of Satan's authority in Matthew 4:8. When Satan offered "all the kingdoms/empires of the world,"[102] Jesus rejected it. Moreover, Jesus did not "exercise his authority in the oppressive manner of the imperial Gentiles" (Matt 20:25–28).[103] If "Jesus comes not as one who lords his authority

99 Mathew, "Indian Biblical Hermeneutics," 108.

100 Overman, *Matthew's Gospel*, 154.

101 Patte, *Gospel According to Matthew*, 400.

102 Warren Carter, *Matthew and Margins: A Sociopolitical and Religious Reading*, ed. Norman K. Gottwald and Richard A. Horsley, The Bible and Liberation (Maryknoll, NY: Orbis, 2000), 551.

103 Carter, 195.

over others, but as one who rejects domination and comes as a servant,"[104] Western missions have misunderstood Jesus's authority, which is different from that of Satan and "the religious elites and Roman imperialism."[105] Significantly, Jesus receives his authority "by the way of suffering obedience."[106] Therefore, "all authority" in Matthew 28:18 does not assure Christians of Jesus's power that can forcefully convert non-Christians into Christians. Instead, it refers to deep insights into the culture and religion in missionary fields and contexts as, for example, in Asia.

Jesus's authority implies that his disciples can "go" all over the world.[107] Jesus's ministry in the Gospels included much travel. For me, "to go" reminds me of the arrival of Western missionaries in Asian countries as agents of Western imperialism. Historically speaking, imperialists also preferred to go to other nations.[108] Without any hesitation, they moved to other countries, entered into other regions, and exercised imperial authority. Imperialism is "a system of economic, political, and cultural force that disavows borders in order to extract desirable resources and exploit an alien people."[109] Vladimir Ilich Lenin defined imperialism as the "highest stage of capitalism."[110] Expanding imperialism had an unlimited visa and could go anywhere. Colonizers freely traveled and entered other colonized nations without any necessary permission to do so.

As Musa W. Dube suggests, the Exodus-Joshua story shows how Israel entered foreign and inhabited lands and destroyed and occupied them.[111] According to Dube, "Jesus is undoubtedly a traveler, whose divinity, class, race, and gender endow him with privilege and authority" (Matt 15:21–28).[112]

104 Stanly P. Saunders and Charles L. Campbell, *The Word on the Street* (Grand Rapids, MI: Eerdmans, 2002), 110.
105 Carter, *Matthew and Margins*, 551.
106 France, *Matthew*, 413.
107 Keener, *Commentary on the Gospel of Matthew*, 718.
108 Chung, "Postcolonial Reading," 284.
109 J. Phillips, "Educating the Savages," in *Recasting the World: Writing after Colonialism*, ed. Jonathan White (Baltimore: Johns Hopkins University Press, 1993), 26.
110 V. I. Lenin, *Imperialism, the Highest Stage of Capitalism: A Popular Outline* (New York: International, 1935), 59.
111 Musa W. Dube, *Postcolonial Feminist Interpretation of the Bible* (St. Louis: Chalice, 2000), 70.
112 Dube, 146.

For her, Jesus is the agent of Roman imperialism throughout Matthew. But she does not consider Jesus's other travels as an itinerant preacher. Indeed, Jesus said, "Foxes have holes, and birds of the air have nests; but the Son of man has nowhere to lay his head" (Matt 8:20). Similar to today's homeless, Jesus did not possess a house to stay a night. Although Dube's is a postcolonial reading of Matthew's story, she does not pay attention to the radical liberative image of Jesus. For instance, Matthew contains many Q documents that describe Jesus as a radical social ethicist against the powers.

The Roman emperor's travels cannot be compared to Jesus's travels. Dube's points, however, are useful to correct the misinterpretation of contemporary Western Christians' mission policy about going to other countries. Western missionaries did not enter Eastern countries as Jesus had done but went to them as subjugators. Therefore, when Jesus said "to go" to the world, he did not mean invasion of other nations. Instead, Jesus also said, "If any man would come after me, let him deny himself and take up his cross and follow me" (Matt 16:24), and this suggests entering other nations with love, modesty, and sacrifice. In this respect, Korea, which is presently "the second-largest missionary-sending country in the world," does not critically analyze their so-called Great Commission initiative when Koreans go to other nations.[113] Yonghan Chung points out, "They have missionized others in the same way that [they] had been missionized."[114]

"Make disciples," "baptize," and "teach" have been read as three imperatives in Matthew 28:19. However, "baptize" and "teach" are grammatically subordinate to "make disciples."[115] "Disciple" is more frequently used in Matthew than in the other Gospels. Although many churches interpreted discipleship as a permanent duty, Overman suggests that discipleship reflects the social situation of Matthew's community and should be understood as a specific mission truth located in a certain community's situation.[116] But Western Christianity has used this status to subordinate other countries and for the expansion of their imperial agenda. Therefore, a postcolonial understanding

113 Chung, "Postcolonial Reading," 277.

114 Chung, 277.

115 David J. Bosch, *Transforming Mission: Paradigm Shift in Theology of Mission* (Maryknoll, NY: Orbis, 1991), 73.

116 Overman, *Matthew's Gospel*, 124–49.

of Christian mission tries to overcome a hidden imperial agenda by getting involved in exclusive Christian mission and participating in the movement of justice and peace in the global scenario.[117]

Confucian Filial Piety and the Respect for the Parents

In Asia, Christianity is not a majority religion. Hinduism, Buddhism, Taoism, Confucianism, and Shamanism dominate the Asian context. However, in the West, when discussing Asian religions, Confucianism often tends to be ignored because Confucianism appears in Asian countries as a life ethic rather than a religious ritual. In fact, Confucianism is the religion of the largest population in Asia. Erin Cline points this out in this way: "No single tradition has had such widespread cultural influence; Confucian values saturate the cultures of East and Southeast Asia, and Confucian religious beliefs and practices are tightly woven into the forms of Buddhism and Daoism, as well as of popular religion, that are practiced throughout East Asia today. People throughout East and Southeast Asia, regardless of whether they would describe themselves as Buddhist, Daoist, Christian, or atheist, are deeply influenced by the Confucian tradition in how they think about and lead their lives."[118] Generally, Confucian values emphasize "respect for elders, an emphasis on family, an appreciation for ritual, and a commitment to learning and education."[119] In particular, loyalty to the country and filial piety, which are called *Chunghyo* (忠孝), are the most important virtues of Confucianism. Confucius, known in East Asia as Kongzi, 孔子 (551–479 BCE), played a crucial role in shaping the tradition and values of *Chunghyo*. Kongzi was born in the state of Lu, located in what is now the Shandong Province in the People's Republic of China. In living and teaching "during a time of violence and warfare both between and within different states," Kongzi tried to recover "the values and practices of earlier times, which he believed could help his society return to a time of peace and stability and help people to lead happier and ethically better lives."[120] He

117 Cho, "Postcolonial Interpretation of Matthew," 11–21.

118 Erin M. Cline, "Confucianism, East Asian Cultures, and the Spiritual Exercises," in *A World on Fire: Sharing the Ignatian Spiritual Exercises with Other Religions* (Washington, DC: Catholic University of America Press, 2018), 228.

119 Cline, 228–29.

120 Cline, 229.

insisted that he was not an innovator of Confucianism; instead, he rediscovered its values and transmitted its tradition to his generation (*Analects* 7.1).[121] Likewise, Jesus did not abolish the Jewish law and invent a new law; he rediscovered the true meaning of the law.

In Confucianism, filial piety—"serving one's parents is one's most pressing ethical obligation"—is the starting point, and it is "a cultivated disposition to attend to the needs and desires of one's parents" by expressing "a deep sense of gratitude, reverence, and love."[122] When we examine Matthew's attitude toward parents and family, we see that there are pros and cons. In Matthew 10:35–37, Jesus said, "For I have come to set a man against his father, and a daughter against her mother, and a daughter-in-law against her mother-in-law; and one's foes will be members of one's own household. Whoever loves father or mother more than me is not worthy of me; and whoever loves son or daughter more than me is not worthy of me." Here, Jesus seems to be against filial piety and family. However, Jesus's utterances in Matthew 15:4–5 reflect a different perspective: "For God said, 'Honor your father and your mother,' and, 'Whoever speaks evil of father or mother must surely die.' But you say that whoever tells father or mother, 'Whatever support you might have had from me is given to God,' then that person need not honor the father."

The two conflicting views indicated above can be explained if we consider the contextual and circumstantial evidence of the texts. In chapter 10, Jesus instructs the twelve disciples concerning the mission to the nation of Israel (Matt 10:2–15), telling them about their mission and the persecution they are likely to face in the mission field (10:16–33). Jesus was prophesying about the conflicts that were going to occur within and between families. He was warning the disciples about both the external and the internal difficulties that they might suffer due to their commitment for mission. These verses can be better understood in relation to Matthew 10:34. Gerry Breshears points out, "Jesus' similar antithesis, 'Do not think that I came to bring peace, but a sword' (Matt 10:34) cannot mean there is no sense in which Jesus brings peace. Similarly, His word here cannot be understood that Jesus means to establish the

121 Cline, 229.
122 Cline, 236.

Law and there is no sense in which He abrogates the Law. One need only think of the termination of the sacrificial system to know this is not true."[123]

On the other hand, in chapter 15, Jesus referred to the honor of parents as contrasted with the traditions of the elders and the Pharisees. The attitude toward the law taken by Matthew's community that we looked at above helps us to interpret Jesus's words regarding respect due to parents. While maintaining the validity of the law, Matthew's community claimed that formative Judaism relied on their traditions to misinterpret the law. In other words, although the law commands respect to parents, formative Judaism does not obey the law with regard to honoring parents. The Gospel of Matthew has a special story about the birth and childhood of Jesus that is not found in other Gospels (Matt 1:18–2:23), which describes how Jesus's parents raised and responded to him.

Whereas Luke's Gospel unfolds the story of Jesus's birth and childhood centered on Mary (Luke 1:26–2:52), the Gospel of Matthew records the events around Jesus's father, Joseph. If the Gospel of Luke interprets the law in a more comprehensive and varied way to be accepted by godly gentiles, Matthew interprets it while maintaining the tradition of Judaism. In this regard, Matthew records the birth of Jesus and his infant years within the scope of Jewish law. In Matthew 15, Jesus's command to respect our parents is the result of a true interpretation of the law related to his birth and the fact that Jesus spent time with his parents in both infancy and adulthood. This interpretation of Jesus is persuasive to many Asians in the Confucian culture because Confucianism emphasizes the need to appreciate parents who give birth to children.

Moses Typology—Jesus as a Liberator

As we have already seen in the discussion on the structure of Matthew, the typology of Moses is one of the important interpretative keys of the Gospel. Like Moses, Jesus is born to experience the threat of death by political forces. Just as Moses went up to Mount Sinai and taught the people of God, Jesus went up the mountain and preached the message of the kingdom to the people. Above all, in the OT, Moses was a liberator who released the people of Israel

123 Timothy J. Hegg, "What Does 'Plerosai' Mean in Matthew 5:17?," 6, cited in Gerry Breshears, "The Place of the Law in the Life of the Believer in Christ" (unpublished paper, n.d.), 3.

from Egyptian oppression. The importance of Moses as a liberator has often been disregarded in the biblical tradition. Although Matthean scholars have emphasized Moses typology, they do not see Jesus as a liberator: "Moses led his people out of slavery rather than just changing a few problems in the system of slavery."[124] This aspect of the Mosaic tradition is also taken into account in the context of the Matthean community.

In the context of many Asian realities, I believe that the liberative image of Jesus is significant. Asia is the largest continent on earth, so Asian contextual realities include diverse political, cultural, and religious backgrounds. Most of the Asian countries became independent from their colonizers during the period between 1945 and 1960.[125] They were economically and politically exploited for a long span of time as colonies of Western countries and Japan. Although they are politically independent in today's context, they are still suffering from economic and cultural domination at the hands of the former colonial powers. This causes systemic poverty for about 80 percent of the Asians in the current scenario. By reflecting Jesus as a Moses-type figure, one considers four major faces of systemic poverty: "exploitative international capitalism," "economic disparity among Asian countries," "the increasing gap between the rich and the poor on a domestic and on an international level," and "the persistence of scandalous poverty among Asian masses."[126] In addition, many Asian countries have withheld the freedom of their own people because of military coups, autocratic governments, war, and militarism.[127] Whereas the oppressive religious ideologies of Christianity, Buddhism, Hinduism, Islam, Taoism, and Confucianism have helped autocratic governments and dictators, intentionally or unintentionally, *Minjung* theology (Korea), *Dalit* theology (India), and Asian feminist theology emphasize Jesus as a liberator.[128]

124 Andrew Sung Park, "Asian American Theology," in *Liberation Theologies in the United States: An Introduction*, ed. Stacey M. Floyd-Thomas and Anthony B. Pinn (New York: New York University Press, 2010), 117.

125 Keun-Joo Christina Pae, "Asian Liberative Ethics," in *A Liberative Approach*, ed. Miguel A. De La Torre (Minneapolis: Augsburg Fortress, 2013), 48–49.

126 Pae, 50.

127 Pae, 50–51.

128 Pae, 51–59.

CONCLUSION

The Gospel of Matthew has long been regarded as a treasure for the Christian life. Although modern biblical scholarship places the Gospel of Mark as the first Gospel to be written, no one denies the importance of Matthew for the study of the historical Jesus and Christian theology. Matthew was written in Koine Greek by using the Sayings source (Q), Mark and Matthew's special materials around 85–90 CE in Syria by an unknown Jewish Christian author. Matthew describes Jesus as the new Moses who keeps the Jewish law and identifies and interprets it based on the principle of mercy and love. Matthew's interpretation of the law is unique compared to that of Mark and the Pauline epistles. Matthew's attitude toward the law is impressive because he keeps its validity and tries to reinterpret its original intention. Alongside of other biblical methodologies, the postcolonial interpretation of the Bible is effective for Asian realities. In particular, Matthew's mission is relevant for both Asian Christians and non-Christians when one sees that the Western mission and imperialism have always been connected to each other. Because the Great Commission of Matthew 28:18–20 has deeply influenced the Christian mission, it needs to be read from a postcolonial perspective.

In many ways, the Gospel of Matthew can be read in the light of Asian hermeneutics. For various practical reasons, I have presented just a few concerns in the above discussion. In addition to them, there are other topics that reflect the reality of Asia. A reader of the Gospel of Matthew can also develop themes like small group ministry in the Gospel (Matt 18:20), Jesus's divinity and personality by yin-yang theory, the Sermon on the Mount and the emergence of Gandhian nonviolence and *Satyagraha* movements, the parables and the miracles in the Asian context, Mathew and the Margins in the Majority World context, Asian folklore traditions and the Matthean folklore, ethical teachings of Jesus in the context of moral degradation, Reign of God in the context of the Roman Empire, and Matthean women in the Asian context with new eyes.[129] I leave these aspects for future Matthean scholars to pursue.

129 I thank Dr. Johnson Thomaskutty for suggesting these topics and giving valuable comments.

FURTHER READING

Balch, D. L. 1991. *Social History of the Matthean Community: Cross-Disciplinary Approaches*. Minneapolis: Fortress.

Carter, W. 2000. *Matthew and Margins: A Sociopolitical and Religious Reading*. The Bible and Liberation, edited by Norman K. Gottwald and Richard A. Horsley. Maryknoll, NY: Orbis.

Ellis, P. F. 1974. *Matthew: His Mind and His Message*. Collegeville, MN: Liturgical.

France, R. T. 1985. *Matthew*. The Tyndale New Testament Commentaries, edited by Canon Leon Morris. Grand Rapids, MI: Eerdmans.

Hamerton-Kelly, R. 1972. *Attitudes toward the Law in Matthew's Gospel: A Discussion of Matthew 5:18*. Chicago: Chicago Society of Biblical Research.

Keener, C. S. 1999. *A Commentary on the Gospel of Matthew*. Grand Rapids, MI: Eerdmans.

Kingsbury, J. D. 1975. *Matthew: Structure, Christology, Kingdom*. Philadelphia: Fortress.

Luz, U. 1992. *Matthew 1–7*. Translated by Wilhelm C. Linss. Minneapolis: Fortress.

Overman, J. A. 1990. *Matthew's Gospel and Formative Judaism: The Social World of the Matthean Community*. Minneapolis: Fortress Press.

Patte, D. 1987. *The Gospel According to Matthew: A Structural Commentary on Matthew's Faith*. Philadelphia: Fortress.

Song, C.-S. 1977. *Christian Mission in Reconstruction: An Asian Analysis*. Maryknoll, NY: Orbis.

FOUR

The Gospel of Mark

Edwin Jebaraj
Gurukul Lutheran Theological College
Chennai, India

Johnson Thomaskutty
The United Theological College
Bengaluru, India

The Gospel according to Mark is the shortest among all the Gospels because the author moves fast in narrating the story of Jesus with his own unique interest and purpose. In the contemporary scholarship, Mark is treated as the first gospel account included in the canonical writings that has been arguably used by other synoptic Gospel writers in their writings. Mark's account of the suffering of Jesus cannot be neglected because it connects with the lived experience of several persecuted Asian Christian communities today. Hence in this chapter, as an Asian reader of the Markan account, the contextual realities will be kept in mind to provide an introduction to the book.

PRELIMINARY CONCERNS OF THE GOSPEL

Authorship

The authorship of the Gospel of Mark is shrouded in mystery. This is because the Gospel does not mention the name of its author. It may be possible that Mark is the real name of the author. However, there is no mention either in the Scriptures or in the tradition as to who this Mark is. William Lane, in his attempt to find out the authorship of the Gospel, cites an "unbroken tradition" that holds the Gospel was written by John Mark, who transcribed the teaching of Simon Peter.[1]

The early church was unanimous in their acceptance that John Mark wrote the Second Gospel and that it was the documentation of the teachings of Simon Peter. Papias (60–130 CE) records the earliest account. Though none of his writings have survived, we come to know of this through the writing of Eusebius of Caesarea (260–340 CE). Eusebius is known as the father of church history and lived about two hundred years after Papias.[2] According to him, Papias affirms that Mark was Peter's interpreter, recorded Peter's memories of Jesus accurately but not in exact order, and took special care not to omit anything he had heard and not to put anything which is untrue. Probably Papias had the immediate concern of ascertaining the apostolic authority of Mark at a time when Marcion was championing the Gospel of Luke.[3] Justin Martyr, an early Christian apologist (150 CE), also writes about the authorship of Mark. He considers the Gospel of Mark as the memoir of Peter. In quoting Mark 3:17, Justin adds that the "sons of thunder" designation for James and John, a phrase unique to Mark, comes from Peter's memory.[4]

Another early tradition, the Anti-Marcionite Prologue to Mark (180 CE), mentions Mark as a Gospel writer and connects him with Peter. It says Mark was Peter's interpreter and that after Peter's death, he wrote down the Gospel in the regions of Italy.[5] Irenaeus (130–200 CE), a disciple of Polycarp who in turn knew the apostle John, agrees with the Anti-Marcionite Prologue. He writes that Mark wrote after the "departure" of Peter and Paul, implying their death.[6]

1 W. L. Lane, *The Gospel According to Mark: The English Text with Introduction, Exposition and Notes*, New International Commentary on the New Testament (1988; repr., Grand Rapids, MI: Eerdmans, 1974), 21.

2 David Oliver Smith, *Unlocking the Puzzle: The Keys to the Christology and Structure of the Original Gospel of Mark* (Eugene, OR: Resource, 2016), 123.

3 W. W. Wessel, "Mark," in *The Expositor's Bible Commentary (Matthew, Mark, Luke)*, ed. Frank E. Gaebelein (Grand Rapids, MI: Zondervan, 1984), 8:606.

4 Mary Ann Beavis, *Mark* (Grand Rapids, MI: Bakers, 2011), 8.

5 Wessel, "Mark," 8:606.

6 Pheme Perkins, *Introduction to the Synoptic Gospels* (Grand Rapids, MI: Eerdmans, 2007), 14.

Clement of Alexandria (195 CE) asserts that Mark, who was Peter's follower, wrote in response to a request from those who heard Peter preached in Rome.[7] The authorship of Mark, the interpreter of Peter, was also affirmed by Tertullian (ca. 200), Origen (ca. 200), Eusebius (ca. 324), and Jerome (ca. 392).[8] From the above traditions, it becomes plain that the authorship of the Second Gospel was attributed to John Mark very early, and that belief was widespread. The tradition of the early church points to another important aspect of her conviction that the Gospel was sourced in the testimony of the apostle Peter.

Date

The question regarding the date of Mark's Gospel is still undecided. Scholars have proposed different dates for the Gospel of Mark, and they can be brought under two sections.

Before 70 CE

For a long time, based on the early Christian tradition, it was believed that the evangelist wrote his Gospel in Rome sometime during the sixties of the first century CE. The Anti-Marcionite Prologue to Mark and Irenaeus inform that Mark wrote down the Gospel after Peter's death.[9] The death of Peter happened during the Neronian persecution of 64–65, and this puts the date of the Gospel prior to 70 CE. Cranfield says the evangelist's frankness in portraying the apostle's failures, the use of Mark by the later Synoptic writers, and the fact that chapter 13 does not presuppose the actual events of the Jewish War of 66–70 point to a date between 65 and 67 CE.[10] Kümmel thinks that Mark was written in 70 CE.[11] Nonetheless, alternative answers with regard to the question of the Gospel's date have been proposed.

7 Mary Healy, *The Gospel of Mark* (Grand Rapids, MI: Baker Academic, 2008), 18.

8 R. H. Stein, *Mark*, Baker Exegetical Commentary on the New Testament (Grand Rapids, MI: Baker Academic, 2008), 4; Beavis, *Mark*, 8.

9 C. E. B. Cranfield, *The Gospel according to St Mark: An Introduction and Commentary*, Cambridge Greek Testament Commentaries (Cambridge: Cambridge University Press, 1959), 4.

10 Cranfield, 8.

11 W. G. Kümmel, *Introduction to the New Testament*, trans. Howard Clark Kee (Nashville: Abingdon, 1996), 98.

James Crossley connects Mark 13:14 with the Caligula crisis when the emperor threatened to set up his statue in the temple.[12] He further argues that Mark's Gospel presents Jesus as one fully observing biblical law, an assumption that could have been possible only at a time when Christianity was largely law observant, and this puts the date of the Gospel not later than the mid-40s.[13] C. S. Mann uses the Griesbach hypothesis to show that Mark's Gospel was composed in two drafts, the first in Rome (55 CE) and the second in Palestine (65 CE). He further says Mark used Matthew and Luke for the second draft and condensed them.[14] However, the number of scholars who support the early date is few.

After 70 CE

Brandon argues that the events described in Mark 13 reflect the situation of the Roman Christians in 71 CE. Brandon contends that there were Christians who were embarrassed by the fact that their founder was crucified for sedition. Consequently, the Gospel of Mark tried to argue that Jesus was not seditious, and it blamed Jesus's death more on Jewish leaders than on the Romans.[15] Thus, the Gospel was written shortly after 71 CE to encourage fellow Christians in Rome at a time of sore perplexity and danger.[16] F. J. Moloney prefers a date after 70 but before 75 CE.[17] However, the dates proposed by Brandon and Moloney have not found acceptance among a majority of NT scholars.

Though the exact date of the Gospel of Mark is uncertain, the external and internal evidence show that the Gospel is the eyewitness account of the life, actions, and teachings of Jesus as delivered by Peter and that it was compiled and distributed after his death (64–65 CE). The overwhelming argument by a majority of scholars favors a date before 70 CE. It can be assumed that Mark was written in the mid-sixties.

12 J. G. Crossley, *The Date of Mark's Gospel: Insights from the Law in Earliest Christianity* (London: T&T Clark, 2004), 19–43.

13 Crossley, 82–124.

14 C. S. Mann, *Mark: A New Translation with Introduction and Commentary*, AB 27 (New York: Doubleday, 1986), 76–77.

15 S. G. F. Brandon, *Jesus and the Zealots: A Study of the Political Factor in Jewish Christianity* (Manchester, UK: Manchester University Press, 1967), 245–46.

16 Brandon, 227.

17 F. J. Moloney, *The Gospel of Mark: A Commentary* (Grand Rapids, MI: Baker Academic, 2002), 14.

Place of Writing

It is difficult to determine with certainty the original place of the writing of the Gospel. At least four places are suggested as possible locations for Mark's composition. The traditional view stands in favor of Rome as the place of the composition of Mark's Gospel. Papias, Anti-Marcionite Prologue, Irenaeus, and Clement of Alexandria believed that the Gospel was written in Rome. On the basis of the patristic evidences, Taylor maintains Rome as the place of origin.[18] The evidence of the Gospel's relation to Peter (1 Pet 5:13) and the presence of Latinisms (5:9; 15:16, 39, 44, 45; 12:15) suggest Rome as the location. Lane points to the Roman method of reckoning time used in Mark in support of Rome (6:48; 13:35).[19] Cranfield connects Mark 15:21 with Romans 16:13 to suggest that the Rufus named by both Paul and Mark is one and the same. According to Cranfield, Mark's mention of Rufus as Simon's son and the references to suffering and persecution (8:34–38; 10:38–39; 13:9–13) that indicate the hostile social conditions the church was enduring under Nero's reign point to the Roman origin of the Gospel.[20] In the past few decades, the traditional view that Mark was composed in Rome was rejected by several influential scholars, and other locations are suggested.

The first scholar who strongly advocated for Syria as a possible location for Mark was Bartlet.[21] According to Bartlet, Papias's knowledge of John the Presbyter, who lived in the East, possibly in Antioch; Peter's connection with the Antiochene church; the reference to Simon of Cyrene (15:21; see Acts 21:20); Mark's use of Aramaic words; Antioch being a great center of Roman culture and the place where Christians first received that name on the model of Roman political factions; the very early use of Mark's Gospel by Matthew and Luke; and Mark's unexplained use of Palestinian geography point to a place other than Rome, and he says Antioch fits into the space.

Two notable NT scholars who set Mark's origin in Galilee are Willi Marxsen and Kelber. According to Ernest van Eck, Marxsen's Galilean setting for Mark is based on two earlier works of Lohmeyer (1936) and Lightfoot (1938),

18 Vincent Taylor, *The Gospel According to St. Mark: The Greek Text with Introduction, Notes, and Indexes* (London: Macmillan, 1963), 32.

19 Lane, *Gospel According to Mark*, 24–25.

20 Cranfield, *Gospel according to St Mark*, 8–9.

21 J. V. Bartlet, *St. Mark: Introduction* (Edinburgh: T. C. & E. C. Jack, 1922), 34–38.

who preferred a Galilean setting of Mark based on the theme of conflict. Lohmeyer and Lightfoot, in their studies of the Gospel, find a direct opposition between Galilee and Jerusalem. While Lohmeyer says Galilee is the center of Jesus's ministry and Jerusalem is the center of opposition toward Jesus's ministry, the sphere of hate and misunderstanding, Lightfoot says Galilee is the sphere of revelation and Jerusalem is the sphere of rejection.[22]

John Chrysostom suggested that the Gospel was composed in Egypt. This is the only contrary witness in the early Christian tradition concerning the origin of Mark.[23] Chrysostom's view that Mark wrote in Egypt has not found acceptance among the NT scholars because many view it as a mistake and based on a misunderstanding of a statement in Eusebius's *Ecclesiastical History* (2.16.1): "They say that Mark set out for Egypt and was first to preach there the gospel which he composed."[24] Despite the various attempts to locate the writing of the Gospel in Antioch or Galilee, the arguments in favor of Rome are too strong. As mentioned earlier, both the external and internal evidences point to the origin of the Gospel in Rome. It makes sense considering Mark's connection with Peter, the use of Latin words, the interpretation of the phrases in Aramaic (5:41; 7:34; 15:34), the explanation of Jewish customs (7:3–4), and the references to persecution.

Reading the Gospel of Mark through an Asian lens reveals the importance of the Gospel's setting in a multilinguistic, multicultural, and multireligious context. The context of Asia is pluriform in nature, where people belonging to different cultures, speaking different languages, and professing different faiths coexist. Though the land of Asia is known as the birthplace of major religions of the world, there are social ills such as casteism, religious fundamentalism, and pseudonationalism in varied forms, and they afflict the society. The Gospel of Mark is written in a pluralistic context of Rome to unite and strengthen the people to withstand social evils, so it has much relevance to the pluriform Asian context.

22 Ernst Van Eck, "A Sitz for the Gospel of Mark? A Critical Reaction to Bauckham's Theory on the Universality of the Gospels," *HTS Theological Studies* 56, no. 4 (2000): 968–1003, esp. 982–83.

23 Wessel, "Mark," 608.

24 Wessel, 608–9; also see Cranfield, *Gospel according to St Mark*, 8–9.

Audience

Identifying the original audience of the Gospel is a complex issue because different views are proposed by scholars.[25] A rapid reading of the Gospel reveals that its audience are gentiles. Apart from the frequent observation of the translation of Aramaic phrases into Greek in several instances and the explanation of Jewish customs and ideas in the Gospel, the rarely noticed reference to the possibility of women initiating divorce (10:12) suggests gentiles as the audience of Mark.[26] The text further gives enough clues for a Christian audience familiar with the gospel traditions.[27] In line with this, Hengel argues that the Gospel is "obviously written for gentile Christians."[28] However, it does not mean that the Jewish Christians are excluded from the audience of Mark. S. H. Smith argues that the controversy stories that are written in the pattern of Rabbinic-style debate with which the Jewish audience would have been familiar points to a mixed audience of Mark.[29] Thus, one can assume that Rome, as a large metropolis, must have had a mixed audience of gentile and Jewish Christians.

The emphasis on suffering in the Gospel as an essential requirement to follow Jesus, Markan theology of the cross, and the frequent failure of the disciples indicate that the audience to whom it is addressed is exposed to persecution and death.[30] It agrees with the persecution of the Christians under Nero, during whose reign Peter was martyred. The Gospel was meant to encourage the Christians suffering persecution under a tyrant. Christopher Bryan says the audience of Mark was people who probably found themselves isolated and insecure, victims of others' violence and dragged before kings and governors, yet who find their security and their very identity in the Christian community and in the fellowship of Jesus Christ.[31]

---

25 W. R. Telford, *Mark* (Sheffield, UK: Sheffield Academic Press, 1995), 151.

26 S. H. Smith, *A Lion with Wings: A Narrative-Critical Approach to Mark's Gospel* (Sheffield, UK: Sheffield Academic Press, 1996), 38.

27 Stein outlines seven evidences to establish the Christian audience of Mark's Gospel. See Stein, *Mark*, 9–10.

28 Martin Hengel, *Studies in the Gospel of Mark* (Eugene, OR: Wipf & Stock, 2003), 13.

29 Smith, *Lion with Wings*, 38.

30 Moloney, *Gospel of Mark*, 12.

31 Christopher Bryan, *A Preface to Mark: Notes on the Gospel in Its Literary and Cultural Settings* (Oxford: Oxford University Press, 1997), 160.

The situation of suffering and persecution of the Christians in Rome as portrayed in the Gospel has deeper significance to the Asian context because Christians living here also endure similar experiences. To remain a true Christian often requires giving up one's rights and privileges, as well as a willingness to suffer and even die. Christianity in the Roman world of Mark's time was considered a subversive movement, and Christians were characterized as the followers of an anti-Roman rebel. In the Asian context, there are instances of Christians being branded as antinational simply for being truthful to their faith convictions. The pluriform nature of the Christian community in Asia is another aspect of comparison with the Markan community. The community of Mark was struggling to maintain unity in the face of hostilities; Asian Christians grapple with the issue of division in the name of caste, tribe, region, and language. The heretical teachings with which the Markan community was struggling can be compared, in the Asian context, with false teachings that often come in the form of false prophecy. On the one hand, Christians in Asia see Jesus as the suffering Son of Man identifying with them in their struggles. On the other hand, they see him as the liberating Messiah who gives them glory in the midst of suffering.

Purpose

Finding the reason for the writing of the Gospel is a complex issue because Mark does not specifically state his purpose in writing the Gospel. Though in the very first verse he indicates that his purpose is to write a "gospel"—that is, an account of the good news about Jesus Christ, the Son of God—the omission of the birth narratives and accounts of Jesus's early life raises questions regarding the historicity of the person of Jesus as the Son of God. According to Martin Dibelius, the purpose of Mark was twofold: on the one hand, to show Jesus as the Messiah, and on the other hand, "to show why He was not recognized as Messiah by the people and why He was opposed, despised, and finally sent to the cross."[32] Therefore, he calls the Gospel of Mark "a book of secret epiphanies."[33] This view is not fully accepted because the Gospel points

32 M. Dibelius, *From Tradition to Gospel* (Cambridge, UK: James Clarke, 1971), 230.
33 Dibelius, 230.

to other factors as well. Scholarly opinions evade consensus, and several views are expressed as probable reasons for the writing of the Gospel.[34]

As Eusebius mentioned, the aging of Peter probably prompted Mark to preserve Peter's personal account of the life of Jesus.[35] This may be due to his concern that after the death of the eyewitnesses, the accounts might be manipulated unless they are put into writing. Clement of Alexandria says Mark recorded Peter's preaching in response to a request made by Peter's hearers in Rome. Mark may be understood as a pastoral response in difficult times. When the church was struggling with twin major problems, both internal and external, Mark wrote with a pastoral concern. Kelber sees Mark's primary purpose as correcting a false Christology that is centered on the understanding concerning the Parousia.[36] Several scholars express the view that Mark was written to strengthen the persecuted Christians of Rome. Guthrie describes the Gospel as a call to extreme discipleship, which requires an acceptance of persecution. He says Mark likely wrote in order to explain why Christians had to suffer.[37] For Culpepper, Mark is a "gospel of hope" because it is written for a persecuted community.[38] Using the redaction-critical analysis of the four passages that speak about the persecution of Christians (4:17; 8:34–35; 10:29–30; 13:9–13), Roskam argues that Mark's purpose is to exhort and encourage the persecuted Christians.[39]

The scholars who are mentioned above are unanimous in their view that the Gospel of Mark was written in response to persecution of the Christians. It makes sense to think that the imminent danger to Christians was caused by the rise of Nero, who used persecution as a ploy to hide his failures. The

34 See Adam Winn, *The Purpose of Mark's Gospel*, WUNT 2 (Tübingen: Mohr Siebeck, 2008), 5–42; Donald Guthrie, *NT Introduction*, rev. ed. (Leicester, UK: Apollos, 1990), 65–71.

35 David E. Garland, *Mark: NIV Application Commentary* (Grand Rapids, MI: Zondervan, 1996), 28.

36 Werner H. Kelber, *The Kingdom in Mark: A New Place and a New Time* (Minneapolis: Fortress, 1974), 130.

37 Guthrie, *NT Introduction*, 70–71.

38 R. A. Culpepper, *Mark*, Smyth & Helwys Bible Commentary (Macon, GA: Smyth & Helwys, 2007), 23.

39 See H. N. Roskam, *The Purpose of the Gospel of Mark in Its Historical and Social Context*, NTS 114 (Leiden: Brill, 2004), 72–74; D. Rhoads, J. Dewey, and D. Michie, *Mark as Story: An Introduction to the Narrative of a Gospel* (Philadelphia: Fortress, 1982), 139–40.

persecution of Christians must have caused a faith crisis that Mark attempted to address. Thus the Gospel is written to encourage Christians who are either being persecuted or about to be persecuted. According to C. F. D. Moule, the main purpose of Mark was evangelistic.[40] Gundry also thinks Mark's purpose was "to convert non-Christians despite the shame of the cross."[41] Kümmel supports a polemic purpose behind the writing of the Gospel.[42] He says Mark defends Jesus against the charge that he abandoned the Jewish law and against the suspicion of Jewish nationalism. Further, he holds the Jewish leaders guilty of Jesus's crucifixion (3:6; 12:13; 14:1, 55).

In the Asian context, persecution of Christians is alarmingly intensifying, false teachings are on the rise, and social evils such as casteism, religious fundamentalism, and pseudonationalism are mounting. The Gospel of Mark has relevance in Asia because it motivates the faithful to remain strong in the face of threats and persecution, bear witness for truth, and work toward the formation of a transformed society. It also offers tools for cross-cultural mission.

Structure

A quick reading of the Gospel will reveal that it has a rigid geographical structure characterized by Jesus's movement from Galilee to Jerusalem. It is because of this reason that Guthrie calls Mark the "Gospel of action."[43] On geographical considerations, Mark's Gospel can be divided into six sections.

1:1–13 . . . . . . Prologue: The preparation of Jesus for ministry

1:14–8:26 . . . . Jesus's ministry in Galilee and the neighboring gentile territories

8:27–10:52 . . . Journey to Jerusalem

11:1–13:37. . . . Ministry in Jerusalem

40 Cited by Guthrie, *NT Introduction*, 65.

41 Culpepper, *Mark*, 24; also see R. H. Gundry, *Mark: A Commentary on His Apology for the Cross* (Grand Rapids, MI: Eerdmans, 1993), 1026.

42 Kümmel, *Introduction to the New Testament*, 93.

43 Guthrie, *NT Introduction*, 61.

14:1–16:8 . . . . Passion, death, and resurrection of Jesus

16:9–20 . . . . . Epilogue: The conclusion of Jesus's ministry[44]

As noted earlier, Galilee is the geographical center for the first half of the Gospel of Mark, whereas in the second part, there is a shift toward Jerusalem as the center of Jesus's ministry. Mark's structure follows the basic pattern of the early Apostolic preaching as seen in Acts 10:37–43. This structural outline is shared by both Matthew and Luke. The scholars who propose a topographical structure of Mark are Cranfield, Guthrie, and Kümmel. An important feature in the Gospel is Peter's confession of faith in Jesus at Caesarea Philippi (8:27–31). Prior to this incident, one can observe Jesus performing many miracles and preaching to large crowds in Galilee, whereas after 8:31, the action shifts from Galilee to gentile areas or hostile Judea, where only a few miracles are performed and Jesus mainly teaches his disciples. However, the passion narrative dominates the second part of the Gospel, and all the teachings and events that happened before are considered as preparatory for the passion.

There is no scholarly consensus for a fixed structure, and this is because the organizing principles on the basis of which a structure is constructed are diverse. For example, S. H. Smith makes comparative analyses of the structures of both Mark and Greek tragedies and argues that the structure of Mark is similar to that of a Greek tragedies.[45] Similarly, apart from topography, structures are also constructed on the basis of theological themes, *Sitz im Leben* of the recipients, literary factors, and lectionary concerns.[46] Despite the diverse structures proposed, the topographical structure stands out as the accepted one among the majority of the scholars.

44 Mark 16:9–20 is generally considered as a later addition because the oldest manuscripts that are considered to be accurate do not contain this section.

45 S. H. Smith, "A Divine Tragedy: Some Observations on the Dramatic Structure of Mark's Gospel," *Novum Testamentum* 37, no. 3 (1995): 227–28.

46 See K. W. Larsen, "The Structure of Mark's Gospel: Current Proposals," *Currents in Biblical Research* 3, no. 1 (2004): 143–64.

MARK AND THE CONTEMPORARY ASIAN REALITIES

The Gospel of Mark serves as one of the significant literary masterpieces that accommodates the individualistic, familial, social, and contextual dynamics of Asian realities. The Second Gospel's setting, characterization, and plot development provide a realistic feeling in the process of reading. At the same time, it reverberates in the literary and situational thought-world of Asian communities.

Markan Jesus and the Asian Realities

The Gospel of Mark provides certain indications that take the attention of the reader toward Asian realities. The setting of the story is delineated with the help of some of the Asian geographical and topographical details. It also presents some of the typical Asian characters and their contextual and behavioral patterns. At the introductory level, the narrator introduces the appearance of John the Baptist (1:1–8), the baptism (1:9–11), and the temptation of Jesus (1:12–13).[47] Thereafter, the readers are drawn to the four major areas of Jesus's ministry: first, ministry around the Sea of Galilee (1:14–5:43); second, further journeys in Galilee (6:1–9:50); third, the Judean period (10:1–13:37); and fourth, the passion and the resurrection of Jesus (14:1–16:20).[48] This development of Jesus's ministry is centrifugal in nature, as it takes the attention of the reader to the Acts 1:8 mission model. For Mark, the starting point of Jesus's mission and ministry is the Galilean province—that is, in Asian realities. In his home state, Jesus engages himself in preaching (1:14–15, 39), teaches and performs miraculous signs (1:16–38, 40–45; 4:35–5:43), engages in discourses (4:1–34), calls the disciples (3:13–19), and establishes his ties with the world (3:31–35).[49] As Jesus's mission takes shape in Asian realities, its centrifugal nature is demonstrated. For Jesus, hometown is the most significant place in the process of missional and ministerial involvements.[50]

47 Guthrie, *NT Introduction*, 100–101.

48 Paul J. Achtemeier, Joel B. Green, and Marianna Meye Thompson, *Introducing the NT: Its Literature and Theology* (Grand Rapids, MI: Eerdmans, 2001), 129–42.

49 See Guthrie, *NT Introduction*, 100.

50 Raymond E. Brown, *An Introduction to the NT* (Bangalore: Theological Publications in India, 2009), 128–38.

Jesus's rejection in Nazareth (6:1–6) and his movements in the regions of Gennesaret (6:53–56), Syro-Phoenicia (7:24–8:10), Bethesda (8:22–26), Caesarea Philippi (8:27–9:29),[51] and other parts of Galilee demonstrate the geographical and topographical expansion of his itinerant ministry.[52] In 10:1–16:20, the ministry of Jesus develops in the Judean province. But in Mark, the ministry of Jesus is mostly restricted within the national boundary with an exception of some of the neighboring towns and villages.[53] The universal mission of Jesus is accomplished through the disciples after the ascension. Jesus's pronouncement to the disciples in Acts 1:8 underscores the paradigmatic mission of the early church.[54] As Jesus was migrated to and relocated in the Jerusalemite context, the mission focus was shifted from the Galilean provinces to the Judean provinces. Hence the starting point of the disciples' mission was Jerusalem.[55] This paradigm of Jesus's mission demonstrates that the early Christian mission started from Asian realities and flourished to the end of the world. Mark focuses on Jesus as an Asian, and his ministry emerged out of the realities of the Asian context.

Michael Amaladoss finds in Jesus some of the Asian images as he demonstrates him as a sage, guru, *satyagrahi* (seeker of truth), *avatar* (incarnation of God), servant, compassionate one, and pilgrim. Asian readers can identify all the previously stated images in their own contexts. They can see the socioreligious and politico-cultural dynamisms of Asian realities at work within the text.[56] In his famous lecture entitled "Jesus Christ: Europe and Asia" (1866), Keshub Chandra Sen identifies Christianity's first form as Asiatic because Jesus was an Asian teacher, and his disciples were Asiatic.[57] Further, P. C. Mozoomdar, in his book *The Oriental Christ*, emphasizes the fact that Christ is of Asia.[58] The Markan portrait of Jesus is one of the significant narrative

51 See Craig S. Keener, *The IVP Bible Background Commentary: New Testament* (Downers Grove, IL: InterVarsity, 1993), 149–63.

52 Guthrie, *NT Introduction*, 101.

53 Guthrie, 101.

54 See D. Edmond Hiebert, *An Introduction to the NT: Three Volume Collection* (Waynesboro, GA: Gabriel, 2003), 100–101.

55 John D. Grassmick, "Mark," in *The Bible Knowledge Commentary: New Testament* (Colorado Springs, CO: Authentic, 2004), 101–2.

56 See Michael Amaladoss, *The Asian Jesus* (Delhi: ISPCK, 2005).

57 Anantanand Rambachan, *Essays in Hindu Theology* (Minneapolis: Fortress, 2019), 98.

58 Quoted in Robin Boyd, *An Introduction to Indian Christian Theology* (Delhi: ISPCK, 2000), 30.

masterpieces that delineate the Asian image of Jesus to the Roman audience. Jesus's migration from heaven to earth at the macrolevel and from Galilee to Judea at the microlevel are important narrative developments to understand the theological master plan of the Gospel.[59] As the Asian Christian theologians in particular and the interpreters of the Scripture across the globe in general constantly deal with the issue of migration, Jesus's movement from the Galilean scenario to the Judean context can be considered a significant indicator for hermeneutical reflections.[60]

Portrait of Jesus as a Powerful Savior

In the first eight chapters of Mark, Jesus is presented as a triumphalist wonder-worker. Guthrie comments, "Mark sees the disciples as spokesmen for a theology of glory linked to the Hellenistic divine man idea."[61] At the outset of the Gospel, the narrator states, "The beginning of the gospel about Jesus Christ, the Son of God" (1:1). After setting the stage and the entry of the Son of God, the narrator invites the attention of the reader toward the public ministry of Jesus. The prologue of Mark (1:1–13) focuses on the baptism of Jesus and the coming of the Holy Spirit upon him (1:12–13).[62] As a Spirit-endowed figure, Jesus engages into a triumphalist ministry that includes healing the sick, performing exorcisms, and teaching the word.[63] His ministry as the "Messiah, Son of God" runs from 1:16–8:26, and his power to heal and exorcise (1:21–28, 29–34, 40–45; 2:1–12; 3:7–12; 5:1–20, 21–43; 6:32–44, 45–56; 7:24–37; 8:1–10, 22–26) and his authority above the teachers of the law (1:27–28; 7:1–23), the Sabbath (2:23–28; 3:1–6), and the natural powers (4:35–41) are exemplified by the narrator to the readers.[64] Pheme Perkins states, "On the human level, Jesus' powerful miracles and teaching attract crowds of followers but they also lead to strong opposition from both religious (scribes, Pharisees) and political (Herodians) authorities. On the cosmic level, Jesus' ministry is pictured as a conflict

59 Brown, *Introduction to the NT*, 128–38.

60 See Songram Basumatary, ed., *Migration in Perspectives: Towards Theology of Migration from the Margins* (Chennai: GLTC, 2018).

61 Guthrie, *NT Introduction*, 68.

62 Brown, *Introduction to the NT*, 128–38.

63 R. A. Guelich, "Mark, Gospel of," in *Dictionary of Jesus and the Gospels*, ed. Joel B. Green, Scot McKnight, and I. Howard Marshall (Downers Grove, IL: InterVarsity, 1992), 516.

64 Guelich, 516.

with Satan."[65] Jesus's appearance as a powerful Savior in the first eight chapters of the Gospel has a lot of significance in the Asian context. His authority over diseases, the powers of darkness, and the natural world has relevance in the contemporary context, which includes people who are afflicted by evil powers, epidemic and pandemic situations, and natural disasters.

Jesus's presence as an authoritative teacher and preacher is obvious in the Gospel of Mark. He teaches in the synagogue as one who has authority (1:22, 38–39; 2:13; 3:22–35; 4:1–34; 6:8–11; 7:14–23; 8:34–38). Jesus demonstrates himself as a teacher who guides his disciples to a divine lifestyle.[66] It is not only the Jewish and the Greco-Roman teachers but also the Asian teachers who are known in the areas of ethical and moral teachings. In Chinese context, Confucius was a great teacher who taught his disciples to be ethically and morally upright.[67] Buddha was popularly known as a teacher who imparted higher knowledge to his disciples.[68] In Sikhism, Guru Nanak, a succession of other gurus, and finally Guru Granth Sahib open ways for a teaching tradition.[69] The guru traditions of India and Asia see the resonances in the Markan tradition. Jesus as a *Sadguru* (Good Teacher) and *swamy* (sage) who walks through the roads of India can be derived out from the annals of the Markan story.

Mark has a unique nature of using resistance language to counter the Roman Empire.[70] Jesus is introduced as the Son of God, a title ascribed to Roman emperors like Augustus, Tiberius, Nero, Titus, and Domitian.[71] Jesus's authority as the Son of God places him above all the powers and principalities of the world. Ched Myers states, "Mark's story of Jesus stands virtually alone among the literary achievements of antiquity for one reason: it is a narrative

65 Pheme Perkins, *New Testament Introduction* (Mumbai: St. Paul's, 2002), 265.

66 R. Riesner, "Teacher," in Green, McKnight, and Marshall, *Dictionary of Jesus and the Gospels*, 807–11.

67 For more details about Confucius's teachings, see *Stanford Encyclopedia of Philosophy*, s.v. "Confucius," accessed July 29, 2020, https://plato.stanford.edu/entries/confucius/.

68 Holger Kersten, *Jesus Lived in India: His Unknown Life before and after the Crucifixion* (Gurgaon: Penguin, 2001), 114–23.

69 Christopher Shackle and Arvind-pal Singh Mandair, eds., *Teachings of the Sikh Gurus: Selections from the Sikh Scriptures* (London: Routledge, 2005), xi–xx.

70 John Drane, *Introducing the New Testament* (Oxford: Lion Hudson, 1999), 199.

71 J. R. Daniel Kirk, *A Man Attested by God: The Human Jesus of the Synoptic Gospels* (Grand Rapids, MI: Eerdmans, 2016), 257.

for and about the common people. The Gospel reflects the daily realities of disease, poverty, and disenfranchisement."[72] In Mark, on the one hand, the narrator foregrounds the socioreligious and politico-cultural realities of the Roman Empire, and on the other hand, he brings to the fore Jesus as a transformer of the social life. As Myers says, "It breaks the 'cultural silence' of the poor by making them—fishers and farmers, the lame and leprous—the central subjects and protagonists of the gospel of the kingdom."[73] The Gospel of Mark substitutes the Roman Empire with the kingdom of God.[74] The Markan contextual realities of the diseased, the poor, and the neglected reverberate in the Asian context in a convincing way.[75] The narrator's portrayal of Jesus as a powerful and authoritative teacher, provider, healer, and social transformer is a significant paradigm in the present realities of Asians.[76]

Suffering Servant Model of Jesus

The last eight chapters (9–16) of the Gospel present Jesus in terms of a suffering servant. Jesus's three predictions about his suffering inaugurate the passion scene in the Gospel (8:31–32; 9:30–31; and 10:33–34).[77] In 8:31–32, Mark speaks about the rejection of Jesus and his death; in 9:30–31, Mark speaks about the betrayal and the death; and in 10:33–34, Mark speaks about the rejection and the resultant suffering in the form of condemnation, mocking, spitting, flogging, and killing. In all these passages, the resurrection of Jesus is also emphasized.[78] The second evangelist presents Jesus as a suffering servant when the Jewish and the Christian minorities in Rome were undergoing persecution under Claudius and his successor, Nero.[79] Though Jesus is a glorious figure (Mark 1–8), his identification with the persecuted sects in the Roman

72 Ched Myers, *Binding the Strong Man: A Political Reading of Mark's Story of Jesus* (Maryknoll, NY: Orbis, 2002), 39.

73 Myers, 40.

74 Paul N. Anderson, *From Crisis to Christ: A Contextual Introduction to the New Testament* (Nashville: Abingdon, 2014), 71–72.

75 See Myers, *Binding the Strong Man*, 91–167.

76 R. S. Sugirtharajah, *The Bible and Asia: From the Pre-Christian Era to the Postcolonial Age* (Cambridge, MA: Harvard University Press, 2013).

77 Perkins, *NT Introduction*, 266.

78 Perkins, 266–67.

79 Anderson, *From Crisis to Christ*, 55–56.

Empire is made obvious.[80] In that sense, there emerges a transition from a dynamic Jesus to a static Jesus. This aspect of the Gospel is an attempt to correct the early church's wrong notion of understanding the Christ event. While the disciples of Jesus were embracing a theology of glory, the narrator teaches them also about a suffering servant model of ministry.[81] This phenomenon of the Gospel cautions the Asian Christians to rejoice even in the midst of their minority status, struggles, persecution, and death-like situations in life.

The theology of glory culminates with the transfiguration account (9:1–29), and the theology of suffering foreshadows thereafter with the three predictions about the passion (8:31–32; 9:30–31; 10:33–34). Keener comments, "In Mark 9:2–13, the glory of Jesus, who is greater than Moses and Elijah, is revealed on the mountain; he is thus the ultimate spokesperson for God (Deut 18:18–19)."[82] When it comes to Mark 10:41–45, the theme of suffering is underscored through Jesus's significant utterance: "For the Son of Man came not to be served but to serve, and to give his life a ransom for many" (10:45).[83] The servant model of leadership in Mark patterns the messianic figure in Isaiah 53. As a messianic servant, Jesus is concerned about the poor, dehumanized, persecuted, and ostracized.[84] In that sense, the arrest, trial, passion, crucifixion, and death of Jesus (14:1–15:47) are dramatic movements and at the same time a parody to the Roman imperial system.[85] The Little Apocalypse in Mark 13 demonstrates Jesus's prophetic vision about the life of the people that combines the present struggles and the future glory.[86] At the macrolevel of the story, the glorious Jesus (chs. 1–8) turns into a suffering Son of Man (chs. 9–15). In chapter 16, the suffering Son of Man is declared as the resurrected Lord.[87]

Asian communities can derive a contextually inclined hermeneutical paradigm from the Markan narrative. First, the story turns from a theology of glory (chs. 1–8) to a theology of suffering (chs. 9–15), and from a theology

80 Guthrie, *NT Introduction*, 68.
81 Guthrie, 68.
82 Keener, *IVP Bible Background Commentary*, 157.
83 Keener, 163–64.
84 Keener, 163.
85 Grassmick, "Mark," 174–92.
86 Grassmick, 166–73.
87 Achtemeier, Green, and Thompson, *Introducing the NT*, 129–43.

of suffering (chs. 9–15) to a theology of glory (ch. 16). Asian Christian communities are encouraged to balance their lifestyles between the glorious and the suffering times in their lives.[88] Second, the transfiguration account (9:1–29), the Little Apocalypse (ch. 13), and the resurrection narrative attune the attention of Asian communities toward a future glorious time. Third, the passion is followed by a resurrection, so Asian communities are motivated to be hopeful about their future. Thus Mark emphasizes a situation of transition, a theology of transformation, and a triumphalist future. As Mark demonstrates the servant model of Jesus as a means to achieve glorification, the Asian church is instructed to implement a suffering servant model in its missional and ministerial involvements.

A Gospel of Action in the Asian Context

Mark presents Jesus's story in a unique style as a gospel of action. In the Gospel, Jesus appears as the protagonist with candor.[89] The evangelist is more concerned about the movements of Jesus rather than his discourses. Guthrie comments, "The vividness of the style gives the impression of a quickly-moving drama with the cross as its climax."[90] The characteristic features such as brevity, action, vividness, and realism take the Gospel more closely to the oral realities.[91] On several occasions, the Gospel presents the preaching and the teaching of Jesus in passing statements as follows: "Jesus went into the synagogue and began to teach" (1:21b; see 2:13); "the people were amazed at his teaching" (1:22a); "so he travelled throughout Galilee, preaching in their synagogues and driving out demons" (1:39).[92] Mostly this tendency is vivid in the Gospel except, for example, in 4:2–32; 7:6–23; and 13:1–37. Otherwise, the narrator is mostly interested in describing the miraculous events centered on Jesus: the driving out of demons (1:21–28) and many healing narratives (1:32–39), like the one of a leper (1:40–45), a paralytic man (2:1–12), and others.[93] Through the means of the Greek parataxis *kai* and the formulaic

88 Guthrie, *NT Introduction*, 68.
89 Guthrie, 61–62.
90 Guthrie, 61.
91 Hiebert, *Introduction to the NT*, 97–99.
92 Keener, *IVP Bible Background Commentary*, 137–43.
93 Keener, 137–43.

expression *euthys*, Mark's Jesus moves as a fast-paced protagonist who exhibits the potential of the kingdom of God among the people.[94] Mary Healy says, "One of the favourite words is *euthys*, 'immediately,' used over forty times (as compared to six times in Matthew and once in Luke), giving his narrative a sense of urgency and fast-paced action."[95] As an action-packed gospel, the narrator shows the authority of Jesus as the powerful Son of Man, his command over the unclean spirit, his potential to heal and transform human lives, and his ability to engage in the mission of God in the world.[96]

Mark's portrayal of Jesus and the events in the Gospel reverberate in several ways in the Asian contextual realities. The narrator emphasizes the movement of Jesus and details the events one after another. The candor of the narrator is a significant aspect. The narrator of the story, the protagonist Jesus, and the disciples together make the events colloquial and plain to the readers. Jesus's emotions of compassion, severity, anger, sorrow, tenderness, and love are expressed in public without any artificiality or coverage (1:41, 43; 3:5; 8:12, 33; 10:14, 16, 21).[97] The stated characteristics like the fast-paced dramatic movement, the candor of the characters, the vividness of the events, and the colorless depiction of the story reveal the realistic nature of the narrative.[98] As the Markan community was a persecuted community with a large number of diseased and demon-possessed people, the narrator records the story without incorporating any stylistic or linguistic flavors.[99] Those who read the Gospel in the Asian context can identify themselves with the persecuted, diseased, demon-possessed, and dehumanized members of the Markan community.[100] The Dalits, the Tribals, and the Adivasis in India; the Minjungs in Korea; the Burakumins in Japan; the plantation workers in Sri Lanka; and the poor and the ostracized in different parts of Asia can side with them.[101] The Jesus of the Gospel who is quickly moving, action oriented, and locally centered can be

94 Hiebert, *Introduction to the NT*, 97.
95 Healy, *Gospel of Mark*, 23.
96 Hiebert, *Introduction to the NT*, 97–99.
97 Guthrie, *NT Introduction*, 62.
98 Hiebert, *Introduction to the NT*, 97–104.
99 Hiebert, 97–104.
100 J. Stanly Jones, *The Jesus Movement and Its Resistance to Oppressive Institutions: A Study of Healing Narrative in Mark's Gospel* (Delhi: ISPCK, 2000), 326–42.
101 Jones, 313.

introduced for social transformation. The boldness of Jesus and the theology of power can be used as hermeneutical tools for witnessing Christ in the Asian context.

Jesus as Redeemer and Healer

The portrait of Jesus in Mark is unique because it has its own implications. At the very outset of the Gospel, the evangelist portrays the purpose of the Gospel in vivid terms. Mark attempts to show the beginning of the gospel of Jesus Christ, who is the Son of God (1:1).[102] The author states the genre of his work as a Gospel of Jesus Christ. Revealing the Son of God to the world through his deeds is one of the very purposes of the Second Gospel.[103] That makes the Gospel a Christologically oriented masterpiece. As the Son of God, Jesus intervenes in the lives of people as a healer and as an authoritative figure from above. Mark also uses the title Son of Man.[104] Through the usage of these titles, the narrator demonstrates the aspects of power and authority of the Son of God and at the same time the suffering Son of Man figure.[105] The Markan evangelist lays a significant emphasis on the passion because Jesus's missional purpose was to be a ransom for many (10:45).[106] The Markan evangelist purposes to show the power of the cross and its salvific effect on the creation. Healy says, "The cross casts its light and shadow over the whole Gospel, as the destination toward which all Jesus' public ministry—and all Scripture—inexorably leads. But in a more subtle way, the resurrection too sheds its radiant light over the Gospel."[107] In Mark, the story of Jesus takes the attention of the readers toward the cross of Jesus, the power of the atoning work on the cross, and the universal redemption through it.[108] As the primitive Christians emphasized the cross and the suffering of Jesus as marks of salvation, reconciliation, and redemption, Mark's Gospel foregrounds such an

102 Guelich, "Mark, Gospel of," 516–17.
103 Healy, *Gospel of Mark*, 23.
104 Guelich, "Mark, Gospel of," 520–21.
105 Healy, *Gospel of Mark*, 24.
106 W. R. Telford, *The Theology of the Gospel of Mark*, New Testament Theology (Cambridge: Cambridge University Press, 1999), 30–114.
107 Healy, *Gospel of Mark*, 24.
108 Telford, *Theology of the Gospel*, 103–16.

emphasis that takes contemporary readers' attention toward the root of early Christianity.

The deeds of power portrayed through the healing narratives in Mark attune the attention of the readers toward the integral relationship between the healer and the healed.[109] Guthrie states, "The miracles are not told to glorify the Healer, but to throw light on his relationships with the sick."[110] Mark's presentation of Jesus as a redeemer and healer enables Asian readers to relate their own stories with the story of Jesus in the Gospel. The image of Jesus as a redeemer and healer can be considered as a potential paradigm in the Asian context in the following ways: first, the liberative mission of Jesus as an "action-oriented Savior" can be used to portray the image of the protagonist among the marginalized communities in the Asian context;[111] second, Jesus as the powerful and authoritative figure with the impartation of the Holy Spirit can be a liberative model in the sociopolitical and religio-cultural realities in Asia;[112] third, the healing and the exorcism narratives in Mark foreground the image of Jesus as a figure from above and against all the powers that emerge from below;[113] and fourth, Jesus's image as the Son of God, Son of Man, suffering servant, martyr, redeemer, and healer reveals his nature as a glorious figure and at the same time a suffering servant intermittingly to comfort the suffering even in the midst of oppressive situations.[114]

Messianic Secrecy in the Asian Context

In Mark, Jesus instructs his disciples and those who follow him to be silent about his identity. This phenomenon is often called the "Messianic Secrecy."[115] Paul Anderson poses a significant question regarding this: "Messianic secrecy is sharply muted in Matthew and Luke, but why would Mark's Jesus proclaim the kingdom of God, perform wonders and call for a response to the

109 Jones, *Jesus Movement*, 127–254.

110 Guthrie, *NT Introduction*, 65.

111 See Yangkahao Vashum, ed., *Tribal Theology and the Bible: A Search for Contextual Relevance*, Tribal Study Series 19 (Jorhat: Eastern Theological College, 2011), 59–110.

112 Jones, *Jesus Movement*, 127–254.

113 Guelich, "Mark, Gospel of," 521.

114 Guthrie, *NT Introduction*, 62–65.

115 See William Wrede, *The Messianic Secret*, trans. J. C. G. Greig (London: James Clarke, 1971).

good news, but then command people to secrecy?"[116] This aspect continues in Mark as a style at various intersections (1:25, 34, 44; 3:12; 5:43; 7:24, 36; 8:26, 29–30; 9:9, 30).[117] The evangelist uses it as a unique rhetorical strategy to make a dichotomy between the "insider" and the "outsider." In non-Jewish locations (5:19), Jesus does not demand for secrecy to be insisted upon.[118] That leads the Markan community to strategize their ministry with a distinction between the insider and the outsider. In Mark, the cross of Jesus is the epitome of the messianic revelation.[119] The messianic secrecy can be considered a Markan community dynamic for their existence in a rival society, and at the same time, they implemented it as a rhetorical strategy for gospel propagation.[120]

In the multireligious and pluralistic Asian context, the Markan messianic secrecy can be considered a unique strategy to implement in Christian witness, mission, and evangelism.[121] Witnessing Christ in Asia cannot be done as it is exercised in other parts of the globe. Even within the Asian context, the method of witnessing Christ requires variation from context to context. The Markan context was antagonistic, there was a dichotomy between the superior and the inferior, and the followers of Jesus were widely persecuted. The *Sitz im Leben* of Jesus inspires the Markan community to initiate a countercultural movement against the imperial policies toward Christ followers.[122] While the community was involved in witnessing Christ in the imperial headquarter, they had to implement a different strategy in propagating the gospel. Messianic secrecy can be considered as a rhetorical strategy that the early Christians implemented in the Roman imperial context.[123] The same method has significance in the Asian context in the following ways: first, an insider and outsider dynamism can work well in the process of witnessing Christ in the Asian context; second, the mission of the Asian church requires certain precautions like messianic secrecy, as it is involved in witnessing Christ in a hostile world; third, as the messianic secrecy was fully revealed on the cross of Jesus, the

116 Anderson, *From Crisis to Christ*, 67.
117 Guthrie, *NT Introduction*, 521–22.
118 Hiebert, *Introduction to the NT*, 100.
119 Guthrie, *NT Introduction*, 522.
120 Anderson, *From Crisis to Christ*, 67–69.
121 Guelich, "Mark, Gospel of," 521–22.
122 Telford, *Theology of the Gospel*, 46.
123 Anderson, *From Crisis to Christ*, 67–69.

Asian church should maintain secrecy until the appropriate time of revelation; fourth, the Asian church, as a minority community, should use the device of suspense in hostile situations and surprise at favorable times as part of its mission strategy; and fifth, the messianic secrecy can be a significant tool to organize and stabilize insiders to engage in witnessing Christ to outsiders.[124]

Markan Discipleship in the Asian Context

Mark is a masterpiece of discipleship. In the Gospel, following Jesus and learning from the guru are considered the hallmarks of a disciple. Jesus calls them to become fishers of people (1:16–20) and invites them to follow him (2:14; 3:13–19). He tells his disciples to deny themselves and take up their own crosses in following him (8:34).[125] On another occasion, he calls for a rich man to sell his possessions and give the money to the poor on his way to following him (10:21). Jesus extends his call to the twelve (3:13–19) to follow him and learn from him. The disciples are sent out as apostles to fulfill the mission of God (6:7–13; also see 3:7; 8:10, 27; 10:32; 11:1, 11; 14:13, 17, 20).[126] Anderson states, "Women also accompany Jesus in some of his ministry; notably, it is they who are present at the crucifixion, while members of the Twelve are not."[127] Mark places the disciples as those who accompany their master through his missionary involvements, right from the beginning of their calling in Galilee until the journey to Judea and the events in Jerusalem.[128] In the Gospel, the disciples appear both in a narrower sense as the twelve disciples who are commissioned to share in the ministry of teaching, healing, and exorcism (3:13–14; see 5:18; 6:7–13, 30) and as a larger circle who are commissioned to do the same tasks (2:15–17; 5:19–20).[129] However, the disciples often show their failure to understand the mystery of Jesus's teaching, performances, and the coming death (4:13, 34; 7:18; 8:32–33; 9:9–13, 32; 10:10–12). As a response to the disciples, Jesus teaches on discipleship to them during his passion predictions in 8:27–10:52. As Jesus demonstrated the glory

124 See Telford, *Theology of the Gospel*, 46.
125 Anderson, *From Crisis to Christ*, 70.
126 Guelich, "Mark, Gospel of," 522–23.
127 Anderson, *From Crisis to Christ*, 71.
128 Guelich, "Mark, Gospel of," 522–23.
129 Guelich, 522.

of God on the cross, the disciples are expected to manifest honor through the means of sufferings, trials, and persecutions.[130]

Discipleship in Mark is unique in its master plan because it takes the attention of the readers toward convincing conclusions. The following things are important to note: first, the Markan community was more concerned about a theology of glory, but the narrator attempts to attune them not only to a theology of glory but also to one of suffering;[131] second, Jesus reveals his glory through his very death on the cross, and in that way, the narrative accommodates the suffering situation of the community;[132] and third, the disciples are called to follow, learn from the teacher, and get involved in the ministry, even to the point of suffering and death.[133] These aspects of the Gospel attune the message well to Asian realities as follows: first, Asian communities are well attached to their respective ideologies and the traditions of the gurus, and that connects with the Markan understanding of following the Master; second, the Markan Gospel attunes the attention of the Asian communities not only to the glorious aspects of Christian living but also to a life even in the midst of suffering;[134] third, the Asian church can identify their struggles, persecutions, and martyrdoms with the death of Jesus on the cross; and fourth, following Jesus and being his disciple even to the point of death have more significance in the Asian context than elsewhere in the world. Thus, the Markan discipleship model has more implications in the contemporary Asian context.

Mark as Story in the Asian Context

The Gospel of Mark delineates the story of Jesus as a collection of self-contained, independent literary units. Its Greek is not of a literary type. Guthrie states, "There is an absence of the carefully chosen periods of the classical models. Indeed, Mark's favorite construction seems to be parataxis, that is, the joining of clauses with a simple conjunction (*kai*)."[135] The appearances of *kai* at

130 Guelich, 523.
131 Guthrie, *NT Introduction*, 68.
132 Guthrie, 68.
133 Guelich, "Mark, Gospel of," 522–23.
134 Guthrie, *NT Introduction*, 68.
135 Guthrie, 94.

the beginning of most of the paragraphs reveal how the redactor assembled folk literature and put them together for liturgical, didactical, and apologetical purposes. The episodic nature of the literary units provides a unique feature in Mark because the pericopes can be interpreted in their own individual terms as well as within the larger framework of the Gospel. The oral nature of the delineation, the simple nature of the language, the action and brevity of the narrative, and the Aramaic flavor of the Gospel make the reader think of its realistic and communitarian outlook. The narrator's role in presenting the vivid natures of the characters through their thoughts, feelings, emotions, and intentions reveals the colloquial nature of the story.[136] The plot of the story revolves around the "good news about Jesus the Messiah, the Son of God"; his words and deeds among the people; and the climax of the story through the execution of the protagonist and the succeeding resurrection.[137] Conflict develops between the protagonist Jesus and the antagonists with demonic possessions (1:12–13, 21–27), Jewish authorities (2:1–3:6; 12:13–44), Roman authorities (15:2–15), his own family (3:20–21, 30–35), and even his own disciples (8:14–21).[138] These features of the Gospel have the potential to persuade all types of people. Jesus's heroic nature as a quickly moving, action-oriented, and authoritative but suffering Messiah attracts the readers for a transformed living.

The oral nature and the storytelling style of Mark are more relevant in the Asian context because people in this part of the world are well connected to folk traditions.[139] As the evangelist attempts to expose the life situation of Jesus and the early Christianity in a plain language, his narrative has hermeneutical significance in the contexts of the Dalit, tribal, and Adivasi struggles in India; the Minjung realities in Korea; and the life situations of the common people in China.[140] The poor, the marginalized, and the ostracized sections of the Asian community express their thoughts, feelings, emotions, and intentions distinctly from that of the elegant rhetoric of the elite groups.[141] As Mark was addressing the persecuted Christians of the Roman Empire, the author

136 Guelich, "Mark, Gospel of," 515.
137 Guelich, 515.
138 Guelich, 515.
139 This is more accurate in the context of the tribal communities in different parts of the Asian context.
140 Hiebert, *Introduction to the NT*, 97–99.
141 Jones, *Jesus Movement*, 299–342.

attempts to communicate the gospel in common language and sympathizes with those who struggle in Asia and other parts of the world. Asians are known for their use of simple parataxis and people-oriented linguistic style.[142] The storytelling style of Mark captures the attention of the Asian readers because its peculiar style has the potential to attract ordinary human situations in today's context. Thus the pool of stories stitched together in Mark connects well with varied life situations of the Asian people.

CONCLUSION

The Gospel of Mark commands a great deal of scholarly and popular attention. A majority of biblical scholars consider it the first written account of Jesus's life. Many readers are captivated by its fast-paced literary style and the use of dramatic irony. In the Asian context, Mark is one of the most admired books of the NT, and the *Sitz im Leben* of Mark is seen as similar, to a large extent, to the contemporary contextual realities. Mark has a message of encouragement and hope for the marginalized sections in the Asian context. The Second Gospel has a lot of images that can captivate the attention of Asian readers. Its fast-paced and action-oriented storyline, its emphasis on healing and redemption, Jesus's appearance as the powerful Savior, the demonstration of his suffering servant model, and the demand for absolute discipleship invite the attention of the readers.

FURTHER READING

Amaladoss, M. 2005. *The Asian Jesus*. Delhi: ISPCK.

Beavis, M. A. 2011. *Mark*. Grand Rapids, MI: Bakers.

Boyd, R. 2000. *An Introduction to Indian Christian Theology*. Delhi: ISPCK.

Cahill, M. 1998. *The First Commentary on Mark: An Annotated Translation*. Oxford: Oxford University Press.

Kersten, H. 1981/2001. *Jesus Lived in India: His Unknown Life before and after the Crucifixion*. Gurgaon: Penguin.

142 Vashum, *Tribal Theology*, 59–91.

Myers, C. 2002. *Binding the Strong Man: A Political Reading of Mark's Story of Jesus.* Maryknoll, NY: Orbis.
Shackle, C., and A. S. Mandair, eds. 2005. *Teachings of the Sikh Gurus: Selections from the Sikh Scriptures.* London: Routledge.
Stein, R. H. 2008. *Mark, Baker Exegetical Commentary on the New Testament.* Grand Rapids, MI: Baker Academics.

FIVE

The Gospel of Luke

Ekaputra Tupamahu
Portland Seminary, George Fox University
Portland, Oregon, USA

Although this introduction to the Gospel of Luke aims to present an Asian point of view of the text, the category "Asian"—being a colonial product itself—is inherently unstable. The internal differences in Asian societies contest such a large and sweeping category. Of course, one short essay will not be able to solve the enigma of what constitutes "Asianness." As one born and raised in Indonesia, I will ground the discussion here primarily in the Indonesian context—not that the category "Indonesia" as a nation-state is free of the categorical problem I just identified. Far from it. But narrowing the context at least roots my discussion in a particular Asian context—one, moreover, that has largely been absent in the English-speaking biblical scholarly conversation.

PRELIMINARY ASPECTS

Authorship

Together with the book of Acts of the Apostles, the Gospel of Luke is the first part of a two-volume work attributed to Luke. But who is this Luke? The name Luke appears only three times in the NT (Col 4:4; 2 Tim 4:11; Phil 24). Though tradition has it that this is Luke the physician, in reality, no one knows who the author of this book is. Western scholars speculate about Luke based primarily on the connection between "him" and Paul (in Pauline letters!)[1] because these scholars are philosophically conditioned to be obsessed with it.

The obsession in Western biblical scholarship with the identity of an author behind the production of a text is born out of a longing for a foundational stability of the meaning of a text. This foundation is grounded primarily in an author's psychological state. Words are a psychological product, so to understand them, one has to examine the state of mind of the author. This strategy of introspecting the internal state of authorial psychology can be traced back to Friedrich Schleiermacher's famous work on hermeneutics that has profoundly influenced Western modern biblical scholarship.[2] However, writing is more distant or detached from the author than speaking. Thus the interpretation of texts does not have to depend on an investigation of an author's psychological state, and the uncertainty regarding the identity of "Luke" should not pose a serious problem for interpretation.[3] Instead, the authorial decentering can, and I think should, open more space for Asian readers to be in a dialogical interaction with the text of the Gospel of Luke such that it does not need to rely on speculative authorship. Thus when I use the name "Luke" here, I refer not to a person but to a book.

Many local stories in Indonesia (e.g., *Batu Badaong*, *Malin Kundang*, *Sangkuriang*)[4] are not thought of as being rooted in a single authorial intention.

1 The earliest witness of the connection between Paul and Luke was found in Irenaeus's statement: "Luke also, the companion of Paul, recorded in a book the gospel preached by him" (*Adversus Haereses* 3.1.1).

2 See Friedrich Schleiermacher, *Hermeneutics and Criticism*, trans. Andrew Bowie (Cambridge: Cambridge University Press, 1998), 5–157.

3 See Joel B. Green, *The Gospel of Luke*, NICNT (Grand Rapids, MI: Eerdmans, 1997), 20.

4 *Batu Badaong* is a story of Maluccas about a mother whose son is constantly disobedient of her. In her sadness, she goes to the beach and gets swallowed by a big stone. *Malin Kundang* is a story from West Sumatra about a son who left his family to pursue his dreams in the city. He became successful and rich. At the end of the story, he denied his mother and told people around him that he did not know the woman who came to him. He was cursed because of that, and his ship was turned to stone. *Sangkuriang* comes from Sunda, West Java. It is about a man who falls in love with his own mother.

Even the tales about great figures like *Wali Sanga*[5] have circulated in society for centuries without the need to ground them in a particular authorship. They are communal stories transmitted through oral tradition. When people in Indonesia hear and learn from these stories, they do not think about the authorial intention of those stories as the only way to understand them—not only because no one has any idea who the author is but also because the notion that only a particular individual author can dictate the meaning of a story is not a consideration for them. This is why folk stories in Indonesia tend to be free and open to adaptation, change, reappropriation, and reinterpretation.[6]

Audience

The text mentions the specific addressee of both Luke and Acts as Theophilus (Luke 1:3; Acts 1:1). Who is this Theophilus? The name itself means "a lover of God" or "a friend of God." Luke adds the modifier "most excellent" (κράτιστος) behind Theophilus. The word κράτιστος appears only here in Luke and three other times in Acts to refer to the governor Felix (Acts 23:26; 24:3) and Festus (26:25). Theophilus therefore might be a high-ranking official in the Roman Empire. However, we should not close off the possibility that this is a generic term to refer to "a wider Gentile-Christian readership," as Luke Timothy Johnson puts it.[7] Beyond this, we do not have much information to imagine more about the specific situation and condition of the earliest audience of this book. In any case, theoretically and practically, the enterprise of imagining, constructing, or inventing the "original" audience is virtually impossible. As Walter J. Ong has shown in his classic essay "The Writer's Audience Is Always a Fiction,"[8] when a writer constructs a literary product, a specific audience is never imagined. Thus the reference to "Theophilus" (God's friend) here should be seen as an abstracted audience.

5 *Wali Sanga* are nine Muslim saints who laid the foundation for Islam in Indonesia, particularly in Java. They are Maulana Malik Ibrahim (aka Sunan Gresik), Sunan Ampel, Sunan Giri, Sunan Bonang, Sunan Drajad, Sunan Kudus, Sunan Kalijaga, Sunan Muria, and Sunan Gunung Jati.

6 See Walter J. Ong, *Orality and Literacy*, 3rd ed. (London: Routledge, 2012).

7 Luke Timothy Johnson, *The Gospel of Luke*, Sacra Pagina (Collegeville, MN: Liturgical, 1991), 28.

8 Walter J. Ong, "The Writer's Audience Is Always a Fiction," *PMLA* 90, no. 1 (1975): 9–21.

That being said, because we still have access to this text today, another set of readers is worth mentioning: Asian readers. Asians are as important as other readers, and this introductory book intends to shed some light on the reality of Asian readership. However, Asian readership has often been marginalized in the larger conversation on the Bible. As R. S. Sugirtharajah notes, "Interestingly when the Bible reached these areas through the modern missionary movement, it did not come as a book echoing an Asian ethos and sentiments but as a book appropriated and interpreted by western Christendom, using tools designed to meet its own Western cultural and ecclesiastical needs. But more importantly, it came as an ideological manifesto of the imperialists, denigrating Asian peoples' stories and sacred texts. This might lead one to suppose that the Bible is accorded only a marginal status in Asia's theological agenda."[9] This is certainly true in the Indonesian context as well. As a former Dutch colony, in Indonesia, the reading of the Bible has been shaped by this long history of colonial relation with the Mother Church in the Netherlands.[10] Indonesian readers, as a consequence, tend to hide behind the dominance of colonial interpretation. It is time now to bring out of the closet the "flesh-and-blood readers," to borrow a term from Fernando Segovia, from Indonesian contexts.[11]

Date

The date of composition suggested for this Gospel usually depends on its relationship to other Synoptic Gospels. According to two major established theories of the Synoptics in Western scholarship, Farrer and the two-source theory, the Gospel of Luke is the last of the Synoptic Gospels to have been written,[12]

9 R. S. Sugirtharajah, "The Bible and Its Asian Readers," *Biblical Interpretation* 1, no. 1 (January 1, 1993): 55.

10 See Yusak B. Setyawan, "Encountering State Ideology: Reading the Bible from an Indonesian Postcolonial Perspective," in *Colonial Contexts and Postcolonial Theologies: Storyweaving in the Asia–Pacific*, ed. Mark G. Brett and Jione Havea, Postcolonialism and Religions (New York: Palgrave, 2014), 99–112.

11 Fernando F. Segovia, *Decolonizing Biblical Studies: A View from the Margins* (Maryknoll, NY: Orbis, 2000), ch. 1.

12 See Mark Goodacre, *The Synoptic Problem: A Way through the Maze* (London: T&T Clark, 2004); Mark Goodacre and Nicholas Perrin, eds., *Questioning: A Multidimensional Critique* (Downers Grove, IL: IVP Academic, 2004).

meaning that Luke was written after Mark and Matthew. This puts the writing of this Third Gospel toward the end of the second half of the first century. Raymond Brown's estimation of the year 85 CE is very probable, though no one can actually establish a definitive date.[13]

Structure

The Gospel of Luke opens with a clear statement that it aims to present "an orderly account" of Jesus (1:1). However, as Tzvetan Todorov reminds us, the act of reading is fundamentally an act of constructing "an imaginary universe on the basis of the text."[14] The European historical critical scholars treat the Gospel of Luke as a book that represents reality and, in so doing, forget that more accurately it "creates reality."[15] They tend to disregard the construction of the novelistic reality of the Gospel in order to get at the objective facts behind the text.[16] They demythologize it in order to get at the *kerygma* of the early Christian movements. Such a strategy of scholarship is not just an act of violence toward the text but also an act of forgetting the readers' role in the process of reading.

Asian readers would take the text seriously as a site of reality construction. In this sense, readers have to become involved in the process of constructing such a reality. It is no surprise, therefore, that when we read different commentaries on Luke, we find many different takes on how the text is structured. The diversity of structures is not only the result of the polysemic nature of the text itself[17] but also the result of the role of readers as coconstructors of the novelistic reality.

13 See Raymond E. Brown, *An Introduction to the New Testament* (New Haven, CT: Yale University Press, 1997), 273–74.

14 Tzvetan Todorov, *Genres in Discourse*, trans. Catherine Porter (Cambridge: Cambridge University Press, 1990), 39.

15 Todorov, 39. For a close analysis of the Gospel of Luke as a "dialogic novel" using a Bakhtinian framework, see Raj Nadella, *Dialogue Not Dogma: Many Voices in the Gospel of Luke*, Library of New Testament Studies 431 (London: T&T Clark, 2011).

16 See David E. Aune, "Historical Criticism," in *The Blackwell Companion to the New Testament* (Hoboken, NJ: Wiley-Blackwell, 2010), 101–15, https://onlinelibrary.wiley.com/doi/abs/10.1002/9781444318937.ch7.

17 Paul Ricoeur, *Interpretation Theory: Discourse and the Surplus of Meaning* (Fort Worth: Texas Christian University Press, 1976).

As a coconstructor of reality, the structure of the Gospel of Luke that I propose here is suggested mainly by my experience as an Indonesian immigrant and by the experiences of many other Asian immigrants who travel from Asia—the place where I was born—to the United States. This is a structure constructed on the basis of various journeys or spatial movements in Luke, particularly the journey of Jesus leaving the place where he was born to go to Jerusalem. This theme of journey is extended further in Acts, which moves from Jerusalem to Rome. My focus here is only on the journeys in the Gospel of Luke.

Introduction (1:1–4)

The nativity narrative (1:5–2:20)

The early life of Jesus (2:21–4:13)

Jesus in Galilee (4:14–9:50)

The journey to Jerusalem (9:51–19:27)

Jesus in Jerusalem (19:28–24:12)

- The arrival and grand welcoming into Jerusalem (19:28–44)
- Jesus in the temple (19:45–21:38)
- The passion narrative (22:1–24:12)

Concluding events (24:13–53)

THE GOSPEL OF LUKE IN AN ASIAN CONTEXT

Most of the Gospel of Luke commentaries are from the West and from the pens of white men, and until recently they have dominated the discussion on the Gospel of Luke.[18] In the past two decades, however, scholars from Asia have begun to publish works in the English language that bring their perspectives

18 See François Bovon, *Luke the Theologian*, 2nd ed. (Waco, TX: Baylor University Press, 2006).

to the fore.[19] The following discussions are some themes that highlight the way an Indonesian reader can appropriate and interpret the Gospel of Luke. I frame these themes in what Sugirtharajah calls "vernacular hermeneutics," which is grounded in a local tongue and local culture.[20] The purpose of the following discussion, therefore, is not to present the existing scholarly debates and discourses about the Gospel of Luke in the Western world. Here they are bracketed. To quote Sugirtharajah again, "Contextual concerns do not necessarily undermine scholarly sharpness. They open up a new relationship between the communal concerns of the people and biblical scholarship."[21] This far-from-complete elaboration should be seen merely as an introduction to the encounter between the Gospel of Luke and the Asian communities, particularly Indonesian communities.

Jesus as a *Perantau*

Jesus's spatial movement from Galilee to Jerusalem in the Gospel of Luke is rarely seen as an act of migration (Indonesian: *perantauan*). In the context of the United States and the Western world, the idea of migration is often understood as a cross- or transnational movement of people. For instance, immigrants are those who move from the Philippines to the United States. Those who move, say, from California to Florida would not be considered immigrants because their movement is within a single nation. This is quite different from the Indonesian context. I grew up in the eastern part of Indonesia, in the province of Moluccas. When people from my province move to Java, we see them as *perantau* (immigrants) because they no longer live in their original *kampung*.[22] Songs from Moluccas are often about those in Java remembering

19 For instance, among others, see Xiaoli Yang, *A Dialogue between Haizi's Poetry and the Gospel of Luke: Chinese Homecoming and the Relationship with Jesus Christ*, Theology and Mission in World Christianity 9 (Leiden: Brill, 2018); Yong-sung Ahn, *The Reign of God and Rome in Luke's Passion Narrative: An East Asian Global Perspective*, Biblical Interpretation Series 80 (Leiden: Brill, 2006); Ranjini Rebera, "Polarity or Partnership? Retelling the Story of Martha and Mary from Asian Women's Perspective," *Semeia* 78 (1997): 93–107.

20 R. S. Sugirtharajah, *The Bible and the Third World: Precolonial, Colonial, and Postcolonial Encounters* (Cambridge: Cambridge University Press, 2001), ch. 6.

21 Sugirtharajah, "Bible and Its Asian Readers," 64.

22 The word *kampung* literally means "village." In Indonesia, particularly in eastern Indonesia, this word also signifies "hometown" and "home village."

their *kampung.* Java is considered a *tanah orang* (a foreign land). Those who live in Java often express their longing for their homeland through song. For instance, the song *Nusaniwe Tanjung Alang*[23] has the following lyrics:

> *Apa tempo kulihat lagi?*
> *Ambon tanah asalku*
> *kalo sudah sampe di tanah Jawa*
> *jangan lupa Nona Kabaya*
>
> When can I see you again
> Ambon, my homeland?
> When you arrive in Java Island
> Do not forget Miss *kabaya.*[24]

This song beautifully expresses the Moluccan view of spatial movement. Here immigration is not about crossing national borders but about leaving one's birthplace, one's hometown. The moment of departure in the harbor, when the ship begins to leave the island, is usually the moment that is filled with many tears. Java is far away. Leaving one's family behind is a moment of painful transition.

In Greek, the word that is often translated as "the Jews" is οἱ Ἰουδαῖοι. This word can also mean "Judeans," or people who live in a geographical area called Judea.[25] It appears five times in Luke (7:3; 23:3, 37, 38, 51). Bracketing the question of Jesus's ethnic identity, Luke does not describe Jesus as a person from Judea. Pilate's question, "Are you a king of the Jews (ὁ βασιλεὺς

23 *Tanjung Nusaniwe* (Nusaniwe Cape) and *Tanjung Alang* (Tanjung Alang) are two main capes in Ambon Island. Every boat that sails to and from Ambon will have to pass through these two capes.

24 *Kabaya* is a female traditional dress in Ambon. A charming video of kids singing this song and playing ukuleles can be seen at "Nusaniwe Tanjung Alang," Nico Tulalessy Ukulele, July 27, 2019, YouTube video, 2:32, https://www.youtube.com/watch?v=M0Lk7popPC8.

25 Ruth Sheridan, "Issues in the Translation of Οἱ Ἰουδαῖοι in the Fourth Gospel," *Journal of Biblical Literature* 132, no. 3 (October 5, 2013): 671–95; Malcolm Lowe, "Who Were the ΙΟΥΔΑΙΟΙ?," *Novum Testamentum* 18, no. 2 (1976): 101–30; David M. Miller, "Ethnicity Comes of Age: An Overview of Twentieth-Century Terms for Ioudaios," *Currents in Biblical Research* 10, no. 2 (February 1, 2012): 293–311.

τῶν Ἰουδαίων)?" (23:3) is a form of mockery. Pilate's inquiry about whether Jesus is a person from Galilee (ὁ ἄνθρωπος Γαλιλαῖός ἐστιν) in 23:6 demonstrates that Jesus is not perceived as a local person. "He's not from around here" is probably a better way to put it. His disciples are also depicted as Galileans (Γαλιλαῖοι; see Acts 2:7), denoting the geographical area from which they came.[26] Peter is recognized as a follower of Jesus because he is a Galilean (22:59). Sometimes the Galileans are considered to be outsiders or others (see 1 Macc 5:14–22). All this is to say that Jesus's spatial movement from Galilee to Judea can be read, at least from an Indonesian point of view, as a *perantauan* (migration). Jesus is a *perantau*.

When Jesus began to leave Galilee, Luke describes it as follows: "He set (ἐστήρισεν) his face to go to Jerusalem" (9:51). The Greek verb ἐστήρισεν can be translated as "strengthen" or "fix." What does "he strengthened [or fixed] his face" mean? It could mean he was determined to begin journeying to Jerusalem. "To strengthen/fix the face" is a very rare expression in the NT; indeed, it appears only here. Craig Evans's study of this idiom, which investigates its Septuagintal roots, argues that it carries a "sense of judgment."[27] However, strengthening the face can also suggest a sense of controlling one's deep sadness. In Jeremiah 21:10, the use of this expression (ἐστήρικα τὸ πρόσωπόν μου ἐπὶ τὴν πόλιν ταύτην; I strengthened my face against this city) can be interpreted as a pronouncement of judgment. The preposition ἐπί does not have to mean "against"; it can also mean "over," "on," or "at" (see Ezek 6:2; 13:17; 21:2; 21:7).[28] So if this statement is translated as "I strengthened my face on this city," it can be understood as God holding or controlling God's emotion or sadness because God knew the city was going to fall into the hands of the Babylonian king. In the case of Luke 9:51, there is no preposition ἐπί, but the idiom is followed by an articular infinitive τοῦ πορεύεσθαι, which

26 See Mark A. Chancey, *The Myth of a Gentile Galilee*, Society for New Testament Studies Monograph Series 118 (Cambridge: Cambridge University Press, 2002). See also Mark A. Chancey, *Greco-Roman Culture and the Galilee of Jesus*, Society for New Testament Studies Monograph Series 134 (Cambridge: Cambridge University Press, 2005).

27 Craig A. Evans, "'He Set His Face': A Note on Luke 9:51," *Biblica* 63, no. 4 (1982): 545–48. See also Craig A. Evans, "'He Set His Face': A Note on Luke 9:51 Once Again," *Biblica* 68, no. 1 (1987): 80–84.

28 All the appearances of this phrase in Ezekiel, which Evans uses to make his case, are followed by the preposition ἐπί.

indicates purpose or cause.[29] This means that Jesus strengthened his face in order to begin his journey to Jerusalem.

Why does he need to strengthen his face? Strengthening one's face usually occurs at the moment of transition, at the threshold of life. The journey of transition from Galilee to Judea takes up about 40 percent of the Gospel of Luke—from 9:51 to 19:28.[30] Jesus strengthening his face signifies not only his determination to go to Jerusalem but also his deep and profound sense of loss, of sadness, at this moment of life transition. At this threshold point, Jesus is about to leave his place of birth and journey to a place where he will experience rejection to the point of death. Just as many Moluccan people leaving for Java have to strengthen their faces, holding their emotion and their sadness, so too Jesus is at that liminal point in his life.

Kingdom of God and Colonization

The Gospel of Luke was probably written in the mid-eighties CE, at a time at which the Roman Empire was under the reign of Domitian (81–96 CE). Compared to other Gospels, this Gospel explicitly connects the stories of Jesus and the Roman empire. The mention of two major Roman emperors, Augustus (2:1) and Tiberius (3:1), is an important indicator that this Gospel invites its readers to see Jesus in the larger context of the political struggle at that time.[31] All the events in the narrative took place in the eastern part of the Mediterranean world. In this sense, the world of Jesus and Luke is a colonized world.

This Gospel pays particularly close attention to the theme of fear. The verb φοβέω and the noun φόβος (and their derivatives) appear thirty times in this Gospel (1:13, 21, 30, 50, 65; 2:9–10; 5:10, 26; 7:16; 8:25, 35, 37, 50; 9:34, 45; 12:4–5, 7, 32; 18:2, 4; 19:21; 20:19; 21:26; 22:2; 23:40). Almost every great event is responded to with fear. When Zechariah saw the angel, fear fell

29 Daniel B. Wallace, *Greek Grammar beyond the Basics* (Grand Rapids, MI: Zondervan, 1996), 610.

30 Floyd V. Filson, "The Journey Motif in Luke-Acts," in *Apostolic History and the Gospel: Biblical and Historical Essays Presented to F. F. Bruce on His 60th Birthday*, ed. W. Ward Gasque and Ralph P. Martin (Exeter, UK: Paternoster, 1970), 70.

31 Pyung Soo Seo, *Luke's Jesus in the Roman Empire and the Emperor in the Gospel of Luke* (Eugene, OR: Pickwick, 2015); Kazuhiko Yamazaki-Ransom, *The Roman Empire in Luke's Narrative*, Library of New Testament Studies 404 (London: T&T Clark, 2010).

upon him (1:12). When people heard about the birth of John the Baptist, fear came to them (1:65). When the shepherds saw an angel, Luke uses an intensified expression to describe their reaction: ἐφοβήθησαν φόβον μέγαν (2:9). Although it is hard to render this expression literally into English, the idea is that the fear that they experienced was great.[32] After Jesus heals the demoniac person in the country of the Gerasenes, Luke explains that the people in that area were "seized with great fear" (8:37). The list can go on. The question is, Why are the people in this Gospel filled with so much fear? The terror of a foreign imperial power would inevitably create a constant existential threat to the community. Fear is a shared condition of colonized subjects. It affects their reaction to almost anything that happens to their lives.

Such fear is understandable because the Romans could do to the colonized communities what they did, for instance, to the city of Corinth: they could raze the entire community. The sting of Roman imperial power struck them in 70 CE, when the Romans destroyed Jerusalem. This book was the product of the aftermath of colonial Roman brutality.[33] Thus, Luke opens his Gospel both by locating the story of Jesus in the larger context of Roman rule and by describing the fear that many were experiencing during that time, particularly those who lived in rural areas like the shepherds in chapter 2.

Asian readers, and specifically Indonesian readers, of the Gospel of Luke can relate well to this political condition, this constant existential fear. Indonesia is a former Dutch colony. The opening line of the Indonesian constitution is a clear declaration of the country's opposition to colonization:

> *Bahwa sesungguhnya Kemerdekaan itu ialah hak segala bangsa dan oleh sebab itu, maka penjajahan di atas dunia harus dihapuskan, karena tidak sesuai dengan perikemanusiaan dan perikeadilan.*
>
> Whereas independence is the inalienable right of all nations, therefore, all colonialism must be abolished in this world as it is not in conformity with humanity and justice.

32 It is hard to translate this expression into English because of its repetitive style.

33 See Miguel A. De La Torre, *The Politics of Jesús: A Hispanic Political Theology* (Lanham, MD: Rowman & Littlefield, 2015), 27.

Indonesia as a nation is built on an explicitly anticolonial foundation. To put it differently, at the heart of Indonesian nationalism is a strong response to Western colonization.

The message not to be afraid declared by the angel to Zachariah (1:13), Mary (1:30), and the shepherds (2:10) in Luke's nativity narrative makes sense within this context of a colonized world. The angel brings Mary a message telling her not to be afraid and reveals a promise of the kingdom. "He will reign over the house of Jacob forever, and of his kingdom (τῆς βασιλείας αὐτοῦ) there will be no end," said the angel (1:33). This is a political promise. It is important to keep in mind that the Greek word βασιλεία can also be translated as "empire."[34] The English phrase "Roman Empire" in Greek is ἡ βασιλεία Ῥωμαίων (lit. the kingdom of the Romans). The promise of an endless kingdom should again be understood in the light of their political condition as colonized subjects. Just as the nation of Indonesia is built on an anticolonial foundation, the kingdom of God is a promise given to replace the Roman imperial power.

The main mission of Jesus is to bring the good news about the kingdom of God (ἡ βασιλεία τοῦ θεοῦ, 4:43; 8:1; 9:11). When Jesus sent the twelve, he commissioned them to proclaim the kingdom of God (9:2). Healing is the mark of the nearness of the kingdom of God (10:9). Jesus teaches his disciples to pray and ask for the kingdom to come (11:2). Jesus's parables are intended to explain the reality of the kingdom of God (13:18, 20). The first beatitude statement of Jesus is, "Blessed are you who are poor, for yours is the kingdom of God" (6:20). Luke does not include the prepositional phrase "in spirit" (τῷ πνεύματι) after describing the poor as Matthew does (Matt 5:3)—although it is worth noting that some ancient scribes ([2]א[a], Q, Θ, f[1.13], 33, 579, 2542, and others) added that phrase to Luke to harmonize it with the Matthean version.[35] The poor (οἱ πτωχοί) in this sense refers not only to spiritual poverty but also, above all, to a sociopolitical reality. The answer to the problem of poverty in Luke is therefore not the Roman imperial system but the kingdom of God.

34 Warren Carter, "Christian Origins and Imperial-Critical Studies of the New Testament Gospels," in *Christian Origins and the Establishment of the Early Jesus Movement*, ed. Stanley E. Porter and Andrew W. Pitts (Leiden: Brill, 2018), 264–82.

35 See Cambry Pardee, *Scribal Harmonization in the Synoptic Gospels* (Leiden: Brill, 2019).

Just as Indonesians in 1945 imagined a new community[36] free from colonial subjugation, the Gospel of Luke presents an imagination of the coming of a new community. The kingdom of God (to borrow a phrase from Kazuhiko Yamazaki-Ransom) is an "anti-imperial ideology."[37]

The Messianic Hope and *Ratu Adil*

Related to the problem of colonization is the hope for the messianic liberation. Within this colonized world, the expectation for the coming of the Messiah is not just a spiritual hope; it is also political. It is a hope for divine intervention in bringing liberation to the colonized community. In Indonesia, particularly in the Javanese context, there is a hope of the coming of *Ratu Adil*. The term *Ratu Adil* means "the Just King."[38] *Ratu Adil* is a reflection of the Javanese hope for a messianic figure who will bring peace, justice, and liberation to the people. The myth originated in the twelfth century during the reign of King Jayabaya of Kediri, East Java.[39] The figure of Ratu Adil is closely connected to *Satrio Piningit* (the hidden knight).[40] The myth's popularity reached its climax in the nineteenth century during the resistance war in Java led by Pangeran Diponegoro against the colonial Dutch Empire (1825–30). Historian Peter Carey writes, "During the course of the Java War, Dipanagara tried to live up to the popular expectation of him as the long-awaited Javanese 'Just King' (*Ratu*

36 See Benedict R. Anderson, *Imagined Communities: Reflections on the Origin and Spread of Nationalism*, rev. ed. (London: Verso, 2006).

37 Yamazaki-Ransom, *Roman Empire*, 98.

38 For a more thorough discussion on *Ratu Adil*, see Peter Carey, "Waiting for the 'Just King': The Agrarian World of South-Central Java from Giyanti (1755) to the Java War (1825–30)," *Modern Asian Studies* 20, no. 1 (February 1986): 59–137; Khoon Choy Lee, *A Fragile Nation: The Indonesian Crisis* (Singapore: World Scientific, 1999), 127; P. B. R. Carey, *The Power of Prophecy: Prince Dipanagara and the End of an Old Order in Java, 1785–1855* (Leiden: Brill, 2015), ch. 10.

39 For the history of the Jayabaya's prophecy of *Ratu Adil*, see Prasetyo, ch. 3; Thomas A. Reuter, "Reading the Future in Indonesia: Javanese Texts of Prophesy as a Popular Genre," 17th Biennial Conference of the Asian Studies Association of Australia, Melbourne, Australia, July 1, 2008, http://citeseerx.ist.psu.edu/viewdoc/download?doi=10.1.1.574.8750&rep=rep1&type=pdf.

40 See Alfian Ade Prasetyo, "The Myth of Satrio Piningit and the Hope of Javanese Society (Philosophical Hermeneutics Analysis)" (bachelor's thesis, Semarang, Walisongo State Islamic University, 2016), http://eprints.walisongo.ac.id/6943/.

Adil) who would institute a period of light taxation and provide a cornucopia of cheap provisions after a time of darkness, oppression and depravity, the classic '*jaman kala bendu*.'"[41] In Javanese history, there is a clear connection between the rise of messianic hope for the coming of the *Ratu Adil* and colonial oppression.

With that in mind, Jesus in the Gospel can be seen through this lens of *Ratu Adil*.[42] Jesus is described as "the Messiah of God" in 9:18. When the angel appeared to the shepherds in the fields, the angel said to them, "Do not be afraid; for see—I am bringing you good news of great joy for all the people: to you is born this day in the city of David a Savior, who is the Messiah, the Lord" (2:10–11). Just like Pangeran Diponegoro, Jesus is the *Ratu Adil*, the Messiah who comes to bring great joy of liberation to all people, especially the oppressed and colonized. As a *Ratu Adil*–like figure, Jesus's messianic proclamation of the good news to the poor and the liberation to the captives, oppressed, and the like in 4:19 should be read as mirroring the Magnificat vision of social reversal in 2:46–56, as Amanda C. Miller has demonstrated.[43] Jesus's status in the Gospel of Luke as a messiah who has been predicted or prophesied by the law of Moses, the prophets, and the psalms (24:44) is strikingly parallel to the prophecy of Jayabaya about the coming of the *Ratu Adil*.

The only significant difference between *Ratu Adil* and the messianic status of Jesus is that there is no hint for a suffering and resurrecting *Ratu Adil* in the Javanese cultural context. Luke describes the Messiah not only as a figure that will bring the kingdom of God, great joy, and social reversals but also as one who will "suffer and . . . rise from the dead on the third day" (24:44; see 24:26).

41 Carey, "Waiting for the 'Just King,'" 65. *Jaman kala bendu* means period of troubles.

42 Some scholars have attempted to construct a Javanese Christology on the basis of the hope for *Ratu Adil*. See Gani Wiyono, "Ratu Adil: A Javanese Face of Jesus?," *Journal of Asian Mission* 1, no. 1 (1999): 65–79; Gabriel Possenti Sindhunata, *Hoffen auf den Ratu-Adil: Das eschatologische Motiv des "Gerechten Königs" im Bauernprotest auf Java während des 19. und zu Beginn des 20. Jahrhunderts* (Hamburg: Kovač, 1992); Karel A. Steenbrink, "Five Catholic Theologians of Indonesia in Search for an International or Local Identity," *Exchange* 29, no. 1 (January 2000): 2–22; Andreas Anangguru Yewangoe, *Theologia Crucis in Asia: Asian Christian Views on Suffering in the Face of Overwhelming Poverty and Multifaceted Religiosity in Asia* (Amsterdam: Rodopi, 1987), 233–37.

43 Michel Foucault, *The History of Sexuality* (New York: Vintage, 1988), 1:92.

Power as *Sakti*

In reading the Gospel of Luke, an Indonesian will not fail to notice the multiple occurrences of the word *power* (Greek: *dynamis*) in this book. Prominent figures in the Gospel are *orang-orang sakti* (powerful people). They are described as being filled with or possessing power. The Gospel begins with the promise of the angel to Zechariah that his son, John, will have "the spirit and power of Elijah" (1:17). The angel also says to Mary, the mother of Jesus, that "the power of the Most High will overshadow" her (1:35). Likewise, Jesus is filled with power (4:14, 36; 5:17). From this perspective, the Christology of the Gospel of Luke cannot be separated from this connection with power. Jesus is an *orang sakti* (a powerful person).[44]

Power in the Javanese worldview is not abstract relation, as commonly understood in the West,[45] but a concrete energy that can fill or leave a person.[46] Power is transferable from one person to another. For the Javanese people, "power exists, independent of its possible users."[47] Thus, power can be acquired, maintained, and transferred. Since power is concentrated on a person, according to Benedict Anderson, "Luke's description of power is parallel to this understanding of power. John received Elijah's power. Jesus' power flows out of him when healing takes place (6:19; 8:46). Jesus gave power (ἔδωκεν αὐτοῖς δύναμιν) to the disciples when he sent them out on their mission (9:1). Because power exists independent of its user, the idea of being clothed (24:49), filled (4:14), or overshadowed (4:14) with power is not something foreign in the Javanese context." Here, we can also see one significant point of difference. In the Javanese context—at least in Anderson's analysis—power can be either diffused or unified. Diffusion of power will result in disorder,

44 Benedict Anderson, stating this in parentheses, writes, "The old usage of the word *power*, which survives in such phrases as 'The Great Powers' or 'Power had gone out of him' [Gospel according to St. Mark, 5:30] approximates the Javanese idea, but by no means coincides with it." It is actually in the Gospel of Luke that we can find a more vivid description of *power*. Benedict R. O'g Anderson, "The Idea of Power in Javanese Culture," in *Language and Power: Exploring Political Cultures in Indonesia*, ed. Benedict R. O'g Anderson (Jakarta: Equinox, 2006), 20n8.

45 See Foucault, *History of Sexuality*, 1:92–93.

46 Anderson, "Idea of Power," 22.

47 Anderson, 22.

whereas the concentration of power will lead to sociopolitical order.[48] The rule of a political dynasty requires a concentration of power. In other words, the power in the Javanese conception is marked by a "highly centripetal characteristic."[49] In the Gospel of Luke, the dispersion of power is not described as a source of disorder. Quite the contrary: Jesus promises his disciples that they will be clothed with power (24:49). The decenteredness of power is the mark of the early Christian movement (see Acts 1:8). The kingdom of God in Luke is established not through the concentration of power in a king or sultan but rather through the dispersal of power.

Invasion of Wind/Spirit

In Indonesia, when someone is affected by a fever or a cold, feels bloated, or has a headache, people believe that they are experiencing *masuk angin*, which literally means "being entered or seized by wind." In their view, wind entering the human body is the major cause of many bodily sicknesses and weaknesses. Even though this belief has been challenged by medical research, it is still widely believed among Indonesians.[50] *Masuk angin* is clearly not a medical explanation of human diseases. It is their cultural understanding of human beings, their relationship with nature. According to anthropologist Atik Triratnawati, in the Javanese worldview, the world is made up of four elements: earth, wind, fire, and water. When it comes to the wind, they believe that the world is covered by four *mata angin* (lit. "the eye of the wind," or cardinal directions) and one center point.[51] Not only does wind play an important role at a cosmic level, but one's body is also animated by *napas* (air). *Masuk angin* is a symptom of the imbalance of these cosmic elements in which the wind takes too much control of one's body and causes sickness. The worst kind of *masuk angin* is the so-called *angin duduk* (sitting wind), which is when the wind enters and completely overtakes or controls one's body. It can cause serious sickness to the point of death. Healing can

48 Anderson, 34–35.

49 Anderson, 42.

50 See Robert Wessing, "Porous Boundaries: Addressing Calamities in East Java, Indonesia," *Bijdragen Tot de Taal–, Land–En Volkenkunde* 166, no. 1 (2010): 49–82.

51 See Atik Triratnawati, "Masuk Angin dalam Konteks Kosmologi Jawa," *Jurnal Humaniora* 23, no. 3 (August 10, 2012): 326–35.

happen through a procedure called *kerok*, which casts out the *angin jahat* (the evil wind).

In reading the Gospel of Luke, it is important to remember that the Greek word *pneuma* means not only "spirit" but also "wind" or "breath." The theme of *pneuma* is prominent in this Gospel because it appears thirty-six times. Luke describes *pneuma* as not having, or the absence of, "flesh and bones" (24:37). The idea that *pneuma* is the cosmic element that animates one's body can be seen in the crucifixion narrative. Jesus's last words before his death on the cross are, "Father, into your hands I commend my spirit (τὸ πνεῦμά μου)" (23:46). In the Javanese view, Jesus here is surrendering his *nafas*, his animating breath, to the Father.

There are two kinds of *pneuma*, or wind, that are at work in the human realm. The wind that has a divine origin is called the "holy wind/spirit" (1:15, 35, 41, 67; 2:26; 3:16; 4:1; 10:21; 11:13; 12:10, 12) or the "wind of the Lord" (4:18). The bad kind of wind is called "unclean winds/spirits" (4:33, 36; 6:18; 8:29; 9:42; 11:24) or "evil winds/spirits" (7:21; 8:2). I grew up in the eastern part of Indonesia. Because we live very close to the sea, we see wind as being either bad or good. The evil wind can cause serious damages to the boats, and sailing becomes extremely dangerous. But when the good wind comes, sailing can get a lot easier. It is no surprise, therefore, that when something good happens, we say in the Indonesian language, "*Angin baik lagi datang*" (the good wind is coming). *Angin baik* signifies good luck, happiness, and prosperity. People's experience on the sea becomes a hermeneutical lens to understand the human body. Thus *angin jahat* can cause bodily dysfunction, and *angin baik* will bring luck.

The site of struggle between these two forces of wind in the Gospel of Luke is also in the human body. In chapter 4, for instance, Luke explains that Jesus is full of the holy wind (4:1) and led by the power of the wind to Galilee (4:14). After the incident in Nazareth where Jesus declared, through the reading of the scroll, that the wind of the Lord is upon him (4:18), Jesus went to Capernaum. There, Jesus, who was filled with the holy wind, met a man "who had the wind of an unclean demon" (ἔχων πνεῦμα δαιμονίου ἀκαθάρτου, 4:32). Jesus rebuked the unclean wind, and it left him without any harm (4:35). The people who witnessed this incident were amazed and said, "With what authority and power he commands the unclean spirits/winds, and out they come!" (4:37). They clearly saw the confrontation between the two forces of wind in the body of this man.

The *pneuma* appears to be a cause of sickness in one's body. The stories of a spirit seizing a boy (9:37–42) and crippling a woman (13:10–19) are the most vivid descriptions in Luke of the role of wind in bringing sickness. Luke also attributes other diseases to the invasion of an unclean wind (see 6:18). Dale Martin calls it the "invasion" theory of sickness.[52] Martin's discussion on this theory is mainly about the invasion of an evil spirit. In the Indonesian context, this is not just an abstract spirit; people believe that when the wind invades one's body, it causes the body to malfunction. Indonesians have a name for this condition: *masuk angin*. Many Indonesians would likely regard the symptoms of *masuk angin* in the Gospel of Luke as being very extreme, and thus they would recategorize it as *angin duduk*. Instead of using *kerok*, Jesus rebukes the unclean spirit, or the bad *angin*, ordering it to go out from the person's body. Jesus has power over sicknesses that are caused by *masuk angin*.

Women in Luke's Gospel

The figure of the mother is important in many communities in Indonesia. The land itself is called *Ibu Pertiwi* (motherland).[53] In Maluku, for instance, many songs are written to praise and adore mothers. Songs are rarely written about fathers. The most famous song about a mother is "Sio Mama e" (Oh Mama!).[54] The song begins with the story of how a mother, Mama, raised her child.[55] The chorus of the song is as follows:

---

52 Dale B. Martin, *The Corinthian Body* (New Haven, CT: Yale University Press, 1999). See also Pamela Shellberg, *Cleansed Lepers, Cleansed Hearts: Purity and Healing in Luke-Acts* (Minneapolis: Fortress, 2015), 78–79; Todd Klutz, *The Exorcism Stories in Luke-Acts: A Sociostylistic Reading*, Society for New Testament Studies Monograph Series 129 (Cambridge: Cambridge University Press, 2004), 67–68.

53 See Dian Lestariningsih and Wariyatun, "'NDuweni Ibu Pertiwi' (Keeping the Motherland): Women's Agency to Resist Cement Plants in Tegaldowo and Timbrangan Villages, Rembang," *Asian Journal of Women's Studies* 21, no. 2 (April 3, 2015): 166–79.

54 The word *sio* in the Maluccan language is really hard to translate into English. It is often used to express sadness or a sigh, but the use of *sio* is far more than just a sigh.

55 *Berapa puluh tahun lalu / Beta masih kacil e / Beta inga tempo itu / Sio mama gendong-gendong beta e / Sambil mama bakar sagu / Mama manyanyi buju-buju / La sampe basar bagini Beta seng lupa Mamae.* (Many years ago / When I was small / I remember that time / Oh Mama was carrying me / While Mama was cooking sago / Mama sang a song of lullaby / Until I am big / I will not forget my Mama.)

Sio mama e
Beta rindu mau pulang e
Sio mama e mama su lia kurus lawang e
Beta balom balas mama
Mama pung cape sio dolo e
Sio Tete Manis e, jaga beta pung mamae

Oh Mama
I want to go home
Oh Mama, you have seemed so thin
I haven't paid back
Mama's past hard work
Oh Jesus, please take care of my Mama.

This song reflects the centrality of a mother figure in the Moluccan families. As anthropologist Hatib Abdul Kadir puts it, "*Pesan-pesan ibu sangatlah sakral dan tidak pantas untuk dilanggar serta tidak dipatuhi*" (The words of a mother are very sacred and must not be violated and disobeyed).[56] Women play a crucial role in shaping the Moluccan imagination.

When one reads the Gospel of Luke, they will not fail to notice the importance of women and mothers in this Gospel. "It is a fact readily acknowledged by all that in Luke's Gospel not only are women mentioned more often than in other Gospels but also, and more importantly, are they seen to play more significant roles," writes Eugene Maly.[57] In the nativity narrative, two female figures are at the center of the story: Mary and Elizabeth. Elizabeth specifically addresses Mary as "the mother of my Lord" (ἡ μήτηρ τοῦ κυρίου μου). Luke describes Mary's embodied experience as "conceiving in the womb" and "bearing" a son (1:31). Mary is blessed among women, and the fruit of her womb (ὁ καρπὸς τῆς κοιλίας) is also blessed. In 11:27, after Jesus cast an unclean wind out of a person, a woman came out of the crowd and shouted that not only his mother's womb but also her breasts that nursed (μαστοὶ οὓς

56 Hatib Abdul Kadir, "Romantisme Anak Muda dalam Lagu-Lagu Ambon," *Jurnal Ilmu Komunikasi* 5, no. 2 (December 4, 2013): 49.

57 Eugene H. Maly, "Women and the Gospel of Luke," *Biblical Theology Bulletin* 10, no. 3 (August 1, 1980): 99.

ἐθήλασας) Jesus are blessed.[58] This description of motherhood rings bells in Moluccan ears. *Air susu mama* (breast milk) is seen as sacred because it is the source of life. In a famous folk song, "*Satu Tetes Air Susu Mama*" (Mama's One Drop of Breast Milk), the lyrics explains this life-giving power of breast milk. One of the stanzas goes as follows:

> *Satu tetes air susu mama*
> *Beta hidop deng puluh tahun mama*
> *Mana bisa beta lupa e*
> *Mana bisa beta manyangkal e*
>
> One drop of Mama's breast milk
> I can live for many years, Mama.
> How can I forget it?
> How can I deny it?

From this perspective, Mary is blessed because she is Jesus's source of life. Her breasts give life to Jesus. Elizabeth also has a similar bodily experience. Upon hearing Mary's greeting, the child leaped in her womb (1:41). Luke uses the word κοιλία (womb or belly) more than any other books in the NT.[59] It shows that Luke stresses this embodied female experience more than any other writers of the NT.

Other women also appear in the Gospel of Luke. Luke's is the only Gospel that talks about the character of Anna, the prophetess (2:36–38). She is a devout worshipper who came out from the temple to praise God and speak about Jesus.[60] Luke includes the story of Mary and Martha in 10:38, the healing of

58 Rachel Conrad Wahlberg offers a critical reading of the bodily images of women in Luke. See Rachel Conrad Wahlberg, "Jesus and the Uterus Image," *Theology Today* 31, no. 3 (October 1, 1974): 228–30.

59 This word only appears twice in Matthew (Matt 12:40; 15:17), once in Mark (Mark 7:19), twice in John (John 3:4; 7:38), four times in Pauline letters (Rom 16:18; 1 Cor 6:13; Gal 1:15; Phil 3:19), and twice in Revelation (Rev 10:9, 10). In the Gospel of Luke, it appears seven times, and it appears two times in Acts.

60 See Sarah Harris, "Letting (H)Anna Speak: An Intertextual Reading of the New Testament Prophetess (Luke 2:36–38)," *Feminist Theology* 27, no. 1 (September 1, 2018): 60–74; Andrés Gracía Serrano, "Anna's Characterization in Luke 2:36–38: A Case of Conceptual Allusion?," *Catholic Biblical Quarterly* 76, no. 3 (2014): 464–80.

a twelve-year-old girl, and a woman who has been suffering from hemorrhages for twelve years (Luke 8:40–56). The number twelve echoes the twelve tribes of Israel and the twelve disciples of Jesus. Israel and Jesus's disciples are feminized in the Gospel. When Jesus went from city to city and village to village, Luke explains that many women give what they have to support Jesus (8:1–3). After Jesus died, the women who followed him from Galilee—which are probably those who Luke lists in chapter 8—came to his tomb to bring spices and ointments for his body. In chapter 24, the women received the news of Jesus's resurrection and came back to tell all the eleven male disciples.

Moreover, the appearance of female characters in Jesus's parable of the Lost Coin (15:8–10) is quite revealing about Luke's gender-inclusive theology. God is described as a woman who has ten silver coins, but when one coin is lost, she sweeps the house in search for that coin. When she finds it, she gathers her friends and neighbors to celebrate it. This female image of God is deeply embedded in a patriarchal imagination. As Susan Durber puts it, the picture we have here is "only an image of a woman in a domestic situation."[61] This is also the case with many songs about mothers or women in Maluku. The female image is still depicted as being in a domestic space. That being said, an Asian reading of this Gospel has to take seriously the significance of female characters in its narrative.

CONCLUSION

The themes discussed in this chapter are not intended to be a comprehensive list or an exhaustive elaboration of an Asian, particularly Indonesian, reading of the Gospel of Luke. I intentionally narrow the discussion to an Indonesian context to show that "Asian" is a big category. Asian culture is never monolithic. Asians are diverse through and through. Similarly, "Indonesia" as a bigger national category also consists of a huge variety of cultures. Thus there are many other ways of reading different themes and passages in the Gospel of Luke in conversation with, and from the point of view of, Indonesian cultural experiences.

61 Susan Durber, "The Female Reader of the Parables of the Lost," *Journal for the Study of the New Testament* 14, no. 45 (January 1992): 70.

As C. S. Song puts it, "The life of Asian peoples is full of political stories. The task of political theology is to discover them, to penetrate into the woes and joys, despairs and hopes behind those stories, and to encounter and experience the human soul possessed and cherished by God."[62] Asian stories are not just rich resources for constructing political theology; they are also for interpreting biblical texts. Every interpretation of biblical text has to be rooted in a particular social location. This introductory essay has a more focused aim: to stimulate more discussions and creative Asian readings of this Gospel.

FURTHER READING

Ahn, Y-S. 2006. *The Reign of God and Rome in Luke's Passion Narrative: An East Asian Global Perspective*. Biblical Interpretation 80. Leiden: Brill.

Brendan, B. 2000. *The Hospitality of God: A Reading of Luke's Gospel*. Collegeville, MN: Liturgical.

Jacob, S. 2015. *Reading Mary Alongside Indian Surrogate Mothers: Violent Love, Oppressive Liberation, and Infancy Narratives*. The Bible and Cultural Studies. New York: Palgrave Macmillan.

Jung, C-W. 2004. *The Original Language of the Lukan Infancy Narrative*. Library of New Testament Studies 267. London: T&T Clark.

Massey, J. 2007. *The Gospel According to Luke*. Dalit Bible Commentary, New Testament 3. New Delhi: Centre for Dalit/Subaltern Studies.

Nadella, R. 2011. *Dialogue Not Dogma: Many Voices in the Gospel of Luke*. Library of New Testament Studies 431. London: T&T Clark.

Orevillo-Montenegro, M. 2010. *The Jesus of Asian Women*. New Delhi: Logos.

Sam, L. R. A. 2008. *The Love Commandment of Jesus Christ in the Gospel of Luke and Its Implication in the Indian Context*. Delhi: ISPCK.

Segovia, F. F. 2000. *Decolonizing Biblical Studies: A View from the Margins*. Maryknoll, NY: Orbis.

Song, C.-S. 2002. *Third-Eye Theology: Theology in Formation in Asian Settings*. Eugene, OR: Wipf & Stock.

62 Choan-Seng Song, *Theology from the Womb of Asia* (Maryknoll, NY: Orbis, 1986), 92.

Sugirtharajah, R. S. 2013. *The Bible and Asia: From the Pre-Christian Era to the Postcolonial Age*. Cambridge, MA: Harvard University Press.

Yang, X. 2018. *A Dialogue between Haizi's Poetry and the Gospel of Luke: Chinese Homecoming and the Relationship with Jesus Christ*. Theology and Mission in World Christianity 9. Leiden: Brill.

SIX

The Gospel of John

Johnson Thomaskutty
The United Theological College
Bengaluru, India

The Gospel of John is considered one of the significant writings of the NT that appeals to the Indian spirituality and the Asian ideals in multifarious ways. The Gospel has unique features as a universalistic literary masterpiece that encompasses the feelings and aspirations of Asian communities from a universal perspective. The Gospel's genre dynamism, features of setting, ideological constructs, character traits, plot structure, and point of view reflect and reveal its assimilative power to reverberate the situational aspects of Asian communities, with a special impression on Indian contextual realities. In this chapter, I attempt to see the preliminary concerns such as authorship, audience, date and place, structure, and the outline of the Gospel in a succinct fashion. In the latter part of the chapter, I place the Gospel in the Indian/Asian context to derive an interpretative dynamism that takes into account the diverse religious and cultural aspects.

PRELIMINARY CONCERNS

The following discussion is an attempt to facilitate a brief discourse on the authorship, audience, date and place, genre, and structure of the Fourth Gospel so a wider understanding of the Gospel might be brought to the foreground.

Authorship

The Johannine author seemingly looks like an Asian with a lot of mystical and ideological resemblances. The Asian mindset of "seeing the realities and reflecting" is at the foreground of the Fourth Gospel as the author declares that "we have seen his glory" (1:14; see 19:35; 21:24–25). The placement of Thomas at the significant narrative intervals (11:16; 14:5; 20:24–28; 21:1) and the *inclusio* that is made between John's thesis statement (1:1: "the Word was God") and its resolution through Thomas's utterance (20:28: "My Lord and my God") can help us to see the link between the Johannine author and the Thomas community in India.[1] The eyewitness in the Gospel is an unnamed disciple who is sometimes referred to as the "beloved disciple" (19:26–35; 20:2). It is believed that he was reclining close to Jesus during the Last Supper (13:23). There are no convincing historical grounds for rejecting the identification of the beloved disciple as John, the son of Zebedee.[2] The Gospel reveals the author's knowledge of Jewish customs (2:6; 7:37; 4:27; 5:10; 7:21–23; 8:12; 9:2, 14), Jewish history (4:9; 7:35; 11:49; 18:13), and Palestinian geography (1:28; 2:1; 3:23; 4:46; 6:1; 12:1; 18:1; 21:1) in lucid fashion. These details make the scholars think of the author's identity as a Jew.[3]

Similarly, church fathers such as Irenaeus, Tertullian, Clement of Alexandria, Origen, and others consider the Gospel as written by John, son of Zebedee.[4] Irenaeus stated, "John, the disciple of the Lord, who leaned on his breast, also published the gospel while living at Ephesus in Asia" (*Adv. Haer.* 3.1.2).[5] Clement of Alexandria considered it as a "spiritual Gospel" (Eusebius, *HE.* 4.17.4).[6] While Eusebius mentions John's association with Polycarp

1 Johnson Thomaskutty, *Saint Thomas the Apostle: New Testament, Apocrypha, and Historical Traditions*, Jewish and Christian Texts Series 25 (London: Bloomsbury T&T Clark, 2018), 84–85, 148–50, 201–2.

2 Donald Guthrie, *New Testament Introduction*, rev. ed. (Leicester, UK: Apollos, 1990), 260.

3 Craig L. Blomberg, *Historical Reliability of John's Gospel: Issues and Commentary* (Leicester, UK: InterVarsity, 2001), 27.

4 Guthrie, *New Testament Introduction*, 269–71; Francis J. Moloney, *The Gospel of John* (Collegeville, MN: Liturgical, 1998), 6–9.

5 Richard Bauckham, *Jesus and the Eyewitnesses: The Gospels as Eyewitness Testimony* (Grand Rapids, MI: Eerdmans, 2006), 452–58.

6 M. M. Thompson, "John, Gospel of," in *Dictionary of Jesus and the Gospels*, ed. Joel B. Green, Scot McKnight, and I. Howard Marshall (Downers Grove, IL: InterVarsity, 1992), 369.

(*HE.* 5.4–8), Polycrates connects him with the city of Ephesus (Eusebius, *HE.* 3.31.3).[7] Papias valued the Gospel of John highly as an authentic source, more highly than other Gospels he knew.[8] The Gospel of John is usually considered as a "Gospel with Indian spirit," so Indians in particular and Asians in general can recognize the Gospel's universalistic significance here and now.[9]

Audience

The audience of the Gospel is usually considered as those who came to faith in Jesus under the leadership of the ideal figure popularly known as the Beloved Disciple. It was during the late first century that the believing community of the Beloved Disciple faced opposition from the synagogue, and they were excommunicated because of their unique faith. The Gospel of John reflects such a challenging situation (see 9:22; 12:42; 16:2). Jey J. Kanagaraj states, "In a context of such hostility, John offers hope of a heavenly life that is available even now for those who believe in Jesus."[10] The purpose statement of the Fourth Gospel (20:30–31) reflects that it is an attempt both to invite faith in Jesus (*missionsschrift*) and to deepen the faith of the believing community (*gemeindeschrift*).[11] In that sense, the author demonstrates both missional and pastoral intent.[12]

Louis Martyn suggests that John can be read as a two-level drama.[13] Following the suggestion of Martyn, Blomberg comments, "This approach has assumed that the characters and issues highlighted in John refer (at least much of the time) not to the historical Jesus and his contemporaries but to the Christians in the Johannine community and their opponents (or other, more interested outsiders)."[14] While Jesus's ministry was mostly concentrated

7 Bauckham, *Jesus and the Eyewitnesses*, 438–52.

8 Bauckham, 423.

9 See Johnson Thomaskutty, *The Gospel of John: A Universalistic Reading*, Biblical Hermeneutics Rediscovered 25 (New Delhi: Christian World Imprints, 2020).

10 Jey J. Kanagaraj, *The Gospel of John: A Commentary* (Secunderabad: OM, 2005), 23.

11 A. Barus, "John 2:12–25: A Narrative Reading," in *New Currents through John: A Global Perspective*, ed. F. Lozada and T. Thatcher (Boston: Brill, 2006), 140.

12 Johnson Thomaskutty, "Glo[b/c]alization and Mission[s]: Reading John's Gospel," in *The Gospel of John: A Universalistic Reading* (New Delhi: Christian World Imprints, 2020), 92.

13 J. Louis Martyn, *History and Theology in the Fourth Gospel*, 2nd ed. (Nashville: Abingdon, 1979).

14 See Blomberg, *Historical Reliability of John's Gospel*, 61–62.

in the Jerusalemite context in John, later on, the community of the Beloved Disciple flourished from its Jerusalem roots to the Ephesus-centric gentile context. The narrator adds the Johannine community situation to the story of Jesus to re-create and retell it according to the new demands.[15] The universalistic language and the literary style of the Gospel attune the attention of the readers toward "everywhere and ever" realities.[16]

Date and Place

As in the case of other writings of the NT, the dating of the Fourth Gospel is a herculean task. The scholarly consensus is between 85 and 110 CE.[17] The second-century manuscripts such as *Rylands Papyrus 457* (P52; 125–175 CE) and *Egerton Papyrus 2* (end of the second century CE) support such a possibility.[18] Though there are arguments concerning the dependency of John upon the Synoptic traditions, there is no convincing evidence to prove such a position. Paul N. Anderson argues that the Johannine traditions were already in existence alongside the Synoptic traditions. As Anderson suggests, the Fourth Gospel would have undergone several editorial processes. The first edition may have finalized around 80–85 CE, but the final edition was probably finalized around 100 CE, after the death of the Beloved Disciple.[19]

As the Johannine community situation is reflected in the Gospel, three periods of the community can be understood as follows: first, in the Palestinian context, it was developing as an autonomous Gospel tradition (ca. 30–70 CE); second, in its earlier Asia Minor period, the forging of the Johannine community took place (ca. 70–85 CE); and third, in the latter Asia Minor period, dialogues emerged between several Christian communities (ca. 85–100 CE).[20] In that sense, there is a shift from the Palestinian context to the Ephesian context. As J. A. T. Robinson dates the Gospel in the sixties CE, he suggests an autonomous development of the Johannine tradition. When Robinson argues for the "priority" of the Fourth Gospel, he was concerned with the Gospel's

15 Thomaskutty, *Gospel of John*, 155–56.
16 Thomaskutty, 3–14.
17 Guthrie, *New Testament Introduction*, 297; see Kanagaraj, *Gospel of John*, 23.
18 Guthrie, *New Testament Introduction*, 297.
19 Paul N. Anderson, *From Crisis to Christ* (Nashville: Abingdon, 2014), 127.
20 Anderson, 138.

closeness to the *Sitz im Leben Jesu*, its deepest theological reflection, and its historical and theological accuracy.[21] Based on these scholarly indications, I suggest the following: first, the Johannine traditions developed from the early stages alongside other gospel traditions; second, it underwent several editorial processes; and third, the canonical Gospel in its current shape probably emerged during the 90–110 CE period. All the indications help us associate the final draft of the Gospel with the Ephesian context. So the context of writing is particular, though the message is universal.

Structure and Outline

Classical Johannine scholarship divides the Fourth Gospel into four parts: two smaller parts (i.e., 1:1–18 as the "prologue" and 21:1–25 as the "epilogue") and two larger parts (i.e., 1:19–12:50 as the "Book of Signs" and 13:1–20:31 as the "Book of Glory").[22] C. H. Dodd considered the entire chapter 1 as the proem that includes the prologue (1:1–18) and the testimony (1:19–51).[23] The Gospel writers had their own criteria when they included materials. Blomberg says, "Whatever does not fit into the structures determined by those criteria is simply omitted."[24] Thus, John has a unique structure that does not match with the Synoptic Gospels. John's structure is more dramatic than that of the other Gospels. After the prologue (1:1–18) within the framework of the proem (1:1–51), the evangelist discusses the first half of the Gospel (2:1–12:50) with seven signs and seven discourses.[25] This major part of the Gospel is concluded in 12:37–50.[26] John 13:1–20:31 reflects on the hour, the lifting up, and the glorification of the Son of Man. This second major section is brought to a climax in the purpose statement of the Gospel in 20:30–31. In 21:1–25, the narrator attempts to bring an epilogue to the entire Gospel.[27]

21 See J. A. T. Robinson, *The Priority of John* (London: SCM, 1985).

22 See Raymond E. Brown, *The Gospel According to John*, vols. 1–2 (Garden City, NY: Doubleday, 1966, 1970).

23 Dodd, *Interpretation of the Fourth Gospel*, 292–96.

24 Blomberg, *Historical Reliability of John's Gospel*, 54.

25 See Blomberg, 55. Also see Leon Morris, *The Gospel According to John*, 2nd ed. (Grand Rapids, MI: Eerdmans, 1995).

26 C. H. Dodd, *The Interpretation of the Fourth Gospel* (Cambridge: Cambridge University Press, 1960), 379–83.

27 See Thompson, "John, Gospel of," 373–74.

Based on the details discussed, a reader can outline the Gospel in the following way. The outline helps a reader to understand the pattern and the narrative mechanism of the Fourth Gospel in a nutshell.

Prologue: The incarnation of the Word (1:1–18)

Book of Signs: The signs and the anticipated hour of Jesus (1:19–12:50)
- Introductory Events: John the Baptist's witness and the call narratives (1:19–51)
- The Public Ministry of Jesus: The encounters and signs of Jesus (2:1–12:50)
  - The revelation of the new order in Jesus (2:1–4:42)
  - Jesus the mediator of life and judgment (4:43–5:47)
  - Jesus feeds five thousand and his status as the bread of life (6:1–71)
  - Jesus the water and the light of the world (7:1–8:59)
  - Jesus the light and shepherd of humanity (9:1–10:42)
  - Jesus the resurrection and the life (11:1–54)
  - Jesus the King: Triumphant through Death (11:55–12:50)

Book of Glory: The Hour of Jesus Is Revealed on the Cross (13:1–20:31)
- Farewell Discourse: The Discourses and the Prayer of Jesus (13:1–17:26)
  - Last Supper and the Coming Departure (13:1–38)
  - Jesus the Way to the Father and the Coming Counsellor (14:1–31)
  - Vine and the Branches, Jesus's Friends, World's Hated (15:1–16:4)
  - Spirit's Work and the Prediction of Changes (16:5–33)
  - High Priestly Prayer of Jesus (17:1–26)
- Passion of Jesus: Hour/Lifting up/Glorification of the Son of Man (18:1–19:42)
- Resurrection of Jesus: Resurrection and the Purpose of John (20:1–31)

Epilogue: The Risen Jesus Reveals Himself to the Disciples (21:1–25)

This outline of the Gospel looks entirely different from the framework of the Synoptic Gospels. As the Gospel demonstrates different layers of meanings, an interpretation based exclusively on the explicit outline may lead the reader to wrong interpretations. Hence both the explicit and the implicit aspects are significant in the process of interpreting the Fourth Gospel.

THE GOSPEL OF JOHN IN THE ASIAN CONTEXT

The Gospel of John, through its four significant parts, provides a persuasive theological framework for Asian communities. A reader who dives deep into the Gospel can derive contextually oriented and universally applicable messages. When an Asian reader approaches the Gospel, the possibility of proximity and the availability of contextual applications are convincing.

The Prologue

We can reread the Prologue of John (1:1–18) as a rhythmical responsive literary piece.[28] It sustains all the features of a quasi-poem (a conglomeration of prose and poem) throughout. The South Indian literary form *Kathāprasangam* has a combination of both the prose and poem in a persuasive way. The orator maintains a rhythmical responsive style in the process of its presentation to the audience.[29] Some of the twentieth-century dramatic arts performed on stages sustain the dialogic and musical compositions. The Johannine narrator introduces the first major part of his book through the means of a trilevel dialogical masterpiece. At the interaction level of the text, the narrator dialogues with the reader from an eternal point of view. As with the *Rāmāyana*, the *Mahabharata*, and other religious writings, the narrator of the prologue presents the events from an omniscient point of view. Though the stories of many of the Asian religious writings sustain mythical and fictional aspects, the readers consider the message with immediate effects. Asian communities integrate the senses of the Scriptures in their contemporary realities.

28 See Thomaskutty, *Gospel of John*, 41–42.

29 The South Indian literary form called *Kathāprasangam* is used to entertain audiences of all levels. The presenters usually take the burning social issues and present them to the intended audience through rhythm, persuasion, sarcasm, and individual and social criticism.

At the intratextual level, the prologue is considered as a wisdom hymn stitched together at the forefront of the Gospel to make the overall message comprehensible to the reader. Some of the thematic words of the Gospel are first introduced in these verses: life, light (1:4), witness (1:7), true (in the sense of "genuine" or "ultimate," 1:9), world (1:10), and glory and truth (1:14).[30] Throughout the Gospel, the Logos is narrated as a divine emissary in conflict with the world (1:9–10; 3:16–17, 19; 6:14; 10:36; 11:27; 12:46; 16:28; 17:18, 21, 23, 37). The narrator also sets an intertextual relationship between the story of Jesus and the story of Moses. Opening with an echo of Genesis 1:1, the prologue goes on to identify its protagonist as the Logos, the Word of God, and thus places the drama in a cosmic setting and against the backdrop of the OT.[31] Comparisons between Jesus and Moses, and between Jesus's death and the Exodus, recur throughout John.[32] The Prologue of John is a unique masterpiece that reverberates in several ways with Asian realities. The literary and philosophical framework of the pericope resonates through conceptual aspects like life (*jîva*), light (*jyoti*), truth (*satya*), witness (*sākshi*), world (*lōkam*), and logos (*vachan*) in an interlocking way.

The Book of Signs

After the prologue in 1:1–18, the narrator introduces the first major part of the Gospel called the Book of Signs (1:19–12:50).[33] Raymond E. Brown divides this part into four subsections: the initial days of the revelation of Jesus to his disciples under different titles (1:19–51); the first and second miracles in Cana (chs. 2–4); a third miracle, OT feasts, and their replacements (chs. 5–10); and a fourth miracle, the raising of Lazarus, and its aftermath (chs. 11–12).[34]

30 Thomaskutty, *Gospel of John*, 45–46.

31 Thomaskutty, 46.

32 Mark W. G. Stibbe, *John*, Readings: A New Biblical Commentary (Sheffield, UK: Sheffield Academic Press, 1993), 23.

33 See Brown, *Gospel According to John*, 1:xxviii–xxxix; see Gilbert van Belle, *The Sign Source in the Fourth Gospel: Historical Survey and Critical Evaluation of the Semeia Hypothesis*, Bibliotheca Ephemeridum Theologicarum Lovaniensium 116 (Leuven: Leuven University Press, 1994); also see Johnson Thomaskutty, *Dialogue in the Book of Signs: A Polyvalent Analysis of John 1:19–12:50* (Leiden: Brill, 2015), 1.

34 Raymond E. Brown, *An Introduction to the NT* (Bangalore: Theological Publications in India, 2009), 338–51.

In the first subsection (1:19–51), Jesus's name is revealed through various witnesses as "the lamb of God" (1:29–35), "Messiah" (1:41), "one about whom Moses and the prophets wrote" (1:45), and "Son of God" and "King of Israel" (1:49). Some of the key revelatory aspects and the universality of Jesus are made obvious in this section.[35] The second subsection (chs. 2–4) describes a circular mission journey of Jesus that begins in Cana (2:1–11), proceeds through Jerusalem (2:13–22) and Samaria (4:1–45), and ends in Cana (4:46–54). Jesus's role and status as giver of joy (2:1–11), great teacher (3:1–21; 4:1–45), and provider of life (4:46–54) are exemplified through the events here.[36] The third subsection (chs. 5–10) focuses on the fulfillment of OT festivals in Jesus's ministry. As Asian people observe festivals like Diwali, Onam, Pongal, Holi, Ramadan, and others, the Johannine narrative offers a friendly and contextually relevant rhetoric to such readers. Whereas the festival of Booths/Tabernacles (7:2, 37) is attached to the symbols of light and water ablution, the festival of Diwali is considered as a festival of light and water ablution and is one of the significant aspects in Hindu spirituality.[37] The fourth subsection (chs. 11–12) is crucial because the death and raising of Lazarus prepares readers for Jesus's death and the resurrection in the second major part of the Gospel.[38] Asians value friendship at multiple levels, so Jesus's friendship with Lazarus and his family energizes readers, and they can identify with Jesus, who mourns at the tomb of Lazarus.

An Indian/Asian can see a lot of contextual and ideological resonances between the Book of Signs (1:19–12:50) and Asian religious literature. Just like the *Rāmāyana* has been a perennial source of spiritual, cultural, and artistic inspiration for thousands of years, the stories of John inspire many with spiritual insights,[39] cultural identification with the Johannine community,[40] and artistic inspiration.[41] As Rāma, Sîtā, and Hanumān have

35 See Thomaskutty, *Dialogue*, 92.

36 Kanagaraj, *Gospel of John*, 97–163.

37 Also see Rana B. P. Singh, "Water Symbolism and Sacred Landscape in Hinduism: A Study of Benares (Vārāṇasi)," *Erdkunde* 48, no. 3 (1994): 210–27.

38 See Thomaskutty, *Dialogue*, 368–404.

39 Clement of Alexandria considers it a spiritual Gospel. See Hypotyposes, cited in Eusebius, *HE* 6.14.7.

40 See Raymond E. Brown, *The Community of the Beloved Disciple* (New York: Paulist, 1979).

41 Refer to *Jyoti Art Ashram* (blog), accessed April 21, 2020, http://jyotiartashram.blogspot.com/.

inspired millions of people with the deepest and tenderest love, reverence, and devotion, John's Jesus, the Johannine community, and the *Paracletos* inspire many across the globe.[42] As the great sage Vālmîki presents Rāma, the ancient idol of the heroic ages, as the embodiment of truth and morality, the ideal son and husband, and above all, the ideal king,[43] the Beloved Disciple presents Jesus as the protagonist, the embodiment of truth (1:17; 14:6) and great morality, the ideal son of God (1:34, 49), the bridegroom figure of the Johannine community (3:29), and the ideal king of Israel (1:49). Kamala Subramaniam says, "'Drama' is the first word which comes to the mind while reading the great epic, *Mahabharata*. 'Bhakti,' on the other hand, is the thread running through the entire narration of the *Bhagavata*. 'Pain' is the predominant emotion in the *Rāmāyana*."[44] The Johannine narrator combines the aspects of drama, bhakti, and pain at their best in the portrayal of Jesus.

The seven signs in the Book of Signs (2:1–11; 4:46–54; 5:1–18; 6:1–15; 6:16–21; 9:1–41; 11:1–54) are told within the framework of the grand sign, the incarnation of the Word (1:1–18). A similar phenomenon is seen in the Hindu scriptures. The *Rāmāyana* and *Mahabharata*, as well as the eighteen Puranas, depict the astonishing power of divine beings. Hayes states, "Whether it was Arjun or Karna of the *Mahabharata* or Rama or Indrajit of the *Rāmāyana*, their accomplishments were miraculous. . . . Lord Vishnu took ten incarnations, or avatars, in human, semi-human, and animal forms in order to cleanse evil from this mundane world."[45] Similarly, Fiordalis states, "Exhibitions of superhuman power are often portrayed as evidence of holiness in Buddhist literature. Superhuman powers of various kinds result from developing the techniques of meditation that lead to the attainment of the highest goals of the Buddhist path."[46] Miracles and superhuman powers are part and parcel of Hindu, Buddhist, and other traditions. Jesus's performance of signs

42 Kamala Subramaniam, *Ramayana* (Mumbai: Bharatiya Divya Bhavan, 2017), v.

43 Subramaniam, v.

44 Subramaniam, ix.

45 See Patrick J. Hayes, ed., *Miracles: An Encyclopaedia of People, Places, and Supernatural Events from Antiquity to the Present* (Santa Barbara, CA: ABC-CLIO, 2016), 172.

46 David V. Fiordalis, "Miracles and Superhuman Powers in South Asian Buddhist Literature" (PhD diss., University of Michigan, 2008), 208–9.

to reveal his identity is identical to Asian realities, and they are presented in a universalistic fashion.[47]

The Book of Glory

After the Book of Signs, the second major part of the Gospel is called the Book of Glory (13:1–20:31). Brown subdivides this section into three parts: first, the Last Supper and Jesus's Last Discourse (chs. 13–17); second, Jesus's passion and death (chs. 18–19); and third, four scenes in Jerusalem and faith in the risen Jesus (20:1–29), followed by the Gospel conclusion or statement of the purpose of writing (20:30 31).[48] As a person influenced by biblical thought, Mahatma Gandhi's speeches reflect the ideals of Jesus. In his *The Story of My Experiments with Truth*, Gandhi emphasizes the aspects of love, truth, nonviolence, integrity, and morality.[49] These are some of the core values of Jesus's teaching in John 13–17.

While the Book of Signs ends with Mary anointing the feet of Jesus (12:1–8), the Book of Glory begins with Jesus washing the feet of the disciples (13:1–20). While the Book of Signs ends with the death and the raising of Lazarus (11:1–54), the Book of Glory takes our attention to the death and the resurrection of Jesus (chs. 18–20). While the Book of Signs ends with Jesus's weeping over Lazarus at his tomb (11:35), the Book of Glory ends with Mary Magdalene's weeping at the tomb of Jesus (20:10–18).[50] Thus, there is an integral connectivity between the two major parts of the Gospel. The longer section in chapters 13–17 follows the literary style of farewell discourses or testaments of famous men.[51] John shares some of the literary features parallel to the *Testaments of the Twelve Patriarchs* that contain the last words of each of the patriarchs to their people.[52] The discourse traditions of

47 For more Indian and Johannine resemblances, see Christopher Duraisingh and Cecil Hargreaves, eds., *India's Search for Reality and the Relevance of the Gospel of John* (Delhi: ISPCK, 1975).

48 See Brown, *Introduction to the NT*, 351–60.

49 M. K. Gandhi, *The Story of My Experiments with Truth* (Ahmedabad: Navajivan, 1968).

50 These striking literary interconnections between the Book of Signs and the Book of Glory is rhetorical in the process of interpreting the Gospel as a whole.

51 R. F. Collins, *The Things Have Been Written* (Louvain: Peeters, 1990), 221.

52 George R. Beasley-Murray, *John*, Word Biblical Commentary 36 (Waco, TX: Word Books, 1987), 222–23.

Sri Buddha,[53] Guru Nanak,[54] Sri Ramakrishna Paramahansa,[55] and Swami Vivekananda[56] are well-known. As Jesus's discourse was a blueprint for his disciples, the Indian religious leaders used their discourses to persuade their followers.

The Farewell Discourse begins with Jesus's foot washing (13:1–20) and ends with his high priestly prayer (17:1–26). As Jesus exemplified his servant leadership through the paradigm of foot washing, the servant leadership of Gandhi and Mother Teresa are popularly known across the globe. In 17:1–26, Jesus prays for himself (vv. 1–5), his disciples (vv. 6–19), and future believers (vv. 20–26). In Asian contexts, prayers are usually done for personal edification and for relatives, friends, and the world at large. One of the Hindu prayers from *Brihadaranyaka Upanishad* (1.3.28) proceeds as follows: "Lead me from untruth (*asat*) to truth (*sat*); lead me from darkness (*tamas*) to light (*jyotih*); and lead me from death (*mrutyu*) to immortality (*amrita*)." While *asat*, *tamas*, and *mrutyu* refer to temporality or impermanence, *sat*, *jyotih*, and *amrita* refer to the eternals and hence to Brahman and Atman.[57] Many scholars connect this prayer with the utterance of Jesus: "I am the Way, the Truth, and the Life" (14:6). The prayers of Jesus in John make God's presence known universally.

The passion narrative in chapters 18–19 describes Jesus's betrayal and arrest (18:1–11), the trial before Annas and Caiaphas (18:12–14), Peter's three denials (18:15–27), the trial before Pilate (18:28–19:15), the crucifixion and death (19:16–37), and the burial (19:38–42). The irony of the cross is revealed through the final utterances of Jesus: first, while his own people did not care

53 Buddha's first discourse contains the Noble Eightfold Paths and Four Noble Truths; see "The First Discourse of the Buddha," Vipassana Research Institute, accessed July 19, 2021, https://www.vridhamma.org/discourses/first-discourse-of-buddha. Also see Maurice Walshe, trans., *The Long Discourses of the Buddha: A Translation of the Digha Nikaya* (Somerville, MA: Wisdom, 1995).

54 Kamala Elizabeth Nayar, *The Socially Involved Renunciate: Guru Nanak's Discourse to the Nath Yogis* (Albany: State University of New York Press, 2012).

55 See more details at "Sri Ramakrishna," Belur Math, accessed July 20, 2021, https://belurmath.org/sri-ramakrishna/.

56 Speech delivered by him on September 11, 1893, at the First World's Parliament of Religion on the site of the present Art Institute in Chicago. In his speech, he introduced Hinduism to America and called for religious tolerance and an end to fanaticism.

57 See "From Darkness to Light," IndiaFacts, accessed April 23, 2020, http://indiafacts.org/from-darkness-to-light/.

for him (1:10–11), he protects his own (17:11–12) and cares for his mother (19:26b); second, at the point of death, he entrusts a divine responsibility to the Beloved Disciple (19:27); third, the giver of living water is thirsty, and the provider of the new wine / the true vine is given sour wine (19:28–29; see 2:1–11; 15:1–5); and fourth, irrespective of the worldly persecution, he accomplishes the task of the Father (19:30).[58] The hour / lifting up / glorification of the Son of Man is demonstrated on the cross. Just as Jesus died as an innocent martyr, the Sikh tradition (especially *Adi Granth*) makes mention of *śahîdî* or *śahādat* (in Punjabi and in Perso-Arabic, respectively), which means a "witness." In the seventeenth- and eighteenth-century history of Sikhism, Sikhs fought against a series of murderous foes whose sole goal was the extermination of Sikhism.[59] Fenech comments, "These were struggles that became a part of a Sikh's *sevā*, or a selfless service to humanity, service that is essential to securing salvation, according to the Sikh Gurus."[60] Jesus's death, which marks the victory of righteousness and truth, is reminiscent of historical events that we see in Sikh history. Indians can also identify the glorious death of Jesus as they cherish the martyrdoms of heroic figures like Mahatma Gandhi, Indira Gandhi, Rajiv Gandhi, and others.

John 20:1–29 describes the resurrection of Jesus and the succeeding events. The section begins with an introduction, consisting of Mary Magdalene's coming to the tomb, finding it empty, and reporting the news to Simon Peter and the Beloved Disciple (20:1–2).[61] There are four scenes reported in the Jerusalem context: first, Simon Peter and the Beloved Disciple run to the tomb and confirm the absence of Jesus's body (20:3–10); second, Mary Magdalene returns to the tomb, where two angels are now present (20:11–18); third, on Easter Sunday night, the disciples are in a place where the doors are locked due to fear of the Jews (20:19–25); and fourth, a week later, the disciples are in the same place with Thomas present (20:26–29).[62] The purpose statement makes it clear

58 Joel B. Green, "Death of Jesus," in Green, McKnight, and Marshall, *Dictionary of Jesus and the Gospels*, 161–63.

59 Louis E. Fenech, "The Tropics of Heroic Death: Martyrdom and the Sikh Tradition," in *Martyrdom, Self-Sacrifice, and Self-Immolation: Religious Perspectives on Suicide*, ed. Margo Kitts (Oxford: Oxford University Press, 2018), 205.

60 Fenech, 205.

61 Brown, *Introduction to the NT*, 359.

62 Brown, 359–60.

that the goal of the Gospel has been to have people come to faith or increase in faith in Jesus as the Messiah, the Son of God, and through this faith to possess eternal life in his name (20:30–31).[63] As the Brahman is presented as the eternal being in the Hindu traditions, the Gospel of John depicts God/Jesus as eternal and universalistic.[64] This aspect of the Fourth Gospel can be aligned within the religious aspirations of the Asian communities.

In the Book of Glory, pain and glory develop simultaneously. Jesus, the protagonist, and those who believe in and follow him are in pain. But Jesus's suffering brings glory; the shameful cross becomes God's way of salvation. The glory of God/Jesus is further revealed through the resurrection placed at the climax of the story. The story of the *Rāmāyana* has a similar narrative dynamic. Subramaniam says, "Pain is the monochord which can be heard throughout [*Rāmāyana*]: and yet, this very pain is ennobling, purifying, and satisfying. *Rāmāyana* is a threnody filled to the brim, with noble thoughts, noble sentiments, noble characters, not one of whom is spared the experience of pain."[65] As in the case of *Rāmāyana*, John's narrative is a threnody that encompasses melody, comedy, and tragedy. In that way, Asian realities and literary features are part and parcel of the Gospel of John.

The Epilogue

The epilogue of John is set in the Galilean context, and this section can be subdivided into three parts: first, the appearance of Jesus and the event of miraculous fishing (21:1–14); second, the saying of the risen Jesus to Peter and the Beloved Disciple (21:15–23); and third, the conclusion (21:24–25).[66] Just as the Gospel has a double introduction (1:1–18; 1:19–51), it has a double conclusion too (20:30–31; 21:1–25, especially vv. 24–25). In the first part of this chapter (21:1–14), the gathering of seven disciples seems symbolical because this group of disciples represents the future community, the church.[67] While

63 Brown, 360.

64 Thomas Egenes and Kumuda Reddy, *Eternal Stories from the Upanishads* (New Delhi: Smriti, 2002), 4–6; Allen Wright Thrasher, *The Advaita Vedānta of Brahma-Siddhi* (Delhi: Motilal Banarsidass, 1993), 6–7.

65 Subramaniam, *Ramayana*, ix.

66 Brown, *Introduction to the NT*, 360–61.

67 Rudolf Schnackenburg, *The Gospel According to St. John* (New York: Herder & Herder, 1982), 3:352; see Thomaskutty, *Saint Thomas the Apostle*, 78–79.

others do not recognize Jesus, the Beloved Disciple exclaims, "It is the Lord!" (21:7). Achtemeier, Green, and Thompson say, "Even after his resurrection, Jesus is not easily recognized, and the disciples must learn to recognize Jesus all over again."[68] The second part of the chapter (21:15–23) focuses on two major characters, Peter and the Beloved Disciple. Even as Peter denied Jesus thrice before a charcoal fire (18:15–27), he is reinstated in love and prepared for future mission (21:15–17). While the Beloved Disciple recognizes the Lord (21:7), Peter is instructed to follow him (21:19, 22). The same command of Jesus ("Follow me") to Philip in 1:43 and to Peter in 21:19, 22 introduces a larger inclusion to the Gospel. After a conclusion in 20:30–31, another recap statement is added (21:24–25). The Beloved Disciple is identified "as the witness who stands behind the Gospel narrative and certifies the truth of his testimony."[69] In that sense, the entire story is narrated through the perspective of the Beloved Disciple.

A comparison may be drawn between the disciples in the Fourth Gospel and the disciples of Confucius who attended to their teacher while following him. Confucius and his disciples endured many hardships, and he encouraged them to stand firm in times of trial.[70] He warned them to keep away from greed and laziness and built in them moral and ethical principles to lead renewed lives in their society. In that way, Jesus and Confucius were teachers of great lessons. Just as the oral thoughts of Confucius spread through his disciples to future generations, the Johannine community developed the oral traditions of Jesus according to the growing demands. As the Beloved Disciple reinterpreted his master's teachings, the teachings of Confucius were later on compiled as *Analects*.[71]

68 See Paul J. Achtemeier, Joel B. Green, and Marianne Meye Thompson, *Introducing the New Testament: Its Literature and Theology* (Grand Rapids, MI: Eerdmans, 2001), 197.

69 See Brown, *Introduction to the NT*, 361.

70 For more details, see *Stanford Encyclopedia of Philosophy*, s.v. "Confucius," accessed April 25, 2020, https://plato.stanford.edu/entries/confucius/.

71 See "Roles of the Disciples in Confucianism," classroom.com, accessed April 23, 2020, https://classroom.synonym.com/roles-of-the-disciples-in-confucianism-12086182.html.

In his 1820 work *The Precepts of Jesus*, Raja Ram Mohan Roy, one of the Hindu Renaissance leaders of India, placed the four Gospels alongside the *Upanishads*. He revered the extracts of Jesus's teaching in the Fourth Gospel with great aptitude alongside the Sermon on the Mount (Matt 5–7).[72] For Sadhu Sundar Singh, the Bible was the primary standard, or *pramāna*, but he had a preference for John's Gospel: "St. John seems to me to have loved Christ more than the other Apostles."[73] As a strong proponent of Indianization of the Gospel, Sundar Singh's interpretation of the Scripture is based on the metaphor of "water of life in an Indian cup."[74] Furthermore, A. J. Appasamy understood "Christianity as Bhakti Marga" based on the devotional traditions of the Fourth Gospel and the philosophical roots of Ramanuja.[75] The following discussion shall give us further details concerning the possible interpretative avenues of the Fourth Gospel in Asian contexts.

The Word as the *Sat/Cit*, the *Avatāra*, and the *Adisabda*

The Fourth Gospel begins with a well-known rhythm as follows: "In the beginning was the Word, and the Word was with God, and the Word was God" (1:1). There are parallels between the Fourth Gospel and the *Chandogya Upanishad*. In the *Chandogya Upanishad*, the sage begins his teaching with the words, "In the beginning, Being (*sat*) alone existed, one without a second" (6.2.1).[76] In that sense, Jesus as the word was fully God. The word becoming flesh and dwelling among humanity is one of the incarnational aspects of the Fourth Gospel (1:14). While Jesus is portrayed as the incarnation of God in the Gospel, a similar concept like *avatāra* is used in Hinduism. The word *avatāra* comes from the root meaning "to descend," and Rama and Krishna are considered *avatārs* of Vishnu (see *Gita* 4.7.8).[77]

72 Robin Boyd, *An Introduction to Indian Christian Theology* (Delhi: ISPCK, 2000), 19–20.

73 Boyd, 96.

74 Boyd, 86–109.

75 Gregory Thomas Basker, *Interpreting Biblical Texts: John and His Tamil Readers* (New Delhi: ISPCK, 2016), 30–33.

76 Kanagaraj, *Gospel of John*, 35.

77 Boyd, *Introduction to Indian Christian Theology*, 81.

There are some similarities between the Johannine *Logos* and the Hindu concept of *Om/Aum*. The divine sound *Om* is derived out of three sounds, *a*, *u*, and *m*, that represent three Vedas and the *trimurti* of Brahman (*a*), Vishnu (*u*), and Shiva (*m*). In the Upanishads, *Om* is considered the primordial sound or *Adisabda* and a symbol of true existence.[78] It is considered to be the totality of the manifested world, *ekaksara* ("the one syllable" or "the imperishable one"), *praṇava* (signifying a droning utterance), symbolism of a sacred syllable, and a prayer or mantra of all other mantras.[79] This understanding of Hinduism goes well with the preincarnate (1:1–5) and incarnate (1:14) forms of Jesus in John's Gospel.

Keshub Chandra Sen considered *Brahman* as *Sat* (being), *Cit* (intelligence), and *Ananda* (bliss). For Sen, in the words of Boyd, "The *Logos*, then, who in eternity lay as it were asleep in God, is the Word of Creation, *Cit* (intelligence, wisdom), ever at work in the development of the created world, and in the fullness of time being born as man in Jesus of Nazareth."[80] Similarly, Brahmabandhav Upādhyāya (1861–1907) considered the Hindu concept of Saccidānanda Brahman on par with the Christian Trinity.[81] In his Sanskrit hymn—the *Hymn of the Incarnation*—Upādhyāya describes Christ as the God-Man and the Logos. Boyd puts it as follows: "Christ is the Image of God (*Brahman*) and in him the eternal Word (Intelligence, *Cit*), the fullness of the Godhead, dwells. In the refrain, victory (*jai*) or glory is ascribed to him who is the true *Nara-Hari* ('Man-God')."[82] Jesus the *Logos* can resonate with the *Sat* because he is one with the Brahman, with *Cit* because he is the divine wisdom from above, with the *avatāra* because he came to establish righteousness and justice in the world, and with the *Adisabda* because he is God's eternal voice in the universe.

78 Kanagaraj, *Gospel of John*, 39–41.

79 Martin Owens, "OṂ," in *Encyclopaedia of Hinduism*, ed. Denise Cush, Catherine Robinson, and Michael York (London: Routledge, 2008), 573.

80 See Boyd, *Introduction to Indian Christian Theology*, 28.

81 Boyd, 63–74.

82 Boyd, 78. See also Paul Anderson, *Following Jesus: The Heart of Faith and Practice* (Newberg, OR: Barclay, 2013).

John and the Jnana, Karma, and Bhakti Margas

The *Bhagavad Gita* describes three paths to salvation: first, the jnana *marga* (a path that emphasizes thoughts and introspection);[83] second, the karma *marga* (a path of ritual action or duties); and third, the bhakti *marga* (a path of devotion).[84] Though John has exclusive claims like "I am the Way and the Truth and the Life" (14:6), its soteriology has much scope to connect with the jnana, karma, and bhakti traditions of Hinduism. In John's Gospel, knowing (*ginōskein*) and believing (*pisteuein*) occur together, and in several passages, they function in relation to other cognates (see 4:53; 6:69; 10:38; 17:8).[85] When Jesus says that "My Father is always at his work to this very day, and I, too, am working" (5:17), the aspect of karma can be identified (also see 4:34–38; 9:3–5; 13:14).[86] As the Father is engaged in works, the Son is working; as Jesus engages in works, the disciples are encouraged to do what he does (13:14).

Alongside knowing and working, the aspect of devoting oneself in discipleship (1:43; 21:19, 22), worship (4:21–24; 9:38), and belief (1:7; 3:15–17; 4:39–42; 6:29–34; 7:38–39; 11:25–28; 16:27–30) is also demonstrated. *Jnana marga* leads people to attain knowledge over ignorance and to understand the truths of ultimate reality.[87] While karma *marga* engages people to do selfless works in the society, bhakti *marga* helps people focus on God.[88] On one occasion, Jesus held up an action as a *hypodeigma* (i.e., an example) for the disciples to follow (13:1–20). Thus John emphasizes the knowing, working, and devoting aspects of Christian living in a dynamic way.

83 See Anantanand Rambachan, "To Recognize and Love God in All: An Introduction to Hinduism," in *Five Voices, Five Faiths: An Interfaith Primer* (Cambridge, MA: Cowley, 2005), 7.

84 See *Encyclopaedia Britannica Online*, s.v. "Hinduism," accessed April 30, 2020, https://www.britannica.com/topic/Hinduism/Karma-samsara-and-moksha#ref50477.

85 See more details at J. Gaffney, "Believing and Knowing in the Fourth Gospel," *Theological Studies* 26, no. 2 (May 1, 1965): 215–41.

86 Expressions like *to ergon* (4:34), *ergadzetai* and *ergadzomai* (5:17), and *ta erga* and *ergadzesthai* (9:3–4) are used to emphasize the aspect of work.

87 Basker, *Interpreting Biblical Texts*, 36.

88 See A. J. Appasamy, *Christianity as Bhakti Marga: A Study of the Johannine Doctrine of Love* (Madras: CLS, 1991), 13, 22. Also see Abraham Philip, *History and Theology of the Gospel According to St. John* (Tiruvalla: CSS, 2018).

Johannine Discipleship and the Asian Realities

The call of the first disciples (1:19–51) provides us with a brief understanding of Johannine discipleship. John the Baptist introduces Jesus to the world: "Behold, the Lamb of God" (1:36; see 1:29). His witness about Jesus resulted in two of his disciples following Jesus. Here we see the first record of people following Jesus (1:37). The verb *follow* serves as a metaphor for discipleship throughout the Fourth Gospel (see 1:37, 43; 8:12; 10:4–5, 15, 27; 12:26; 21:19, 22).[89] Nicodemus and the woman at the well bring to the fore two models of discipleship, one of them a member of the Jewish religious elite (3:1–21) and the other a woman living in a Samaritan village (4:1–26). Andrew (1:35–42; 6:8; 12:22), Philip (1:43–44; 6:8; 12:22), Peter (1:40–42; 6:66–70; 13:6–10; 18:15–26; 20:1–10; 21:1–23), the man born blind (9:1–41), Thomas (11:16; 14:5; 20:24–28; 21:2), the family of Lazarus (including Mary and Martha; 11:1–54; 12:1–8), the Beloved Disciple (13:23; 19:26–27; 20:2; 21:7, 20), Mary Magdalene (19:25; 20:1–18), and others follow Jesus.[90] The disciples are those who believe, follow, and worship Jesus. The entire Gospel is placed in an *inclusio* of Jesus's commands to follow him in 1:43 and in 21:19, 22.

In the Chinese context, Confucius was an influential guru with a large following. To Confucius, the main objective of being an educator was to teach people to live with integrity. Through his teachings, he strove to resurrect the traditional values of benevolence, propriety, and ritual in Chinese society.[91] The guru-shishya tradition of India is old and takes us back to the Upanishadic period.[92] Just as Jesus was a walking teacher and the disciples followed him in a Peripatetic style,[93] the Asian religious teachers like Dronacharya,

89 See Johnson Thomaskutty, "Reading John's Gospel in the Nepali Context," *Journal of Asian Evangelical Theology* 20, no. 1 (March 2016), 5–21.

90 See M. J. Wilkins, "Disciples," in Green, McKnight, and Marshall, *Dictionary of Jesus and the Gospels*, 176–82.

91 "Confucius," biography.com, accessed May 1, 2020, https://www.biography.com/scholar/confucius.

92 Surinder Singh Kohli, *The Sikh and Sikhism* (New Delhi: Atlantic, 1993), 18.

93 Peripatetic School is "the school founded by Aristotle in Athens in 336 BCE, supposedly named after the peripatos or covered walk in the garden of the Lyceum, where he lectured. Apart from Aristotle, its important members were Theophrastus, Eudemus of Rhodes, and Strato of Lampsacus." See "Peripatetic School," Oxford Reference, accessed May 2, 2020, https://www.oxfordreference.com/view/10.1093/oi/authority.20110803100317855.

Buddha, Mahavira, and the Sikh gurus imparted knowledge to the disciples while they walked together. Guru Dronacharya was a legendary and illustrious teacher in the *Drona Parva* of the *Mahabharata*.[94] He taught royal princes of both the clans Pandavas and Kauravas. The guru-shishya relationship was emphasized in the Sikh religion. The Punjabi word *sikh* (learner) is related to the Sanskrit *shishya* (disciple). After a succession of ten gurus beginning from Guru Nanak, the *Guru Granth Sahib* became the final guru.[95] Similarly, Mahavira and Buddha had a large number of followers.

The Signs and Their Significance in Asia

The signs recorded in the Fourth Gospel function in a dynamic way as they contribute semantically to its narrative framework. Jesus turns water into wine at a wedding to solve a family's pressing problem in an honor-and-shame sociocultural context and to launch his public ministry (2:1–11).[96] By healing an official's son, he encourages the official to progress in his journey of faith (4:46–54).[97] By feeding the five thousand, he demonstrates his compassion for all of humanity (6:1–15), and by walking on the water, he reveals his power and authority over all of nature (6:16–21).[98] In healing a man born blind, he shows the reader how such a sign can nurture a person's faith development (9:1–41),[99] and by restoring Lazarus to life, he gives the reader a sense of his concern for all who belong to the community of God (11:1–44).[100] By enabling a miraculous catch of fish, he reveals his Lordship to the disciples (21:6–11).[101] The mentioned situations are echoed in the Asian context, where divine signs are significant.

94 See Krishna-Dwaipayana Vyasa, *The Mahabharata of Krishna-Dwaipayana Vyasa Book 7 Drona Parva* (London: Bottom of the Hill, 2013); Basker, *Interpreting Biblical Texts*, 78.

95 *Encyclopaedia Britannica Online*, s.v. "Guru, Sikhism," accessed May 1, 2020, https://www.britannica.com/topic/Guru-Sikhism.

96 Beasley-Murray, *John*, 32–37.

97 C. K. Barrett, *The Gospel According to St. John: An Introduction with Commentary and Notes on the Greek Text* (London: SPCK, 1978), 205–8.

98 Beasley-Murray, *John*, 85–96.

99 Barrett, *John*, 292–304.

100 See Johnson Thomaskutty, "Reading John's Gospel in the Bangladeshi Context," *Journal of Asian Evangelical Theology* 21, no. 2 (March–September 2017), 67–68.

101 Above all, the resurrection of Jesus from the dead reveals his glory to the world (20:1–29).

In the words of Blackburn, the Synoptic *dynameis* (deeds of power) and the Johannine *sēmeia* (signs) function in different ways. While the Synoptic evangelists present *pistis* on the part of the suppliants (or their representatives) as a prerequisite for receiving miraculous help (Mark 2:5; 6:5–6), in John, the signs ideally result in *pistis*.[102] As John's Jesus is open-ended and unconditional in performing miraculous signs, the multicultural and pluralistic Asian communities can embrace him wholeheartedly. The Asian context is known for the large numbers of sick and the poor, who seek a healer and a provider like Jesus. While Jesus engages in the mission of God, he uses the signs as a means of revealing his glory and to build a holistic community.[103] In a context of social isolation, quarantine, global shutdown, and death and bereavement due to the pandemics like Covid-19, the Johannine Jesus can be introduced as a paradigmatic healer to Asian communities.[104]

The "I Am" Sayings of Jesus in the Asian Context

In his ministry, the Jesus of John's Gospel grounds his public discourses in equally public actions.[105] His actions and speech develop simultaneously within the Johannine narrative framework. One who feeds five thousand people with physical bread (6:1–15) declares himself to be bread from heaven (6:22–59).[106] The feast of Tabernacles is actualized by the presence of Jesus as "the light of the world" (8:12).[107] One who gives physical sight to the blind (9:1–7) is introduced, again, as "the light of the world" (9:5).[108] When the sheep are sent out of the synagogue (9:34), Jesus is ready to receive them as

102 B. L. Blackburn, "Miracles and Miracle Stories," in Green, McKnight, and Marshall, *Dictionary of Jesus and the Gospels*, 550.

103 Thomaskutty, "Bangladeshi Context," 67–68.

104 See Johnson Thomaskutty, "Reading John's Gospel in the Context of Pandemic Covid-19," academia.edu, accessed May 2, 2020, https://www.academia.edu/42734341/Reading_Johns_Gospel_in_the_Context_of_Pandemic_Covid-19.

105 Gary M. Burge, "'I Am' Sayings," in Green, McKnight, and Marshall, *Dictionary of Jesus and the Gospels*, 354–56.

106 Jan G. van der Watt, "I Am the Bread of Life: Imagery in John 6:32–51," *Acta Theologica* 27, no. 2 (2007): 186–204.

107 David Mark Ball, *"I Am" in John's Gospel: Literary Function, Background, and Theological Implications*, JSNTSS 124 (Sheffield, UK: Sheffield Academic Press, 1996), 155.

108 Ball, 80–93.

"the door of the sheep" (10:7).[109] The leaders of the synagogue are mere hirelings (10:12–13), but Jesus shows himself to be "the good shepherd" (10:11, 14, 16) by resolving the struggles of the man born blind.[110] One who raises the dead (11:38–44) is himself "the resurrection and the life" (11:25). One who is "the way, the truth, and the life" (14:6) prepares a way and a place in heaven for those who follow him (14:2–3).[111] One who provides the best wine (2:1–11) is himself "the true vine" (15:1–11).[112] Thus, Jesus's utterances are backed up by his actions.

In the Asian context, people highly value those who walk their talk. In religion, politics, and culture, such people are given heroic images in society. Politicians who make promises but remain unable to fulfill them are not considered respectable figures. Asian figures like Mahatma Gandhi,[113] Malala Yousafzai,[114] Pandita Ramabai,[115] and Mother Teresa[116] are known not only for their rhetoric but also for their actions for community development. In this context, the Johannine Jesus can be identified as an ideal model for human transformation in the pluralistic context of Asia.[117]

Johannine Characters in the Asian Context

Within the Gospel's narrative framework, John's characterization is extremely effective. The various characters are memorably presented with the help of a wide range of literary devices and narrative techniques.[118] One who reads the Johannine story paradigmatically may identify its characters from one's own

109 Thomaskutty, *Dialogue*, 341–45.

110 See Thomaskutty, 310–40.

111 Ball, *"I Am" in John's Gospel*, 119–28.

112 Ball, 60–145.

113 B. R. Nanda, "Mahatma Gandhi," *Encyclopaedia Britannica Online*, accessed April 3, 2020, https://www.britannica.com/biography/Mahatma-Gandhi.

114 Refer to "Malala Yousafzai," Nobel Prize, accessed April 3, 2020, https://www.nobelprize.org/prizes/peace/2014/yousafzai/facts/.

115 See Aisha Khan, "Overlooked No More: Pandita Ramabai, Indian Scholar, Feminist and Educator," *New York Times*, November 14, 2018, https://www.nytimes.com/2018/11/14/obituaries/pandita-ramabai-overlooked.html.

116 See "Mother Teresa," Nobel Prize, accessed April 3, 2020, https://www.nobelprize.org/prizes/peace/1979/teresa/biographical/.

117 Basker, *Interpreting Biblical Texts*, 75–77.

118 See Thomaskutty, "Nepali Context," 17.

context. For example, an Indian or a Nepali reader may identify Nicodemus with a higher-caste Hindu or a Buddhist who seeks to understand Jesus.[119] When a reader ministers in a village, addressing the lower-caste women of the region, they may identify them with the Samaritan woman.[120] "Secret" Christians, those who believe in Jesus but do not take the public step of identifying with the Christian community, seem much like Joseph of Arimathea (19:38–42). The blind man, the family of Lazarus, Mary Magdalene, Thomas, Nathanael, Peter, Philip, and other characters bear a strong resemblance to people we come across on a daily basis. This is the peculiar narrative dynamic of John's storytelling.[121] In our own reading, we find the Johannine characters to be quite Asian.

The story of Nathanael (1:43–51) resembles very much the story of Buddha, and the story of the Samaritan woman (4:1–26) resembles in many ways various Buddhist traditions. Similarly, the invalid at the pool of Bethesda (5:1–18) and the man born blind who was healed in Jerusalem (9:1–41) are like the poor beggars in and around the temples, mosques, pagodas, gurudwaras, and other religious centers in Asian countries. Nathanael, as a person who sits under the fig tree (1:48b) and is enlightened to recognize Jesus as the "Son of God" and the "King of Israel" (1:49), resembles in many ways Buddha, who sat under the Bodhi tree in Bodh Gaya and was enlightened.[122] Jesus, who comes to the Samaritan village and asks a woman for water, corresponds in many ways to Ananda, a famous disciple of Buddha who asked a Matanga Caste woman for water at a well.[123] The social distancing between communities is seen in her question, "How do you ask water of me, an outcaste who may not touch thee without contamination?" (see John 4:9).[124] Ananda replied, "My sister, I ask not of thee thy caste, I ask for water to drink" (see John 4:10,

119 Blomberg, *Historical Reliability of John's Gospel*, 91–95.

120 Moloney, *Gospel of John*, 113–50.

121 See Thomaskutty, "Nepali Context," 18.

122 See Blomberg, *Historical Reliability of John's Gospel*, 83.

123 See Kumaranasan, "Chandalabhikshuki—Kumaran Asan," malayalamkavithakal.com, November 9, 2018, https://malayalamkavithakal.com/chandalabhikshuki-kumaran-asan/. Also see Biju Chacko, "Samaritan Woman, *Chandalabhikshuki* and a Third Space of Hermeneutics: Reading the 'Well-Encounter' in John 4 from an Intercultural Perspective" (academic paper, Senate of Serampore College, Kolkata, 2018), 3.

124 P. Lakshmi Narasu, *The Essence of Buddhism* (New Delhi: Gautam, 2009), 84.

13–14). He breaks the sociocultural and religious barriers in drinking the water.[125] The othering by social distancing is transcended, and this daring action crossed the binary spaces of *me* and *you* to a third space where both could engage in their conversation and interaction.[126] Ananda thanked her, showered on her a blessing from Buddha, and went away. This girl, attracted by the defiant action of the Buddhist Bhikshu, followed his footprints and reached the Buddhist Sangha Viharam (Ashram).[127] Encounters near wells are usual in Asian village contexts, as women are expected to fetch water for the whole day from the village well. The local and the universal are interwoven throughout this Gospel. This peculiar feature of the Gospel makes it both local and universal in the context of Asia.[128]

Mysticism in John and in the Asian Religions

The spirituality reflected in John's Gospel has much in common with the mystical traditions of the Asian religions. The following aspects can be considered significant in that regard: first, at the heart of Johannine theology, we witness a union between God/Jesus and human beings (6:56; 15:1–17);[129] second, Jesus's vertical and horizontal relationships are reflected through his mystical expressions like "All that is mine is yours; all that is yours is mine" (17:10; also see 17:21–23; see 14:7–12);[130] third, as a Gospel of belief and love, the aspects such as believing in and loving God are emphasized to sustain the union between God and believers (3:16; 6:47; chs. 14–16);[131] fourth, the language John uses like "'having fellowship' (*koinōnia*) with the Father and the Son," "to be born of God," or to be "children of God" (1:13), and "I know mine and mine know me" (10:14; 17:3) reveals an integral relationship;[132] fifth, the knowing, seeing,

125 This story is described in the Matangi Sutra of Buddhist Sources. This encounter gave birth to Shurangana Sutra.

126 Chacko, "Samaritan Woman," 3; also see Johnson Thomaskutty, "Biblical Interpretation in the Global-Indian Context," *Fuller Magazine*, no. 8 (2017): 64–68.

127 Chacko, "Samaritan Woman," 3.

128 See Thomaskutty, *Gospel of John*, 3–14.

129 James McPolin, "Johannine Mysticism," theway.org.uk, accessed May 3, 2020, 26–27, https://www.theway.org.uk/back/18McPolin.pdf.

130 McPolin, 27–30.

131 Basker, *Interpreting Biblical Texts*, xvii.

132 McPolin, "Johannine Mysticism," 31–32.

and believing aspects of the Gospel make it more contemplative as it demands a deeper level of reflection on the meaning of Christ for our lives;[133] sixth, the imageries like "light" (1:9; 8:12; 9:5), "vine and the branches" (15:1–15), and others express the intimacy of communion with Christ forcefully;[134] and seventh, the binding communion between the Father, the Son, the Holy Spirit, and the believer and the inseparable unity is emphasized through the formula of immanence.[135] These aspects of the Fourth Gospel resonate in several ways in the Asian thought-world.

The Johannine idea of oneness with God has resonances in the Asian religious and philosophical traditions. While Hinduism expresses the view of "Atman is Brahman" ("the soul is one with God"),[136] Mahayana Buddhism has the idea of *tathātā*, which can be described as "thisness of reality."[137] The teachings of Confucius and the Sufi tradition of Islam emphasize mystical experiences. Sankara, one of the Indian classical proponents of *Advaita* (nondualism) philosophy, see an eternal union between Brahma the Absolute and the Atman or pure consciousness (*chaitanyam*).[138] The *Advaita* interpretation of Sankara was later modified by Ramanuja through his *Vishishtadvaita* (qualified nondualism) interpretation of Vedanta.[139] Ramanuja was critical of Sankara's impersonal *nirguna* Brahman concept.[140] S. Radhakrishnan states, "Shankara and Ramanuja were both great exponents of Vedanta, examined the same texts, and based their ideas on the same assumptions, yet reached different conclusions."[141] While Sankara emphasized God's existence as the absolute reality over against the relatively real status of human beings and the world, Ramanuja concluded that a personal relationship between God and human beings is possible. John perceives God as the supreme or ultimate reality, but the evangelist neither portrays God as nirguna nor presents human beings as

133 McPolin, 32–33.

134 McPolin, 33–34.

135 Rudolf Schnackenburg, *The Gospel According to Saint John* (New York: Seabury, 1980), 2:63.

136 See Roshen Dalal, *Hinduism: An Alphabetical Guide* (Gurgaon: Penguin, 2014), 234.

137 Lisa Jo Rudy, "What Is Mysticism? Definition and Examples," Learn Religions, accessed May 3, 2020, https://www.learnreligions.com/mysticism-definition-4768937.

138 Dalal, *Hinduism*, 6.

139 See Philip, *History and Theology of the Gospel.*

140 See Dalal, *Hinduism*, 334–35.

141 Dalal, 457–58.

totally dependent to God.[142] John teaches that human personality can either accept or reject God, but a union is possible between God and human beings through the initiative of knowing God, doing his work, and devoting oneself in faith.[143] Though John sustains certain commonalities with the nondualistic and the qualified nondualistic trends of Sankara and Ramanuja, the narrator expounds his thought-world within a dualistic framework.

Dualism in John and in the Asian Context

The Fourth Gospel is well-known for its dualistic framework. In John, this trend begins with the pair of light and darkness being placed at the outset (1:5).[144] Other dualistic pairs in John include above and below (8:23), spirit and flesh (3:6), life (eternal) and death (3:36), belief and disbelief (3:18), truth and falsehood (8:44–47), heaven and earth (3:31), God and Satan (13:27), and Israel and "the Jews" (1:19 and 47).[145] As in Judaism, John develops a modified dualism that affirms God's sovereign rule as an overcomer of evil.[146] Scholars, including Bauckham, observe similarities between Johannine dualism and that of the OT (Gen 1:3–5; Isa 9:2; 42:6–7; 60:1–3), Qumran (1QS 3.3–4.26), and Gnostic writings.[147] John's trend of dualism has many parallels in the Asian context.

Among the Asian religions, Zoroastrianism reflects a complete separation of good and evil at the cosmic and the moral levels. Cosmic dualism refers to the ongoing battle between good (*Ahura Mazda*) and evil (*Andra Mainyu*) within the universe. Moral dualism refers to the opposition of good and evil in the mind of humankind. In Zoroastrianism, good and evil are equal and opposite realities.[148] In that sense, the propositions of three Asian religious/

142 McPolin, "Johannine Mysticism," 25–26.

143 Dalal, *Hinduism*, 457–58.

144 Jan G. van der Watt, *An Introduction to the Johannine Gospel and Letters* (London: T&T Clark, 2007), 30–32.

145 Robert P. Vande Kappelle, *Truth Revealed: The Message of the Gospel of John Then and Now* (Eugene, OR: Wipf & Stock, 2014), 84.

146 Vande Kappelle, 85.

147 See Richard Bauckham, *Gospel of Glory: Major Themes in Johannine Theology* (Grand Rapids, MI: Baker Academic, 2015), 117–18.

148 See "Dualism in Zoroastrainism," BBC, accessed May 5, 2020, https://www.bbc.co.uk/religion/religions/zoroastrian/beliefs/dualism.shtml.

philosophical schools are noteworthy: Zoroastrianism follows an unqualified dualism; Sankara's *Advaita* philosophy advocates an unqualified nondualism; and Ramanuja proposes a qualified nondualism. John maintains a dualistic framework as in Zoroastrianism, but he distances himself from Zoroastrianism through his creativity of setting in the foreground a qualified dualism.

John interprets God as the absolute reality and suggests a union between God and the human beings, as it is in *Advaita*. However, he considers neither a nondualistic existence of God nor that God is nirguna or without attributes.[149] John proposes a personal relationship between God and human beings and suggests a bhakti *marga*, as in Ramanuja, but John goes beyond the qualified nondualism of *Vishishtadvaita*.[150] In his propositions, John is closer in many ways to the principles of Madhava, a twelfth-century CE interpreter of Vedanta, who suggested a *Dvaita* philosophy.[151] Madhava considered the supremacy of Brahman and the separate existence of human beings and the world. His dualism was not true dualism in the sense of two equal powers.[152] Here, we see a connection between the qualified dualism of John (1:5) and the qualified dual existence suggested by Madhava. This comparison of various religious and philosophical traditions helps us understand John's accommodation of ideas and his distinctive emphasis in relation to the Asian thought-world.

Other Johannine Bridges with the Asian Realities

Alongside the above-mentioned observations, some of the following aspects also need to be considered: First, as the Johannine community was treated as a minority sect and was expelled from the Synagogue (9:22, 34; 16:2), Asian Christian communities suffer discrimination and rigorous persecution due to their minority status.[153] Second, in Roman Palestine, Jesus worked among the masses, especially those who were poor, marginalized, and ostracized (4:1–26; 5:1–18; 9:1–41); in Asia, the church, in her mission, focuses on the

149 In Sankara's *Advaita* philosophy, God is considered as the single reality without a second, and for him God is nirguna Brahman.

150 Ramanuja proposes a qualified nondualism that is distinct from the qualified dualism of John.

151 Dalal, *Hinduism*, 227–28.

152 See Dalal, 128.

153 See Thomaskutty, "Nepali Context," 9–10.

poor sections of the society.[154] Third, as John portrayed women with respect to and on par with men characters (2:1–11; 4:1–42; 12:1–8; 20:1–18), the Asian churches have started to adopt the method of a hermeneutics of suspicion to make the voice of women heard in the church and in the society.[155] Fourth, as dialogue is the preferable literary genre within John,[156] Asian Christians are dialogical and interactional in the public arena.[157] Fifth, as in the case of the Johannine community situation, the Dalit communities in India, the Minjung in Korea, and other poor sections across Asia endure economic deprivation, social vulnerability, and religious dehumanization.[158] Sixth, as Mary of Bethany exemplified her devotion through superabundant generosity (12:1–8), the Asian communities are benevolent in hospitality and care even toward strangers. And seventh, as the Johannine Jesus expresses mission concerns both at the public level (1:19–12:50) and in the private sector (13:1–17:26), Asian communities can be approached in both their private and public sectors. These aspects of the Fourth Gospel can bridge the gulf between the *Sitz im Leben* of the Johannine community and the *Sitz im Leben* of Asians.

The Gospel of John has genuine global significance. It speaks equally to pluralistic Indians, communist and Confucian Chinese, Muslim Bangladeshis and Pakistanis, Buddhist Burmese and Cambodians, Shamanistic Koreans and Philippines, Taoistic Japanese, and others in Asian contexts. Its messages of peace, love, faith-centered life, holistic salvation, and the mission of God have the potential to liberate and transform the societies across the Asian continent. In Asia, a missional hermeneutic that crosses the traditional boundaries of interpretation and that builds dialogical bridges between the world of John and that of our own time may be very effective. Such boundary crossing and bridge building will enable Asian readers of John to direct their communities to a "third space" for dialogue. This should be paradigmatic for Asians as a whole.

154 See Thomaskutty, 11–12.
155 See Thomaskutty, 12–13.
156 See Thomaskutty, *Dialogue*, 1–20.
157 See Thomaskutty, "Nepali Context," 16–17.
158 See Basker, *Interpreting Biblical Texts*, 124–43.

CONCLUSION

In sum, the Fourth Gospel has a large number of terminological and conceptual parallels with Asian socioreligious and philosophical traditions. This quality of the Gospel fits well within the spectrum of Asian realities. The universalistic linguistic and literary style, the appearance of characters as representative figures, the conceptual linkage between the Asian religions and philosophical ideologies, and the open-ended outlook of the signs can go well with the contextual aspects of Asia. John's nature as a "riddle" is obvious when it appears mystical and at the same time dualistic, *advaitic* and *dvaitic*, Indianizing and indigenizing, local and universal, and divine and human. Asian religious and philosophical thought-worlds like Hinduism, Buddhism, Jainism, Sikhism, Confucianism, Shamanism, Zoroastrianism, Sufism, and others have Johannine parallels. In the Gospel, we see that the narrator echoes a number of Asian concepts and ideologies, and at the same time, he distances himself from them to recreate everything in a "third space." By crossing the traditional boundaries, creating ideological constellations, and building dialogical relationships, the narrator of the story aims to direct Asian minds toward a "third space."[159] The Johannine Jesus appears as a friend of the socially vulnerable, religiously expelled or persecuted, and spiritually thirsty such as the Dalits, Minjungs, tribals, Adivasis, and other sections of society.

FURTHER READING

Anderson, P. N. 2011. *The Riddles of the Fourth Gospel: An Introduction to John.* Minneapolis: Fortress.

Appasamy, A. J. 1991. *Christianity as Bhakti Marga: A Study of the Johannine Doctrine of Love.* Madras: CLS.

Barrett, C. K. 1978. *The Gospel According to St. John: An Introduction with Commentary and Notes on the Greek Text.* London: SPCK.

Basker, G. T. 2016. *Interpreting Biblical Texts: John and His Tamil Readers.* New Delhi: ISPCK.

159 See Thomaskutty, *Gospel of John*, 151.

Bauckham, R. 2006. *Jesus and the Eyewitnesses: The Gospels as Eyewitness Testimony.* Grand Rapids, MI: Eerdmans.

Beasley-Murray, G. R. 1999. *John.* Word Biblical Commentary 36. Nashville, TN: Thomas Nelson.

Duraisingh, C., and C. Hargreaves. 1975. *India's Search for Reality and the Relevance of the Gospel of John.* New Delhi: ISPCK.

Kanagaraj, J. J. 2005. *The Gospel of John: A Commentary.* Secunderabad: OM.

Namita, 2000. *A New Paradigm for Evangelisation in the Third Millennium: In the Light of Mission in the Gospel According to St. John and the Early Upanishads.* Bangalore: St. Peter's Pontifical Institute.

Subramaniam, K. 2017. *Mahabharata.* Mumbai: Bharatiya Vidya Bhavan.

Thomaskutty, J. 2020. *The Gospel of John: A Universalistic Reading.* Biblical Hermeneutics Rediscovered 25. New Delhi: Christian World Imprints.

Van der Watt, J. G. 2007. *An Introduction to the Johannine Gospel and Letters.* London: T&T Clark.

SEVEN

The Book of Acts

Esa Autero
South Florida Bible College and Seminary
Deerfield Beach, Florida, USA

The Acts of the Apostles is one of a kind among the NT writings. It narrates Jesus's ascension to heaven, the outpouring of the Spirit, and the early days of the church in Jerusalem and beyond. It tells of miraculous healings, deliverance from evil spirits, narrow escapes from prisons, and hair-raising adventures at sea. The early church experienced victories and triumphs as well as failures, tragic losses, and intense persecution. Yet more than merely telling a history of the early church, Acts narrates a story that resonates closely with the experiences of many Christians in Asia today. Many identify with the life-giving hope and dignity that the gospel brings to the marginalized, as well as the comfort and strength it gives to suffering Christians in several Asian countries.[1] Reading the stories about suffering and oppression that the early church went through in Acts gives strength, hope, and guidance to many believers today. As such, it is not just a book of yesteryears but a life-giving narrative to which the church returns again and again.

1 See also Bindulata Barik, *Persecution and Hope: Exploring Suffering in the Book of Revelation* (Bangalore: SAIACS, 2015), 109–32; Vikas Ram and Kay Higuera Smith, "Christian Response to Violence in India," in *Christianity in India: Conversion, Community Development, and Religious Freedom*, ed. Joel Carpenter and Rebecca Samuel Shah (Minneapolis: Fortress, 2018), 198–227.

PRELIMINARY DETAILS ABOUT THE BOOK

Though Acts speaks to Asian Christians today, its original purpose and historical setting are important for a proper understanding of its message for present-day readers.[2] For that reason, the first part of this essay focuses on genre, authorship, historical background, literary patterns, and other pertinent information.

Purpose and Genre of the Book

Though many Christians today can identify with stories found in Acts, its specific purpose has been disputed by scholars.[3] Some of the main suggestions include catechesis for Christians, history about the beginning of Christianity, apologetic motif, mission, evangelism, and the legitimation of gentile inclusion.[4] Nevertheless, Acts cannot be reduced to a single purpose. On the contrary, it weaves together various themes and foci.

Perhaps the most obvious purpose of Acts is to demonstrate the "work of his [Jesus's] followers in the post-resurrection era" (see 1:1–2).[5] Other important emphases are salvation historical continuity (with a view to God's ancient promises) and mission of the church in the power of the Holy Spirit. The former roots the church into the history of God's mighty acts in the past. Connection with the past calls forth a redefinition of identity in light of gentile inclusion, place of Torah observance, and conflict with the ancestors (nonbelieving Jews). The latter highlights the mission of God's people. Good news of the kingdom is to be proclaimed from Jerusalem to the end of the earth in the power of the Spirit (1:8). As such, Luke intended to inspire his audience to continue the mission of God in the power of the same Spirit that empowered the apostles.

Using past narratives to speak to subsequent generations is also part and parcel of Indian literary tradition and religious heritage. The great stories of

2 See George Soares-Prabhu, "The Historical-Critical Method," in *Readings in Indian Christian Theology*, ed. R. S. Sugirtharajah and Cecil Hargreaves (Delhi: ISPCK, 1993), 1:186–94.

3 Options are summarized in Jacob Jervell, *The Theology of the Acts of the Apostle* (Cambridge: Cambridge University Press, 1996), 11.

4 See presentations of views in, e.g., Howard I. Marshall, *Acts. Tyndale New Testament Commentaries* (Downers Grove, IL: IVP Academic, 1980), 17–23.

5 Babu Immanuel, *Acts of the Apostles: An Exegetical and Contextual Commentary*, India Commentary on the NT (Bangalore: Primalogue, 2016), 5.

Indian epics (*Mahabharata* and *Rāmāyana*) and the *Puranas* have been (and still are) retold, adapted, and applied in various settings throughout generations. In this process, they become "an eternal present" speaking to present audiences in various ways.[6] As the church in Asia reads (and listens to) the Acts today, the Spirit of God fuses the biblical story with the stories of God's people, creating "an eternal present" that gives life, hope, strength, and guidance.

What type of literature is the Acts of the Apostles? Babu Immanuel states that Acts has affinities with great Indian Sanskrit epics known as *itihasa*.[7] G. Ayyaneth adds that *itihasic* literature, especially *Mahabharata* and *Rāmāyana* (the two great Indian epics), mix history and legend with dharmic (ethical) and religious teachings.[8] Much of the classic Indian literature features storytelling with a goal of reaching *moksha* (liberation/salvation).[9] As such, *itihasic* literature bears some similarities with Acts. As was indicated, Acts is filled with stories of healings, exorcisms, miraculous rescues, angelic appearances, and heavenly dialogues, and the entire book is framed with God's kingdom and salvation (1:6–8; 28:28–31). Similar features are found in India's ancient literature (e.g., *Mahabharata*).[10] It is significant that Luke chose to write a narrative account (Gk. *diēgesis*, Luke 1:1) because this form resonates with ancient Indian literature and with many present-day readers and hearers throughout Asia.[11] Of course, it is important to note that Acts and *Mahabharata* (and other Indian epics) include a number of differences as well, not least the enormous difference in length.

How would Luke's audience (or an ancient librarian) have categorized Acts? In the ancient world, as today, genre and purpose are connected.[12] Yet Acts does not fit squarely into any ancient genre category.[13] Some think Acts is like an

6 See G. Ayyaneth, *Indian Poetics (Kāvya Śāstra) and Narratology towards the Appreciation of Biblical Narrative* (New York: Peter Lang, 2016), 25–26.

7 Babu Immanuel, "Acts," in *South Asia Bible Commentary: A One-Volume Commentary on the Whole Bible*, ed. Brian Wintle et al. (Udaipur, Rajastan: Open Door, 2015), 1450.

8 Ayyaneth, *Indian Poetics*, 24–25, 65–66, 137–42.

9 Ayyaneth, 47–48.

10 See Bushra Admed et al., *The Illustrated Mahabharata: The Definitive Guide to India's Greatest Epic* (Laxmi Nagar: DK, 2018).

11 See Ayyaneth, *Indian Poetics*, 45.

12 Of course, genre categories are never pure, hard, and fast.

13 See David E. Aune, *New Testament in Its Literary Environment* (Philadelphia: Westminster, 1987), 138–53.

ancient novel or epic with adventures and entertaining scenes.[14] Others liken Acts to ancient biographies (pace Luke's Gospel).[15] Most scholars state that Acts most closely resembles ancient histories—perhaps with apologetic innuendos (esp. Acts 22–28).[16] Be that as it may, Luke is able to weave historical narrative, rhetorically persuasive speeches, exciting adventures, miraculous deliverances, and vivid storytelling into his literary work. Acknowledging this enables readers to appreciate Luke's narrative aesthetic and spiritual dimensions at greater depth. An evaluation of Luke-Acts' literary aesthetics and theology from various Asian perspectives might also reveal other previously unappreciated dimensions.[17]

The Question of Authorship

Who wrote the Acts? The literary work does not identify its author, yet scholars agree that the same person who wrote Luke's Gospel also wrote Acts. This is deduced by comparing the prologues of Luke and Acts (Luke 1:1–4; Acts 1:1–2) as well as stylistic, theological, and other features.

Though many modern Bibles have a superscription "Acts" or "Acts of the Apostles,"[18] the original document does not include it.[19] Church tradition from the late second century calls the author of the Third Gospel and Acts "Luke," while some add that he is closely connected to Paul.[20] Some further identify this Luke as "the beloved physician" and the companion of Paul mentioned in Colossians 4:14 (see Phlm 24; 2 Tim 4:11).[21] Based on this, many scholars

14 See Helmut Koester, *History and Literature of Early Christianity*, 2nd ed. (Berlin: Walter de Gruyter, 1982), 2:310–15.

15 See Charles H. Talbert, "The Acts of Apostles: Monograph or 'Bios'?," in *History, Literature, and Society in the Book of Acts*, ed. Ben Witherington (Cambridge: Cambridge University Press, 1996), 58–72.

16 See Craig S. Keener, *Acts: An Exegetical Commentary, 1:1–2:47* (Grand Rapids, MI: Baker Academics, 2012), loc. 5948–8488 of 100446, Kindle.

17 Ayyaneth, *India Poetics*, 50.

18 This seems to be the trend in most translations that I have seen, including all the Standard English translations that I am aware of (NRSV, KJV, NIV, NASB, NKJV, and others).

19 The best of the early manuscripts of Acts (P^{45}, *Codex Sinaiticus*, and *Vaticanus*) do not include an original superscription.

20 See Irenaeus, *Ad. Haer.* 3.1.1; 3.14.1; *Muratorian Fragment*, lines 34–39; *Anti-Marcionite Prologue* [to Luke].

21 Irenaeus and *Anti-Marcionite Prologue*. The "we" passages in Acts (16:10–17; 20:5–15; 21:1–18; 27:1–28:16) are then understood as further support for this theory.

uphold the traditional ascription of authorship.[22] Others doubt the authenticity of the tradition and emphasize the novelistic character of Acts and the differences between Paul's epistles and Acts.[23] Despite the differing perspectives between Acts and Paul, the traditional authorship may be affirmed.[24] Yet since Acts (or Luke's Gospel) does not mention who penned it, one should not be dogmatic about the question of authorship.

If Luke indeed was the author of the Acts, can anything else be said of him? Though Luke-Acts does not exhibit any specific "medical language" (as was thought earlier),[25] there is little reason to doubt the tradition of Luke as a physician (esp. Col 4:14; *Anti-Marcionite Prologue*).[26] More noteworthy is that he is listed among Paul's gentile coworkers (Col 4:14), though some think that Luke was a Hellenistic Jew.[27] Nevertheless, it seems difficult to maintain that both Colossians and church tradition ascribed him gentile status if he was a Jew.

Luke occupied a high socioeconomic status.[28] This is indicated particularly by Luke's sophisticated use of the Hellenistic literary style, his interest in socioeconomic themes, and his knowledge of formal proceedings of the Roman elite (Acts 23:23–25:27).[29] In light of this, it is noteworthy that Luke is critical of wealth in the Gospel (Luke 1:52–53; 6:20–26; 12:32–34; 14:12–14, 32–33; 16:19–31) and portrays the early Jerusalem community's spiritual and socioeconomic equality as a theological ideal (Acts 2:16–18, 42–48; 4:32–37).

Luke also criticizes Roman power and ideology as he records how the apostles preach the gospel (Acts 2:34–36; 4:25–30; 12:1–24; 23:11; 28:31).

22 See Immanuel, *Acts of the Apostles*, 2–3.

23 See, for example, Helmut Koester, *History and Literature*, 321–27.

24 See especially the evidence marshaled by Keener, *Acts*, loc. 11581–3046 of 100446.

25 See Joseph A. Fitzmyer, *The Gospel According to Luke I–IX*, Anchor Bible Commentary 28 (New York: Doubleday, 1982), 51–53.

26 After all, many (though not all) physicians in the ancient world were slaves (*Diog. Laert.* 6.2.30; see, e.g., Keener, *Acts*, loc. 19588–707 of 100446).

27 Karl Kuhn, *Luke: The Elite Evangelist* (Collegeville, MN: Liturgical, 2010), loc. 198–251 of 2182, Kindle.

28 See Esa J. Autero, *Reading the Bible across the Contexts: Luke's Gospel, Socio-economic Marginality, and Latin American Biblical Hermeneutics*, Biblical Interpretation Series 145 (Leiden: E. J. Brill, 2016), 155–64.

29 Kuhn, *Luke the Elite*, loc. 1226–51 of 2182.

The message about the kingdom of God and Jesus's Lordship was offensive to many Jews and made the apostles suspicious in the eyes of Roman officials and pro-Roman enthusiasts (esp. Acts 16:19–21; 17:6–9; 19:23–40). After all, Jesus was put to death and accused of rebellion against Roman political order (Luke 23:1, 5, 18–25, 38). Luke also openly exposes unjust and corrupt practices of the Roman officials (16:35–40; 18:16–17; 24:24–27; 25:9). Yet this does not make Luke flatly anti-Roman.[30] On the contrary, he takes pains to demonstrate the innocence of the apostles (Acts 18:12–16; 23:9, 29; 25:25; 26:31–32), records conversions of prominent people (6:7; 10–11; 13:12; 17:4, 12, 34), and indicates that, at times, God uses Roman law and order to protect the apostle Paul (Acts 16:37–38; 22:22–29; 23:26–28). As such, Luke also weaves an apologetic motif into Luke-Acts.

It is difficult to know why Luke portrays the Roman Empire in such ambivalent terms. Perhaps it is a sort of survival strategy, or it reflects Luke's struggles with his own privileged status. Yet similar ambivalence is evident as Christian minorities position themselves in many Asian countries—a combination of (sometimes subtle) criticism and apologetics. One may try to imagine how Luke's family and neighbors would have reacted to the counterintuitive and somewhat subversive message in Luke-Acts. After all, he lived in a world where honor and status were intricately bound to family, status, and social networks. Despite this immense social pressure—something many in Asia are painfully aware of—Luke articulates his message with conviction and breaks with many of the upper-class values of the time. He not only includes gentiles into God's people but also grants access to salvation and the Spirit to those who come from the socially marginalized segments of the society (2:16–21, 43; 3:4–10; 4:13, 32–37; 6:1–6; 8:4–8; 9:32–46; 10–11; 15:1–30). As a result, he must have experienced the shame of associating with the crucified—yet now vindicated—Jewish Messiah (see Tac. *Hist.* 5.5).[31]

30 Raymond Pickett, "Luke and the Empire: An Introduction," in *Luke-Acts and Empire*, ed. David Rhoads, David Esterline, and Jae Won Lee (Eugene, OR: Pickwick, 2011), 1–19.

31 It is commonly known that, in general, Jews did not feel comfortable mixing with gentiles (10:28; 15:8–11; John 18:18; *Jub* 22:16; 3 *Macc* 3:4–7; *Tob* 1:10–13; *CD* XI, 14–15; Josephus, *Ag. Ap.* 2.257); however, many gentiles, especially of the upper classes, did not look favorably on Jews either (Tac. *Hist.* 5.5); see Craig S. Keener, *Acts: An Exegetical Commentary, 3:1–14:28*, vol. 2 (Grand Rapids, MI: Baker Academics, 2013), loc. 20067–169 of 105811, Kindle.

Nevertheless, if Luke's addressee, Theophilus, was a real person,[32] one must reckon that Luke maintained some connections with the higher echelons of society and perhaps wanted to call them to follow the Lord Jesus Christ.[33]

Sources and Text of the Acts of the Apostles

Where did Luke receive the traditions to write Acts? It is commonly acknowledged that Luke received information from "eyewitnesses and servants of the word" (Luke 1:2) to compose the Gospel. This most likely included Mark, Q, and the L (Luke's own material) sources. Nevertheless, there is no agreement on what sources he used to compile Acts. Luke's use of sources in the Gospel indicates that he adapts, reworks, and polishes them. This was probably the case with Acts as well.

Most scholars postulate that though Luke uses sources (see Luke 1:1–4; Acts 1:1–2), it is impossible to specify them. Common suggestions include a Jerusalem source (perhaps partially in Aramaic) for the early chapters;[34] an Antiochene source for the sections connected to the church in Antioch; and the "we section," which was either a travel journal or an eyewitness account.[35]

Luke may also have had access to information regarding the early church in other ways. If the "we section" betrays Luke as a genuine traveling companion to Paul, he could have obtained oral traditions (via interviews) from Philip (21:8–10; see 6–8 [Hellenists]) during his stay in Caesarea (21:8–10; see 10:1–48 [Cornelius episode]) and from Jerusalem apostles (and others) during his two-year stay in Jerusalem (21:15–16; 24:27; 27:1).[36] As a traveling companion to Paul, he also had a chance to speak with and observe Paul's ministry firsthand even if he did not accompany him on all his journeys. Finally, the social networks among the early Christian communities probably

32 Autero, *Reading the Bible*, 159.

33 Kuhn, *Luke the Elite*, loc. 1717 of 2182; Autero, *Reading the Bible*, 155–64.

34 Ernst Haenchen, *The Acts of the Apostles: A Commentary*, trans. Bernard Noble and Gerald Shinn (Oxford: Basil Blackwell, 1971), 72–77; Ben Witherington, *The Acts of the Apostles: A Socio-rhetorical Commentary* (Grand Rapids, MI: Eerdmans, 1998), 44.

35 See, e.g., Haenchen, *Acts*, 81–90; C. K. Barrett, *A Critical and Exegetical Commentary on the Acts of the Apostles: Preliminary Introduction and Commentary on I–XIV*, International Critical Commentary (Edinburgh: T&T Clark, 1994), 1:49–56.

36 See Barrett, *Critical and Exegetical*, 51–56; Keener, *Acts*, loc. 9539 of 100446.

played an important role (11:28–29; 21:16–18).[37] Whatever materials Luke had, he skillfully weaved them into a narrative to convey his message in a form of creative historical narration.

Acts poses a unique challenge regarding its textual history.[38] Unlike other NT writings, it has two textual traditions, Alexandrian and Western. Most scholars maintain the Alexandrian text type as primary, though some readings from the Western text may betray a more authentic tradition.[39]

The questions of historical traditions and textual/manuscript accuracy is not equally important for all Asian Christian traditions. For example, much of India's sacred literature has developed across the span of hundreds (or thousands) of years. Especially the two great epics *Mahabharata* and *Rāmāyana* evolved with numerous layers added over centuries. They include numerous textual versions, recensions, editions, and traditions.[40] Many stories also contain variety of local forms.[41] Further, they freely include narrative retellings, legends, and the like. Some of the *Puranas* follow the same pattern.[42] Also, the textual integrity and transmission of the Qur'an has been important for Muslims from at least the time of Caliph Uthman (d. 655/6 CE).[43] For some Christians, a consideration of variant readings is relevant in popular apologetics—even if the Christian view of biblical inspiration differs from the Muslim understanding of Qur'anic inspiration and the Indian sacred

37 See Rom 1:8; 15:26; 16:1–5; 1 Cor 11:16; 16:10–12, 17; 2 Cor 8–9; Phil 2:25; 1 Thess 1:7–9.

38 Barrett, *Critical and Exegetical*, 2.

39 See Bruce M. Metzger, *A Textual Commentary on the Greek New Testament*, 2nd ed. (Stuttgart: German Bible Society, 1994), 222–36.

40 Ayyaneth, *Indian Poetics*, 13; Adluri, "Introduction," in *Argument and Design: The Unity of Mahabharata*, ed. Vishwa Adluri and Joydeep Bagchee (Leiden: Brill, 2016), 1–21; Joydeep Bagchee, "The Epic's Singularization to Come," in Adluri and Bagchee, *Argument and Design*, 83–126; John Brockington, "Ramayana," in *Encyclopedia of Hinduism*, ed. Denise Cush, Catherine Robinson, and Michael York (London: Routledge, 2008), 667–69; Lynn Thomas, "Mahabharata," in *Encyclopedia of Hinduism*, 469–71; see 83–85.

41 Ravi Gupta and Kenneth Valpey, *Bhagavata Purana: Selected Readings* (New York: Columbia University Press, 2016), 19–20.

42 Gupta and Valpey, 25.

43 See Muhammad Mustafa Al-Azami, "The Islamic View of the Quran," in *The Study Quran: A New Translation and Commentary*, ed. Seyyed Hossein Nasir et al. (New York: Harper One, 2015), loc. 92924–3366 of 126722, Kindle; Michael Cook, *The Koran: A Very Short Introduction* (Oxford: Oxford University Press, 2000), 119–42.

literature. Nevertheless, it must be kept in mind that critical study of the biblical manuscripts is older than the study of Qur'anic manuscripts or textual traditions of India's sacred books.[44] For many Asian Christians, knowledge of the historical details and manuscript variations is less important than knowing and experiencing the message of the text.

Date and Place

When, where, and to whom did Luke write the Acts? There is no unanimity among scholars. Later tradition indicates that Luke comes from Antioch (*Eccl. Hist.* 3.4.7; Jerome, *De Viris Illustribus* 7). Eusebius further surmised that Luke completed Acts while Paul was facing martyrdom in Rome (*Eccl. Hist.* 2.22.4–8; 2 Tim 4:18).[45] Though Irenaeus quotes liberally from Acts, he does not give details (*Adv. Haer.* 12–14). Beyond these two locations, scholars have suggested that Luke wrote Acts from Achaia (see *Anti-Marcionite Prologue to Luke*), Macedonia, or Caesarea. The specific addressee was Theophilus, though Luke envisioned a broader audience as well.

Scholars posit three possible dates for Acts: the early date (pre-70 CE, usually c. 62–64 CE), the midrange (ca. 70s–95 CE), and the late date (ca. 100–130 CE). Any of these is possible, but the last is least likely. The late date has difficulties explaining the early second-century allusion to Acts by Polycarp (*Phil* 1.2/Acts 2:24) and Justin Martyr (*Apol.* I 39.2/4:13; I 1.50.12/1:8; II 10.6/17:23).[46] The midrange seems agreeable to most scholars. The appeal of the early date is the abrupt ending of Acts, with its seeming open-endedness and the lack of references to the temple's destruction (but see Luke 21:20–24). The midrange date focuses on Luke's dependence on Mark and the dating of Mark to the late sixties, among other things. It also recognizes that narrating Paul's death would be anticlimactic in light of the triumphant nature of the gospel in Acts. That Luke was Paul's traveling companion fits both the middle and early dates.[47]

44 See Bruce M. Metzger, "Trends in the Textual Criticism of the Illiad, Mahabharata, and the New Testament," *JBL* 65, no. 4 (1946): 339–52; see also Adluri, "Introduction," 1–21.

45 Eusebius, however, maintains that Paul was released from the Roman imprisonment described in Acts 28 but was (shortly?) afterward captured again and put to death by the emperor Nero as alluded to in 2 Timothy 4:18 (*Eccl. Hist.* 2.22.3–8).

46 See Haenchen, *Acts*, 9–10; Keener, *Acts*, loc. 18808–83 of 100446.

47 For detailed surveys of the views, see Keener, *Acts*, loc. 18500–926 of 100446.

Literary Patterns, Symbolism, and Outline

Acts is part of Luke's two-volume literary work that includes the Gospel of Luke and Acts. The two are related on a literary level as well as historical and theological levels. Perhaps the most obvious literary connections between Luke and Acts are the recapitulation of Jesus's ascension (Luke 24:50–51; Acts 1:9–11)[48] and the fulfillment of the outpouring of the Spirit according to Jesus's promise (Luke 3:16; 11:13; 24:49; Acts 1:8; 2:1–4). As such, Luke wants to narrate how God's divinely orchestrated plan unfolds through the risen Christ and takes shape through the early church in the power of the Spirit. Talbert indicates twelve parallels between Luke's presentation of Jesus in the Gospel and church (or the apostles) in Acts. Here are some of the most obvious ones:[49]

The Spirit descends on Jesus after a prayer (Luke 3:22)	The Spirit falls on the early church after prayer (Acts 1:13, 24; 2:1–4)
Jesus's ministry begins with the Spirit's anointing and Scriptural fulfillment (4:16–30)	The church's ministry begins in the fullness of the Spirit and with Scriptural fulfillment (2:1–40)
Scriptural fulfillment is exemplified by preaching, acts of compassion, and healings; conflicts illustrate rejection (4:31–8:56)	Scriptural fulfillment is exemplified by preaching, healings, and miraculous deeds; persecution illustrates conflict and rejection (2:41–12:17)
Jesus goes through four trials (before the Sanhedrin, Pilate, Herod Antipas, Pilate; 22:26; 23:1, 8, 13)	Paul goes through four trials (Sanhedrin, Felix, Festus, Herod Agrippa; 23; 24; 25; 26)

An important implication of the parallels is that the life of Jesus's followers is patterned after their Master. The church replicated the pattern of preaching, healing, compassionate action, and suffering. Yet there are also differences that reflect historical particularities of each volume, such as the Gospel's focus on rural Galilee and Acts' focus on cities of the Roman Empire.[50]

48 It is worth noting that Luke is the only NT writing that narrates Jesus's ascension.

49 Charles H. Talbert, *Reading Acts: A Literary and Theological Commentary*, rev. ed. (Macon, GA: Smyth & Helwys, 2005), xxiv–xxv.

50 Jesus stilling the storm hardly qualifies as a parallel (8:22–25)—Luke omits the story of Jesus walking on the water recorded by Matthew (14:22–32) and Mark (6:45–52).

The overall literary pattern of Acts may be viewed in more than one way, though the perspectives are not necessarily mutually exclusive. Perhaps the most common is the geographical scheme. According to it, the structure of Acts is based on Jesus's command to take the gospel from Jerusalem to the ends of the earth (1:8). Luke's narrative shows how the gospel moves from Jerusalem to Judea (Acts 1–7), Samaria (Acts 8:4–25), and the ends of the earth (Acts 13–28). Other scholars divide Acts based on the summary statements (2:41, 47; 4:4; 5:14; 6:7; 9:31, 42; 11:21; 12:24; 13:48; 16:5; 19:20; 28:31) or the two key characters, namely Peter (Acts 1–12) and Paul (Acts 13–28).[51] As such, the overall structure may be organized in more than one way. A sample outline of Acts may be presented as follows:

Prologue, commissioning of the disciples, and preparation for Pentecost (1:1–26)
- Prologue (1:1–2)
- Commissioning by the risen Christ and preparation for Pentecost (1:3–26)

Pentecost and its aftermath (2:1–47)
- Outpouring of the Spirit and crowd's response (2:1–13)
- Peter's sermon and crowd's response (2:14–42)
- Life of the Jerusalem church (2:43–47)

Church in Jerusalem—victories and opposition (3:1–5:42)
- Healing of the lame man and its explanation (3:1–26)
- The arrest of Peter and John (4:1–22)
- Unified prayer and united hearts of the Jerusalem church (4:23–47)
- Ananias and Saphira—threat from within (5:1–11)
- Summary of miraculous deeds and church growth (5:12–16)
- Apostles' arrest, release, and persecution (5:17–42)

Expansion of the Church beyond Jerusalem (6:1–9:31)
- Dissention over widows and the seven deacons (6:1–7)

51 Witherington, *Acts*, 74; Talbert, *Reading Acts*, xxvii–xxx; Keener, *Acts*, loc. 26158–375 of 100446.

Persecution, defense, and martyrdom of Stephen (6:8–8:1a)
Ministry of Philip in Samaria and beyond (8:1b–40)
Conversion of Saul and the beginning of his ministry (9:1–31)

The Beginning of the gentile mission (9:32–12:25)
Peter's power ministry in Lydda and Joppa (9:32–43)
Conversion of Cornelius and Peter's defense (10:1–11:18)
Expansion of the church and famine relief (11:19–30)
The imprisonment and miraculous deliverance of Peter (12:1–25)

Paul's first missionary journey and the Jerusalem council (13:1–15:35)
The Spirit sends Paul and Barnabas from Antioch (13:1–3)
Ministry in Cyprus, Pisidian Antioch, Iconium, and Lystra (13:4–14:21a)
Return journey to Antioch (14:21b–28)
Jerusalem Council (15:1–35)

Paul's second missionary journey (15:36–18:22)
Separation of Paul and Barnabas (15:36–41)
Strengthening churches and Spirit's guidance (16:1–10)
Ministry in Macedonia and Achaia—and return to Antioch (16:11–18:22)

Paul's third missionary journey and return to Jerusalem (18:23–21:16)
Apollos and Paul in Ephesus (18:23–19:41)
Paul travels through Greece and Macedonia to Miletus (20:1–17)
Paul's speech to Ephesian elders (20:18–38)
Paul's journey to Jerusalem (21:1–16)

Paul's arrest in Jerusalem and journey to Rome (21:17–28:31)
Paul in Jerusalem (21:17–23:22)
Paul in Caesarea (23:23–26:32)
Paul's journey and ministry in Rome (27:1–28:31)

Some Asian scholars have criticized Acts' narrative pattern for focusing exclusively on the westward movement of Christianity (that is, to Europe).[52] This direction is undoubtedly true (except 8:26–40); however, it is noteworthy that Luke depicts early Christians as a marginalized sect of Judaism that hails from the "east," or Asia (see *Ant.* 5.220). From the ancient perspective, Luke is Asian and reflects "Asian historiography."[53] He promotes values that revise "key . . . Roman social values" and advocates ethnic equality and inclusivity. Asians and other non-Greeks (or Romans) are not inferior because "God shows no partiality" (see Acts 10:34b–35).[54] Some scholars have even seen in the westward movement of early Christians—especially 16:6–10—a deliberate contrast to Alexander the Great's crossing of the Hellespont (narrow straight between Greece and Turkey) to conquer the East.[55] As such, Luke depicts this tiny band of "apostles from the east" turning the mighty Roman Empire in the west "upside down" (17:6). God's election of "uneducated and ordinary men" (see 4:13) to advance the kingdom and the inclusion of ritually impure gentiles (10–11; 15:1–30) into God's people also resonates with today's Dalit (and other marginalized) communities in India and beyond.[56]

Luke uses a literary pattern of repetition to emphasize and highlight important themes in Acts. For example, the apostles are arrested, interrogated, and released twice in the early chapters (Acts 4:1–22 and 5:17–42). In both instances, the apostles' arrests are preceded by miracles and proclamation (3:1–10; 5:12–16). Unity of the early church and the Spirit-prompted sharing of possessions are repeated twice (2:42–47; 4:32–37); both are preceded by the outpouring of the Spirit (2:1–4; 4:31). Paul's conversion is repeated thrice, with each narration revealing new dimensions of God's intentions (9:1–19;

52 R. S. Sugirtharajah, *Postcolonial Reconfigurations: An Alternative Way of Reading the Bible and Doing Theology* (St. Louis: Chalice, 2005), 13–36, esp. 25.

53 See David L. Balch, "ΜΕΤΑΒΟΛΗ ΠΟΛΙΤΕΙΩΝ. Jesus as the Founder of the Church in Luke-Acts: Form and Function," in *Contextualizing Acts: Lukan Narrative and Greco-Roman Discourse*, ed. Todd Penner and Caroline Vander-Stichele (Atlanta: SBL, 2003), 139–88. See also Craig S. Keener, *Acts: An Exegetical Commentary, 15:1–23:35*, vol. 3 (Grand Rapids, MI: Baker Academics, 2014), loc. 7041–175 of 112687, Kindle.

54 See Balch, "ΜΕΤΑΒΟΛΗ ΠΟΛΙΤΕΙΩΝ," 150–54.

55 See Balch, 150–54, esp. 152; Keener, *Acts*, loc. 7041–150 of 100446, is more cautious.

56 See James Massey, "Acts of the Apostles," in *One Volume Dalit Bible Commentary: New Testament*, ed. T. K. John (New Delhi: Center for Dalit/Subaltern Studies, 2010), 331–33, 340–42.

22:1–21; 26:2–23). Some of the key characters in Acts are also introduced briefly before the narrative spotlight focuses on them more extensively (e.g., Paul in 7:58–8:3; 9:1–30; 13–28). Acts employs linear movement and repetitions to establish and reinforce important points in the narrative.[57] Yet, Acts' linear movement (Jerusalem to Rome) also includes circularity and dialogues, patterns commonly found in ancient Indian literature.[58]

Revelatory dialogues and miracle stories abound in Acts. In fact, they are more numerous in Acts than in standard ancient historiographies.[59] This pattern finds many parallels in *Mahabharata* and *Bhagavad Purana*, as well as many folk stories and traditions.[60] Indian classics are particularly known for their dialogues between gods (*devas/devis*) and human beings.[61] Perhaps the best known example is the lengthy dialogue between Krishna and Arjuna in the field of Kurukshetra depicted in the *Bhagavad Gita*.[62]

Biblical scholars have not paid much attention to the function and extent of revelatory dialogues in Acts. Risen Christ, Holy Spirit, and angels do not merely give direction; Acts also records many lengthy revelatory dialogues (1:4–11; 9:3–6, 10–16; 10:3–6, 10–16, 19–20; 11:5–13; 22:7–11, 17–21; 26:13–19).[63] Ananias, an ordinary believer, has one of the lengthiest dialogues with the risen Christ in Acts (9:10–16). He is commissioned and given revelatory insight into God's intentions. Though Ananias initially protests (9:13–14), he is finally persuaded by the heavenly voice. Similar patterns are also evident in Peter's and Paul's revelatory dialogues (10:13–17; 26:14–16). In addition to the pattern of narrative and speeches, readers ought to pay attention to the heavenly dialogues in Acts. Though dialogues do not abound in Acts like in Indian literature, they are an important revelatory feature of Acts that merits more attention.

57 See Keener, *Acts*, loc. 25873–6156 of 100446.

58 See Ayyaneth, *Indian Poetics*, 52–90.

59 Keener, *Acts*, loc. 7025–673 of 100446.

60 See Govind Chatak, *The Folk Tales of Uttarkhand*, trans. Arun Pant (Delhi: Jaykay Enterprises, 2015); Ayyaneth, *Indian Poetics*, 26–29.

61 Ayyaneth, *Indian Poetics*, 52–90; Adluri, "Introduction," 1–21.

62 It is perhaps worth noting that both *Upanishads* and *Bhagavad Purana* are largely written in dialogical format, whereas the epics (*Mahabharata* and *Rāmāyana*) include large narrative sections interspersed with dialogues.

63 Some sections are not explicitly narrated as dialogues but include repetitive commands and corresponding responses (8:26, 29, 39–40; 12:7–11; 16:6–10).

In addition to the above, other important literary patterns in Acts include the use of speeches as a way to communicate important theological themes and miracle stories that demonstrate God's compassion and authenticate the gospel message.[64] Retelling old narratives and including quotes and allusions from Hebrew Scripture further grounds the gospel in Israel's past revelation. The pattern of using past narratives in new settings is reminiscent of the way Indian epics and *Puranas* draw from, allude to, and retell older Vedic materials.[65]

Some Indian scholars have highlighted the importance of employing the tools of classical Indian literary appreciation (Kāvya Śāstra), such as *dhvani* hermeneutics to biblical texts.[66] Though that is not the only Indian approach to hermeneutics,[67] *dhvani* readings could open up new vistas in Acts. The above-mentioned revelatory dialogues are an example.[68] The thrice repeated Paul's conversion narrative dialogue (9:3–19; 22:6–21; 26:12–18) could be appreciated from a new angle: not as a series of contradictory accounts needing resolution but as a potential to open up a vision of new spiritual reality to a perceptive audience.[69] According to Luke's narrative depiction, Paul genuinely thought he was following God by violently persecuting followers of Jesus (23:1; 24:16). Yet despite his ignorance of Jesus's identity (9:5; 22:8; 26:15) and his obstinacy (9:4; 22:7; 26:14),[70] God met him in a surprising way. The power of this new spiritual reality is not just individual conversion but God's way of demonstrating the power of his kingdom to overcome evil, protect vulnerable Christians, and create new Christ-centered communities through a former evildoer.[71]

64 Wendy Cotter, *Miracles in Greco-Roman Antiquity: A Sourcebook for the Study of New Testament Miracles Stories* (New York: Routledge, 1999), 1–3.
65 See Ayyaneth, *Indian Poetics*, 60–66; Gupta and Valpey, *Bhāhavata Purana*, 9–16.
66 Francis D'Sa, "'Dhvani' as a Method of Interpretation," *Bible Bhashyam* 5, no. 4 (1979): 276–94.
67 See Mathew, "Indian Biblical Hermeneutics," 100–126; Ayyaneth, *Indian Poetics*, 11–32.
68 Ayyanoth, *Indian Poetics*, 30–32.
69 Ayyaneth, 255.
70 Suggested perhaps by Paul's falling on the ground and blindness.
71 For similar implications of Paul's conversion for Dalits, see Peniel J. R. Rajkumar, "'Texts of Life' and 'Texts for Life': The Bible as the Living and Life-Giving Word of God for Dalits," in *Text and Context: Vernacular Approaches to the Bible in Global Christianity*, ed. Melanie Baffes (Eugene, OR: Pickwick, 2018), loc. 3204–26 of 7585, Kindle.

THEOLOGICAL THEMES AND HERMENEUTICAL ANALYSIS

This last section will explore some of the major theological themes and reiterate hermeneutical issues mentioned earlier. Emphasis is on relevance for Asian Christians. As Acts is a narrative and teaches spiritual truths through a story, subsequent readers may draw different inferences from it. Yet this relative ambiguity is simultaneously the richness of Acts, especially for Asian readers accustomed to inferring spiritual guidance from narratives and stories.

God's Mission and Salvation History

God is the foundational character of Acts. He is the cosmic Creator guiding history and movement of the nations, as Paul's sermon in Athens eloquently attests (17:24–28; see 4:24–28; 7:2–50; 10:15; 11:19; 13:17, 22, 47; 14:15–17). Luke shows throughout Acts that God's plan of salvation is foretold in Scripture and hence fulfilled "according to Scripture" (1:16; 2:17–36; 3:13–26; 4:10–12, 25; 8:32–38; 10:39–43; 11:15–16; 14:26–41; 28:25–28). God's redemptive plan was set in motion through Israel (2:5–12, 39; 3:24–26; 5:31; 10:36; 13:17, 23–24, 46; 28:20) and moved forward in stages from Jerusalem toward the "ends of the earth" (1:8). Yet the church struggled to follow the plan to create an inclusive, multiethnic community. This is exemplified by Peter's meeting with Cornelius's household as he hesitates to share table fellowship with "impure" gentiles (10:15, 28, 34–35). The process was a struggle of collective identity as much as salvation. God's Spirit was needed to resolve the resulting conflict between Jewish Christians and representatives of gentile Christians (15:1–29). Yet the decision of the apostolic council was a "compromise" between Jewish Christians (represented by James) and advocates of gentile Christians (represented by Paul).

The apostolic council (15:23–29) and events leading to it (Acts 10–11) resonate closely with Christians in Asia. It demonstrates the importance of finding solutions to intra-Christian (and interreligious) conflicts. In India and elsewhere in Asia, an important line of disagreement among Christians is faith-propagation and conversion. This is particularly acute between Pentecostal-type churches and the mainline denominations[72]. These disputes

72 Sarbeswar Sahoo, *Pentecostalism and Politics of Conversion in India* (Cambridge: Cambridge University Press, 2018), 43–86.

are often connected to social, caste, and cultural distinctions as well. Careful reading of the apostolic council (10–11; 15:1–29) and the events leading up to it from various Asian perspectives could point a way forward to dialogue, peace building, and greater unity.

Despite conflicts and human weakness, Acts portrays God's plan of salvation and how difficult it is for humans to keep up with God's intentions (Acts 1:6; 2:12; 5:34–39; 9:4–5; 10:4, 13–16; 15:1–29; 26:14).[73] God chose lowly and uneducated men and women (esp. Acts 1–12) and a well-educated religious zealot (Paul; 13–28) to advance his plan. Though Acts is rather optimistic in its outlook, it frequently depicts sin and human failings (e.g., 5:1–9; 6:1–3; 15:36–41). Nevertheless, nothing can thwart God's purposes, be it violent persecution (4:3–22; 5:17–39; 6:11–16; 7:54–58; 8:1–4; 14:19–20; 16:19–24; 17:5–9; 18:13–17; 19:23–41; 21:27–36; 23:12–22), sin, weaknesses, temptations, or even disputes within the church (5:1–11; 6:1–16; 8:18–21; 10:13–16; 15:1–2, 36–41).

The narrative world of Acts depicts God's actions directly and indirectly. Luke uses special vocabulary to indicate "divine necessity/purpose" (Gk. *dei; anagkaion*)[74] and "divine plan" (Gk. *boulē*).[75] This is often connected to God's plan of salvation (e.g., 2:23; 3:21). Yet God's action is also implied through divine "coincidences," such as paired visions of Paul and Ananias (9:3–19), an earthquake opening prison doors (16:16), and acts of benevolence and protection (5:33–34; 16:26; 19:30–31, 35–41; 21:31–32; 22:23–29; 23:17–22, 29–35; 26:22; 27:30–31, 42–44; 28:2, 7–10).[76] Even the subtle ending in Acts 28 leaves the audience wondering what God will accomplish through his people before he will finally come to "restore all things" (3:21).

The tension between God's sovereignty and human freedom is evident in Acts, especially regarding salvation. The conundrum has been resolved differently in various Christian and Hindu traditions. Vaiṣṇava schools have used monkey and cat illustrations, respectively, to emphasize either human

73 Luke Timothy Johnson, *The Acts of the Apostles*, Sacra Pagina 5 (Collegeville, MN: Michael Glazier, 2006), 15.

74 See *dei* in Acts 1:21; 3:21; 4:12; 5:29; 9:6, 16; 14:22; 15:5; 16:30; 19:21; 20:35; 23:11; 25:10; 27:24, 26; see *anagkaion* in 13:46.

75 For *boulē*, see 2:23; 4:28; 13:36; see 5:38 and 27:42 for the human plan in contrast to God's.

76 Darrell L. Bock, *A Theology of Luke and Acts* (Grand Rapids, MI: Zondervan, 2012), 125–28, 139–40.

participation (Northern school) or total surrender of the devotee (Southern school).[77] This is reminiscent of the Calvinist-Arminian disputes in Protestant Christianity. More generally, though, the idea of karma in many Asian traditions emphasizes human effort in achieving this-worldly benefits and ultimate salvation.[78] Yet unmerited favor is not absent from some strands of Hinduism and Buddhism. Total surrender of the devotee in *Bhagavad Gita* (e.g., *Gita* 12.7, 20) and grace in Pure Land Buddhism find close parallels with "salvation by grace" as depicted in Acts (e.g., 15:9–11) and later Christian tradition.

Universal Salvation through the Risen Jesus

If God is the foundational character, Jesus takes the center stage in the narrative. As indicated earlier, Acts continues the story about Jesus where Luke's Gospel ends (Luke 24:51–53; Acts 1:9–11). Acts shows Jesus's transition from the earthly to the heavenly realm (1:6–11; 2:22–36; 9:3–9) and spells out what that means for Jesus's followers. Jesus is the Messiah, Son of God, Savior, and Lord from the beginning (Luke 1:31–33; 1:76; 2:11), yet resurrection and ascension signals his enthronement and exaltation to the right hand of God (Acts 2:24–36). His claims are vindicated after the shameful crucifixion as foretold in Scripture (Ps 16:8–11; 110:1; Isa 53:7–8; Acts 2:16–36; 8:32–33).

At Pentecost, Peter makes an extraordinary claim that everyone must call upon the Lord Jesus to be saved (2:34–36; Ps 110:1; see Joel 2:28; Acts 2:16) and be baptized "in the name of Jesus Christ" (2:38). This same Lord also pours out the eschatological Spirit on all who believe in him (2:33, 38–39; see 16:6–8). Though Jesus is often portrayed in his human role as suffering and vindicated God's servant (2:22; 3:13, 26; 4:25–26, 30), his role as the Savior, exalted Lord, dispenser of the Spirit, and eschatological judge (2:21, 24, 32–38; 3:6, 15–16, 20–23; 4:12; 10:36; 15:17, 26; 16:6–10, 31; 17:30–31; 28:31) indicates that he is on par with the supreme God (see 2:21; 2:32–36, 38; 10:36; 15:17, 26; 20:21).[79]

77 Pratap Kumar, "Vaiṣṇavism," in *Encyclopedia of Hinduism*, 926–27.

78 Swami Bhaskarananda, *The Essentials of Hinduism: A Comprehensive Overview of the World's Oldest Religion* (Seattle: Viveka, 2002), 79–97.

79 Bock, *Theology*, 173–75. For a less exalted view of Jesus in Acts, see Jacob Jerwell, *The Theology of the Acts the Apostles*, New Testament Theology (Cambridge: Cambridge University Press, 1996), 131–32.

The revelation of Christ's glory (1:9–10; 9:3–9) and the movement from earthly to glorified status resonates with revelatory stories in India's sacred literature. *Mahabharata* and *Bhagavad Purana* abound with stories where Krishna and other gods reveal their glorified form, at times unexpectedly.[80] Yet theologically, Christians affirm that only Jesus Christ is at the level of the supreme God (John 1:1–3, 14, 18; Col 2:9) or *Brahman* (according to Indian tradition).[81]

Jesus's role in Acts is most apparent as Savior and Lord. To be saved, everyone must repent and believe in him (2:38; 3:16; 4:12; 5:30–31; 8:12, 22; 10:42–43; 11:18; 16:31; 20:21; 24:24). Receiving salvation in "the name of Jesus" is holistic and includes forgiveness of sins and rescue from eschatological judgment (2:38; 5:31; 10:42–43; 13:38; 17:31). Yet salvation also grants the gift of divine Spirit (2:38–39; 5:32; 8:14–17; 9:17; 10:44–48; 19:6), healing (3:16; 4:9–10, 22, 30; 8:6–7; 9:34; 10:38; 14:8–10), inclusion into God's people regardless of one's socioeconomic status or ethnicity (2:16–17; 4:32–37; 10–11; 10:34; 11:20; 15:8–10), deliverance from evil spirits (5:12–16; 8:6–7; 16:16–18; 19:11–20), and rescue from evil and danger (23:12–22; 25:1–5; 27:21–44; 28:1–6).[82] As Lord and Savior, Jesus may be communicated in an Indian context as the supreme *avatāra*. He is not one among the many but in the "very heart of Brahman" who may be discovered only through a spiritual transformation of the heart.[83]

Faith in the Lord Jesus also challenges other lords, gods, saviors, and healers (16:20–21; 17:7–8; 19:13–41). Because believers refused to accommodate or worship other gods/lords, they experienced ridicule (2:13; 17:6, 17; 19:9), threats (4:17–18; 5:40), imprisonment and social ostracism (5:17–18; 19–24; 8:3; 9:1–2; 12:3–5; 16:23–24; 21–28), communal/mob violence (16:19–24; 17:5–8; 19:23–41; 21:27–31; 22:22–24), prolonged court cases (24:26–27; 22–28), and even martyrdom (7:57–60; 9:1–2; 12:1–2; 14:19–20; 20:36–38).

A person's honor (and shame) was considered of utmost value in ancient society, so public ridicule and imprisonment would have seemed like a social

80 *Bhagavad Gita* 10–11; esp. 11.47–55.

81 See Robin Boyd, *An Introduction to Indian Christian Theology* (Delhi: ISPCK, 1975), 80–82, 127–29.

82 Traditional words for "healing" or "salvation/rescue" are not used in each case (e.g., 21:12–22; 25:1–5).

83 Klaus L. Klostermaier, "What Do Men Say about the Son of Man," in *Readings in Indian Christian Theology*, ed. R. S. Sugirtharajah and Cecil Hargreaves (Delhi: ISPCK, 1993), 1:116–27.

death sentence. However, early Christians had turned the values of the society upside down following Jesus's teaching (Luke 6:22–23). Instead of succumbing to shame, the apostles rejoiced over public beating, ridicule, and shame (5:40–41).[84] They practiced nonviolent resistance, or *ahimsa*, also known in Jain and Hindu traditions. Forgiving one's adversary is also not unknown in Hindu writings, as depicted by *Mahabharata* hero Yudhishthira at his final test in the afterlife (see Acts 7:59–60).[85] On other occasions, Paul used his rights as a Roman citizen to partially regain his dignity (16:22–24, 35–40; 22:25–29). Acts depicts the church's varied responses to persecution. These included witnessing openly and boldly, enduring patiently, appealing to the rule of law, and taking advantage of divinely assisted escapes (4:19–21, 31; 9:23–25; 12:7–17; 16:37–39; 22:25–29; 28:17).

Unfortunately, many Christians in Asia also face oppression and persecution. Some carry a sense of shame for being considered second-class citizens;[86] others face imprisonment and even potential death. As a result of the sociocultural pressure, some who are drawn to Christ do not formally convert. They are known as *Yeshu bhaktas* (Jesus devotees) in India and Jesus *Imandars* in Bangladesh. They stand in the liminal space between formal Christianity and their mother religion (Hinduism or Islam), somewhat like the "God-fearers" (10:1–11:18; 18:7; see 13:12) in Acts stood between Judaism and Greco-Roman religions.[87] Acts gives encouragement to discouraged Christians and provides a good starting point to reflect on theologies of suffering and practical responses to social exclusion and persecution.

Sometimes Acts has been accused of toning down the concern for the poor and the marginalized in contrast to Luke's Gospel. While Acts does emphasize evangelism and establishing new churches, it is not at the expense of caring for the marginalized. The newly established kingdom communities were called to embody just and compassionate actions that Jesus

84 In an informal interview, a newly converted believer in Myanmar told me he "felt honored" as I inquired about his views on Matthew 5:11–12.

85 See Mahabharata, *Svargarohanika Parva* 18.1–3.

86 See Esa Autero, "Ghosts, Women, and Evangelism: A Dialogue between Bolivia and Indonesia," in *Bible and Transformation: The Promise of Intercultural Bible Reading*, ed. Hans de Wit and Janet Dyk (Atlanta: SBL, 2015), 267–89.

87 Vidush Bhandari, "The 'God-Fearers': Significance of the Gentile Worshippers in Luke-Acts as a Paradigm of Mission among Yeshu Bhaktas" (unpublished manuscript, September 2020).

demonstrated (Luke 4:17–18)—though now applied in a new sociocultural setting in the power of the Spirit (2:44–47; 3:2–6; 4:32–37; 6:1–6; 9:32–43; 10:2; 11:28–30; 20:33–35; 24:17). As such, Luke's social concern in Acts focused on the inclusion of the "impure" gentiles who were now cleansed through faith in Jesus (Acts 1:8; 10–11; 15:1–33; 28:28). Salvation is now offered to all nations, ethnicities, and socioeconomic statuses without distinction. One of the great challenges of Asian churches is to bridge the gap between social classes, castes, and other forms of social discrimination in society and in the church.

As "the Way" became universally available to everyone, salvation was exclusively available through Jesus Christ according to the Acts narrative (2:38; 3:16; 4:12; 15:11; 16:31). This exclusivity was considered disruptive and offensive (16:20–21; 17:6–8; 19:23–41).[88] Despite its universal scope, the exclusive view of salvation is also difficult to accept today, both in Asia and elsewhere. As a result, a number of hermeneutical approaches has been suggested to be more inclusive. Tatsiong Liew states, "Acts is . . . more interested in conversion than conversation."[89] As such, he prefers to focus on the "more tolerant thread in Acts." He highlights cooperation on the sea voyage (27:1–28:16) and Acts' anticolonial dynamics.[90] Others have suggested hermeneutical tools that negotiate exclusive claims of Christian salvation or explore alternative ways to maintain their religious traditions.[91] As difficult as the question is, Christians can hardly escape the exclusive claims found in Acts (and elsewhere in the NT) without neglecting (or rejecting) large parts of the narrative.[92] K. K. Yeo

88 See Keener, *Acts*, vol. 2, loc. 6313–49 of 105811.

89 He also states, "Paul promotes in Acts . . . the elimination of all other ethnic/religious identities for all people" (p. 424).

90 Benny Tatsiong Liew, "Acts," in *Global Bible Commentary*, ed. D. Patte et al. (Nashville: Abington, 2004), 423–28.

91 See S. J. Samartha, "The Cross and the Rainbow: Christ in a Multireligious Culture," in *Readings in Indian Christian Theology*, ed. R. S. Sugirtharajah and Celcil Hargreaves (Delhi: ISPCK, 1993), 1:102–15.

92 See Ivan Satyavrata, "Jesus and Other Faiths," in *Asian Christian Theology: Evangelical Perspectives*, ed. Timoteo D. Gener and Stephen T. Pardue (Cumbria: Langham Partnership, 2019), loc. 4732–5203 of 9260, Kindle; K. K. Yeo, "Asian and Asian American Biblical Interpretation," in *Scripture and Its Interpretation: A Global, Ecumenical Introduction to the Bible*, ed. Michael J. Gorman (Grand Rapids, MI: Baker Academics, 2017), 332–38.

takes a more affirming stance to the Acts narrative as a whole and calls for "ethic of humility" and dialogue while maintaining Christ's primacy.[93] He highlights Paul's Areopagus speech (Acts 17:22–34), where "the gospel is indigenized by the use of native words, concepts, and expressions," as a model of dialogue with other religions.[94]

Paul's example in Athens is a good resource of contextualization for the philosophically minded; however, the sections that highlight the tangible power of the Spirit are equally important. Many adherents of popular religion/culture in Asia are drawn to Christ as a healer and deliverer from evil spirits (e.g., *Yeshu bhaktas*). Particularly people with little or no access to medical care and those oppressed by the caste system, evil spirits, and other forms of marginality find hope and dignity in Christ.[95] As the marginalized segments in Asia, such as Dalits and Adivasis in India, find a new sense of dignity in Christ, it will inevitably cause sociopolitical disruption much like in the Roman Empire and beyond.[96]

Life-Giving Spirit and the Empowered Church

One of the decisive moments in the Acts narrative is the outpouring of the Spirit on the day of Pentecost (2:1–4). The same Spirit who inspired the Scripture and spoke through the prophets (1:16; 2:17; 4:25; 28:25) was poured out regardless of gender, ethnicity, or socioeconomic status (2:16–18; 10:44–45). Pentecost has traditionally been celebrated as the "birthday of the Church," yet in Acts, it signals the inauguration of the "last days" (see Joel 2:28; Acts 2:17) and the beginning of the church's worldwide mission as evidenced by the language miracle (2:1–13). Further, Peter's shift from a cowardly disciple (Luke 22:34, 54–62) to a fearless evangelist (2:14–39; 3:11–26; 4:8–20; 5:29–32) signals the importance of the Spirit's power for everyone.

93 Yeo, "Asian and Asian American," 332–38; K. K. Yeo, *What Has Jerusalem to Do with Beijing? Biblical Interpretation from a Chinese Perspective*, 2nd ed. (Eugene, OR: Pickwick, 2018), 173–93.

94 K. K. Yeo, *What Has Jerusalem*, 167–93; Satyavrata, "Jesus and Other Faiths," loc. 5048–108 of 9260.

95 See Massey, "Acts," 313–60; Rajkumar, "Texts of Life," loc. 3165–348 of 7585; Sahoo, *Pentecostalism and Politics*.

96 See particularly the insightful research of Dalit conversion to Christianity in Rajastan from a Hindu perspective by Sahoo, *Pentecostalism and Politics*.

Acts narrates five dramatic outpourings of the Spirit, each at a decisive moment (2:1–4; 4:28–31; 8:15–17; 10:44; 19:6).[97] Yet the Spirit's involvement is palpably felt throughout Acts. The "Spirit of prophecy" given by the risen Christ guides the church in mission (1:8; 8:26–29, 39; 10–11; 16:6–8), enables various ministries (6:3, 5; 8:17; 9:17; 19:1–6), and gives revelatory knowledge (5:3, 9; 6:3, 5, 10; 7:55; 10:19; 11:12; 15:1–34). Further, the Spirit empowers and directs individuals, both apostolic leaders (10:19; 16:6–8; 20:23) and ordinary believers (7:55; 8:29, 39; 9:10–18; 21:4, 8–9). This guidance is often supernatural, as indicated by heavenly visions and dreams (9:3–18; 10:9–20; 16:6–8), Spirit's direct speech (8:29; 20:23), and in-filling and promptings (4:31; 5:32; 9:17, 31; 21:4).[98] Though Acts does not include a clear pilgrimage motif, Paul's journeys echo the idea (13:1–3; 14:22; 18:18; 19:21). R. S. Sugirtharajah has pointed out that Paul's missionary journeys were not finely tuned mission strategies as depicted by later history;[99] rather, they betray a sense of spiritual calling and practical urgency. For many Asian traditions, pilgrimage is an important religious practice, especially for merit accumulation and spiritual purification.[100] Though Paul's journeys do not include the idea of merit accumulation, his hardships (14:22), uncertainty regarding the route (16:6–10), and sense of fulfilling an inner call (19:21; 20:22; 26:17–20) are important motives in many pilgrimage traditions.

The Spirit is also indispensable because he enables the church to continue witnessing about "the Lord Jesus" under immense pressure and persecution (4:8–10, 31; 5:27–32; 6:8–15; 7:55–57; 8:1–3; 9:1–2; 20:22–23, 28; 21:11). The Spirit's power is closely connected to healings, victory over demonic powers, and prophecies in conjunction with the "name of Jesus" (1:8; 2:17–18; 8:18, 39; 9:17; 10:45; 13:9–10; 16:18; 19:13–17). Manifestations of the Spirit are so visible and tangible that the church can readily testify about "what you see and hear" (2:13; see 8:7, 15–18; 10:44–45). As such, the Spirit's presence enables a vivid and powerful *anubhava* (experience) of Christ.

97 Johnson, *Acts*, 14.

98 God's guidance is of course not limited to supernatural events. For example, Paul's second missionary is prompted by his desire to "visit the believers" (15:36).

99 Sugirtharajah, *Postcolonial Reconfigurations*, 21–34.

100 René Gothóni, "Pyhiinvaellus," in *Uskonnot maailmassa*, ed. Katja Hyry and Juha Pentikäinen (Helsinki: WSOY, 1999), 468–78.

As indicated above, Acts portrays the Spirit as God's empowering presence and experience of Christ. Yet the Spirit also takes on characteristics of a personhood (1:16; 5:3, 32; 7:51; 13:2, 4; 15:28; 16:6; 20:23, 28; 21:11; 28:25). Though most Asian traditions are very spiritual, Indian tradition regarding spirit is somewhat difficult to relate to Acts and Christian faith. One of the difficulties is the multifaceted understanding of spirit and spiritual. The foundational word for *spirit* in Hindu philosophy is *Atman* (and *paramatman*); it refers to an impersonal *Brahman* and soul/self.[101] Other words, such as *shakhti*, *antaratman*, and *antaryamin* (and others) for spirit add to the confusion. Indian theologian Chenchiah connected the Holy Spirit to great spiritual power (*mahashakti*) as cosmic energy and divine person.[102] Chakkarai states that Spirit is the active and real power of Christ connecting the believer's *atman* to the *atman* of Christ, who energizes within it.[103] As such, spirit *shakti* is "the power which made the blind to see, the coward to preach, and . . . turned the world upside down." This spirit is given to everyone equally and without distinction, regardless of caste, wealth, or position (see 2:16–21). He comes from outside of a person to all who ask but remains within, transforming the self, communities, and beyond. Finally, the Spirit in Acts is connected to joy (2:46; 13:52; see 3:8; 8:8, 39; 15:3; 16:34), somewhat like joyful devotion in bhakti tradition and *Ananda* (bliss) in the Hindu "trinity" *Saccidananda* (*Brahman* as *Sat*, *Cit*, and *Ananda*, or being, consciousness, and bliss, respectively).[104]

Acts' portrayal of the Spirit-empowered church is crucial for God's people today. Christians throughout Asia are living out the miraculous power of the Spirit as they give witness to the risen Christ.[105] As Ayyaneth, Yeo, Satyavrata, and many others testify, Asians are thoroughly spiritual and do not disbelieve the miraculous, nor are they limited by reductionist scientism.[106] The crucial question for Asian believers is not the existence of God or spiritual powers but

101 See, e.g., *Chandogya Upanishad* VI 8.7; *Brihadaranyaka Upanishads* I 4.1, 10; II 5.1–2.

102 See Boyd, *Introduction*, 155–56; B. J. Kristie Kumar, "An Indian Christian Appreciation of the Doctrine of Holy Spirit," *Indian Journal of Theology* 30 (1981): 29–35.

103 Boyd, *Introduction*, 172–75.

104 See Boyd, 241–43; Kumar, "Indian Christian Appreciation," 29–35.

105 See Massey, "Acts," 313–60; Sahoo, *Pentecostalism and Politics*, 49–86.

106 "Intellectual study of the Bible in Asia does not exclude belief in the supernatural world" (Yeo, "Asian and Asian American," 327). Still, India (as many other Asian countries) has venerable and stimulating intellectual and philosophical traditions.

rather their identity. Acts is an indispensable resource of spiritual discernment because it actualizes the presence of the Spirit and highlights the importance of Scripture among God's people (see 15:1–29). The Spirit bears witness to the reality in front of the text in our present contexts by building a bridge between past works of God and his desire to commune with his people today. According to the Acts narrative, the enemies of the gospel are defeated by the "Gospel of peace" as the Spirit reconciles different ethnicities and social classes (10:36). The witnessing community that embodies kingdom lifestyle thereby demonstrates joy-filled communion with the risen Christ and one another (2:42–47; 4:32–37).

There are numerous parallels between Acts and Asian context, some of which were highlighted earlier. Examples were also given of Indian hermeneutics (e.g., *dhvani* and Dalit), texts, experiences, and practices in hopes of reading Acts from an Asian perspective. More could be explored if space permitted. Asian hermeneutics is not just about exegeting a biblical text in its historical context; rather, it must involve worldview considerations and spiritual sensitivity in addition to dialogue between biblical texts and various Asian traditions.

An important area for further research is the perspectives of the ordinary Bible readers (and listeners).[107] By carefully listening to ordinary readers in various socioeconomic and cultural contexts in Asia, scholars may gain a better understanding of their perspectives (vernacular hermeneutics). This in turn will help develop robust Asian theologies and pastoral practices.

CONCLUSION

Acts is unique among the NT writings. Its narrative presentation gives a glimpse into the experiences, beliefs, and practices of the earliest Christians. The focal point of Acts is the commissioning of the church to diffuse the message of God's kingdom to the ends of the earth in the power of the Holy Spirit. This includes gospel proclamation and acts of justice—and potential conflict with those who oppose it. Whether one accepts the vision of Acts fully (Yeo) or in part (Liew) depends on one's conviction regarding its status

107 See Autero, *Reading the Bible*, 49–116.

as God's word and applicability for theology and practice today. Be that as it may, part of the appeal of Acts lies in its ability to touch believers of all sorts, even those who disagree with its message. Yet perhaps the greatest appeal of Acts is reserved for Asian believers who live among their non-Christian neighbors experiencing hardship and oppression. They can most readily identify with narrative depictions and draw strength from its stories as they worship the living God and bear witness to the reality of the risen Christ in their lives.

FURTHER READING

Barrett, C. K. 1994. *A Critical and Exegetical Commentary on the Acts of the Apostles: Preliminary Introduction and Commentary on I–XIV.* International Critical Commentary 1. Edinburgh: T&T Clark.

Bik, E. Z. 2014. "Universal Salvation in the Context of Interfaith Dialogue in Myanmar." In *Theology under the Bo Tree: Contextual Theologies in Myanmar*, edited by Samuel Ngun Ling and Daniel K. Zau Nan, 415–431. Yangon: Myanmar Institute of Theology.

Bock, D. L. 2012. *A Theology of Luke and Acts.* Grand Rapids, MI: Zondervan Academic.

D'Sa, F. 1979. "'Dhvani' as a Method of Interpretation." *Bible Bhashyam* 5, no. 4: 276–294.

Johnson, L. T. 1992. *The Acts of Apostles.* Sacra Pagina. Collegeville, MN: Liturgical Press.

Keener, C. S. 2012–2014. *Acts: An Exegetical Commentary. Introduction and Vols. 1–3.* Grand Rapids, MI: Baker Academics.

Massey, J. 2010. "Acts of the Apostles." In *One Volume Dalit Bible Commentary: New Testament*, edited by T. K. John, 313–360. New Delhi: Center for Dalit/Subaltern Studies.

Yeo, K. K. 2017. "Asian and Asian American Biblical Interpretation." In *Scripture and Its Interpretation: A Global, Ecumenical Introduction to the Bible*, edited by Michael J. Gorman, 332–338. Grand Rapids, MI: Baker Academics.

EIGHT

The Letter to the Romans

Arren Bennet Lawrence
Asia Theological Association
Bengaluru, India

> A soldier named Nobushige came to [a Zen monk] Hakuin, and asked: "Is there really a paradise and a hell?"
>
> "Who are you?" inquired Hakuin. "I am a samurai," the warrior replied.
>
> "You, a soldier!" exclaimed Hakuin. "What kind of ruler would have you as his guard? Your face looks like that of a beggar." Nobushige became so angry that he began to draw his sword, but Hakuin continued: "So you have a sword! Your weapon is probably much too dull to cut off my head."
>
> As Nobushige drew his sword Hakuin remarked: "Here open the gates of hell!" At these words the samurai, perceiving the master's discipline, sheathed his sword and bowed.
>
> "Here open the gates of paradise," said Hakuin.[1]

There are several stories like this in Asia that address how one could go to heaven and how one could live a moral life. Similarly, Paul addresses issues such as how one could be justified, how one could avoid the wrath of God, how one could live a holy life, and the like in his epistle to the Romans.

1 Nancy Wilson Ross, *The World of Zen: An East-West Anthology* (New York: Random House, 1960), 80.

The book of Romans is a concise, comprehensive, captivating, and carefully constructed Gospel presentation found in the Bible.[2] The famous Reformer Martin Luther called it the "purest Gospel."[3] It is not an easy task to write an introduction to Romans because there are numerous writings on the book. This introduction is concentrated on explaining the epistle to the Romans for Asian readers without sacrificing the content of the book.

PRELIMINARY ASPECTS

Authorship

The epistle to the Romans was written by Paul (Rom 1:1). Tertius, the one mentioned in Romans 16:22, was probably an amanuensis or a scribe to Paul.[4] Though it is fashionable in recent times to question the traditional authorship of some of the books of the NT, it remains certain that this book was written by Paul.[5]

Addressees

Paul identifies the recipients as the believers in Rome (Rom 1:7). Ambrosiaster (fourth century CE) says that the Romans had "embraced the faith of the Christ, albeit according to the Jewish rite, without seeing any sign of mighty work or any of the apostles" (Ambrosiaster, *PL* 17.46). Ambrosiaster's depiction of the Roman church is possibly close to the truth.[6] By seeing the significant Christian presence by 49 CE, it is fair to assume that the church at Rome was formed by the Jews who accepted Christ on the Day of Pentecost (Acts 2:10–11). The significant presence of Christians is highlighted through two

2 Norman L. Geisler, *A Popular Survey of the New Testament* (Hyderabad: Authentic, 2007), 127; Luke Timothy Johnson, *The Writings of the New Testament* (Bangalore: Theological Publications in India, 2009), 343.

3 Martin Luther, "Preface to the Epistle to the Romans, 1522," in *Word and Sacrament*, LW 35, ed. E. Theodore Bachmann (Philadelphia: Fortress, 1960), 365.

4 D. A. Carson, Douglas J. Moo, and Leon Morris, *An Introduction to the New Testament* (Manila: OMF Literature, 1992), 241.

5 James R. Edwards, *Romans*, UBCS (Grand Rapids, MI: Baker, 1992), 5.

6 Carson, Moo, and Morris, *Introduction*, 242.

historical incidents in Rome. While Claudius was the emperor (ca. 49 BCE), he evicted the Jews out of Rome on the account that they were constantly creating "disturbances" in the name of "Chrestus" (Suetonius, *Claudius*, 25.4). *Chrestus* could have been the Latin transliteration of the Greek name *Christos*.[7] Therefore, Jews, including Jewish Christians, were expelled from Rome in 49 CE. However, when Nero became the emperor (after the death of Claudius in 54 CE), the Jews (including Christians) slowly came back and settled in Rome because Nero did not implement the "Edict of Claudius." On the contrary, Nero turned violent against the Christians in 64 CE, and he blamed them for starting the fire that consumed half of Rome (64 CE). Roman historian Tacitus reports the mass persecution of the Christians in Rome in this period.[8] Therefore, it is possible that this letter could have arrived in Rome between these two historically significant incidents.[9]

In this context, it is plausible to think that the majority of the church was gentile in nature while a significant number of Jewish Christians were present, as is indicated by the Jewish names in Romans 16. This notion is also strengthened by Paul's words in Romans 1:5–6, which says, "Among all *the nations* including you . . . to the Romans." The term *nations* could also be read as gentiles from the Greek word *ethna*. This gentile majority seems to have controlled the leadership of the church after the Jews left the city.[10] However, when the Jewish settlers came back, these gentiles might not have given opportunities to the Jews to practice their gifts and leadership in the church. Paul could have written Romans 12–15 against this, exhorting them to accommodate the weak. This shows the presence of both gentiles and Jews in the church, though the gentiles could have been the majority at the time the letter was written.

7 Edwards, *Romans*, 9.

8 Tacitus, "Annals Book XV," in *Complete Works of Tacitus*, trans. Alfred John Church, William Jackson Brodribb, and Sara Bryant (New York: Random House, 1873), 395.

9 Paul favoring the governing authorities shows that this persecution under Nero had not begun at the time of the reception of the letter (Rom 13).

10 Scot McKnight, *Reading Romans Backwards: A Gospel of Peace in the Midst of Empire* (Waco, TX: Baylor University Press, 2019), 18–21.

Provenance and Date

It is possible that when he wrote the letter, Paul was in Corinth or in Cenchreae.[11] As Paul was traveling to Jerusalem by the end of his third missionary journey (Acts 19:21; 20:16), he spent three months in Greece (Acts 20:3).[12] He probably stayed at Corinth on his way (see 2 Cor 13:1, 10). At this time, he could have penned this epistle to the Romans as a way of addressing the problems in the church that he had heard about.[13] In addition, he would have wanted to tell his travel plans to the Roman believers. Moreover, he would have wanted to present the Gospel beyond Rome so he could prepare them to support him in his mission trip to Spain.

A few other details that strengthen this hypothesis come from the names Paul mentions toward the end of the letter. Paul's mention of Phoebe and his commendation of her to the Romans are significant. Phoebe was a "deacon" of the church at Cenchreae, the city that was close to Corinth (Acts 18:18; Rom 16:1). Paul asks the church to "help her in whatever she may need" (Rom 16:2). Phoebe could have been the courier of the letter.[14] Paul asks the Romans to show hospitality to Phoebe because she had shown hospitality to Paul and his company, as "she has been a patron to many and me" (Rom 16:2). As Paul received hospitality, he expects to repay her by exhorting his friends in Rome to return the favor. In Asia, this return of hospitality is a common sociological phenomenon. This "debt of gratitude" is called *utang na loob* in Filipino,[15] *Nandri Kadan* in Tamil, and *Prathyupakaram* in Malayalam. This sense of gratitude is a sociological response for a favor received. Paul's increased "debt of gratitude" could also have come from the fact that Phoebe possibly helped him in the delivery of the letter to the Roman recipients.[16]

---

11 Raymond E. Brown, *An Introduction to the New Testament* (Bangalore: Theological Publications in India, 2009), 559.

12 Carson, Moo, and Morris, *Introduction*, 241.

13 Douglas J. Moo, *Romans*, NICNT (Grand Rapids, MI: Eerdmans, 1996), 18.

14 Colin G. Kruse, *Paul's Letter to the Romans*, PNTC (Grand Rapids, MI: Eerdmans, 2012), 553.

15 Isabel S. Panopio and Relidad Santico Rolda, *Society and Culture: Introduction to Sociology and Anthropology* (Quezon: Katha, 2007), 86.

16 James A. Stifler, *The Epistle to the Romans* (Chicago: Moody, 1960), 244; Brown, *Introduction*, 559.

Further, Paul also names Gaius, who was his host at the time of the writing of the letter (Rom 16:23). Gaius was one of the prominent members of the Corinthian church (1 Cor 1:14), with whom Paul spent the winter of 57/58 CE at Corinth.[17] In addition, Paul also sends greetings from Erastus, "the city treasurer" of Corinth (Rom 16:23).[18] These details support the fact that Paul probably wrote the letter from Corinth, during 57/58 CE.

Occasion

According to Romans 15:22–29, three places are listed in Paul's travel plans—namely, Jerusalem, Rome, and Spain. Paul was traveling to Jerusalem in the immediate future as he was writing this letter (Rom 15:25).[19] He plans to go to Spain to preach the Gospel in the near future (Rom 15:24). On his way to Spain, he wanted to visit the Roman believers and minister to them (Rom 15:24; 1:15). In Romans 1:13, he says his intention to come to Rome is to "reap some fruit" among the Romans, as he had received among the rest of the gentiles.[20] In Romans 15:24, he says, "I hope to see you in passing as I go to Spain, and to be helped on my journey there by you." Therefore, one of the possible reasons for Paul's visit to Rome was to be supported by the Romans in his missionary journey to Spain. *Sadhus* and monks in India and Buddhist countries receive alms from the people for their livelihood and travels. Similarly, Paul is requesting help from the Roman church for his missions and travels (Rom 15:24). This could be one of the reasons for Paul's writing of the letter.

Another possible purpose of the letter is to present the Gospel in a coherent way so that people could understand his position better. Due to the Galatian controversy and other encounters with the Jews, Paul could have been seen by others as an antinomian.[21] As Paul was traveling to Jerusalem, he would have anticipated presenting himself to his fellow Jewish brethren and having to explain the statements he made earlier. Therefore, it is possible that

17 Brown, *Introduction*, 560.

18 Craig S. Keener, *Romans*, NCCS (Eugene, OR: Cascade, 2009), 191–92.

19 Paul seems to be returning from his third missionary journey (Acts 19:21; 20:16).

20 Arren Bennet Lawrence, "Eisegetical Fallacies: A Polemic against Certain Word Study Fallacies," *Hindustan Evangelical Review* 4 (2010–11): 107–25.

21 Moo, *Romans*, 21.

this letter could be seen as Paul's logical presentation of the Gospel with explanations combined to explicate his stand on obedience to the law. This is validated by Paul's exhortation on obedience to the law and fulfillment of the law in the sanctification process through pneumatic nomism and *agapal* nomism (discussed later).[22] In addition, Paul could have presented this Gospel as a good introduction of himself, as he had not visited the Roman church as yet.[23]

In his recent book on Romans, Scot McKnight stresses that the epistle should be read "backwards."[24] While reading the book from the beginning, it appears as though Paul was presenting the Gospel systematically, devoid of many contextual affinities.[25] However, when the book is read backward—that is, when read in the light of the last few chapters of the book—it could be understood differently. When the first few chapters are read in light of the last few chapters (i.e., Rom 12–16), it appears that Paul was primarily concerned about the leadership crisis created by the gentile-Jewish tensions.

Therefore, the immediate needs of the church could have included the following: first, a clarification on why the church ought to believe in the Gospel, which emphasizes faith in Jesus as the means of attaining righteousness (Paul addresses this in Rom 1:18–5:21); second, why and how one should not continue in sin (Rom 6:1–15:13); third, the importance of gentile church leadership sharing the responsibilities with the Jews (Rom 12); fourth, submitting to the governing authorities (Rom 13); and fifth, accepting the weak brethren (probably the Jews; Rom 14:1–15:13). For all these issues, Paul finds an answer in the Gospel, and he structures the book in such a way that these issues are addressed with clarity. Therefore, he penned sixteen chapters in a meticulously constructed rhetoric, placing the Gospel as the answer, which enables the believer to live a righteous life.

Structure of Romans

The structure of Romans could be seen as follows:

1:1–17 . . . . . . Introductory remarks

22 *Pneumatic* in this article means "by the Spirit" (that is, with the help of the Holy Spirit).
23 Moo, *Romans*, 17–18.
24 McKnight, *Reading Romans Backwards*. 1–4.
25 Stifler, *Epistle to the Romans*, 15.

1:18–3:31	Righteousness is attained only by faith in Christ
4:1–25.	Both Abraham and David attained righteousness through faith
5:1–21	Righteousness through faith results in great spiritual blessings
6:1–7:6	Having been made righteous is not a license to sin
7:7–25	Obedience to the law produces sins because of the flesh
8:1–34.	Live a holy life with the help of the Spirit
9:1–11:36	God has not rejected the nation of Israel, and they will be restored
12:1–15:13. . . .	Live a holy life by loving one another
15:14–16:27 . . .	Final remarks with an appeal to come to Rome and greetings to Roman churches

Paul starts his book with the problems (1:18–3:20). Then he gives solutions to the problems (3:21–31). Further, he gives the benefits of the solution (Rom 4–5). In Romans 6–16, he gives the ways in which a person can live a holy life.

OVERVIEW OF ROMANS

Instead of introducing his Gospel first, Paul begins the letter by comparing his Gospel with the two other ways of attaining righteousness, by worshipping idols (Rom 1:18–32) and by obeying the law (Rom 2:1–3:20). He compares his Gospel to help understand it better and to show the inefficacy of the other ways in providing justification. *Upamana* in Indian philosophy indicates comparison as a source of knowledge. For example, a better understanding of a cow could be attained by observing the similarities and differences between a domestic cow and a wild cow.[26] A. Parthasarathy says, "You gain the knowledge of an unknown entity by comparing it with something known to you."[27] Comparison is common in Asian culture and literature. In Greek it was called as *synkrisis*, and in rhetoric it was called *camparatio*.[28] Paul compares the other two ways of attaining righteousness to emphasize the way he suggests to attain righteousness, by having faith in Jesus Christ alone. For example, Buddhism propagates a middle path, which is against the other way of attaining liberation of its time—that is, "extreme asceticism" of Hinduism.[29] For Buddha, the followers need not follow extreme asceticism or "unrestrained sensuality."[30]

Marketing imageries could be used to explain what Paul does in Romans. In the streets of Asia, marketing a product may involve several strategies. When there is much competition, the seller may use various strategies to market the products. If Paul's product is the Gospel (i.e., righteousness by faith in Jesus Christ), he talks about it only in Romans 3:21–31. He gives his product as the answer to the problems. Like a competitive salesman, Paul puts down the other two ways of attaining righteousness, worshipping idols (Rom 1:18–32) and obeying the law (Rom 2:1–3:20). He shows that both the other products cannot deliver the desired result of righteousness. In fact, they will produce only sins, the opposite of the desired result. Therefore, Paul promotes his Gospel and elevates it against the other two ways of attaining righteousness.

Apart from this, to sell a product, big companies use well-known people as product ambassadors. On the roads of Manila or Bangkok, one can see huge billboards with colorful lights showing celebrities promoting various products. Similarly, Paul says even Abraham and David, the two great leaders of the Jewish nation, were declared righteous by faith (Rom 4). Abraham and David function as the brand ambassadors for Paul's Gospel. Moreover, to

26 Anantanand Rambachan, *Accomplishing the Accomplished: The Vedas as a Source of Valid Knowledge in Sankara* (Honolulu: University of Hawaii Press, 1991), 27.

27 A. Parthasarathy, *Choice Upanishads* (Delhi: Parthasarathy, 2014), n.p.

28 Arren Bennet Lawrence, *Comparative Characterization in the Sermon on the Mount: Characterization of the Ideal Disciple* (Eugene, OR: Wipf & Stock, 2018), 98, 99.

29 Fritz Ridenour, *So What's the Difference? A Look at 20 Worldviews, Faiths and Religions and How They Compare to Christianity* (Ventura, CA: Regal, 2001), 100.

30 Ridenour, 100.

sell a product, an expert marketing person would talk about all the positive aspects of the product. Similarly, Paul says in Romans 5 that by having the righteousness by faith in Jesus Christ, the believer will have peace with God (v. 1), will rejoice in the hope of the glory of God (v. 2), and will receive the grace of God (v. 15). Therefore, Paul promotes his product through comparisons (Rom 1:18–3:20), putting down his competitive products (Rom 1:18–3:20), bringing in ambassadors from the history of Judaism (Rom 4), and identifying the benefits of using his product (Rom 5).

After successfully promoting his product (i.e., his Gospel), Paul finds a potential problem in his argument. If we are declared righteous before God by having faith in Jesus Christ, can we continue in sin (Rom 6:1)? Paul uses the rest of the chapters in the book to show how one could live a sanctified life after becoming righteous by the Gospel. In Hinduism, law or *dharma* is important for holiness. Performance of *dharma* (obedience of the law) is the means of holiness.[31] For Paul, we need not obey the law to be holy. In Romans 6–7, Paul says that the believer should not continue in sin. He argues that because we are dead to sin and the law (Rom 6:1–14; 7:1–6), and as we have become slaves to righteousness (Rom 6:15–23), we should not continue in sin. This is an exhortation to actively shun sin.[32] This is not a passive activity. In Romans 7:1–25, Paul identifies the problem of blaming the law as the causative agent of producing sins (Rom 5:20 and 7:8). Therefore, he rescues the law by showing how the law is holy, but when it is applied on human flesh, it only produces sin because it does not have the capacity to transform the flesh (Rom 7:13–25). Flesh thus overpowers the law and produces sins. In this way, Paul protects the law, which is considered one of the important essentials of Judaism.

If the law cannot transform flesh, how can the believer live a holy life? To answer this, Paul suggests two solutions. Believers can live holy lives with the help of the Holy Spirit (Rom 8) and through loving one another (Rom 12–14). With the help of the agency of the Holy Spirit and by loving one another, believers are expected to fulfill the requirements of the law (Spirit, Rom 8:4; love, 13:8). This could be called pneumatic nomism (fulfilling the

31 Shivesh Chandra Thakur, *Christian and Hindu Ethics* (Abingdon, UK: Routledge, 2019), 132.

32 I call this kinetic holiness (or kinetic *hagiosune*). Here Paul is exhorting the believer to be active (kinetic) in being holy.

law by the Spirit) and *agapal* nomism (fulfilling the law through love). Though there are ways in which a person could live a holy life in Hinduism, there is no direct agent like the Holy Spirit who can help a person live a holy life.

As mentioned earlier, Paul seems to have written the letter to exhort the church to accept the Jewish leaders by treating them as equal members. In one sense, Romans is quite the opposite to the Letter to the Galatians. In Galatians, Paul was writing the letter emphasizing how the gentiles are to be treated as equal members of the body of Christ to the Jews.[33] Here, Paul seems to exhort the gentiles to treat the weak Jews equally in the church by giving them equal opportunities to use their leadership and other gifts (Rom 12:4–8). Paul predominantly seems to take the side of the weak and serves as an advocate on their behalf. He is like Mahatma Gandhi, who frequently fought for the weak and powerless, whether for the Indians as a whole against British Empire, for the Muslims against the Hindu majority in India, or even for the people of Czechoslovakia, Poland, and Denmark against Hitler in a letter written to Hitler on December 24, 1940. Similarly, Paul stood for the weak in the Roman church and exhorted them to be holy and practice loving one another (Rom 12:1–15:13). In the remaining verses, Paul identifies his interest in coming to Rome after his visit to Jerusalem (Rom 15:14–33).

NO OTHER WAY BUT THE GOSPEL

In the introduction, Paul introduces himself as "the bond-servant of Christ Jesus" (Rom 1:1). In Asia, though slavery is not prevalent, housemaids (or *yayas* in Filipino) are quite common. Paul, who would brag about his apostolic credentials elsewhere (Gal 1:1), displays his humble side here, as it is not required in the context. The Gospel is going to be the key in this book, as he describes what this Gospel is in detail later.

33 Arren Bennet Lawrence, *Legalistic Nomism: A Socio-rhetorical Reading of Paul's Letter to the Galatians* (Delhi: ISPCK, 2016), 131–33.

Paul's Gospel: Righteousness by Faith in Jesus Christ

In many parts of Asia, pluralism is a prevailing worldview. For example, in India, Hinduism is considered a "conglomerate of cults and creeds."[34] Many creeds and cults come together to form Hinduism. However, for Paul, there is only one Gospel, and there is only one way of being righteous by faith. The other two ways of attaining righteousness that were significant in his time are addressed and put down in the beginning of the book.

From Romans 1:18–3:20, Paul emphasizes that all human beings have failed to attain righteousness before God. In Romans 1:18–32, he has to downplay the gentile attempt to attain righteousness (i.e., idol worship) so he can emphasize his Gospel (i.e., faith in Jesus Christ) as the means of attaining righteousness. While doing so, Paul begins his argument by emphasizing the result that idol worship leads them to—namely, the wrath of God (Rom 1:18). Though the gentiles knew God (Rom 1:19–21), they neglected him and did not honor him as God, but they exchanged that glory to the idols resembling humans, birds, animals, and others (Rom 1:23).

In Asia, idol worship is one of the prevalent practices among the people. Hindu temples in the streets of India and Nepal, Buddhist shrines in the streets of Singapore and Malaysia, and Buddhist temples in the streets of Sri Lanka and Thailand are common in Asian geography. However, for Paul, idol worship will not lead a person to righteousness. For him, it brought forth only excessive sins into their world, including sexual immorality and homosexuality (Rom 1:26–27). For Paul, sexual immorality and homosexuality constitute the ultimate evidence of the presence of sin among the gentiles. Along with these, Paul also names other sins in a list in Romans 1:29–31. Further, for Paul, these sins bring forth the wrath of God because they lead the people to death. Paul's chiastic structure[35] from Romans 1:18–32 emphatically identifies the failure of idol worship to provide righteousness because it could lead the people only to the wrath of God.

34 L. S. S. O'Malley, *Popular Hinduism: The Religion of the Masses* (Cambridge: Cambridge University Press, 1935), 2.

35 Chiastic structure is formed by having similar ideas formed in a chiastic manner, i.e., A, B, C, C^1, B^1, A^1, similar to X (Chi), the Greek alphabet. Here A=18; B=19–23; C=24–25; while C^1=26–27; B^1=28–31; A^1=32.

Sins, *Moksha*, and Righteousness

In Asian philosophies, including Hinduism and Buddhism, the result of an evil deed incurs bad karma, while the opposite will bring forth good karma. Similarly, Paul says evil deeds like sexual immorality will bring forth the wrath of God. Whereas in Paul, sins are defined as actions mentioned in the list (Rom 1:29–31), in Hinduism, sins are defined as bad actions or inaction of one's assigned duties (i.e., dharma). In popular Hinduism, each person is expected to perform her/his duties based on the caste in which he/she is born. If a person is born in a barber caste, he/she is expected to cut the hair of the people of the village. This is her/his dharma. When a person goes against her/his dharma, he/she commits sins and incurs bad karma. This bad karma can lead people far away from salvation (i.e., *moksha*, which is the release from the cycle of rebirth—samsara). For Paul, the sins are caused by idol worship, and these sins further lead a person far away from justification.

For Paul, the evidence of the presence of sins is homosexuality (1:26–27). In India, homosexuality is not always seen as a sin. Aravan is a minor character in the Hindu epic *Mahabharata*.[36] He was the son of Arjuna, one of the protagonists of *Bhagavad Gita*. In the Tamil folk versions of the epic, Aravan was prophesied to die on the eighteenth day of the Kurukshetra war, fought between Pandavas and Kauravas.[37] Knowing that he was about to die to make his side win the war, Aravan expressed his desire to marry someone before the fight in the battle and eventual death. No woman came forward to marry a dying man. Knowing this, Krishna the lead protagonist of the epic and a chief god of Hinduism, became a woman called Mohini and married him the day before his death. Therefore, many in India consider homosexuals as Aravani, the wife of Aravan, an avatar of the god Krishna. In many parts of India, it is considered auspicious to donate money or goods to homosexuals. Contrary to this, Paul considers homosexuality as the epitome of sin (Rom 1:26–27). The presence of homosexuality, for Paul, indicates the extreme presence of sin that leads to the wrath of God. In Romans 2:1–3:20,

36 *Mahabharata*, Book 6: *Bhisma Parva*, chs. 45, 56, 75, 81, 83, 90, 91, 96.

37 Alf Hiltebeitel, *The Cult of Draupadi: On Hindu Ritual and the Goddess* (Chicago: University of Chicago Press, 1991), 284–85; Alf Hiltebeitel, "Dying before the Mahabharata War: Martial and Transsexual Body-Building for Aravan," *Journal of Asian Studies* 54 (May 1995): 447–73.

Paul makes similar arguments, but his concentration is pointed to the Jewish people.

From Romans 2:3–5, Paul emphasizes that even the Jews are susceptible to the wrath of God because they also are committing the same sins as the gentiles. The concept of karma could be used here to explain Romans 2:6–10, where Paul beautifully narrates how good works will produce good karma, while the sins of the Jews will eventually bring forth the wrath of God (Rom 2:3, 5, 9). For Paul, though the Jews judge others as sinners, they also commit the same sins listed in Romans 1:29–31. The Jews, who are "instructed by the law" (Rom 2:1), also steal though they preach against stealing (2:21); they commit adultery though they speak against adultery (Rom 2:22). Therefore, the presence of sin is also evident among the Jews. Though the Jews boast in their law, they break the law (Rom 2:23) and commit sins. Therefore, Paul emphatically concludes in Romans 3:9, "For we have already charged that all, both Jews and Greeks are under sin." This functions as the key theme of the passage (Rom 1:18–3:20). Therefore, the Jews also sin, and therefore, they also are susceptible to the wrath of God (Rom 2:5).

Further, Paul moves on to explain why and how the Jews are sinners. In Romans 3:10–18, he uses many quotations from the Jewish Scriptures to show how all (both Jews and gentiles) are sinners in their flesh. This also provides a way to strengthen Paul's thesis that the source of sinfulness of the human being could be traced to the flesh of the human beings, which he will bring forward in Romans 7:14–25. In Romans 3:13–18, Paul points out the sins that are present in the throat (13), tongue (13), lips (13), mouth (14), feet (15), and eyes (18). Therefore, Paul quotes Psalm 14:1–3 and 53:1–3 to state, "None is righteous, no, not one." In this way, he proves that both the Jews and the gentiles are not made righteous by the law or by idol worship, respectively. In Romans 3:21–31, Paul stresses that a person can be justified by having faith in Jesus Christ.

In Indian philosophy, a human soul (*atman*) is considered caught in the material world (*maya*). This *maya* is similar to the evil material world of Platonic thought. The goal of the *atman* is to be released from the unending rebirth called samsara in the material world of *maya*. In other words, the ultimate destiny of the *atman* is to be released from samsara and to be enjoined with the all-encompassing universal spirit, called *Brahman*.[38] This

38 Klaus K. Klostermaier, *A Survey of Hinduism*, 3rd ed. (Albany: State University of New York Press, 2007), 166–67.

is equivalent to salvation in Christianity. There are many philosophical traditions in Hinduism, which emphasize several ways of attaining salvation or release (i.e., *moksha*).

The three common ways of attaining salvation are called *gnana*, karma, and *bakhti margas* (*marga* means way).[39] In *gnana marga*, when a person knows that his/her soul (*atman*) is part of the universal soul (*Brahman*) through knowledge (*gnana*) and through yoga, he/she can attain this release from rebirth and *maya*.[40] In *gnana marga*, the devotee should leave his/her home, live an ascetic life, and practice concentrated meditation for years. In karma *marga*, a person may have to perform dharma (duties) to attain good karma so that he/she can be born in a higher caste in the next birth.[41] Through several rebirths and through continually fulfilling the dharma, and by performing other good works such as giving alms to the Brahmin (highest caste person), the individual may be able to attain *moksha*. This may take several births and sometimes even thousands of births. The third is *bakhti marga*. In the *Bhagavad Gita*, Krishna says to Arjuna that a person could attain *moksha* by showing *bakti* (devotion) to Krishna (*Bhagavad Gita* 12.9). By having undivided devotion to the deity, a person could attain *moksha*, according to *bakhti marga*.

Though these are the three popular philosophical traditions showing different routes to the same end, there are also a few other philosophical trends that show different paths as ways of resistance movements to the three *margas*.[42] For example, Charvaka philosophy (from the eighth to twelfth centuries CE) said that the material world is not *maya* and therefore is not evil.[43] The ultimate goal of this life is not to get the release from this world but to enjoy this world.[44] This is similar to Cyrenaics of the Greeks, who

39 Mariasusai Dhavamony, *Hindu Spirituality* (Rome: Editrice Pontificia Università Gregoriana, 1999), 23–24.

40 Klostermaier, *Survey of Hinduism*, 167.

41 There are four major caste classifications in Hinduism: Brahman, Kshatriyas, Vaishyas, and Shudras (in hierarchical, descending order).

42 Braj Ranjan Mani, *Debrahmanising History: Dominance and Resistance in Indian Society* (Delhi: Manohar, 2005).

43 Wendy Doniger, *Against Dharma: Dissent in the Ancient Indian Sciences of Sex and Politics* (New Haven, CT: Yale University Press, 2018), 124–25.

44 Y. V. Satyanarayana, *Ethics: Theory and Practice* (Delhi: Pearson, 2010), 30.

emphasized "eating, drinking and being merry."[45] Another interesting philosophy that came as a resistance movement was called Aghorism.[46] In this movement, the sadhus (saints) rearranged the purity codes of the Brahmanical philosophies to point out that all things in this world are pure and holy. In one sense, the *aghoris* (saints) inverted the purity codes of the Brahmins. Though the *aghoris* may be seen as a subsect of the *gnana marga*, due to their austere lifestyle, they practice things that were regarded as disgusting by the higher-caste sadhus. The *aghoris* would eat anything that is described as unclean by the Aryan system. They would eat dirt, corpses, and anything else.[47] This was regarded as giving power for them because they assumed all things are pure and clean. They would even have tantric sex with a menstruating woman, who was considered unclean by the Brahmins. In the history of Hindu philosophy, there seem to be several philosophies that come together and form what is known as Hinduism. No one form takes precedence, and no one form rejects the other as a heresy, but each one is seen as a path to the same goal.[48] However, in Romans, Paul emphasizes that his Gospel and his way (i.e., by faith in Jesus Christ) are the means of attaining salvation.

The Gospel, the Way

In Romans 3:23, Paul summarizes his argument made in Romans 1:18–3:20 as follows: "All have sinned and fall short of the glory of God." In Romans 3:29, he says God is the God of both Jews and the gentiles. Therefore, God must have only one means of justification for both Jews and the gentiles (Rom 3:30). For Paul, as there is no distinction, the righteousness of God is made available to all "through faith in Jesus Christ for all who believe" (Rom 3:22). This justification is actualized through the grace of God (Rom 3:24). This justification is an act of "redemption" of God through Christ (Rom 3:24). God actualized this by making Jesus as the propitiation, by his blood, so that

45 Everett Ferguson, *Backgrounds of Early Christianity* (Grand Rapids, MI: Eerdmans, 1987), 295–96.

46 Robert L. Hardgrave, *Portrait of the Hindus: Balthazar Solvyns and the European Image of India, 1760–1824* (Oxford: Oxford University Press, 2004), 257.

47 Hardgrave, 259.

48 This could be considered an overstatement in one sense, but this is applicable to most of the philosophical traditions of Hinduism.

this gift of God (i.e., justification) could be received by the believer in faith. In this way, God's righteousness is revealed to all. God, with his righteousness (i.e., through the righteousness of Christ) and by the death of Christ on the cross, made us righteous through his blood so we may be declared righteous by simply believing in him rather than working out for salvation.

An important theme running through Romans 3:21–31 is that the righteousness of God was not available through obedience to the law (Rom 3:21, 28, 31) but was acquired through faith in Jesus Christ. For Paul, this ultimate justification is manifested "apart from the law although it was witnessed in the law and prophets" (Rom 3:21). Paul stresses that this justification is given apart from the law and that it is given through faith in Jesus Christ. In this way, God's righteousness is made universal, where both Jews and gentiles are justified through this faith. Therefore, Paul stresses that righteousness for all is received neither through idol worship nor through obedience to the law but through faith in Jesus Christ. In this way, Paul seems to counter the idea of karma. For Paul, one cannot receive righteousness through the obedience of the law but by faith in Christ alone.

FOLLOWING THE ELDERS AND FOLLOWING THE GOSPEL

In chapter 4, Paul shows that even Abraham and David authenticated the Gospel that emphasized justification by faith. In Asian societies, respecting elders is given a significant place.[49] The high respect given to elders results in the conviction that things decided by the forefathers are considered unbreakable or even infallible.[50] When the elders decide something, the younger ones simply follow them. In addition, the community is expected to follow the tradition of the forefathers.[51] In Romans 4:3, Paul supports the statement that Abraham was declared righteous by faith with a quotation from Genesis 15:6. He connects this from the previous verse, saying Abraham was not justified

49 Sarah Lamb, *White Saris and Sweet Mangoes: Aging, Gender, and Body in North India* (Berkeley: University of California Press, 2000), 65–67.

50 William Theodore De Bary, ed., *Sources of East Asian Tradition: The Modern Period* (New York: Columbia University Press, 2008), 2:292.

51 Kyu-t'ak Sŏng, *Respect and Care for the Elderly: The East Asian Way* (Lanham, MD: University Press of America, 2007), 65.

by works of the law (Rom 4:2). Abraham goes through circumcision in Genesis 17 (works of the law), but he is identified as one who receives righteousness (Gen 15:6). Both these chapters are about God ratifying the covenant with Abraham. However, before the obedience of the law (i.e., circumcision) in Genesis 17, Abraham was already justified by having faith (Gen 15:6). Therefore, Paul says Abraham is made righteous not by the law but by faith. Abraham, the father of the Jewish nation, is set as an example for Paul's Gospel, which stressed becoming righteous by faith alone.

Similarly, Paul quotes David from Psalm 32:1–2 to show that "blessed is the man against whom the Lord will not count his sins" (Rom 4:8). By this quotation, Paul could have implied that David's sins were forgiven not by the law but by his faith. Therefore, the readers ought to acknowledge that the message of their forefathers who emphasized justification by faith validated Paul's Gospel.

HOPE IN THE MIDST OF SUFFERING

Romans 5 could be regarded as Paul's enunciation of the advantages of believing in the Gospel. He gives three major benefits in believing in the Gospel. Believers have peace with God (Rom 5:1; 6–11), receive grace (Rom 5:2a; 12–21a), and have hope (Rom 5:2b–5; 21b). In this chapter, Paul uses a parallel structure such as A, B, C, A^1, B^1, C^1 (Peace [1]; Grace [2a]; Hope [2–5]; *Peace* [6–11]; *Grace* [12–21a]; and *Eternal life* [Hope: 21b]). Paul departs from his usual chiasmic structure and creates this beautiful pericope with parallels emphasizing the benefits of receiving his Gospel.

In 5:1, Paul says that by having been justified by faith in our Lord Jesus Christ, we have peace with God. This peace was brought by Christ, who died for us when we were still his enemies (Rom 5:10). In addition, through faith, we have access to his grace (Rom 5:2) that abounded all the more (Rom 5:20) to make many righteous (Rom 5:19). Whereas sin and death came through one man (Rom 5:12), Jesus's death and righteousness brought forth grace, which brought forth justification to all who believe in him (Rom 5:16). These lead to the third major benefit of receiving Paul's Gospel, the hope of the glory of God. The hope of the glory of God could be considered to be the hope of receiving eternal life (Rom 5:21). For Paul, through the Gospel, the believer is assured of the gift of eternal life. However, the realization of this hope is not easy or automatic. Paul says hope is achieved through character (Rom 5:4b), character is produced by endurance (Rom 5:4a), and endurance is produced by suffering (Rom 5:3b). Therefore, for Paul, we must rejoice in suffering because it leads us to the hope of the glory of God (Rom 5:3). Buddhism's ultimate goal is to end the suffering of this world. The Four Noble Truths of Buddhism are as follows: first, the existence of suffering (*dukka*); second, the reason for suffering (*samudaya*); third, the cessation of suffering (*nirodha*); and fourth, the way leading to that cessation of suffering (*marga* or *magga*).[52] However, for Paul, suffering is the way to the hope of the glory of God.

Asians live in a context of persecution. According to ADF India, there are 292 cases of persecution in India in 2018 compared to 147 incidents reported in 2014.[53] Christians in India today are going through organized persecution more than ever before in history. The vigilantism of Saffron parties in India targets house churches and smaller Christian groups, destroys the properties, and engages in violence against Christians. In August 2007, in Kandhamal district in Odisha, India, Christians in several villages underwent large-scale persecution. At that time, "more than 600 villages were ransacked, 5,600 houses were looted and burnt, 54,000 people were left homeless . . . [and] at least 39 Christians were killed and 232 churches destroyed, though human rights groups quote higher numbers."[54] These records amply inform us of the hard situations of the Christian communities in Asia.

In addition, Christians in communist-ruled China have been going through oppression for several years. The *Guardian* reported on January 13, 2019, "In China, they are closing churches, jailing pastors—and even rewriting scripture. China's Communist party is intensifying religious persecution as Christianity's popularity grows."[55] The *Christian Post* reported on January 5, 2020, "China announced it will soon implement harsh new

52 Masao Abe, "Buddhism," in *Our Religions*, ed. Arvind Sharma (New York: HarperOne, 1993), 86.

53 Vijesh Lal, *Persecution Conference*, UBS Pune, December 2–4, 2019.

54 "'They Don't Feel Sorry': Revisiting Kandhamal 10 Years after the Violence against Christians," Scroll.in, accessed February 1, 2020, https://tinyurl.com/b65uwzn4.

55 "In China, They Are Closing Churches, Jailing Pastors—and Even Rewriting Scripture," *Guardian*, accessed February 1, 2020, https://www.theguardian.com/world/2019/jan/13/china-christians-religious-persecution-translation-bible.

measures requiring all religious personnel to support and implement total submission to the Chinese Communist Party, sparking concern among Chinese Christians."[56] In this context, Paul's words would come to life for the Asian Christians. Paul says we must rejoice in suffering as it leads one to endurance, which will produce character, which will further produce the hope of the glory of God. He then assures that believers will not be put to shame, as they will attain the hope by the help of the Holy Spirit and by loving one another (Rom 5:5).[57]

SANCTIFICATION: THE ART OF HOLY LIVING

In Romans 1–3, Paul emphasizes justification by faith in Christ alone. In chapters 4 and 5, he showed the importance of this Gospel. From chapter 6 onward, he clarifies how justified persons should live a sanctified life.[58] In Romans 6–7, Paul concentrates on the question of whether a Christian can continue in sin after being justified by faith. Paul's answer is an emphatic no. In Romans 6:1–7:6, Paul gives three ways a justified person could continue living a holy life: first, by being dead to sin (Rom 6:1–14); second, by being a slave to righteousness (Rom 6:15–23); and third, by being free from the law (Rom 7:1–6). Romans 6:1 and Romans 15 show that Paul is writing strongly against a hypergrace ideology. For Paul, because a believer is made righteous by having faith in Christ, they should not assume that they have attained perfection and continue in sin. For him, the believer should now make conscious efforts to be holy (Rom 6:2).

For Paul, by being dead to sin, a believer can avoid sin reigning in the mortal body (Rom 6:12). Is this an automatic result of believing in Christ?

56 "China Imposes Harsh New Rules Governing Religious Groups in 2020," *Christian Post*, accessed February 1, 2020, https://www.christianpost.com/news/china-imposes-harsh-new-rules-governing-religious-groups-in-2020.html.

57 "And hope does not put us to shame, because *God's love* has been poured into our hearts through the *Holy Spirit* who has been given to us" (Rom 5:5; emphasis mine).

58 An exception to this is Romans 9–11. In 7:7–25, he addresses the role of law in the sanctification process. From Romans 8, he deals with being holy by fulfilling the law through Spirit and love. Therefore, from Romans 6:1 onward, Paul deals with the art of holy living (i.e., sanctification).

Paul says being dead to sin means "not presenting the members of the body to sin as instruments for unrighteousness" (13a). Moreover, the believers must present themselves and their "members to God as instruments of righteousness" (13b and c). These imperatives in Romans 6:13 show that the believer is exhorted to consciously put efforts to act so that they can live a holy life. Consequently, holy living is not passive sanctification or auto sanctification, where a believer does not do anything to be holy. In addition, Paul does not use active verbs to exhort them to live a holy life. He does not say that holy living involves active sanctification, where a believer puts in much effort to live a holy life. Paul's language in Romans 6:1–7:6 includes concepts like being dead to sin and being a slave to righteousness. There is an active element there, but it is also presented as passive activity. Therefore, Paul is quite careful to say that holiness is not a purely human effort. For him, being holy is guided sanctification, which involves being guided by the Spirit and love in the sanctification process (Rom 8; 12–15).

How can the believer be dead to sin? In South Asia, *biriyani* is a famous dish. It includes meat and rice cooked together with a variety of spices. The aroma of biriyani with all the spices is enticing and salivating. South Asians may get tempted to eat biriyani if they are alive and the dish is kept in front of them. However, if they are dead, there will be no salivating or urge to eat the biriyani. Similarly, Paul wants the believer to be holy by being dead to sin so the members of the body will not be tempted by sin. This involves conscious efforts from the believer.

Similarly, in Romans 6:15–23, Paul says until one received Christ he was a slave to sin (6:16–17). However, by obeying the teachings of the Gospel (Rom 6:17), when he is justified by faith in Christ, he is set free from sin and becomes a slave of righteousness (6:18). Likewise, Paul uses the imagery of divorce to show how to be holy apart from the law in Romans 7:1–6. For him, one cannot be holy by being under the law (Rom 7:5). Being holy means being released from the condemnation of the law (Rom 7:4, 6). Hence Paul uses an imagery of divorce to stress that as the believer is dead to the law, the law is now dead to the believer. Consequently, the believer can live a holy life by being released from the law and by "serving in the new way of the Spirit" (Rom 7:6). This is further explained in Romans 8.

For Paul, the law cannot bring forth holiness in the life of a believer. Paul frequently makes mention of the negative aspects of the law in his epistles (Rom 3:20; 5:20; 6:14; 7:5; 7:7; 7:8; 10:4; Gal 3:13, 21–22). If so, why was the law given? For Paul, the law was given for cognitive and causative purposes;[59] cognitive because the law brought forth the knowledge of sin (Rom 3:20; 7:7), and causative because it produced "all kinds of covetousness" in us (Rom 7:8; see also 5:20). For him, the law was never given for justification.

Paul shows that it was not the law that brought forth sin; it was the sin in the flesh that brought forth sins (Rom 7:13). The law does not have the power to transform the flesh or sin. When a person in the flesh is confronted by the law, more sin is produced, so the sin will be made visible, and the person will be identified as a sinner. Only a sinner could look for a Savior. Moreover, Paul brings forth another person along with Christ in Romans 8, the Spirit. For Paul, in Christ, the believer is set free from the bondage of sins as the Spirit transforms the flesh and brings forth holiness by helping in the fulfillment of all the requirements of the law.

PNEUMATIC NOMISM

In Romans 6:1–7:6, Paul shows the importance of believers living a holy life. In Romans 8 and 12–15, he shows how a believer could successfully live a holy life. For him, though obedience to the law is not the basis for salvation, the believer must fulfill the requirements of the law to be holy.[60]

In Romans 8, Paul brings in the Spirit as the agent who could help the believer in living a holy life. The law is not able to help the believer because it cannot transform the flesh (8:3). However, the Spirit is able to help the believer because it is the Spirit of life. In Romans 8:3–4, Paul introduces a series of phrases through which he is conveying some important truths. He says what the law could not do (i.e., bring forth obedience), God did through the sending of his own Son. By sending him in the likeness of sinful flesh and by offering him as an offering for sin, he condemned sin in the flesh so the requirement of the law will be fulfilled in us (8:3–4). It means that our

59 Richard Longenecker, *Galatians*, Word Biblical Commentary 41 (Grand Rapids, MI: Zondervan, 1990), 138–39.

60 E. P. Sanders, *Paul, the Law, and the Jewish People* (Minneapolis: Fortress, 1983), 93–114.

sanctification process is complete in the death of Jesus Christ. However, Paul continues in saying the fulfillment of the requirements of the law happens in the believers "who do not walk according to the flesh but according to the Spirit" (8:4). This means though the fulfillment of the requirement of the law is complete through the death of Jesus Christ, the realization of the holiness in the believer happens only when the believer "walks according to the Spirit and not according to the flesh." This means the believer is required to do his/her part when God had done his part (i.e., sending the Son to die on the cross). It also means there are some imperatives involved in the sanctification process. Inferentially, the believer is expected to live in a certain way to bring forth the realization of the holiness in the life of the believer. This could be considered as imperative for the fulfillment of the law. In addition, as the Spirit is the one who helps in the fulfillment of the law, it is possible to call this obedience pneumatic nomism (*pneuma*, Spirit; *nomism*, obedience of the law).

For Paul, the requirements of the law must be fulfilled in the life of the believer in the sanctification process (Rom 8:3–4). In addition, one cannot obey the law on their own because the law applied directly to the flesh will bring forth only sins. However, the law obeyed with the help of the Spirit would bring forth fulfillment of the requirements of the law (Rom 7:6; Gal 5:18–24). This is called pneumatic nomism (fulfilling the law with the help of the Spirit). How could the believer fulfill the requirements of the law with the help of the Spirit? The believer is expected to "walk according to the Spirit" (*Pneumatic Peripateism*; Rom 8:4). This involves conscious walking according to the Spirit and not according to the flesh (Rom 8:4). This is not a passive activity but a guided walking where, with the help of the Spirit, the believer consciously walks in the direction of the Spirit (Gal 5:17) so that he/she can avoid sinfulness. Further, Paul says the believers must not set their mind on the things of the flesh but on the things of the Spirit (*Pneumatic Phroneoism*; Rom 8:5).[61] He says, "For the mind set on the flesh is death, but the mind set on the Spirit is life and peace" (Rom 8:6; also Gal 6:7–8). Therefore, the believer can live a holy life by setting his/her mind on the things of the Spirit.

61 In Colossians 3:2, Paul says, "Set your mind on the things above, not on the things that are on earth."

In Zoroastrianism, one can be holy by having "pure thoughts, pure words, and pure deeds." Zoroaster says, "It is these that lead us to salvation. If you will always keep your thoughts pure, that is, if you will think of nothing but what is true and proper, and if after such true and good thoughts you will speak nothing but the truth, and if after speaking nothing but the truth you will do nothing but what is good and righteous, the Ahura Mazda [the chief god] will reward you for all that, you will pass a happy life."[62] Similarly, in Buddhism, the first of the *Ariya Atthangika Magga* (the Noble Eightfold Path) is "right thought," which would bring forth "right understanding," which would further lead to "right speech," "right actions," "right livelihood," "right effort," "right mindfulness," and finally, "right concentration" (i.e., the state of enlightenment). Therefore, in Buddhism, right thoughts lead a person to enlightenment (i.e., salvation in Buddhism). However, in both Zoroastrianism and Buddhism, there is no agent like the Spirit (as in Pauline thought) to enable and empower the believer to facilitate right thought. For Paul, the Spirit empowers the believer when they keep the mind on the Spirit so that they can live a holy life.

In Romans 8:8–11, Paul points out that the believer should be in the Spirit and not in the flesh (*En Pneumati*).[63] If the believers are in the flesh, they cannot please God (Rom 8:8). When the believer dwells in the Spirit, the Spirit will dwell in the believer and will also help in the transformation. For the people in Wetu Telu of Lombok in Indonesia, the ancestral spirits help people in every way.[64] However, to seek help, they need to contact the spirits by reciting a secret formula, which is called a mantra. In addition, they need "certain power transferring media" such as betel, sacred water, and sacred cloths.[65] They also need religious officials who can help in contacting the spirits.[66] However, for Paul, the Holy Spirit lives in the believer. As the Spirit dwells in the believer, the believer also lives in the Spirit. Therefore, there is no need for an external

62 Cited in James Bisset Pratt, "Parsees," in *India and Its Faith* (New York: Cosimo, 2005), 322.

63 See also 1 Cor 3:16 and 1 Cor 6:19.

64 Sven Cederroth, "Gods and Spirits in the Wetu Telu Religion of Lombok," in *Animism in Southeast Asia*, ed. Kaj Arhem and Guido Sprenger (New York: Routledge, 2016), 238.

65 Cederroth, 238.

66 Cederroth, 239.

agent or "power transferring media." The Spirit is readily available to enable the believer to live a holy life.

In Romans 8:12–13, Paul uses more imagery: living according to the Spirit and not according to the flesh (*Pneumatic Zoeism*). In Romans 8:13, he says that the believer must put his/her deeds of the flesh to death (*Pneumatic Thanatism*; Rom 8:13; see also Col 3:5–10). In Romans 8:13, Paul says the believer must kill the deeds of the body. A possible comparison could be a Cowboy shooting a gun at something that pops up. Similarly, when believers find a deed of the flesh rising up, they should shoot and kill the deed to remain holy. The Holy Spirit will help in this regard as well (Rom 8:13). Further, in Romans 8:14, Paul says that to keep oneself holy, the believer must be led constantly by the Spirit of God (*Pneumatic Agomaism*[67]).

In the animist worldview of the Katu people of central Vietnam, spirits are consulted to help with their needs.[68] The spirits for the Katu people are omnipresent, and therefore, nothing important is done without consulting them.[69] However, Nikolas Arhem says, "The spirits help the villagers but also demand their due."[70] In contrast, for Paul, the Spirit helps the believer live a holy life just because they believe in the Gospel. The believer needs not appease the Spirit by donating human blood or a sacrifice.[71] For Paul, the Holy Spirit is the moral guide for the believer and helps them to live a holy life.

Through Romans 8:14, Paul explains how the Holy Spirit helps a believer to be holy. Further, in the remainder of the chapter, Paul narrates the other functions of the Holy Spirit. As the Holy Spirit helps the believer to be holy, it also testifies who the children of God are (Rom 8:14). The Spirit helps the believer cry out to God as "Abba! Father!" (Rom 8:15; Gal 4:6). The Holy Spirit testifies with our spirit that we are the children of God (Rom 8:16;

67 Derived from the passive form of *agō*.

68 Kaj Arhem, "Animism and Hunter's Dilemma," in *Animism in Southeast Asia*, ed. Kaj Arhem and Guido Sprenger (New York: Routledge, 2016), 91.

69 Arhem, 91.

70 Nikolas Arhem, "Wrestling with Spirits, Escaping the State," in *Animism in Southeast Asia*, ed. Kaj Arhem and Guido Sprenger (New York: Routledge, 2016), 115.

71 Like a person called Balang Pelaba from Sarawak, Malaysia, was asked by the Great Spirit (Pun Tumid) to sacrifice human blood to help him in his endeavors. Monica Janowski, "The Dynamic of the Cosmic Conversation," in *Animism in Southeast Asia*, ed. Kaj Arhem and Guido Sprenger (New York: Routledge, 2016), 189.

Heb 10:15–18). Further, the Spirit helps in our adoption as the children of God (Rom 8:16). The whole creation is waiting to see the adoption of the children of God (Rom 8:19). This will happen at the time of the redemption of our bodies (Rom 8:23). The Spirit helps in the adoption by continually interceding for us (Rom 26–28; 1 Cor 2:10–15). Moreover, in the context of the Spirit's activity in the life of the believer, it is better to know that the Spirit also helps the believer in the process of perfection. Paul says, "For those whom he foreknew, he also predestined . . . and those whom he predestined, he also called; and those whom he called, he also justified; and those whom he justified, he also glorified" (Rom 8:30). Hence the Spirit helps in the perfection of the believer.

Therefore, in Romans 8, Paul shows how the Spirit helps a believer in being holy and how it helps the believer in the adoption and in the perfection process. Paul may be expected to continue his explanation on how to be holy by loving one another, as he has done in the book of Galatians.[72] However, Paul takes a diversion and concentrates on the status of the Jews in Romans 9–11.[73] In Romans 9–11, he deals with the status of the Jews in the plan of God. For him, just because salvation has come to everyone who believes in Jesus Christ, the Jews by birth are not rejected by God. For Paul, God's promise of salvation is not given to Abraham's children through flesh but to the children of the promise (9:6–9). In addition, God's promised salvation was not given to Israel as a whole, but only to the chosen and called from among Israel and the

72 In Galatians, through 5:12, Paul explains how a person is justified by faith and not by the works of the Law. And from 5:13 onward, he brings being led by the Spirit and loving one another as the two ways the believer could live a holy life. Interestingly, he keeps them in parallels as follows:

> 5:13–15, Loving one another
> *5:16–26, Walk in the Spirit*
> 6:1–6, Loving one another; restoring the brother
> *6:7–8, To sow in the Spirit and reap in the Spirit*
> 6:9–10, Loving one another; to fulfill the law by doing good to others

73 When Paul asserts that no one can separate the believer from the love of Christ (8:35), he must have thought about the status of the Jews. And he must address the status of the Jews in detail. Therefore, he concentrates on the Jews in Romans 9–11 and then he comes back to being holy by loving one another in Romans 12–15.

gentiles (9:10–33). God sent his prophets to Israel, but they rejected him and his salvation (10:1–21). However, God will not leave Israel. A remnant such as Paul and others received God's promised salvation through faith and not through works (11:1–10). For Paul, when the fullness of the gentiles has come in, Israel will eventually be saved (11:11–36).

BE HOLY BY LOVING ONE ANOTHER

From Romans 12 onward, Paul describes loving one another as one of the two ways of sanctification. If Romans 9–11 is a digression, Romans 12:1 should have followed Romans 8, which dealt with the other way of sanctification (i.e., fulfilling the law with the help of the Spirit). In Romans 12:3–8, he asks the Roman church leaders to give opportunity to all believers in using their gifts in the church. In 12:9–21, Paul exhorts them to do good to all. In 13:1–7, he asks the believers to submit to the governing authorities. In 13:8–14, he asks them to be holy by loving one another. In 14:1–15:13, he exhorts the majority to accept the weak brethren and accommodate them. In all these, loving one another is the strong theme that unites them all. Moreover, Romans 13:8–14 shows Paul's exhortation on fulfilling the law by loving one another (*agapal* nomism), which is similar to Paul's teaching on fulfilling the law by the Spirit (Rom 8).

In Romans 13:8, Paul says, "The one who loves another has fulfilled the law." For him, the law must be fulfilled in the life of the believer. This is not a onetime event but something that must be practiced continuously by the believer. Paul explains it further by using certain laws from the Ten Commandments, such as "You shall not commit adultery, you shall not murder, you shall not steal, and you shall not covet" (13:9). For him, all these commandments are connected with loving one another. If the believer loves his neighbor, he would not commit adultery with his wife or covet his property. Similarly, if he loves him, he would not murder him or steal from him. For Paul, the believer could live a holy life by fulfilling the laws through loving one another (Rom 13:10).

If McKnight is right, then most of the things Paul writes in Romans are connected to the gentile-Jewish problem in Roman churches.[74] Romans was

74 McKnight, *Reading Romans Backwards*, 1–19.

possibly written at a time when the expelled Jews (at the time of Claudius, at 49 CE) were returning to Rome in the time of Emperor Nero.[75] McKnight says, "If we date Romans right in that time period, the tension between returning Jewish believers and the empowered Gentile believers is all but a certainty."[76] It is possible that the strong gentile believers despised the weak Jewish believers.[77] Therefore, Paul exhorts the Roman church to accommodate the weak (Rom 15:1–7) and share responsibilities with them in the church (Rom 12:3–8).

Paul exhorts his Roman believers "not to think of themselves more highly than one ought to think" (Rom 12:3). He is possibly addressing the so-called strong believers in the church. The strong should not be proud but they must be humble. Thirukkural 978 says, "The great will always humble himself in self-admiration." If the strong should be identified as strong, they must humble themselves. The strong gentiles should have accommodated the weaker Jews in the church by utilizing their talents and gifts (Rom 12:6). In many parts of Asia, casteism and classism divide the people and polarize them. The powerful people in the church do not share responsibilities with the low caste or lower-class people. However, for Paul, both the strong and the weak are equal members of one body in Christ (Rom 12:5). Therefore, he exhorts the strong to accommodate the weak and to share power by loving one another. In addition, in Romans 12:9–21, Paul shares many exhortations, but a key theme that runs through these exhortations is loving one another. For Thiruvalluvar, love is essential to righteous living (*Kural* 76). He says, "The ignorant says that love is an ally to virtue only but it is also a help to get out of vice." This means that similar to Paul, Thiruvalluvar says through love, people can keep themselves holy.

In Asia, Christians in many countries live under persecution either directly sanctioned by the government or indirectly targeted at the Christians. For these Christians, Paul's words about submitting to the governing authorities are very important. For Paul, the governing authorities are "instituted by God" (Rom 13:1). Here Paul stresses the sovereignty of God, and even the rulers are instituted by God (13:4).[78] For him, as the rulers facilitate good conduct, the

75 McKnight, 18.
76 McKnight, 18.
77 McKnight, 19.
78 Richard N. Longenecker, *The Epistle to the Romans*, NIGTC (Grand Rapids, MI: Eerdmans, 2016), 960.

believers should not have any problem in obeying them. Particularly, this submission should be extended by paying taxes to the government (Rom 13:7).[79] In several parts of Asia, submitting to the persecuting governments is a concern for present-day Christians. Paul's logic in exhorting the believers to obey the government lies in his stress that the government he is referring to is "not a terror to good conduct but to bad" (Rom 13:3). In Romans 13, he is not exhorting his Roman audience to submit to an oppressive government. It is not clear what Paul would have said regarding an oppressive government.

We are living in a world where the majority and the powerful dominate the others. In most cases, the powerful dictate the terms for the others. When the majority comes to power and dictates terms against the minority and powerless, the powerless are oppressed or even persecuted. McKnight shows how the gentile majority in the Roman churches could have taken power from the Jewish leaders who were fleeing Rome because of the decree of Emperor Claudius.[80] The "return" of the former leaders to the church could have created "tensions" among the present gentile leaders.[81] The ones in power at the time of writing seem to be reluctant in sharing it with the minority. The powerful may not have given opportunity to the minority to practice their gifts in their fullest capacity in the church (Rom 12:5–11). In addition, the powerful majority could have imposed rules about eating non-kosher food on the Jewish minority (Rom 14:1–6). For Paul, both observing the day and eating certain kinds of food are not major problems because both are done for the Lord (Rom 14:16). Therefore, Paul exhorts that the majority should not "put an obstacle or a stumbling block in a brother's way" (Rom 14:3). He says, "For if because of food your brother is hurt, you are no longer walking according to love" (Rom 14:15). Paul again brings the imperative of love to exhort the majority to accommodate the minority.

Majoritarian politics is commonly seen in the world today. In the book called *Majoritarian State*, the authors identify how majoritarian politics oppress the minorities in India.[82] This could be extended to a few other Asian

79 McKnight, *Reading Romans Backwards*, 8.

80 McKnight, 8.

81 McKnight, 9.

82 Angana P. Chatterji, Thomas Blom Hansen, and Christophe Jaffrelot, *Majoritarian State: How Hindu Nationalism Is Changing India* (Oxford: Oxford University Press, 2019).

countries such as China, Israel, Syria, and the like. Christophe Jaffrelot says, "Ethnic democracy is first the product of ethnic nationalism, the ideology of a majoritarian group based on racial, linguistic, religious or, more generally speaking, cultural characteristics that implies a strong sense of belonging and often superiority. This identity goes along with a rejection of the minorities, generally perceived as threats to the survival and integrity of the ethnic nation."[83] The minorities are branded as terrorists or proselytizers.[84] They are persecuted in the name of vigilantism, cow protection, protection of the majority's religion, and more. Some are beaten up, even to the point of being killed.[85] Laws are changed to restrict or oppress the minority. If the situation continues, the minority will be persecuted badly while the majority will enjoy the power at the expense of the minority.

Paul, addressing the majoritarian politics in the Roman church, says that the strong should accommodate the weak (Rom 15:1). Further, he says the strong should build up the weak (Rom 15:2). He introduces Christ as the example who gave himself up for humanity (Rom 15:3). The strong should not trample or oppress the weak. Paul envisions a world where both strong and weak, majority and minorities, live "in harmony with one another," loving one another and building up one another so "God and the Father of our Lord Jesus Christ will be glorified."

In Confucianism, the term *sheng* is considered as holiness or sanctification.[86] A sheng-jen is a holy person or sage.[87] For Confucius, "the perfect moral character of a sage" is reflected in loving one another.[88] *The Analects* says, "Fan Chih [a disciple of Confucius] asked about 'Jen.' The Master [Confucius] said 'Love your fellow men'" (Confucius, *The Analects* 12.22). Seung-an Im says, "The Confucianists believed that the way to be 'sheng' [holy] does not depend

83 Christophe Jaffrelot, "A De Facto Ethnic Democracy? Obliterating and Targeting the Other, Hindu Vigilantes and the Ethno State," in *Majoritarian State: How Hindu Nationalism Is Changing India*, ed. Angana P. Chatterji, Thomas Blom Hansen, and Christophe Jaffrelot (Oxford: Oxford University Press, 2019), 42.

84 Jaffrelot, 64–65.

85 Jaffrelot, 64.

86 Seung-an Im, "A Dialogue between Wesley and Confucius on the Theme of Sanctification," *Didache: Faithful Teaching* 4, no. 1 (June 2004): 7.

87 Im, 8.

88 Im, 7–8.

on some mysterious spiritual power, but on humanity itself."[89] However, for Paul, loving others alone is not enough to be holy. The believers should also be guided by the Spirit. Through addressing these issues, Paul presented his Gospel with a strong exhortation to love another and live in harmony "for the glory of God."

CONCLUSION

Paul's epistle to the Romans is structured in such a way that Paul could establish the equality of the Jews and gentiles in sin, redemption, justification, and sanctification. For Paul, all were sinners (1:18–3:20). When a person believes in Jesus, they are justified (3:21–31). This saved person should live a holy life (Rom 6–7). The Holy Spirit is given to help the believer live a holy life (Rom 8). In addition, the believer should love others and live in harmony "for the glory of God" (Rom 12–15). This whole presentation of the Gospel could be called Paul's exhortation to live a holy life through loving one another and through the help of the Spirit. This message is needed even today. In many parts of the world, borders are closed toward "others," and violence is promoted against minorities. Paul's message of being holy through loving one another is important for Asia today. The minorities should be loved and accepted. The powerless should be accommodated. These words should be voiced loudly in Asia and beyond.

FURTHER READING

Käsemann, E. 1994. *Commentary on Romans*. Grand Rapids, MI: Eerdmans.

Keener, C. S. 2009. *Romans: A New Covenant Commentary*. NCC 6. Eugene, OR: Cascade.

Kruse, C. G. 2012. *Paul's Letter to the Romans*. PNTC. Grand Rapids, MI: Eerdmans.

Lawrence, A. B. 2016. *Legalistic Nomism: A Socio-rhetorical Reading of Paul's Letter to the Galatians*. Delhi: ISPCK.

89 Im, 8.

McKnight, S. 2019. *Reading Romans Backwards: A Gospel of Peace in the Midst of Empire*. Waco, TX: Baylor University Press.
Moo, D. J. 1996. *The Epistle to the Romans*. NICNT. Grand Rapids, MI: Eerdmans.
Schreiner, T. R. 1998. *Romans*. BECNT. Grand Rapids, MI: Baker Academic.
Talbert, C. H. 2002. *Romans*. SHBC. Macon, GA: Smyth & Helwys.
Thielman, F. 1994. *Paul and the Law: A Contextual Approach*. Downers Grove, IL: InterVarsity.
Witherington, B. 2003. *Paul's Letter to the Romans: A Socio-rhetorical Commentary*. Grand Rapids, MI: Eerdmans.
Wright, N. T. 2004. *Paul for Everyone: Romans*. 2 vols. Louisville: Westminster John Knox.

NINE

The Letters to the Corinthians

Rolex M. Cailing
Asia Graduate School of Theology
Quezon City, Philippines

The Christian life is about transformation. Paul's answers and counsel to the issues raised in the Christ-assembly in Corinth may assist Asian Christ-assemblies in discovering a more genuine vision for community life and for leadership practices in the church. Paul's letters to the Christ-assembly in Corinth are still in many ways as relevant today as they were when he wrote them. The competitive, social-climbing, status-obsessed, morally decadent society and cultural ideologies of the Greco-Roman world of Paul's time have remarkable parallels with some Asian cultures, and Paul offers timely teachings on how to remain faithful Christ followers in such a world. Hence an Asian reading of Paul's letters attempts to reflect on engaging culture in the light of the gospel (1 Cor) and on doing theology in the context of ministry (2 Cor). This goal coheres well with Paul's own goal for his ministry and writing: to help transform the Christ believers' hearts and minds entirely so they will truly understand that they are God's temple in Christ and live as those in whom the Spirit of God dwells (1 Cor 3:16–17). Yet our practical and theological concerns must necessarily build upon our historical data to which we now turn.

CORINTH AND THE CHRIST-ASSEMBLY

This section introduces Paul's initial visit to Corinth with the message of the gospel, how the first encounter of the city led to the founding and formation of the Christ-assembly, and what prompted Paul to write his letters after he left Corinth and the brewing Christ movement.

Paul's Founding Visit to Corinth

Paul's initial visit to Corinth (1 Cor 1:19; 15:1–3; 2 Cor 10:14) is narrated by Luke (Acts) and amplified at points by Paul's own reflections (1 and 2 Corinthians), providing us two contemporary sources from differing perspectives for Paul's first mission in Corinth (2 Cor 10:14; 1:19).[1] As Paul entered Macedonia and traversed most of Greece from north to south, organizing Christ-assemblies and entrusting them in the hands of local leaders, he was challenged by new and different cultures. Nowhere was this challenge more dramatic than in the large metropolis of Corinth, the capital of Achaia, the southern half of Greece.[2] Corinth's location made it strategic to the east-west shipping lanes of the Mediterranean. The city had a port to the east (Cenchreae) and a port to the west (Lechaeon) connected at the narrowest point on the Isthmus by only 4.8 kilometers of land. Corinth was a terminal city and consequently had an international and intercultural population with a constant flow of traders.[3] This is the city Paul entered in 50 CE with the intention of offering Christ to one and all.

Paul found the people at Corinth quite different from Athenians and other Greeks. At least part of the reason was the fact that the Greek city of Corinth had been destroyed, and its citizens had been disbanded in 146 BCE.[4] Corinth quickly became the Roman commercial center and cosmopolitan culture that

1 Paul W. Barnett, *The Corinthian Question: Why Did the Church Oppose Paul?* (Nottingham, UK: Apollos, 2011), 21; E. Schnabel, *Early Christian Mission* (Downers Grove, IL: IVP, 2004), 1181–97.

2 Scot J. Hafemann, *2 Corinthians*, NIVAC (Grand Rapids, MI: Zondervan, 2000), 22–23.

3 In detail, see David A. deSilva, *An Introduction to the New Testament: Contexts, Methods and Ministry Formation* (Downers Grove, IL: IVP, 2004), 555–60. Likewise, see Gerd Theissen, *The Social Setting of Pauline Christianity: Essays on Corinth* (Eugene, OR: Wipf & Stock, 2014), 99–101.

4 See Elizabeth R. Gebhard and Matthew W. Dickie, "The View from the Isthmus, ca. 200 to 44 BCE," *Corinth* 20 (2003): 261–78.

Paul encountered when he began what turned out to be an eighteen-month stay there (Acts 18:11). In choosing Corinth as his missionary base, Paul was prepared to accept the challenge "to plant the gospel in the most difficult of all environments."[5] In Corinth, there were gymnasiums and athletic fields, testimonies both to the Roman love for spectator sports and to the Greek love for participation in track and field games. The Isthmian Games had been held in Greek Corinth before its destruction and were being revived by the citizenry of Roman Corinth. There were both indoor and outdoor theaters for the staging of dramas and other performances. Paul found an *agora* (a kind of early shopping center) with several blocks of shops and booths along a paved road leading from the main city to the seaport. The extent and variety of religious practices in Corinth must have fascinated Paul: temples had been built, priests had been ordained, and worshippers had been secured for many different cults.[6] Indeed, the strategic position of Corinth offered Paul avenues and provided him the soil for the planting of the gospel seed and the formation of Christ-assemblies.

Paul's Christ-Assembly in Corinth

Upon his arrival in Corinth from Athens in 50 CE, Paul met Priscilla and Aquila, who had been among those in the Jewish community in Rome who had heard the Christian gospel preached by missionaries from the mother church in Jerusalem. Priscilla and Aquila seem to have had workshops and sales offices at various times in three great cities: Rome, Corinth, and Ephesus. During his first few weeks in Corinth, Paul attended the meetings of the Jews in their synagogue and began to proclaim to them his conviction that Jesus of Nazareth was the Messiah spoken of by the Jewish prophets.[7] The Jews found what Paul said to be offensive and became hostile toward him. When they denied him further opportunity to teach in the synagogue, a respected man named Titius Justus extended hospitality to Paul and offered his house as a meeting place for those who wanted to hear more of Paul's message.[8]

5 Jerome Murphy-O'Connor, "1 and 2 Corinthians," in *The Cambridge Companion to St Paul*, ed. James D. G. Dunn (Cambridge: Cambridge University Press, 2003), 74.

6 See Benjamin Powell, "The Temple of Apollo at Corinth," *AJA* 9, no. 1 (1905): 44–63.

7 Carl R. Holladay, *A Critical Introduction to the New Testament* (Nashville: Abingdon, 2005), 306.

8 Although not a Jew, Titius was a "god-fearer" or "worshiper of God," which meant that he admired the faith of the Jews and often attended synagogue meetings and activities.

The gatherings in the home of Titius Justus included many non-Jews as well as those Jews from the synagogue who were attracted by Paul's message. It seems that one of the first Christ followers to declare himself a believer in Jesus as the Christ was Crispus, a former synagogue authority. Paul was soon joined by Silas and Timothy, two of his young partners who facilitated the formation of the Christ-assemblies Paul had established in the towns of Macedonia such as Thessalonica, Philippi, and Beroea.[9] With the hospitality of Priscilla and Aquila, the daily meetings with interested Jews and gentiles in the home of Titius Justus, and the services of Silas and Timothy, Paul gave shape to an emerging Christ-assembly in Corinth.

Providentially, amid intense opposition, some synagogue attenders joined the Christ movement. Sosthenes, the leader of the synagogue in Corinth, was beaten in front of the judge's bench and later came to Christ (Acts 18:17; 1 Cor 1:1), as had Crispus, the leader who preceded him (Acts 18:8; 1 Cor 1:14). This same Sosthenes was with Paul later in Ephesus when Paul wrote a letter to the Christ-assembly in Corinth (1 Cor 1:1). When Paul moved on from Corinth (Acts 18:18–19; 20:31), he left a community that was vibrant and growing but also very open to a wide range of ideas from inside or outside of the Christ-assembly. In their openness, however, the Christ-assembly developed various schisms that were expressed in leadership factions, class structure issues, and conflicting worship styles.[10] These schisms created problems for the Christ-movement that Paul needed to address in his letters.

Paul's Letters to the Christ-Assembly

After Paul left Corinth and moved on to other ministry opportunities, he heard something that raised concerns about the welfare of the Christ-assembly, and he felt the need to write a letter to deal with the issue (e.g., of sexual immorality; 1 Cor 5:9). This first letter from Paul is no longer extant and is therefore sometimes referred to as the "lost letter."[11] Yet Paul continued to guide the Christ-assembly by corresponding with them. Chloe's people from Corinth brought a report to him while he was ministering in Ephesus (1:11–12).

9 George H. Guthrie, *2 Corinthians*, BECNT (Grand Rapids, MI: Baker, 2015), 19.

10 Holladay, *Critical*, 307; Edward W. Watson and Martin M. Culy, *Quoting Corinthians: Identifying Slogans and Quotations in 1 Corinthians* (Eugene, OR: Pickwick, 2018), 13.

11 Watson and Culy, *Quoting*, 15.

Around the same time, the Christ-assembly wrote a letter to him to ask several questions about a variety of issues (7:1).[12] As a result of the oral reports from Chloe's people and the Christ-assembly's letter, Paul wrote his second letter, which we now know as 1 Corinthians. This letter was likely written during the Ephesian sojourn (see Acts 19) that stretched from 54 through 56 CE because Paul anticipates his soon departure for Corinth.

Paul's relationship with the Christ-assembly does not end with what we see in 1 Corinthians and Acts. Second Corinthians reflects a strong opposition that had emerged in Corinth and motivated Paul to make an emergency visit to Corinth from Ephesus, across the Aegean Sea (ca. 55 CE). Unfortunately, Paul was significantly wronged by some individual, likely through slander (2 Cor 2:5–11), and he refers to this time as a "painful" visit (2 Cor 2:1–2). Following this painful visit, with his apostolic authority in question, Paul wrote a third letter to defend his apostleship. This letter was apparently very polemical, as he sought to rebuke the Christ-assembly for their openness toward those who would oppose him.[13] Paul refers to this letter as the "tearful" letter (2 Cor 2:3–4; 7:8–12), which he likely wrote around 55 CE. Some scholars believe that this letter has been lost, but others have suggested that the "tearful" letter has been preserved in 2 Cor 10–13, which would account for the significant shift in tone between 2 Corinthians 1–9 and 2 Corinthians 10–13.[14] Rightly so, the nature of the relationship between these two sections is disputed, but chapters 10–13 seem to depict Paul's response to a fresh outbreak of opposition at Corinth.[15]

Paul's "tearful" letter rebuking the Christ-assembly for their openness to those who opposed him seems to have been effective in bringing repentance from their rebellion (2 Cor 7:8–12). When his relationship with the Christ-assembly had been restored, Paul confidently wrote a fourth letter, which has been referred to as the "cheerful" letter (2 Cor 2:12–14; 7:13–15). This letter

12 Holladay, *Critical*, 307; Craig S. Keener, *1–2 Corinthians*, NCBC (Cambridge: Cambridge University Press, 2005), 62.

13 See C. K. Barrett, *2 Corinthians*, BNTC (London: A&C Black, 1973), 28–30; see Jerry L. Sumney, *Identifying Paul's Opponents: The Question of Method in 2 Corinthians*, JSNTSS 40 (Sheffield, UK: JSOT, 1990), 149–79.

14 Holladay, *Critical*, 305.

15 D. A. Carson and Douglas Moo, *An Introduction to the New Testament*, 2nd ed. (Grand Rapids, MI: Zondervan, 2005), 430–44; Keener, *1–2 Corinthians*, 143–51.

(2 Cor 1–9) seems to have been written while Paul was traveling from Macedonia, before he arrived in Corinth in 56 CE to pick up the collection that the Christ-assembly had been gathering for the poor in Jerusalem (see Acts 20:2–3; 2 Cor 8:1–15; 9:1–15).[16] Paul stayed for three months under Gaius's hospitality (Rom 16:23) during the winter of 56 or 57 CE, and likewise he penned his letter to the Romans (Rom 15:22–33). Paul's interaction with the Christ-assembly over the course of approximately five years illustrated the intimate nature of their relationship established during the extended period of time Paul was establishing the Christ-assembly, and that relationship continued to be shaped through oral and written discourses over a span of several years.[17] During this time, we know that Paul wrote at least four letters to the Christ-assembly.

STRUCTURAL INTRODUCTION AND OUTLINE

Now that we have seen some of the important issues that form the background to Paul's letters to the Christ-assembly in Corinth, we are ready to look at the content of these letters. We will briefly explore each canonical letter to the Christ-assembly by providing a structural overview and outline of the major sections.

Structural Introduction of 1 Corinthians

First Corinthians is the second letter that Paul wrote to the Christ-assembly in Corinth. He indicated that a prior letter (i.e., first letter) existed by including the words, "I have written you in my letter" (1 Cor 5:9). The Christ-assembly also sent Paul a letter (1 Cor 7), and 1 Corinthians appears at many points to respond to issues raised in their letter. First Corinthians is arranged in four major sections. The salutation (1:1–3) is fairly brief, stating that the letter is from Paul and Sosthenes and that the Christ-assembly in Corinth is the intended audience. It also includes a short blessing that serves as a greeting.

16 Gary M. Burge, Lynn H. Cohick, and Gene L. Green, *The New Testament in Antiquity: A Survey of the New Testament within Its Cultural Contexts* (Grand Rapids, MI: Zondervan, 2009), 313; H. D. Betz, *2 Corinthians 8 and 9* (Philadelphia: Fortress, 1985), 3–36.

17 See Watson and Culy, *Quoting*, 16.

The thanksgiving (1:4–9) is also rather short, expressing Paul's gratitude for the faith and spiritual giftedness of the Christ-assembly as well as his confidence in their salvation.[18] The main body (1:10–16:12) consists of two large subsections, consisting of responses to letters and reports. Chapters 1:10–6:20 include Paul's responses to reports he had received from Chloe's household, and 7:1–16:12 contains Paul's responses to the letter he had received from the Christ-assembly. He addressed three main issues that had come to his attention through the messages from Chloe's household: divisions within the church, immorality, and Christian associations.[19] The closing (16:13–21) contains several general exhortations, an endorsement of Stephanas and his household, a final greeting, a blessing, and a note in Paul's own hand verifying the letter's authenticity.

The Christ-assembly in Corinth was fragmented by allegiance to particular leading figures such as Paul, Peter, Apollos, and Jesus (1:12). They were divided against one another in lawsuits and had become arrogant toward the weak among them and toward the poor in Jerusalem. Paul tackled these errors in a few different ways. For instance, he argued that if they had only looked to Jesus as their primary leader and regarded the apostles and teachers as Christ's servants, the Corinthians would not have clashed over their preferences for certain apostles and teachers. By honoring their human leaders too highly, they had lost sight of Jesus, who far outshined all others (1:13).[20] Paul then wrote extensively on the total ineptitude of worldly wisdom at handling spiritual matters. Evidently the influential minority in the Christ-assembly was largely composed of those whom the secular society would have respected, such as the wealthy and the educated. Under their leadership, the rest of the Christ believers followed suit in adhering to worldly values (e.g., 1:19–20). He told them they were foolish for thinking like the world, were mere infants in Christ (3:1–2), and were not even close to being qualified to lead God's people.

Paul also reprimanded the Christ-assembly for the immorality reported to him. He addressed the issue of a man who was cohabiting with his stepmother (5:1–13). He also wrote more generally about the issue in 6:12–20,

18 Carson and Moo, *Introduction*, 415–16.

19 Carson and Moo, 416–17.

20 deSilva, *Introduction*, 566; Craig L. Blomberg, *From Pentecost to Patmos: An Introduction to Acts through Revelation* (Nashville: B&H, 2006), 169–72.

where we learn that the Christ-assembly had apparently misappropriated the slogan "Everything is permissible for me." Paul responded directly to this error by qualifying the slogan in 6:12–13 (see 10:23).[21] Elsewhere in chapter 6, Paul mentions a number of sexual sins that had characterized the Christ followers prior to their coming to Christ, including fornication, adultery, male and female prostitution, and homosexuality. The Christ-assembly's toleration of the man who cohabited with his stepmother clearly demonstrated their laxity in this area. Finally, Paul clarified some instructions he had previously given to the Christ-assembly concerning Christian associations. He wanted them to maintain their relationships with non-Christ followers in the world, but he wanted them to distance themselves from those who claimed to be Christ followers but brought disrepute to God's people, such as the man who lived in a sexual relationship with his stepmother. In such cases, the Christ-assembly was to practice proper church discipline,[22] even excluding the offenders if necessary (5:9–11).

The second major section of the main body of 1 Corinthians runs from 7:1 to 16:12. This is where we find Paul's responses to the Christ-assembly's questions on marriage (7:1–40), meat sacrificed to idols (chs. 8–10), worship (11:2–34), spiritual gifts (chs. 12–14), resurrection (ch. 15), and the collection for the church (16:1–12). The first questions to which Paul responded dealt with marriage, remarriage, and singleness (see 7:1–40). Some Christ believers in Corinth adopted asceticism and sexual abstinence even within marriage, which led to questions about sexual behavior within marriage and about the sanctity of marriage itself. In response to this, Paul affirmed both marriage and singleness, and he insisted that marriage must include a sexual element. But he also taught that singleness is more advantageous than marriage because singleness allows believers to focus more on "the things of the Lord" (i.e., on the interests of Christ's kingdom).

In chapters 8–10, Paul addressed the subject of meat sacrificed to idols. In common practice, pagan temples did not eat or serve all of the meat from

21 Roy E. Ciampa and Brian S. Rosner, *The First Letter to the Corinthians*, PNTC (Grand Rapids, MI: Eerdmans, 2010), 251–55; Andrew B. Spurgeon, *Twin Cultures Separated by Centuries: An Indian Reading of First Corinthians* (London: Langham Global Library, 2016), 109–13, 184–85.

22 Keith R. Krell, *Temporal Judgment and the Church: Paul's Remedial Agenda in 1 Corinthians* (Dallas: Biblical Studies, 2011), 137; see 130–36.

the animals they butchered, and they often sold the remainder. In chapter 10, Paul wrote about meat purchased in the *agora*. He defended Christ believers who ate this meat, so long as they did not do so as an act of pagan worship or in violation of their conscience. But he also taught them not to eat when their actions were likely to be mistaken for idolatry. In chapter 9, he explained his own willingness to restrict Christian freedom, implicitly asking others to do the same.[23] Paul turned to two matters relating to worship in chapter 11: gender roles (vv. 2–16) and the mistreatment of the poor during the Lord's Supper (vv. 17–34). The same arrogance and egocentrism that had led to schism in the Christ assembly, to lawsuits, and to stumbling and weak Christ followers with food had also produced Christ followers who dishonored one another in worship. Not surprisingly, Paul's solution was not only to stop the offending behaviors but also to change the attitudes of the heart.

In chapters 12–14, Paul addressed problems related to the use of *charismata*. He explained that the Holy Spirit did not give gifts in order to enhance the status of those gifted or as a reward to the righteous. Rather, he gifted people according to the needs of the Christ-assembly (ch. 12). In what is commonly known as the "love chapter" (ch. 13), Paul explained that all spiritual gifts were to be used in love, and if they were not used in this way, they were worthless. Finally, in chapter 14, Paul reprimanded the Christ followers for their disorderly worship gatherings, and he gave instructions on how they were to restrain their use of gifts in public worship.

Chapter 15 introduces the subject of the resurrection of all Christ believers. Evidently, some in the Christ-assembly denied that believers would be raised bodily from the dead. In response to this error, Paul explained that Christ's resurrection was key to the gospel and that for Christ believers to receive final salvation, they would have to be raised just as Jesus was. Paul completed his response to the Christ-assembly's questions in 16:1–12 by giving them instructions on how to take up the collection for the needy in Jerusalem and by making a few comments about Apollos.

Outline of 1 Corinthians: Engaging Culture in the Light of the Gospel

The following outline introduces the overall content of the letter, reflecting the inevitable interaction between gospel and culture, the challenge of individual

23 Watson and Culy, *Quoting*, 84–85.

and group identity formation, and the potential tension in the exercise of rights and freedom.

Introduction (1:1–9)

Responding to news from Chloe (1:10–6:20)
- Concerning divisions (1:10–4:17)
- Concerning incest (5:1–13)
- Concerning pagan court-related issues (6:1–11)
- Concerning sexual immorality (6:12–20)

Responding to the Christ-assembly's letter (7:1–16:18)
- Concerning marriage (7:1–40)
- Concerning food sacrificed to idols (8:1–11:1)
- Concerning worship (11:2–14:40)
- Concerning the resurrection (15:1–58)
- Concerning the collection for Jerusalem (16:1–4)
- Concerning Paul's travel plans (16:5–18)

Conclusion (16:19–24)

Now that we have looked at the structural flow and outline of the content of 1 Corinthians, we should turn our attention to Paul's second canonical letter to the Christ-assembly.

Structural Introduction of 2 Corinthians

Second Corinthians can be structured under four major headings. The salutation (1:1–2) states that the letter is from Paul and Timothy, and it identifies the church in Corinth and the saints in the surrounding region of Achaia as the intended audience. It includes a short blessing that serves as a greeting. The inclusion of an introduction (1:3–11) is somewhat atypical of Paul, but it describes the intense suffering that Paul underwent for the sake of his ministry as well as the comfort he received from God. While it primarily functions to make the Christ followers sympathetic toward Paul's arguments, it also offers great consolation to all who suffer for the sake of the gospel, even referring to the Lord himself as "the God of all comfort." Moreover, it encourages those who suffer to learn from their experience how to comfort others who suffer.[24] The main body (1:12–13:10) takes up the bulk of the letter and includes five major subsections: a defense of Paul's conduct (1:12–2:11), a defense of Paul's ministry (2:12–7:1), instructions regarding the collection for Jerusalem (7:2–9:15), a continuing defense of Paul's ministry (10:1–12:13), and a discussion of Paul's upcoming visit (12:14–13:10).[25] The brief closing (13:11–14) consists of a few general exhortations and a final greeting.

In 2 Corinthians 1:12–2:11, Paul defended his conduct, first by explaining why he had not visited Corinth as he had previously planned, and second by addressing a wrong that had been done to him by one of the Christ-followers. Due to a conflict that had arisen between him and some within the Christ-assembly, Paul knew that if he were to visit them, he would have to be confrontational. Hence he opted to change his travel plans. Some got offended, questioned his credibility, and failed to realize that this was an act of forbearance. Paul addressed a far more serious issue in 2:12–7:1: certain individuals within the Christ-assembly continued to doubt Paul's apostleship. Although Paul addressed this issue in 1 Corinthians, from his words in 2 Corinthians, it is obvious that a number of Christ believers in Corinth had not repented of their error. Hence as an extensive defense of the nature of his ministry, Paul proclaimed that his call and authority both came from God, and he clarified the grave consequences of not recognizing this. He suggested that those who doubted his apostleship were not even saved, had not been reconciled to God, and still bore the weight of their sins (5:18–20; see Luke 10:16).

In 7:2–9:15 Paul provided instructions regarding the collection for Jerusalem. In response to the crisis, the Christ-assembly, along with many other Christ-assemblies, had committed to sending funds to aid them. But the Christ-assembly had failed to finish collecting their contribution. Therefore, Paul engaged in a lengthy discussion of the value of sacrifice for the sake of others. He appealed to both the exemplary giving of the Macedonian Christ-assemblies, who gave even more than they could afford to give and were honored to serve in this manner, and the example of Christ, who gave up his very life that the Christ followers might enjoy abundance. Beyond this, he

24 Guthrie, *2 Corinthians*, 62.

25 See Carson and Moo, *Introduction*, 430–34; Mark A. Siefrid, *The Second Letter to the Corinthians*, PNTC (Grand Rapids, MI: Eerdmans, 2014), xxix–xxxi.

encouraged the Christ-assembly that God would bestow great blessings on them if they followed through with their prior intentions.

Paul returned to defending his apostleship in 10:1–12:13. The Christ-assembly apparently valued eloquent speakers and expected their leaders to draw a salary of sorts. Because Paul did not practice professional rhetoric, and because he chose to support himself financially while in Corinth so as not to burden the Christ-assembly, he was considered inferior.[26] In response, Paul laid out his qualifications, both to assert the legitimacy of his ministry and to rebuke the Christ-assembly for holding to improper values. Among other things, he mentioned his tremendous sacrifices for the sake of the gospel ministry. Moreover, he went on the offensive, attacking and discrediting the false apostles who spread their lies in Corinth but who nevertheless carried earthly credentials that the Christ-assembly respected (2 Cor 11:13).[27] By calling the false apostles servants of Satan, Paul made it clear that they were unbelievers and liars and that those who listened to them did so at their own peril.

Finally, in 12:14–13:10, Paul turned to the matter of his upcoming visit. He was now planning to come to Corinth regardless of whether or not it would mean judgment upon the Christ-assembly. Paul's apprehension led him to instruct his readers to examine or test themselves to make sure that they were in "the way of the messiah" (2 Cor 13:5). Paul knew that many who professed faith did not actually trust in Christ for their salvation. So he earnestly preached the gospel of repentance, faith, and salvation to the Christ-assembly in the hopes that his opponents would become genuine followers of Jesus Christ.

Outline of 2 Corinthians: Doing Theology in the Context of Ministry

The following outline introduces the overall thrust of the letter highlighting Paul's theological, ethical, and conciliatory stance for ministry where opposition, affliction, and foregoing of rights are necessary and paradoxically embedded.

26 See E. A. Judge, "Paul's Boasting in Relation to Contemporary Professional Practice," in *Social Distinctives of the Christians in the First Century: Pivotal Essays*, ed. David M. Scholer, 57–71 (Peabody, MA: Hendrickson, 2008), 60–61. Likewise, see David E. Briones, *Paul's Financial Policy: A Socio-theological Approach*, LNTS 494 (London: T&T Clark, 2013), 180.

27 Paul Barnett, *Paul: Missionary of Jesus* (Grand Rapids, MI: Eerdmans, 2008), 170–75.

Introduction (1:1–11)

Paul's ministry with the Christ-assembly (1:12–7:16)

- Paul's confidence in his motives (1:12–22)
- Paul's sorrow (1:23–2:11)
- Paul's travels to Macedonia (2:12–13)
- The saved versus the perishing (2:14–4:6)
- Present affliction versus future glory (4:7–5:10)
- The core of ministry: Reconciliation (5:11–21)
- Present afflictions versus present glory (6:1–10)
- Appeal to the Spirit people (6:11–7:4)
- Paul's travel report resumed (7:5–7)
- The Christ-assembly's sorrow (7:8–13)
- Paul's confidence in the Christ followers (7:13–16)

Paul's collection for Jerusalem (8:1–9:15)

Paul's response to opposition (10:1–13:10)

Conclusion (13:11–14)

After looking briefly at the background and content of Paul's canonical letters to the Christ-assembly, we should turn our attention to our third concern: Paul's theological and missional outlook as reflected in 1 and 2 Corinthians, which also serve as points of contact with Asian readers.

POINTS OF CONTACT BETWEEN CORINTH AND ASIAN REALITIES

Paul's letters to the Christ-assembly in Corinth, including his other letters, are full of challenges to contemporary ways of thinking. Paul was carrying the good news beyond the Jewish community, and this move inevitably resulted in cultural and sociopolitical tensions.[28] Yet it also provided points of contact with the gentile world. Asian Christ-assemblies may not stand in the same footing as the web of problems in Corinth—factions, incest, lawsuits, prostitution, debates over marriage and celibacy, food sacrificed to idols, gender roles, the abuse of the Lord's Supper, spiritual gifts in worship, questions about the resurrection, and fundraising for Judeans[29]—but definitely some common grounds provide fruitful engagement for the relevance of Paul's letters today. Just as Paul believed it is appropriate to mine the Jewish Scriptures for typological analogies of the kind of behavior to imitate or avoid for the Christ followers in Corinth (1 Cor 10:6, 11), likewise the Asian church needed to interact with Paul to find points of relevance (e.g., for pastoral care, ministry, mission, identity formation, and the like). Here I offer some of these scores hinted in his letters to the Christ-assembly.

Honor and Shame

Written in the middle of the first century, Paul's letters to the Christ-assembly in Corinth are not only relevant but perhaps the most contemporary of Paul's letters, at least from the vantage point of ministry. The letters reveal that the Christ-assembly was not yet comfortable in living out the shame (or scandal) of the cross, but Paul kept calling them back to Christ crucified (1 Cor 1:17; 2:2). Paul consistently attempts to reverse the honor-shame convention that corrupts the Christ-assembly's grasp of the gospel in order to root out arrogance and divisive activities.[30] For instance, Paul's activities are not done in secret. And concerning the apostles, there had been a renunciation of trickery

28 Spurgeon, *Twin Cultures*; Hafemann, *2 Corinthians*, 25–28.

29 See Anthony C. Thiselton, *First Corinthians: A Shorter Exegetical and Pastoral Commentary* (Grand Rapids, MI: Eerdmans, 2006), 62. For a recent entry on social identity formation, see J. Brian Tucker, *Remain in Your Calling: Paul and the Continuation of Social Identities in 1 Corinthians* (Eugene, OR: Pickwick, 2011).

30 David E. Garland, *2 Corinthians*, NAC 29 (Nashville: B&H, 1999), 30–31.

(Fil. *panloloko sa kapwa*) in their methods and message. They did not falsify the gospel they proclaimed. Hence they were not guilty (Fil. *nagkasala*) of withholding significant parts of the truth (2 Cor 4:2).[31] That said, dishonor and slander are still inescapable dimensions of a faithful ministry that Paul models in 2 Corinthians, and faith and resilience are integral to the way in which God's power is unleashed in the world. Catherine M. Jones is insightful here: "On a first-century view, manual labour testified not to virtue but to lack of integrity; not to legitimate authority but to shameful servility. The life of a manual labourer was analogous to a theatre of shame, a picture that is confirmed by Paul himself,"[32] with regard to the character of Paul's ministry.

Moreover, Paul's ability to identify with his Greco-Roman audiences and communicate to them in culturally relevant ways made his mission flourish. Part of the conventions that guided life in the first-century Mediterranean region was this culture of honor and shame.[33] Paul appealed to this convention in person and through his letters as he attempted to "become all things to all people" and used whatever appropriate method he could to win them (1 Cor 9:22). His letters address the division, false teachings, and immoral living that disturbed many early Christ-assemblies. He purposefully attempted to isolate, shame, and motivate sinners to change their ways (1 Cor 4:14; 6:5; 15:34) and conform to what he considered the place of honor before God.[34] He did this to preserve the purity and integrity of the Christ-assembly, and he was confident that the erring Christ followers would realize their anomalies, repent, and return to the Christ-assembly with restored honor.

Furthermore, Paul also addresses issues that spring from the members' continued allegiance to their previous social networks. The Christ followers still seek to establish their honor and evaluate the honor of others in terms of external appearance, social and spiritual precedence, and successful competition. In response, Paul encourages them to distance themselves from their

31 Garland, 205–6.

32 Catherine M. Jones, "Theatre of Shame: The Impact of Paul's Manual Labor on His Apostleship in Corinth" (PhD diss., Toronto School of Theology, 2013), ii.

33 Other examples of honor-related issues include Paul's teachings on honoring God (1 Cor 10:31–32), head coverings (1 Cor 11:2–16), and honorable behavior (1 Cor 12:23–25).

34 Jackson Wu, "Does Paul Use Shame to Challenge or Correct the Corinthians?," Patheos, accessed March 2, 2020, https://www.patheos.com/blogs/jacksonwu/2017/11/08/shame-paul-corinthians/.

former values, embrace new standards for claiming honor, and replace competition within the group with cooperation and mutuality (1 Cor 10:31–32). Ascriptions of honor and dishonor before "the righteous court of God" should alone guide the believers in their desire for honor and in their estimation of the value of individual Christ followers.[35] The Philippine setting is not far from this scenario within the *padrino* system. In this system, social transactions are both constrained and enabled by such Filipino cultural codes as the ethics of "debt of gratitude" (Fil. *utang na loob*) and the psychosocial notion of shame (Fil. *hiya*).[36] The desire for praise (Fil. *parangal*) is at the root of the Christian way of living out their religion. To praise meant to bestow honor (Fil. *karangalan*); to blame meant to take away honor and cause shame (Fil. *kahihiyan*). It was through honor that a person's rightful place in society was defined. Honor provided a person with a status in society. It was like a social rating that entitled the person to act and be treated in certain ways.[37] People knew how to locate themselves and behave toward superiors, inferiors, and equals because of the system of honor. Honor-shame cultures tend to be more sensitive to hierarchy and social rank.

Within the honor-shame (Fil. *dangal at hiya*) culture of Asia, two things matter to Spirit-indwelt Christ followers: integrity (or authenticity) and divine appraisal or approval. Hence there should be no dichotomy in what we consider honorable and shameful before God and people; there should be no double standard in our talk and walk. Cracks occur in Christ-assemblies when our personal and interpersonal lives lack integrity. Narry Santos rightly posits, "Breakdowns in faithful and compassionate relationships happen when we move toward becoming Christians who are *makasarili*, *walang pakiramdam*, and *manhid*."[38] The vision and voice of Paul still remain: a kinship that builds integrity and authenticity, enriches loyal and compassionate relationships,

35 Ciampa and Rosner, *First Letter*, 495–97.

36 See F. Landa Jocano, *Filipino Social Organization: Traditional Kinship and Family Organization* (Quezon City: PUNLAD, 1998), 43–46.

37 Jaime C. Bulatao, "Hiya," *Philippine Studies* 12, no. 3 (1964): 426–28. See Jeremiah Lasquety-Reyes, "In Defense of Hiya as a Filipino Virtue," *Asian Philosophy* 26, no. 1 (2016): 1–13.

38 That is, selfish, insensible, and numb. Narry F. Santos, *Turning Our Honor into Shame: Transformation of the Filipino HIYA in the Light of Mark's Gospel* (Quezon City: Lifechange, 2003), 273.

nurtures harmony and unity, and transforms our society. Perhaps more than any other Pauline letter, the Corinthian letters address the basic issue of what constitutes honor for the Christ follower and within the Christ-assembly. Paul does not discard honor and shame, including suffering, as moral rubrics; he reframes them for the good of the Christ-assembly. His example can help us reconstruct a more concrete and biblical social morality for God's people, whether Jews, gentiles, Westerners, or Asians in Christ.

Suffering and Mission

Like the apostle Paul, Asian Christians should embrace suffering as part of their Christian witness: it is suffering in, for, and with Christ. I will focus here on suffering as Christian formation and discipleship. Shaped and inspired by the Hebrew Scriptures (e.g., Isa 49:8 in 2 Cor 6:2) for his mission to the gentiles, Paul identified his sufferings with the sufferings of Christ (2 Cor 1:5; 4:10–11; 13:4). Hence we are certain that Paul's sufferings for the Christ-assembly resulted in the awakening of their lives.[39] Suffering remains instrumental to making God's glory known. Although Paul provides the most detailed description of his apostolic suffering in 2 Corinthians (11:16–33), his other letters also bear the evidence.[40]

The bearing of this paradigm of suffering on Asian realities depends on one's social location. For instance, it is one thing if we are situated in Malaysia, "where we find strong Islamic resurgence and rapid Islamization are being experienced," and it is another if we live in the war zone areas in Mindanao, Philippines.[41] Nevertheless, I concur with Lim that Paul's situational theological framework for the community in Corinth still contributes to our understanding of "what it means to be faithful Christ-followers in Asia."[42] Suffering is intrinsic to knowing the God who suffered. The cross not only shows us God's solidarity with us in our struggles but also guarantees that we can only come to know the true God through sharing in Christ's sufferings. As such,

39 See, for instance, 2 Cor 1:6; 2:15–16; 4:10–12; 13:4.

40 See Siu Fung Wu, ed., *Suffering in Paul: Perspectives and Implications* (Eugene, OR: Pickwick, 2019).

41 See Kar Yong Lim, "A Theology of Suffering and Mission for the Asian Church," in *Asian Christian Theology*, ed. Timoteo D. Gener and Stephen T. Pardue (Carlisle, UK: Langham, 2019), 189–94.

42 Lim, "Theology of Suffering," 194.

the sociopolitical conventions and experiences of Asia, including the Philippine concept of struggle, India's Dalit theology, Korea's Minjung theology, and Myanmar's concept of Dukkha,[43] seem to resonate very much with Paul's concept of suffering.

Nonetheless, suffering in Asia is not hopeless and final—it is resilient and hopeful (2 Cor 1:3–7). Paul's teaching that Christian suffering will lead not to shame but to hope (Fil. *pag-asa*) bears much upon the Asian experience of resilience in suffering. Just as Paul's perception of suffering is transformed by his understanding of the cross of Christ, so is his heart filled with his deep desires, hopes, and joys as he struggles to secure the Christ followers' sincere and pure devotion to Christ.[44] Paul claims that he could resort to force and domination to exercise his rightful authority (2 Cor 10:6; 1 Cor 4:20–21), but he prefers that the Christ followers respond willingly. Hope controls Paul's ethics (7:29–31) and mission. It contrasts the fading nature of this world, which is seen as oppressive, evil, and antithetical to God's purposes in the world. He is always confident that God will ultimately establish a renewed political structure (his reign) that will be characterized by order, peace, and justice.

Poverty and Ministry

The apostle Paul portrays a vision of a renewed humanity in Christ where all are restored to be full partakers of God's provisions (2 Cor 5; Isa 40–66). This vision can serve as the basis not only of ministry engagements in Asia today but also of following Jesus in light of their embeddedness in their own social locations defined, for instance, by poverty and oppression.[45] Hence Paul's collection campaign initially comes to mind. His concern for the Judean communities (1 Cor 16:1–4; 2 Cor 8–9; Gal 2) appeals to the Asian church's concern for poverty within and outside her constituents.[46] Indeed, Paul's missional

43 For explorations, see James R. Whelchel, *The Path to Liberation: Theology of Struggle in the Philippines* (Quezon City: New Day, 1995).

44 Robert L. Plummer, "The Role of Suffering in the Mission of Paul and the Mission of the Church," *SBJT* 17, no. 4 (2013): 6–19.

45 See John Malcolm Dowling and Yap Chin-Fang, *Chronic Poverty in Asia: Causes, Consequences and Policies* (Singapore: World Scientific, 2009).

46 Scot McKnight, "The Collection for the Saints," in *DPL*, ed. Gerald F. Hawthorne, Ralph P. Martin, and Daniel G. Reid (Downers Grove, IL: IVP, 1993), 143–47.

concern permeates the Asian landscape for social concerns. Before the first missionary journey in Acts 13, Paul delivered funds to Jerusalem collected by the Christ-assembly in Antioch (see Gal 2:1–10). The "poor" in mind here are the members of the Jerusalem church, the very people the famine visit was intended to help.[47]

Moreover, what a person really thinks about poverty is articulated most clearly by how they live. Paul and his colleague Sosthenes were unafraid and unbashful, and they were willing to do whatever it took to spread the good news to different ethnicities. They were willing to be poor, and even homeless, for the same cause (1 Cor 4:11–13). Paul's life and ministry were characterized by "boldness" and points at how Asian Christians should live their lives and conduct their ministry. Later on, Paul notes that he may be sorrowful but is rejoicing, and he may be poor but is making many spiritually rich through telling others of the saving message of Jesus. He goes on to say that he may have nothing but actually possesses everything: he possesses salvation and the Holy Spirit through Jesus (2 Cor 6:10).[48]

Yet from Paul's missional campaign (2 Cor 8–9), two primary motivations for the offering emerge that also resonate the concerns of the Asian churches: to alleviate the needs of the poor Christians there and to offer a kind of tribute to the "mother church" from which all early Christian communities were ultimately derived. In fact, these motivations correspond to the two major purposes of Christian giving throughout church history: "to help the physical and spiritual needs of people and to remunerate ecclesiastical authorities."[49] Likewise, it is a message for most Christ-assemblies today to overcome sticking to just preaching the gospel, and it has left human needs to social workers and government agencies.

As the number of poor communities in Asia continues to rise at an alarming rate, Christ followers need to examine their missional role in sharing the hope, joy, healing, and servanthood of Christ to those in despair. If Paul were alive, he would invite Christ-assemblies to continue to wrestle with the question of how to address with compassion and conviction the stark realities of

47 See Bruce W. Longenecker, *Remember the Poor: Paul, Poverty, and the Greco-Roman World* (Grand Rapids, MI: Eerdmans, 2010), 135–56.

48 Hafemann, *2 Corinthians*, 271–72.

49 See Rom 15:26–27. Blomberg, *From Pentecost*, 198.

urban poverty in, for instance, Manila or Kolkata.[50] And without hesitation, he would continue to advocate generosity, equality, and unity (2 Cor 8–9; see 2 Thess 3:6–15) among God's people, which requires obedience and imitation. We could learn from Paul in matters such as mutual support instead of competition, caring for the needy and rejecting materialism, spiritual gifts and their appropriate use for serving others, and future accountability for present actions. Clearly enough, pastoral care from a Pauline perspective for Asian communities concerns the hurting, the shamed, the marginalized, the displaced, the weak, the poor, the traumatized, and the like.[51]

Patronage and Community

In Paul's Corinthian letters, he deals with disputes of status and power. The Christ-assembly was split along social status lines, with the divisions evident at the Lord's Supper, eating meat offered to idols, Christians' use of Corinthian courts, and reactions to Paul's means of self-support.[52] However, to retain his status of leadership and independence, Paul often had to avoid appearing to be their client or in-house philosopher—a paradigm he calls on the strong, and all of us in Asia, to imitate. This is Paul's overall strategy of rejecting the status symbols of upper-class ideology and of disrupting the hierarchical assumptions of those in power. Likewise, Asia possesses this culture of power and recognition, which we call the *padrino* system in the Philippines, which encompasses the Filipino bilateral kinship system within which patron-client relations often take place. Indeed, Asian politics revolves around interpersonal relationships and factions composed of personal alliances that reflect one's social status, and this is also true within the ecclesial structures. In Corinth, Paul speaks not only of the need for the Christ-followers to "discern the body" (1 Cor 11:29) but also of forming an alternative community or "space" with a distinct ethos, hence "the body of Christ" (1 Cor 12:12–14). Instead of constructing personal alliances, the Christ followers' identity and symbolic unity

50 Scott Bessenecker, ed., *Quest for Hope in the Slum Community: A Global Urban Reader* (Waynesboro, GA: Authentic, 2005).

51 Paul A. Barker, *Tackling Trauma: Global, Biblical, and Pastoral Perspectives* (Carlisle, UK: Langham, 2019).

52 Dale B. Martin, *The Corinthian Body* (New Haven, CT: Yale University Press, 1999), 86. See John Kin-Man Chow, "Patronage and Power: Studies on Social Networks in Corinth" (PhD diss., Durham University, 1991), 91–129.

allow the existence of diversity and difference (1 Cor 1–4).[53] This is a corrective to the stifling effect of a kinship structure of social relations in the Philippines made up by the *compadrino* system.

Another occasion relevant for Asian Christ-assemblies relates to how charisma (gifts) and order operate among and within God's people. Paul insists that they were not granted to individuals primarily for their personal, subjective enjoyment but rather for the building up of the community (1 Cor 12:7; Eph 4:12). He recognizes the legitimacy of a private use, albeit in a very limited way, of charisma within the Christ-assembly (1 Cor 14:28), but the service of others, not oneself, is in view (1 Cor 14:12).[54] This reverses the practice that was apparently in operation at Corinth—where the charismatic aspirations of the individual, rather than the common good of the community, were paramount—because the Spirit does not arbitrarily force his gifts upon individual persons but acts rather as the agent of God who is "not a God of confusion but of peace" (1 Cor 14:33).[55]

Again, in a culture that judges people by reputation and achievements, Paul is counterintuitive: Christ followers have to resist the lure of living for professional recognition and advancement.[56] Moreover, Paul urges the Christ-assembly, especially those Christ followers with high status, to arrive at a transformation of behavior that will support the position of the lower-status Christ followers. His call for Christ followers, including us, does not change, and it serves to enact what he spoke about the substitution of the values of the "other realm" for the values and status indicators of "this world" and the reversal of normal status indicators. Although it remains a struggle to recognize the alternative value system of the "in Christ" space, nonetheless, the upper-class "hierarchical realm" is repeatedly turned on its head.[57] To Paul, kinship in Christ encourages communal action and defense for the right of the weak.

53 Adam G. White, *Where Is the Wise Man? Graeco-Roman Education as a Background to the Divisions in 1 Corinthians 1–4*, LNTS 536 (London: Bloomsbury, 2015).

54 Ciampa and Rosner, *First Letter*, 667–68; Keener, *1–2 Corinthians*, 112, 116.

55 Robert Banks, *Paul's Idea of Community* (Exeter, UK: Paternoster, 1980), esp. 102–12. See "new politics" in Scot McKnight, *A Fellowship of Differents: Showing the World God's Design for Life Together* (Grand Rapids, MI: Zondervan, 2014), 186–92.

56 Nancy Pearcy, *Total Truth: Liberating Christianity from Its Cultural Captivity* (Wheaton, IL: Crossway, 2008), 357.

57 Martin, *Corinthian Body*, 86.

Paul's revolutionary vision is to integrate people from various social strata of society into the Christ-assembly of God in Corinth.

God and Deities

Corinth, like the other Greco-Roman cities or villages, was very religious. Inscriptions, coins, and statuary from the city attest to the worship of more than fifty deities in the area. Scores of lesser deities likewise governed the affairs of everything from the household to the sheepfold.[58] How were Christ followers to live their lives as believers in the context of the religious and social life of their community? Part of the problem Paul counters in Corinth includes the tendency to reduce Christ to leadership factions, and he addresses the Christ-assembly as the *ekklesia* of God. He saw the need to maintain his view of one God but through the lens of the Christ. For Asians, the question remains thus: "How do we make sense of the Christian understanding of God in contexts filled with a plethora of vastly different conceptions of deity."[59] One feature of Asia is its diversity or plurality. It is a diverse world of faiths, cultures, and races, very much like that of Corinth. It is the birthplace of the world's major religions. Indeed, "religious pluralism is at the heart of Asian empirical reality. It fills every geographic nook and cranny of her soils and waters."[60] So I imagine what this view of one God looks like for Christ followers in a multifaith society where many deities exist, such as the gurus of Sikhism, the Allah of Islam, the Buddhas of Buddhism, the Hindu deities, the Korean deities, the Filipino concepts of spirits, and the many faces of Jesus.

First Corinthians gives us a sense of the challenges the early Christ followers faced as they shifted their loyalties away from their traditional gods to the God of Israel. The issue of idol food in Asian countries has many similarities to that of ancient Corinth (see 1 Cor 8:4–13; 10:27–33). While Paul did set up behavioral boundaries, he did not impose an absolute rule concerning eating idol food as such. He sought rather to transform the attitude of "strong" Christ followers toward a forgoing of one's rights out of concern

58 See Moyer V. Hubbard, *Christianity in the Greco-Roman World: A Narrative Introduction* (Peabody, MA: Hendrickson, 2010), 20–22.

59 Simon Chan, *Grassroots Asian Theology* (Downers Grove, IL: IVP Academic, 2014), 48.

60 See Peniel Rajkumar, ed., *Asian Theology on the Way: Christianity, Culture and Context* (London: SPCK, 2012).

for the "weak" Christ followers and for the Christ-assembly, and he sought to create in them a desire to do all things for the glory of God.[61] For Filipinos, food is both culture and history, and it is embedded in our religious practices. Traditional healers always associate healing with offerings (e.g., meat, rice, liquor) to spirits or deities. Should Paul write to Asian Christ-assemblies today, he would undoubtedly wrestle with the issues of animism and syncretism prevalent in the Asian (and especially Southeast Asian) society and culture.[62]

Asian Christ followers can no doubt identify with Paul's polemic against false religion in 1 Corinthians 8–10.[63] Kevin Higgins is right as he perceives that Christ believers "remain engaged in the socio-religious dimensions of their birth culture."[64] But he explains further, "Instead of simply asking whether certain actions or rituals or places are inherently idolatrous (e.g., 'Can a believer regularly go to the mosque or a Hindu temple?'), it might be more important to ask what activities, rituals, ceremonies, or rites result in the believer, as a participant, actually seeking to commune with another spiritual being other than the One True God."[65] The syncretism reflected in 1 Corinthians 10:21 finds parallels in numerous contemporary contexts in Asia, some more akin to paganism.[66] Paul's approach is relevant here: while seeking points of contact, Paul felt responsible to move the Athenians far beyond their polytheistic beliefs and into a knowledge of the one true and living God uniquely revealed in Jesus Christ (Acts 17; 1 Cor 8–10).[67]

61 Alex T. Cheung, *Idol Food in Corinth: Jewish Background and Pauline Legacy*, JSNTSS 176 (Sheffield, UK: Sheffield Academic Press, 1999); Derek Newton, *Deity and Diet: The Dilemma of Sacrificial Food at Corinth*, JSNTSS 169 (Sheffield, UK: Sheffield Academic Press, 1998), 392–93.

62 See Alfred McCoy, "Baylan: Animist Religion and Philippine Peasant Ideology," *Philippine Quarterly of Culture and Society* 10, no. 3 (1982): 141–94.

63 Trent Alan Rogers, "The Representation of God in 1 Corinthians 8–10: Understanding Paul in the Context of Wisdom, Philo, and Josephus" (PhD diss., Loyola University Chicago, 2015), 220–300.

64 Kevin Higgins, "At Table in the Idol's Temple? Local Theology, Idolatry, and Identification in 1 Corinthians 8–10," *International Journal of Frontier Mission* 31, no. 1 (2014): 27.

65 Higgins, 35.

66 See John Hick and Paul Knitter, *The Myth of Christian Uniqueness: Toward a Pluralistic Theology of Religions* (Maryknoll, NY: Orbis, 1987).

67 See Craig L. Blomberg, *1 Corinthians*, NIVAC (Grand Rapids, MI: Zondervan, 1994), 197–201.

Reflecting on gentile converts who turn from dumb idols (1 Cor 12:2), Bruce Winter is instructive: "It did not however extract converts from life in cities where religious pluralism was woven into the very fabric of every daily life."[68] This is an example of what it means to engage culture in the light of the gospel.

Love and Hospitality

Clearly enough, Paul desired that the Christ-assembly would understand that the nature of his apostleship and ministerial style (2 Cor 2:14–4:12; 1 Cor 13) was transformed by his understanding of the cross of Christ (1 Cor 1–4; Rom 5:8). To him, covenant love is the essence of the cross. At the cross, Brian K. Blount reflects, "God takes what humans intend to be the definitive act of disfigurement and dishonor (capital punishment, death, end of life) and reclaims it as something uniquely revelatory." Yet in that case, "the cross is the consummate act of divine irony," and "what the Romans believed to be the cessation of life and meaning, God claims as the marker that defines the possibilities of life" for gentiles, Jews, and the rest of us.[69] Consequently, "the cross becomes the ultimate apocalypse, that is, the revelation of God's intention for humankind. Through struggle and even death, God reveals life."[70] This is life's destiny in the new creation, at least from a Pauline point of view. Ultimately, the eschatological hope of new creation in Paul's world and ours still revolves around the lordship of Christ, the love of God, and life in the Spirit (1 Cor 15). The missing practice of this kind of cruciform frame of Christian life should be recovered and embraced afresh in our fragmented and polarized communities (sociopolitical and ecclesial). Instead of being Corinthianized (reflecting the prevailing problem of self-centeredness), we should be Christianized, meaning we continue to be gospelized in order to conform to the image of God's Son and to truly be His *ekklesia* in the cosmos.

68 Bruce W. Winter, "Theological and Ethical Responses to Religious Pluralism—1 Corinthians 8–10," *Tyndale Bulletin* 41, no. 2 (1990): 209–26.

69 Brian K. Blount, *Invasion of the Dead: Preaching Resurrection* (Louisville: Westminster John Knox, 2014), xii.

70 Blount, xii; N. T. Wright, *Surprised by Hope* (New York: HarperOne, 2008), 293–95.

There is more to reflect on for the Asian discourse.[71] Love is both the ethics and destiny of the new creation "in Christ." In Christ, God has provided a liberating space or welcoming home for the have-nots and the weak, those who lost their way in the realm of Adam (see 1 Cor 15:45; 2 Cor 3:17). New identities are formed in Christ, especially for the shamed, the poor, the suffering, the slave, and the disadvantaged. Paul's vision of community formation shaped by love, compassion, acceptance, peace, and justice stands as a corrective[72] and offers freedom from our present confinements. That vision is missing in the current entrepreneurial approach to pastoral ministry and mission, which lacks biblical and theological grounding. Concurring with Paul, our intention should be to unite Christ followers in truth as expressed in loving and kind gestures, welcoming and serving one another (see Rom 12:13; Gal 5:13–15).[73]

Also, Paul builds his cross-ethic of freedom and love upon the kerygma of the divine mystery (1:18–2:16). The intention is to provide ways to avoid being fleshly (*sarkikoi*) and ways to be spiritual (*penumatikoi*) in Christ.[74] He demonstrates this by foregoing his rights as an apostle and refusing to patronize the Christ-assembly for his support. Yet there is another lesson to learn from Paul's attempt to foster and regulate community life: love and kindness could heal the fractious nature of the Christ followers' behavior and could sustain unity within the God-ordained diversity in the Christ-assembly (see 2 Cor 9:6–8). Not all the Christ followers may have divisive, shameful behavior, but Paul's solution for any conflict is inclusive of all, much more than just those who are honored "in Christ." Paul models for them how not to seek one's own good but to seek the good of all Christ followers, and he expects them to follow his example (1 Cor 10:23; 11:1) for the glory of God.[75] The evangelical

71 Amos Yong is convinced that "the practice of hospitality holds one of the keys to life in a global context of twenty-first century." See Yong, preface to *Hospitality and the Other: Pentecost, Christian Practices and the Neighbor* (Maryknoll, NY: Orbis, 2008).

72 See James W. Thompson, *Pastoral Ministry according to Paul: A Biblical Vision* (Grand Rapids, MI: Baker, 2006), 119–48, esp. 131–34.

73 Barnett, *Corinthian Question*, 213.

74 See Thompson, *Pastoral*, 125.

75 For God, and Paul, there is no "second-class" citizen in the Christ-assembly. See J. Paul Sampley, *Walking between the Times: Paul's Moral Reasoning* (Minneapolis: Fortress, 1991), 60–61.

world, not just Asia, needs communities that practice hospitality or embody theology. For Paul, the ultimate test of a projected action is whether it shows love to others, whether it edifies others (1 Cor 8:1). Therefore, any Christian gesture must be reckoned inappropriate if it does not give expression to love for the others within the community. Again, we may recall Paul accepted hospitality and benefaction only as it advances the gospel and his mission to form Christ-assemblies.

CONCLUSION

The power of Paul's message in 1 and 2 Corinthians to transform communities could not be reduced to the selected themes from our Asian context. However, the points of contact introduced here provide some starting ground to engage Paul's responses to pressures inside and outside Christ-assemblies in order to form and transform them. Paul's theological, ethical, and relational parameters remain an invaluable guide. Hence a clear portrait of the assembly of God's people is reintroduced: first, a Christ-assembly that maintains diverse individual and group identities but learns to navigate conflict in order to promote cohesion within the body; second, a Spirit-indwelt community where Christ believers are vividly aware of the Spirit's presence in their midst and of being endowed with spiritual gifts for edification; third, a gospel-driven community that is free to relate with one another in the ways of Christ; and fourth, a distinct missional community that carries out the mandate to engage culture with the light of the gospel and to do theology in the context of ministry.

FURTHER READING

Barnett, P. W. 2011. *The Corinthian Question: Why Did the Church Oppose Paul?* Nottingham, UK: Apollos.

Bessenecker, S., ed. 2005. *Quest for Hope in the Slum Community: A Global Urban Reader*. Waynesboro, GA: Authentic.

Chan, S. 2014. *Grassroots Asian Theology: Thinking the Faith from the Ground Up*. Downers Grove, IL: IVP Academic.

Cheung, A. T. 1999. *Idol Food in Corinth: Jewish Background and Pauline Legacy*. JSNTSS 176. Sheffield, UK: Sheffield Academic Press.

Ciampa, R. E., and B. S. Rosner. 2010. *The First Letter to the Corinthians*. PNTC. Grand Rapids, MI: Eerdmans.

Cosgrove, C. H., H. Weiss, and K. K. Yeo. 2005. *Cross-Cultural Paul: Journeys to Others, Journeys to Ourselves*. Grand Rapids, MI: Eerdmans.

Keener, C. S. 2005. *1–2 Corinthians*. NCBC. Cambridge: Cambridge University Press.

Lim, K. Y. 2019. "A Theology of Suffering and Mission for the Asian Church." In *Asian Christian Theology*, edited by Timoteo D. Gener and Stephen T. Pardue, 181–198. Carlisle, UK: Langham.

Rajkumar, P., ed. 2012. *Asian Theology on the Way: Christianity, Culture and Context*. London: SPCK.

Thiselton, A. C. 2006. *First Corinthians: A Shorter Exegetical and Pastoral Commentary*. Grand Rapids, MI: Eerdmans.

Tucker, J. B. 2011. *Remain in Your Calling: Paul and the Continuation of Social Identities in 1 Corinthians*. Eugene, OR: Pickwick.

TEN

The Letter to the Galatians

Roji Thomas George
SAIACS
Bengaluru, India

Galatia refers to a region in modern-day Turkey. Among the undisputed letters of Paul, this is the only letter that was sent by the apostle to the churches in Asia. Galatians occupies a vital space among the letters of Paul. To some extent, Galatians contains the essence of Paul's theology, which is expanded in his other letters. For example, Paul's letter to the Romans includes an elaborate discussion on the key themes present in Galatians like "justification by faith," "the law versus the grace of God in human salvation," "flesh versus the Spirit antithesis," "freedom in the Spirit," and others. Paul weaves them all skillfully in shaping and sharpening his argument against the agitators in Galatia not only to defend the purity of the gospel he preached and his apostleship but also to safeguard his converts from getting entrapped in a new web of slavery. Hence the tone of the apostle is fierce and sharp. Paul pours out his heart in anger, fervent emotional appeal, and stern warnings to the believers while wishing the worst for those who were disturbing his new converts by preaching a perverted version of the gospel with hidden self-interest (Gal 1:7–9; 5:12). In Galatians, Paul's defense of an inclusive gospel and his vision to form a community in Christ beyond every social polarity within a culturally hybridized context of Galatia are important aspects for us in our preaching and practicing our faith in the contemporary Asian setting.

In the ensuing discussion, I will explore issues relating to the general background like authorship, date, purpose, occasion, and others. Even select vital theological themes emerging in the letter will be discussed as much as they may relate to the Asian social, cultural, religious, and political realities.

Authorship

There is an unparalleled unanimity among Pauline scholars regarding Paul's authorship of the letter to the Galatians. The internal evidence names Paul as the author and sender of the letter (1:1; 6:11). As Donald Guthrie observes, except for the eighteenth-century Dutch school with radical claims, there has been little doubt on the authorship of Paul.[1] Such rare claims have been generally overlooked in the study of Galatians because of the unparalleled support to Paul's authorship.

Audience

According to the internal evidence, the letter was sent "to the churches of Galatia" (1:2; see 3:1). It is an encyclical letter sent to a group of churches established in the region of Galatia who shared similar challenges. However, the identity of "Galatians" is disputed. Traditionally, the ethnic Galatians, inhabiting the northern part of Galatia, were identified as Paul's original audience. J. B. Lightfoot argued that for both Paul and Luke, Galatia refers to a geographical location inhabited by the Galatian ethnic stock in the northern region. The reasons are numerous. First, the names of the regions mentioned along with Galatia, like Mysia, Phrygia, and Pisidia, are strictly geographical terms, and this requires treating "Galatia" in the same sense (Acts 14:24; 16:6–8; 18:23). Second, the identification of Lystra and Derbe, the cities in the Roman provincial Galatia, as "cities of Lycaonia" (Acts 14:6) and Antioch as Pisidian (Acts 13:14) proves that Galatia stands for the ethnic Galatian region. Third, the expression "the regions of Phrygia and Galatia" in Acts 16:6 (see 18:23) stands for the two adjacent regions.[2] Fourth, Paul's reference to

1 Donald Guthrie, *New Testament Introduction*, rev. ed. (Leicester, UK: Apollos, 1990), 485–86.

2 J. B. Lightfoot, *Saint Paul's Epistle to the Galatians: A Revised Text with Introduction, Notes, and Dissertations*, 8th ed. (London: Macmillan, 1884), 19–20.

the earlier visit in Galatians 4:13 (which implies another visit sometime later) attests Luke's mention of his two trips in Acts 16:6 and 18:23.[3] And fifth, the similarity of the auditors' general temperament about the ethnic Gauls (fickleness and superstition), referred to by Paul in the letter (1:6) and the ancient witnesses, supports the North Galatian audience of the apostle.[4] Therefore, they conclude that Paul wrote to the churches of Ancyra, Pessinus, Tavium, and Juliopolis in the north of Galatia.

In modern times, this hypothesis has been questioned in favor of the South Galatian audiences by Ramsay, Bruce, Hemer, Dunn, and many others based on vital historical pieces of evidence.[5] First, arguing against Lightfoot's contention, Bruce points out that according to Luke, the Lycaonians shared with Gauls similar behavioral characteristics.[6] Second, Paul's mission trips to North Galatia during his second and third missionary journeys (see Acts 16:6; 18:23) are not supported by any positive evidence from the period. We have no evidence supporting the existence of Pauline churches in the region. In contrast, a detailed narration of Paul's evangelistic activity in the Roman provincial Galatia and the available positive evidences in favor of the churches existing in the southern region lend more weight to the South Galatian auditors of Paul.[7] Third, Paul's mention of Barnabas and his inconsistent behavior in Galatia (2:1, 9, 13) is meaningful only to those who knew Barnabas very well (see Acts 20:4) and did not expect such behavioral inconsistencies in him. Fourth, Paul's mention of the "marks of Jesus" in his body (6:17) could be a reference to the event of being stoned in Lystra (Acts 14:19).[8] Finally, the proponents of the South Galatian audience contend that

3 Lightfoot, 22–25.
4 Lightfoot, 14–17.
5 William M. Ramsay, *A Historical Commentary on St. Paul's Epistle to the Galatians* (London: Hodder & Stoughton, 1900), 308–24; F. F. Bruce, *The Epistle of Paul to the Galatians: A Commentary on the Greek Text*, NIGTC (Exeter, UK: Paternoster, 1982), 3–18; Colin J. Hemer, *The Book of Acts in the Setting of Hellenistic History* (Winona Lake, IN: Eisenbrauns, 1990), 305; Richard N. Longenecker, "Introduction to *Galatians*," Word Biblical Commentary 41 (Dallas: Word Book, 1990), lxxii.
6 Bruce, *Galatians*, 8.
7 Guthrie, *Introduction*, 469.
8 Guthrie, 471; D. A. Carson, Douglas J. Moo, and Leon Morris, *An Introduction to the New Testament* (Manila: OMF Literature, 1992), 291.

Luke preferred to use imperial nomenclatures while referring to geographical locations.[9]

In summary, the weight of evidence seems to favor a South Galatian readership living in different cities in the Roman province (see Gal 1:2) rather than a North Galatian one. Although either position taken makes no significant difference to the interpretation of the letter, recognizing the weight of the argument in support of the South Galatian audience helps us understand the related historical details correctly. Paul evangelized South Galatia during his first missionary journey. If so, when did Paul write this letter?

Date

The proponents of the North Galatian theory have traditionally argued for a later post–Jerusalem Council date (55–58 CE).[10] However, if Paul's audience was the South Galatians, then there are two possible options, pre– and post–Jerusalem Council dates, for our consideration. Scholars like Longenecker and Fung contend in favor of a pre-Jerusalem date and equate Galatians 2:1–10 with Acts 11:27–30. The reasons for their arguments are as follows:[11] first, it renders unnecessary the theory that Paul failed to mention all his visits to Jerusalem; second, Paul's omission of any reference to the decision of the Jerusalem Council is merely because the Jerusalem Council had not taken place at the time of writing of Galatians; and third, Peter and Barnabas don't need to be seen in a bad light (hypocrisy). Their inconsistent behavior is easily explainable as a result of a situation without explicit rules governing the extent of table fellowship between Palestinian Jewish Christians and native Christians.[12]

9 Carson, Moo, and Morris, *Introduction*, 291.

10 Raymond E. Brown, *An Introduction to the New Testament* (Bangalore: Theological Publications in India, 2004), 477; Joseph A. Fitzmyer, "The Letter to the Galatians," in *The New Jerome Biblical Commentary*, ed. Raymond E. Brown, Joseph A. Fitzmyer, and Roland E. Murphy (Bangalore: Theological Publications in India, 2000), 781.

11 Longenecker, "Introduction to Galatians," lxxii–lxxxviii; Ronald Y. K. Fung, *The Epistle to the Galatians*, NICNT (Grand Rapids, MI: Eerdmans, 1988), 9–28; R. A. Cole, *The Epistle of Paul to the Galatians: An Introduction and Commentary*, TNTC 9 (Grand Rapids, MI: Eerdmans, 1974), 20–23; Guthrie, *Introduction*, 472–81; Carson, Moo, and Morris, *Introduction*, 293–94.

12 Longenecker, "Introduction to Galatians," lxxxi–lxxxii.

In contrast, those who argue for a post–Jerusalem Council date rely upon the visible similarities between Galatians 2:1–10 with Acts 15:1–30.[13] Further, Paul clearly distinguishes his earlier visit (Gal 1:18) from the second one by saying "again" in Galatians 2:1. Then, the first visit was undertaken immediately after his conversion (see Acts 9:26), whereas the second visit was fourteen years later, along with Barnabas and Titus. The post–Jerusalem Council date helps us fit Titus quite well among "some of the others" that Luke mentions in Acts 15:2.[14] If so, Paul wrote Galatians between 50 and 52 CE from Corinth,[15] where he stayed for eighteen months (Acts 18:11) during his second missionary journey. Thus the letter would be one of the earliest letters of Paul, though not the first.

Occasion, Purpose, and Identity of the Agitators in Galatia

The identity of the agitators in Galatia is a hotly debated issue. Paul himself does not identify them with their teaching. In the light of a lack of any reliable alternate modern reconstruction of the identity of the opponents in Galatia by scholars, the traditional theory that they were Jewish Christian Judaizers appears to be correct. Paul recounts that those of high reputation (2:6) in Jerusalem acknowledged the grace given to him. He says, "I had been entrusted with the task of preaching the gospel to the uncircumcised just as Peter had been to the circumcised" (2:7). Paul's words point to two types of early Christian mission: first, the Law-observing mission, and second, the Law-free mission.[16]

The Law-observing missionaries are called Judaizers, who were probably the agitators in Galatia. In the absence of Paul, they disturbed the Galatian churches (1:2) by preaching "a different gospel" (1:6; see 4:10; 6:12) based on Jewish cultural requirements like circumcision. Paul found them to be in

13 Carson, Moo, and Morris, *Introduction*, 293–94; Donald Guthrie, *Galatians*, CBN Series (Greenwood, SC: Attic, 1969), 29–30.

14 G. Walter Hansen, *Galatians*, IVPNTC (Leicester, UK: IVP, 1994), 1.

15 See J. D. G. Dunn, *The Theology of Paul's Letter to the Galatians* (Cambridge: Cambridge University Press, 1993), 8, 16; Herman N. Ridderbos, *The Epistle of Paul to the Churches in Galatia: The English Text with Introduction, Exposition and Notes*, NICNT, trans. Henry Zylstra (Grand Rapids, MI: Eerdmans, 1953), 31.

16 See J. Louis Martyn, "A Law-Observant Mission to Gentiles," in *Theological Issues in the Letters of Paul* (Nashville: Abingdon, 1997), 8.

direct opposition to the gospel that he preached among non-Jews. Although the agitators are painted in a dark light by Paul in Galatians, we are unsure whether they deliberately undertook a mission to oppose the apostle.[17] Paul's arguments give us an impression that these agitators questioned his apostleship (1:1, 12, 17; 2:2) and falsely pictured him as practicing circumcision (see 5:11). They also seemingly claimed to have the support of the Jerusalem apostles. It necessitated Paul explaining to the Galatians his relationship with the leaders in Jerusalem (see 2:6–14). In contemporary Galatian studies, the Judaizers are commonly considered to be the Galatian opponents but with minor modifications or variations based on one's interpretation of the words of Paul. Individual scholars reconstruct the situation in Galatia and the identity of the opponents differently.[18] According to Dunn, the men from James and the other missionaries operated with the single aim of Judaizing the non-Jewish Christians—that is, by having the men circumcised.[19]

If so, what was their relationship to the apostles in Jerusalem? How does it help us to envision why Paul sent this letter to the Galatians? Paul links the opponents to the Jerusalem apostles by mentioning them as "certain men from James" (Gal 2:12). Howard, Borgen, and others explain the relationship between the agitators in Galatia and the Jerusalem apostles in the light of the events transpiring in Judea and Galilee.[20] Jewett maintains that the growing Zealot campaign in Judea and Galilee in the late forties CE, which eventually led to the Jewish revolt in 66 CE, created a threat to everyone in Palestine who mingled with non-Jews. The danger forced the Jewish Christians in Judea to

17 George Howard, *Paul: Crisis in Galatia*, SNTSMS 35 (Cambridge: Cambridge University Press, 1979), 9; Joseph B. Tyson, "Paul's Opponents in Galatia," *Novum Testamentum* 10, no. 4 (1968): 252–54; Dunn, *Galatians*, 11–12.

18 Gerd Lüdemann, *Opposition to Paul in Jewish Christianity*, trans. M. Eugene Boring (Minneapolis: Fortress, 1989), 97–103; Tyson, "Paul's Opponents in Galatia," 241–54; Howard, *Paul*, 1–19; Martyn, "Law-Observant Mission," 7–24; Robert Jewett, "The Agitators and the Galatian Congregation," *New Testament Studies* 17, no. 2 (1971): 198–212; Walt Russell, "Who Were Paul's Opponents in Galatia?," *Bibliotheca Sacra* 147, no. 587 (1990): 329–50. Daniel Hayden King, "Paul and the Tannaim: A Study in Galatians," *Westminster Journal of Theology* 45, no. 2 (1983): 340–70.

19 Dunn, *Galatians*, 14–15.

20 Howard, *Paul*, 3; Peder Borgen, "Paul Preaches Circumcision and Pleases Men," in *Paul and Paulinism: Essays in Honour of C. K. Barrett*, ed. M. D. Hooker and S. G. Wilson (London: SPCK, 1982), 37–46.

undertake a nomistic mission to the other native Christians for the sake of their safety in Palestine (see 6:12). Therefore, they undertook the task of convincing the non-Jews in Galatia concerning the need to accept circumcision purely in theological terms (for example, the reference to Abraham in 3:6–18) and by misrepresenting Paul as a preacher of circumcision (see 5:11). They did not insist that the Galatians ought to keep the whole law after being circumcised. Paul urges the Galatians to recognize this hidden truth in explicit terms (5:2–3). Such a reconstructed scenario is supported by Acts 15:1–5. If so, probably some out of this group created the problem in Galatia.[21]

The internal shreds of evidence prove that some who entered the churches in the region taught a version of the gospel contrary to what Paul had taught them, and they had questioned Paul's apostleship. Hence Paul purposed to defend his apostleship and the gospel, claiming to be directly appointed by Christ (1:1, 11–12, 15–16) and accepted by "those esteemed as pillars" in Jerusalem (2:9). According to Luke, Paul and Barnabas founded the churches in South Galatia during their (first) missionary journey (Acts 13:1–14:27), before the Jerusalem Council (Acts 15:1–30) took place. They established churches among the non-Jewish native population in the cities of the region. However, after they left the region, the preachers of another gospel followed them into the churches, teaching an ideologically colored gospel. They came with approval from the leaders in Jerusalem and claimed authority to teach their version of the gospel. As a result, they appear to have misunderstood Paul's position on the validity of circumcision for believers in Christ. They sought to impose coercively Jewish identity markers like circumcision, Kosher laws (i.e., the rules governing table fellowship between Jews and others), and Sabbath laws upon the Galatians for particular selfish political interests. They were concerned about their safety under emerging threats from Jewish nationalists in Palestine and the local Galatian authorities.

After Paul came to know about the turn of events taking place among the churches he planted, he sent the letter on his behalf appealing and warning them about the danger that lay close to them. He thought that the version of the gospel they preached was irreconcilable with the pattern of life according to the gospel that he preached to them. The apostle encouraged them to reject the agitators' teachings and lead a cruciform lifestyle in

21 Jewett, "Agitators," 198–212.

Christ Jesus. Hence he educated them about their identity as the real people of the circumcision. They did not require to submit to the "weak and miserable forces" (4:9) by returning to live under the law. He encouraged them to live in the freedom that is in Christ as the heirs of the Abrahamic promises (4:21–5:1).

Genre of Galatians

Literary studies of Paul's Letter to the Galatians in recent decades may be broadly classified under two general categories: first, identifying epistolary form and structure, and its functions, and second, rhetorical analysis of the letter. From the latter group, H. D. Betz marshaled assigning Paul's letter to Galatians to the "'apologetic letter' genre."[22] He reads it in the light of rhetorical techniques, mainly as explained by Quintilian. He separates the epistolary framework, namely "The Prescript" (1:1–5) and "The Postscript" (6:11–18) of Galatians, from the "body" of the letter. Betz divides the "body" of the letter under five parts: *exordium* (1:6–11), *narratio* (1:12–2:14), *propositio* (2:15–21), *probatio* (3:1–4:31), and *paraenesis* (5:1–6:10). Each of these sections has been explained in relation to the rhetorical argumentation in Galatians. However, Betz finds it difficult to explain *probatio* (4:21–31) as part of an apologetic letter based on Quintilian. He switches over to Pseudo-Demetrius to explain the rhetoric of Paul in the section.[23]

The contention of Betz has not gone unchallenged, though some, like Troy Martin[24] and James D. Hester,[25] have followed him. He is critiqued for placing undue reliance upon Quintilian, who wrote around 90 CE—that is, after Paul wrote Galatians—to prove his thesis rather than on his an earlier compatriot like Cicero, who wrote around 85 BCE.[26] His argument is thought

22 Hans Dieter Betz, "The Literary Composition and Function of Paul's Letter to the Galatians," in *The Galatians Debate: Contemporary Issues in Rhetorical and Historical Interpretation*, ed. Mark D. Nanos (Peabody, MA: Hendrickson, 2002), 4.

23 Betz, 23.

24 Troy Martin, "Apostasy to Paganism: The Rhetorical Stasis of the Galatian Controversy," in Nanos, *Galatians Debate*, 73–94.

25 James D. Hester, "The Rhetorical Structure of Galatians 1:11–2:14," *Journal of Biblical Literature* 103, no. 2 (1984): 223–33.

26 Joop Smit, "The Letter of Paul to the Galatians: A Deliberative Speech," in Nanos, *Galatians Debate*, 43.

to work at best for the first two chapters (1–2), whereas the following four chapters (3–6) fail to fit naturally within the apologetic letter genre.[27] Betz confesses this limitation, but he attributes it to Paul's great rhetorical skill "in disguising his argumentative strategy."[28]

As the proposal of Betz is associated with difficulties, scholars like Hall,[29] Witherington,[30] and Smit[31] have argued in favor of Galatians as deliberative rhetoric. For them, Paul aimed neither at justifying some past actions nor at defending his apostleship. Instead, the goal was to persuade his audience to cleave to him in the future. To do that, they had to reject the other gospel brought to them by the agitators. Deliberative rhetoric seems to be a useful rhetorical tool to Paul because it was often used to produce unity and peace while addressing a congregation plagued by discord and strife.[32]

Paul adopted the then standard Hellenistic and Greco-Roman epistolary conventions. Epistolary analysis of the form and structure of Galatians proves it. However, he modified them to serve his immediate purpose.[33] Clavin J. Roetzel, drawing a parallel between the papyrus letter and the Pauline letters, proposes a fivefold structure: salutation, thanksgiving, body, closing command, and conclusion.[34] Paul deliberately modified the conventional epistolary traditions to address the specific situation of his readers. For Roetzel, Paul's modified salutation (1:1) provides a clue to the author's purpose in the

27 Longenecker, "Introduction to Galatians," cxi; Robert G. Hall, "The Rhetorical Outline for Galatians: A Reconsideration," in Nanos, *Galatians Debate*, 30.

28 Betz, *Galatians*, 129.

29 Hall, "Rhetorical Outline for Galatians," 29–38.

30 Ben Witherington, *Grace in Galatia: A Commentary on St Paul's Letter to the Galatians* (Grand Rapids, MI: Eerdmans, 1998), 27.

31 Smit, "Paul to the Galatians," 39–59.

32 See Margaret M. Mitchell, *Paul and the Rhetoric of Reconciliation: An Exegetical Investigation of the Language and Composition of 1 Corinthians* (Louisville: Westminster John Knox, 1991), 60–64; Witherington, *Grace in Galatia*, 35; Smit, "Paul to the Galatians," 58.

33 An important contribution in epistolary structural study was by Deissmann. For him, epistles are carefully constructed literary works formed in the then known epistolary forms. Adolf Deissmann, *Light from the Ancient East: The New Testament Illustrated by Recently Discovered Texts of the Graeco-Roman World*, trans. Lionel R. M. Strachan, 2nd ed. (London: Hodder & Stoughton, 1910), 225.

34 Calvin J. Roetzel, *The Letters of Paul: Conversations in Context*, 2nd ed. (Atlanta: John Knox, 1982), 30–31.

letter—that is, the defense of his apostleship independent of the Jerusalem apostles and the authenticity of the gospel that he preached.

A more in-depth analysis of Galatians reflects the adoption of a wide range of Hellenistic and Greco-Roman epistolary conventions, which does not fit perfectly with any one form or genre. It is generally accepted that Galatians, unlike Paul's other letters, lacks a thanksgiving report immediately following the salutation and his travel plan in the body of the letter.[35] Paul's adoption of and adaptation to the Hellenistic and Greco-Roman epistolary traditions are proved beyond doubt. However, Roetzel, Dahl, and others see a Jewish epistolary and liturgical influence upon the letter in Paul's announcement of peace upon his audience (6:16).[36] Similarly, Paul's biblical exegesis in Galatians 3–4 is viewed as "Jewish rhetorical conventions."[37] In other words, Galatians reflects a hybridized or eclectic form originating from Paul, who himself moved freely in the intermediate space between the three dominant cultures—Jewish, Hellenistic, and Roman.

In recent years, James D. Hester, B. C. Lategan, and Robert M. Berchman refrained from labeling Galatians under any one particular rhetorical type.[38] Berchman argues that Paul employs all three forms of rhetoric (forensic, deliberative, and epideictic) within Galatians 1:1–5.[39] Based on the complex nature of Paul's rhetoric, Lategan pictures the audience of the Galatians.[40] For him, the intrusion of Judaizers complicates the situation in Galatia because they exploited the latecomer state of non-Jews with an incisive break from their past lifestyle. Such a break from the past made them a vulnerable target of Judaizers who claimed to teach them a practical dimension of the newfound Christian faith from its mother religion, Judaism. Paul's paraenetic

35 Roetzel, 32–34.

36 Roetzel, 37; Nils A. Dahl, "Paul's Letter to the Galatians: Epistolary Genre, Content, and Structure," in Nanos, *Galatians Debate*, 140.

37 Longenecker, "Introduction to Galatians," cxi.

38 James D. Hester, "Epideictic Rhetoric and Persona in Galatians 1 and 2," in Nanos, *Galatians Debate*, 181–96; B. C. Lategan, "The Argumentative Situation of Galatians," in Nanos, *Galatians Debate*, 385; Robert M. Berchman, "Galatians (1:1–5): Paul and Greco-Roman Rhetoric," in Nanos, *Galatians Debate*, 60–72; Robert A. Bryant, *The Risen Crucified Christ in Galatians*, SBL Dissertation Series 185 (Atlanta: SBL, 2001), 52–54.

39 Longenecker, "Introduction to Galatians," cxix; Hansen, *Galatians*, 24.

40 Lategan, "Argumentative Situation," 385.

section hinges on the two central motifs, "freedom in Christ" and "walk in the Spirit," and instructs the non-Jewish converts to refrain from accepting "the works of the law."[41] Thus, we may conclude that Paul exercised freedom in employing rhetorical tools and epistolary types from across the full range of genres of rhetoric and letter-writing practices to achieve his purpose among the Galatians.

Structure of Galatians

Epistolary greeting and introduction of the key issues (1:1–10)

Autobiographical statement of Paul (1:11–2:14)

Bridge passage: the central affirmation (2:15–21)

The OT basis of gentile incorporation in Christ (3:1–4:31)

Set free to live by the Spirit (5:1–6:10)

Signature line and summing-up of arguments (6:11–18)

GALATIANS THROUGH AN INDIAN/ASIAN PERSPECTIVE

The theology of Paul and his view on relationships within the Christian community and in society at large have significance in the Asian context. It is beyond dispute that his thoughts bear similarities with the philosophical thought patterns of multiple Asian philosophies. Several parallels can be drawn from Buddhist, Hindu, and Islamic religious philosophical traditions. Here it is not intended to be exhaustive either in highlighting all the possible points of contacts between Paul's theology and other religious traditions in Asia or in critically analyzing them from a Christian theological standpoint, though that would be a worthwhile exercise. Hindu and Indian religious and social contexts are given priority here over other vital religious traditions to

41 Lategan, 387–95.

view the apostle's theology contextually. I seek to do that in relation to the existing framework of contextual Christian theological discourses in India, Hindu religious-ethical philosophical traditions, and the prevailing influence of the Varna system both within and outside the church.

Christian Theology beyond Cultural Binaries

Paul, the theologian par excellence, articulated his theology within a Jewish and Greco-Roman pluralistic context in the first century that is similar to contexts in Asia today. He manifests significant traits of a theologian who is contextually grounded but operates consciously beyond cultural binaries. He resists beliefs and native traditions that clash with the gospel he received directly on the road to Damascus. This fine balance in Paul the theologian can be a standard for biblical scholars and Christian theologians in Asia to strive for. He was deeply sensitive toward his missional, sociocultural contexts and the background of his new converts. However, he resisted every attempt to cage the Christian faith in polarizing religious-cultural categories. Hence unlike many modern attempts to articulate Christian theology from a local context, Paul's theological reconstruction is inclusive-exclusive, nonpartisan, and aimed at nurturing local churches through a liberative Christological-soteriological lens within the ecclesial space.

The critical issue of contention between Paul and the Galatian agitators was the purity of the gospel he preached to the gentile Galatians. While those who later entered the Galatian churches sought to teach, in Paul's words, "a different gospel" (1:6), the apostle passionately resisted such attempts. He urged his audience not to accept such a culturally ridden gospel because it would confuse the believers. It was a corrupt version of the gospel because it subtly imposed the requirement of circumcision upon gentiles. For Paul, requiring the gentile Galatians to undergo the process of circumcision meant their submission to the enslaving Mosaic law. Paul refers to a Jew's life under the law, analogically, in 4:1–2. In the first century, Jews believed that God put nations under guardian angelic beings, and the Jews lived directly under the Sovereign God. Hence Paul says that the Galatians were under enslaving elemental spiritual forces of the world in their former life.

Similarly, Jews live in slavery by their absolute submission to a particular lifestyle under the law (4:1–2). They live under the guardian elemental spiritual forces of the world (4:3). Hence they are no different from the gentile nations' submission to slavery under the oversight of their guardian angel in a different context.[42] According to Caird, Jews repeated the error of the gentiles to live under "the elemental spiritual forces of the world" by giving absolute status to the law.[43] Thus, like the gentiles, Jews who slavishly live under the law and require others to do so are enslaved to the spiritual forces that are not by nature god.

If the condition of the Jews living under the law is such, then Paul does not want anyone among his Galatian audience to be deceived into slavery by accepting the gospel taught by the agitators in Galatia. He encouraged the gentile believers to continue to retain their unique gentile cultural identity while living in tune with the gospel of grace appropriated through faith. The struggle to relate the gospel to any culture is neither new nor exceptional.

In the past, Indian Christian theologians have attempted to articulate Christian theology in native religious and cultural terms. In that process, a dominant approach has been developed to articulate Christian theology in the Hindu Brahmanical tradition. Since the time of foreign missionaries like Robert De Nobili to the modern times, such efforts have been made with a missionary purpose, to present Christianity as a religion on par with the Hindu Vedic tradition,[44] or to prove that Christianity is more noble than Hinduism.[45] In the present Indian Christian theological discourse, K. P. Aleaz employs the *Advaitic* philosophical approaches and categories[46] to interpret the person and

42 Roji T. George, *Paul's Identity in Galatians: A Postcolonial Appraisal* (New Delhi: CWI, 2016), 202.

43 G. B. Caird, *Principalities and Powers: A Study in Pauline Theology* (Oxford: Clarendon, 1956), 49.

44 R. S. Sugirtharajah, "Complacencies and Cul-de-sacs: Christian Theologies and Colonialism," in *Postcolonial Reconfigurations: An Alternative Way of Reading the Bible and Doing Theology* (London: SCM, 2003), 152.

45 J. N. Farquhar, *The Crown of Hinduism*, 2nd ed. (New Delhi: Oriental, 1971).

46 Aleaz, after analytically approaching the Christian responses to Indian philosophy, concludes by explaining the positive role of the Indian philosophical categories in interpreting the biblical text. K. P. Aleaz, *Christian Responses to Indian Philosophy* (Kolkota: Punthi Pustak, 2005). See also K. P. Aleaz, "Indian Philosophy and the Method of an Indian Christian Philosophy," in *For a Christian Philosophy from India: Cambridge Teape Lectures, 2005* (Tiruvalla: CSS and BTTBPSA, 2006), 37–64; K. P. Aleaz, "The Sabda-Dhvani Methods of Biblical-Theological Hermeneutics," in *Christian Philosophy from India*, 108–32.

work of Christ.[47] This strand of Christian theologizing has proved to be very useful in explaining Christian theology in Indian philosophical categories. However, an inherent problem is that it speaks in the tongue of the dominant minority,[48] the Brahmanical Hindus, excluding the majority of the deprived section of people (*Avarnas* and tribals). It is also untouched by their concerns. Sugirtharajah alleges that the religious and philosophical categories they use are "of the elite and high culture in which Dalits hardly figure."[49] Such theological efforts have failed to articulate an inclusive theology beyond cultural binaries. The assertion of equality of all at the metaphysical level only co-opts non-Brahmins into alien categories of Christian theology that does not serve justice and equality here and now. Not surprisingly, many such advocates of contextualization—for example, De Nobili—have ended up enslaving Christ and the gospel within the Hindu caste practices.

In 4:8–11, Paul argues that the Galatian believers' submission to the gospel, as advocated by the agitators, would be like their return into slavery under elemental spirits who, by nature, are not gods. The Galatians who submitted to such a demand, Paul says, would be required to keep the whole law (see 5:3). But Paul contends vehemently that the Galatians are saved by faith and not by "the works of the law," which served as shorthand for all that stood as Jewish cultural "identity markers" like the law, circumcision, food laws, and the Sabbath.[50] Paul repeatedly refutes such a perversion of the gospel of Christ by the subtle imposition of a mother missionary culture upon the new gentile converts by the Jewish Christian teachers in Galatia (1:8–9). Similarly, a "dalit Christian's"[51] return to Christian theology via Brahmanical tradition is very similar to a gentile Galatian's return to cultural slavery

47 K. P. Aleaz, *Christian Thought through Advaita Vedānta* (Delhi: ISPCK, 1996); K. P. Aleaz, "Indian Philosophy and the Content of an Indian Christian Philosophy," in *Christian Philosophy from India*, 65–94.

48 The Brahmanical Hinduism is the religion of a minority, the Aryans, who invaded the Indian subcontinent and subjugated the religion of the natives, who were animists. Dalit intelligentia has repeatedly argued for their non-Hindu status.

49 Sugirtharajah, "Complacencies and Cul-de-sacs," 154.

50 J. D. G. Dunn, "The New Perspective on Paul," in *Jesus, Paul and the Law: Studies in Mark and Galatians* (Louisville, KY: Westminster John Knox, 1990), 192, 196.

51 It is a misnomer in every sense to say "Dalit Christian" in Christ, but such identification also highlights the existing social reality in the Indian Christianity.

under Judaism. In India, the gospel of Christ ought to be contextualized in hybrid cultural terms, just as Paul did. That would enable Dalits' self-actualization for liberation. In contrast, a return to Brahmanical Vedic traditions to articulate the gospel of liberation from oppressive social-religious powers is a subtle return to alien dehumanizing cultures and is spiritual and intellectual slavery.

However, liberation theologies have rightly drawn our attention to oppressive social hierarchies as requiring careful Christian theological response. Hence many have sought to formulate a *Dalit* quest for liberation through Dalit hermeneutics. The goal is to liberate the dehumanized sections of Indian society from centuries of slavery. While the intent of such a hermeneutical-theological exercise is noble, it has also operated on polarized hermeneutical principles. For example, Dalit theology is "a people's theology, and a particular people's theology, i.e., that of the Dalits, therefore, a theology *of* the Dalits, *by* the Dalits, *for* the Dalits."[52] As a countertheology, it essentializes the Dalit identity by holding pathos as the hermeneutical key over praxis. Thereby, it privileges a Dalit alone as the sole agent of reconstructing an authentic Dalit theology.[53] It is suspicious[54] of every form of dominant theological/power discourse due to its tendency "to accommodate, include, assimilate and finally conquer other theologies."[55] As a result, Dalit theology gathers steam by its methodological exclusivism,[56] which has successfully brought the hitherto overlooked historical reality of the Dalit oppression to the center of the Christian theological reflection. However, the methodological exclusivism of Dalit theology subjects it, like a victim, to the "proverbial Wittgensteinian 'mental cramp'"—that is, one trying to hold on to something as a solution which itself is the

52 M. E. Prabhakar, "The Search for the Dalit Theology," in *Indigenous People: Dalits. Dalit Issues in Today's Theological Debate*, ed. James Massey (Delhi: ISPCK, 1994), 210. Emphasis original.

53 See A. P. Nirmal, "Doing Theology from a Dalit Perspective," in *A Reader in Dalit Theology*, ed. A. P. Nirmal (Madras: Gurukal Lutheran Theological College & Research Institute, n.d.), 142.

54 See A. Maria Arul Raja, "Reading the Bible from a Dalit Location: Some Points for Interpretation," *Indian Theological Studies* 36, no. 1 (1999): 81–82.

55 Nirmal, "Doing Theology," 143; A. P. Nirmal, "Towards a Christian Dalit Theology," in Massey, *Indigenous People*, 219.

56 Nirmal, "Doing Theology," 142; Nirmal, "Towards a Christian Dalit Theology," 219.

problem.[57] Rightly, Samuel observes that it leads Dalit theology "into the discursive trap of an oppositional discourse with an apparent default of what may be called 'repetition *despite* displacement.'"[58]

If so, how should the gospel of Christ be contextualized in the Asian context? What is the role of culture in articulating Christian theology? When Paul rejects a "different gospel" preached by the agitators, he is not denying the role of the culture in interpreting the gospel within a cultural context. Instead, Paul is fighting against the subtle imposition of certain cultural elements that were not in tune with the core of the gospel. Paul occupied an in-between cultural space between the three dominant cultures—Jewish, Hellenistic, and Roman.[59] Hence he resisted the imposition of one culture above others to define the gospel. In Galatians 3–4, Paul used the OT traditions, like Abrahamic and Mosaic, to articulate the essence of the gospel—that is, a holistic liberation but beyond cultural binaries.

Even in formulating Dalit Christian theology, it is possible to operate from an in-between cultural location, like Paul sought to do in Galatians. Ayrookuzhiel points out, based on historical details from Kerala, that down through the history of religious colonization by the Brahmanical tradition, there has been a mutual exchange between caste Hindu and Dalit religious traditions, a process of cross-fertilization and hybridization. The conquering Vedic Hindu religion assimilated the Dalit places of worship; the Dalit deities as part of Brahmanical gods, like Vishnu or Shiva; Dalit worship patterns (blood offerings); Brahmin *Saantis* performing worship in Dalit shrines; and specific forms of dance in worship. Nevertheless, they invariably perceived Dalit deities as subordinate and inferior and imposed a new or modified form of religion and culture upon the latter.[60]

57 Bali Sahota, "The Paradoxes of Dalit Cultural Politics," in *Claiming Power from Below: Dalits and the Subaltern Question in India*, ed. Manu Bhagavan and Anne Feldhaus (New Delhi: Oxford University Press, 2008), 189–90.

58 Simon Samuel, "Reading the Postcolonial Creative Discourses: Towards Modelling a Strategic Postcolonial Theology of/for the Marginalia," *Doon Theological Journal* 5, no. 2 (2008): 167, emphasis original.

59 George, *Paul's Identity in Galatians*, 1–8.

60 A. M. Abraham Ayrookuzhiel, "A Proposal for the Study of the Religious Heritage of the Dalits: Some Methodological Considerations," in *Essays on Dalits, Religion and Liberation* (Bangalore: Asia Trading Corporation, 2006), 24–31; A. M. Abraham Ayrookuzhiel, "Religion and Culture in Dalits' Struggle for Liberation," in *Essays on Dalits*, 62–63.

Similarly, even religious traditions imposed by the caste Hindus valorized or subordinated the colonized Dalit religious traditions. Nonetheless, subsumed within them lay "myths and songs of protest against caste and untouchability."[61] In other words, both the Brahmanical Hindu religion and the native Dalit traditions have undergone a cultural and religious transformation. Neither religious tradition was destroyed; both retained some primitive elements. Hence we must remind ourselves of Sugirtharajah's prophetic voice in this context. He says, "Rather than striving to redeem India, Indian Christian theology's future would lie in its ability to evolve a hybridized style of identity. Its relevance will be measured not by its ability to invoke lost authenticates of ancient India or to superintend the purity of the gospel, but by its ability to create an allegory of theological hybridity."[62] In other words, the pure gospel of Paul articulated in the Indian context, or even Asian context, is not a gospel untouched by cultural elements or a gospel soaked in polarizing cultural categories; it is a gospel soaked in hybrid cultural terms that are assimilative and disruptive simultaneously toward culture.

Salvation through Faith or the Works of the Law

The agitators in Galatia taught a gospel of Christ that required gentile Galatians to accept Jewish circumcision to inherit the Abrahamic blessings available through Christ. Paul disagrees with them because he sees the availability of salvation, the promised Abrahamic blessing, via circumcision as leading to righteousness through good human works. Paul was rejecting, in Hindu terms, *moksha* through karma *marga*. In Hindu understanding, karma *marga* is one of the three ways, along with bhakti *marga* and jnana *marga*, to get liberation from the samsara (cycle of births). Just as in Hindu traditions a karma *margi* ought to perfectly perform every rule of karma yoga to attain salvation, in Galatians 5:3, Paul declares loud and clear that "every man who lets himself be circumcised . . . is obligated to obey the whole law." But the event in Antioch with Peter proves that no human, including Jews, can

61 Ayrookuzhiel, "Proposal for the Study," 38; A. M. Abraham Ayrookuzhiel, "Dalits' Challenges to Religious Systems–A People Ignored by Church History," in *Essays on Dalits*, 134.

62 R. S. Sugirtharajah, "Postcolonialism and Indian Christian Theology," in *Postcolonial Reconfigurations: An Alternative Way of Reading the Bible and Doing Theology* (London: SCM, 2003), 125.

keep the law perfectly (2:11–21). The flesh (*sarx*) is incapable of satisfying the requirement of the law perfectly. Hence "by the works of the law no one can be justified" (2:16).

If so, Paul claims that a person is justified by faith in Jesus Christ (2:16). In *Gita* 17:2–3,[63] Krishna explains that faith is based on three modes of nature. He says, "According to the modes of nature acquired by the embodied soul, one's faith can be of three kinds—in goodness, passion or ignorance. Now hear about this. O son of Bharata, according to one's existence under the various modes of nature, one evolves a particular kind of faith. The living being is said to be of a particular faith according to the modes he has acquired." Here, the term *shraddha* (faith) refers to that which originates from the mode of goodness.[64] However, under the influence of these mixed modes of nature, faith that is not out of pure goodness is not transcendental faith. The transcendental faith is to realize that one is part of the Supreme Being. Thus he is independent of three modes of material nature.

Unlike the teachings of Krishna in *Gita*, Paul does not understand "faith" as self-realization of the transcendental self. Instead, "faith" is in the gracious availability of the salvific divine offer to the sinful human beings. For Paul, one is justified and made righteous before God only through human acceptance of salvation with humility in total surrender to God. An idea in Hindu philosophy that comes close to explaining the attitude of a believer, as in Paul's concept of faith, is *prapatti*.[65] John says that "by centering on *prapatti* . . . a seeker without exceptional capacities can simply transfer the weight of one's burden (*bhara-samarpana*) to God and thereby seek refuge under God's feet (*saranagati*)."[66] Faith is humbly surrendering to God while seeking refuge in God's offer of salvation in and through Christ Jesus and transferring the burden of one's sin to God. Faith, as *prapatti*, in Paul's understanding, is trusting in God's mercy to provide a solution to sins that a human is otherwise

63 Every following citation and reference to Gita is from *Bhagavad-Gita as It Is*, ed. and trans. A. C. Bhaktivedanta Swami Prabhupada (Los Angeles: Bhaktivedanta, 1986).

64 *Gita*, 772.

65 In Hindu Vaishnavite tradition, the term *prapatti* in Sanskrit means "surrender"—that is, a total surrender to God.

66 Varughese John, "Being in the Truth: Climacus' Devout Idolater from Within Ramānujā's Visiśtādvaitic Tradition," in *Kierkegaard East and West*, Acta Kierkegaardiana 5, ed. Andrew Burgess et al. (Toronto: Kierkegaard Circle, Trinity College, 2011), 81.

incapable of scripting. In short, both Jews and gentiles stand equally before God to be justified by faith through grace available in Christ Jesus (3:15–16).

Further, if *prapatti* as faith in Paul's theology is a sinner transferring the burden of sin to God by surrender before the gracious gift of salvation from God, then the centrality of the divine act in bringing salvation through Christ to us gets deeper. The death of Christ is meaningful for human salvation only if the grace is appropriated in the attitude of *prapatti* by a believer. Paul declares in Galatians 2:21, "I do not set aside the grace of God, for if righteousness could be gained through the law, Christ died for nothing." An excellent example of a Hindu *bhakta* approaching God in repentance to receive divine mercy is Saint Tukaram in Marathi Bhakti tradition.[67] He prays yearningly, "Do not fail to do Thy duty, O compassionate God! It becomes us to commit sins, but it becomes Thee to succor the unholy. I have done my duty, and it behoves Thee to discharge Thine. Do not fail to accomplish Thy traditional task, says Tuka."[68] It is notable that a *saranagati* (surrendered person) is saved not by the act of *prapatti* but solely by the grace of the deity.

In short, the expression "justification by faith" must always be suffixed with "through grace." If not, seen through the *prapatti* lens, faith is another human effort to attain salvation from God. It would fall short of God's grace to attain salvation. Faith as *prapatti* in God's grace is effective only by God's reciprocation by grace toward a *saranagati* who approaches in humility and repentance to receive the divine offer. Then the process of *shraddha* or *bhava* or *vishwas* is a mere invocation for the grace of God, but one is saved solely by the saving grace of God.

Virtues and Hindu Understanding of *Guna*

In Galatians 5–6, Paul moves on to speak about the life of a believer in the Spirit. He stresses the ethical aspect of a believer's life in Christ. Paul does not want to send out a wrong impression to Galatians that by arguing vehemently against their submission under the law, he is approving a libertine lifestyle

67 See Roji T. George, "Divine Grace in the Making of Paul, the Yesu Bhakta: Re-claiming the Role of Grace in the Self-Consciousness of Paul as a Bhakta in the Light of St. Tukaram's Bhakti Thought," *Bangalore Theological Forum* 45, no. 1 (2013): 74–96.

68 Thomas Darbe, *The God-Experience of Tukaram: A Study in Religious Symbolism* (Pune: Jnana-Deepa Vidyapeeth, Institute of Philosophy and Religion, 1987), 12.

among Christians (5:13). His advocacy to "freedom" is limited to overthrowing "the yoke of slavery" (5:1) under the law because it is incompatible with "justification by faith" in Christ Jesus.

Paul's articulation of Christian ethics before Galatians rests on the idea of love (*agape*). He says, "For in Christ Jesus neither circumcision nor uncircumcision has any value. The only thing that counts is *faith expressing itself through love*" (5:6; emphasis added). In Dunn's words, it is Paul's "love-energized-faith,"[69] which means that Christian faith in God is actualized visibly only though love. If not, "faith" is dead, it is passive, and it is invisible and unnoticed. There is an inseparable bond between faith and love, according to Paul, in a "new creation" existence in Christ (6:15).

The idea of "new creation" refers to a believer's spiritual existence in Christ, having been justified by his death. Neither external bipolarities (circumcised/uncircumcised; 5:6; 6:15) nor passive hope of future justification based on the present status of being justified in Christ (5:5) is relevant in this new spiritual existence. Instead, the spiritual "new creation" state of a believer is manifest only in a corporate setup in and through love. It is a conscious human choice, aided by the Spirit, of a believer to perform acts of love in one's new creation mode of spiritual existence. Paul exhorts the Galatian believers to "serve one another humbly in love. For the entire law is fulfilled in keeping this one command: 'Love your neighbor as yourself'" (5:13–14). Later, Paul declares that by serving one another in love, "you will fulfil the law of Christ" (6:2). In fact, "'the law of Christ' signifies its unique space within the new dispensation of Christ where the Christ modeled self-sacrificial love redefines the law itself."[70] The primacy of "love" in Paul's characterization of one's existence as a "new creation" is further evident in his discussion on the "fruit of the Spirit" (5:22–23). "Love" stands first in the list of virtues. The list of virtues is contrasted with "the acts of the flesh" associated with "the desires of the flesh" (5:16). Hence Paul articulates his ethical teaching within the framework of two bipolar spheres of human existence where one makes a conscious choice of act.

Hindu philosophical discussion on virtues (*Gunas*) recognizes three modes of material nature: *sattva*, *rajas*, and *tamas* (Gita 14:5). *Sattva* is essentially

69 Dunn, *Galatians*, 272.

70 George, *Paul's Identity in Galatians*, 225.

goodness and harmony, whereas *rajas* is dynamic being associated with passion. The former leads to happiness, but the latter causes "fruitive action" (Gita 14:9) that is the active potential to actualize, in Paul's words, "the desires of the flesh." *Tamas* is generally associated with destructive force—that is, darkness and chaos. It produces "madness." These three are usually understood to be always coexistent in every person. But they are in constant opposition to each other for supremacy (Gita 14.10). The dominance of any one at a point of time in a human being characterizes someone's conduct. However, in the teaching of Krishna, the only way for one to elevate from the *tamasic* to the *sattvic* state is when an individual is aided by the spiritual master's right guidance to realize the transcendental mode of Brahman ultimately. In such an elevated state of being, one is liberated from the deeds of lower modes of existence and begins to see things in their real state untouched by the material nature (Gita 14:19). It brings the realization that the activities performed have no performer/agency but are the interplay of the three *gunas*. It coincides with the realization of the Ultimate Being as one beyond the three modes.

In other words, beyond the influence of the three modes, the real self can function to attain freedom. In reply to Arjuna, Krishna says, "O son of Pandu, he who does not hate illumination, attachment, and delusion when they are present or long for them when they disappear" (Gita 14:22). Such a detached state of existence, in a sense, absolves humans of their responsibility of any action because the inner self is independent of the modes of material nature while realizing that the Ultimate One transcends the material nature. Thus "human actions are amoral. After all, an action may be deemed moral only if the actor has moral agency to choose freely actions that are judged to be moral or immoral."[71] However, Paul's view of the human role in sin is quite contrary.

For Paul, the "desires of the flesh" are the result of the fallen human nature that is corrupted by sin. Human beings are responsible for their actions. Hence the exhortation to the Galatians is to learn to live being "led by the Spirit." For Paul, the human self is not independent of the material nature but is enslaved and corrupted by the power of sin or *tamas*. It is the *tamas* that controls a sinful, unregenerated human self. Hence for Paul, one in the active *rajas* state desires to perform acts of ignorance and madness. Humans

71 Aruthuckal Varughese John, "The Ethical Requirement in Hinduism and Christianity," *Doon Theological Journal* 17, no. 1 (2020): 68.

are responsible moral agents of actions who willfully choose to perform any act. In their postconverted state, the Galatian believers are urged to practice *sattvic* virtues "in Christ." Here, a regenerated believer is aided by the Spirit to perform *the sattvic gunas*, the "fruit of the Spirit." However, as for Paul, human beings are responsible moral beings. As free moral agents, they ought to operate in freedom (Gal 5:13). They ought to make a conscious choice not to "indulge [in] the flesh; [but] rather, [to] serve one another humbly in love" (Gal 5:13). In short, unlike in Krishna's teaching, in material nature, humans are not merely under the influence of *sattva* on the way to gain intellectual realization of being beyond three modes of material nature. Instead, believers "in Christ" have the capacity to desire (*rajas*) to act responsibly for the prompting of the Spirit, although they are made helpless by the *tamasic* mode of nature active in the flesh. They are aided by the Spirit to actualize their *sattvic* state of existence as a new creation in Christ to visibly demonstrate their "love-energized-faith," here and now, in a social context.

Community "in Christ" beyond Social Binaries

Battling against the divisive forces operating within the Galatian churches, Paul not only defends his apostleship and the purity of the gospel that he directly received from Christ but also explains the Jew-gentile equality "in Christ." Paul uses the "in Christ" phrase in Galatians to create an imaginary space of self-emancipation for the disenfranchised. Paul uses "Christ" or "the Lord" with different Greek prepositions like "in" (1:22; 2:4, 17; 3:14, 26, 28; 5:6; see 5:10 for "in the Lord"), "into" (3:27; see 3:24), and "of" (3:29; 5:24) within Galatians. Together, they form the apostle's mystical or participatory language. While the former two prepositions imply a shared imaginary space of existence or a movement into it, the third preposition refers to belongingness or ownership. The apostle repeatedly uses these prepositional phrases in relation to the church because the community of believers shares life in Christ. In other words, Christ is the imaginary space in or into which all believers, Jew or gentile, are brought in to share in the divine offer of salvation.

The significance of participatory language in Galatians is that for Paul, "in Christ" is an inclusive space where all social, cultural, political, and other polarities get deconstructed. In Galatians 3:28, Paul declares, "There is neither Jew nor Gentile, neither slave nor free, nor is there male and female, for you are all one in Christ Jesus." The reason for such a bold claim is that for the apostle, "all" are children of God through Christ Jesus (3:26). The dividing wall, represented by the law, between Jews and the rest of the nations is demolished in Christ. Now, in the "new creation" (5:16) in Christ, there is no hierarchy, no polarity, and no narrow social-cultural specificities that celebrate exclusivism of any sort. As a result of God's redemptive grace, made available to every human through the sacrificial death of Christ, the ultimate identity visible is one that is being clothed with Christ (3:27).

Paul's words are countercultural when read in the context of the Hindu *Varna* system. Traditionally, Hindu society was divided into four major *Varnas* (castes) as part of the social labor division: "Each one is separate from the other by strict purity-pollution rules along with other rules guiding socio-religious reciprocity between the four major castes and subcastes."[72] However, the system degenerated later and became a highly oppressive system that privileged the high castes like the *Brahmins* and dehumanized the oppressed lower class called the *Shudras*. Swami Bhaskarananda claims, "Caste, originally determined by the qualities and aptitudes of the individual, was made hereditary by self-interested people in positions of power and authority. They wanted to perpetuate their caste-based social privileges. As a result, the caste system degenerated."[73] The plight of those left outside the *Varnas*, like the *Adivasis* (tribals) or *Dalits*, was very bad because they were not even accorded a human status. The religious explanation for the existing caste system is that the four *Varnas* originate from the body of Brahma: the *Brahmins* (priests) from the head, the *Kshatriyas* (warriors) from the breast, the *Vaishyas* (merchants) from the thighs, and the *Shudras* (untouchables) from the feet. Paul's understanding of all believers equally sharing in the body of Christ is contrary to Manu's rationalization of the Hindu *Varna* system as originating from the body of *Brahma*. While Paul deconstructs polarities "in Christ," Manu constructs hierarchy, justifying division and inequality in Hindu society.

Another vital Hindu ritual *Janeu* (or *Yagyovati*) is a distinct mark of a male *Brahmin* or *Kshatriyas* child's superior status as "twice born" (*Dwija*). The rite

72 Roji T. George, "The Northern Indian Context," in *Christian Higher Education in Northern India and Nepal as Revitalization Movements: Report on the Revitalization Conference Held in Dehradun, India, July 2014*, ed. Robert A. Danielson et al. (Wilmore, KY: First Fruit, 2017), 19.

73 Swami Bhaskarananda, *The Essentials of Hinduism: A Comprehensive Overview of the World's Oldest Religion*, Indian ed. (Mylapore: Sri Ramakrishna Math, 1998), 25.

affirms and initiates the male child into formal training in Hindu religious scriptures, rites, and rituals. As *Janeudhari*, he is superior and socially privileged over other castes' male members due to his religious pedigree, and he is expected to flawlessly fulfill all the religious-ethical requirements. Although it is not an identical practice, the rite of circumcision as a mark of Abrahamic covenant performed on the body of male children in Jewish society in the first century entitled male children to a ritualistic Jewish pedigree implying superior status before gentiles. For Paul, in the mystical Christ space ("in Christ") of liberation, the polarizing Jewish religious pedigree like circumcision was redundant. In Galatians 6:15, Paul says, "Neither circumcision nor uncircumcision means anything; what counts is a new creation."

The condition of Indian Dalit Christians in Indian churches is not much better than that of believers in Galatians under pressure from the Jewish Christian Judaizers who came with a culturally colored gospel that erected a hierarchy within the body of Christ. The church in India is not untouched by the non-Christian religious and cultural practice of the caste system. While there are community-based, homogenous Christian groups that exist, dividing the body of Christ across the caste system, the marginalization of Dalit Christians within the churches in India is widespread.

CONCLUSION

Paul sent the letter to a group of churches in the South Galatian region. He had founded these churches during his first missionary journey before the Jerusalem Council. In the first century, the basis of incorporation of gentile Christians into the church became a contentious issue among the Jewish Christians. Hence Paul, along with Barnabas, went up to Jerusalem to counsel with the apostles. The issue was seemingly settled with few guidelines agreed upon to foster Jew-gentile table fellowship. However, the political upheavals in Jerusalem had its share in igniting the issue again. As Paul, and later Peter, returned to Antioch (Syria), some who were sent from James caused Peter to buckle under the pressure upon realizing the hidden threat. Peter's hypocritical act of moving away from the table fellowship with gentiles at Antioch caused Paul to directly confront Peter.

Meanwhile, the spread of the Law-observant mission in Galatia caused trouble in the churches. In this context, Paul sent the letter between 50 and 51 CE, appealing to the gentile Christians to resist the other gospel preached among them by the agitators. The theological themes that we find developed by Paul in the letter have vital implications in the Asian context. Within the Hindu context in India, the theology of Paul in Galatians is theologically similar but dissimilar. It does challenge the social-cultural value systems, but it is also possible to explain Paul's theology through Hindu philosophical categories. The challenge is to appropriate Paul and his theology in the traditional Hindu thinking system to explain Christian theology in native Vedic philosophical systems. The church needs to stand against the oppressive religious-cultural systems and practices to script liberation for the oppressed and the dehumanized in the space of self-emancipation, "in Christ."

FURTHER READING

Aleaz, K. P. 2006. "Indian Philosophy and the Content of an Indian Christian Philosophy." In *For a Christian Philosophy from India: Cambridge Teape Lectures, 2005*, 65–94. Tiruvalla: CSS and BTTBPSA.

Bruce, F. F. 1982. *The Epistle of Paul to the Galatians: A Commentary on the Greek Text.* NIGTC. Exeter: Paternoster.

Deissmann, A. 1910. *Light from the Ancient East: The New Testament Illustrated by Recently Discovered Texts of the Graeco-Roman World.* 2nd ed. Translated by Lionel R. M. Strachan. London: Hodder & Stoughton.

Dunn, J. D. G. 1990. "The New Perspective on Paul." In *Jesus, Paul and the Law: Studies in Mark and Galatians*, 183–206. Louisville, KY: Westminster John Knox.

Farquhar, J. N. 1971. *The Crown of Hinduism.* 2nd ed. New Delhi: Oriental Books Reprint.

Fung, R. Y. K. 1988. *The Epistle to the Galatians.* NICNT. Grand Rapids, MI: Eerdmans.

George, R. T. 2016. *Paul's Identity in Galatians: A Postcolonial Appraisal.* New Delhi: CWI.

Hansen, G. W. 1994. *Galatians.* IVPNTC. Leicester, UK: IVP.

Howard, G. 1979. *Paul: Crisis in Galatia*. SNTSMS 35. Cambridge: Cambridge University Press.

Martyn, J. L. 1997. "A Law-Observant Mission to Gentiles." In *Theological Issues in the Letters of Paul*, 7–24. Nashville: Abingdon.

Witherington, B. 1998. *Grace in Galatia: A Commentary on St Paul's Letter to the Galatians*. Grand Rapids, MI: Eerdmans.

ELEVEN

The Letter to the Ephesians

Jayachitra Lalitha
Ekklēsia Centre for Biblical Research and Pastoral Accompaniment
Bengaluru, India

The Letter to the Ephesians offers very interesting readings and poses many challenges to Asian NT scholarship because it resonates with the Asian cultures and societies in its faith articulations and theological postulations. Every literary work is a product of the author's interaction with the local culture, language, social practices, and political allegiances. The Ephesian narrative has evolved from the colonial experiences of the author and the readers immediately from the Roman captivation of Ephesus in the first century CE. Ephesus was one of the prime centers of Christianity in general and was the third epicenter of Christianity, trailing only Rome and Alexandria. Therefore, Ephesians reveals the struggle of the early Christians to adhere to their new-found Christian faith without compromising to the then surrounding Greco-Roman sociocultural and stringent Roman political ideological impositions. Present-day Asia, with a varied history of colonization in its different regions, can easily identify with the struggle of the author of Ephesians to articulate Christian theology in a more relevant manner to the believers in Ephesus, who were in constant colonial encounter with the Greco-Roman cultures. In this chapter, Asian perspectives are applied by inferring the unique Asian sociocultural and political nuances in the text.

HISTORICAL AND LITERARY ANALYSIS OF EPHESIANS

The Letter to the Ephesians, in the opinion of many scholars, is not really a letter but a theological discourse addressed to a larger audience irrespective of location, time, and space. There are clear and distinct similarities between Colossians and Ephesians, and it is believed that Ephesians is dependent on Colossians. Besides, these two letters probably were written as covering letters for traditional Pauline letters with an intention to make the early Pauline theology relevant for post-Pauline times in the latter half of the first century CE. The major thrust of the letter is the unity of the church, and it runs through the letter because the Ephesian communities "would formerly have been part of the Pauline mission but are now jeopardized by the outside teachings of unknown origin and content."[1]

Authorship

Traditionally, the letter to the Ephesians is attributed to Pauline authorship. The internal evidences in support of Pauline authorship are drawn from the implied author's allusions to apostolic authority (1:1) and suffering for the cause of Christ, his gospel, and the gentiles (3:1, 13; 4:1; 6:19–20). The author calls himself Paul, a point which is sufficient in general case to approve the authenticity of the letter; nevertheless, critical research has raised suspicion on this claim of Pauline authorship. It is worth noting that the attestation of Pauline authorship of Ephesians draws strong support from the writings of early Christian teachers as well.[2]

A majority of NT scholars is doubtful of the Pauline authorship of the Letter to the Ephesians. Erasmus of Rotterdam initiated the critical study on the authorship of Ephesians in the sixteenth century (1519), followed by Edward Evanson (1792) and W. de Wette (1847). According to Evanson, the letter is very impersonal in its tone as the author says, "I have heard of your faith . . . and your love" (Eph 1:15), which is unlikely from a person who spent a little more than two and a half years in Ephesus (see Acts 18:18–21; 19:1–20:1). The

1 E. Elizabeth Johnson, "Ephesians," in *Women's Bible Commentary Expanded Edition with Apocrypha*, ed. Carol A. Newsome and Sharon H. Ringe (Louisville: Westminster John Knox, 1998), 429.

2 Harold W. Hoehner, *Ephesians: An Exegetical Commentary* (Grand Rapids, MI: Baker Academic, 2002), 2–4.

author assumes that the addressees have most probably heard of his ministry (3:2). There are no individuals mentioned by name or greeted. Further, the epistle ends with a brief, impersonal farewell.[3]

The arguments against Pauline authorship, postulated by W. M. L. de Wette, are significant because they have influenced the research ever after. Wette had highlighted three points: the literary dependence of Ephesians upon Colossians; the distinctive style of the epistle, in particular the use of relative clauses, participles, prepositional phrases, and genitival constructions; and the presence of certain expressions such as "on the foundation of the apostles and prophets" (Eph 2:20) and "the holy apostles and prophets" (Eph 3:5).[4] Thereafter, a number of scholars questioned the authenticity of Pauline authorship.[5] A comprehensive discussion on authorship is found in the work of C. L. Mitton.[6] Mitton has highlighted the new words and phrases in Ephesians that are lacking in the Pauline corpus;[7] the literary style (with long sentences); literary dependence on Colossians; and the different use of words like "mystery" (1:9; 3:3; 5:32; 6:19), "fullness" (1:10, 23; 3:19), and "plan" (1:10; 3:2, 9). He further points out the historical arguments—for instance, the issue of the place of gentiles in churches is replaced by the way the gentiles have to treat Jews. This historical context refers to a later period than Paul himself.[8]

Finally, Mitton sheds light on three doctrinal arguments: the reference to "universal church" (1:22; 3:10, 21; 5:23, 24, 27) replacing the issue of circumcision by the unity of the church; apostles and prophets replacing Christ (Eph 3:5; see 1 Cor 3:11) as the foundation of the church; and the denial of an

3 Edward Evanson, *The Dissonance of the Four Generally Received Evangelists and the Evidence of Their Respective Authenticity Examined* (Ipswich, MA: George Jermym, 1792), 261–62; Hoehner, *Ephesians*, 21.

4 W. M. L. de Wette, *An Historico-critical Introduction to the Canonical Books of the New Testament*, 5th ed., trans. Frederick Frothingham (Boston: Crosby, Nichols, 1858), 88–92, cited by Martin Kitchen, *Ephesians* (London: Routledge, 1994), 5.

5 H. J. Holtzmann (1872), G. Bornkamm (1948), C. Maurer (1951), M. Dibelius (1953), D. E. Nineham (1956), E. Käsemann (1958), and H. Conzelmann (1962). M. V. Abraham, *Theology of St. Paul: An Introduction* (Tiruvalla: Christava Sahitya Samiti, 2008), 10–11.

6 C. L. Mitton, *The Epistle to the Ephesians: Its Authorship, Origin and Purpose* (Oxford: Oxford University Press, 1951), 11; C. L. Mitton, *Ephesians* (London: Oliphants, 1976), 15.

7 While Ephesians has the word *devil* (4:27; 6:11), Paul would be more likely to use the word *Satan*.

8 Mitton, *Ephesians*, 17, cited by Kitchen, *Ephesians*, 6.

imminent Parousia (Eph 2:7; 3:21; 4:13), resulting in household codes differing from Pauline teaching on marriage.[9]

From the various scholarly opinions discussed earlier, the arguments weigh more in favor of non-Pauline authorship of the letter to the Ephesians. This letter could be attributed to post-Pauline authorship on the basis of the lack of the author's familiarity with the Ephesian church, the author's familiarity with the traditions of holy apostles and prophets (see 2:20; 3:5), non-Pauline literary style and vocabulary, and the historical reality of gentile Christians outnumbering Jewish Christians.

Date

In line with the arguments favoring post-Pauline authorship, a proposed date between 80 and 90 CE might be acceptable.[10] This would substantiate the Ephesian author's postapostolic perspective and knowledge of Paul's letters. Further, the early Christian teachers' familiarity with the Ephesian text can also be rationalized.[11] Clement of Rome, Ignatius, Bishop of Antioch, Polycarp, Bishop of Smyrna, Irenaeus, Bishop of Lyons, Clement of Alexandria, and Tertullian of Carthage have quoted heavily from Ephesians, authenticating the quoted words as words of the disciples or the school of Paul, thus reiterating the possibility of a date after Paul's death.[12]

Destination

Ephesians 1:1 mentions the destination of the letter as Ephesus. There are manuscripts that omit the name Ephesus in the text; however, they retain it in the title. The scholars who attribute the letter to Paul are against the Ephesian destination for the reason that Paul stayed in Ephesus during his second missionary journey and knew the church he founded very well (see Acts 19–20). This appears to contradict the reference to Paul having heard of the faith of the addressees (1:15) and the addressees having heard of Paul's mission (3:3).[13]

9 Mitton, *Ephesians*, 17, cited by Kitchen, *Ephesians*, 7.

10 W. G. Kümmel, *Introduction to the New Testament*, ed. and trans. H. C. Kee (Nashville: Abington, 1975), 366.

11 Andrew T. Lincoln, *Ephesians*, Word Biblical Commentary 42 (Nashville: Thomas Nelson, 1990), lxxiii.

12 Hoehner, *Ephesians*, 2–4.

13 Kitchen, *Ephesians*, 35.

But for those who opt for a post-Pauline origin of the letter, Ephesus is undeniably the destination of the letter.

The city of Ephesus had "a Greek connection as early as 1100 BCE. It was the chief of the twelve Ionian cities in Asia Minor's west coast. Croesus conquered it in 560 BCE., Antiochus captured it around 196 BCE., it was incorporated into the Roman province of Asia in 133 BCE., Mithridates had a brief stronghold there in 88 BCE., but it was returned to the Romans, and was eventually sacked by the Goths in 263 CE."[14] With an estimated population between 200,000 and 250,000 people, Ephesus stood as the third largest city in the Roman Empire behind Rome and Alexandria. It was the capital of the Roman province of Asia and the main port of its region. The temple for Artemis in Ephesus was considered one of the seven wonders of the ancient world. This city was held with considerable importance for both Greek and Roman interests.[15]

With regard to the origin and progress of Christianity, it may be noted that Ephesus under Roman rule was a sufficiently significant city for scholars like Von Harnack to call it the third capital of Christianity.[16] Emperor worship and Roman-imposed orders in Ephesus had tremendously influenced the lives of Christians as well as incorporated Roman imperial social and moral codes into Christian ethic. The Roman government tried to bring about external political and economic unity; however, it was difficult to achieve social integration of all the cosmopolitan people who lived under Roman imperialism.[17] In this chapter, it is presupposed that the author is post-Pauline, and therefore, the destination is invariably identified as Ephesus.

14 Accessed October 22, 2008, http://www.novumtestamentum.com/acts/Ephesus/index.html (URL inactive).

15 Accessed October 22, 2008, http://www.novumtestamentum.com/acts/Ephesus/index.html (URL inactive); accessed October 22, 2008, http://ancienthistory.about.com/od/artarchaeologyarchitect/qt/Ephesus.html (URL inactive).

16 Adolf Von Harnack, *Marcion: Das Evangelium vom fremden Gott. Eine Monographie zur Geschichte der Grundlegung der Katholischen Kirche*, vol. 45, 2nd ed., ed. Adolf von Harnack and Carl Schmidt (Leipzig: J. C. Hinrichs'sche Buchhandlung, 1924), cited by Ernst Best, *Essays in Ephesians* (Edinburgh: T&T Clark, 1997), 14.

17 Lincoln, *Ephesians*, lxxxiv.

Purpose

The Letter to the Ephesians retains its ambiguity regarding the purpose of its writing and the historical context even after many years of NT research. This has in turn led to the popularity of the view that it is a circular letter, a view held mostly by those who propose Pauline authorship.[18]

In 1933, E. J. Goodspeed claimed that the Ephesians was written by a follower of Paul to serve as an introduction to a collection of Paul's letters. He based this on the observation that there is no reference in Acts to Paul's writings. This author, being familiar with the Pauline letter to Colossians probably because he himself was from Colossae, wrote the Letter to the Ephesians with key terms and themes derived from the Letter to the Colossians.[19] Mitton, despite his disapproval of Goodspeed's theory of treating Ephesians as an introduction to the Pauline corpus, accepted the possibility of the author's relation with the Pauline letters and the intention of presenting the message of the collected writings of Paul to the communities of new believers.[20]

Andrew T. Lincoln[21] and R. Schnackenburg[22] have rejected outright the proposal of Goodspeed and Mitton mainly because it is difficult to argue that a single author attempted to collect all the letters of Paul while accepting the possibility of gradual spreading of the Pauline writings as realistic. Further, Goodspeed's theory fails to address the pseudonymity of the letter.[23] N. A. Dahl believes that Ephesians was written by Paul and was originally delivered as a homily for a baptismal occasion, instructing young gentile Christians regarding the importance of their faith and baptism. Ephesians 1:3–5 can be easily understood as a blessing on the gentile believers before undergoing the

18 John Muddiman, *The Epistle to the Ephesians*, Black's New Testament Commentaries, ed. Morna D. Hooker (London: Continuum, 2001), 12.

19 Edgar J. Goodspeed, *The Meaning of Ephesians* (Chicago: University of Chicago Press, 1933), 3–17, cited by Muddiman, *Ephesians*, 12; Margaret Y. MacDonald, *The Pauline Churches: A Socio-historical Study of Institutionalization in the Pauline and Deutero-Pauline Writings* (Cambridge: Cambridge University Press, 1988), 93.

20 Mitton, *Ephesians*, 17, cited by MacDonald, *Pauline Churches*, 93.

21 Lincoln, *Ephesians*, xlvii–lxxiii.

22 Rudolf Schnackenburg, *Ephesians: A Commentary*, trans. Helen Heron (Edinburgh: T&T Clark, 1991), 24–37.

23 Muddiman, *Ephesians*, 13.

rite of baptism.[24] G. Schille highlights the presence of a hymn of baptismal thanksgiving and catechesis in the letter attesting to its liturgical origin.[25] J. C. Kirby did an elaborate study along the same line of thinking and concludes that the baptismal sermon in Ephesians has links with the festival of Pentecost influenced by Jewish liturgical traditions.[26]

A major stream of NT scholarship has dealt with the relation of Jewish and gentile Christians mentioned in Ephesians (2:11–21). H. Chadwick proposed that this letter was an apologetic piece of writing reiterating the antiquity of the Christian faith by linking the church's continuity with its Judaistic roots. His interest was to show the church as universal so the Christian church could be viewed as "a metaphysical entity encompassing all generations."[27] Ernst Käsemann proposed that the context may have been that of the gentile Christian majority despising the Jewish Christian minority.[28]

K. M. Fischer added an ecclesiastical crisis to the presumed Jewish-gentile crisis. He argued that the letter responded to "a crisis of authority in the Church caused by the change from Pauline itinerant missionary structures . . . to the residential hierarchical organization that [was] threatening to supplant them."[29] In his argument, the letter was written during the period when the new Episcopal order was promoted in the gentile Christian congregations in Asia Minor. The reference to "the foundation of the apostles and prophets" in 2:20 is a call to reverting to the charismatic structure of Pauline mission.[30] But MacDonald and Lincoln question the impact of the supposed crisis on

24 Nils Alstrup Dahl, "Gentiles, Christians, and Israelites in the Epistle to the Ephesians," *HTR* 79, nos. 1–3 (January/April/July 1986): 38.

25 G. Schille, *Fruhchristliche Hymnen* (Berlin: Evangelische Verlagsanstalt, 1965), cited by Muddiman, *Ephesians*, 14.

26 J. C. Kirby, *Ephesians: Baptism and Pentecost* (London: SPCK, 1968), cited by MacDonald, *Pauline Churches*, 93; Muddiman, *Ephesians*, 14; Kitchen, *Ephesians*, 8.

27 H. Chadwick, "Die Absicht des Epheserbriefes," in *ZNW* 51 (1960): 145–53, cited by Lincoln, *Ephesians*, lxxx.

28 E. Käsemann, "Ephesians and Acts," in *Studies in Luke-Acts*, ed. L. E. Keck and J. L. Martyn (London: SPCK, 1968), 291, cited by Lincoln, *Ephesians*, lxxx; MacDonald, *Pauline Churches*, 94.

29 K. M. Fischer, *Tendenz und Absicht des Epheserbriefs* (Gottingen: Vandenhoeck & Ruprecht, 1973), 21–25, cited by Muddiman, *Ephesians*, 14.

30 Fischer, *Tendenz und Absicht, 79–94*, cited by Lincoln, *Ephesians*, lxxx.

the unity of Jewish and gentile Christians.[31] Care must be taken that such speculation about the hostile attitude of gentile Christians toward Jewish Christians does not sideline research on understanding the implied social situation in Ephesians 2:11–21.

Recipients

A concern that emerges here is about the identity of the recipients of the letter. Are they exclusively gentile Christians in composition? In that case, what is their relation to Jewish Christians? What was the sociocultural and political necessity that persuaded the author to inculcate Jewish religious and cultural elements in the paraenesis of the letter? These questions need urgent attention if the embedded Jewish nature of the letter is to be unraveled. Dahl's comment is significant: the author does not seem to take into account the presence of Jewish Christians among the recipients of the letter. By doing this, despite the author's keen interest in the Jewish origin of the church, the letter fails to "show any concern for the relationship of his audience to contemporary Jews in or outside the church."[32] Therefore, in the following section, we shall probe the explicit references in the letter to the Greek term *ta ethne*, which literally means "the nations" but is generally translated as "gentiles" in English versions.

In Ephesians, the term *ta ethne* (the nations) occurs thrice (2:11; 3:6; 4:17); however, Greek words from the same root appear in 3:1 and 3:8 as well. The author uses the term *ta ethne* to refer either to non-Jewish Christians or to non-Jews (3:1; 4:7). The phrase *ta ethne* is generally translated in English as "gentiles," referring to nations other than Israel. Yet it emphasizes the non-Jewish part of humanity instead of a collective plurality of nations.[33] From pre-Christian periods, *ta ethne* had gained the significance of "nations other than one's own," mainly in contrast to Israel or the church.[34] In a nonsociological sense, this word is used to refer to the people who are not part of the chosen people of Israel.[35] Interestingly, Jews were not the only ones who used *ethne* to denote foreigners,

31 MacDonald, *Pauline Churches*, 94; Lincoln, *Ephesians*, lxxx.

32 Dahl, "Gentiles, Christians, and Israelites," 31, cited by Lincoln, *Ephesians*, lxxxiv.

33 Dahl, 31–33.

34 D. R. de Lacey, "Gentiles," in *Dictionary of Paul and His Letters*, ed. Gerald F. Hawthorne, Ralph P. Martin, and Daniel G. Reid (Downers Grove, IL: InterVarsity, 1998), CD-ROM.

35 Bertram, "*Ethnos/Ethnikos*," in *Theological Dictionary of the New Testament*, 3rd ed., ed. Gerhard Kittel, trans. Geoffrey W. Bromiley (Grand Rapids, MI: Eerdmans, 1968), 2:367.

because prior to the Romans, Greeks called those who were alien to their nation *ethne* to distinguish them and their national identity. The Greeks used this term to refer to non-Greek peoples in a disparaging sense.[36] So it may be inferred that the term *ethne* was generally used in a derogatory sense.

In Ephesians, there is an overall negative impression about the gentiles, who are neither Jews nor Christians. In 2:1–3, the gentiles are dead in their trespasses and sins, and they remain as the followers of the ruler of the power of the air. They are the children of disobedience (see 5:6), and they follow the desires of their flesh and senses. In verses 11–13, they are referred to as gentiles in the flesh or by birth and uncircumcised. In verse 12, an allusion is made to the gentile Christians' way of life before they believed in Christ—they were aliens from the commonwealth (citizenship) of Israel, they were strangers to the covenants of promise, and they had no hope and were without God in the world. The phrase "ones who are far off" (see 2:17) in 2:13 is originally derived from Isaiah 57:19 but is used here in the sense of exclusion in terms of sacred law rather than geographical distance.[37] So the gentiles were far off from the privileges set for the Jews and Jewish Christians.

Ephesians 4:17–19 mentions the general perception of Jews about gentiles. The gentiles live in the futility of their minds, are darkened in their understanding, are alienated from the life of God because of their ignorance and hardness of heart, have lost all sensitivity and have abandoned themselves to licentiousness, and are greedy to practice every kind of impurity. The author of Ephesians also denotes the various characteristics of gentiles in a subtle manner in 5:3–20. Moral integrity and sensitivity are expected from the Christian recipients of the letter in contrast to the behavior of gentiles.

This hostile approach to gentiles is not the end of the matter, however. The author deals with the reconciliation of gentiles with Jews through the salvific act of Jesus Christ. In Ephesians 2:14–22 in particular, the author narrates the reconciliatory act of Jesus, which transformed gentiles from being strangers and aliens to a state of being citizens with the saints and members of the household of God (see v. 19). Moreover, this united household of God

36 K. L. Schmidt, "*Ethnos* in the NT," in *Theological Dictionary of the New Testament*, 3rd ed., ed. Gerhard Kittel, trans. Geoffrey W. Bromiley (Grand Rapids, MI: Eerdmans, 1968), 2:371.

37 Dahl, "Gentiles, Christians, and Israelites," 32.

is built upon the foundation of the apostles and prophets with Christ as the cornerstone (v. 20).

Jesus has abolished the hostility between Jews and gentiles and created a new humanity beyond the liability of the Law. Because of the power of the gospel, the gentiles have now become fellow heirs, members of the same body, and sharers in the promise in Christ Jesus (Eph 3:6). Therefore, the overall negative impression about nonbelieving gentiles is changed once they believe in Christ and become members of the church. For the author, this is a great mystery of God (3:9–12).

Interesting enough, there are no anti-Jewish sentiments expressed in this epistle.[38] Further, by the time this epistle was written by the end of the first century CE, the churches were largely made of Christians of gentile origin rather than of Jewish origin. This clearly indicates a social context of Jewish hostility toward gentiles being replaced by gentile domination over Jewish Christians in the churches. By now, the Greek and Roman converts to Christianity would have outnumbered the Jewish Christians. Therefore, the gentile Christian majority would not have been viewed from a hostile point of view, but unlike the earlier communities of Christians, the contemporary generation of Christians may not have been aware of its Jewish roots. This view may be supported by the lack of anti-Semitic ideas and the presence of Jewish ideas embedded in the epistle.

Outline

1:1–2 . . . . Introductory greetings

1:3–14 . . . . The author's thanksgiving for spiritual blessings through Christ

1:15–23. . . . . . . The author's prayer for the readers of the letter to experience "the riches of Christ's glorious inheritance" and "immeasurable greatness of Christ's power"

2:1–10 . . . . Moving from death to new life

38 Dahl, 37.

2:11–22. . . . . . . New relationship through reconciliation

3:1–13 . . . . Mystery of God's plan revealed in bringing together the Jews and gentiles

3:14–21. . . . . . . Prayer for the readers

4:1–16 . . . . Responsibility to retain unity in the body of Christ

4:17–32. . . . . . . Responsibility to live the new life

5:1–20 . . . . Socially responsible to the world

5:21–6:9 . . . . . . Household codes and familial mutual relationships

6:10–20 . . . . . . Spiritual responsibility of standing firm in the Lord

6:21–24 . . . . . . Closing remarks and benediction

THE LETTER TO THE EPHESIANS: AN ASIAN CRITIQUE

It is quite evident that emperor worship in Rome and the imperial social codes have tremendously influenced the writing of the letter to the Ephesians. The Jews in Ephesus had been forced to absorb and affirm the sociopolitical hierarchical system that the Roman government had designed for civil society in general. Against their religious and moral codes of living, the Jews had to constantly accommodate the demands of the Roman administration to have peace.

Asia is a continent of different religions, ethnicities, and languages living in unity for centuries together. However, the hierarchical systems based on divisive factors such as religion, ethnicity, and language are very similar to what the Letter to the Ephesians projects. Jews, Greeks, Romans, and Christians were the major divisions of people groups based on religion, ethnicity, and language in and around Ephesus.

Religious pluralism, multiple ethnic identities, and linguistic diversity are uniquely characteristic of everyday life in Asia. For instance, my own

Asian identity that belongs to a country like India has wired in a mindset that allows constant and consistent negotiation with the surrounding socioreligious and linguistic realities. It has never been easy to coexist with people who are totally different from oneself, especially considering the sociocultural pressure to compromise with the faith and ideology of others in order to live in harmony.

Growing up in a locality of Hindu neighbors and temples, participating in Hindu festivals, and co-dining with them have been very integral to my upbringing. I am a third-generation Christian with an ancestry that goes back to a very progressive Renaissant Hindu family in the temple city of Madurai, so it has always been a challenge to be a progressive Christian with liberationist ideologies without falling prey to Hindu socioreligious and cultural practices. However, hierarchical dominations on the basis of Hindu caste identity and *Manusmṛiti*-based male chauvinism are not so easy to shed from personal and ecclesial life. Even though the majority of Indian church members belong to the previously untouchable caste communities of the Hindu religion, the ecclesial power rests with the brutally oppressive minority of Christians who converted from a Shudra caste background. This is a vicious cycle of continuing oppression of the people belonging to the margins of the caste system that favors a small group of Christians who have better opportunities of English education and economic empowerment.

As far as the Ephesian Jewish Christians were concerned, there were clear indications of heresies creeping into the Ephesian church (Eph 4:17–32; 5:10–20) due to the overarching impact of the Roman religions, the imperial cult, and their social codes of living.[39] The Epistle to the Ephesians reflects overtones of an imperial ideology as it struggles to keep the pressures from the colonial environment in check. As far as the author is concerned, God's empire is in the heavenly realms with all the spiritual blessings (1:3), which in fact becomes the starting point for narrating the whole theology against the colonial backdrop. The superior power of God is manifested in raising Jesus from the dead and placing him at his right hand in the heavenly realms (1:20). The members of the Ephesian ecclesial community are already seated with Christ in the heavenly realms (2:6). Pheme Perkins makes an interesting comment that if Ephesians 2:11–22 is read against the ideology of the Roman emperor

39 C. I. David Joy, *Revelation: A Postcolonial View Point* (Delhi: ISPCK, 2001), 7–10.

cult, the exalted Christ resembles the emperor who was exalted through the speeches in favor of him.[40]

India, like many other Asian countries, was a British colony for more than two hundred years until political independence was achieved in 1947. The British colonial India, apart from fighting the imperial political and economic exploitation of the British East India Company rule, had to constantly resist the native elitist traitors who sided with the British for vested gains. Even though the Ephesian church by the end of the first century CE consisted more of Christians from a Greco-Roman religious background, the number of Christians from a Jewish ethnic and religious background was not insignificant. The very fact that those Jewish Christians could withstand Roman persecution indicates that they had already been living in collaboration and negotiating with their sociopolitically hostile neighbors and rulers. While those Jewish Christians publicly benefited from an education in Greek language, arts, martial arts, music, dance, and civilization, their adherence to Hebrew language and Judaism remained unadulterated in their private spheres of existence.

Traditionally, Indian Christians are heavily indebted to white colonial missionaries for the imperially colored Gospel, antioriental biblical interpretations, ecclesial denominations, English education and liturgies, and four-part music notations and pipe organs. However, contemporary Christian thinkers and theologians are very critical in their approaches to the Euro-American colonization of Indian minds. Any such Indian/Asian reader of the Letter to the Ephesians will instantly identify similar anti-imperial and anticolonial nuances in the text that resonate with their own postcolonial Asian context. As the author of the Ephesians deals very sensitively with the church in Ephesus, which is predominantly made up of mixed racial and ethnic identities, the Asian/Indian church is motivated to ensure the peace that Jesus achieved by abolishing the dividing walls that tangibly separated the Jewish and "gentile" Christians. The Indian church can certainly derive from this letter spiritual and ethical strength in tackling brutal caste-based discriminations. However, caste and patriarchy seem to exist as long as the world exists! It is only the

40 Pheme Perkins, *Ephesians*, Abington New Testament Commentaries (Nashville: Abington, 1997), 51, cited by J. G. Bird, "The Letter to the Ephesians," in *A Postcolonial Commentary on the NT Writings*, ed. F. F. Segovia and R. S. Sugirtharajah (London: T&T Clark, 2007), 267.

mindset that can be changed toward the hegemonic forces that control the universe and keep people divided. Yet the portrayal of unity and harmony anticipated from those who claim to be followers of Christ in the Ephesian church remains a continuing challenge to the hypocritical, faith-based hierarchical powers in India/Asia.

The empire of God's spiritual/heavenly realm is now incarnated in the household of God (2:19), where no one remains a foreigner or alien but everyone is a fellow citizen with God's people. Interestingly, terms like *citizen*, *foreigner*, and *stranger* are all relevant in a political context of an empire. The concept of household is familiar to Asian families. Asian households share a similar vision of family members living together in unity and harmony. A study of the ethnic, religious, and linguistic groups in the multicultural Rome of the first century CE supports the idea that the Jewish and Christian communities were treated as foreign to Roman culture and social life.[41] But in the Epistle to the Ephesians, the empire is replaced by the household while retaining the other political terms. A household in a Roman society plays a significant role in that the social order is being established beginning from the smallest unit of the society. The concept of the household of God comprising all the members of the Ephesian church closely relates to the author's intention of making God's empire relevant for the church in a colonial environment. The household of God comprises all those who were treated as aliens and foreigners but who have now become fellow citizens with God's people (Eph 2:19). This household is built on the foundation of the apostles and prophets, with Christ himself as the chief cornerstone. So it is Christ who holds together the whole building of the household of God, making it a holy temple, in which God dwells by his Spirit (2:20–22).

The concept/institution of family is foundational to the stability of Asian societies. Mutual submission (Eph 5:21), sacrificial/self-giving love (Eph 5:25), and one-flesh mutuality in marital relationships are intrinsically related to Asian social bonding. The household codes in Ephesians, especially related to wives and husbands in 5:21–33, portray mutuality and submission existing among believers in the household of God as similar to the relationship of a wife and husband. By interpolating Genesis 2:24 in Ephesians 5:31,

41 Beryl Rawson, "'The Roman Family' in Recent Research: State of the Question," *Biblical Interpretation* 11, no. 2 (2003): 131.

the author affirms the mutual one-flesh relationship as more authentic than a domination-subjugation model for a Christian marriage. Genesis 2:24 in Ephesians 5:31 serves as the great mystery of union of wife and husband in comparison with the union of church and Christ.

In such a consummation of mutual one-flesh union, while the distinctiveness of both the sexes is cherished, the dichotomy of gender ceases to exist. This denotes an ideal rejection of gender dichotomy and in turn of gendered sexes. Therefore, a liberative marital union with mutual coexistence of wife and husband as one flesh can become an Asian/Indian reality. In Asia/India, where patriarchy rules in human minds, the notion of the one-flesh union provides the ground for replacing the hierarchical gender roles with a marital relationship of justice and love where "the justice will require that traditional male dominance cannot be tolerated and love will assure that the relationship does not degenerate into a sterile competition of control."[42]

All the members who were saved by the Gospel of Christ have been sealed with the mark of the Holy Spirit (1:13). Jennifer G. Bird comments that once they are marked with the Holy Spirit of promise, they are claimed by God and "are given the assurance that this counter-emperor will be true to the promise of redeeming them and offering them the inheritance of the empire of G(o)d. Instead of the emperor's gospel of salvation, we have the counter-gospel of a different deity, whose salvation is far greater than that offered by the Roman Empire."[43] Therefore, one can easily identify the sealing of the Holy Spirit as a subversive, anticolonial act. The seal of a king constantly reminds the subjects about him "as both the maintainer of justice and order and the source of authority; it also indirectly referred to the power of his kingdom, which sustained him in his role."[44] Now the loyalty of a believing person is changed from the Roman emperor to God Almighty through the gospel of Jesus Christ and by the sealing of the Holy Spirit.

Generally, the Letter to the Ephesians presents a new movement in the sense of a counterempire to the existing Roman imperial power. This is well manifested in the choice of terms like *ecclesia*, *politeia*, *aliens* and *strangers*,

42 A. T. Lincoln and A. J. M. Wedderburn, *The Theology of the Later Pauline Letters* (Cambridge: Cambridge University Press, 1993), 162.

43 Bird, *Ephesians*, 269.

44 Irene J. Winter, cited by Bird, *Ephesians*, 269.

and *peace*. "In the face of an empire that rules through military and economic control, what is the shape of a community that serves a ruler who brings reconciliation and peace by sacrificial death rather than military might? . . . How does a Christian community . . . live its life in empire?"[45] MacDonald reiterates that such terminologies highlight the points of contact of the letter with the imperial ideology; it could be of both appropriation and rejection. Unless the Ephesian church is a colonized community in itself, the thrust of the letter will not make sense to the readers.[46] It also should be noted that in the process of creating a counterempire, the Ephesian church tends to become imperial by mimicking the strategies of the imperial power. The author's inclination to use Greco-Roman terminologies and concepts like household, ekklesia, powers, and authorities, and the imagery of army/soldier in the Letter to the Ephesians attests to this.

In general, colonial discourses were prominent during the colonial period as a means of propagation of knowledge, producing texts that were invariably "colonialist" in their endorsement and thus demanding conformity to the existing dominant imperial ideologies. These texts represented the social existence of colonial relations, which were shaped by dominant imperial notions of hierarchy, competency, and absolute power and had the supreme target of consolidating the unity of the empire/imperialism.

The Letter to the Ephesians is not different because it exhibits a tendency to write back to the empire, adopting a colonial language and culture while at the same time intending to resist it from a standpoint of Christian ethical values. While there is cultural appropriation of colonial values in their socio-religious and political life, there are also elements of resistance to the Roman imperial agenda. Therefore, the outcome is not just an exact imitation of colonial ideologies; instead, there is a combination of acquiescence and resistance in relation to imperial agenda.

45 Brian J. Walsh and Sylvia C. Keesmaat, *Colossians Remixed. Subverting the Empire* (Downers Grove, IL: InterVarsity, 2004), 61.

46 Margaret MacDonald, "The Politics of Identity in Ephesians," *Journal for the Study of the New Testament* 26 (2004): 422.

CONCLUSION

The Ephesian text itself is a weaving together of different stands. On the one side, it yields to the pressing pressures from around the Roman sociopolitical powers. On the other side, it attempts to deconstruct the reliance on a framework of hierarchical domination prevalent in the Roman colonial era. As such, colonial texts cannot be seen to express the dominant ideology alone because they are a tapestry of heterogeneous cultures and discourses. This is applicable for the Letter to the Ephesians, written in the sociopolitical context of Roman imperialism. The faith community portrayed in the Letter to the Ephesians seems to project a "third space of enunciation,"[47] in which the hybridization of multicultures (Jewish, Greco-Roman, and Christian) takes place and provides a transcultural space where the colonial domination has been continually challenged. This Christian document exhibits narrative ambivalence by which the Asian/Indian reader encounters anti-imperial strategies of a fine blend of hybridity and colonial mimicry. The close inferences to Asian/Indian sociocultural and political realities make the Letter to the Ephesians an indispensable NT document in faith journey as well as academic research.

FURTHER READING

Abraham, M. V. 2008. *Theology of St. Paul: An Introduction*. Tiruvalla: Christava Sahitya Samiti.

Bird, J. G. 2007. "The Letter to the Ephesians." In *A Postcolonial Commentary on the New Testament Writings*, edited by F. F. Segovia and R. S. Sugirtharajah, 265–280. London: T&T Clark.

Dube, M. W. 2000. *Postcolonial Feminist Interpretation of the Bible*. St. Louis: Chalice.

George, M., 2004. "Domestic Architecture and Household Relations: Pompeii and Roman Ephesos." *Journal for the Study of the New Testament* 27, no. 1: 7–25.

Helton, S. N. 2005. "Ephesians 5:21: A Longer Translation Note." *Restoration Quarterly* 48, no. 1: 33–41.

47 Bill Ashcroft, Gareth Griffiths, and Helen Tiffin, *Key Concepts in Postcolonial Studies* (London: Routledge, 2004), 118.

Hezser, C. 2003. "The Impact of *Household* Slaves on the *Jewish Family* in Roman Palestine." *Journal for the Study of Judaism* 34, no. 4: 375–424.

Hoehner, H. W. 2002. *Ephesians: An Exegetical Commentary*. Grand Rapids, MI: Baker Academic.

Pui-lan, K. 2002. "Postcolonialism, Feminism and Biblical Interpretation." In *Scripture, Community and Mission*, edited by Philip L. Wickeri, 161–176. Hong Kong: CCA & CWM.

Segovia, F. F., and R. S. Sugirtharajah, eds. 2009. *A Postcolonial Commentary on the New Testament Writings*. New York: T&T Clark.

TWELVE

The Letter to the Philippians

Naw Eh Tar Gay
Myanmar Institute of Theology
Yangon, Myanmar

The Letter to the Philippians is a joyful and thankful missive of Paul. However, it was written in a difficult situation that was different from what most contemporary readers know. It was written to a church in turmoil while Paul himself was in prison. It is both a letter of suffering and a letter of hope. The letter suggests ways to be happy even in the midst of suffering. Herewith, the Letter to the Philippians will be introduced first with its author, date, city, community and occasion, and literary form and structure. Later on, some themes of the letter will be discussed in the context of Myanmar Buddhism in particular and the contemporary Asian context in general. Then I will discuss how the political situation and the traditions and teachings of Theravada Buddhism in Myanmar share some similarities with Paul's ideas and teachings. I will also exemplify how a letter written in the first century CE can be reread from an Asian perspective, shedding light on the contemporary context.

AUTHOR, DATE, AND PLACE

Historically, the church fathers like Polycarp of Smyrna, Irenaeus, Clement of Alexandria, Tertullian, and others assigned the Letter to the Philippians to

Paul.[1] But some of the modern scholars doubted the authenticity of Philippians and wondered whether it ought to be considered a Pauline letter.[2] Hawthorne states, "In spite of the great power and erudition with which Baur argued, his arguments were not convincing nor widely adopted."[3] Similarly, Guthrie also considers it as an "undisputable [Pauline] letter."[4] Paul was born and raised in Tarsus, one of the colonized cities of the Roman Empire. Philippians was probably written from a Roman prison, where Paul was in chains (1:14).[5] Paul does not mention where he was imprisoned but indicates that he was imprisoned several times (2 Cor 11:23). However, Acts mentions three places of Paul's imprisonment: Philippi (16:23–40), Caesarea (23:23–26:32), and Rome (28:16–31).[6] In addition, imprisonment in Ephesus has also been suggested.[7] Where was Paul imprisoned—in Ephesus, three hundred miles away from Philippi, or in Rome, eight hundred miles away? Internal references such as the Praetorian Guard (Phil 1:13) and the household of Caesar (4:22) could refer to people anywhere in urban centers like Ephesus and Philippi, which were widespread in the Roman Empire.[8] Such offices were located in different provinces and colonies and in major economic and administrative centers like Ephesus.[9]

1 G. F. Hawthorne, "Philippians, Letter to the," in *Dictionary of Paul and His Letters*, ed. Gerald F. Hawthorne, Ralph P. Martin, and Daniel G. Reid (Downers Grove, IL: InterVarsity, 1993), 709.

2 See F. C. Baur, *Paul, the Apostle of Jesus Christ: His Life and Works, His Epistles and Teachings* (Peabody, MA: Hendrickson, 2004).

3 Hawthorne, 709.

4 Donald Guthrie, *New Testament Introduction* (Downers Grove, IL: InterVarsity, 1990), 545; also see Craig S. Keener, *The IVP Bible Background Commentary: New Testament* (Downers Grove, IL: InterVarsity, 1993), 556; Robert P. Lightner, "Philippians," in *The Bible Knowledge Commentary: New Testament*, ed. John F. Walvoord and Roy B. Zuck (Hyderabad: Authentic, 2004), 647.

5 Joseph A. Marshal, "Imperial Intersections and Initial Inquiries toward a Feminist, Postcolonial Analysis of Philippians," in *The Colonized Apostle*, ed. Christopher D. Stanley (Minneapolis: Fortress, 2011), 154.

6 Dennis C. Duling, *The New Testament History, Literature, and Social Context*, 4th ed. (Singapore: Thomson Wadsworth, 2002), 209.

7 M. Eugene Boring, *An Introduction to the New Testament History, Literature, Theology* (Louisville: Westminster John Knox, 2012), 219–21.

8 Guthrie, *New Testament Introduction*, 550–55.

9 See Hawthorne, "Philippians," 710; Reymond E. Brown, *An Introduction to the New Testament* (Bangalore: Theological Publications in India, 2009), 495–96.

Those who favor the Ephesian imprisonment hypothesis argue that the Latin term *praetorianum* could mean any Roman military guard or a provincial Roman governor's residence and thus indicates that Paul's imprisonments were in a province outside of Rome.[10] Therefore, it is believed that he was imprisoned in Ephesus and wrote two undisputed prison letters, Philippians and Philemon, during 54 and 55 CE.[11] According to Philippians, he was also waiting for his imminent execution (1:19–26; 2:17, 23).[12] He was probably charged as a person who disturbed the civil peacefulness and created the riots mentioned in Acts 16:16–24; 17:1–9; and 19:23–41.[13] In two other undisputed letters (1 Cor 15:30–32; 2 Cor 1:8–10), Paul mentions that he was facing death in Asia and "fought with beasts at Ephesus."[14] Such references suggest that Roman prisons were terrifying places with unbearable methods of punishment (Phil 1:19–26).[15]

THE CONTEXTUAL REALITIES

It is also important to know the destination of a letter to find out its setting. Moreover, it is important to know the issues or occasions behind the letter to understand the intention of the author as much as possible.

The City of Philippi

The ancient city of Philippi was located in Macedonia, north of Greece proper, and northwest of the region known as Asia Minor (modern-day Turkey), across

10 Efrain Agosto, "Philippians," in *A Postcolonial Commentary on the New Testament Writings*, ed. Fernando F. Segovia and R. S. Sugirtharajah (London: T&T Clark, 2009), 285.

11 Duling, *New Testament*, 209; also see Hawthorne, "Philippians," 711. Lightner suggests a date of 61 or 62 CE; Lightner, "Philippians," 647.

12 Carla Swafford Works, "Philippians," in *Women's Bible Commentary*, 3rd ed., ed. Carol A Newsom, Sharon H. Ringe, and Jacqueline E. Lapsley (Louisville: Westminster John Knox, 2014), 582.

13 Neil Elliott, *Liberating Paul, the Justice of God and the Politics of the Apostle* (Minneapolis: Fortress, 2006), 196–97.

14 Duling, *New Testament*, 209.

15 Agosto, "Philippians," 285.

the Aegean Sea.[16] According to Acts 16:12, this city was a leading district of Macedonia and was a Roman colony.[17] It was originally a Greek city named after Philip II of Macedon, father of Alexander the Great.[18] In the second century BCE, it came under the control of the Romans, and from 40 BCE, Philippi was settled by Roman veteran soldiers.[19] Acts 16 mentions that around 49 CE, Paul visited this city, and the church here was the first church he established in Europe.[20] As a Roman colony, Philippi displayed typical colonial characteristics of that time. It was a place where retired soldiers were resettled and where Rome's influence was particularly strong.[21] The city played a role in Rome's civil wars and saw the development of the imperial cult.[22] It was adorned with imperial images and was proud of the Roman citizenship.[23] The people of Philippi were privileged with Roman citizenship and tax exemption and emulated Roman institutions.[24]

The Community and Its Circumstances

The community in Philippi was composed of non-Jewish Christ believers. According to Acts, Paul's usual custom was to visit the synagogue when he arrived in a city; but unlike in other cities, there was no synagogue in Philippi.[25] Acts mentions that a few women gathered at a river site on the Sabbath day (16:13–15).[26] Paul brought to faith and baptized Lydia and her household from the city of Thyatira, who was a seller of purple goods. There, he also met

16 Paul J. Achtemeier, Joel B. Green, and Marianne Meye Thompson, *Introducing the New Testament: Its Literature and Theology* (Grand Rapids, MI: Eerdmans, 2001), 391–92.

17 Ian Paul, Brian Rosner, and Carl Mosser, "Letters [of Paul]," in *The IVP Introduction to the Bible*, ed. Philip S. Johnston (Downers Grove, IL: IVP Academic, 2006), 235.

18 See more details in Hawthorne, "Philippians," 707–8.

19 Brown, *Introduction to the New Testament*, 483–85; Duling, *New Testament*, 208.

20 Duling, *New Testament*, 208.

21 Guthrie, *New Testament Introduction*, 541–45; Warren Carter, "The Gospel of Matthew," in *A Postcolonial Commentary on the New Testament Writings*, ed. Fernando F. Segovia and R. S. Sugirtharajah (London: T&T Clark, 2009), 69–70.

22 Marshal, "Imperial Intersections," 154.

23 Works, "Philippians," 581–84; Paul, Rosner, and Mosser, "Letters," 235.

24 D. Edmond Hiebert, *An Introduction to the New Testament* (Waynesboro, GA: Gabriel, 2003), 282–85; Agosto, "Philippians," 285.

25 Brown, *Introduction to the New Testament*, 485–89.

26 See Hawthorne, "Philippians," 708.

and exorcized a spirit from a slave girl who could tell the future.[27] According to Acts 16:16–24, because of this incident, Paul and Silas were charged as anti-Roman and thrown in jail.[28] But they were miraculously freed and subsequently brought to faith a jailer and his household (Acts 16:25–40).[29]

In the letter to the Philippians, Paul mentions four people by name (Epaphroditus, Euodia, Syntyche, and Clement) among other fellow workers in Philippi who were actively involved in the Jesus movement.[30] The Christ community in Philippi consisted largely of non-Jews (3:3), and its leaders were organized as bishops ("overseers") and deacons ("helpers"; 1:1).[31] Both Acts and Philippians 4:2–3 mention the significant roles of women as patrons, leaders of the church, and coworkers in the Pauline communities (see Rom 16).[32] Paul seems to have had a good relationship with the Christ believers in Philippi since the beginning (1:5).[33] He also expresses that he was both dependent and independent of the Philippians. Though he received some aid from them, he never asked for it, and he viewed himself as a self-supporting missionary (4:11).[34]

Paul's relationship with the Christ-believing community in Philippi was good, but they were troubled by the outsiders (3:2) whom Paul called dogs, evildoers, and mutilators (3:2–11).[35] Paul's vehement warning against them and condemnatory argument in 3:18–21 indicate that there was a group of people who were continually disturbing the congregation (3:18–19).[36] Paul implied that the Philippians should, just as he himself did, regard those who advocate the protective camouflage of a Judaizing way of life (3:2, 18–19) as dogs and enemies of the cross of Christ.[37] There might have been some

27 Achtemeier, Green, and Thompson, *Introducing the New Testament*, 392–99.

28 Pheme Perkins, *New Testament Introduction*, 3rd ed. (Mumbai: St. Paul's, 2002), 199–200.

29 See Hawthorne, "Philippians," 708.

30 Guthrie, *New Testament Introduction*, 541–42; Duling, *New Testament*, 209; Lightner, "Philippians," 647.

31 Duling, *New Testament*, 209.

32 Agosto, "Philippians," 287.

33 See Perkins, *New Testament Introduction*, 199–201.

34 Marshal, "Imperial Intersections," 154–55.

35 Agosto, "Philippians," 281.

36 See John Drane, *Introducing the New Testament* (Oxford: Lion Hudson, 1999), 358–59; Marshal, "Imperial Intersections," 154–55.

37 Elliott, *Liberating Paul*, 196–97; Marshal, "Imperial Intersections," 154–55.

Jewish Christian believers who required non-Jewish members to undergo circumcision and follow the dietary laws.[38] Such influences may have disturbed the community.[39]

Another obstacle for Paul and the community was the sociopolitical persecution toward the Christian community in some of the Greco-Roman cities.[40] Christians were often in a vulnerable position and faced persecutions such as imprisonment and physical punishments. Paul himself was a prisoner in a Roman colonial prison, and the Philippian Christians were subjects of a Roman colony.[41] The widespread threat alluded to in Philippians 1:28–30 may have been related to Christian antagonism to the imperial cult.[42] Their neighbors in the Roman colony were suspicious of them (see 1 Thess 2:2).[43] The suffering mentioned in Paul's letters is exemplified in the lives of both Paul and the church.[44] Paul makes mention of his affliction and weakness through persecution (Phil 3:10; 2 Cor 13:4) and even death (1 Cor 15:31).[45] It is essential to note that Paul lived, worked, and died during the time of Nero. Probably, he and his fellow Christians were persecuted because of their confession of Christ as Lord over Caesar.[46]

There are many other pieces of evidence that the believers suffered from distress (Rom 5:3–5; 8:12–39; 2 Cor 1:6), affliction (2 Cor 8:1–2; 1 Thess 1:2–7), persecution (1 Thess 1:6; 2:14; 3:3–4, 7), and adversity (Rom 12:12).[47] Even though the status of citizens was a part of *pax Romana*, the "others" such as immigrants, various diaspora groups, and refugees were persecuted. The Roman Empire used massive violence, slaughtering or enslaving, and horrific gladiatorial

38 Agosto, "Philippians," 287–88.
39 Hiebert, *Introduction*, 285–86.
40 Achtemeier, Green, and Thompson, *Introducing the New Testament*, 392–99.
41 Drane, *Introducing the New Testament*, 358–59.
42 Elliott, *Liberating Paul*, 196–97.
43 Elliott, 196–97.
44 D. A. Carson, Douglas J. Moo, and Leon Morris, *An Introduction to the New Testament* (Leicester, UK: Apollos, 1993), 317.
45 S. J. Hafemann, "Suffering," in *Dictionary of Paul and His Letters*, ed. Gerald F. Hawthorne and Ralph P. Martin (Leicester, UK: InterVarsity, 1993), 919–20.
46 Elliott, *Liberating Paul*, 196–98.
47 Hafemann, "Suffering," 919–20.

games to maintain "peace" in the Empire.[48] This was done in collaboration with the elite.[49] Romans 8:35–38 confirms that oppression, distress, persecution, starvation, destitution, peril, and the sword come from human powers.[50]

A BRIEF OUTLINE OF THE BOOK

Philippians is a letter of friendship, following patterns found in such letters in Paul's day. Except for Galatians, which has no thanksgiving, the undisputed letters of Paul share a similar pattern. Philippians includes a greeting, a thanksgiving, the occasion, theological arguments, ethical teachings, a conclusion, and a benediction.[51] The structure of Philippians can be outlined as follows:

Introduction (1:1–2)

Greeting and thanksgiving (1:3–11)

Paul's present circumstances (1:12–26)

Exhortation to steadfastness (1:27–30)

Jesus as suffering servant (2:1–11)

Ethics: Live right in suffering (2:12–16)

The examples of Paul and Timothy (2:17–24)

The example of Epaphroditus (2:25–30)

The power of resurrection to share suffering (3:1–16)

48 Brown, *Introduction to the New Testament*, 498–500.
49 Elliott, *Liberating Paul*, 94–99.
50 Elliott, 122–23, 138.
51 Paul, Rosner, and Mosser, "Letters," 235–36.

Citizenship of heaven (3:17–4:1)

Ethics: Live right in the congregational fellowship (4:2–9)

A note of thanksgiving (4:10–20)

Conclusion (4:21–23)[52]

LITERARY CONTEXT AND AN ASIAN COMPARISON

Many Christians believe that it is a joyful letter. However, the internal evidence, such as Paul's imprisonment and his conflicts and suffering, suggests that this is rather a letter of suffering. According to Efrain Agosto, the Letter to the Philippians has a classical rhetorical form with an *exordium* (introduction), a *narratio* (statement of facts), and a *propositio* (statement of purpose) in chapter 1, followed by a *probatio*, or proofs, in chapters 2 and 3 and a *peroratio*, or recapitulation, in chapter 4. This is a Roman letter of friendship expressed between Paul and the Philippian Christ believers. He encourages them to unite and be faithful as they face opposition by following the example of Jesus, Paul himself, and other ministers.[53] However, the letter is not free from harsh words because it includes warnings and disappointments (3:2–11).

For Agosto, the letter resists and at the same time accommodates imperialism.[54] The literary context of this letter has affinities with the sociopolitical and religiocultural situations in many Asian countries. Particularly, the concept of suffering and ways to annihilate suffering can be found in all religions and their literatures. As the Philippians has included how and why the Christ's believers were suffering and how to overcome it, we can also see parallels to the four noble truths of Buddhism: the existence of suffering, the cause of suffering, the truth of the end of suffering, and finally, the way to end

52 See Guthrie, *New Testament Introduction*, 561–63; Achtemeier, Green, and Thompson, *Introducing the New Testament*, 393; also see Keener, *IVP Bible Background Commentary*, 558–67; Lightner, "Philippians," 648.

53 Agosto, "Philippians," 282–83.

54 Agosto, 282–89.

suffering.[55] The first noble truth (*dukkha*) mentions that there is suffering of pain, suffering of change, and pervasive suffering. The second noble truth (*samudaya*) is the truth of the cause of suffering, such as ignorance, anger, attachment, pride, doubt, and wrong view. The third noble truth (*nirodha*) is the truth of the cessation of suffering through Nirvana.[56] The fourth noble truth (*magga*) is the truth of the path to the cessation of suffering.[57] The fourth noble truth of Theravada Buddhism contains the eightfold noble path, consisting of correct view, correct intention, correct speech, correct action, correct livelihood, correct effort, correct mindfulness, and correct concentration or single mindedness.[58] Rhetorical literature of Paul's time suggests certain parallels to the teachings of Buddhism. Both take the problem of suffering seriously. Therefore, it is meaningful to read and interpret the letter both in the light of political suffering and in relation to the Buddhist realities of suffering.

In comparing the contents of the Philippians with the Asian Buddhist reality, we focus on two main themes: the existence and the causes of suffering and the path that leads to the end of suffering. The letter reveals the reality of the suffering faced by the church. In other words, the existence of the suffering is real, and the causes of the suffering are colonial, political, and patriarchal exploitation and oppression. Conversely, ending oppression and exploitation means the end of suffering. Resistance would be a way to end the suffering described in the letter.

THE EXISTENCE AND THE CAUSES OF SUFFERING

Political Reality and Suffering

Myanmar (formerly known as Burma) is a Southeast Asian and predominantly Buddhist country (89 percent of the total population of 53 million). I

55 See Geshe Tashi Tsering, *The Foundation of Buddhist Thought: The Four Noble Truths* (Somerville, MA: Wisdom, 2005), 28–63.

56 Carol S. Anderson, *Pain and Its Ending: The Four Noble Truths in the Theravāda Buddhist Canon* (London: Routledge, 1999), 55–84.

57 Tsering, *Foundation of Buddhist Thought*, 121–46.

58 Anderson, *Pain and Its Ending*, 55–84.

am a Karen Christian who represents both a minority religion and a minority ethnic group. There are 135 subethnic groups, including eight major groups: Bamar (69.0 percent), Shan (8.5 percent), Kachin (2.4 percent), Karen (6.2 percent), Chin (2.2 percent), Mon (2.4 percent), Rakhine (4.5 percent), and Karenni (0.4 percent).[59] Myanmar was once colonized by Japan for three years and by the British for more than one hundred years until 1948. Since its colonial days, Myanmar has become a poor country and has been ruled mostly by military dictators with their various parties, such as the Burma Socialist Party, State Law and Order Restoration Council (SLORC), and State Peace and Development Council (SPDC), for almost sixty years. It has been plagued by many civil wars between ethnic groups and the military regime.[60] The country also faced several religious conflicts such as a conflict between the Rohingya or Bengali (Muslims) and the military regime (majority Buddhists). Other Southeast Asian countries, except for Thailand, were also colonized by Western countries. Even though the contexts of the colonization of countries in the first century CE and of Asian countries in the eighteenth to twentieth centuries are different, some of the structures of colonization are similar.[61] The causes of suffering mentioned in the Letter to the Philippians have some affinities with those who suffer in Myanmar and other Asian countries.

Brian Wintle observes that like the Philippians, Christians in South Asia are a minority and are also constantly under pressure from other religious communities. These pressures from the outside can bring conflicts among Christians themselves. Asian peoples are suffering under political, social, and economic oppression.[62] Even though the orthodox Buddhists hold the tradition of the Four Noble Truths firmly and try to be free from suffering, from a popular Buddhist perspective, suffering is a reality of life, and the fate of

59 Pum Za Mang, "Religion, Ethnicity, and Nationalism in Burma," *Journal of Church and State* 59, no. 4 (August 2016): 626–48.

60 Mang, "Religion, Ethnicity, and Nationalism," 626–48; Rudy Guyon, "Violent Repression in Burma: Human Rights and the Global Response," *Pacific Basin Law Journal* 10, no. 2 (1992): 410–59.

61 Carl Cavanagh Hodge, ed., *Encyclopedia of the Age of Imperialism, 1800–1914* (Westport, CT: Greenwood, 2008), 796–99.

62 Brian Wintle, "Philippians," in *South Asia Bible Commentary*, ed. Brian Wintle (Udaipur, India: Open Door, 2019), 1648–59.

individuals is due to their karma.[63] Unlike the popular Buddhist understanding of the concept of karma, orthodox Buddhists believe in the tradition of the Four Noble Truths, stating that the cause of suffering is desire or attachment.[64] As an example, the craving of a powerful group can cause the exploitation and oppression of other groups. This results in the suffering of people who are underprivileged. Similarly, the Philippians were facing suffering that was not due to their good or bad deeds (as popular Buddhists view); it came from outside and was for the sake of the gospel of Jesus (Phil 1:19; 3:8). This interpretation is more in line with the views of the orthodox Buddhists in Myanmar. The suffering came from persecution (Phil 3:10) and could be compared to the suffering of Jesus on the cross (2:8).

Paul's interpretation of the cross of Christ reflects the terror of that time. The crucifixion of Christ was displayed to the public (Gal 3:1). This incident is "one of the most unequivocally political events recorded in the NT."[65] Crucifixion is imperial terror and the supreme penalty for lower-class people and slaves. The Roman lawyer Gaius Cassius mentions that four hundred slaves were crucified as a punishment of a slave who murdered his master, a prefect of Rome. In *Jewish War* 2.13.2, Josephus reported that the Roman procurator Felix also suppressed the protest by crucifying many robbers in the fifties CE. *Jewish War* 5.11.1–2 also mentions that after seizing Jerusalem, the Roman general Titus crucified no less than five hundred refugees a day until there was no place to keep the crosses outside the city wall. The Romans also practiced other kinds of punishments or penalties such as beating, burning, torturing, and hanging. Neil Elliot lists penalties such as "whipping, torturing . . . the burning out of the eyes and maiming often preceded the actual hanging."[66] Most of these punishments were done publicly. Likewise, the death of Jesus on the cross became a taboo and a humiliation (Phil 2:8).

In Asia, especially in Myanmar, tribal or ethnic people like the Kachin, Kayar, Karen, Chin, and others (mainly Christians) have been treated as second-class citizens by the Myanmar government, which is dominated by the majority Bamar ethnic group (mainly Buddhists), while other Indian-like

63 Tsering, *Foundation of Buddhist Thought*, 121–46; Anderson, *Pain and Its Ending*, 55–84.
64 Anderson, *Pain and Its Ending*, 55–84; Tsering, *Foundation of Buddhist Thought*, 121–46.
65 Elliott, *Liberating Paul*, 93.
66 Elliott, 94–99.

people such as the Rohingyas or Bengalis (mainly Hindus or Muslims) have been treated as noncitizens or people without a country.[67] Buddhism, as a leading religion, is given special priority in the constitution, and the majority Bamar Buddhists have a primary citizenship in the country.[68] This is *samudaya*, or attachment to power by the military government, which causes *dukkha* to the people.[69]

Patriarchal and Hierarchal Reality and Suffering

Patriarchal structures are universal. Asian countries, their cultures, and their religious beliefs condone gender inequality and discrimination. The Pauline letters and other NT writings discern this in detail. Moreover, Asian culture and beliefs enforce the hierarchal structures of any institutions or organizations. Central patriarchal themes can be found in various forms of masculine imagery in Philippians: athletic contests (3:12–16; see 1 Cor 9:24–27), the expression of fatherly affection for Timothy (2:22; see 1 Cor 4:14–17), military imagery ("fellow soldier," 2:25), and the reference to "the true circumcision" (3:3). These terms are mostly used for men. Almost all athletes were men in ancient times, and this also applied to the military field.[70]

It is clear that although Luke describes Lydia as an instrumental figure in the Philippian context, later on she becomes a mere hostess for Paul and Silas. Some scholars think that although Luke relates traditions about important women in the early Christ movement, he minimizes their official leadership roles to accommodate Roman imperial values and policies. Also, he portrays the early Christ movement as well organized according to Roman standards, with men, not women, in the organization. Paul's letter to the Philippians shows us the real situation during Paul's time in terms of gender issues. The whole letter is dominated by his rhetorical model (1:3–11, 12–14, 24–26; 2:16–18; 3:7–11, 14–17; 4:2, 8–9), which is specifically a male-gendered model, as he uses the phrase "we ourselves are the circumcision" (3:3). Languages and traditions are created by patriarchal norms. Paul's plea for unity

67 William J. Topich and Keith A. Leitich, *The History of Myanmar*, Greenwood Histories of the Modern Nations (Santa Barbara, CA: Greenwood, 2013), 1–10.

68 Anderson, *Pain and Its Ending*, 55–84; Mang, "Religion, Ethnicity, and Nationalism," 626–48.

69 Topich and Leitich, *History of Myanmar*, 1–10.

70 Works, "Philippians," 582–83.

between women leaders in 4:2 is a hierarchical argument. Those who imitate him are mature (3:15) and will gain safety. Paul encourages them to accept his authority within a subordinating structure.[71]

Women in leadership positions, such as Euodia and Syntyche (4:2–3), are mentioned in Philippians. However, their conflict has been misinterpreted and misrepresented by many to mean that female leadership can bring conflicts. Therefore, their portrayal implies that they were not good leaders for the congregation, whereas the leadership of Timothy and Epaphroditus is praised. Then the theme of imitating male models is promoted by Christians. They are asked to follow the models of Jesus, Paul, Epaphroditus, and Timothy. Asian people, especially in Myanmar, read the incident of the two women leaders according to a stereotype of the nature of women who are always in conflict and hardly see the leadership role of women in this incident. Romans 16:1–11 mentions the lists of women leaders, such as Phoebe as a deacon, Prisca as teacher, and Junia as an apostle. Actually, Paul recognized female leadership roles in his letters, and Philippians 4:2–3 provides one example.

Female leadership is not absent in Asian religions such as Hinduism and Buddhism. There were woman leaders in these religious orders. There were bhikkhuni, an order of female ordained monks, in Theravada Buddhism since the time of Buddha. However, this order disappeared in the middle of the eleventh century CE from Sri Lanka and in the thirteenth century CE from Myanmar. Movements of reviving the order have taken place since the 1920s and 1930s in Myanmar and in Thailand. These movements were widely supported even among the liberal scholars. They recalled the ordination procedure done by Buddha and his bhikkhu (male monks) to five hundred bhikkhuni. The ordination of nuns to become bhikkhuni is still not possible because the majority of the monks think that the lineage of bhikkhuni is already extinct and cannot be revived.[72] It is clear that female leadership is a problem not only for Christianity but for Buddhism as well—there is a long history of attempts to support and reject the idea. The ordination of women and female leadership roles in Asian Christian societies are also in jeopardy. Domestic violence, gender

71 Marshal, "Imperial Intersections," 146–60.

72 Hiroko Kawanami, "The Bhikkhuni Ordination Debate: Global Aspirations, Local Concerns, with Special Emphasis on the Views of the Monastic Community in Burma," *Buddhist Studies Review* 24, no. 2 (October 2007): 229–33.

inequality, and gender stereotyping are Asian realities. Christian women are asked to follow Jesus's example by emptying themselves and showing obedience and submission instead of responding with resistance and resilience.

WAYS TO END SUFFERING FROM POLITICAL AND RELIGIOUS AFFAIRS

Coping Strategies

The theological themes that particularly respond to suffering in Philippians are the call to rejoice in the gospel, the call to have hope, the call to be a community with identity, and the call for partnership.[73] From a political perspective, these are known as survival and accommodationist responses to the causes of suffering. The first three chapters of Philippians offer coping strategies and ways to end suffering. These coping strategies or ways of resistance share some similarities with Asian realities and traditions. According to Buddhism, with the help of *nirodha* and *megga*, human beings can be freed from suffering.[74]

A Community of *Sukha*

In Philippians, Paul instructs the people to rejoice as he was rejoicing in the midst of suffering.[75] This theme appears nine times in Philippians: 1:18, 19; 2:17 (twice), 28; 3:1; 4:4 (twice); and 4:10. While this theological theme may seem irrelevant or unhelpful for anyone suffering from hardship, violence, and discrimination, this would be a misreading of Paul. He is not minimizing the significance of their suffering and speaking as one who is safe and secure. Rather, his instructions come out of his own personal experience of learning how to cope with suffering. He writes as one who rejoices in the midst of suffering. Further, his call to rejoice is not a passive response to suffering, but an active one. He is rejoicing in suffering because he is actively defending the gospel of salvation.[76]

73 Works, "Philippians," 582–83.
74 Anderson, *Pain and Its Ending*, 55–84.
75 Sukha (Sanskrit, *pali*) means happiness or joy.
76 Works, "Philippians," 582–83.

Likewise, Paul is calling the Philippians to rejoice for freedom from bondage and suffering. It is an exhortation to endure suffering and transform it into joy. This is to stand firm in the Lord (1:27; 4:1). The call to rejoice is to share suffering and joy together. It is to stand together in unity and cope with suffering and hardship, without giving up the hope for the future. The Philippians are not masochists and are not complaining and mourning, but they choose to rejoice in the midst of their suffering. Paul finds that the Philippians are experiencing joy because of their faith (1:25). Rejoicing is a virtue that can unsettle opponents or enemies. Usually, Roman citizens rejoiced in the peace of Rome, confirming that there was peace and security under the care of the Roman emperor.[77] Likewise, the Philippians should rejoice in the Lord, as they live securely under God's control. This becomes a kind of counteraction of Paul and other Christ believers in the Roman Empire.

According to Buddhist teachings, a controlled and cultured mind is a source of happiness. There are steps to happiness. The first step is to practice Buddhist triple gems by paying homage to and worshipping Buddha, following the teaching of *Dhamma*, and paying homage or respect to Sangha. The second step is to cultivate and practice loving-kindness (*Metta*), compassion (*Karuna)*, appreciative joy (*Mudita*), and equanimity (*Upekkha*).[78] Buddhists in Myanmar try to practice this to gain happiness in the midst of suffering.

Asia is famous for religious traditions that encourage adherents to endure pain and suffering in life. Hinduism encourages asceticism, which is seen as a way to liberate the soul. Accordingly, Gandhi formulated nonviolence as a virtue in response to suffering. Many Buddhist monks, including monks in Myanmar, demonstrated against the political regime by fasting or refusing to receive food from the regime's representatives. They engage in such hunger strikes to make the abusive government feel guilty. This becomes a strategy to end suffering.[79] Buddhist monks seek or gain happiness through this practice.

77 Elliott, *Liberating Paul*, 196.

78 Mu Mu Win, "The Way to Happiness in Buddhism," *Hinthada University Research Journal* 4, no. 1 (2012): 129–34.

79 Sylwia Gil, "The Role of Monkhood in Contemporary Myanmar Society," *Research Paper of Friedrich Ebert Stiftung*, September 2008, 1–12; Pum Za Mang, "Buddhist Nationalism and Burmese Christianity," *Studies in World Christianity* 22, no. 2 (August 2016): 148–67.

A Community of *Apekkha*

The political, social, religious, and economic situations of Asia can lead to feelings of hopelessness. The people of Myanmar often feel hopeless because there is no way to remove the military government from holding power in brutal ways. However, Christians still hope that one day, their country will be freed from all discrimination, violence, war, and injustice. In Philippians, Paul offers hope to people in view of sociopolitical and religious persecution by giving examples and models.[80] Paul himself was facing not only harsh treatment but also death. He hopes for his release to continue his mission. Paul encourages the Philippians to endure and move forward in the midst of conflict and opposition.[81] He offers hope to them by explaining that his imprisonment is not a failure but serves the advance of the gospel (1:12–14).[82]

For Paul, the power of this evil age is unmasked and challenged by the death of Christ. He confirms that he has his freedom from the threats of those powers. He keeps his hope in justice, which is to prevail (Gal 5:5).[83] Moreover, his greatest hope is the end of suffering. In other words, he hopes that the end of the opponents or persecutors will come soon. Philippians 3:19 says, "Their end is destruction, their god is their belly, and they glory in their shame with their mind set on earthly things." In contrast, the end of Christ believers is the opposite. The Christians will live as citizens of heaven and with glory (Phil 3:20–4:1).

Liberation from reincarnation (Hinduism) and liberation from attachment or suffering (Buddhism) are the greatest hopes in Asian religions. Buddhists believe that if they do good and earn merits, they will go to better lives after they die.[84] Actually, hoping for a better life is not an original Buddhist philosophy, as their ultimate goal is Nirvana, which is nothingness. This is a wish for final freedom from rebirth, desires, and death through detachment. To become human again is the second most desirable hope for Buddhists, from which they can try to attain Nirvana, their ultimate hope. To fulfill

80 According to the Pali-English dictionary, *Apekkha* means "waiting for," "looking for," "hope," "desire."

81 Agosto, "Philippians," 285.

82 Elliott, *Liberating Paul*, 196–97.

83 Elliott, 123, 139.

84 Anderson, *Pain and Its Ending*, 55–84; Tsering, *Foundation of Buddhist Thought*, 121–46.

these hopes, ethical, moral, and religious deeds should be practiced and performed with justice, compassion, and loving-kindness.[85] Good karma will bring good things, and bad karma will bring bad things in life. Buddhists also believe that there is a judgment or penalty for the evildoers in this life or in the next. Similar kinds of belief can be seen in all other religions, including Christianity.

A Community with Identity: Citizens of Heaven

Group identity was important for the early Christ believers during the first century CE. The different colonized ethnic groups, including diaspora Jews, were struggling for their identity. People today in Myanmar are also questioning their own identity and their roles in society. Minority groups in particular, such as ethnic groups, religious groups, women, children, and disabled people, are doubly oppressed and treated as secondary citizens. Rohingya people are not granted any identity as a people in Myanmar, and they long to be recognized as citizens so they can live with full human dignity and rights.[86]

In the first century, Roman citizenship was given to only a few privileged people, and only 15 percent of the population during that time were citizens. Citizens had the right to vote, marry, make contracts, pay taxes, and serve in the military. They were free from degrading forms of punishments and had the right to appeal to Rome.[87] Christianity was thought of as a Jewish sect and was not recognized as a separate religion. Paul encourages his fellow Christ believers, assuring them that they are citizens of heaven. Christian identity is defined as citizenship of heaven rather than as citizenship of Rome.[88] This is conceived of as a new identity or community, an alternative society (in postcolonial terms). In this new community, both men and women are called to be citizens of God in a commonwealth under the lordship of Christ

85 John D'Arcy May, "May Buddhists Hope? A Christian Enquiry," University of Divinity, accessed March 18, 2020, 1–5, 16, https://repository.divinity.edu.au/2071/.

86 Htoo Htet Naing and Kyaw Zin Lin, "Hidden Truths of the Invisible: The Experiences of Double Minorities in Northern Rakhine State during Violent Conflict" (research paper of the Peace Leadership and Research Institute, Friedrich Ebert Stiftung Myanmar Office, Yangon, 2019), 3–12.

87 Everett Ferguson, *Background of Early Christianity*, 3rd ed. (Grand Rapids, MI: Eerdmans, 2003), 62–63.

88 Works, "Philippians," 582.

(2:9–11). They should behave like citizens of heaven (1:27), and this citizenship is deemed higher than Roman citizenship (3:20) because the kingdom of God is greater than Rome.[89]

How can one's body be transformed into a body of glory? Here, we must pay attention to the notion of honor and shame. Earthly achievements, such as following practices of Jewish law or receiving Roman citizenship, were seen as matters of honor for Jews throughout the empire. He also asks for loyalty to God from his congregations because they are considered heavenly citizens. Roman citizenship is secondary.[90] Even the names of the two women leaders and other male leaders, referred to in the letter, are thought of as recorded in the book of life in heaven (Phil 4:2–3). Struggle for religious identity in a political setting is not a new thing. Any new religion shall struggle for its identity. Christianity, Hinduism, and Islam in Myanmar are minority religions, trying in various ways to survive in the country. Sometimes they are resistant in nature, and sometimes they accommodate the Buddhist traditions and culture as well as government laws.[91]

A Community of a Suffering Servant Leader

People of Myanmar, especially the Bamar ethnic people who suffer under the military regime, look to Aung San Suu Kyi, the state counselor, as their role model who has suffered with them for several decades. Many ethnic minority groups also have their own role models or martyrs who give their lives for the people and resist the regime. For example, Karen has Saw Ba Oo Gyi as their martyr.[92] For the people, these persons are heroes and heroines. In Philippians, Paul holds up Jesus Christ as a role model and someone to be imitated (2:6–11).[93]

On the one hand, Paul calls his readers to follow the models of himself and his coworkers by enduring suffering with the ultimate hope of heavenly citizenship and glory. On the other hand, the kenotic model of Jesus calls

89 Works, 582–83.

90 Agosto, "Philippians," 288.

91 Mang, "Buddhist Nationalism," 148–67.

92 Paul Keenan, *Saw Ba U Gyi*, Voices of the Revolution Series (n.p.: Karen History and Culture Preservation Society, 2008), 1–24.

93 Elliott, *Liberating Paul*, 196–97.

the people to display a servant leadership model (2:6–11).[94] As Jesus exemplified, people are called to show the same willingness to sacrifice themselves in response to human suffering. It was an act of self-sacrifice for the sake of others. Jesus did it in obedience to God and to serve humanity. Similarly, emptying or denouncing oneself is the essence of both Hinduism and Buddhism. Many monks and ascetics from Hinduism and Buddhism denounce themselves and live lives of asceticism. Emptiness or selflessness (*Annata*) is a state of being and a way of life. Nonself is the essence of Nirvana, and that is cultivated through meditation. The meditation through nonself can be helpful in three ways: becoming mindful of the present reality; being attentive to the study of the dharma; and having good friends.[95] The highest achievement of nonself is enlightenment, or Nirvana. Practicing kenosis, or emptiness, is suggested as a requirement for leaders.

A Community of Resurrection or Reincarnation

The people of Myanmar always recall the day the country attained independence from British colonialism on January 4, 1948. The works of General Aung San, the late father of Daw Aung San Suu Kyi, are praised and retold. Recently, statues of General Aung San were erected in many major cities to revive his spirit of freedom.[96] In Philippians and in other letters of Paul, resurrection is a core theological theme. Jesus's death and resurrection form the foundations of Christianity. Theological meanings of resurrection include ideas of transformation, incorruption, exaltation, and glorification (Phil 2:8–11). Death is not the end, but with resurrection, there is glorification and exaltation. The people of God share Christ's resurrection as glorification and exaltation (3:10, 11).

Both Buddhists and Hindus believe in reincarnation of many different lives. To be reborn to a better life, they live their current lives meaningfully

94 Andrew Barnaby, "'The Form of a Servant': At (-)onement by Kenosis in Paradise Lost," *Milton Quarterly* 52, no. 1 (March 2018): 1–12; Karl Inge Tnagen, "Leadership as Participation in Christ: Paul's Theology of Leadership in the Letter to the Philippians," *Journal of Biblical Perspectives in Leadership* 8, no. 1 (Fall 2018), 276–90.

95 Matthew Kosuta, "Theravada Emptiness: The Abhidhammic Theory of Ajaan Sujin Boriharnwanaket," *Contemporary Buddhism* 8, no. 1 (May 2007): 20–22.

96 Aung Thu Ya, trans., "President U Win Myint Attends Bogyoke Aung San Statue Unveiling Ceremony," *Global New Light of Myanmar* 6, no. 303, 6th Waning of Tabodwe 1381 (February 14, 2020).

and try to earn as much merit as they can. They expect to be reborn in a different body with a different status.[97] This is quite different from the Christian concept of resurrection. In terms of martyrdom, animists believe that the dead who are violently killed will stay alive as spirits, and these spirits, known in Myanmar as *Nats*, will help people in need of justice. There are some Nats who emerged due to the unjust killing of princesses and princes. In animist rituals, a medium invites these spirits to possess their body and then recalls their life and death.[98]

The Nats in Myanmar are worshipped by many rural people. Nat worship in Myanmar was suppressed by King Anawratha (1044–1977) because he was afraid of the king being inferior to the Nats.[99] The belief in Nats may not be similar in character to faith in the resurrection of Jesus Christ, but for animists, their spirits live on and are present with them. In Myanmar, almost all pagodas and temples have shrines for the Nats. People believe that Nats can help their well-being and welfare on this earth while Buddhism helps them with their lives after death. Therefore, they pay homage to Nats in daily life in order to be helped by them in their struggles.

A Community of Egalitarian Partnership

Unity and partnership can challenge patriarchal and hierarchical structures, while divisions and frictions can lead to weakness (1:27–28).[100] A partnership model can be seen in the letter to the Philippians in four ways. The first one is partnership in ministry and sharing the gospel (1:5, 7; 4:14, 15). Here Paul claims that he and the Christ believers share suffering and troubles (1:5, 7; 4:15). The second one is partnership in sharing resources. Paul uses the term *koinōnia* not only to refer to personal fellowship but also in reference to the Jerusalem collection (Rom 15:26; 2 Cor 8:4; 9:13). His congregations are

97 Noble Ross Reat, "Karma and Rebirth in the Upanishads and Buddhism," *Numen* 24, no. 3 (December 1977): 163–85.

98 David Thang Moe, "Nat-Worship and Paul Tillich: Contextualizing a Correlational Theology of Religion and Culture in Myanmar," *Toronto Journal of Theology* 31, no. 1 (2015): 123–36.

99 Moe, 123–36.

100 Nathan Mizzell and Russell L. Huizing, "When Servant Leadership Fails: The Importance of Aligning Values," *Journal of Biblical Perspectives in Leadership* 8, no. 1 (Fall 2018): 12–24; Tnagen, "Leadership as Participation in Christ," 276–90.

also his business partners according to Roman commercial understanding. That is why the church supported his mission through the means of finances (4:14–20), donations to the poor (2 Cor 8:1–5), and the service of Epaphroditus (2:25–30; 4:19). Their partnership will end only when one party dies.[101] Paul thanks the congregation for being part of this divine economy that is an alternative system to that of Rome.

The third aspect is their partnership with Christ. This is the church's communion in Christ (1 Cor 1:9; 10:16).[102] The fourth is sharing of leadership roles. Philippians 4:2–3 is about the inclusion of Paul's coworkers Euodia and Syntyche in the partnership of his ministry. If this is indicative of his core understanding of the partnership and leadership of workers regardless of their gender, it is contrary to the standards of the Roman Empire.

Asian people have a strong sense of unity, and they promote kinship. They value collectiveness more than individualism. Besides, unity is one of the particular virtues and characteristics of minority ethnic groups. The kinship system is practiced and preserved generation by generation through marriage, adoption, and family trees.[103] Burmanization is a strategy used by the military government to favor the majority Bamar ethnic group's involvement in decision-making and to force the minorities into assimilation of the majority culture and religion through laws, policies, and activities. The military rarely recognizes the cultural practices and values of ethnic minority groups.[104] Therefore, being united and promoting kinship is very essential to them. First-century Christians were encouraged to be united as partners and work together for the common good of the group (Acts 4:32–37).

101 Works, "Philippians," 581; Agosto, "Philippians," 288–89.

102 Works, "Philippians," 581–84.

103 Nyunt Nyunt Win and Htu Ra, "Changes in the Kinship System of Diaspora Kachin Groups in Myanmar" (paper, 2nd International Conference on Burma/Myanmar Studies, University of Mandalay, February 16–18, 2018), 674–83, https://umoar.mu.edu.mm/handle/123456789/450 (URL inactive).

104 Naw Wai Hnin Kyaw and Soe Soe Nwe, *From Margin to Center: Experiences of Political Social Marginalization of Ethnic Minorities in Karenni State*, ed. Radka Antalikova (Yangon: Friedrich-Ebert-Stiftung Myanmar Office, 2019), 1–12, http://library.fes.de/pdf-files/bueros/myanmar/15641.pdf.

CONCLUSION

The Letter to the Philippians shares Asian realities such as social, political, and patriarchal struggles and ambiguities. It includes different kinds of resistance and coping strategies. Paul and the Philippians were facing imprisonment and other forms of suffering and oppression. By using a political rhetorical method, Paul encourages his readers. The letter portrays a community struggling with questions of identity, leadership, and unity. Paul responds to the situation by calling the readers to be a community of joy, hope, new identity, and coequal partnership. The letter could be very helpful to guide Asian Christians who suffer in many ways and struggle to cope and respond. The themes of the letter have certain affinities with the Four Noble Truths of Buddhism, which are about causes and reasons of suffering and how to overcome and become liberated from them. Some Asian communities, especially many ethnic minorities, do not have a strong sense of identity and lack leadership models. However, there are leaders who gave their lives for the people and practiced the servant leadership as Jesus did. Hence the community is not without hope but carries a hope for a bright future.

FURTHER READING

Agosto, E. 2009. "Philippians." In *A Postcolonial Commentary on the New Testament Writings*, edited by Fernando F. Segovia and R. S. Sugirtharajah, 281–293. London: T&T Clark.

Bronkhorst, J. 2011. *Buddhism in the Shadow of Brahmanism*. Handbook of Oriental Studies, Section Two: South Asia 24. Leiden: Brill.

Elliott, N. 2006. *Liberating Paul, the Justice of God and the Politics of the Apostle.* Minneapolis: Fortress.

Gil, S. 2008. "The Role of Monkhood in Contemporary Myanmar Society." *Research Paper of Friedrich Ebert Stiftung*, September 2008, 1–12.

Kawanami, H. 2007. "The Bhikkhuni Ordination Debate: Global Aspirations, Local Concerns, with Special Emphasis on the Views of the Monastic Community in Burma." *Buddhist Studies Review* 24, no. 2: 226–244.

Keenan, P. 2008. *Saw Ba U Gyi*. Voices of the Revolution Series. n.p.: Karen History and Culture Preservation Society.

Topich, W. J., and K. A. Leitich. 2013. *The History of Myanmar.* The Greenwood Histories of the Modern Nations. Santa Barbara, CA: Greenwood.

Wintle, B., ed. 2019. "Philippians." In *South Asia Bible Commentary*, 1648–1659. Udaipur, India: Open Door.

Ya, A. T., trans. 2020. "President U win Myint Attends Bogyoke Aung San Statue Unveiling Ceremony." *Global New Light of Myanmar* 6, no. 303, 6th Waning of Tabodwe 1381 (February 14, 2020).

THIRTEEN

The Letter to the Colossians

Finny Philip
Filadelfia Bible College
Udaipur, India

Among the extended letters of Paul, the Epistle to the Colossians is most captivating because of its proximity to Philemon and Ephesians[1] in its theological focus, the geographical connectivity, and the striking social networking that is centered on Christ. The church in Colossae and probably those other churches in the Lycus Valley[2] have been infiltrated by diverse religious beliefs as some attempt to combine facets of local folk religion, Hellenistic piety, and Jewish mystical traditions with Christian beliefs and practices. The comprehensive communication and social networking among Paul, his coworkers, and the Colossian congregation(s) confront these false teachings and affirm the sufficiency of Christ. Though a small letter in comparison to the other NT letters, it contains distinctive teachings about the person and work of Christ, Christian living and relationship, and Paul's conception of ministry.

1 See discussions on the connection between Colossian and Ephesians in Margaret Y. MacDonald, *Colossians, Ephesians* (Collegeville, MN: Liturgical, 2008), 4–6; C. H. Talbert, *Ephesians and Colossians* (Grand Rapids, MI: Baker Academic, 2007), 3–6.

2 Paul Trebilco, "Christians in the Lycus Valley: The View from Ephesus and from Western Asia Minor," in *Colossae in Space and Time: Linking to an Ancient City*, ed. Alan H. Cadwallader and M. Trainor (Göttingen: Vandenhoeck & Ruprecht GmbH, 2011), 180–82.

PRELIMINARY CONCERNS

Author

The explicit author mentioned in the prescript of the letter is Paul (1:1; 4:18). Pauline scholarship denies authenticity due to his use of different vocabulary and mature theological view compared to other letters of Paul.[3] However, an increasing number of scholars have abnegated these arguments by suggesting that the specific language style could reflect Paul's reaction to the Colossian heresy or his extensive use of traditional materials.[4] Others have argued that it was a pseudepigrapher[5] or a scribe who was given the freedom to write Paul's thoughts in his own style.[6] The pseudepigrapher argument has difficulty working on historical grounds because the cities in Lycus Valley were destroyed in an earthquake in 60–61 CE.[7] Such a factor would mean a pseudepigrapher sent a letter to an empty recipient location. It will also be anachronistic to place pseudepigraphy as a device used by later generations who attempted to contemporize the thoughts of their master for new situations and audiences.[8]

The questions on theology are a primary deterrent to consider Colossians as a genuine letter of Paul.[9] However, a few following points also need to be considered in furthering the discussion. One of the features of the ancient epistolography[10] is the conversation between a sender and a recipient who share intimate sentiments across distances of space and time, mainly when it

3 For a discussion on language and style differences in Colossians when compared to other authentic Pauline letters, see E. Lohse's excursus: "The Language and Style of Colossians," in *Colossians and Philemon* (Minneapolis: Fortress, 1988), 84–91.

4 George E. Cannon, *The Use of Traditional Materials in Colossians* (Macon, GA: Mercer, 1983).

5 C. Leslie Mitton, *Ephesians* (London: Marshall, Morgan & Scott, 1976), 11; Andrew T. Lincoln, *Ephesians* (Dallas: Word, 1990), xlix.

6 See Eduard Schweizer, *The Letter to the Colossians* (Minneapolis: Augsburg, 1982), 23–24; see James D. G. Dunn, *The Epistles to Colossians and to Philemon: A Commentary on the Greek Text*, The New International Greek Testament Commentary (Grand Rapids, MI: Eerdmans, 2014), 38.

7 See *Sibylline Oracles* 12:280; Tacitus, *Annals* 14.27; Eusebius, *Chron.* 2.154.

8 Richard Bauckham, "Pseudo-Apostolic Letters," *Journal of Biblical Literature* 107, no. 3 (1988): 469–94.

9 Richard R. Melick, *Philippian, Colossians, Philemon* (Nashville: B&H, 1991), 165–68.

10 See discussions in Paola Ceccarelli et al., eds., *Letters and Communities: Studies in the Socio-political Dimensions of Ancient Epistolography* (Oxford: Oxford University Press, 2018).

is read in public as communal reading.[11] When Paul wrote to the Colossians and other congregations in the Lycus Valley, these intimate sentiments were conveyed. For example, in Colossians 1:29 and 2:1 (see 1 Tim 6:12; 2 Tim 4:7), Paul calls his life an *agōn* (struggle) and his daily activity a continuous *agōnizomai* (struggling). His own personal agony is revealed to his network participants like Epaphras and Archippus as comrades in arms (Col 4:12; Phil 1:30; 2:25; see 2 Cor 10:4). Similarly, the intensity reflected in the prayer of Paul for recipient community suggests such an intimacy is consistent with Paul as one sees in his other letters (Col 1:9–11; see Phil 1:9; Phlm 4–7; 1 Thess 1:2–3; 3:9–10; 2 Thess 1:11–12; Rom 1:9–10; Eph 1:15–16). Such a collective experience is paralleled in other genuinely Pauline letters and is hard to ignore in this conversation.

Similarly, if the Letter to the Colossians is considered in a narrow sense as a *Gattung*, where a letter is a written message from an author to an addressee, marked by an opening and greeting formulae, the potential to see the matrix for community building is missed. However, if the approach is to see it as a form of communication (*Kommunikationsform*),[12] then the interactive elements and the epistolary affiliations for mission and ministry reflected in Colossians 1:3–8 and 4:7–18 show the genuine interest of the author to shape church life through his network and beyond. It fits well into the community-building protocols of the genre.[13] As the real author, Paul's input in managing the networks mainly through at least four earlier or later residents of Colossae is remarkable: Epaphras, who had founded the congregation, who had told Paul how much its members loved one another, and who continuously was praying for the Christians in Colossae, Laodicea, and Hierapolis[14] (Col 1:7–8; 4:12–13;

11 See Abraham J. Malherbe, *Ancient Epistolary Theorists* (Atlanta: Scholars, 1988).

12 For the letter as a form of communication, see Klaus Brinker, *Linguistische Textanalyse: Eine Einführung in Grundbegriffe un Methoden* (Berlin: Erich Schmidt Verlag GmbH, 2010), 137–38.

13 Lutz Doering, *Ancient Jewish Letters and the Beginnings of Christian Epistolography*, WUNT 298 (Tübingen: Mohr Siebeck, 2012), 383–93; Michael B. Thompson, "The Holy Internet: Communication between Churches in the First Christian Generation," in *The Gospel for All Christians: Rethinking the Gospel Audiences*, ed. Richard Bauckham (Edinburgh: Eerdmans, 1998), 49–70.

14 See F. F. Bruce, *The Epistles to the Colossians, to Philemon, and to the Ephesians* (Grand Rapids, MI: Eerdmans, 1984), 90n7.

see Phlm 23); Archippus, who according to Colossians 4:17 was far from perfectly fulfilling his ministry in and to the church in Colossae; Onesimus, who, when he left Colossae, was not yet a member of the local congregation; and Mark, the cousin of Barnabas, who may travel with Tychicus and Onesimus (4:20; see Phlm 12). Such social network relationships indicate genuineness of authorship.[15]

Various locations like Caesarea, Ephesus, and Rome were considered as the provenance for the Epistle of Colossians. In the case of the first two, scholars argue that it is Caesarea at the Sea, a Roman provincial center, because of Paul's two-year captivity (Acts 23:23–26:23)[16] and Ephesus[17] because of its proximity to Colossae. However, nowhere in Paul's letters is Caesarea ever mentioned, nor Ephesus, where much is told of Paul's activities but nothing of his imprisonment (Acts 19).

However, expositors favor Rome.[18] Colossians, a genuinely Pauline letter, was dispatched from Rome. The Colossian Epaphras, who founded the congregation at Colossae and whom the imprisoned Paul informed about the life and love of Christians in Colossae (Col 1:7–8), is not called as a fellow prisoner in Colossians 4:12 but shares the prison with Paul according to Philemon 23. The presence of Luke, Aristarchus (Acts 27:2), Timothy, and other coworkers (2 Tim 1:17; see 4:17) with Paul at the time of writing are essential clues for the provenance of Colossians. If Paul wrote the letter from Ephesus, then it was during his third missionary journey and is dated 52–55 CE. If it was written from the imprisonment in Caesarea, the date is 57–59 CE. The probability for Rome is greater, so one must place the composition of the letter at around 58–60 CE.[19]

15 See N. T. Wright, *Colossians and Philemon: An Introduction and Commentary* (Downers Grove, IL: InterVarsity, 1986), 163.

16 E. Lohse, *Colossians and Philemon: A Commentary on the Epistles to the Colossians and to Philemon* (Philadelphia: Fortress, 1971).

17 C. F. D. Moule, *The Epistles to the Colossians and Philemon* (Cambridge: Cambridge University Press, 1957), 22.

18 J. B. Lightfoot, *St. Paul's Epistles to the Colossians and Philemon* (Grand Rapids, MI: Zondervan, 1959).

19 Peter T. O'Brien, *Colossians, Philemon*, Word Biblical Commentary 44 (Dallas: Word, 1982); Bo Reicke, "The Historical Setting of Colossians," *Review and Expositor* 70, no. 4 (December 1973): 429–38.

Readers

Paul's letters, like other ancient Mediterranean letters, were part of a complex social performance, particularly for the constitution and celebration of community identity and more so the larger communities in the Lycus Valley. The explicit addressees of the letter are "the holy people in Colossae" (1:2), and it is also to be shared with Laodicea and possibly Hierapolis, where the network of the Jesus communities was located.[20]

Colossae was one of the smallest cities in the Lycus Valley, in the Roman province of Asia and in proximity to Laodicea and Hierapolis. Prior to NT times, Colossae was famous for its textiles. But during NT times it was clearly in decline due to its competitive neighbor, Laodicea, because it grew as the administrative and financial center of the region and was noted for its woolen textile industry and medicines. Likewise, Hierapolis became prominent through its hot mineral spring, which attracted visitors. As noted, Colossae was destroyed in a devastating earthquake alongside Hierapolis and Laodicea; however, Laodicea survived.[21]

The region had people from a wide variety of ethnic and cultural backgrounds (3:11). Many ethnic groups entered the region through the major road to the Lycus Valley. The natives were Phrygians.[22] Because of the military and commercial heritage of the valley, Greeks settled in the area during their period of dominance.[23] There was a substantial Jewish community presence in Colossae.[24] Thus, there existed for about three hundred years

20 See Trebilco, "Christians in the Lycus Valley," 180; Brian Wintle and B. J. Nicholls, *Colossians and Philemon: A Pastoral and Contextual Commentary* (Carlisle, UK: Langham Global Library, 2019), 5–7.

21 Alan H. Cadwallader, "Refuting an Axiom of Scholarship on Colossae: Fresh Insights from New and Old Inscriptions," in *Colossae in Space and Time: Linking to an Ancient City*, ed. Alan H. Cadwallader and M. Trainor (Göttingen: Vandenhoeck & Ruprecht, 2011), 151–79.

22 Morna Hooker, *Colossians* (Grand Rapids, MI: Eerdmans, 2003), 1404.

23 Alan H. Cadwallader, "Greeks in Colossae: Shifting Allegiances in the Letter to the Colossians and Its Context," in *Attitude to Gentiles in Ancient Judaism and Early Christianity*, ed. David C. Sim and James S. McLaren (London: Bloomsbury, 2013), 224–41.

24 Paul R. Trebilco, *Jewish Communities in Asia Minor*, SNTSMS 69 (Cambridge: Cambridge University Press, 1991), 14; F. F. Bruce, "Jews and Christians in the Lycus Valley," *Bibliotheca Sacra* 141 (1984): 3–15.

a conglomerate of ethnicities and wide-ranging beliefs.[25] The response to the gospel seemed more successful in Colossae and Laodicea than Hierapolis. The real readers were primarily gentiles (1:19–22; 1:27; see 1:23–29), though they did not undermine the presence of Jews among the network of believers.[26]

Very little information is available about the founding of the Colossian church. Paul himself refers to this in Colossians 2:1, stating that he did not found it, and a majority of Christians there had not seen him in the flesh.[27] However, he considers it part of his network.[28] Several scholars suppose that Philemon himself established the congregation in Colossae.[29] Apart from Philemon being a person of great importance, he supported the mission efforts in Colossae, mostly in a lay capacity.

However, a majority of scholars suggest that Epaphras founded it. Paul identified his fellow prisoner as a native of Colossae, as "one of you" (Col 4:12), and from him, the Colossian Christians had "learned" (Col 1:7) the "grace of God in truth" (Col 1:6). The church most likely began during Paul's third missionary journey, while he taught in the school of Tyrannus in Ephesus (Acts 19:9–10). Epaphras, one of many who came into contact with the gospel in Ephesus, and probably Philemon with him, carried the good news back to their homes. The work of Epaphras resulted in the formation of the Colossian church and perhaps also the churches in Laodicea and Hierapolis (Col 4:13; see 4:15–16).[30]

The real readers are members of churches who met in private homes,[31] in the Lycus Valley (Col 1:2; 4:13; see 4:15–16). It is implied from the letter that there were multiple house churches in either or both in Colossae and Laodicea. Paul refers to the church in Philemon's home (Phlm 1–2) in

25 See David M. Hay, *Colossians* (Nashville: Abingdon, 2000), 25.

26 Trebilco, "Christians in the Lycus Valley," 180–211.

27 See discussions in James D. G. Dunn, *The Epistles to the Colossians and to Philemon: A Commentary on the Greek Text* (Grand Rapids, MI: Eerdmans, 1996), 129.

28 Reicke, "Historical Setting of Colossians," 429–38.

29 O'Brien, *Colossians, Philemon*, 273.

30 F. F. Bruce, "Epaphras," in *New Bible Dictionary* (Downers Grove, IL: InterVarsity, 1996), 326.

31 See Rom 16:5; 1 Cor 16:19; Phlm 2; Acts 2:46; 5:42; 12:12; 16:15, 40; 18:7–8; 20:8, 20; Rom 16:14–15, 23.

Colossae,[32] while Nympha's was in Laodicea (Col 4:15).[33] Paul also indicates that both Onesimus and Tychicus were visiting the Colossians (4:7–9) and that Onesimus was "one of you" (Phlm 16). This would suggest Philemon probably lived either in or near the city of Colossae. It looks odd when Paul leaves out Philemon and Apphia from the greeting list in his letter to the Colossians, possibly to indicate a different location than to the one which Paul was writing.[34] Again, Archippus (Phlm 1–2) is mentioned in Colossians (Col 4:17), but not as "one of you," which suggests he would not be reading the letter with the other Colossians. This might suggest Archippus, who is addressed in the letter of Philemon, as being part of Philemon's home church, and he probably attended a second congregation in the Colossae proximity.

When Paul refers to a congregation in Laodicea (Col 4:15), he identifies it by mentioning that Nympha's[35] house as the meeting place. It is possible to assume that Nympha's home church was only part of "the brothers in Laodicea," and one needs to assume at least one more house church in Laodicea itself.[36] If this is so, none of these congregations were more than thirty kilometers away from one another, and each congregation probably had been founded by Epaphras.[37]

Thus, by writing to these multiple Jesus communities in the Lycus Valley, Paul's letter to the Colossians was an extension of his influence through Epaphras, embodied as an authoritative theological document that shaped church

32 See Vicky Balabanski, "Where Is Philemon? The Case for a Logical Fallacy in the Correlation of the Data in Philemon and Colossians 1.1–2; 4.7–18," *JSNT* 38 (2015): 141–43, 145–48.

33 Joachim Gnilka, *Der Kolosserbrief*, Herders theologischer Kommentar zum Neuen Testament (Freiburg: Herder, 1980), 244, 248, suggests that Nympha's house church was in Hierapolis.

34 See discussion in Peter Arzt-Grabner, "Everyday Life in a Roman Town like Colossae," in *The First Urban Churches 5. Colossae, Hierapolis, and Laodicea*, ed. J. R. Harrison and L. L. Welborn (Atlanta: SBL, 2019), 213.

35 See discussion on Nympha (woman) or Nymphas (a man) in Lucy Peppiatt, *Rediscovering Scripture's Vision for Women: Fresh Perspectives on Disputed Texts* (Downers Grove, IL: InterVarsity, 2019), 127.

36 W. A. Meeks, *The First Urban Christians: The Social World of the Apostle Paul* (New Haven, CT: Yale University Press, 1983), 143.

37 H. Armin Moellermg and Victor A. Bartling, *1 Timothy, 2 Timothy, Titus, Philemon* (St. Louis: Concordia, 1970), 249.

life and community identity, connected them in networks, and provided them with the language in which to envisage themselves.[38]

The Representative and *Tātparya*

A tenuous relationship between the Lycus valley congregations and their founding father, Epaphras (1:7; 4:12–13), is evident when Paul expresses support for Epaphras and his ministry. However, it is Epaphras and not Paul who is under attack in Colossae (Col 4:12–13). Since Paul did not found the church at Colossae, he needs to take into consideration how he comes across as a person and meet the real readers' expectations. Paul mirrors Epaphras's communications with him in Rome in this letter (1:7–8; 4:12–13). Even more when Paul considers Epaphras mirroring his own self-description. By doing so, Paul brings forth a vivid and coherent portrayal of Epaphras as his representative.[39] In all probability, Paul had commissioned Epaphras initially to bring the gospel to the entire Lycus Valley,[40] and then during the time of controversy, Epaphras represented Paul's position in Colossae.

What was Paul's *tātparya* (the intention of the real author) in writing? Although the Lycus Valley was a well-known haven for Diaspora Jews, apparently Epaphras's ministry was exclusive to gentiles (Col 4:11–12) and was viewed by Paul as an extension of his gentile mission (1:24–2:3). Should one understand the specific crisis in Colossae as related to Paul and his mission to the gentiles? The text suggests Paul moved to write the epistle based apparently on Epaphras's report (1:8) of conditions in the churches of the Lycus Valley.

Five years or so had passed since the founding of the Colossian church. False teachings or the philosophy of "empty deceit" have begun to manifest themselves in Colossae. The new teaching claimed to be Christian but was undermining the gospel by robbing Christ of his unique nature and authority. It was probable that Epaphras felt unable to refute this new teaching effectively, so he visited Paul during his Roman captivity.[41]

38 For ancient parallels, see Lutz Doering, *Ancient Jewish Letters*, 383–93.

39 Meeks, *First Urban Christian*, 134, refers to Epaphras as a "local leader." Michael F. Trainor, *Epaphras: Paul's Educator at Colossae* (Collegeville, MN: Liturgical, 2008), 53, considers Epaphras as having a "quasi-apostolic status."

40 Lohse, *Colossians and Philemon*, 174.

41 Lohse, 174; Paul E. Deterding, *Colossians* (St. Louis: Concordia, 2003), 3.

From the report of Epaphras, a few characteristics are evident about these false teachings (Col 2:8–3:17).[42] The "hollow and deceptive philosophy" that "depends on human tradition and the elemental principles of this world" (2:8) that shape "fine-sounding arguments" (2:4) suggests that a Hellenized form of religiosity was persuading the congregations (2:9, 18, 21, 23). This philosophy further added restrictions on food and drink (2:16a) and participation in religious festivals (2:16b), which corresponds well with the first-century Jewish kosher laws and calendric customs. However, none of this provides an exact parallel to the Colossian controversy, and it is rather important to consider the first-century Colossae as an ideological swamp formed by Hellenism, Judaism, and local pagan folk religious culture.

The exponents of this philosophy are attracted to the "worship of angels," into the details about their visions,[43] and were "puffed up with idle notions" (2:18). Their teaching included the existence of cosmic "rulers and authorities" (1:16; 2:10, 15) and the need to depend upon "the elements of the world" (2:8, 20). Apparently, they taught ascetic practices that characterized "false humility" and its essence as a "harsh treatment of the body" (2:23). Other "human commands and teachings" (2:20–22) like "Do not handle! Do not taste! Do not touch!" (2:21) were part of it, without paying attention to basic morality (3:5–10).

For Epaphras and Paul, this new charm toward the deceptive philosophy by some of those in Lycus Valley churches led to a lack of interest in Christ's universal preeminence and his defeat of adverse cosmic powers at his death (1:18–20; 2:2–4; 2:19). Against this understanding, Paul advances a case for the superiority of Christ over the universe and the powers, the sufficiency of Christ's death for the forgiveness of human sin, the inclusion within God's covenant people, and the reconciliation to God. The sufficiency of Christ's death, Paul argues, restrains the need for any ascetic lifestyle as a means of appeasing divine powers. Contrary to the harsh treatment of the body by the proponents of the false teaching, Paul propounds an ethical routine that reflects Christ's reconciliation of the whole world to God through his death on the cross.

42 Scholars have proposed this false philosophy as a pagan cult of Pythagoreanism. See discussions on the affinities to Pythagorean philosophy: F. O. Francis and W. Meeks, eds., *Conflict at Colossae* (Atlanta: SBL, 1975).

43 See Rebecca Macy Lesses, *Ritual Practices to Gain Power: Angels, Incantations, and Revelation in Early Jewish Mysticism* (Harrisburg, PA: Trinity, 1998), 64–75, 117–60.

The Letter Carrier and the Letter

Paul sends Tychicus to Colossae.[44] He must have briefed him on the complexities of the Colossian situation because a courier delivering a letter would decisively influence how the letter was read and interpreted.[45] For the sender, the courier exerted a particular influence on the potential content of the letter to be delivered. And for the recipient, the courier functioned as a living paratext of the message they transported. In Colossians 4:7–9, Tychicus looked over the potential contents as an inevitable frame of authority in his relationship with Paul. Paul's commissioning of the letter carrier indicates that Paul withheld personal information from the letter and instead entrusted the carrier with communicating it orally (4:8).[46] Like Timothy, Tychicus is called a "brother," and like Epaphras, he is called "beloved," "faithful servant," and "fellow-slave" (Col 4:7–9). These Pauline terminologies suggest Tychicus's authoritative position in Pauline circles (Eph 6:21; 2 Tim 4:12; see Acts 20:4), particularly to Colossae and beyond.

Outline

Greeting, thanksgiving, and prayer (1:1–14)

Christ is supreme (1:15–23)

Paul's ministry and his burden for the Colossians (1:24–2:7)

False philosophy and freedom from human regulations through life in Christ (2:8–23)

Warning concerning false teaching (2:8–15)

---

44 Dunn, *Colossians and Philemon*, 271–72.

45 Bianca-Jeanette Schröder, "Couriers and Conventions in Cicero's Epistolary Network," in *Letters and Communities: Studies in the Socio-political Dimensions of Ancient Epistolography*, ed. Paola Ceccarelli and others (Oxford: Oxford University Press, 2018), 81–100.

46 Adam Copenhaver, *Reconstructing the Historical Background of Paul's Rhetoric in the Letter to the Colossians* (London: T&T Clark, 2018).

Rituals and asceticism are not standards of maturity (2:16–19)

The false practice of asceticism (2:20–23)

Household codes (3:1–4:6)

Put to death the old self and put on the new self (3:1–7)

Instructions for Christian households (3:18–4:1)

Further instructions (4:2–6)

Final greetings and conclusion (4:7–18)

LYCUS VALLEY CHRISTIANS AND ASIAN CHRISTIANS

As Paul and his network of leaders together help redefine the contours of theology purely centered on Jesus Christ to those in Colossae, several themes speak to Asian cultures and worldviews. Such realities, ranging from the questions of "elemental spirits" controlling the fate and the supremacy of Christ, churches' attitudes toward suffering and Christ-centered suffering, overcoming cultural and social discriminations, and the ethical conduct in the community, are important for our purpose.

Christ's Supremacy (1:15–20)

The "false philosophy" that Paul counters implied that Christ did not have the stature that was claimed. Contrary to the worship of Christ, the philosophy touted the worship of "the elements of the world," including the angels who controlled the universe and the fate of each person.[47] By gaining "knowledge,"[48] the Colossian church could gain control over their fate and gain access to a deep Christological understanding.

47 See parallel thoughts in 4Q510:4–5 (4Q510–511 Songs of the Sage).

48 Robert McLachlan Wilson, *A Critical and Exegetical Commentary on Colossians and Philemon* (London: T&T Clark, 2005), 100–102.

In response, Paul reminds the Colossian church that they are filled with the proper knowledge of God (1:9–11).[49] One aspect of that knowledge in Colossians 1:13–14 is that God provided redemption and deliverance from sin, and he granted the believers in the Lycus Valley entrance into the kingdom of his son. Paul develops the thought with a hymn[50] that explores the nature of the Son of God at length—a sketch of Christocentrism. Christ is assigned a central role in creation (1:17) as the image of God (1:15). He is the source, focus, and culmination of the whole cosmos, including its various "principalities and powers." All things were fashioned in him, through him, and for him (1:16; 2:15); he was in existence before the universe and created all of creation (1:16), and he continues to sustain them (1:17). Christ stripped all such powers at his crucifixion. Therefore, there is no need to worship the cosmic powers; one should worship God for what he has accomplished in Christ (3:16–17).[51]

Further, in Colossians 1:18–20, Paul elaborates on the primacy of Christ in God's plan. Christ took on the function of the cosmic reconciler. Christ reconciled all creation to himself and also as the authoritative head of the church on a cosmic scale. However, it is important that one must not lose sight of its effects on the church at Colossae and Laodicea, as well as the churches in Asia.

One of the challenges among the newly growing Christianity in Asia is the tendency to maintain the pregospel beliefs as part of their newfound identity as Christians. Though the majority makes a clear break out from the past, others would maintain "persistence of past" beliefs and practices in their present. Their pregospel beliefs are built on a three-tier worldview,[52] which is based on a close relationship among nature, human beings, and various spirits.[53] There is a priority in their life order of material things first, then the spirits,

49 Lohse, *Colossians and Philemon*, 55–56.

50 N. Frank, *Der Kolosserbrief im Kontext des paulinischen Erbes* (Tübingen: Mohr Siebeck, 2009), 126–38.

51 Gordon D. Fee, "Wisdom Christology in Paul: A Dissenting View," in *The Way of Wisdom: Essays in Honor of Bruce K. Waltke*, ed. J. I. Parker and Sven K. Soderlund (Grand Rapids, MI: Zondervan, 2000), 251–79.

52 See Abraham T. Cherian, "Contribution of Churches and Missions to the Bhils of Rajasthan" (unpublished PhD thesis, Asian Institute of Theology, 2005); Shaibu Abraham, "Ordinary Pentecostal Theology" (unpublished PhD thesis, University of Birmingham, 2011).

53 See Paul G. Hiebert, "The Flaw of the Excluded Middle," *Missiology* 10, no. 1 (1982): 35–47.

and ultimately a high God, who is known as *Maalik* or *Ooparwala*.[54] They believe in several spirits, both benevolent and malevolent. They consider these spirits as powerful enough to keep their children from sickness, make them fertile, provide rain, and maintain the welfare of domestic animals.[55] The fear of these spirits motivates the people to worship and offer sacrifices to them.[56] If these spirits are not propitiated, they get angry and are believed to cause harm to life and property.[57] Their material needs or physical problems are immediately attached to spirits; the benevolent high God is sought only as a last resort.[58] Even though tribals believe in a benevolent high God, no offering or sacrifice is made for such a God because *Ooperwala* does not harm them.[59]

However, the Gospel provided a new identity to these new believers, making them feel empowered and self-assured from the past. The Christological articulation they cherish stems from their profound contextual and spiritual experiences. In the context of illness and lack of health care, Jesus is their healer; in the wake of oppression from evil spiritual forces, Jesus comes as the deliverer; amid poverty, Jesus is the provider; during persecution, Jesus comes as the protector.[60] Due to a lack of more profound Christological convictions like Christ's supremacy and lordship, very often the converts maintain a hybrid identity, where they oscillate between the past and the present.[61] It is very similar to the tendency that one finds among the Lycus Valley communities. Paul's deeper reflection on Christ's supremacy is apt for these Asian challenges.

54 Sathianathan Clarke, *Dalits and Christianity: Subaltern Religion and Liberation Theology in India* (New Delhi: Oxford University Press, 1999), 71.

55 Ghanshyam Shah, "Conversion, Reconversion and the State: Recent Events in the Dangs," *EPW* 34, no. 6 (February 6, 1999): 315, https://www.jstor.org/stable/4407620.

56 See Shah, 315.

57 Daniel Katapali, "Indigenous Missions and the Savara Tribal Church of Srikakulam," in *Christianity Is Indian: The Emergence of an Indigenous Community*, ed. Roger E. Hedlund (Delhi: ISPCK, 2004), 270.

58 Cherian, "Contribution," 42.

59 Hiebert, "Excluded Middle," 35–47.

60 Abraham, "Ordinary Pentecostal Theology," 185–257.

61 Sarbeswar Sahoo, *Pentecostalism and Politics of Conversion in India* (Cambridge: Cambridge University Press, 2018), 160.

Sufferings of Christ and Persecution in Asia (1:24–29)

Paul refers to his distinct labor as an apostle to the non-Jewish world, where reconciliation between gentiles and Jews in Christ was revealed (1:24–2:7). For him, it is an agonizing work (1:24–29) that fills up in his flesh what is still lacking in Christ's affliction.[62] The suffering to which Paul refers—which completes the afflictions of Christ—is seen in light of the "messianic woes" that were expected to accompany the last days.[63] In this view, Paul's sufferings are sometimes seen as vicarious (but not redemptive), reducing the degree of suffering to be endured by the churches.[64] However, this argument is not without difficulties, many of which concern the use of the concept in the life-setting of the church in Colossae.[65]

More probable is to see the suffering Paul endured as a result of completing the apostolic mission.[66] The term used for Paul's sufferings is *thlipsis*, which is never used for Christ's sufferings but is rather frequently applied to the hardships of those who proclaim the Gospel.[67] Here, Paul is not presenting himself as a model for the reader to follow,[68] and his sufferings are not related to the problems of living in a broken world, but they are unique to Christian experiences of discipleship and evangelization.[69] He is illustrating one's faithful obedience and the demonstration of the value of the message of the Gospel. Such an understanding would be critical in light of the syncretistic teachings referred to in the letter. Either way, Paul is not endorsing a deficient atonement but is merely showing that Jesus's suffering did not eliminate the need for his followers to suffer.

Asian Christians continue to suffer death, torture, rape, and discrimination for their faith. Christians are regarded with suspicion as followers of a foreign religion, and in many places they are considered second-class citizens. But

62 See Ralph P. Martin, *Colossians and Philemon* (Grand Rapids, MI: Eerdmans, 1973), 69–70.

63 See Dan 12:1; *4 Ezra* 4:36–38; *1 Enoch* 41:1–4; *2 Baruch* 30:2.

64 Wright, *Colossians and Philemon*, 87–88.

65 See O'Brien, *Colossians, Philemon*, xxviii.

66 MacDonald, *Colossians, Ephesians*, 79.

67 F. F. Bruce, *Epistle to the Colossians, to Philemon, and to the Ephesians*, NICNT (Grand Rapids, MI: Eerdmans, 1984).

68 See Talbert, *Ephesians and Colossians*, 202.

69 Marianne Meye Thompson, *Colossians and Philemon* (Grand Rapids, MI: Eerdmans, 2005), 45–46.

persecution also takes place at the grassroots levels of society, where Christianity is seen as a threat to a particular community's way of life. In many places where the gospel is seen as a threat to economic and social structures and an obstacle to exploitation, people resort to mob violence and lynching. Some Christians, both in Lycus and in Asia today, "worship angels" and engage in food rituals (Col 2:18), hoping to lessen their suffering and persecution. Paul's affirmation that the church engaged in representing Christ and continuing the ministry described in the gospel and inevitably faced sufferings will bring encouragement to the churches in Asia. Mission and suffering are inherent elements whenever the church functions as the church. Suffering is so enmeshed within the nature of the church as to constitute a mark of the authentic Asian church.

Overcoming Social and Cultural *Bhedabhaav* (3:11–14)

With a general redirection and dismissal of the old vices, Paul indicates that the Colossians who are gentiles were once dead in their transgressions, but now they have a new identity. To God, they are now alive with Christ (2:11–13; 3:3).[70] As a result, they ought to put to death their former, sinful way of life (3:5–8) and strip off their "old human being practices" (3:9). Christians are clothed in the new garment of "compassion, kindness, humility, friendliness, patience," mutual tolerance, readiness to forgive, and above all, love (3:12–14).[71]

One of the consequences of reorientation toward Christ is the elimination of all social and cultural barriers. The meaning of living in the knowledge of the image of the Creator (Col 3:10) is that there are neither Greeks nor Jews, neither circumcision nor uncircumcision, neither barbarians nor Scythians, neither slaves nor free. Christ is all in all (3:11).[72] This reflects the composition of Christian communities in the Lycus Valley.[73] Paul affirms that before and in Christ, all are equal; even the gulf between the highly sophisticated of the Greeks and the less sophisticated world are eliminated.

The Lycus Valley is depicted with an elaborate network of prejudice, suspicion, and arrogance, and it so ingrained as to be thought so natural and normal.

70 The Hindi expression *Bhedabhaav* used in the title means "discrimination."

71 Frank, *Der Kolosserbrief*, 276.

72 See parallels in 1 Cor 12:13 and Gal 3:28.

73 R. Strelan, "The Languages of the Lycus Valley," in Cadwallader and Trainor, *Colossae in Space and Time*, 77–103, esp. 82–98.

Later, as Paul concludes the Letter to the Colossians, he mentions three men who shared his Jewish heritage: Aristarchus; Mark, the cousin of Barnabas; and Jesus, who was called Justus (4:10–11). He says that they were the only Jews still working with him. Even though Paul was "the apostle to the Gentiles," he still cherished his Jewish roots. No gentile could fully appreciate what it meant to grow up and live with the traditions of Judaism, but Aristarchus, Mark, and Justus could. No wonder Paul calls them "a comfort" to him. For Paul, this ethnic distinction does not cease to exist, but they become irrelevant in Christ, for the love, honor, and respect to be shown to these individuals and groups.

Contemporary counterparts in Asia have seen prejudice, suspicion, and arrogance. Some examples include the most massive and brutal episode of ethnic cleansing of the Rohingya minority by the Myanmar government, concentration camps, the ethnic removal plans through urban renewal and rural development in East Asia, the long-endured injustice and indignity imposed on Dalits in South Asia by the caste system (*unch-neech*), the urban-rural divide, and the plight of migrant laborers in India. These are a few present-day social barriers that generate hatred, social immobility, envy, unfairness, and conflict, creating obstacles to the smooth functioning of everyday living. Paul's direction to the Lycus valley is significant for Asians: when redemption in Christ restores relationship to a person, as one practices the virtues itemized in 3:12–17, God will give one the power to overcome cultural and social barriers.

Conduct and Community Code (3:18–4:1)

In Colossians 3:18–4:1, Paul elaborates on to the so-called *Haustafel*, or domestic code—a catalogue of duties arranged according to social groups that stands in contrast to the elimination of all social barriers proclaimed (3:11–14). Paul is possibly attempting to stabilize the existing social order and thus help the Christian community adapt to its environment in the Lycus Valley.[74]

Colossians features a passage (Col 3:18–4:1, echoed in Ephesians 5:22–6:9 and 1 Peter 2:13–3:7) that is general advice on how a Christian household should behave. These codes are deeply patriarchal documents, accepting without question a traditional view of male superiority, and many scholars argue that they are scarcely different from the general moral framework in society at

74 MacDonald, *Colossians, Ephesians*, 108–10; Petr Pokorný, *Colossians: A Commentary* (Peabody, MA: Hendrickson, 1991), 150.

large—a hierarchical worldview and the familiar topic of philosophers as the ethical teachers of the Greco-Roman world.[75]

Paul reviews the social relationships involved in a household and gives instructions to each group of persons. Working in pairs, he regulates mutual relationships between wives and husbands, children and parents, and finally slaves and their masters.[76] There is a balance in them, encouraging those who have authority (husbands, fathers, masters) to use it responsibly and wisely (Col 3:19, 21; 4:1) and encouraging those who are subject to authority (wives, children, slaves) to accept it "in/for the Lord" (Col 3:18, 20, 23), implying a degree of mutual dependence.[77] What is unique here is that the personal interest of those involved must not guide interpersonal behavior.[78] Further, Paul does not legitimize his household order by finding something intrinsically inferior about its subordinate members. Common equality undergirds the ordering of relationships because "Christ, is all, and is in all" (3:11).

Asians are familiar with societal and ethical codes. In South Asia, the *Dharmaśāstras*, *Manusmṛiti*, and other codified catalogues[79] define and determine social and ethical conduct, from rituals to relationships. In Asian societies, women struggle from the denial of freedom in their homes, repression and unnatural indoctrination, an unequal and inferior status, rigid caste hierarchy, and even untouchability. Children, particularly girls, grew up with gender inequality. Slavery is everywhere in Asia—at brick kilns, teashops, rice mills, stone quarries, farms, brothels, and private homes. The domestic environment that served as the background for the *Haustafel* presupposes a social structure that was common in the Lycus Valley and throughout the entire Greek cultural sphere. However, Paul's usage of phrases "fitting to the Lord" concerning the wives (3:18), "please the Lord" for children (3:20), and "what is

75 See David L. Balch, *Let Wives Be Submissive: The Domestic Code in 1 Peter*, SBLMS 26 (Atlanta: Scholars, 1981), 23–24, 33–49.

76 Hatice Erdemir, "Woollen Textiles: An International Trade Good in the Lycus Valley in Antiquity," in Cadwallader and Trainor, *Colossae in Space and Time*, 104–29.

77 J. D. Crossan and J. L. Reed, *In Search of Paul, How Jesus' Apostle Opposed Rome's Empire with God's Kingdom* (New York: HarperCollins, 2005), 118, 122.

78 John M. G. Barclay, *Pauline Churches and Diaspora Jews* (Tübingen: Mohr Siebeck, 2011), 245–48.

79 For discussion on similar codes in Confucian ethics, see K. K. Yeo, *Musing with Confucius and Paul: Toward a Chinese Christian Theology* (Eugene, OR: Wipf & Stock, 2008).

right and fair" for the slave (3:23) is the counternarrative for modern Asian communities.[80]

CONCLUSION

The Letter to the Colossians is written by Paul the apostle and is addressed to the churches in the Lycus Valley. In the Lycus Valley, as elsewhere in the Mediterranean world, Paul brought critical stimuli for solidification of their beliefs and practices. It is significant to note the contribution of others who surrounded him as representatives, like Epaphras or Nympha and authorized letter carriers like Tychicus. Together, they sought to establish the foundation of norms purely centered on Jesus Christ and the Gospel. Paul helped define the contours of Christianity more clearly, though he had not visited Colossae, and he placed any competitors of "false philosophy" under check. The epistle provides a fresh appreciation for Christ as the fullness of God and the only source for living the Christian life. Against this backdrop of practical Christian living, the love for Christ should translate into love for others—friends, fellow believers, spouses, children, parents, slaves, and masters—as a new narrative for Christian witness and life in Asia.

FURTHER READING

Barclay, J. M. G. 2011. *Pauline Churches and Diaspora Jews*. WUNT 275. Tübingen: Mohr Siebeck.

Cherian, A. T. 2005. "Contribution of Churches and Missions to the Bhils of Rajasthan." Unpublished PhD thesis, Asian Institute of Theology.

Clarke, S. 1999. *Dalits and Christianity: Subaltern Religion and Liberation Theology in India*. New Delhi: Oxford University Press.

Dunn, J. D. G. 1996. *The Epistles to the Colossians and to Philemon: A Commentary on the Greek Text*. Grand Rapids, MI: Eerdmans.

Iralu, S. 2015. "Colossians." In *South Asia Bible Commentary*, edited by Brian Wintle, 1660–1668. Udaipur, India: Open Door.

80 For further discussion, see Wintle and Nicholls, *Colossians and Philemon*, 144–56.

Margaret, Y. M. 2008. *Colossians, Ephesians*. Sacra Pagina. Collegeville, MN: Liturgical.
Moo, D. J. 2008. *The Letters to the Colossians and to Philemon*. PNTC. Grand Rapids, MI: Eerdmans.
Talbert, C. H. 2007. *Ephesians and Colossians*. Paideia Commentaries on the New Testament. Grand Rapids, MI: Baker Academic.
Thompson, M. M. 2005. *Colossians and Philemon*. The Two Horizons New Testament Commentary. Grand Rapids, MI: Eerdmans.
Wintle, B., and B. J. Nicholls. 2019. *Colossians and Philemon: A Pastoral and Contextual Commentary*. ABCS. Carlisle, UK: Langham Global Library.
Witherington, B. 2007. *The Letters to Philemon, the Colossians, and the Ephesians: A Socio-rhetorical Commentary on the Captivity Epistles*. Grand Rapids, MI: Eerdmans.
Yeo, K. K. *Musing with Confucius and Paul: Toward a Chinese Christian Theology*. Eugene, OR: Wipf & Stock, 2008.

FOURTEEN

The Letters to the Thessalonians

Andrew B. Spurgeon
Singapore Bible College
Singapore

Paul's letters to the church in Thessalonica often go unnoticed and unpreached. Byron writes, "Apart from readings of 1 Thess 4:13–18 at funerals and a preoccupation by some with the 'end times' (1 Thess 4:13–5:11; 2 Thess 2:1–12), these two letters do not always receive the level of attention they should."[1] His assessment has some accuracy. The Thessalonian letters do fade in the shadows of the mighty letters such as Romans, 1 and 2 Corinthians, and Galatians. Yet these letters offer practical teachings that are invaluable for Asian Christians.

BASIC INFORMATION

What is the setting for these letters, who wrote them, who were the recipients, when were they written, and what do they contain? Acts of the Apostles, 1 and 2 Thessalonians, and extrabiblical materials answer these questions.

Settings of the Letters

After a successful first missionary journey, Paul and Silas started another missionary journey from Antioch of Syria, their mission base (Acts 15:40–41).

1 John Byron, *1 and 2 Thessalonians*, Story of God Bible Commentary, ed. Tremper Longman III and Scot McKnight (Grand Rapids, MI: Zondervan, 2014), 1.

When they reached Lystra, Paul took in a young protégé, Timothy. The three of them traveled to Troas, the western end of Asia Minor (Acts 16:1–8). Because of an invitation through a vision, Paul and his friends left for Macedonia, the eastern edge of the Western world. The author of Acts possibly joined them, as evidenced by the frequent reference to "we" in Acts 16:9–12. In Macedonia, they ministered at Philippi, Amphipolis, and Apollonia (Acts 16:13–17:1a). When chased from Philippi, they went to Thessalonica for the first time (Acts 17:1b).

Thessalonica had a synagogue (Acts 17:1b). As was his custom, Paul went to the synagogue and reasoned with those in the synagogue that the Messiah had to suffer, die, and resurrect from the dead; and Jesus was that Messiah (Acts 17:2–3). Paul's message convinced some of the Jews and many of the God-fearing Greeks (Acts 17:4). Their conversion to Paul's message raised jealousy among some of the Jews, who took actions against Jason, thinking he was sheltering Paul and his friends (Acts 17:5–9). Fearing further ill-treatment, the new believers in Thessalonica sent Paul and friends to Berea, a neighboring city with a Jewish settlement (Acts 17:10).

Paul continued preaching the resurrected Christ Jesus in Berea. When the Bereans accepted Paul's message, the same jealous Jews went to Berea to agitate the crowd against Paul (Acts 17:11–13). The believers in Berea encouraged Paul to leave the city and travel south via the coastal regions (Acts 17:14). Then Paul traveled to Athens (Acts 17:15–34) and Corinth (Acts 18:1–4). In Corinth, Aquila and Priscilla sheltered him and offered him a job as a tentmaker (Acts 18:2).

While staying in Corinth, Paul was anxious about the Thessalonians: Were they growing in faith? Were they facing further persecution and suffering? Were they doing the work of evangelism? While he anxiously waited in Corinth, Silas and Timothy returned from Berea and said that the Thessalonians were doing well (Acts 18:5).[2] Upon hearing that good news, Paul, Silas, and Timothy penned them a letter, 1 Thessalonians. Several months passed. Persecutions persisted in Thessalonica. Some believers lost their lives, others were tempted to return to their past comfortable living, and some gave up hope and became lazy, even when it came to working for their own food. They had more questions about the coming of the Lord: Has he already come?

2 See Gene L. Green, *The Letters to the Thessalonians*, Pillar New Testament Commentary, ed. Don Carson (Grand Rapids, MI: Eerdmans, 2002), 52.

How will they know when he comes? So Paul and friends, who were still in Corinth, wrote a second letter, 2 Thessalonians.

Authors

First and 2 Thessalonians have three authors: Paul, Silas, and Timothy (1 Thess 1:1; 2 Thess 1:1). Paul, the apostle, shared the gospel with them and established them in their faith (Acts 17:2–3). Silas, a member of the Jerusalem church, colabored with Paul in discipling the young church in Thessalonica. Timothy was Paul's protégé. When Paul was sent away from Berea, Timothy and Silas stayed in Berea and continued to minister to Thessalonians, building on the foundation Paul laid (Acts 17:14–15; 1 Thess 3:1–2). All three had invested their lives in Thessalonians, so they wrote these letters together. Holmes writes, "The conjunction of the three names . . . and the frequent use of the first-person plural ('we') throughout the letter indicate that all three are co-senders of the letter."[3] Yet Paul is the leading apostle behind the message of the letter.

Addressee

These letters were addressed to the "church of the Thessalonians" (1 Thess 1:1; 2 Thess 1:2). Because the term *church* (*ekklēsia*) would not have had "any sacral association in the mind of the recent converts from paganism,"[4] the authors clarify it as "church . . . in God the/our Father and the Lord Jesus Christ" (1 Thess 1:1; 2 Thess 1:2). They were a congregation that met in the name of God the Father and the Lord Jesus Christ.

Thessalonica (also Thessaloniki or Saloniki) was the capital of the Macedonian province and a prosperous city. Cara writes, "Thessalonica's economy was aided by it being a major harbor on the Aegean Sea and a major stop on the Via Egnatia, which was an important east-west road connecting western Greece to Byzantium (modern-day Istanbul)."[5] The city had existed since 5000 BC as *Therma*, meaning "Hot Springs." But when Cassander reestablished it as a

3 Michael W. Holmes, *1 and 2 Thessalonians*, NIV Application Commentary: From Biblical Text to Contemporary Life, ed. Terry Muck (Grand Rapids, MI: Zondervan, 1998), 36.

4 F. F. Bruce, *1 and 2 Thessalonians*, Word Biblical Commentary 45 (Grand Rapids, MI: Zondervan, 1982), 6.

5 Robert J. Cara, *A Study Commentary on 1 and 2 Thessalonians*, EP Study Commentary (Durham, UK: EP, 2009), 21.

Greek city in the fourth century, he named it after his wife, Thessalonice ("victory of Thessaly"), who was a daughter of Philip of Macedon and a half sister of Alexander the Great.[6] The city has kept that name since then. In Greece, only Thessalonica and Athens still stand where they stood two thousand years ago, in Paul's time.[7] Thessalonica minted its own coins, proving its autonomy within the Empire.[8]

Date

Paul and friends wrote these Thessalonian letters from Corinth. Paul's stay in Corinth is one of the undisputed dates in the NT chronology because his trial took place before Gallio, the proconsul of Achaia (Acts 18:12–17). Beale writes, "Documentary evidence indicates that Gallio's time in office lasted at least from July 51 to June 52."[9] Paul's stay in Corinth coincided with Gallio's stay, so Paul wrote the Thessalonian letters sometime in 51–52 CE.

Contents of the Letters

First Thessalonians has two major sections. The first section, 1:1–3:13, is a recollection of the missionaries' time with the Thessalonians.[10] The second section, 4:1–5:24, has exhortations for the Thessalonians to live godly lives in light of the certainty of their future with Christ.

Paul and friends began the letter by thanking God because the Thessalonians accepted the gospel as if it were from God and believed it even when it caused them severe suffering and persecution (1:3–6). By suffering well, they became examples for the believers in Macedonia and Achaia (1:7–8). The pinnacle of their faith was leaving idols to worship the true and living God (1:9–10). The Jews in the audience might have resented being accused of worshipping

6 Gordon D. Fee, *The First and Second Letters to the Thessalonians*, New International Commentary on the New Testament (Grand Rapids, MI: Eerdmans, 2009), 5.

7 Byron, *1 and 2 Thessalonians*, 10.

8 Ben Witherington, *The Acts of the Apostles: A Socio-rhetorical Commentary* (Grand Rapids, MI: Eerdmans, 1998), 503.

9 G. K. Beale, *1–2 Thessalonians*, IVP New Testament Commentary Series, ed. Grant R. Osborne (Downers Grove, IL: InterVarsity, 2003), 14.

10 See David Luckensmeyer and Bronwen Neil, "Reading First Thessalonians as a Consolatory Letter in Light of Seneca and Ancient Handbooks on Letter-Writing," *New Testament Studies* 62 (2016): 31–48.

idols, but any inaccurate picture of God amounts to worshipping a false god, an idol. Gorospe and Ringma write, "Asian societies, which have deep and differing religious systems, tend to emphasize the honoring of cultural and family traditions, social conformity, and the maintenance of a group ethos. In honoring these values, we may indirectly honor the false 'gods' of excessive filial piety, disproportionate commitment to a family business, conformity to corrupt practices in the workplace, or the elevation of persons with social and economic status above the general needs of the Christian community."[11] When Thessalonians heard the gospel of a resurrected savior whom Lord God sent, they accepted the gospel, even when it brought them sufferings.

Paul and friends then recollected their visit, chase, and continued desire to visit the Thessalonians (2:1–20). They first visited the Thessalonians after being persecuted and driven out of Philippi (2:1–2). There, they preached without using trickery or flattering words to convince them of the gospel. They were gentle as nursing mothers who cared for their children (2:3–7). Further, they did not satisfy their own greed by living off of the Thessalonians; instead, they worked night and day with their own hands so they would not be a burden. They were like fathers who provide for their children (2:8–12). Because of their honesty and industry, the Thessalonians accepted God's word and excelled beyond the apostles' expectations. They imitated the actions of the churches in Judea, who too suffered for Christ Jesus's sake from their own people (2:13–16). Tamil speakers advise children with a four-word phrase: *matha, pitha, guru, theivam* (mother, father, teacher, god). Ramakrishnan explains that Tamils set this order because mothers teach the children first, then fathers, then teachers, and ultimately god.[12] Paul, Silas, and Timothy were such mothers and fathers to the Thessalonians, teaching them basic teachings for them to grow to maturity.

Before the apostles could invest more time with the Thessalonians, unbelieving Jews chased the apostles away and orphaned the believers in Thessalonica (2:17). The apostles went to Berea. Whenever Paul tried to return to Thessalonica from Berea, the evil one blocked his way (2:18). But he truly longed for them because they were his hope, joy, and crown (2:19–20). Paul's

11 Athena E. Gorospe and Charles Ringma, *Judges: A Pastoral and Contextual Commentary*, ABC (Carlisle, UK: Langham Global Library, 2016), 143.

12 Usha Ramakrishnan, *Matha Pitha Guru Theivam* (Chennai: Thavan, 2008), 2.

reluctance to leave the Thessalonians and constant desire to see them set a precedent for Christians worldwide not to desert a ministry halfway. In Asia, when Nepali Christians were chased out of Nepal and couldn't return to their homeland, they sang a prayer: "Lord, open the gates of salvation for Gurkhalis [Nepalis] to find salvation."[13] In 1952, their missionaries—who had been debarred from entering the country since 1769—were permitted to return to Nepal.

Paul and friends continued the narrative (3:1–13). When they could no longer know how the Thessalonians were doing, they sent Timothy back to them (3:1–2). Timothy's goal was to encourage and strengthen the Thessalonians' faith so they would endure trials (3:2–3). Paul's fear was that the tempter would tempt them, and they would fall prey to his schemes (3:4–5). But Timothy's visit wasn't disastrous. He returned to Paul and Silas with the news that the Thessalonians' faith was firm and their love was extensive (3:6).

Paul and Silas were relieved upon hearing that God protected the Thessalonians (3:7–9). At the same time, it increased their desire to see the Thessalonians; night and day, they prayed that they would return to Thessalonica (3:10). While they waited for God to open the way, they prayed that God would continue to increase the Thessalonians' love for one another and strengthen their hearts to live blameless lives (3:11–13). These recollections concluded the first part of 1 Thessalonians.

In the second part of the letter, Paul and friends encouraged the Thessalonians to godly living (4:1–18). They also answered questions that the Thessalonians had and gave instructions pertinent to their situation (5:1–28). First, Paul and his friends reminded the Thessalonians to continue to walk in a lifestyle that is pleasing to God (4:1–2). They had earlier instructed them on these issues, and the Thessalonians had been faithfully following those instructions. But Paul and friends continued to exhort Thessalonians, "an intentional process of testifying, teaching, training and transmitting our convictions and our lives to those who would pass it on to others."[14]

13 Ramesh Khatry, "Romans," in *South Asia Bible Commentary*, ed. Brian Wintle (Udaipur, India: Open Door, 2015), 1532.

14 Edmund Chan, *A Certain Kind: Intentional Disciplemaking That Redefines Success in Ministry* (Singapore: Covenant Evangelical Free Church, 2013), 38.

Second, the Thessalonians ought to avoid sexual immorality (4:3–5). Because sexual immorality often abuses and takes advantage of others, the Thessalonians ought to shun such practices (4:6a). Luis Antonio Tagle, the archbishop of Manila, explains that when ordained ministers abuse children, they inflict "wounds not only on the victims, but also on their families, the clergy, the Church, [and] the wider society."[15] The Thessalonians should not be like those who abuse others because God will punish such people (4:6b). Instead, they should live according to their calling: "to live a holy life" (4:7–8).

Third, the Thessalonians ought to continue to excel in love for one another, including living a quiet life of hard work that will have an impact on the outsiders (4:9–12). A quiet life does not mean an idle life; instead, it is a life that avoids "disrupting or intruding into other people's lives and so imposing an unnecessary burden."[16] There were political ramifications for Christians in Thessalonica if they were open and boisterous in their opinions concerning government and politics.[17] Nations with Hindu, Muslim, or Buddhist majorities do not appreciate Christians attacking their practices and beliefs. Even if they don't speak against the government, they could be imprisoned, as in the case of Wang Yi, who was sentenced to nine years of imprisonment in China.[18]

Fourth, the Thessalonians ought not to grieve without hope concerning Christians who have died since those Christians were alive, just as Christ himself died and was raised again (4:13–18). As proof, they would return with Christ when he reappeared. The Thessalonians might have thought spirits of the dead roamed around on earth, as many in Asian cultures do. In a "traditional Buddhist and Taoist festival, observed in certain Asian countries including Malaysia, Singapore, Taiwan and Hong Kong . . . it's believed that the gates to the netherworld are flung open, sending forth restless spirits of the

15 Beuna Bernal, "How the Catholic Church in the Philippines Deals with Clergy Sex Abuse of Children," accessed January 15, 2020, https://tinyurl.com/4vd6vssv.

16 Jacob Cherian, "1 Thessalonians," in *South Asia Bible Commentary: A One-Volume Commentary on the Whole Bible*, ed. Brian Wintle (Udaipur, India: Open Door, 2015), 1674.

17 Callia Rulmu, "Between Ambition and Quietism: The Socio-political Background of 1 Thessalonians 4:9–12," *Biblica* 91, no. 3 (2010): 393–417.

18 Amy Gunia, "Prison Sentence for Pastor Shows China Feels Threatened by Spread of Christianity, Experts Say," *Time*, January 2, 2020, https://time.com/5757591/wang-yi-prison-sentence-china-christianity/.

dead, lost souls, ghosts and demons to seek food and entertainment in the realm of the living."[19] The Thessalonians, however, were not to grieve like others (4:14).

Fifth, they ought not to be alarmed about the timing of the Lord's coming, but they should be alert because it would come unexpectedly. While people promised peace and safety, sudden destruction would come upon them. But unlike the world that would be surprised by the Lord's coming, the Thessalonians would not be surprised because they were "children of light." Whereas Buddhism teaches that a devotee can gain a "luminous mind" (*prabhāsvara-citta*) by discipline and hard work,[20] believers become "children of light" by believing in Christ. As children of light, believers need not fear the Lord's coming, but they should anticipate it and live accordingly (5:1–11).

Sixth, the Thessalonians ought to value those who work hard among them in sharing the gospel and teaching them. But they should avoid those who are idle and disruptive (5:12–14a). Laziness has no place in Christianity. When Christians slack in their work at the workplace, they shame Christ. So the Thessalonians ought to excel in working, encouraging the weakhearted, helping the weak, being patient with one another, not doing wrong, rejoicing, praying, giving thanks, encouraging prophecy, and rejecting every kind of evil (5:14b–22).

Paul and friends conclude the letter with a benediction that assures their readers of God's peace, sanctification, and blamelessness at the coming of the Lord Jesus Christ because God has always been faithful to the Thessalonians (5:23–24). No doubt, this letter would have encouraged the Thessalonians. They had the second-best thing to seeing Paul and his friends: hearing their voices and wisdom through this letter. In Asia, Christians are in the minority, but they can still have a great impact in society by living responsible lives that fear neither persecution nor death. Violent persecutions against Christians erupted in the Indian state of Odisha in 2008. One newspaper reported one hundred people were killed and 250 churches and 6,500 houses were looted and burned, leaving fifty-six thousand homeless. Many women were raped, including a Catholic

19 Alan Teh Leam Seng, "When the Dead Roam among the Living," *New Straits Times*, accessed February 25, 2020, https://www.nst.com.my/lifestyle/sunday-vibes/2018/09/409792/when-dead-roam-among-living.

20 Steven Collins, *Selfless Persons: Imagery and Thought in Theravada Buddhism* (Cambridge: Cambridge University Press, 1982), 238.

nun.[21] The challenge for all Asian Christians is to stand firm in their faith in the midst of severe persecution, just as the Thessalonians did.

2 Thessalonians has three sections. Chapter 1 speaks of the Thessalonians' faith and love. Chapter 2 has answers to questions that the Thessalonians raised concerning the coming of the Lord. In chapter 3, the authors ask for prayers for themselves and exhort the Thessalonians to godly living. Paul and his friends started 2 Thessalonians by thanking God for the faith and love of the believers in the midst of persecution (1:1–4). Then they assured the Thessalonians that God would repay them for their struggles by punishing the oppressors (1:5–10). At the same time, God would also strengthen their faith (1:11–12).

In chapter 2, the apostles answered questions that the Thessalonians had concerning the coming of the Lord (2:1–12). No false claims should alarm them as if the Day of the Lord had arrived. It would come only after the rebellion, the man of lawlessness, and the man doomed for destruction came—none of their visitations have occurred (2:1–5). When the Day of the Lord finally comes, the Lord would return and defeat his enemies with the righteous words of his mouth (2:7–10). Shoko Asahara founded a Japanese religious movement called "Aum" and predicted that the world will end in 1997. He even staged a preview with a sarin gas attack on the Tokyo subway that killed 12 people and injured 5,500 people in 1995. Unlike what he predicted, the world didn't come to an end; instead, he was sentenced to death for the murders he committed.[22] Christians should be leery of those who predict the timing of the end days. Instead, they should wait for the Lord himself to come and prove his coming.

The apostles continued the narration and said that until the Lord comes those who sided with the evil one would be in a delusion, believe the lie the evil one told them, and be condemned for not believing the truth (2:11–12). But God was sanctifying the Thessalonians, through the Spirit, in order to share in the glory of the Lord Jesus Christ (2:13–14). Therefore, they should stand firm and hold fast to the apostles' teachings. God would give them the grace needed for every good work and deed (2:15–17). Even now, there

21 "Christian Beheaded in India's Odisha State," Union of Catholic Asian News, accessed February 25, 2020, https://www.ucanews.com/news/christian-beheaded-in-indias-odisha-state/84576.

22 "Notorious Doomsday Prophets and Cults," CNBC, accessed February 1, 2020, https://www.cnbc.com/2011/04/06/Notorious-Doomsday-Prophets-and-Cults.html.

are alarmists. A website has a rapture index that "is designed to measure the type of activity that could act as a precursor to the rapture."[23] Instead of worrying about the end days, Christians should focus on what really matters: encouraging the weakhearted, helping the weak, and being patient with one another.

In chapter 3, Paul and his friends solicited the Thessalonians' prayers for them: for the gospel to spread through them, and for the apostles to be delivered from the evil people who suppressed the truth (3:1–2). The apostles believed in the prayer of the saints. Korean Christians created a unique prayer style called *Tongsung Kido*, which literally means "praying together out loud."[24]

The apostles also expressed their assurance in the Thessalonians because the Lord was faithful to protect them and work in their hearts (3:4–5).[25] The Thessalonians were to stay away from Christians who refused to work because idleness was not in accordance with the gospel or the examples the apostles themselves gave them. The Thessalonians should never cease from doing good (3:6–13). If someone refused to follow these instructions, the Christians in Thessalonica should take note of them and not associate with them so they would be shamed into changing their ways. But they should not treat them as enemies (3:14–15). Paul, Silas, and Timothy concluded the letter with two benedictions and Paul's signature (3:16–18). Both benedictions affirmed the Lord's peace, and God's grace abided with them.

Outline

First Thessalonians

- A Recollection of Past Events (1:1–3:13)
  - Paul's reason to leave Thessalonica (1:1–3:1)
  - Paul's reason to send Timothy to them (3:2–9)
  - Timothy's message concerning them (3:10–13)

23 "Rapture Ready Index," Rapture Ready, accessed January 1, 2021, https://www.raptureready.com/rapture-ready-index/.

24 Yohang Chung, "Tongsung Kido (a Unique Korean Prayer)," Upper New York Conference of the United Methodist Church, May 10, 2017, https://www.unyumc.org/news/article/tongsung-kido-a-unique-korean-prayer.

25 Nijay Gupta, "An Apocalyptic Reading of Psalm 78 in 2 Thessalonians 3," *Journal for the Study of the New Testament* 31, no. 2 (December 2008): 179–94.

Exhortations to Godly Living (4:1–5:24)

Avoid sexual immorality and abuse of others (4:1–8)

Continue to love and work quietly (4:9–12)

Not to grieve without hope about the Christians who have did (4:13–18)

Confidently believe in the coming of the Lord (5:1–11)

Work and provide for the needy believers (5:12–24)

Second Thessalonians

Assurance That God Will Reward Them for Their Suffering (1:1–12)

Answers to Questions Concerning the Lord's Coming (2:1–17)

Request for Prayer and Exhortation to Work Hard (3:1–18)

THEMES

There are four major themes that outshine the others in the Thessalonian letters: simplicity, suffering, hope, and industry. An understanding of these themes shall provide a perspectival framework for these epistles.

Simplicity

Simplicity is a conscious effort to minimalize one's belief or lifestyle in an affluent society or culture. Mahatma Gandhi and Mother Teresa could have remained in South Africa and Venezuela, respectively, and enjoyed the pleasures of life. Yet they chose India and simple living. They weren't ensnared by the luxuries of life; they preferred simple clothing and diets.

The Thessalonians chose a simplicity of faith and life after hearing the gospel. Rome chose Thessalonica to be the capital city of the province of Macedonia even with a military base in the north at Philippi, noble people in the south in Berea, and philosophers, art, and culture in the farthest south at Athens. One hundred thousand people lived in Thessalonica, making it a large metropolis.[26] Besides commerce and politics, Thessalonians had a rich religious history. In the sixth century BCE, Thessalonians

26 Byron, *1 and 2 Thessalonians*, 11.

brought from Aenea the temple of the goddess Aphrodite.[27] They also built temples for Dionysus, Serapis and Isis, Osiris, Harpocrates, Anubis, and Roma. Cabirus—a god holding a hammer in his right hand and a lit staff in his left—became their patron deity.[28] Thessalonians truly lived in a rich religious and political context, and they could have taken great pride in their culture and ethnicity. Yet the Christians in Thessalonica chose simplicity of faith and life.

First, they expressed their simplicity in choosing to worship a single God in a polytheistic society (1 Thess 1:9). In India, a devotee worships Ganesh for wisdom, Lakshmi for wealth, and Vishnu for health. Similarly, Thessalonians worshipped different gods for different needs. But when Paul preached the gospel of a monotheistic creator God to them, they chose the simplicity of worshipping him alone.

Second, they expressed their simplicity in choosing a single resurrection rather than multiple reincarnations. Some in Thessalonica worshipped the goddesses of Demeter and Gore, who died and were reborn every season. Their concept of rebirth was similar to Hinduism, Jainism, Buddhism, and Sikhism, which believe in some form of reincarnation or rebirth of the same individual in multiple generations. But upon hearing that God raised Jesus from the dead and that Jesus shall never die again, the Christians in Thessalonica chose a single resurrection of life (Acts 17:2–3).

Third, they chose the simplicity of loving everyone equally. Castes, creeds, and classes divide people, separating noble from ignoble, freed from slaves, males from females, and landowners from the poor. Segregating people into different statuses keeps a person on the edge of not knowing when to bow, when to say "sir" or "madam," when to accept or give salutations, and whom to appoint to a job vacancy. Such complexity of life vanishes when one values everyone equally. In India, a Hindu priest defied the caste system by carrying an untouchable (who are forbidden from entering the temple) on his shoulder and by entering into the temple to visibly demonstrate that everyone

27 "The Archaic Greek Temple of Aphrodite in Thessaloniki, Macedonia, Greece," Archaeology News Network, May 14, 2010, https://archaeologynewsnetwork.blogspot.com/2010/05/archaic-greek-temple-of-aphrodite-in.html.

28 Charles Edson, "Cults of Thessalonica (Macedonia III)," *Harvard Theological Review* 41, no. 3 (July 1948): 200.

was equal.[29] Mother Teresa loved the unlovable poor in the streets of Kolkata. Long before them, Thessalonians chose the simplicity of loving everyone equally. They were so good at loving one another that Paul acknowledged that God himself taught them such love (1 Thess 4:9). Their love overflowed to the neighboring districts, and they became models to those in Macedonia and Achaia (1 Thess 1:7–8; 4:10).

Fourth, their simplicity was expressed in their single-mindedness in faith (1 Thess 1:5). Opposite to single-mindedness is wavering in one's faith (Jas 1:6–8). A Chinese proverb says, "Indecisiveness breeds confusion."[30] Thessalonians weren't indecisive or confused in their faith; they wholeheartedly believed the gospel because it came to them with the power of the Holy Spirt. They had previously lived in a world of relativism, distrust of authorities, and suspicion, but then they chose the simplicity of believing univocally as followers of Jesus.

Fifth, they expressed their simplicity in their fidelity in sexuality (1 Thess 4:3–7). Often societies challenge and question gender identities and relationships. The Supreme Court of India overturned a sodomy law, section 377 of the Indian Penal Code, in September 2018, making sodomy no longer a crime among consenting adults.[31] Thessalonians were no strangers to such lifestyles. Emperor Nero married two of his freed male slaves.[32] Yet the Thessalonians chose the simplicity of fidelity in one's sexuality. God's will for all Christians is sexual purity (1 Thess 4:3). Each person ought to treat their own body in a holy and honorable way, avoiding passions that nonbelievers embrace (1 Thess 4:4–5). Further, illicit sexual acts take advantage of others (1 Thess 4:6). Often women and children are the victims. In 2017, one billion minors (between the ages of two and seventeen years old) endured physical, emotional, or sexual violence.[33] Chiam tells the story of a young girl, Priya (fictional name), who was married off at the age

29 "Why This India Priest Carried an 'Untouchable' into a Temple," BBC, April 20, 2018, https://www.bbc.com/news/world-asia-india-43807951.

30 Theodora Lau, *Best-Loved Chinese Proverbs*, 2nd ed. (New York: HarperCollins, 2009), 73–74.

31 Krishnadas Rajagopal, "SC Decriminalises Homosexuality," *Hindu*, accessed September 20, 2019, https://www.thehindu.com/todays-paper/sc-decriminalises-homosexuality/article24887363.ece.

32 Seutonius, *Nero*, 29.

33 "The Protection of Minors in the Church," pbc2019, accessed September 29, 2019, https://www.pbc2019.org/protection-of-minors/child-abuse-on-the-global-level.

of fourteen and later fell victim to human trafficking and sexual exploitation until a Christian organization freed and rehabilitated her.[34] Christians should avoid sexual promiscuities in their lives and fight for the oppressed. The attitude of the Thessalonians in their sexual behavior is a paradigm to the contemporary realities.

Sixth, the Thessalonians expressed their simplicity in giving freedom to each believer to exercise the Spirit's gifts, without quenching them. They carefully examined the gifts to make sure they were genuine (1 Thess 5:19–21). Complexity, in contrast, is refusing to be examined, making unnecessary claims, or distrusting that God uses the Spirit's gifts for the edification of the church (Eph 4:12). The Thessalonians not only believed in the Spirit's gifts but also exercised them properly after evaluating their authenticity.[35]

Seventh, the Thessalonians exercised simplicity by caring for those who served them (1 Thess 5:12–13). Whether menial servants or Christian ministers, simplicity means honoring them for their service. Complexity is expecting them to serve others without reward or respect. Jesus taught that he did not come to be served but to serve (Mark 10:45). He demonstrated his servitude by washing the disciples' feet (John 13). Jesus did not grab honor and seek privilege. He lived a simple life, and so did the Thessalonians. In Singapore, often elderly people work in hawker centers (food courts) collecting trays and dishes from tables, even though the signs say, "Please return your tray to the designated place." We should honor these workers for their simplicity.

By choosing these aspects of simplicity, the Christians in Thessalonica set an example for other Christians in Asia. Christians should be strongly convinced of their faith and exercise the Spirit's gift carefully and faithfully.

Suffering

Suffering comes in various forms. Gandhi's trials began even before he reached India: he was on a train voyage to Pretoria, South Africa, when he was "forcibly

34 Michael Chiam, "What If She Was Your Daughter or Sister?," in *The Servant at the Fringes: Christians Serving Foreign Workers in Singapore*, ed. Calvin Chong (Singapore: Singapore Bible College, 2018), 90–94.

35 Yabbeju Rapaka, *Dalit Pentecostalism: A Study of the Indian Pentecostal Church of God* (Lexington, KY: Emeth, 2013), 1–159.

removed by the rail authorities at Pietermaritzburg from the first class compartment and thrown off the train."[36] William Riead, in the movie *The Letters* (2014), graphically describes Mother Teresa's fight with loneliness and depression, including a fear of abandonment from God. Christians in Thessalonica were familiar with suffering, including abandonment and beating (Acts 17:5–7). But they did not give up; instead, they became examples for Christians in Macedonia and Achaia (1 Thess 1:7–8). Five principles motivated them.

First, the Thessalonians suffered because they identified with Christ, the one who suffered. They heard the message that Jesus Christ suffered and died, and they accepted that message for their salvation and endured suffering (Acts 17:3). Jason was such an example—he endured suffering when jealous Jews beat him and dragged him before the city officials, accusing him of causing trouble (Acts 17:5–9). Others followed his example (1 Thess 1:5). *BBC News* catalogs a partial list of sufferings Christians in Pakistan endured in recent years: 14 killed and 70 injured in two bomb blasts in March 2015; 70 people killed and 340 worshippers injured in an Easter Sunday suicide attack in 2016; 9 people killed and 57 injured in an attack on a church in December 2017; 80 people killed in a Peshawar church in twin bomb suicides in 2018; and 40 houses and a church burned, with 8 people burned alive, in 2019.[37] Asian Christians endure such suffering as minority communities spread across the continent.

Second, the Thessalonians suffered because Paul modeled endurance for them. Paul came to Thessalonica after being stripped naked, beaten with rods, severely flogged, imprisoned, and chased out of Philippi, 160 kilometers north of Thessalonica (1 Thess 2:2; Acts 16:16–40). In Thessalonica, he endured insults and persecutions and was a living example of enduring suffering well. By watching God's messenger suffer, the Thessalonians learned the path of suffering. In the process, they set examples for other churches, including those in Asia. *The Korean Pentecost* outlines some of the sufferings early missionaries in North Korea endured for sixty years.[38]

36 "S. Africa, India to Commemorate Gandhi Train Incident," Xinhuanet, accessed October 5, 2019, http://www.xinhuanet.com/english/2018-06/07/c_137235527.htm.

37 "Why Are Pakistan's Christians Targeted?," BBC, accessed January 29, 2020, https://www.bbc.com/news/world-asia-35910331.

38 William Blair and Bruce Hunt, *The Korean Pentecost and the Sufferings Which Followed* (Edinburgh: Banner of Truth, 2015).

Thirdly, the Thessalonians imitated the Judean churches while their people persecuted them (1 Thess 2:14–16). Persecution was common for the Jews—their prophets were persecuted and driven out of their cities, and their apostles were killed (Acts 12). As a former persecutor of Christians, Paul would have informed the Thessalonians of Judean persecutions and perseverance. The Thessalonians imitated them and endured persecution from their own people, both Jews and gentiles, setting a model for other churches to imitate. Asian churches have followed both Judean and Thessalonian Christians and have endured suffering for centuries.

Fourth, some Thessalonians paid the ultimate price of persecution of losing their lives in martyrdom (1 Thess 4:13). Their deaths grieved other Christians, who wondered whether they had run the race without a purpose. Paul assured them that those who had "fallen asleep" in the Lord were with him and would return with him (1 Thess 4:14–18). Therefore, the living Christians shouldn't grieve without hope. They would see again the Christians who died. Martyrdom is the ultimate price many Christians in Asia pay, but the hope is that God will resurrect them and bring them with Christ when he returns.

Fifth, by faithfully suffering and persevering, Thessalonians left an example for other churches (2 Thess 1:4–7). Paul himself boldly spoke of the Thessalonians' endurance to other churches. And their endurance wasn't without hope: God himself would defend them (2 Thess 1:6).

Thessalonians faithfully endured sufferings and left others examples of endurance. They followed the examples of the Lord Jesus Christ, Paul, Silas, Timothy, and the churches in Judea. In this way, they are examples for churches worldwide. Asian Christians face many trials—poverty, loss of jobs, insults, beating, imprisonment, and death. In August 2017, the US Commission on International Religious Freedom (USCIRF) ranked persecution against Christians in India at "Tier 2," along with Iraq and Afghanistan.[39] The Covid-19 virus started in Asia but has become a pandemic affecting the world. In a heart-wrenching article, Friedman recollects the many sufferings people in rural Asia face every day.[40] For them, Christianity

39 Sarah Erkhoff Zylstra, "State Department's Unusually Short Religious Freedom Update: ISIS is Bad," *Christianity Today*, accessed August 30, 2018, https://tinyurl.com/3s9mr6uw.

40 Edward Friedman, "The Persistent Invisibility of Rural Suffering in China," *Indian Journal of Asian Affairs* 22, nos. 1–2 (June–December 2009): 19–45.

offers hope, not relief from suffering (although relief might be possible in a few cases). Whatever sufferings may come their way, they should endure, knowing that prophets, apostles, the Thessalonians, and even Jesus endured suffering.

Hope

Hope gives a person the needed strength to endure insults, sufferings, and persecutions. Gandhi's hope of a free nation began with peaceful protests at the Dharasana Salt Works, where he refused to pay salt tax to the British.[41] He was a man with a small army of nonviolent protesters against an army that claimed the sun did not set on its empire, but he had a hope that he would free India. Mother Teresa saw the vastness of poverty and said, "I alone cannot change the world, but I can cast a stone across the waters to create many ripples."[42] With hope, they changed India and impacted the world.

In the same way, the Christians in Thessalonica had hope in God. Cara writes, "If these letters could be boiled down to one main theme, it is the ongoing need for the Thessalonians to put their hope in God."[43] They exercised hope from the onset (1 Thess 1:3). But hope, unless fanned, could die like a flame that doesn't have enough oxygen. So Paul exhorted them to continue in their hope that stood firm on six principles.

First, the Thessalonians' hope centered on the Lord Jesus Christ (1 Thess 1:3). The word *Lord* (*kurios*) was a pregnant term religiously and politically in those days. Religiously, it equated Jesus with the YHWH-God of the OT because the Greek translations used *kurios* to translate his name. Such a declaration that Jesus was equal with YHWH-God would have been blasphemous to the Jews (1 Cor 1:23), yet it alone brought them salvation (Rom 10:9–10). Politically, by calling Jesus Lord (*kurios*), the Christians were replacing Emperor Claudius as their "Lord," which would have endangered their

41 "Salt March," History, accessed October 1, 2019, https://www.history.com/topics/india/salt-march.

42 Mother Teresa, "I Alone Cannot Change the World, but I Can Cast a Stone across the Waters to Create Many Ripples," goodreads.com, accessed October 26, 2019, https://www.goodreads.com/quotes/49502-i-alone-cannot-change-the-world-but-i-can-cast.

43 Cara, *Study Commentary*, 21.

lives in the society.[44] Yet the Thessalonians accepted Jesus Christ as their Lord, both religiously and politically. Thai people call their king *Pho Luang*, "Royal Father." As such, calling God Father could be considered offensive to the Royal Father.[45] Yet they have chosen to refer to God as Father and Jesus as Lord, following the examples of the Thessalonians.

Second, the Thessalonians' hope rested in the assurance of resurrection (1 Thess 4:13). Whereas persecution ended in martyrdom for some Christians, the Thessalonians weren't to despair. In actuality, the dead Christians were with Christ, and God would bring them back to the Thessalonians; thus, they would precede the living Christians in their resurrection (1 Thess 4:14–17). Christians believe in a bodily and material resurrection just as Christ arose in bodily resurrection (Luke 24:39). This teaching varies from Buddhism, which does not "believe in the resurrection of Buddhas and bodhisattvas as much as in producing mindfulness, understanding, and love in ourselves."[46] But the Thessalonians believed in a resurrected Messiah and the bodily resurrection of people.

Third, the Thessalonians' hope was in the return of the Lord Jesus Christ (1 Thess 4:16–17). After his resurrection and when the Lord Jesus was taken up into the clouds, the angels assured the people of Galilee, "This same Jesus, who has been taken from you into heaven, will come back in the same way you have seen him go into heaven" (Acts 1:11; see Matt 24:27–31). Early Christians, including the Thessalonians, hoped in his assured return.

The Thessalonians, however, were confused about the timing of his coming. Outsiders tried to deceive them into thinking the Lord had already come (2 Thess 2:3), so Paul explained to them the sequence of events. When people were so self-confident, saying, "There is peace in the land and everyone is safe," then the Lord would come quickly and surprise them all (1 Thess 5:3). Christians themselves knew this fact—the Lord's coming will be similar to the coming of a thief in the night, unannounced and unexpected. So if the Thessalonians remained alert, they had nothing to fear.

44 N. T. Wright, "God and Caesar, Then and Now," speech delivered on June 30, 2003, accessed January 19, 2019, http://ntwrightpage.com/files/2016/05/Wright_God_Caesar.pdf (URL inactive).

45 Christians in Chiang Mai told me this.

46 Thich Nhat Hanh, *Living Buddha, Living Christ* (New York: Riverhead, 2012), 57.

In addition, there were warning signs to prepare them before the coming of the Lord, just as vultures gathered where there were dead carcasses (Matt 24:28). One of the vultures was the lawless one, whose destruction was certain (2 Thess 2:3). The lawless one would oppose every government and god, demand worship, and take the seat in God's temple, proclaiming to be God (2 Thess 2:4). Then the Lord would destroy the lawless one with the breath of his mouth at the splendor of his coming (2 Thess 2:8). Although that lawless one's deceptive works were already present (2 Thess 2:7), they hadn't yet come. Therefore, the Thessalonians should be watchful. The second vulture was Satan, who was instrumental in the lawless one's works (2 Thess 2:9). Upon seeing those vultures roam, one should take caution of the end time, for they were here to feast on the dead bodies. Christians in Thessalonica themselves were alive in the Lord. As such, they had nothing to fear of the vultures, but they should nevertheless pay attention to their works and live as children of light (1 Thess 5:5).

Christians in Asia must live with such assurance: "We are not like everyone else . . . our hope is focused not on the circumstances of today, but on the future return and victory of Jesus. Like the Thessalonians, we are caught in the eschatological tension."[47] Even with the present crisis of Covid-19, Christians should be in the forefront without fearing, strengthening the weakhearted and serving the afflicted. They should do that because they are children of light and have the hope of resurrection and eternal life.

Fourth, the Thessalonians' hope was in their salvation (1 Thess 5:8–9). They believed that Jesus suffered, died, and resurrected, and therefore, he was their Messiah (Acts 17:3–4). That salvation protected them from destruction just as a helmet protects a soldier in a war (1 Thess 5:8). They were to guard themselves by always wearing that helmet of salvation. God appointed them not to suffer his wrath but to receive salvation through the Lord Jesus Christ (1 Thess 5:9).[48] Asian Christians are afraid to share the gospel with their neighbors in countries where other religions are in the majority, but sharing the good news of salvation along with helping the needy can bring a lot of positive changes in the society. Without attacking others' religions, Christians can witness Christ in company with people of other faiths.

47 Byron, *1 and 2 Thessalonians*, 10.

48 For a detailed study of Thessalonians letters and sanctification, see Preben Vang, "Sanctification in Thessalonians," *Southwestern Journal of Theology* 42, no. 1 (Fall 1999): 50–65.

Fifth, the Thessalonians' hope was in the justice of God (2 Thess 1:6–10). God would not ignore people's violence against Christians; he would pay back trouble to those who troubled them (2 Thess 1:6). God would give relief to the suffering Christians, if not then, the Lord himself would return to them with his powerful angels (2 Thess 1:7). At that hour, the Thessalonians would also see the Lord Jesus in his everlasting glory (2 Thess 1:10). Knowing God's justice, the Thessalonians continued to hope in him.

Sixth, the Thessalonians' hope rested on the inability of the enemies to shut down the gospel (1 Thess 2:14–16). Whereas the enemies of the gospel repeatedly tried to shut it down—Paul himself was once a part of this movement—it kept spreading. The gospel spread out irrespective of the death of the Lord, his prophets, and everyone who believed in him. That gave the Thessalonians hope. When missionaries were expelled from China, people feared that Christianity would perish. Instead, it flourished amid persecutions, just as it flourished in Thessalonica.

When the Christians in Thessalonica had such unquenchable hope, they gave hope to others, including Paul. Thessalonians were Paul's joy, crown, glory, and hope (1 Thess 2:19). There were times when Thessalonians' hope wavered; but the Lord Jesus Christ and God the Father strengthened them (2 Thess 2:16). God and Lord stood by them, encouraged them, and gave them hope. As such, the Thessalonians were constantly encouraged in their hope. They were firm and unshaken. An article in the *Guardian* says, "One in three Christians face high level of persecution in Asia, with India entering the top 10 for the first time."[49] It could increase in the years to come. Thus, there are several resemblances between the experiences of the Thessalonian believers and the Asian Christians.

Industry

The final theme is industry, or hard work. Gandhi, who introduced the world to the concepts of *ahimsa* (nonviolence) and *satyagraha* (peaceful civil disobedience) and *khadi* (actively growing cotton). He wore clothes that he himself made, even when others weighed him down as a half-naked fakir (religious

49 Harriet Sherwood, "One in Three Christians Face Persecution in Asia, Report Finds," *Guardian*, accessed February 21, 2020, https://www.theguardian.com/world/2019/jan/16/one-in-three-christians-face-persecution-in-asia-report-finds.

ascetic).[50] Likewise, Mother Teresa was known for her industry. Raghu Rai states, "Her daily act and *sewa* [selfless service] were so intense and powerful; her eyes held compassion, concern and love. If you look at any image in the show, there is so much strength in her very being. I always felt: here was a person who was absolutely 100% human . . . here was a person who did only two things—being in prayer and looking after the sick."[51] The Thessalonians were industrious, working faithfully with their own hands. When they failed, Paul exhorted them to work without faltering or depending on others. If they didn't work, they shouldn't eat. Industry was key in the lifestyle of the Thessalonians.

First, Paul and his companions modeled that lifestyle of industry for the Thessalonians: "Surely you remember, brothers and sisters, our toil and hardship; we worked night and day in order not to be a burden to anyone while we preached the gospel of God to you" (1 Thess 2:9). They lived in a time when itinerant preachers traveled through cities and villages, taught theologies, and expected people to provide for their needs. Paul, Silas, and Timothy were not so with the Thessalonians, although they had the right to impose on them (2 Thess 3:9). Instead, they worked hard (2 Thess 3:6–10) to not be a burden to the Thessalonians (1 Thess 2:7). They were like nursing mothers to the Thessalonians and fed them (1 Thess 2:7). Also, like fathers who sustain and provide for families, the apostles sustained themselves and ministered to the church (1 Thess 2:11). With Peter and friends' examples, the Thessalonians too worked hard and made their own living. Mukti Mission (started by Pandita Ramabai) and Dohnavur Fellowship (started by Amy Carmichael) are self-sustaining missions. These missionary organizations have gardens in which they grow products needed for the orphanage, milking cows for the sake of children, and farm animals for food.[52] They leave an example for other orphanages and ministries to be industrious in all their actions, just as the Thessalonians were.

Second, not all Thessalonians followed the apostles' examples and were industrious (2 Thess 3:6–12). Instead, some were idle and disruptive to the

50 R. R. James, ed., *Winston S. Churchill: His Complete Speeches, 1897–1963* (New York: Chelsea, 1974), 5:4985.

51 Raghu Rai, "Mother Teresa: Mother of Mercies," *Economic Times*, accessed October 25, 2019, https://economictimes.indiatimes.com/mother-teresa-mother-of-miracles/articleshow/6435509.cms.

52 "Dairy Farming," Dohnavur Fellowship, accessed August 3, 2020, http://dohnavurfellowship.org/project/how-to-feed-the-world/.

community (2 Thess 3:6, 11). Paul instructed the Thessalonians to keep away from such lazy Christians (2 Thess 3:6). If they weren't willing to work, they shouldn't eat (2 Thess 3:10). The church was alerted to ask such believers to stop wandering house to house and begging for food. They were instructed to work with their own hands for daily sustenance (2 Thess 3:12). The Christians were asked not to have fellowship or eat with such people (2 Thess 3:14). The Thessalonians, however, should not think of them as enemies of God or of themselves. They were still fellow believers—they were simply lazy (2 Thess 3:15). The hardworking believers should set them an example of doing good so the lazy believers would return from their folly and work diligently (2 Thess 3:13). One Chinese proverb accompanies a story: When a young girl was asked to choose between two potential husbands, she chose both—a rich but ugly suiter on the eastern side of the village and a poor but handsome suiter on the western side. The proverb says, *Dōng shí xī sù* (East food, west night), which means "Taking full advantage of a person in a selfish way."[53] Christians shouldn't be like this young girl, taking advantage of others without working with their own hands for their living. Only by industrious means can Christians set an example for the world around them, just as the Thessalonians did in both Macedonia and Achaia.

People who study world trends propose that by 2025, millennials will form 75 percent of the work force in this world.[54] Millennials bring new approaches, ideas, and values to the workplace. In addition, they bring different styles, including living in the parents' home until their late thirties and forties, staying up late at night playing video games, emphasizing friendship more than long working hours, and partnering with one another to accomplish tasks. Instead of quickly dismissing them as "lazy," "unconcerned about work," or "people with poor work-ethics"—accusations older generations toss at them—we should see the good in their work styles.[55] As long as they work for their own food and are committed to work in their own fashion, we should treat them as industrious although different in style. Regardless, we should be

53 "Eat in the East, Sleep in the West," chinesetimeschool.com, September 26, 2012, http://www.chinesetimeschool.com/en-us/articles/eat-in-the-east-sleep-in-the-west/ (URL inactive).

54 Jacob Morgan, "The Five Trends Shaping the Future of Work," IE University, accessed October 25, 2019, https://www.ie.edu/insights/articles/the-five-trends-shaping-the-future-of-work.

55 The Asia Theological Association's Consultation held in Singapore, 2019, addressed these issues.

committed to a high work ethic in everything they do—ministry, labor, spreading the gospel, or raising a family. God is an industrious God, and the church imitates him.

PRACTICAL ISSUES

Contemporary Asian Christians live in uncertain times, as did the Christians in Thessalonica. Weekly protests in Hong Kong, gang rapes of women in India, and Covid-19 and the economic disaster associated with it are some of the uncertainties Christians in Asia face. How will the Letters to the Thessalonian help them cope with these troubling situations?

First, Christians shouldn't ask the question, "Who sinned?" as did the disciples when they saw a visually impaired person (John 9:2). When they ask this question, they reflect the mindset of Eliphaz, who said to the afflicted Job, "Consider now: Who, being innocent, has ever perished? Where were the upright ever destroyed? As I have observed, those who plow evil and those who sow trouble reap it" (Job 4:7–8). Eliphaz's conclusion was Job must have sinned. When faced with calamities, it is natural to ask, Who sinned? But in reality, God allows calamities for his power to be displayed (John 9:4). Paul too reminded the Thessalonians: "He called you to this [suffering] through our gospel that you might share in the glory of our Lord Jesus Christ" (2 Thess 2:14). Christians will share in the Lord's glory provided they also suffer for him.

Second, Christians should be proactive in their societies to correct the wrongs and challenge injustices. Just as William Carey fought against *sati* (burning of widows on the pyre of their husbands) in India, and as Joni Eareckson Tada fights for the physically challenged throughout the world, Christians worldwide must be in the forefront of social justice.[56] Many Asian Christians are already involved in fighting for migrant workers and their rights,[57] preserving God's creation,[58]

56 Dibin Samuel, "Wiliam Carey Played Significant Role in Abolishing Sati System," *Christian Today*, December 4, 2009, https://tinyurl.com/4k8k76v3.

57 Calvin Chong, ed., *The Servant at the Fringes: Christians Serving Foreign Workers in Singapore* (Singapore: Singapore Bible College, 2018).

58 Melissa Ong and Prarthini M. Selveindran, eds., *God's Gardeners: Creation Care Stories from Singapore and Malaysia* (Singapore: GraceWorks, 2020).

and speaking for people with special needs.[59] Christians and churches can no longer remain silent. The Thessalonian letters challenge them: "Encourage the disheartened, help the weak, be patient with everyone. Make sure that nobody pays back wrong for wrong, but always strive to do what is good for each other and for everyone else" (1 Thess 5:14–17). Christians must remain always in the forefront of social justice.

Third, Christians should strive to live sanctified lives. Whereas the world constantly challenges the status quo of morality, Christians must rely on God: "May God himself, the God of peace, sanctify you through and through. May your whole spirit, soul and body be kept blameless at the coming of our Lord Jesus Christ" (1 Thess 5:23). Also, they must rely on God's word and avoid those who refuse the instructions: "Take special note of anyone who does not obey our instruction in this letter. Do not associate with them, in order that they may feel ashamed. Yet do not regard them as an enemy but warn them as you would a fellow believer" (2 Thess 3:14–15). With divine strength, Christians can live morally pure and remain examples to others.

Fourth, Christians should be industrious. A Chinese proverb says, *Jīnrì shì, jīnrì bì*, which roughly means "Never put off what you can do today for tomorrow." Christians should be known for honest labor, hard work, and reliability. Those actions will speak louder than words.

Fifth, Christians should anticipate the coming of the Lord without speculating about it. Whereas the world lives for the day and doesn't pay attention to eternal life, Christians must believe in the resurrection and live in the light of that. At the same time, they shouldn't be relaxed, thinking every disaster implies the end of days. Instead, they should walk as children of light in the midst of pain, suffering, and persecution.

CONCLUSION

In a world filled with greed and a "grab everything" mentality, the Thessalonian letters instruct believers to simplicity of life. These letters encourage believers to endure suffering and persecutions. Further, they instruct people

59 Leow Wen Pen and Anne Wong-Png, eds., *Call Me by Name: Stories of Faith, Identity, and Special Needs* (Singapore: Family Inclusion Network, 2018).

to have hope in God, Christ, salvation, and eternal life in the midst of suffering, trials, and uncertainties of life. They teach believers to work diligently and faithfully so they are not accused of laziness. Basically, these letters are practical and relevant for the Christians in Asia who face discontentment, easy-believe-ism, avoidance of suffering, life without any hope, and lethargy in one's attitude to life.

FURTHER READING

Beale, G. K. 2003. *1–2 Thessalonians*. The IVP New Testament Commentary Series. Downers Grove, IL: InterVarsity.

Boring, M. E. 2015. *I and II Thessalonians: A Commentary*. The New Testament Library. Louisville: Westminster John Knox.

Byron, J. 2014. *1 and 2 Thessalonians*. The Story of God Bible Commentary. Grand Rapids, MI: Zondervan.

Cara, R. J. 2009. *A Study Commentary on 1 and 2 Thessalonians*. EP Study Commentary. Durham, UK: EP.

Cherian, J. 2015. "1 Thessalonians." In *South Asia Bible Commentary: A One-Volume Commentary on the Whole Bible*, edited by Brian Wintle, 1669–1676. Udaipur, India: Open Door.

Fee, G. D. 2009. *The First and Second Letters to the Thessalonians*. The New International Commentary on the New Testament. Grand Rapids, MI: Zondervan.

Furnish, V. P. 2007. *1 Thessalonians. 2 Thessalonians*. Abingdon New Testament Commentary. Nashville: Abingdon.

Green, G. L. 2002. *The Letters to the Thessalonians*. The Pillar New Testament Commentary. Grand Rapids, MI: Eerdmans.

Malherbe, A. J. 2004. *The Letters to the Thessalonians*. The Anchor Yale Bible Commentaries. New Haven, CT: Yale University Press.

FIFTEEN

The Letters to Timothy

Asish Thomas Koshy
SAIACS
Bengaluru, India

First Timothy, 2 Timothy, and Titus are called the Pastoral Epistles (PE)[1] because they deal with issues of doctrines, household codes, and church order related to the congregations at Ephesus and Crete,[2] as well as responsibilities in the church and society at large. Although addressed to individuals, these letters predominantly focus on the public and social behavior of the community.[3] This essay critically looks at the preliminary aspects of 1 and 2 Timothy such as authorship, recipients, occasion and purpose, date, structure, and an Asian interpretation of some of the motifs such as the status of women, domestic codes, Christology and soteriology, and the process of handing on tradition. The letters reflect Paul's pastoral oversight through his involvement in the crisis at Ephesus, and such an understanding gives insight into ministry in today's Asian context. We shall analyze some of these preliminary aspects and some of the concerns in relation to Asian realities.

1 D. N. Bardot coined the term "Pastoral Letters" in 1703. The earliest manuscript (P32) containing Titus 1:11–15 and 2:3–8 originated in Oxyrhynchus, Egypt. Raymond F. Collins, *1 & 2 Timothy and Titus: A Commentary*, 1st ed., New Testament Library (Louisville: Westminster John Knox, 2002), 1.

2 Frances M. Young, *The Theology of the Pastoral Letters*, New Testament Theology (Cambridge: Cambridge University Press, 1994), 1.

3 Young, 4.

PRELIMINARY ASPECTS

In the following section, we deal with some of the critical aspects pertinent to the authorship, recipients, occasion and purpose, date and structure of 1 and 2 Timothy.

Authorship

The issue of Pauline authorship of the PE has affected both the approach to the letters as well as the interpretative processes related to them. Luke Timothy Johnson brings out the detrimental effect of scholarship's wide assumption that Paul is not the author of the PE.[4] The early church fathers unanimously affirmed the authenticity of the PE and cited them frequently.[5] I. Howard Marshall and Philip H. Towner note that "there is no evidence of rejection of them by any (Early Christian) writers except for Marcion."[6] Questioning of the authenticity of the PE began in the early nineteenth century CE with J. E. C. Schmidt, followed by Friedrich Schleiermacher, Johann Gottfried Eichorn, and Heinrich Julius Holtzmann.[7] Toward the end of the twentieth century, most of the NT scholars argued that the PE were written after Paul's

4 Luke Timothy Johnson, *The First and Second Letters to Timothy: A New Translation with Introduction and Commentary*, 1st ed., Anchor Bible 35A (New York: Doubleday, 2001), 52.

5 Paul's correspondence to Timothy was known to Polycarp (ca. 117 CE cited in Phil 4:10) and is also found in second-century writers such as Athenagoras (ca. 180 CE; Supplication 37/1) and Theophilus (later second century), who cite 1 Timothy 2:1–2. The church fathers Irenaeus and Clement of Alexandria are also aware of the writings, and it is included in the Pauline letters in the Muratorian canon (later second century CE). Andreas J. Köstenberger, "Hermeneutical and Exegetical Challenges in Interpreting the Pastoral Epistles," in *Entrusted with the Gospel: Paul's Theology in the Pastoral Epistles*, ed. Terry L. Wilder and Andreas J. Köstenberger (Nashville: B&H, 2010), 2.

6 Ian Howard Marshall and Philip H. Towner, *A Critical and Exegetical Commentary on the Pastoral Epistles*, International Critical Commentary on the Holy Scriptures of the Old and New Testaments (Edinburgh: T&T Clark, 1999), 8.

7 Both Schmidt and Schleiermacher stated that the vocabulary of 1 Timothy was unrelated to 2 Timothy and Titus and thus was not written by Paul. Schmidt, *Historical-Critical Introduction to the New Testament* (1804/5), cited in Collins, *1 & 2 Timothy and Titus*, 3; Friedrich Schleiermacher, *Über den sogenannten ersten Brief des Paulus an den Timotheus: ein kritisches Sendschreiben*; J. C. Gass, *Realbuchhandlung*, 1807, cited in Collins, *1 & 2 Timothy and Titus*, 3; Eichorn, *Introduction to the New Testament* (1812) and Heinrich Julius Holtzmann (1885), cited in Collins, *1 & 2 Timothy and Titus*, 3–4.

death, citing "stylistic and lexical issues, the theological views, the biographical data, and skeletal elements of church structure" that arise in the study of the epistles.[8] Despite a majority of scholars arguing against the authenticity, George W. Knight and Luke Timothy Johnson continue to argue for Pauline authorship.[9]

There are five alternative theories for the authorship of the epistles: fictional hypothesis, pseudonymous writing, fragmentary hypothesis, allonymity, and amanuensis. The advocates of the fictional hypothesis view the PE as pure fiction without a trace of genuine Pauline content. They suppose the author was an admirer of Paul who produced the three letters in the beginning of the second century CE. Personal details were added to create authenticity. The defenders of this theory (Dibelius, Conzelmann, Bultmann, and others) belong to the Tübingen School.[10] The fragmentary hypothesis does not reject the Pauline authorship outright. It supposes that the PE contain fragments that were put together by an anonymous person (or an editor) who had access to the notes written by Paul or found fragments of Paul's letters after his death. The authentic material includes the personal and historical references. The proponents of this theory include P. N. Harrison, R. Falconer, A. Strobel, G. Holts, and P. Bornier.[11] The pseudonymous writing thesis is that the letters are "writing in which a later follower attributed a given piece of writing to his revered teacher in order to perpetuate that person's teaching and influence."[12] The proponents of this view are M. Dibelius, H. Conzelmann, N. Borx, V. Hasler, B. S. Easton, F. D. Gealy, J. B. Higgins, C. K. Barrett, and J. H. Houlden.[13]

The allonymity theory was proposed by Marshall and Towner, who proposed that the terms *allonymity* and *allepigraphy* be used to denote the

8 Collins, *1 & 2 Timothy and Titus*, 4.

9 George William Knight, *The Pastoral Epistles: A Commentary on the Greek Text*, New International Greek Testament Commentary (Grand Rapids, MI: Eerdmans, 2008); Johnson, *Letters to Timothy*.

10 William D. Mounce, *Pastoral Epistles*, Word Biblical Commentary 46 (Nashville: Thomas Nelson, 2000), cxix.

11 Anthony Tyrrell Hanson, *The Pastoral Epistles: Based on the Revised Standard Version*, New Century Bible Commentary (Grand Rapids, MI: Eerdmans, 1982), 10.

12 Andreas J. Köstenberger, "Hermeneutical and Exegetical Challenges in Interpreting the Pastoral Epistles," *SBJT* 7, no. 3 (Fall 2003): 2.

13 Hanson, *Pastoral Epistles*, 11.

activity of writing in another person's name, though the intent was not to deceive. They contend that 2 Timothy was "written up" by an unknown compiler of Pauline material. Titus and 1 Timothy were written later to address "growing opposition to Paul in some of his congregation."[14] As time went by, the origin of these letters got buried, and they were taken as written by Paul himself.[15] The amanuensis hypothesis argues that Paul's thoughts were determined and conveyed through one of Paul's scribal secretaries. Scholars conclude that the elements that are not Pauline were added by the secretary and that the Pauline aspects were contributed by Paul, who did make use of amanuenses in his other letters (Rom 16:22; Gal 6:11). Also, if Paul was in strict Roman imprisonment while writing 2 Timothy, it is plausible to assume that it was written by a secretary. According to Mounce, "The Amanuensis Hypothesis best explains the internal and external evidence. It accounts for the differences between the PE and the other Pauline letters and does not introduce its own set of problems."[16] The weighty list of scholars who argue for this hypothesis include J. Jeremias, W. Metzger, and C. F. D. Moule. Though several hypotheses exist concerning the composition of the PE, it is significant to note that Paul's thoughts frame the overarching ideology of these epistles.

Identity of the Opponents

Scholars have objected to Pauline authorship on the grounds that the heresy detailed in the PE and the supposed opponents belong to the second century and are not characteristic of Paul's time.[17] The other major contention is that the author attacks the opponents and not their teachings, which is unlike the earlier letters of Paul. In this regard, Johnson observes that no reconstruction of the letters' evidence matches any known heresy. He notes that the heresy presented in the PE is a combination of several aspects—the doctrine that the resurrection has already happened, abstaining from marriage and food

14 Marshall and Towner, *Critical and Exegetical Commentary*, 86.

15 Marshall and Towner, 92.

16 Mounce et al., *Pastoral Epistles*, cxxix.

17 H. J. Holtzmann, *Die Pastoralbriefe, kritisch und exegetische Behandelt* (Leipzig: W. Engelmann, 1880), cited in Thomas D. Lea and Hayne P. Griffin, *1, 2 Timothy, Titus: An Exegetical and Theological Exposition of Holy Scripture*, The New American Commentary 34 (Nashville: Holman Reference, 1992), 22.

(1 Tim 4:3), implementing physical asceticism (1 Tim 4:3), observance of the Law (1 Tim 1:7)—that seem to imply that the PE address the issue of deviance from orthodoxy.

Johnson identifies three other difficulties in attempting to locate the opponents in the second century:[18] first, the elements seen in the PE can also be traced in other individual letters; second, a lot of it has to do with the ancient rhetorical rules regulating defense between opponents; and third, the other difference from the PE and the undisputed letters is that the PE employ polemic, whereas the others use theological disapproval of the opponents. The polemic makes use of generalities, especially in 1 and 2 Timothy. Mounce adds the following: first, Paul also lashed out at individuals when the occasion demanded it (Gal 1:8–9; Phil 3:18–19); second, Paul responds to the Ephesian opponents by theological disapproval as well as personal critique; third, the real issue was not theological but immorality, where the conscience is put aside; fourth, the actions are the result of their beliefs; and fifth, the letters are addressed to Paul's delegates, who knew Paul's theology and were capable of evaluating false teaching.[19] Taking into consideration the arguments of Johnson and Mounce, it is fair to say that the identity of the opponents and the heresy discussed in the PE need not be taken as a later development.

Church Structure

A further objection to Pauline authorship is that the church structure advanced in the PE betrays a second-century development such as that of Ignatius of Antioch (35–107 CE), who outlines a monarchical bishopric and a three-layered hierarchy (Eph 2:2).[20] Hanson states that the PE focus on the distinctive ordained offices of the church, which marks them "as belonging to a later generation than Paul's."[21] Marshall and Towner argue that there was movement from charismatic communities to appointments of offices.[22] MacDonald states that the organization of Paul's communities was a development in the

18 Johnson, *Letters to Timothy*, 73.

19 William D. Mounce et al., *Pastoral Epistles*, Word Biblical Commentary 46, ed. Ralph P. Martin (Nashville: Nelson, 2009), xcvii.

20 Köstenberger, "Hermeneutical and Exegetical Challenges," 7.

21 Hanson, *Pastoral Epistles*, 31.

22 Marshall and Towner, *Critical and Exegetical Commentary*, 93.

Pauline tradition after Paul's death.[23] Hanson concludes, "In them we see the church as it sets out in the second century, tackling its practical problems with vigour and success."[24]

In looking at these objections, Johnson states there seems to be an assumption in scholarship that there was a historical development from a church centered on spiritual gifts to a structured household of God having the offices of bishops, elders, and deacons, as well as women deacons and widows.[25] Knight contends that interest in "the form or order and authority in the church" and who "may rightly designate spiritual leaders" is evident in Paul's early letters.[26]

Another objection concerns the use of the terms *overseer* and *elder*. These terms refer to the same office and thus reflect a two-layered rather than three-layered structure and thus presuppose an earlier structure.[27] Paul, in his letter to Thessalonians, mentions a group of leaders who have persevered in ministry. He tells the church to hold them in high regard (1 Thess 5:12). There is also no formalization of offices. Johnson observes that the church structure Paul describes is comparable to that of first-century synagogues and Pauline *ekklēsia*.[28]

Mounce gives four reasons why the organizational structure of the PE is not of a later generation. He states that from the beginning, Paul followed the synagogue tradition of appointing elders; Timothy and Titus were not part of the church structure but rather were apostolic delegates sent on Paul's authority to deal with the local problems; the aspect of church structure is very less in Titus (five out of forty-one verses) and absent in 2 Timothy (except 2 Tim 2:2); and there are significant differences among the three letters, so one cannot speak of church structure in the PE.[29] The objection that the PE present a development in church order seems to have significant limitations.

23 Margaret Y. MacDonald, *The Pauline Churches: A Socio-historical Study of Institutionalization in the Pauline and Deutero-Pauline Writings*, 1st paperback ed., Society for New Testament Studies Monograph Series 60 (Cambridge: Cambridge University Press, 2004), 9.

24 Hanson, *Pastoral Epistles*, 51.

25 Johnson, *Letters to Timothy*, 74.

26 Knight, *Pastoral Epistles*, 29.

27 Andreas J. Köstenberger, L. Scott Kellum, and Charles L. Quarles, *The Cradle, the Cross, and the Crown: An Introduction to the NT* (Nashville: B&H, 2009), 780.

28 Johnson, *Letters to Timothy*, 76.

29 Mounce et al., *Pastoral Epistles*, lxxxvi–lxxxviii.

Historical Situation

The historical information mentioned in the PE is absent from the Acts of the Apostles and the other Pauline letters and appears to some to be fabricated (2 Tim 4:19–21). Certain incidents mentioned in the PE are not found in Acts: Titus in Crete; Paul leaving his belongings in Troas (2 Tim 4:13); and Onesiphorus's courageous conduct (2 Tim 1:16). Hanson states, "We cannot a priori rub out all apparent historical references in the PE as fictional, any more than we can a priori declare all to be genuine."[30] Paul's travels to the eastern parts of the Roman Empire, such as his journey to Crete and his visit to Nicopolis (Titus 3:12), do not appear in Acts.[31] The historical details in the PE cannot be reconciled with the other Pauline letters and Acts. Further, scholars who hold to the authenticity of the PE need to presume a two-year delay at the end of Paul's career. The reference to Paul's delegate Timothy does not fit with the historical Timothy.

In opposition to the above, Johnson rightly states, "Although Acts is generous in its attention to Paul, devoting most of chapters 13–28 to his mission, it is a notoriously selective source, providing considerable detail for certain movements and scenes." Further, the portions where the incidents are mentioned have to be separated from the ethical aspects. The difficulty of aligning the biographical information of Paul in Acts is not limited to the PE but also includes Galatians, Philemon, and Philippians. Johnson proposes that rather than taking the additional information in the PE as incongruent, if "turned another way, they also provide the basis for expanding our understanding of Paul's movements in exactly the same way the other letters do."[32]

Another theological problem often identified is the issue of orthodoxy. The PE appeal to "sound teaching," "the faith," and "the truth," which are taken to mean a set of doctrines. However, Romans 16:17, 1 Corinthians 11:2, and 2 Thessalonians 2:15 also refer to teachings of Jesus and the apostolic *kerygma*. Mounce states, "The author of the PE does not say that the body of doctrine is complete, closed, and that nothing is to be added; he says that the gospel teaching is true and is to be adhered to."[33] Thus the PE make no claim to the sort of orthodoxy found in later times.

30 Hanson, *Pastoral Epistles*, 15.

31 Lea and Griffin, *1, 2 Timothy, Titus*, 32.

32 Johnson, *Letters to Timothy*, 68.

33 Mounce et al., *Pastoral Epistles*, xcv.

Use of Theological Motifs

The PE lack some of the common terms used in the undisputed letters of Paul,[34] and these include preexistence of Christ, the Holy Spirit, the cross, flesh versus spirit, mystery, and the Fatherhood of God.[35] The themes are also used differently in the PE. The phrase "in Christ" refers not to a mystical relationship in the PE but to a quality that is obtainable by those who are "in Christ." Similarly, the term *faith* in the PE is not related to belief but is defined as a deposit.[36] The incarnation is presented as an epiphany and not as divine humiliation.[37] Much stress is given to societal virtues such as temperance, common sense, seriousness, integrity about money, modesty, domestic fidelity, and respectability.[38] The Christian doctrine is termed as *parathēkē*, "what has been entrusted to you" (1 Tim 6:20). This deposit of faith has been delivered by Paul to Timothy and must in turn be handed on by Timothy to trustworthy successors (2 Tim 1:13–14; 2:2; 3:14).

There seems to be an assumption that there is a central idea in Paul's theology by which the PE can be evaluated. On the contrary, what we find is fluidity in Paul's thought. We can account for the missing themes: Paul was writing to his delegates, and the PE are not a church manual. Moreover, the PE are different in size and subject matter and therefore need to be treated independently. Just as differences in 1 and 2 Thessalonians are treated as insignificant because of their size and subject matter, in the Pauline letters, the theme in one letter may be less significant than in another.[39] Lastly, there seems to be no uniformity in the way Paul deals with themes. Mounce notes the variations in the use of *faith* in the Pauline writings. In 2 Corinthians 13:5, Galatians 1:23, and Philippians 1:27, *faith* refers to the gift of Christian faith, but in Romans 1:8, *faith* connotes the proclamation that they are Christians.

34 Collins, *1 & 2 Timothy and Titus*, 3.

35 Mounce et al., *Pastoral Epistles*, lxxxviii–lxxxix.

36 Hans Conzelmann states, "There is no thought of the evolution of a deposit of faith (*depositum fidei*) in the sense of the Catholic 'living tradition' (*traditio viva*)." Martin Dibelius and Hans Conzelmann, *The Pastoral Epistles: A Commentary on the Pastoral Epistles*, Hermeneia—A Critical and Historical Commentary on the Bible (Philadelphia: Fortress, 1972), 9.

37 Hanson, *Pastoral Epistles*, 3.

38 Hanson, 4.

39 Refer to the arguments in Mounce et al., *Pastoral Epistles*, xci–xcii.

Mounce responds to the claim that the PE use certain Pauline themes in a contradictory manner by saying he cannot find one example that cannot be explained by "Pauline usage elsewhere" or because of "differing recipients and historical situations."[40]

Recipients

Timothy is named as the recipient of 1 and 2 Timothy. The author makes clear that Timothy was in charge of Ephesus, where the cult and temple of Greek goddess Artemis was well-known, a sizeable Jewish population resided, and many house churches existed (1 Tim 1:3). His father was Greek, but Timothy was brought up in the faith tradition by his grandmother and mother (2 Tim 1:5; 3:14–15). Paul uses several terms to describe Timothy: son (1 Tim 2:18; 2 Tim 1:2; 2:1), beloved and "faithful" (1 Cor 4:17), and fellow-worker with God (1 Thess 3:2). He was sent on several assignments to Thessalonica (1 Thess 3:1–10), Corinth (1 Cor 4:17), Macedonia (Acts 19:22), Philippi (Phil 2:19–24), and Ephesus (1 Tim 1:3).

There seems to be a division among scholarship regarding the primary recipient of the letters. Marshall and Towner argue that the primary recipients were the church leaders. This is based on two reasons: first, the basic instructions stated in the letters were needless for Timothy, who was part of Paul's ministry for many years, and second, the letters were addressed to the congregation as suggested by the plural form of the benediction. In contrast, Knight states that the recipients are described as Timothy (1 Tim 1:2; 2 Tim 1:2) and Titus (Titus 1:4) at the beginning of the letter.[41] The personal remarks about the individuals throughout the letters also substantiate the idea that they were written to individuals; added to this is the use of second-person singular imperatives and personal pronouns. However, the instructions are also for the church members at times directly (1 Tim 2:1–15): women (2:9–15), bishops and deacons (3:1–16), and slaves (6:1–10). As the personal elements are abundant in these letters, especially in 2 Timothy, Knight's view seems to be convincing.

40 Mounce et al., xciv.
41 Knight, *Pastoral Epistles*, 6.

Occasion and Purpose

Paul's Letters to Timothy were written to respond to the situation of house churches in Ephesus that were plagued by false teachings not detailed by Paul. The false teachings probably came up from within the churches and not from outside (1 Tim 1:3; 6:2; 2 Tim 2:14; 4:2).[42] The important texts are 1 Timothy 1:3–7, 18–20; 4:1–5, 7a; 6:2–5, 20–21; Titus 1:10–16; 3:9–11; and 2 Timothy 2:14–18, 22–26; 3:6–9. The false teachings in 1 Timothy include "myths and genealogies" (1:4), "bragging about being interpreters of the law" (1:8), "prohibition of marriage" (4:3), and "refraining from particular food" (4:3).

In the Christian Ephesian community, asceticism was evident in disallowing of marriage or particular food (1 Tim 4:1–5) and doctrines stating that resurrection had already taken place (2 Tim 2:17–18). These may refer to Greek-style dualism that gives importance to spirituality over natural order. There was also emphasis on speculation (1 Tim 1:4, 6; 6:4, 20; 2 Tim 2:14, 16, 23), deceptiveness (1 Tim 4:1–3; 2 Tim 3:6–9, 13), immorality (1 Tim 1:19–20; 2 Tim 2:22; 3:3–4), and greed (1 Tim 6:5; 2 Tim. 3:2, 4). Paul conceptualizes the teachings of the opponents as follows: "unholy chatter" and "senseless babble" (1 Tim 2:16), "endless" (1 Tim 1:4), "foolish" (1 Tim 6:2), "totally lacking in love" (1 Tim 1:5), "advancing foolishness and speculation" (2 Tim 2:23; 1 Tim 6:4), "empty words" (1 Tim 6:4; 2 Tim 2:14), "only appearing to have godliness" (2 Tim 3:5; 1 Tim 6:20), and "ruining those who listen" (2 Tim 2:14).[43]

While Mounce categorizes the heresy into three types (Jewish, protognostic, and Hellenistic),[44] Marshall and Towner rule out any form of Gnosticism and point to "a group of Jewish Christian, perhaps travelling teachers with an ascetic streak, who were active within the Pauline mission area."[45] The heresy, however, does seem to have a residue of both Jewish and Hellenistic elements. The purpose of Paul's writing to Timothy (1 Timothy) is to delegate him to carry out Paul's responsibilities in his absence. These include understanding the false teachings that were prevalent in the churches (5:2–6:2), addressing issues at Ephesus (6:3–21a), instructing how the church ought to conduct itself, opposing the opponents and their teachings, and serving as an example of right conduct and teaching.

42 Köstenberger, Kellum, and Quarles, *Cradle, Cross, and Crown*, 782.
43 Mounce et al., *Pastoral Epistles*, lxxiii.
44 For more details, refer to Mounce et al., lxix–lxxii.
45 Marshall and Towner, *Critical and Exegetical Commentary*, 51.

The context of 2 Timothy is different from 1 Timothy and Titus. Here Paul is arrested again after a preliminary hearing (4:16–18). Paul sees death as imminent (4:6–8). Some of his friends sacrificed much for him, others mistreated him and left him (4:14–16), and he experienced loneliness (4:10–12). The situation at Ephesus had worsened from its earlier situation, when Paul wrote 1 Timothy. Hymenaeus, who had been excommunicated, continued to spread his own version of teaching (1:17–18). Timothy was to follow Paul's pattern of guarding the gospel and entrusting the gospel to faithful men (2:1–2; 4:1–2). Tomlinson states, "Second Timothy is the most personal letter within the Pauline archive."[46] Paul uses the imagery of the father-son relationship in 2 Timothy (1:4). Paul wrote 2 Timothy for several reasons: first, he wanted Timothy to finish up a few details in Ephesus and come to see Paul before his death; second, in the midst of opposition, he encourages Timothy to remain true to the gospel message and be willing to suffer for it; and third, Paul wanted a report from Timothy about him and his coworker's activities.

Date

Scholars who support Paul's authorship date the letters to 63–66 CE. It is possible that Paul was released after his first Roman imprisonment and undertook his second Aegean ministry. This then provides the background for 1 and 2 Timothy and Titus. Paul was released from his first imprisonment possibly in 61 or 63 (Acts 28:30), and his execution happened during the rule of Nero, possibly between 64 and 67. Most probably 1 Timothy was penned from Macedonia (1 Tim 1:3). Second Timothy mentions that Paul is a captive, and this probably refers to his second imprisonment, when execution was imminent (4:6–8, 13–18).[47] The close similarities between 1 Timothy and Titus suggest they were written at the same time. Lea and Griffin propose the following chronology: 61–63 CE, first imprisonment; 63–65/66 CE, writing of 1 Timothy and Titus; 65/66 CE, Paul's second arrest, writing of 2 Timothy, and imprisonment and execution.[48]

46 F. Alan Tomlinson, "The Purpose and Stewardship Theme within the Pastoral Epistles," in *Entrusted with the Gospel: Paul's Theology in the Pastoral Epistles*, ed. Terry L. Wilder and Andreas J. Köstenberger (Nashville: B&H, 2010), 63.

47 Lea and Griffin, *1, 2 Timothy, Titus*, 41.

48 Lea and Griffin, 41.

Scholars who dispute Paul's authorship place the letters at a later date. Collins dates the PE after 80 CE because he holds that the language is similar to that of the Hellenistic authors of the early second century, it was at this later time that the Parousia was a pressing factor, and 2 Timothy appears to be a testimony in nature.[49] These arguments for dating presuppose that the letters are not Pauline.

Structure

Hanson views the letters to Timothy as having no unifying theme and no development of thought.[50] However, as Köstenberger notes, there has been a shift in scholarship since 2010 from the view that did not see any structure in the PE to "a high level of cohesion in each of the Pastoral Epistles."[51] Marshall states that the letters "demonstrate signs of a coherent structure and of theological competence."[52] The letters can be seen as personal paraenetic letters and farewell discourses comprising encouragement and pieces of advice to Timothy.[53] There is a lot in common between the proposed structures of 1 and 2 Timothy of both Mounce and Köstenberger:[54]

1 Timothy

- Salutation (1:1–2)
- Personal warning (1:3–20)
    - Problem of false doctrine (1:3–7)
    - The function of the law (1:8–11)
    - Paul's personal example (1:12–17)
    - Exhortation to Timothy (1:18–20)

49 Collins, *1 & 2 Timothy and Titus*, 9.

50 Hanson, *Pastoral Epistles*, 42.

51 R. Van Neste, *Cohesion and Structure in the Pastoral Epistles*, JSNTSup 280 (London: T&T Clark, 2004), 285, cited in Köstenberger, "Hermeneutical and Exegetical Challenges," 12.

52 I. H. Marshall, "The Christology of Luke-Acts and the Pastoral Epistles," in *Crossing Boundaries: Essays in Biblical Interpretation in Honour of Michael D. Goulder*, ed. S. E. Porter, P. Joyce, and D. E. Orton (Leiden: Brill, 1994), 171, cited in Köstenberger, Kellum, and Quarles, *Cradle, Cross, and Crown*, 786.

53 Johnson, *Letters to Timothy*, 97.

54 Köstenberger, "Hermeneutical and Exegetical Challenges," 12.

- Directions for the congregation (2:1–4:16)
    - Prayer (2:1–7)
    - Men and women at prayer (2:8–15)
    - Overseers (3:1–7)
    - Deacons (3:8–13)
    - Enigma of faith (3:14–16)
    - Prediction of apostasy (4:1–5)
    - Timothy an example (4:6–16)
- Duties toward various groups (5:1–6:2a)
    - The old and the young (5:1–2)
    - Widows (5:3–16)
    - Elders (5:17–25)
    - Slaves (6:1–2a)
- Final directions (6:2b–21)
    - Discussions on false teachers (6:2b–10)
    - Instructions to Timothy (6:11–16)
    - Instructions to the rich (6:17–19)
    - Final instructions to Timothy (6:20–21)

2 Timothy

- Opening greetings (1:1–2)
- Thanksgiving (1:3–7)
- Personal encouragement (1:8–18)
    - Follow Paul's example of suffering (1:8–14)
    - Good and bad examples (1:15–18)
- Metaphors of ministry and trustworthy saying (2:1–26)
    - Metaphors of ministry: soldier, athlete, and farmer (2:1–7)
    - Trustworthy saying (2:8–13)
    - Metaphors of ministry: workman, vessel, and servant (2:14–26)
- Description of the opponents (3:1–9)
- Exhortation to Timothy (3:10–4:8)
    - Directive to Timothy (3:10–17)
    - Proclaim the Word (4:1–8)
- Personal instructions (4:9–18)
- Closing greetings (4:19–22)

Lea and Griffin contend that these letters should not be treated as a "church manual" but contain ad hoc statements to direct Timothy and Titus as to how to address their churches' issues and grant them authority to serve as Paul's agents and not as "permanently resident pastors."[55] The response of 1 and 2 Timothy to some of the issues can be interpreted as follows.

Status of Women

First and 2 Timothy deal with some of the issues related to women in the first century CE. Those issues need to be adequately discussed to see their resonances in the contemporary Asian context.

Women's Role in 1 Timothy 2:8–15

Subsequent to Paul's instruction to Timothy on prayers being offered for all people (including rulers), he deals with guidelines for the behavior of both men and women in worship. Worship for Paul should model a "peaceful and quiet life" (2:2).[56] The first set of instructions pertains to men who are to pray with reverence and not be given over to anger and argument. The next instruction is to women, who are to dress modestly and pay more attention to good works than to personal appearance.[57] The third set of instructions dealing with women's participation and authority in worship (2:11–15) has been the bone of contention in terms of women's leadership and participation in worship.[58] The PE in general and this text in particular have played a major role in the silencing of leadership roles of women in the church and the silencing of women's voices. Paul discusses five aspects concerning directives regarding the behavior of women in worship:

- "Let a woman learn in quietness with all submissiveness." (2:11; RSV)

55 Lea and Griffin, *1, 2 Timothy, Titus*, 50.

56 Johnson, *Letters to Timothy*, 204.

57 Padgett states that the concern for modesty in attire was taken as a regular feature of Greco-Roman virtue for women. Alan Padgett, "Wealthy Women at Ephesus: 1 Timothy 2:8–15 in Social Context," *Interpretation* 41, no. 1 (1987): 19–31, 23.

58 The focus here is on 1 Timothy. Nevertheless, the related issues are seen in 2 Tim 2:14–18, 23–26; 3:1–9, 13; 4:3–4, 14–15.

- "I permit no woman to teach or to have authority over men; she is to keep silent." (2:12; RSV)

Paul backs these statements with theological endorsements from biblical texts:

- primacy of Adam in creation (2:13)
- Eve's greater vulnerability to deception and ethical failure (2:14)[59]
- women's "biological function of child bearing"[60]

The mentioned text has generated a plethora of interpretation, with many scholars taking extreme views. On the one side stands Köstenberger, who treats 1 Timothy as a church manual: "Paul did not permit women to serve in roles of ultimate authority and responsibility in the church." He further states, "God so chose to order male-female relations in the family and in the church that wives submit to husbands and the church to male elders."[61] On the other side stands Klyne Snodgrass, who does not see this as "a universally applicable prohibition of teaching of women."[62] Some have totally rejected the text as patriarchal and androcentric in its interpretation of biblical texts. K. Zamfir states, "The provisions concerning women in 1 Tim 2 match the ancient model of female deportment, characterized by concealment and self-effacement."[63]

A more plausible interpretation of the text is possible when the cultural and literary contexts of the text are taken into account. Texts are culturally specific, and the present text is more descriptive rather than normative or prescriptive.[64] Marshall and Towner rightly state, "The restrictions on the women teaching are to be understood against a cultural background and the involvement of

59 Johnson, *Letters to Timothy*, 205.

60 Johnson, 205.

61 Köstenberger, "Hermeneutical and Exegetical Challenges," 22.

62 Klyne Snodgrass, "A Case for the Unrestricted Ministry of Women," *Covenant Quarterly* 67, no. 2 (2009): 26–44, esp. 39.

63 Korinna Zamfir, "The Topos of Female Hiddenness: A Contextual Reading of 1 Tim 2:9–15," *Ephemerides Theologicae Lovanienses* 88, no. 4 (2012): 486.

64 There are some who hold that the text is normative. For example, Bray states, "Paul based his argument not on cultural considerations but on the basic doctrine of the creation and the fall, neither of which has changed in the slightest." Gerald Lewis Bray, *The Pastoral Epistles: 1 Timothy, 2 Timothy, Titus*, A Theological Commentary (London: T&T Clark, 2019), 174.

some women with the writer's opponents and therefore are related to a particular situation." They also state that some women were teaching children (2 Tim 1:5; 3:15) and younger women (Titus 2:4)—hence the need for the prohibition in 1 Timothy 2—and that some women were acting as deacons.[65] There is one more reason other than the disorderliness in the church—that is, the presentation of the church to the Roman world in the context of Roman persecution. Young rightly states, "To a fair extent the teaching in these epistles seems very culture-specific, concerned as they are with the practical outworking of Christian living at the time and in the social environment in which they were written."[66] Alan Padgett also supposes that Timothy was written during a period of growing opposition from Roman authorities.[67]

Paul's instruction to Timothy is a response to the presence of a different teaching that invaded the church at Ephesus. Heidebrecht details five characteristics of the teaching: first, the teaching was different from the proclamation of the gospel; second, Paul's response was directed to those within the church itself; third, the problem primarily had to do with disparity between teaching and lifestyle through their rejection of conscience; fourth, the false teaching typified meaningless talk and vain gossip; and fifth, the false teaching had a substantial influence on the households (Titus 1:11).[68] These five aspects help in navigating Paul's directives to men and women in worship, especially the use of ἡσυχίᾳ in 1 Timothy 1:12. Women were leaders and teachers when the pastoral epistles were written.[69] We will take up the five aspects just mentioned and attempt to interpret them in context.

First, the Greek word translated as "silence" (ἡσυχίᾳ 1 Tim 1:12) can mean "quietness," "rest," or "silence." The context seems to suggest that

65 Marshall and Towner, *Critical and Exegetical Commentary*, 56; Lilian Portefaix, "'Good Citizenship' in the Household of God: Women's Position in the Pastorals Reconsidered in the Light of Roman Rule," in *A Feminist Companion to the Deutero-Pauline Epistles*, ed. Amy-Jill Levine and Marianne Blickenstaff, Feminist Companion to the New Testament and Early Christian Writings 7 (London: T&T Clark, 2003), 151.

66 Young, *Pastoral Letters*, 2; Vergeer calls this a "strategy of accommodation." Wim C. Vergeer, "The Redeemer in an 'Irredeemable Text,'" *Neotestamentica* 50, no. 1 (2016): 76.

67 Padgett, "Wealthy Women at Ephesus," 20. Also see Portefaix, "'Good Citizenship,'" 151.

68 Doug Heidebrecht, "Reading 1 Timothy 2:9–15 in Its Literary Context," *Direction: A Mennonite Brethren Form* 33, no. 2 (Fall 2004): 173–74.

69 Padgett, "Wealthy Women at Ephesus," 20.

"quietness" is suitable here. Padgett suggests that Paul had wealthy women in mind.[70] This comment has its limitations, but it is clear that Paul is not intending to disallow speech that is conveyed through the term *silence* but more so in terms of orderliness and scope for willingness to receive the teaching. Wiebe notes that Paul uses the word ἡσυχίᾳ in 1 Tim 2:2 to denote "quietness."[71] Paul qualifies the learning "with all submissiveness" but does not state to whom the women need to submit in the learning process. Instead of succumbing to the false teachers,[72] they are to heed to those who teach aspects of the faith (1:3–6; 4:6).[73]

Second, the problem at Ephesus was about false teaching in both form and content. Timothy was directed by Paul to instruct some not to teach matters of faith that were against correct teaching (1:3, 4; 6:2–4). First Timothy 2:12 excludes women from all aspects of teaching, while in Titus 2:3–4, women are required to be teachers in other circumstances. Paul is not universalizing the exclusion of women from their teaching role. In Acts 18:26, Aquila and Priscilla accurately explain the way of God to Apollos. Though some would distinguish teaching from explaining, clearly instruction is given to Apollos by both Priscilla and Aquilla.[74] In the second part of Paul's directive, Paul deals with the behavior of women in connection with men.[75] Women are not to "exercise authority over" (the term for authority is *authentein*) men. *Authentein*

70 Padgett, 23.

71 Ben Wiebe, "Two Texts on Women (1 Tim 2:11–15; Gal 3:26–29): A Test of Interpretation," *Horizons in Biblical Theology* 16, no. 1 (1994): 58.

72 Kimberley takes the view that the Paul is restoring the "womanly vocation to its rightful place in contrast to the manner in which it was depreciated in the gnostic circles." This theory presents a difficult proposition. David R. Kimberley, "1 Tim 2:15: A Possible Understanding of a Difficult Text," *Journal of the Evangelical Theological Society* 35, no. 4 (1992): 486.

73 Padgett, "Wealthy Women at Ephesus," 24.

74 Hughes states, "Apollos learned his theology from both of them (Acts 18:26)." R. Kent Hughes, "Living Out God's Order in the Church," *Master's Seminary Journal* 10, no. 1 (1999): 107.

75 Saucy takes the view that teaching and exercising authority over are not two different activities but two aspects of one idea. This is less possible as the object changes in the second aspect. Robert L. Saucy, "Women's Prohibition to Teach Men: An Investigation into Its Meaning and Contemporary Application," *Journal of the Evangelical Theological Society* 37, no. 1 (1994): 90.

is a *hapax legomenon* in the NT. It has different connotations in terms of its usage. In classical usage, it referred to murder or suicide; in the Hellenistic period, it referred to an aggressive action or power against others. Essentially, the word *authentein* has a connotation of mastery over others and not just authority (the common Greek word is *exousia*). Wiebe states that *authentein* denotes "some kind of self-centered and disruptive behaviour stands behind this instruction."[76]

Third, in 1 Timothy 2:13, the primacy of Adam is mentioned from a temporal perspective and does not seem to signify superiority in authority in terms of the order of creation. Here the reference is in terms of typology. Just as Adam was created first but did not act on his own, so too the women in Ephesus are warned not to yield themselves to the imperious spirit of the false teachers.[77]

Fourth, the statement in verse 14 needs not be interpreted in terms of greater vulnerability of women to deception. Here again Paul continues to use typology. Just as Eve was deceived by the serpent and was overcome by transgression, the women of Ephesus could also fall into the same trap by listening to the false teaching (1 Tim 4:1–5; 5:14–15).[78]

Fifth, in 1 Timothy 2:15, as an alternative to reading this as salvation through childbirth, the NIV reads "will be kept safe through child bearing" with reference to the birth of the messiah. Paul concludes this section with a statement on women living out their faith. The context helps throw light on the interpretation of the text. The false teachers advocated asceticism that rejects marriage (4:1–5); therefore, Paul encourages women to put their faith into practice by bearing children, and he gives direction to the family (5:14). Padgett states, "The wealthy women of Ephesus followed the false teachers, who taught that marriage was tainted and that one should neglect family duties." Padgett rightly concludes the articles by stating, "We have not found anything in these verses to indicate that women were not leaders in the early church, nor anything that would limit their role in the church today." He continues by arguing that we cannot overlook the social context of the letters "when interpreting this pericope today."[79]

76 Wiebe, "Two Texts on Women," 60.
77 Wiebe, 61.
78 Wiebe, 61.
79 Padgett, "Wealthy Women at Ephesus," 30.

Status of Women in South Asia

South Asia presents a grim picture on the status of women. The twin representation of women in Hinduism as goddess and slave is also prevalent in other religious traditions. The Vedas, considered the oldest scripture, present women as having equal status with men during the Vedic period.[80] The important epics *Rāmāyana* and *Mahabharata* depict women positively. God is conceptualized in Hinduism as both male and female. Sugandha Rawat and Pradeep Kumar state, "God is shown as *ardhanarishvara* or 'God who is half woman.'"[81] Unlike the Vedas, the *Smritis* denigrate women in various ways. Manu, the oldest lawgiver (in *Manusmṛiti*), teaches that women must be submissive in their different life stages such as in childhood to their fathers, in youth to their husbands and his relations, and to the sons when they become widowed. In that sense, the first-century thought-world was not different from that of the South Asian contexts.

Unlike the Brahmanical tradition, where male Brahmin priests dominate, the goddess tradition gives women status as leaders with ritual authority. This is seen in the *Adhiparasakthi* tradition, where Devī, the supreme universal goddess and Divine Mother, is worshipped and given daily offerings and prayers in India and Sri Lanka. The goddess is the epitome of authority, sovereignty, and power. Nanette R. Spina states, "More specifically, attention was drawn to the efficacy of the goddess' power to make things happen, influence circumstances, and to act on behalf of her devotees. The image of the Divine Mother in this setting focuses on her power in action, protection, and the fortification of her devotees."[82] In the goddess tradition, a woman is a "*prakṛti*, the mother or source of all; *śakti*, the indomitable potency and fecundity; and finally *māyā*, the seductress. All three aspects of Goddess deal with her sexuality and reflect the two accepted roles of women in society—namely, wife and mother."[83] Each person has to engage in specific social and religious duties

80 Sugandha Rawat and Pradeep Kumar, "Hindu Women in the Mirror of Time: At Once a Goddess and a Slave?," *Journal of Indian Research* 3, no. 3 (2015): 83.

81 Rawat and Kumar, 83.

82 Nanette R. Spina, "In Relationship with the Goddess: Women Interpreting Leadership Roles and Shaping Diasporic Identities," in *Modern Hinduism in Text and Context*, ed. Lavanya Vemsani (London: Bloomsbury Academic, 2018), 140.

83 Samjukta Gombrich Gupta, "The Goddess, Women and Their Rituals in Hinduism," in *Faces of the Feminine in Ancient, Medieval, and Modern India*, ed. Mandakranta Bose (New York: Oxford University Press, 2000), 95.

known as dharma, and a woman's dharma is designated as *strī-dharma*.[84] In that sense, the Hindu-Indian context is very similar to the context of Ephesus, where Artemis was venerated. Paul's pro-women and household instructions in 1 Timothy 3:11–15 need to be understood from this socioreligious and cultural perspective.

The presentation of woman as Divine Mother in the theological expression of Hinduism is only one aspect of the entire understanding of women. Women's social roles proceed from a patriarchal and caste-dominated society, where genealogy is defined through male terms. Samjukta Gombrich Gupta states, "In this society, the role models for women are such epic and *purāṇic* characters such as Sītā, who followed her husband into his forest exile, leaving behind the luxury of the palace of Ayodhyā, and Sāvitri, who followed her dead husband when the god of death was taking him to the land of the dead and tricked the god into returning her husband alive and well."[85] There are three primary roles that a woman is required to fulfill in Indian society: wife, mother, and daughter. As David G. Mandelbaum puts it, "A young wife, of any *Jāti* or region, usually has the lowest status in the family and is given the most onerous chores."[86] For a Hindu woman, marriage is a movement from instability to stability and a means of acquiring the prestigious status of motherhood. Kana Mitra notes that a married woman models her life after the classical ideal wives such as Sita, Sävitri, and Satï. A married woman serves her husband, who is both her lord and god.[87] First Timothy 2:8–15 reflects a similar situation in the ministry of Paul and Timothy. As Ephesus was situated on the west coast of Asia Minor (modern-day Turkey), and as Paul spent nearly three years of his ministry in this center of Asian life, a reader of the letter can understand the apostles' awareness about Asian realities.[88]

Motherhood holds an esteemed position in Hindu society, especially in their sacred literature. Gupta states, "Mothers are more sacred. In motherhood,

84 Gupta, 88.

85 Gupta, 87–88.

86 D. G. Mandelbaum, *Society in India: Continuity and Change* (Berkeley: University of California Press, 1970), 1:86, cited in Kana Mitra, "Women in Hinduism," *Journal of Ecumenical Studies* 20, no. 4 (1983): 586.

87 Mitra, "Women in Hinduism," 591.

88 C. E. Arnold, "Ephesus," in *Dictionary of Paul and His Letters* (Downers Grove, IL: IVP, 1993), 249.

women achieve symbiosis with the earth and nature on the one hand and with the Great Goddess, the cosmic mother, on the other."[89] Mitra postulates, "In Hindu traditions women are venerated as mothers. Säkta Hindus worship God as Mother—the *Säkti* and her different manifestations."[90] The birth of a daughter is not a welcome sign in a Hindu family, especially in the *Ṛg Veda* that has many blessings for conceiving a son. The preference for the son over the daughter affects not only this life, often seen as an indebtedness, but also the next life because the last rite has to be done by a male descendant for a safe passage to the next world. Mitra states, "'*Putra,*' the Sanskrit word for 'son,' is derived from the fact that the son delivers from hell *(put)*."[91] These representations of wife, mother, and daughter have a sustained bearing on the psyche of women, promoting an understanding that they are inferior to men. As Paul was dealing with the issues of Ephesus and the wider Asian contexts, the mixed realities of the Asian attitude toward women are echoed in his writings.

Despite all the advancement in technology, education, and scientific capabilities, the status and treatment of women in India have not improved proportionately. The Indian church is also shrouded with issues of ordination and leadership of women. Texts such as 1 Timothy 2:8–15 have been used as a tool to deny meaning and significance of women in the church today. It is a sad state of affairs, though God created man and woman alike in God's image.

Domestic Codes

The PE deal with stipulations on community behavior in groups. They belong to a literary form called household codes (see also Col 3:18–4:1; Eph 5:22–6:9; 1 Pet 2:18–37; 5:1–6) that typically include the following pairings: husbands and wives, parents and children, older people and younger people, and slaves and slave owners. The texts that deal with these in the PE are 1 Timothy 2:9–15 (women), 1 Timothy 6:1–2 (slaves), and Titus 2:1–10 (older men, older women, younger women, younger men, slaves). Hanson explains that these

89 Gupta, "Goddess, Women and Rituals," 92; Mitra, "Women in Hinduism," 592; Alleyn Diesel, "Hindu 'Amman' Religion as a Post-patriarchal Women's Spirituality," *Journal for the Study of Religion* 17, no. 1 (2004): 13–14.

90 Mitra, "Women in Hinduism," 592; Gupta, "Goddess, Women and Rituals," 92.

91 Mitra, "Women in Hinduism," 594.

codes did not originate in Christianity but are borrowed from pagan literature and then "thoroughly Christianised."[92]

The domestic codes advocated by Paul can be compared to the concept of dharma in Hinduism. Dharma consists of social and religious duties that a person performs individually (*sva-dharma)* and as a member of a particular *jāti* (*jāti-dharma*)—that is, the caste community into which one is born.[93] Women have *strī-dharma*, generally associated with household duties. The household codes of the PE demonstrate the social dynamics and the community-centered lifestyle of first-century Asian communities. A reader of the PE can see several resemblances between the Ephesian realities and contemporary Asian communities.

Christology and Soteriology

Salvation in the PE begins with God as Savior and the salvation God provides in Christ. There are several references in the PE to God as a Savior (1 Tim 1:1; 2:3–4) who wants everyone who believes to be saved (1 Tim 4:10), affirming that "Christ Jesus came into the world to save sinners" (1 Tim 1:5). In 2 Timothy, Paul states God has saved us (2 Tim 1:8–9) through "the appearance of our Saviour Christ Jesus" (2 Tim 1:10) by the believer's faithfulness and perseverance in the faith (2 Tim 2:10). Salvation includes preservation in this life and the passage into the next (1 Tim 2:15; 4:16; 2 Tim 4:18). The concept of a savior was widely prevalent in Ephesus and appears in Scripture as a title or description of "gods, emperors, provincial proconsuls, and local patrons."[94] Köstenberger states, "Rather than salvation being found by adhering to various myths and genealogies, Paul contended that it was for 'all people' (1 Tim 2:4) and came through Christ the Saviour (1 Tim 1:15; 2:3–4; 4:10)."[95] The PE identify the universal problem of sin (1 Tim 1:15; 5:2; 2 Tim 3:2–5) and God's desire to save humanity from sin's power and penalty (1 Tim 2:4). Salvation is God's work alone and promised by God before the beginning of time.

92 Anthony Tyrrell Hanson, *Studies in the Pastoral Epistles* (London: SPCK, 1968), 43.

93 Gupta, "Goddess, Women and Rituals," 88.

94 S. M. Baugh, "'Savior of All People': 1 Tim 4:10 in Context," *Westminster Theological Journal* 54, no. 2 (1992): 331–40, esp. 335.

95 Köstenberger, Kellum, and Quarles, *Cradle, Cross, and Crown*, 405.

In contrast, Hindu *Moksha* (salvation), liberation from the cycle of rebirth (*saṃsāra*), is the ultimate goal of human existence. This can be achieved through practices including tantric rituals and *marga* or paths that are combined as karma yoga (selfless action or service), jnāna yoga (knowledge of one's union with the divine), and bhakti yoga (awakening through loving devotion). Spina states, "Within the Adhiparasakthi tradition, cultivating a relationship with the divine by adhering to this path, which combines these three aspects in one, one comes to understand the goal of *yoga*: awakening, liberation, *mokśa*, or in other terms, union with the divine."[96] Though the conceptual framework of salvation is different in Hinduism, it is important to note that the concept of salvation is at the base of both the religious traditions.

Handing Over of Traditions

Christian doctrine is termed as *parathēkē*, "what has been entrusted to you" (1 Tim 6:20). This deposit of faith has been delivered by Paul to Timothy and must be in turn be handed on by Timothy to trustworthy successors (2 Tim 1:13–14; 2:2; 3:14). To the objection of the use of *parathēkē*, Knight states that the similar concept of handing over is seen in the use of the terms *received* and *deliver* present in 1 Corinthians 15:1–3. Paul exhorts the Thessalonians to hold on to the tradition that they were taught (2 Thess 2:15) and take disciplinary action according to the tradition (2 Thess 3:6). The difference is in the pronounced emphasis on the handing over of the tradition. This could be because the recipients of the PE were Paul's delegates especially put in charge of teaching ministry and not the churches of the earlier letters.[97]

The handing over of tradition by Timothy (*parathēkē*) can be seen in the light of the concept of dharma in Hinduism. Dharma has two basic forms—namely, *śruti* and *smṛti*. Both of them are considered as sacred texts and primarily the source of knowledge.[98] *Śruti* (lit. hearing), unlike *smṛti*, is taken as the most sacred and important articulations listened to by the

96 Spina, "Relationship with the Goddess," 140.

97 Knight, *Pastoral Epistles*, 35.

98 Shlomo Biderman, "Authority and Action: An Indian Perspective," in *Scripture and Knowledge: An Essay on Religious Epistemology*, Studies in the History of Religions 69 (New York: Brill, 1995), 175.

sages, who fully understood what was communicated.[99] *Śṃrti* (lit. remembrance) comprises various collections of traditions such as the two great epics, *Purānas,* and others. In Hinduism, *śruti* takes more importance than *sṃrti;* what is heard is more valuable than what is remembered. The oral aspect of the Vedas is essential for its authority and power because orality preceded the written text.[100]

In this regard, Lucius Nereparampil states, "*Sruti* Scriptures are considered to be the most sacred as they were written down by the rishis who 'heard' from God and passed down orally and thus were 'heard' by succeeding generations. It is through *Sruti* that 'Veda,' namely the 'knowledge' of God reached mankind."[101] He further states that the seers are only "introducing apt language to translate their experience of the true Word, they are only imitating the true Word itself in its move to self-manifestation. Here the seers are only trying to translate their experience of 'seeing' the True Word into understandable human language. They are not composing Veda, but enacting it. So they are not the authors of the Veda, but only its agents."[102]

Paul instructing Timothy to hand over tradition to trustworthy successors can be seen in the light of the guru-shishya[103] relationship in Hinduism. The Veda is handed over orally from a teacher to a disciple. Here there is a continuing tradition as well as a relationship between the teacher and the disciple that facilitates the understanding of scripture.[104] In ancient India, disciples stayed in *Gurukula* (Home of the Teacher), where importance was given to relationship and imitation in the learning process. The guru, through personal contact, had a substantial influence on the shishya's life.[105]

99 Biderman, 175.

100 Biderman, 178.

101 Lucius Nereparampil, "Sruti and Revelation: Indian and Christian Approaches to Scripture," in *Indian Interpretation of the Bible: Festschrift in Honour of Prof. Joseph Pathrapankal,* ed. Augustine Thottakara (Bangalore: Dharmaram, 2000), 150.

102 Nereparampil, 154.

103 Sam P. Mathew, "Discipleship in the Gospel of Mark and the *Guru-Sishya* Relationship in Sankara's Teaching," in *Indian Interpretation of the Bible: Festschrift in Honour of Prof. Joseph Pathrapankal,* ed. Augustine Thottakara (Bangalore: Dharmaram, 2000), 368–69.

104 Biderman, "Authority and Action," 178.

105 Anil Sooklal, "The Guru-Shishya Parampara: A Paradigm of Religio-Cultural Continuity," *Journal for the Study of Religion* 3, no. 2 (1990): 17.

CONCLUSION

Many scholars argue against Pauline authorship of the letters to Timothy and Titus, but the external and internal evidences suggest otherwise. Paul instructs Timothy to stay at Ephesus because the situation was critical, especially due to the false teaching that emerged from within the church. The issues that Paul addresses have similarities with the South Asian contextual issues such as women's role in religion, domestic codes, soteriology, and passing down traditions. The Ephesian Artemis and the cultic elements associated with it also have many similarities with the South Asian context. The challenge is the interaction between faith and context and related aspects.

FURTHER READING

Bray, G. L. 2019. *The Pastoral Epistles: 1 Timothy, 2 Timothy, Titus.* A Theological Commentary. London: T&T Clark.

Collins, R. F. 2002. *1 & 2 Timothy and Titus: A Commentary.* 1st ed. The New Testament Library. Louisville: Westminster John Knox.

Gupta, S. G. 2000. "The Goddess, Women and Their Rituals in Hinduism." In *Faces of the Feminine in Ancient, Medieval, and Modern India*, edited by Mandakranta Bose, 87–106. New York: Oxford University Press.

Johnson, L. T. 2001. *The First and Second Letters to Timothy: A New Translation with Introduction and Commentary.* 1st ed. The Anchor Bible 35A. New York: Doubleday.

Knight, G. W. 2008. *The Pastoral Epistles: A Commentary on the Greek Text.* The New International Greek Testament Commentary. Grand Rapids, MI: Eerdmans.

MacDonald, M. Y., 2004. *The Pauline Churches: A Socio-historical Study of Institutionalization in the Pauline and Deutero-Pauline Writings.* 1st ed. Society for New Testament Studies Monograph Series 60. Cambridge: Cambridge University Press.

Marshall, I. H., and P. H. Towner. 1999. *A Critical and Exegetical Commentary on the Pastoral Epistles.* The International Critical Commentary on the Holy Scriptures of the Old and New Testaments. Edinburgh: T&T Clark.

Mounce, W. D., B. M. Metzger, D. A. Hubbard, G. W. Barker, and W. D. Mounce. 2009. *Pastoral Epistles.* Word Biblical Commentary 46. Nashville: Nelson.

Rawat, S., and P. Kumar. 2015. "Hindu Women in the Mirror of Time: At Once a Goddess and a Slave?" *Journal of Indian Research* 3, no. 3: 82–91.

SIXTEEN

The Letter to Titus

Xiaoli Yang
Charles Sturt University
University of Divinity Australia

"Small is beautiful." Titus, considered part of the Pastoral Letters together with 1 and 2 Timothy, is one of the shortest of all the letters that the apostle Paul wrote to his young disciples. In a very short space, the letter gives practical suggestions to different groups of believers on how to live out their faith in church and society, without extensive instructions in more fundamental areas as his letters to the Romans, Colossians, or Corinthians (see 1 Cor 3:1–3). Addressed to his junior missionary, this letter shows Paul's apostolic leadership and pastoral concerns toward the Cretan church in both internal and external affairs. Without overriding the diverse traditions and cultures in Asia, this chapter attempts to read the book of Titus from Asian backgrounds, especially those influenced by Confucian tradition. Asian minds in this tradition would quickly find reminiscence with the *Analects* (*Lunyu*, 论语), an ancient classic composed of a collection of teachings by Confucius and his contemporaries. It contains practical instructions from a master to his disciples concerning life and how to be a perfect human—a sage.

Authorship and Authenticity

Although the style and vocabulary of the Pastoral Letters differ from those in other Pauline letters, it has been traditionally accepted that the apostle Paul is the author.[1] Biblical scholars since the late nineteenth century have raised questions about Pauline authorship. Some think that the book was written by one of his disciples. Some hold that it is a collection of Paul's teaching, just like the *Analects* (论语) were compiled and written by Confucius's students. Some take the view that Paul's followers wrote the letter but used Paul's name for the sake of honoring him. Others believe that the compilers are in fact those of a later generation instead of Paul's followers.[2] Walter L. Liefeld thinks most evangelicals hold that Paul himself wrote the letter.[3] I. H. Marshall offers the term *allonymity* to define an authorial process that might close the gap between the apostle and the author who co-opts his name.[4]

The rhetorical difference between the Pastoral Letters and other Pauline letters can be explained by the personal nature of the letter and the possibility of the composition by an editor or a secretary. As a mentor and spiritual father, Paul writes to Titus in a personal manner. After much suffering and pain, Paul, now in his sixties, shows that the fiery temper of his early years seems to have been tamed. Confucius measures human development by a person's age: "At fifteen, I had my mind bent on learning. At thirty, I stood

1 Thomas C. Oden, *First and Second Timothy and Titus*, Interpretation, a Bible Commentary for Teaching and Preaching (Louisville: J. Knox, 1989), 10–15.

2 Timothy Yu, ed., *Zhongwen Shengjing Qidaoben* [*The Chinese study bible*] (Hong Kong: Rock, 2002); David A. Ackerman, *1 & 2 Timothy/Titus: A Commentary in the Wesleyan Tradition*, New Beacon Bible Commentary (Kansas City, MO: Beacon Hill, 2016), 35–43; Walter L. Liefeld, *1 and 2 Timothy/Titus: The NIV Application Commentary from Biblical Text . . . to Contemporary Life*, NIV Application Commentary Series (Grand Rapids, MI: Zondervan, 1999), 24–27; Philip H. Towner, *The Letters to Timothy and Titus*, New International Commentary on the New Testament (Grand Rapids, MI: Eerdmans, 2006), 9–26.

3 Liefeld, *Timothy/Titus*, 24–27; see also John R. W. Stott, *The Message of 1 Timothy & Titus*, The Bible Speaks Today (Downers Grove, IL: InterVarsity, 1996), 33–34.

4 Towner, *Timothy and Titus*, 25; I. Howard Marshall and Philip H. Towner, *A Critical and Exegetical Commentary on the Pastoral Epistles*, International Critical Commentary (Edinburgh: T&T Clark, 2004), 83–84.

firm. At forty, I had no doubts. At fifty, I knew the decrees of Heaven. At sixty, my ear was an obedient organ for the reception of truth. At seventy, I could follow what my heart desired, without transgressing what was right."[5] Christian maturity cannot be easily measured by age, although Asians tend to pay respect to their seniors because they are assumed to carry the wisdom of life. Paul has grown to maturity in the likeness of Christ through many trials and suffering. His letter now exhibits much fruit of gentleness, humility, and perseverance.

It is likely that Paul dictated the letter with the help of a secretary (see 1 Cor 16:21; Gal 6:11; Col 4:18; 2 Thess 3:17; Phlm 19), or an "active amanuensis."[6] This was a common practice for well-educated writers as recorded by the Romano-Jewish historian Josephus (37 CE–100 CE).[7] Naturally, changes of style and expression were unavoidable. These factors do not diminish the probable authenticity of Paul's authorship.

However, as Charles J. Bumgardner laid out in his literature review (2009–15), the debates among contemporary scholars are far more comprehensive and exhaustive than this chapter can show.[8] As such, the date and venues of the letter become disputable. Suggestions vary from the Second Imprisonment Theory in the traditional paradigm to pseudonymity in the modern paradigm.[9] Stott states that the most likely scenario is that Paul wrote the PE toward the end of his life.[10] The date therefore could be anywhere between 63 CE and 67 CE, which was at the start of the First Jewish-Roman War (66 CE–73 CE), or the early period of the Eastern Han or Later Han period (25 CE–220 CE) in China.

5 Confucius, "Lunyu, Wei Zheng," Analects, accessed October 2, 2019, https://ctext.org/analects/wei-zheng/zhs?en=on. The Chinese version is the following: "吾十有五而志于学, 三十而立, 四十而不惑, 五十而知天命, 六十而耳顺, 七十而从心所欲, 不逾矩."

6 Stott, *Message*, 30–33.

7 Flavius Josephus and H. St John Thackeray, *Josephus: The Life—Against Apion*, vol. 1 (London: Heinemann, 1966).

8 Charles J. Bumgardner, "Paul's Letters to Timothy and Titus: A Literature Review (2009–2015)," *Southeastern Theological Review* 7, no. 2 (2016): 77–116.

9 Towner, *Timothy and Titus*, 9–26.

10 Stott, *Message*, 34.

Purpose

As one of Paul's early Greek converts (1:4; Gal 2:3) and coworkers (Gal 2:1), Titus is mentioned thirteen times in Paul's letters (2 Cor 2:13; 7:6, 13, 14; 8:6, 16, 23; 12:18; Gal 2:1, 3; 2 Tim 4:10; Titus 1:4). Clearly, he is Paul's trusted ministry partner, having been assigned to help resolve the problems of the church in Corinth (2 Cor 2, 7, 8, 12) and now in Crete. These churches faced enormous challenges both internally and externally. It appears that Titus was able to complete the assignment faithfully, showing his great leadership gifts and capacity (2 Cor 7:6–7, 15; 8:16; 2 Tim 4:10; Titus 3:12). In this letter, Paul wrote Titus to

- provide guidelines for the selection of elders (1:5–9),
- warn against false teachers and their doctrine (1:10–16; 3:9–11),
- emphasize the relationship between the doctrinal truth and ethical living of believers (2:1–3:8), and
- give him some specific instructions on personal matters (3:12–14).

As someone in a position of seniority, Paul gave clear guidance to his junior missionary on these key issues of the Cretan church instead of writing to the entire church as in his normal pattern of writing. Like a wise master seeking to train his disciples, Paul's words are filled with sternness and care.

Outline

The letter is clearly structured in the form of a Hellenistic letter. The following outline of the letter demonstrates the development of the epistle in a clear fashion.

Salutation (1:1–4)

Leaders and false teachers (1:5–16)
- Criteria for the selection of elders (1:5–9)
- Exposing false teachers (1:10–16)

Believers' ethical living (2:1–15)
- Godly character and behavior of believers of different age groups (2:1–10)
- Gospel grounding (2:11–15)

Believers' social responsibilities (3:1–7)
  Responsibilities to the state and society (3:1–2)
  Gospel grounding (3:3–8)

Warnings against rebels (3:8–11)

Personal instructions and greetings (3:12–15)

HERMENEUTICAL ANALYSIS FROM ASIAN PERSPECTIVES

Several selected hermeneutical aspects are highlighted as one reads the letter from an Asian lens—namely, mentorship, morality, relationships, worldviews, and poetry.

Mentorship: Instructing in Love

Paul is not only a senior missionary giving instructions on church ministry but also a spiritual father to Titus, calling him τέκνον (1:4), meaning a male child ("my true son" in NIV; "my loyal child" in NRSV). It signifies "an intimate and reciprocal relationship formed . . . by the bonds of love, friendship, trust, just as between parents and children."[11] This affectionate address is also used to suggest how Paul's teaching has given birth to Titus's conversion and nurtured and molded his Christian growth. On the one hand, with the longest salutation and most self-reference (1:1–4), Paul stresses his spiritual authority and status to the church (3:15) when dealing with "many rebellious people" (1:10) and those who "cause divisions" (3:10). On the other hand, he emphasizes his special personal intimate relationship with Titus (1:4). It appears that Paul's seniority to exercise his authority as "an apostle of Jesus Christ" (1:1) is coupled with a loving relationship with the recipient as a father to a son.

This dual relationship bears much resemblance to the reciprocal way of relating that Confucius invites his disciples to use. He humbly admits, "When I walk along with two others, they may serve as my teachers" (三人行, 必有

11 "The Online Greek Bible," Greek New Testament Resources, accessed October 4, 2019, http://www.greekbible.com.

我师焉).[12] He stresses the harmonious relationship between a teacher and a student through the ethic of *ren* (仁, human love), which forms the foundation of all human relationships. The ethic of "honoring the teacher and loving the Dao (the truth)" (尊师重道) in Confucian classics has been emphasized throughout the ages. A teacher is often called *enshi* (恩师), someone to whom one is greatly indebted. A student is to honor their teacher, and a teacher is to love their students. A teacher not only holds certain authority but also must love their student like a loving parent. This is taken to an extreme when combined with filial piety in Asian tradition—hence the well-known phrase "A day as a teacher, a lifetime as a father" (一日为师, 终身为父). A teacher can abuse a student, and a student can become a subservient servant. This tradition also influences Asian church leadership in the way that senior leaders tend to be authoritarian. As Paul Cornelius indicates, they are reluctant to pass the baton to the younger generation.[13]

For Christians, it is through the mutuality of *ren* expressed in the action of humble service that a healthy and authentic relationship can be developed. K. K. Yeo uses a Confucian term *Renren* (仁人, human beings who love) to explain that Jesus is the perfect manifestation of an I-Thou relationship in two dimensions—with God and with human beings.[14] It is precisely in the common faith in Jesus (see 1:4) that Paul's relationship with Titus as a mentor, a teacher, a senior missionary, and a loving father is firmly grounded.

Morality: Grateful Responses

Paul's criteria for the selection of leaders in the church is mentioned three times in his Pastoral Letters. The list here for an elder and a bishop or "overseer" (1:6–9, common terms for leadership in antiquity) is similar to the list in 1 Timothy 3:2–7 for a "bishop." The list in 1 Timothy 3:8–12 for "deacons" can also be found in the other two passages, except for "not double-tongued." Among the list, two things stand out for contemporary Asian eyes. First, facing

12 Confucius, "Lunyu, Shuer," Analects, 22, accessed September 5, 2019, https://ctext.org/analects/shu-er/zhs.

13 Paul Cornelius, "Titus," in *South Asia Bible Commentary*, ed. Brian C. Wintle (Udaipur, India: Open Door, 2015), 1701.

14 Khiok-Khng Yeo, "Chinese Christologies: Images of Christ and Chinese Cultures," in *The Oxford Handbook of Christology*, ed. Francesca Aran Murphy (Oxford: Oxford University Press, 2015).

rampant divorce, concubinage, and prostitution in the Greco-Roman world, Paul points out the importance of honoring the marital union between a man and a woman (1 Tim 3:6; see Gen 2:24; 1 Cor 6:16; Eph 5:21–6:9). In Paul's mind, sexual liaison with one outside of marriage—whether married or unmarried, in the form of a concubine or prostitute—is the same as polygamy. These are regarded as shameful behaviors that dishonor God (see 1 Tim 4:3).

This countercultural call is as challenging in Asia as it was to ancient Greeks and Romans. The ancient Confucian and Daoist ideal of harmony through the correlation of yin and yang is achieved by a "husband of one wife." As "Doctrine of the Mean" (中庸) records, "The Dao of a gentleman [sage] starts from the relationship between a husband and a wife" (君子之道,造端乎夫妇).[15] Concubinage, however, was highly popular in East Asia until the early twentieth century, whether via the system of *qie* (妾) in feudal China, the Nair caste females with Nambudiri males of Kerala in India, concubinage among the nobility before the Meiji period in Japan, or different ranks of concubines in a harem of Joseon monarchs in Korea. Today, following widespread economic growth, there is a return of mistresses interconnected with an explosion in corruption all over Asia. The cultures of sexual perversion and adultery have also penetrated the church. Leaders often fall due to sexual immorality, along with other lapses like greed and power. Here Paul reminds Titus of an important qualification to be an elder of a church with regard to marriage.

Second, Paul's list stresses twice the quality of a leader being "blameless" (ἀνέγκλητος) followed by a set of character traits (Titus 1:6–7). They resonate with the ideal picture of a "'sage" (*junzi*, 君子) in Confucian tradition, who possesses four main characteristics: "In his conduct of himself, he was humble; in serving his superior, he was respectful; in nourishing the people, he was kind; in ordering the people, he was just" (其行己也恭, 其事上也敬, 其养民也惠, 其使民也义).[16] Similarly, in the following chapter, Paul gives instructions to different groups of people in the church with specific character traits listed that resonate with some listed for leaders (2:1–10). In particular, the character trait of being "prudent" or "self-controlled" (σώφρονα; 1:8; 2:2; see 2:5–6) and

15 Confucius, "Liji, Zhongyong," Book of Rites, accessed November 11, 2019, http://ctext.org/liji/zhong-yong/zh.

16 Confucius, "Lunyu, Gong Ye Chang," Analects, accessed October 11, 2019, https://ctext.org/analects/gong-ye-chang/ens.

"upright" (δίκαιον, 1:8; 2:12) would draw the attention of Asian eyes. It is rendered a quality of thoughtful care in one's behavior, as well as chastity and faithfulness of women prized by the ancient Greeks and Romans.[17] In the eyes of Paul, these are important countercultural qualities of a Christian leader in the lying and cunning culture of Crete. Surprisingly, in another ancient context, Confucian tradition develops its way of living in the world with similar qualities: "Intelligent is he and *prudent*, and so preserves his person" (既明且哲, 以保其身).[18] Confucius's student Zi Gong also described his master as "benign, *upright*, courteous, temperate, and complaisant" (温、良、恭、俭).[19]

These outward behavior resemblances are derived from different motivations. In Confucian tradition, it is to achieve the ideal of harmony with Dao (道), in the language of ethics—"perpetual unity of the Self with Heaven" (*tianren heyi*, 天人合一). Confucianism teaches that the goal of unity can be achieved by self-cultivation and self-determination. As Tu Wei-ming states, "Being religious, in the Confucian sense, is being engaged in ultimate self-transformation as a communal act. Salvation means the full realisation of the anthropocosmic reality in our human nature."[20] Out of this tradition, Asians, including those in ministry, tend to be hard workers. The assumption is that people need not depart from selfhood and humanity to become fully realized. It is through a deepening and broadening awareness of ourselves as humans that we serve heaven.

Paul does not deny the full human flourishing that exhibits godly character, but he stresses that the source of such full realization comes from the Lord Jesus Christ. He insists that chosen leaders must have "a firm grasp of the word" and teach sound doctrine (1:9). To clarify this further, he reiterates the gospel (2:11–15; 3:3–8) after a list of character traits for believers (2:1–10; 3:1–2). Salvation is demonstrated by the redemptive death of Jesus Christ for our sins (2:14) and the renewal of the Holy Spirit (3:5–6). Of note, the notion

17 Steven M. Baugh, "1 and 2 Timothy, Titus," in *1 & 2 Thessalonians; 1 & 2 Timothy, Titus*, ed. Clinton E. Arnold (Grand Rapids, MI: Zondervan, 2002), 102–3.

18 Confucius, "Liji, Zhongyong," 28.

19 Confucius, "Lunyu, Xueer," Analects, accessed October 11, 2019, https://ctext.org/analects/xue-er/ens.

20 Tu Wei-ming, "The Confucian Tradition: A Confucian Perspective in Learning to be Human," in *The World's Religious Traditions: Current Perspectives in Religious Studies*, ed. Frank Whaling (London: Bloomsbury Academic, 2016), 70.

of sins is understood not only from the perspective of a perpetrator in Asia. It needs to be discussed in terms of its effect on the victim. For Koreans, the concept of *han* (anger, resentment, and bitterness), a kind of bondage of a victim, also requires freedom by the saving work of Christ.[21] For Chinese, the concept of sin (*zui*, 罪), though appearing in Confucian classics, is difficult to comprehend because it is connected with crime or punishment of crime. The lying culture of the Cretans would be seen not necessarily as absolute sin but as mistakes that bring shame. Regardless of its historical and contextual interpretations, salvation is not by one's own behavior or good works but through the grace (χάρις, 2:11; 3:7) of God and his mercy (ἔλεος, 3:5). For Paul, good works are the outward expression of a genuine Christian faith. Rather than Confucian humanistic endeavor, Paul's listed qualifications for leaders and godly character traits for believers derive from deep gratitude toward the benefaction of God.

How do Asians express their gratitude in a culture founded in relationship? As social scientists and missiologists point out, *patronage* is an etic term to describe a "reciprocal, asymmetrical relationship" between social unequals in collectivistic and honor-shame societies.[22] Asians traditionally perceive that the protection and provision of a patron demand moral obligations and the gratitude of a client. They will in turn create an ongoing reciprocity that deepens the relationship. It is not the rules that define relationships; rather, relationships define the rules. The reciprocity (*lishangwanglai*, 礼尚往来) arising from relational debt in Asian cultures indicates that people first need to experience the unconditional love of God through life and ministry of Jesus; only then can they express reciprocal love to God with thanksgiving and ethical living with their neighbors through mutual sharing, support, and submission.

Relationship: Being inside and outside of Home

This short letter of Paul to Titus is read not as a doctrinal document but rather as a personal letter about home matters. Asian eyes would immediately note that this home is grounded in relationship with Jesus Christ, other family members, and those outside family. This relational emphasis echoes with

21 Andrew Sung Park, *The Wounded Heart of God: The Asian Concept of Han and the Christian Doctrine of Sin* (Nashville: Abingdon, 1993).

22 Jayson Georges, *Ministering in Patronage Cultures: Biblical Models and Missional Implications* (Downers Grove, IL: InterVarsity, 2019), 9–11.

much non-Abrahamic Asian tradition, whether it is the pragmatic integration of heaven, society, community, family, and self in Confucianism; the communal, generational, and relational dharma sought in Hinduism; or the way of nonaction (*wuwei*, 无为) in relation to humans and nature in Daoism. Here is a relational list throughout the letter:

1:4. . . . . Calling Titus his "loyal child"

1:6 . . . . Elders' marriage and parenthood at home ("married only once . . . children are believers")

1:8. . . . . A bishop as God's steward

1:11 . . . . "Whole families" upset by the teaching

1:13–14 . . . . . Relationship with false teachers

2:2 . . . . Older men's character and behavior

2:3–4 . . . . . . Older women's behavior especially in relation to young women

2:4–5 . . . . . . Young women's behavior in relation to their husbands and children at home

2:6 . . . . Younger men's character and behavior

2:9 . . . . Slaves' character and behavior in relation to their masters

2:11, 14 . . . . . Relationship with God as "a people of his own"

3:1–2 . . . . . . Character and behavior in relation to "rulers and authorities"

3:7. . . . . Relationship with God as "heirs"

3:10 . . . . Relationship with those engaged in divisions and controversies

3:13–14 . . . . . Personal care of those in need

The overarching thread of Paul's letter is that relationship matters. It forms the basis of Christian witness both inside and outside the family of God. It appears that there are three key layers of relationship with which Paul deals.

Relationship with Those in Faith—That Is, the Members of the Household

Because of their primary relationship with God, who bestows on them the grace of the gospel through the redemptive work of Jesus Christ, members of the household are now reconciled with God as heirs and with each other as family members. Christian kinship is coupled with the attitude of honor, respect, self-control, and love for one another. Within the household, Paul has multilayers of relationships with other members: he shows a personal intimate relationship with Titus, he holds elders and bishops accountable, he gives general instructions to believers of different age and social status, and he shows personal care to those in need.

In the "high context" of Asian cultures, relationship, collectivism, intuition, and contemplation are greatly valued. People see themselves as part of a close-knit web of community and cannot be separated from a network of interpersonal relationships.[23] Their faith is not privatized in a particular secluded setting; instead, it is largely defined by the sociopolitical community to which they belong. For instance, Hindu communities in India are composed of close-knit families and communities, and often a hindrance to being converted is their fear of being ostracized from their family because without community, life becomes "rootless, homeless, anchorless."[24]

Paul's stress on "family values" (1:6; 2:4–5), which was promoted by the first-century emperor Augustus,[25] is also an important cultural ingredient in Asia where family and community are emphasized in social ethics. The

23 Mary Ellen Guffey and Dana Loewy, *Essentials of Business Communication* (Nashville: South-Western College, 2016).

24 Choan-Seng Song, *Theology from the Womb of Asia* (Maryknoll, NY: Orbis, 1986), 123.

25 Baugh, "Timothy, Titus," 102–3.

Hebrew mindset in Paul is very close to Asian thinking that largely focuses on relationship (*guanxi*, 关系). Mengzi (372–289 BCE) articulates the five main relationships (*wulun*, 五伦) that form the basis of human connectiveness. The relationships are between father and son, ruler and minister, husband and wife, old and young, and friends. He teaches, "How, between father and son, there should be affection; between sovereign and minister, righteousness; between husband and wife, attention to their separate functions; between old and young, a proper order; and between friends, fidelity" (父子有亲, 君臣有义, 夫妇有别, 长幼有序, 朋友有信).[26] Among the five, three of them (father and son, husband and wife, old and young) are directly connected with members of a household. These five human relationships were promoted later in the Song and Ming dynasties, forming the essence of traditional Chinese morality. Even religious rites are useful "to cultivate kinship values like filial piety, family loyalty, and continuity of the family lineage."[27]

By reading Paul from Asian perspectives, one grasps not only the importance of Christian kinship but also how these relationships are redefined when rooted in the unconditional love of Christ. Ethical behavior toward one another is not based on moral code or blood relationships; rather, it is a response to the one who draws believers to the common faith through "the water of rebirth and renewal by the Holy Spirit" (3:5; see Isa 32:15; 44:3; Ezek 39:29; Joel 2:28–29). The language used in the "baptismal hymn" (3:4–8) is likely part of a preexisting hymn, expressing the basic truth of Christian faith on salvation.[28] To become "heirs" is to inherit eternal life (v. 7) by the work of Christ, not to carry on the family lines and fulfill duty to honor ancestors. This new family of God is defined by kingdom values, not by bloodline but rather by doing the will of God (see Matt 12:48–50).

26 Mengzi, "Tengwengong Shang," Chinese Text Project, accessed November 11, 2019, 4, https://ctext.org/mengzi/teng-wen-gong-i.

27 Ralph R. Covell, *Confucius, the Buddha, and Christ: A History of the Gospel in Chinese*, American Society of Missiology Series (Maryknoll, NY: Orbis, 1986), 9.

28 Terence J. Keegan, *First and Second Timothy, Titus, Philemon*, New Collegeville Bible Commentary New Testament (Collegeville, MN: Liturgical, 2006).

Relationship with Those in Authority

There was an increasingly nationalistic sentiment in first-century Judea under the ruling of the Roman Empire. Here Paul instructs submissive relationships with rulers and authorities, who are likely pagans (Titus 3:1; see 1 Tim 2:2; Rom 13:1–7). He gives clear, active instructions here: "be obedient" (πειθαρχεῖν), which indicates "readiness of persuasion—an attitude of cooperation."[29] He repeats himself twice to Christians to "be ready for every good work" (Titus 3:1) and "devote themselves to good works" (v. 8). "To speak evil of no one, to avoid quarrelling, to be gentle, and to show every courtesy to everyone" (v. 2)—these are Christian virtues toward those who govern them in society. Clearly Paul is not encouraging revolts or revolution; instead, he is promoting good deeds and a humble attitude toward "everyone" (ἀνθρώποις, vv. 2, 8)—male and female, Jews and gentiles, the rich and the poor. All should be treated with consideration and respect. Paul's teachings here are particularly relevant to the sociopolitical reality of Asia today. Since the time Western missionaries brought the gospel to many Asian countries, Asian Christianity has been deeply entangled with the state, foreign involvement, and social changes. Christian faith for Asian Christians is not a private matter but rather involves public engagement. The ecclesiological forms also reflect their relationships with the state and are rooted in historical complexity. Asian Christians should remember that the authorities exist and are appointed by God (Acts 17:26). They need to pray for them and live peaceful, quiet lives (1 Tim 2:2–4).

However, Asian history has shown the prevalent oppression and persecution toward believers during different periods. What does it mean for Asian Christians to be obedient to the state while maintaining their solidarity to Christ, standing with the oppressed and advocating the kingdom values of justice and peace? Some groups in Asia suffer from exclusion and discrimination such as the Lumads (indigenous Mindana) in the Philippines, the Rohingyas (Muslim) in Myanmar, or the Dalits (broken ones) in India. Both "water buffalo theology" of Southeast Asia and "Minjung theology" of South Korea speak of the Christian experience of struggle for social justice. The "suffering theology" (*shouku shenxue*, 受苦神学) of the "silent majority" in China was developed out of much painful and cross-bearing experience of millions

29 Reggie M. Kidd, "Timothy and Titus," in *The Baker Illustrated Bible Commentary*, ed. Gary M. Burge and Andrew E. Hill (Grand Rapids, MI: Baker, 2012), 1480.

of Christian believers, especially during the cultural revolution. With the rise of religious and ethnic nationalism in places like Malaysia, Indonesia, India, and Pakistan, Christians suffer from enormous pain, persecution, and even death for the sake of their faith. They often have to pay a high price because of their alignment with Jesus Christ in the public sphere of secular atheist regimes, or among religious/cultural/ethnic dominants as "the other." While Paul's instructions to the first-century Cretan Christians are clearly expressed here, Asian Christians of the twenty-first century are to live out such godly lives without compromising their faith so they can be "salt and light" and good citizens in the midst of an increasingly challenging world (Matt 5:13–14).

Relationship with False Teachers and Those Engaged in Controversies

This short letter demonstrates that Paul's reproof toward those rebels is firmly unyielding. Twice in this short letter, Paul warns against false teachers (1:10–16) and those causing controversies (3:9–11). The rebels Paul refers to are those who disobey the apostles' teachings, especially with regard to circumcision (1:10) in Jewish tradition. The lies of these false teachers focus on the empty "Jewish myths" (1:14) and "genealogies" (3:9, see 1 Tim 1:4) that promote speculations. Paul rebukes them for personal gain and "upsetting whole families" (1:11). They are given over to corrupt behaviors (1:13–16), because bad roots bear bad fruit. To those false teachers who insist on the law of the OT and quarrel about it, Paul points out their talks are "unprofitable and worthless"; he even warns to "have nothing more to do" with them (3:9–10). In the Jewish community, this form of expulsion is the strictest toward the offender.[30] Paul's concerns for the effect on the whole household of God shows his collective mindset (resonant in Asian thinking) that all relationships are interconnected.

Although Asia faces different kinds of challenges in today's reality, various forms of false teaching not in alignment with the Scriptures are common. As Jesus predicted, "false messiahs and false prophets will appear" and deceive even believers (Matt 24:23–24). As in the first and second centuries, the rise of various cults and heresies have caused damaging controversy, corruption, and

30 John H. Walton and Craig S. Keener, *Cultural Backgrounds Study Bible: Bringing to Life the Ancient World of Scripture*, New International Version, Red Letter Edition (Grand Rapids, MI: Zondervan, 2016), 2131.

destruction in many regions of Asia, especially in rural areas. Local people are easily lured into false teaching due to the influence of folk religions or superstitious beliefs. Many of these cults elevate their leaders to godlike figures. They are involved in sexual misconduct, commit crimes, and bring social disorder and threats. Some of them are extremely dangerous—for example, the Sai Baba movement in India, the Sky Kingdom and Al-Arqam in Malaysia, the Wat Dhammakaya in Thailand, the Providence and Shincheonji Church of Jesus in South Korea, the Jakartas's Eden in Indonesia, and the Aum Shinrikyo in Japan.

Among Chinese in the Mainland, Hong Kong, Taiwan, and diasporas overseas, one of the dangerous cults is Eastern Lightning (also called Church of Almighty God, or Seven Spirits), with a claim of a female Christ already returned. Another, the Cry Cult, believes that one must cry to be cleansed and saved. In 2009, the Chinese government denounced fourteen cults, and twelve of them were in the name of Christianity. There are also some extreme teachings in Asia within the mainline churches that are equally dangerous. In addition, syncretic beliefs are prevalent as the churches are yet to articulate their own theological reflections in the postcolonial context. Their negative impact affects both the body of Christ and the society as a whole.

Like Paul, these false teachers and their doctrines need to be seriously warned against. They cause chaos, confusion, and misunderstanding for both believers and nonbelievers. People are easily lured into these cults or unable to determine which one is the true gospel and true church. Therefore, we should not only warn believers but also separate ourselves from these kinds of people. Paul's warning is a good reminder of the importance of the sound belief of the good news of Jesus Christ, and of raising up leaders who can teach the word, so many can withstand cults, heresies, and foolish teachings today. The Asian reading of Paul's letter grounded in relationships both within and outside of church family is inseparable from the dominant culture of honor and shame in Asia.

Worldviews: Honor and Shame

The cultural value of honor and shame is underlined in Paul's words. He requires elders and bishops of the church to be "blameless" (1:6–7) before the community so they may be respected and honored. The purpose of the instruction to older women is that "the word of God may not be discredited"; this means we should honor the Word (2:5). The fidelity of submissive slaves may be an "ornament" to God, showing a form of honor to God (2:9–10).

In contrast, the opponents of the missionaries will be "put to shame" (ἐντραπῇ, 2:8), and their reputation will be disgraced. The expulsion of the offenders as the strictest way of discrediting the opponents in a community clearly shames them. The family life of a church leader is to be above reproach, and one's character is more important because it is tested with or without public eyes. Polygamy; nonbelieving children; debauchery; being rebellious, arrogant, or quick-tempered; being addicted to wine; being violent or greedy for gain (1:6–7)—all are regarded as shameful behaviors unworthy of one leading a community.

Unlike countries and regions such as North America or Western Europe, the worldview of an honor-shame culture and collectivistic mindset is deeply rooted in 75 percent of the world's population.[31] Biblical scholars have studied this important cultural value in the ancient Near East. Bruce Malina defines honor as "the value of a person in his or her own eyes . . . plus that person's value in the eyes of his or her social group."[32] In contrast, shame reflects the diminishment of self-worth as a result of "failure or inadequacy to reach or live up to a socio-parental goal or ideal."[33]

Confucian tradition also believes that a gentleman "may be killed, but he cannot be dishonoured" (可杀而不可辱也).[34] "He who has no shame is no human" (无羞恶之心, 非人也).[35] The symbol of honor is *face*, which can be called *mianzi* (面子) in terms of one's social worth, or *lian* (脸) in terms of one's moral worth. There are more than fifty references of "loss of *lian*" in Confucian

31 Walter "Bud" Simon, "Honor-Shame Cultural Theory: Antecedents and Origins," *Global Missiology* 1, no. 16 (2018): 1–8.

32 Bruce J. Malina, *The New Testament World: Insights from Cultural Anthropology*, rev. ed. (Louisville: Westminster John Knox, 1993), 31.

33 Lyn M. Bechtel, "Shame as a Sanction of Social Control in Biblical Israel: Judicial, Political, and Social Shaming," *Journal for the Study of the Old Testament* 16, no. 49 (February 1991): 49.

34 Confucius, "Liji, Ruxing," Book of Rites, 8, accessed November 11, 2019, http://ctext.org/liji/ru-xing/ens.

35 Mengzi, "Gongsunchou I," Chinese Text Project, 6, accessed November 12, 2019, https://ctext.org/mengzi/gong-sun-chou-i/ens.

texts,[36] and there are 144 instances of words for *shame*.[37] They believe that domestic shame should not be made public (家丑不可外扬). If things don't function properly, it will cause shame on the entire home, and one will be regarded as a "lost person" (*diuren*, 丢人) or having "lost face" (*diulian*, 丢脸)—"disgraced" without dignity.

The traditional family is the fundamental value in Asian social structure. The chapter "Family" (家人卦) in the *Book of Changes* says, "A kingdom is stable if a home is in order" (正家而天下定矣).[38] How can a home be in order? It is when every family member is performing their function rightly. In such a context, hospitality is a vital practice to welcome guests and show honor toward them so the face of the family or community is preserved.

An Asian reading of the passage would immediately grasp why Paul puts family affairs as the first criteria for the choosing of leaders. The way they conduct themselves within a home bears consequence that brings either honor or shame to them individually and as a community. As Gordon D. Fee asserts, a man's family life speaks volumes of his character and ability to his leadership capacity in the church.[39] Yet leaders are prone to hypocrisy and may live a double life for the sake of "saving face" (*baomianzi*, 保面子). Paul's list for the selection of a leader requires consistency of character every moment of their life. Hospitality is also a vital qualification. Behaviors such as bribery, drunkenness, sectarianism, and consumerism need to be brought into question as cultural norms. Paul's encouragement to the members of the household and his rebukes to the rebels speak loudly that God honors those who honor him and shames those who shame him. Through the life and work of Jesus Christ, God "saves the faces" of those who humbly come to him.

---

36 Jane Geany, "Guarding Moral Boundaries: Shame in Early Confucianism," *Philosophy East and West* 54, no. 2 (2004): 120.

37 J. Li, Q. Wang, and K. W. Fischer, "The Organization of Chinese Shame Concepts," *Cognition and Emotion* 18, no. 6 (2004): 767–97.

38 "Yijing, Jiaren," Book of Changes, 1, accessed October 10, 2019, http://ctext.org/book-of-changes/jia-ren/zh.

39 Gordon D. Fee, *1 and 2 Timothy, Titus*, New International Biblical Commentary, ed. W. Ward Gasque (Peabody, MA: Hendrickson, 1988), 173.

Poetry: Prophetic Insight

As an effective cross-cultural missionary, Paul's evangelistic strategy is to find ways to introduce people to the good news in their heart language. From Homer to Aristotle and Plato, poetry plays a key role in ancient Greek civilization. Clearly, as an educated Jew, Paul knows not only the Jewish Scriptures but also the cultural background of his audiences—in this case, the words of poets and prophets in Greek tradition. Paul is able to find the cultural key that opens their hearts to hear the gospel. Earlier, while walking around the pagan city of Athens, Paul preaches to the people of Athens and refers to the poets they are familiar with: "In him we live and move and have our being" (Acts 17:28), a line that resembled Epimenides's seventh- to sixth-century BCE poem *Cretica*.[40] Now again, Paul offers the words of "their very own prophet" (1:12) and affirms that it is true (v. 13). He recognizes that the Spirit is already working in Cretan culture and speaking through the prophetic critique of their poets about justice, morality, and truthfulness. This allows Paul to go further and warn against the Cretan's cunning and self-serving nature that makes them receptive to a counterfeit gospel (vv. 14–16).

As in Greek culture, poetry has a long historical, cultural, and religious tradition in many Asian countries. Over the centuries, places like Iran, India, and China have been the birthplace of poetry and have given us some of the finest poets who speak truth and beauty not only into their own cultures but also to the rest of the world. The Confucian classic, the "Book of Poetry" (or "Poetry," Shijing, 诗经) is dated from the tenth to the seventh century BCE and includes a total of 305 poems of the Zhou dynasty (1046–256 BCE). The most distinguished early poet, Qu Yuan 屈原 (340–278 BCE), is known for his work "Questions to Heaven" (*Tianwen*, 天问). This poem has been regarded by the Chinese throughout the ages as the most magnificent work of its kind. Today the Bible Museum in Washington, DC, reveals that the most searched keyword in China is "poem" (诗篇). This heart language, or language of the heart, has become a daily embodied expression of life because it has the capacity to trigger imagination, creativity, and emotions.

40 David W. Pao, "Acts," in *The Baker Illustrated Bible Commentary*, ed. Gary M. Burge and Andrew E. Hill (Grand Rapids, MI: Baker, 2012), 1200.

Like Paul, we can affirm the prophetic insight of these poets and go further to either invite our audiences to respond to the gospel as in Acts or warn against the danger of receiving false teaching as in Titus. Missiologists have learned this from Paul and attempt to find connecting points. Throughout Chinese intellectual history, a poet's sacrifice is unavoidable to fulfill the benevolence of the sage—in the form of self-sacrificing death to show faithfulness toward the heavenly righteousness. This prophetic action echoes with Jesus's sacrifice for the whole of humanity. In addition, by using poetry as a cultural lens, conversations can be created to find common language between culture and faith so the gospel can be understood within a given culture. For example, in a dialogue between contemporary Chinese poet Haizi (1964–1989) and Jesus Christ in the Gospel of Luke, some common yet powerful terms are identified: "homelessness," "table fellowship," "brokenness," and "surrender." They become a crucial and rich source of data for an ongoing conversation on a homecoming journey. It also offers how the gospel complements a generation of Chinese soul-searching expressed in Haizi's poetry.[41] This is precisely Paul's open, humble, and loving evangelistic strategy in and through a particular cultural context.

This contextualization is vital because the Asian world is seeking to find expressions of faith in their own culture and language. Indonesians' oral culture gives space for proverbs, songs, or stories to be discussed in their social interaction. Storytelling in the form of poetry or songs is a key to communicating in India. Art forms like *Kathakali* and *Mohiniyattam* incorporate poetry, enactment, and other forms together. Paul's evangelistic strategy affirms the prophetic insight of the poets in the culture of the day, therefore providing a prime example to engage culture intelligently without compromising the gospel message.

CONCLUSION

Drawing from ancient texts of Confucian tradition and contemporary experience in Asia, this chapter has attempted to read Paul and his writing from

41 Xiaoli Yang, *A Dialogue between Haizi's Poetry and the Gospel of Luke—Chinese Homecoming and the Relationship with Jesus Christ*, Theology and Mission in World Christianity 9 (Leiden: Brill, 2018).

Asian perspectives. While anachronism is carefully avoided, an Asian reading of Titus sheds new light without imposing the experiences onto the text. Following some contextual and structural analysis, this chapter has highlighted a few aspects from an Asian lens: Paul's dual relationship with Titus as both a mentor and a father; morality as a grateful response toward the unconditional love of God; layers of relationships with those inside and outside the household of God; the worldview of honor and shame undergirding Paul's instructions; and poetry as a cultural key to unlock the listeners' hearts to the gospel.

Many examples of an Asian reading of Titus can be explored further. For example, an important cultural quality of being hospitable is listed among the criteria for a bishop (1:8), bearing much resemblance to many Asian cultures. Paul's instruction on keeping peace with fellow believers and those in authority also resonates with the Asian idea of *He* (和), which implies "unity and harmony." An Asian Christian theology can be developed here as the text of Titus interacts with Asian tradition, culture, and the sociopolitical reality of today. Paul's pastoral letter to Titus in first-century Crete continues to speak to Asian churches today, showing that the gospel of Jesus Christ is the enduring ground of our common faith and ethical living.

FURTHER READING

Ackerman, D. A. 2016. *1 & 2 Timothy/Titus: A Commentary in the Wesleyan Tradition*. New Beacon Bible Commentary. Kansas City: Beacon Hill.

Cornelius, P. 2015. "Titus." In *South Asia Bible Commentary*, edited by Brian C. Wintle, 1701–1704. Udaipur, India: Open Door.

Fee, G. D. 1988. *1 and 2 Timothy, Titus*. Edited by W. Ward Gasque. New International Biblical Commentary. Peabody, MA: Hendrickson.

Keegan, T. J. 2006. *First and Second Timothy, Titus, Philemon*. The New Collegeville Bible Commentary New Testament. Collegeville, MN: Liturgical.

Kidd, R. M. 2012. "1–2 Timothy and Titus." In *The Baker Illustrated Bible Commentary*, edited by Gary M. Burge and Andrew E. Hill, 1454–1482. Grand Rapids, MI: Baker.

Marshall, I. H., and P. H. Towner. 2004. *A Critical and Exegetical Commentary on the Pastoral Epistles*. The International Critical Commentary. Edinburgh: T&T Clark.

Towner, P. H. 2006. *The Letters to Timothy and Titus*. New International Commentary on the New Testament. Grand Rapids, MI: Eerdmans.

Yang, X. 2018. *A Dialogue between Haizi's Poetry and the Gospel of Luke—Chinese Homecoming and the Relationship with Jesus Christ*. Theology and Mission in World Christianity 9. Leiden: Brill.

Yeo, K. K. 2015. "Chinese Christologies: Images of Christ and Chinese Cultures." In *The Oxford Handbook of Christology*, edited by Francesca Aran Murphy, 393–407. Oxford: Oxford University Press.

SEVENTEEN

The Letter to Philemon

Thawng Ceu Hnin
Hindustan Bible Institute
Chennai, India

Philemon is Paul's shortest letter, having only 25 verses and 335 words in Greek. In the history of NT research, scholars did not lavish much attention to this letter because it does not address the problem of the early church. The letter does not offer Paul's profound theology as we see in Romans, Galatians, and others. Nor does it offer explosive polemics and ethical exhortation as seen in the Corinthian letters, 1 Thessalonians, and Philippians.[1] One major issue Paul addresses in Philemon is slavery. Nevertheless, this was not a new thing for the early Christians because slavery was a common social reality in the Greco-Roman world.[2] Hence this letter suffers neglect from the time of its inception until the nineteenth century. This chapter revisits a precise history of research on Philemon.

1 Demetrius K. Williams, "No Longer as a Slave: Reading the Interpretation History of Paul's Epistle to Philemon," in *Onesimus Our Brother: Reading Religion, Race, and Culture in Philemon*, ed. Matthew V. Johnson, James A. Noel, and Demetrius K. Williams (Minneapolis: Fortress, 2012), 11.

2 Williams, 10.

John Knox's doctoral dissertation entitled *Philemon among the Letters of Paul*, written in 1935 and later revised in 1959, ignited the curiosity of scholars.[3] In his dissertation, Knox argued that Archippus was Onesimus's master and that the letter that we call Philemon today was the letter from Laodicea that Paul mentioned in Colossians 4:16.[4] Knox also insisted that in fact Onesimus was set free from slave bondage so he would assist Paul in his mission. Onesimus then became the bishop of Ephesus who preserved Paul's letter and the framer of a primitive Pauline letter corpus.[5] The subsequent Pauline scholars nonetheless challenged Knox's position. For instance, John G. Nordling, in response to Knox, argues that Onesimus was a fugitive slave.[6]

In recent years, we have witnessed several journals and articles written to explore Philemon.[7] In 1985, in his monograph *Rediscovering Paul: Philemon and the Sociology of Paul's Narrative World*, Norman Petersen contributes numerous insights into the study of Philemon, particularly from Paul's sociological perspective.[8] In 2016, Sung Uk Lim, a South Korean biblical scholar, considered Philemon through the eyes of the marginalized.[9] Using postcolonial reading as his hermeneutical lens, Lim reads Paul's letter to Philemon not from "the central perspective of Paul or Philemon" but from "the marginalized perspective of Onesimus."[10] He argues that most of the Western interpretations have the tendency to ignore the agency of Onesimus and set aside the voice of the marginalized Onesimus. He classifies two lenses:

3 See John Knox, *Philemon among the Letters of Paul: A New View of Its Place and Importance* (Chicago: University of Chicago Press, 1935).

4 Knox, 69.

5 Knox, 103, 107.

6 For John G. Nordling's response to Knox, see his book and article: *Philemon* (Saint Louis: Concordia, 2004), 9–19; Nordling, "Onesimus Fugitivus: A Defense of the Runaway Slave Hypothesis in Philemon," *JSNT* 41 (1991): 97–119.

7 See John M. G. Barclay, "Paul, Philemon and the Dilemma of Christian Slave-Ownership," *NTS* 37 (1991): 161–86; Nordling, "Onesimus Fugitivus," 97–119.

8 See Norman R. Petersen, *Rediscovering Paul: Philemon and the Sociology of Paul's Narrative World* (Philadelphia: Fortress, 1985).

9 Sung Uk Lim, "The Otherness of Onesimus: Re-reading Paul's Letter to Philemon from the Margins," *Theology Today* 73, no. 3 (2016): 215–29.

10 Lim, 215.

"reading for" and "reading with" Onesimus. The "reading for" Onesimus lens pays attention only to the character interplay between Paul and Philemon. Responding to this Western lens, he proposes and uses a lens "reading with" Onesimus, which places the marginalized Onesimus as the protagonist of the show.[11]

Commentators have exegeted Philemon in light of Jewish and Greco-Roman backgrounds.[12] The immense exegetical and theological contributions of the West have laid the foundation for our understanding Philemon in particular and the NT books in general. In addition, Western scholars have penned books that are introductions to the NT.[13] At this juncture, what is the purpose of the current work? The purpose is not to disparage the Western contributions. Rather, this paper is complimentary in nature. In doing so, a question is posed: How can we, as Asians, interpret Philemon in the light of Asian social, religious, and cultural realities? Nevertheless, the paper also concisely discusses authorship, recipient, occasion and purpose, date and place of writing, and several major themes of Philemon through Asian eyes.

INTRODUCING PAUL'S LETTER TO PHILEMON

This section offers the traditional historical critical analyses of Philemon. Accordingly, I precisely discuss some of the most important areas of the letter, such as authorship, recipient, occasion and purpose, place and date of composition, and the structure and outline.

11 Lim, 216–17.

12 J. B. Lightfoot, *Saint Paul's Epistles to the Colossians and to Philemon*, CCGNT (London: Macmillan, 1875); William Hendriksen, *Exposition of Colossians and Philemon*, NTC (Grand Rapids, MI: Baker, 1964); Peter T. O'Brien, *Colossians, Philemon*, Word Biblical Commentary 44 (Dallas: Word, 1982).

13 W. G. Kümmel, *Introduction to the New Testament*, trans. Howard Clark Kee (London: SCM, 1975); Donald Guthrie, *New Testament Introduction* (Downers Grove, IL: Inter-Varsity, 1990); Raymond E. Brown, *An Introduction to the New Testament* (London: Doubleday, 1997).

Authorship

Paul identifies himself as the author of this epistle (Phlm 1). Today, there is no serious challenge on the authenticity of Pauline authorship on Philemon.[14] However, it was F. C. Baur who challenged the historicity of Paul's authorship on Philemon.[15] Marvin Vincent explains that Baur repudiates Philemon as Paul's authentic letter because the content of the letter does not have commonality with the other writings of Paul and that Paul's favorite theme, the "righteousness of God," is missing from the letter.[16] Daniel Wallace comments, "F. C. Baur's extreme Hegelianism as applied to the NT prevented him from seeing Philemon as authentic."[17] For Baur, Philemon was a second-century document written to teach the Christians how to deal with slavery.[18] James D. G. Dunn, however, argues that the style and vocabulary found in the opening and closing (vv. 1–7, 21–25) of Philemon are Pauline.[19] The absence of Paul's major theological themes in Philemon does not validate the inauthenticity of the letter because Paul's letters were occasional in nature and addressed to specific churches. Hence Philemon can be considered as Paul's authentic letter.

Recipient(s)

Philemon is the recipient of the letter (v. 1b). Paul addresses him as "beloved and fellow worker" (v. 1b).[20] In addition, Paul also mentions other addressees: Apphia, who was a female member; Archippus, who was a fellow soldier; and

14 C. F. D. Moule, *The Epistles of Paul the Apostle to the Colossians and to Philemon: An Introduction and Commentary* (Cambridge: Cambridge University Press, 1957), 13.

15 Ferdinand Christian Baur, *Paul, the Apostle of Jesus Christ: His Life and Work, His Epistles and His Doctrine*, trans. Eduard Zeller (Eugene, OR: Wipf & Stock, 1876).

16 Marvin R. Vincent, *A Critical and Exegetical Commentary on the Epistles to the Philippians and to Philemon* (Edinburgh: T&T Clark, 1897), 159.

17 Daniel B. Wallace, "Philemon: Introduction, Argument, and Outline," bible.org, accessed November 4, 2019, https://bible.org/seriespage/18-philemon-introduction-argument-and-outline.

18 F. F. Bruce, *The Epistles to the Colossians, to Philemon, and to the Ephesians*, NICNT (Grand Rapids, MI: Eerdmans, 1959), 191–92.

19 James D. G. Dunn, *The Epistles to the Colossians and to Philemon*, NIGTC (Nashville: Eerdmans, 2014), 298.

20 See Knox, *Philemon*, 70.

the church who were gathering at the house of Philemon (v. 2). Hence this letter is both private and public, intended for a broad audience.[21] Considering Colossians 4:9 and 4:17, Eduard Lohse contends that Philemon and Archippus belong to the community at Colossae.[22] It is suggested that Philemon lived in Colossae.[23] Dunn deduces about Philemon the following: He was well-to-do and had a large house that hosted the Christians (v. 2) and provided a guest room (v. 22); he was a slave owner who owned several slaves; and he was a successful businessman (vv. 17–18). It is also inferable that he was a leader of the church that gathered in his home.[24]

Occasion and Purpose

A plain reading of Philemon discloses the occasion of the letter.[25] Although Paul has the apostolic or the spiritual fatherhood authority to command Philemon (v. 8), he instead appealed him on the basis of love (v. 9). The content of the letter indicates that Onesimus was a slave of Philemon and that he fled from his owner. By the will of God, he happened to meet Paul in a prison. After meeting Paul, Onesimus became a spiritual son of Paul (v. 10). Now that Onesimus has become a believer, Paul wants Philemon to reconsider and accept Onesimus no longer as a δοῦλος (slave) but as a ἀδελφός ἀγαπητός (beloved brother; v. 16). In addition, Paul appeals Philemon to receive Onesimus in the same manner as he would receive Paul (v. 17), and Paul will repay the debts of Onesimus (v. 18).[26]

Several issues remain obscure, however. First, the specific reason for Onesimus's fleeing from his owner remains unknown.[27] The traditional explanation is that Onesimus had stolen certain belongings of his master and then

21 Markus Barth and Helmut Blanke, *The Letter to Philemon: A New Translation with Notes and Commentary*, ECC (Grand Rapids, MI: Eerdmans, 2000), 112.

22 Eduard Lohse, *Colossians and Philemon*, trans. William R. Poehlmann and Robert J. Karris (Philadelphia: Fortress, 1968), 186.

23 Lohse, 186.

24 Dunn, *Epistles to the Colossians*, 301.

25 Douglas J. Moo, *The Letters to the Colossians and to Philemon*, PNTC (Nashville: Eerdmans, 2008), 364.

26 See Richard R. Melick, *Philippians, Colossians, Philemon*, The New American Commentary 32 (Nashville: Holman Reference, 1991), 338–39.

27 Lohse, *Colossians and Philemon*, 187.

absconded (v. 18).[28] Others hold that Onesimus owed Philemon "the value of the work that would have been done in his [Philemon] absence."[29] In other words, there were some works that Onesimus has to do in the absence of his master. Still others suggest that Philemon sent Onesimus to Paul, but he overstayed his time. Hence Paul appeals Philemon to count him responsible rather than Onesimus. Second, no one knows whether Philemon obeys Paul on the matter of receiving back Onesimus.[30] However, we can assume that Philemon did accept Onesimus as appealed by Paul himself. If, in the history, Philemon did not respond positively to Paul's request, then the letter would probably have been destroyed and would not have been included in the biblical canon of the NT.

Place and Date of Composition

Phrases such as "Paul, a prisoner of Christ Jesus" (v. 1), "I, Paul . . . a prisoner of Christ Jesus" (v. 9), "my imprisonment" (v. 10), "my imprisonment for the gospel" (v. 13), "I [Paul] am hoping through your prayers to be restored to you" (v. 22), and "Epaphras, my fellow prisoner in Christ Jesus" (v. 23) specify that Paul was in prison when he wrote this letter. But the question remains, Where was he imprisoned?

In response to this question, scholars have proposed three plausible places: Ephesus (55 or 56 CE), Caesarea[31] (57–59 CE; see Acts 23:23–26:32), and Rome[32] (60–62 CE; see Acts 28:14–21).[33] Geographically, Caesarea and Rome are far away from Colossae. Hence Lohse states, "It is difficult to imagine how a runaway slave would have travelled so far without being detected."[34] Today, the majority of scholars are in favor of the Ephesus hypothesis due to its geographical closeness to Colossae.[35] Verse 22 is used to strengthen

28 O'Brien, *Colossians, Philemon*, 266.

29 Melick, *Philippians, Colossians, Philemon*, 337.

30 Melick, 337.

31 Martin Dibelius and Heinrich Greeven, *An die Kolosser, Epheser, an Philemon*, HNT 12 (Tübingen: J. C. B. Mohr, 1953), 52, 102, cited in Lohse, *Colossians and Philemon*, 188.

32 Lightfoot, *Saint Paul's Epistles*, 310–12.

33 Brown, *Introduction*, 507.

34 Lohse, *Colossians and Philemon*, 188.

35 Dunn, *Epistles to the Colossians*, 307.

this hypothesis that Philemon makes ready a guest room for Paul.[36] Thus it is possible and more convincing to locate Ephesus as the place where Paul wrote this letter and met the runaway slave Onesimus.

The dating of the letter is based upon the place of composition. The Rome hypothesis dates the epistle at 61 CE,[37] the Ephesus hypothesis dates it at 55 CE,[38] and the Caesarean hypothesis dates it at 58 CE.[39] Although there are three possible dates, the mid-fifties seems to be more probable because the letter probably would have been composed at the city of Ephesus.

The Structure of Philemon

Mirror reading of Philemon reflects something about its structure. The first three verses contain the names of five people: Paul, Timothy, Philemon, Apphia, and Archippus. The last three verses also have the names of five people: Epaphras, Mark, Aristarchus, Demas, and Luke. The second significant structure we can observe is that the first five names are followed by the phrase "the grace . . . from the Lord Jesus Christ" (v. 3). A similar construction is found in verse 25: "the grace of the Lord Jesus Christ." Paul's greeting ends with "the Lord Jesus Christ," and he also concludes the letter with "the Lord Jesus Christ." Here, it is plausible that Paul is utilizing a literary device called *inclusio* to plea on behalf of Onesimus.

Outline of Philemon

Epistolary Greeting (vv. 1–3)

Thanksgiving and Intercession (vv. 4–7)

Love as a Means for Appealing (vv. 8–9)

Paul's Plea for Onesimus (vv. 10–20)

36 D. A. Carson and Douglas J. Moo, *An Introduction to the New Testament* (Grand Rapids, MI: Zondervan, 2009), 593.

37 O'Brien, *Colossians, Philemon*, 269.

38 Lohse, *Colossians and Philemon*, 188.

39 Melick, *Philippians, Colossians, Philemon*, 337.

Additional Remarks (vv. 21–23)

Doxological Greeting (v. 25)

MAJOR THEMES OF PHILEMON: AN ASIAN APPROACH

Several vital themes of Philemon signal a remarkable commonality with Asian cultures and worldviews. Here the selected themes are honor and shame, slavery, brotherhood, and friendship.

Honor and Shame

People of the first-century Mediterranean world valued one another in terms of social basis such as "gender-based roles" and the particular groups to which a person is socially rooted. They were always mindful about "public awards of respect and honor."[40] Unlike the West, whose culture is classified as an innocence-and-guilt culture, the first-century world was classified as an honor-and-shame culture. Whether gentile or Jew, regardless of one's ethnicity, a person from childhood was trained and taught to hunt honor and evade shame and disgrace.[41] Their social stratification was built upon "the foundational social values of honor and dishonor."[42] Honor is a social status awarded on the basis of the individual's capability to maintain the social virtues and attributes that their society values.[43] In the Roman world, a wealthy person receives public honor.[44] The poor are the "shabby people," as Tacitus calls them (*Histories* 1.4). In the social order of the first-century world, everyone knew their place.[45]

The Asian culture resembles the honor-and-shame culture of the Ancient Mediterranean world. While the West embraces the spirit of individualism,

40 Bruce J. Malina, *The Social World of Jesus and the Gospels* (London: Routledge, 1996), 35.

41 D. A. deSilva, "Honor and Shame," in *Dictionary of New Testament Background*, ed. Stanley E. Porter and Craig A. Evans (Downers Grove, IL: InterVarsity, 2000), 518.

42 David A. deSilva, *Honor, Patronage, Kinship and Purity: Unlocking New Testament Culture* (Downers Grove, IL: IVP Academic, 2000), 23.

43 deSilva, "Honor and Shame," 519.

44 James S. Jeffers, *The Greco-Roman World of the New Testament Era: Exploring the Background of Early Christianity* (Downers Grove, IL: IVP Academic, 1999), 188.

45 Jeffers, 180.

to the headship of their owners.[57] Orlando Patterson defines slavery as "social death."[58] J. A. Harrill defines social death as "denying a person all dignity . . . and ties of birth in both ascending and descending generations."[59] Slaves were also considered as "property . . . capable of being bought and sold by private owners."[60] They were also "deracinated outsiders."[61] In the Greco-Roman world, as William Warwick Buckland writes, "Captives, it is said, may be slain: to make them slaves is to save their lives."[62] Slavery was part of not only the Romans and the Greeks but also the "nomadic groups." The ancient nomadic groups had slaves.[63] Hence slaves were marked as living tools, social death, and properties.[64]

In ancient India, slavery was well established since the birth of the Common Era.[65] In ancient Indian texts, the term *dasa* is used to refer to a slave. Apparently, the term is derived from the word *das*, which means "to finish" or "to terminate something."[66] However, during the Rig Vedic era, the term *dasa* was used to refer to different people groups apart from the Aryas. By the later Vedic period, the Sanskrit *dasa* was used to mean "slave."[67] In *Arthashastra* (3.13, 14), Kautilya uses different expressions: *dasa* (a slave), *dasatava* (the

57 S. S. Bartchy, "Slaves and Slavery in the Roman World," in *The World of the New Testament: Cultural, Social, and Historical Contexts*, ed. Joel B. Green and Lee Martin McDonald (Grand Rapids, MI: Baker, 2013), 169.

58 O. Patterson, *Slavery and Social Death: A Comparative Study* (Cambridge, MA: Harvard University Press, 1982), 27.

59 J. A. Harrill, "Slavery," in *DNTB*, ed. Stanley E. Porter and Craig A. Evans (Downers Grove, IL: InterVarsity, 2000), 1124.

60 J. Albert Harrill, "Paul and Slavery," in *Paul in the Greco-Roman World*, ed. J. Paul Sampley (London: Bloomsbury, 2017), 2:303.

61 Jeremy Punt, *Postcolonial Biblical Interpretation: Reframing Paul* (Leiden: Brill, 2015), 160.

62 William Warwick Buckland, *The Roman Law of Slavery: The Condition of the Slave in Private Law from Augustus to Justinian* (Cambridge: Cambridge University Press, 1970), 1.

63 Daniel C. Snell, "Slavery in the Ancient Near East," in *The Cambridge World History of Slavery*, ed. Keith Bradley and Paul Cartledge (Cambridge: Cambridge University Press, 2011), 1:4.

64 See Bartchy, "Slaves and Slavery," 169–78.

65 Scott C. Levi, "Hindus beyond the Hindu Kush: Indians in the Central Asian Slave Trade," *JRAS*, 3rd ser., 12, no. 3 (2002): 277–88.

66 Dev R. Chanana, "Slavery in Ancient India: As Depicted in Pāli and Sanskrit Texts," in *Subordinate and Marginal Groups in Early India*, ed. Aloka Parasher-Sen (Oxford: Oxford University Press, 2004), 27.

67 Upinder Singh, *A History of Ancient and Early Medieval India: From the Stone Age to the 12th Century* (Chennai: Pearson, 2009), 321.

concept of slavery), *dasabhava* (the state of being a slave), and *dasakalpa* (the rules regarding slavery). The *Narada Smriti* (5.26) states that a slave can be pledged or mortgaged. It also talks about the freeing of slaves. Accordingly, a slave could be freed only when the master willed to release. On the manumission of a slave, the master removes "a jar of water from the shoulder of the slave and break[s] it." He sprinkles some parched grain and flowers over his head and utters thrice, "You are no longer a *dasa*."[68]

As slaves in the Greco-Roman world were considered property, ancient Indian slaves were also categorized as some form of object.[69] Three types of slaves existed during this era: *kara-mara-anito* (slaves brought from foreign countries), *antojatako* (children of female slaves), and *dhankito* (bought slaves).[70] In addition, there are subtypes of slaves: *dhvajahrita* (prisoners of war), *dayagat* (inherited slaves), *labadha* (gifted slaves), *atmavikraya* (those who sold themselves as slaves), *ahitaka* (mortgaged slaves), and *danda-pranita* (criminals whose punishment for their crime was to serve as a slave).[71] They are prohibited from running away from the household of the master. If they flee, they will lose their right to redemption (*Arthashastra* 3.13.6).

In ancient Buddhism, there is no absolute Buddhist source, scripture, or document that plausibly supports the institution and the practice of slavery.[72] However, in the later period, both male and female slaves were mentioned and were considered "gifts." The institutional monastic ownership of slaves was practiced in Sri Lanka, Cambodia, Myanmar (aka Burma), Thailand, Korea, China, and Japan. The individual monks privately owned slaves. For instance, in the Koryo period of Korea (918–1392 CE), the Buddhist monastic institution was one of the major slaveholders on the Korean peninsula.[73]

From the Greco-Roman context, the fugitive slave Onesimus can be classified as a living tool, a social death, and a property of Philemon that can be

68 Singh, 812.

69 Singh, 204.

70 Chanana, "Slavery in Ancient India," 97–98.

71 Aditi Trivedi, "Slavery in Ancient India: Vedic Times to Gupta Period," academia.edu, accessed November 12, 2019, https://xdocs.net/preview/slavery-in-ancient-india-aditi-trivedi-5c74494f17b4e.

72 Jonathan A. Silk, "Slavery," in *Encyclopedia of Buddhism*, ed. Robert E. Buswell Jr. (New York: Thomson, 2004), 780.

73 Silk, 780.

bought and sold. The text is silent about how Onesimus became Philemon's slave. Ostensibly, we can assume that Onesimus was a bought slave, because Philemon 22 indicates that Philemon was a wealthy Christian possessing an inn to host the itinerants.

From the Asian (Indian) context, one may perceive Onesimus as *dasa* in general and *dhankito* in particular. Onesimus can be classified as *dhankito*, meaning a bought slave. Onesimus the *dhankito* is both a property that can be bought and sold and a gift that can be presented to others. Socially, Onesimus the *dhankito* has no status and is dead, religiously deserted, and politically voiceless; economically, he lives at the spoon of the master. In his letter to Philemon, Paul appeals Philemon to accept him no more as *dhankito* but as ἀδελφός ἀγαπητός (beloved brother; v. 16). In appealing Philemon, Paul does not command him. Rather, Paul uses ἀγάπη (love) as a means for appealing (v. 9). Considered that Philemon acted as Paul appealed, the social status of Onesimus is reversed from the state of private property to a human being. The reversed social status of Onesimus from a *dhankito* to a member of the body of Christ signposts to the theological reality that in Christ, there is no social pyramid that stratifies human beings. It is a divine call to become humane.

Brotherhood

After his conversion (v. 10), the social status of Onesimus shifts from δοῦλος to a spiritual τέκνον (child) of Paul, from ἄχρηστος (useless) to εὔχρηστος (useful; v. 11), and from δοῦλος to ἀδελφός ἀγαπητός (v. 16). In Philemon, Christian brotherhood is a pivotal theme embedded with social status transformation of the fugitive slave Onesimus.

Brotherhood is something exceedingly celebrated in the Asian cultural milieu. The concept of Christian brotherhood reverberates in the "We World." In Islam, the word *brotherhood* denotes a "faith-based community that includes both men and women as brothers and sisters."[74] Surat al-Hujurat 49:10 says, "The believers are but brothers, so make reconciliation between your brothers and fear Allah that you may receive mercy." It is also written in Surat Ali Imran 3:103: "Hold firmly to the rope of Allah all together and do not become divided. Remember the favor of Allah upon you, when you

74 Qamar Islam Khan, "The Concept of Brotherhood in Islam," qamarislamkhan.com, accessed November 13, 2019, http://qamarislamkhan.com/concept-of-brotherhood-in-islam/.

were enemies and He brought your hearts together and you became brothers by his favor." Believers are to consider and address one another as "brothers." Brotherhood in Islam is based upon a pleasing personality with others, treating others the way one wants to be treated, and the treasuring of common values.[75] In Islamic brotherhood, oppression, forsaking, and despising are extremely prohibited.[76] Hence brotherhood on the basis of faith is indispensable. Every believer (i.e., brother/sister) experiences justice and equality. In the eyes of Allah, there is no social status pyramid. These aspects lie at the heart of the Asian morality.

In the teaching of Buddha, the brotherhood concept is meticulously associated with renunciation. When a person is converted to Buddhism, they become a renunciant. It requires them to willingly give up familial relationships, social relationships, and all dependence upon wealth.[77] Renunciants are to strictly follow the four rules: the wearing of old and cast-off garments, survival through alms begging, homelessness (their home is where night finds them, as under a tree or on a rock), and the use of special medicine made from cattle urine.[78]

In light of the aforementioned background, there are similarities between biblical brotherhood and the Asian religious brotherhood. The social status of Onesimus from a slave to a beloved brother after his conversion resonates with the Islamic understanding of brotherhood. As a non-Muslim becomes a brother when he believes in Allah, Onesimus becomes a Christian beloved brother when he believes in the Lord Jesus Christ. The "then" of Onesimus was useless. The "now" of Onesimus is useful. He shares the common values, experiences justice and equality, and gains his rights as a human.

From the Buddhist religious window, Onesimus is summoned to the path of renunciation, and he then becomes a renunciant. Forsaking one's rights for the benefit of others is a Christ-centered act, and this act is expected of him. Buddha's teaching of renunciation echoes Jesus's teaching to some extent. In conversing

75 Qamar Islam Khan.

76 Ruth Starkman, "The Concept of Brotherhood: Beyond Arendt and the Muslim Brotherhood," *Critical Review of International Social and Political Philosophy* 16 (2013): 595–613.

77 Bukkyo Dendo Kyokai, *Teaching of Buddha* (Tokyo: Kosaido, 2005), 194.

78 Kyokai, 195. Also see Vitthal V. Parab, "A Search for Universal Love and Brotherhood in Rabindranath Tagore's 'Gitanjali,'" *International Journal of Applied Research* 1, no. 9 (2015): 266–69.

with his disciples, Jesus teaches that self-denial and taking up one's cross are inevitable prerequisites of a disciple (Matt 16:24; Luke 9:23). Without taking up one's own cross, a person cannot become a disciple of Jesus (Luke 14:27). Although Paul does not explicitly mention the notions of self-denial and carrying one's own cross, these nonnegotiable prerequisites are implicitly entrenched in the text. In the eyes of Paul, Onesimus's headship shifts from Philemon to Christ.

Friendship

Being a collectivist culture, Asians value friendship to its highest level. Asian religions teach the significance of having a good friend and avoiding an evil friend. Confucianism teaches six kinds of friendship: friendship with those who flatter, those who are meek, those who compromised the truth, those who are upright, those who are truthful, and those who are well formed.[79] The first three are considered harmful friendship, and the second three are considered beneficial friendship. Rig Veda talks about friendship terms such as *mitra sakha* (those who eat together) and *suhra* (good or kindhearted).[80] These expressions denote intimate friendship. Cicero calls a friend (*amicus*) a "divine gift" (*De amicitia* 6.20), and the classical Indian literature also defines *mitra* (friend) as a "divine gift" (*Hitopaeśa* 1.210).[81]

Buddhism teaches three types of friends: *Kalyana Mitta* (the good friend), *Papa Mitta* (the evil friend), and *Mitta Patirupaka* (a foe in the guise of friend).[82] *Kalyana Mitta* is a friend with sympathy and audacity, and they speak the truth even if it is hurtful for their friend. They are ideal friends. In the *Sigalovàda Sutta*, Buddha listed the virtues of a good friend. The list includes giving more than what one asks, reassuring when one is frightened, being constant through good and bad times, rejoicing in one's success, looking after one another, keeping the other from evil doing, encouraging the other to do good, and keeping secret as secret.[83] *Papa Mitta* is a friend who encourages the weakness of their friend. *Mitta Patirupaka* is a type of friend

79 Lay Nwe, "The Concept of Friendship in Theravada Buddhist Thought," *JMAAS* 11, no. 9 (2013): 1–9.

80 Minoru Hara, "The Hindu Concept of Friendship," *RDSO* 75, Fasc. 1/4 (2001): 157–87.

81 See John T. Fitzgerald, ed., *Greco-Roman Perspectives on Friendship* (Atlanta: Scholars, 1997).

82 Sita Arunthavanathan, "Buddhist Concept of Friendship," maithri.com, accessed January 10, 2021, https://www.maithri.com/links/articles/buddhist-concept-of-friendship/.

83 Nwe, "Concept of Friendship," 4.

who only takes from others, renders lip service, flatters, and leads his friend to the demise of his wealth.[84]

In light of the previous discussion, we can recognize Philemon as Paul's *kalyana mitta* or *mitra*. The absence of the term φίλος in Philemon does not dismiss the presence of the idea of friendship. Instead of φίλος, Paul addresses Philemon as κοινωνός (partner), "companion," or "sharer" (v. 17) and as ἀδελφός (v. 20). Κοινωνός means "fellow" or "participant" and carries the idea of fellowship or sharing with someone or in something.[85] Conceptually, κοινωνός is related to φίλος and συνεργός (fellow-worker). This implies "sharing of a common enterprise."[86] Κοινωνός particularly expresses an "inner relationship."[87] This suggests that Philemon has been Paul's mission partner in carrying out the good news. Friends benefit each other. Through his partnership and friendship with Philemon, Paul let Onesimus benefit.

The letter does not give Philemon's response to Paul's appeal. Nonetheless, if Philemon was Paul's *kalyana mitta* or *mitra*, he would positively respond to Paul's request. As Buddha enumerates "giving more than what is asked" as a virtue of *kalyana mitta*, there is no doubt Philemon would do even beyond Paul's petition on behalf of Onesimus. As good friends, Paul always thanks God on behalf of Philemon (v. 4), and he rejoices in Philemon's unceasing love and unshaken faith (vv. 5–7). Here Paul's act of rejoicing in the success of Philemon is a virtue of *kalyana mitta* as listed by Buddha. In the light of Confucianism, Philemon's act of loving the saints and believers and his unfading faith in the Lord Jesus signpost uprightness, truthfulness, and faithfulness, which are also virtues of an ideal friend.

CONCLUSION

While the Western scholarship has enormously reconnoitered Philemon through historical critical methods and the traditional exegesis, the letter concomitantly has its commonalities with Asian realities. In the narrative framework

84 Nwe, 3.
85 Hauck, "κοινωνός," *TDNT* 3:797–98.
86 Hauck, 3:797.
87 Hauck, 3:797.

of Philemon, though Onesimus is a minor character, he plays a significant role. The themes of honor and shame, slavery, brotherhood, and friendship are significantly common to the Asian religious literatures (Hinduism, Buddhism, Confucianism, and the like). To sum up, Paul's letter to Philemon provides a way through which we can relate to people from the Christian faith and other religious faiths. Philemon, as a letter, calls for the restoration of the shamed Onesimus from shame to honor, from slavery to brotherhood, from a slave to a friend, and from uselessness to usefulness. We as Asians should embrace the messages of deserting one's rights for the good of others, considering fellow Christians as brothers and sisters in Christ regardless of color, race, clan, and denomination; maintaining egalitarianism; placing God above our culture; letting God transform our cultural practices that are antibiblical; and hunting for the message of reconciliation amid hostility. Thus Philemon as a letter establishes the equality of every individual in the family of God.

FURTHER READING

Barth, M., and H. Blanke. 2000. *The Letter to Philemon: A New Translation with Notes and Commentary*. ECC. Grand Rapids, MI: Eerdmans.

Dunn, J. D. G. 1996. *The Epistles to the Colossians and to Philemon: A Commentary on the Greek Text*. NIGTC. Grand Rapids, MI: Eerdmans.

Glancy, J. A. 2002. *Slavery in Early Christianity*. Oxford: Oxford University Press.

Harrill, J. A. 2017. "Paul and Slavery." In *Paul in the Greco-Roman World*, edited by J. Paul Sampley, 2:301–345. London: Bloomsbury.

Kreitzer, J. J. 2008. *Philemon*. Sheffield, UK: Sheffield Phoenix.

Kyokai, B. D. 2005. *Teaching of Buddha*. Tokyo: Kosaido.

Levi, S. C. 2002. "Hindus beyond the Hindu Kush: Indians in the Central Asian Slave Trade." *JRAS*, 3rd ser., 12, no. 3: 277–288.

Lim, S. U. 2016. "The Otherness of Onesimus: Re-reading Paul's Letter to Philemon from the Margins." *Theology Today* 73, no. 3: 215–229.

Moo, D. J. 2008. *The Letters to the Colossians and to Philemon*. PNTC. Grand Rapids, MI: Eerdmans.

Nordling, J. G. 2004. *Philemon*. Saint Louis: Concordia.

Petersen, N. R. 1985. *Rediscovering Paul: Philemon and the Sociology of Paul's Narrative World*. Philadelphia: Fortress.

EIGHTEEN

The Letter to the Hebrews

Gilbert Soo Hoo
Singapore Bible College
Singapore

Many commentaries on the Letter to the Hebrews covering basic introductory matters have been written.[1] This introductory chapter will not repeat what has been covered but will instead move in a different direction. Anticipating an Asian readership, this chapter will deal specifically with Asian realities that find expression in the text in more detail.

Seven Asian realities, to be enumerated later, emerge from reading Hebrews and invite Asian readers to see personal relevance and applicability in the text. The concerns, interests, and challenges that characterize their life situations take center stage. They no longer need to feel marginalized; rather, they can regard the letter to have been addressed specifically to them. In that sense, Hebrews is an Asian text. To facilitate the reading experience, a suggested Asian hermeneutics is presented that incorporates a number of recent reading strategies: the yin-yang principle, diasporic hermeneutics, and metaphorical reading.

1 See Thomas R. Schreiner, *Commentary on Hebrews*, Biblical Theology for Christian Proclamation (Nashville: B&H, 2015); Paul Ellingworth, *The Epistle to the Hebrews*, NIGTC (Grand Rapids, MI: Eerdmans, 2015).

Unlike most of the other NT letters, Hebrews lacks the usual greeting that identifies the author and readers and that sometimes previews themes developed later in the body of the text. In the early church, some leading scholars claimed Paul as the author, especially in the Eastern church, but others, particularly in the Western church, doubted Pauline authorship. Yet there was near universal acknowledgment of the letter's authority and place in the canon.

Readership

Because the author does not name his readers, their historical identity remains shrouded in mystery. In spite of the numerous OT references and their inclusion in the argument of Hebrews, one cannot automatically assume that the readers were Jewish because gentile believers also would have been quite familiar with the Jewish Scriptures. The significant use of the OT in Romans and the Corinthian correspondence, for example, demonstrates that gentile converts were quite at home with Jewish history and teachings.

Evidence of closeness between the author and his readers suggests a familial relationship. Like a father whose voice invokes instant recognition, the author finds no need for greeting or salutation. He plunges directly into the subject. He is authoritative and gives strong warning against the consequences of apostasy in the manner of an Asian parent scolding his children.

Date of Composition

Without the identity of the author and the readers to provide clues as to the time of the letter, one can situate it broadly between the time of Christ's death and the letter's reference by 1 Clement, which is traditionally dated toward the end of the first century. The letter's silence about the temple's destruction in 70 CE does not necessarily imply that it should predate that event. The author's use of the Levitical priesthood and references to the tabernacle serve to advance his discussion about Christ's priesthood whether or not the actual temple continued to stand.

Likely, both the author and his readers were second-generation Christians without a firsthand encounter with the Lord (Heb 2:3). The readers had sufficient time to mature and become teachers (Heb 5:12). Therefore, a possible date in the second half of the first century seems as reasonable a conjecture as any other.

Genre

Hebrews conveys a loving communiqué from an authoritarian father to his children. The formality of expression creates a sense of distance—what sociologists call a power distance. This characteristic typifies how Asian fathers relate primarily through teaching and admonition. They have their children's best interests in mind and so set high expectations to which they should aspire. No sentimentality dilutes the letter's forceful exhortations and warnings. Deeply concerned that his children have slackened in their spiritual progress, the father shames them (Heb 5:11–14), exhorts them to get back on track (Heb 6:1–3), and offers encouragement (Heb 6:9–12). The motif of honor and shame permeates this Asian letter describing the family dynamic. No opportunity is given for rebuttal; the father has the final say.

The orality of Hebrews emerges through a number of features. First, the use of the first-person plural pronoun *we* shows the author identifying with his readers (e.g., Heb 2:1; 3:6; 4:2, 14; 8:1; 10:19, 21; 12:1). Second, the author employs verbs like *speak*, *say*, and *heard* (e.g., Heb 2:1–3; 3:7; 5:11; 6:9; 8:1; 12:25). Third, the repeated refrain of exhortation and warning throughout pictures the father who alternately urges and scolds his children.

Outline

The flow of thought in Hebrews traces the development of the familiar Asian honor-and-shame motif. It is outlined below:

God honors Jesus as the Son (1:1–3:6)

Stern warning: beware of the shame of a sinful, unbelieving heart (3:7–4:16)

God honors Jesus by appointing him high priest (5:1–10)

Stern rebuke: shame on you for being spiritual slackers (5:11–6:12)

As glorious high priest, Jesus is more effective than Levitical priests (6:13–10:25)

Stern warning: eternal shame for rejecting God's truth and Son (10:26–31)

Exhortation to persevere in order to receive the glorious promise (10:32–12:13)

Stern warning: beware of the shame of facing God's judgment (12:14–29)

Exhortation to remain faithful to earthly responsibilities (13:1–25)

POINTS OF CONTACT WITH ASIAN REALITIES

A sensitive reading of Hebrews brings to the surface points of contact with the realities we readers situated in Asia face on a daily basis. With such an approach, we affirm that this letter speaks yet again to our time and social location, as it has to previous generations of readers. Specifically, seven Asian realities emerge, each of which I will discuss briefly in turn.

Asian Reality One: Pilgrimage

Four categories of pilgrims populate the Letter to the Hebrews. One, the letter portrays Jesus on a cosmic journey starting with the incarnation (Heb 2:6–17), then moving to the cross before returning to heaven at the right hand of God's throne (Heb 1:3; 12:2). He has entered the holy place (Heb 6:19–20; 8:1–2; 9:11–14, 24–26), passing through heaven (Heb 4:14) to Mount Zion (Heb 12:22–24). Later, he will appear a second time on earth (Heb 9:28). Two, the letter provides a number of OT exemplars of faith, all of whom were on a pilgrimage (Heb 11:8–40). Three, the writer of Hebrews warns his readers about the unbelief of the wilderness generation as they journeyed to the promised land (Heb 3:7–11, 16–19). Four, the readers of Hebrews run "the race of life" (Heb 12:1, 13), with their ultimate destiny being the inner sanctuary (Heb 6:19–20; 10:19–22) in the heavenly Jerusalem (Heb 12:22–24). In the meantime, they ought to go outside the camp in bearing the reproach Jesus bore (Heb 13:13). Their hope lies in the promise of entering God's rest (Heb 3:12–15; 4:1–11), the holy place (Heb 10:19–22).

The pilgrimages covered by Hebrews find their modern analogy in migration. Migration transcends the boundaries of Asia to become a global phenomenon.[2] Normally, however, migration studies deal with significant numbers of people from a given country of origin or ethnicity going to another country because of work or study or as refugees. In recent years, many women participate in marriage migration.[3] The people movement in Hebrews differs from the categories of migration today, but I believe a number of similarities warrant comparison to provide perspective on the pilgrimages in Hebrews. A closer analogy, however, can be found in the religious pilgrimages of, for example, devout Hindus and Muslims, in which the outward and inward aspects of the journey coalesce—going to a sacred site and at the same time experiencing an inner spiritual transformation.[4] Similarly, Buddhists must renounce worldly desires to maximize the benefits of pilgrimages.[5]

Pilgrimage can mean a journey covering significant distances, leaving the familiar to enter the unfamiliar, whether it be culturally, linguistically, ethnically, or even morally. The distance between heaven and earth marks an unbridgeable divide only Jesus could traverse. He was made lower than angels (Heb 2:9) and faced temptation, yet he was without sin (Heb 4:15). While struggling, Jesus petitioned with loud cries and tears "in the days of his flesh" (Heb 5:7).

Abraham left his home country to travel to a foreign land about which he knew nothing (Heb 11:8–10). He and Sarah acknowledged their status as strangers (Heb 11:13). Undoubtedly, the local inhabitants regarded them as such, and the social distance between them proved too much to bridge. Insightfully, Hebrews penetrates into their perspective to comment that this couple saw no earthly place as home because their true home was heaven, where God has prepared for them a city (Heb 11:14–16). Ancient Buddhist monks traveled on

2 Stephen Castles, Hein de Haas, and Mark J. Miller, *The Age of Migration: International Population Movements in the Modern Word*, 5th ed. (New York: Guilford, 2014), 147–70.

3 Castles, de Haas, and Miller, 154–55.

4 See Rana P. B. Singh, "Pilgrimage in Hinduism: Historical Context and Modern Perspectives," in *Tourism, Religion, and Spiritual Journeys*, ed. Dallen J. Timothy and Daniel H. Olsen (London: Routledge-Taylor, 2006), 220–36; Nadia Caidi, "Pilgrimage to Hajj: An Information Journey," *International Journal on Information* 3, no. 1 (2019): 44–76.

5 Chan Khoon San, *Buddhist Pilgrimage* (Selangor Darul Ehsan: Subang Jaya Buddhist Association, 2001), 10–19, 67–130.

foot as Abraham did, going through great distances and inhospitable lands, with some dying on the way.[6]

Long-term missionaries experience something similar.[7] After a while on the foreign field, their former home no longer feels like home as before. The field has become more like a home, yet it is not home because the locals see them as foreigners. The duration of work migration depends on the employment contract. The host country does not want foreign workers to become a social liability or to change the native culture should the contract end and they stay.[8] Similarly, once Jesus completes his mission objective, he immediately returns to heaven to begin the new phase of his intercessory ministry as high priest.

Whereas the sojourners of Hebrews measure their journey within a single lifespan, Hindu or Buddhist sojourners may require an innumerable amount of cycles (samsara) before achieving Nirvana.[9] The latter's fate depends on karma, not faith, as in Hebrews. A superficial resemblance between the Hindu pursuit of union with Brahma and Christians entering the inner sanctuary (Heb 6:19–20; 10:19–22) suggests commonality, but Christians retain individuality in eternity. In today's context, companies and host countries see the economic necessity of foreign workers to satisfy labor requirements. Hebrews argues for the need to replace an ineffective covenant with a new covenant (Heb 8:7–13). Jesus's sacrifice proves more effective (Heb 9:11–14, 25–26; 10:1–18). Thus Hebrews depicts the redemptive necessity of Jesus's journey to earth (Heb 10:7). As for the OT saints, the writer infers their wanderings showcase persevering faith (Heb 11:39).

Pilgrims must possess qualifications before embarking on their journey. Recently, a large number of highly skilled professionals moved overseas within Asia.[10] India, Japan, Taiwan, Singapore, South Korea, and Malaysia

6 Chan, 17–18.

7 Karl Dahlfred, "Why Missionaries Can Never Go Home Again," dahlfred.com, accessed April 26, 2019, https://www.dahlfred.com/index.php/blogs/gleanings-from-the-field/747-why-missionaries-can-never-go-home-again.

8 Castles, de Haas, and Miller, *Age of Migration*, 156.

9 G. B. Nandan and Nasir Ahmed M. Jangubhai, "The Comparative Study between Hinduism and Buddhism," *International Journal of Humanities and Social Science Invention* 2, no. 5 (2013): 27–31.

10 Castles, de Haas, and Miller, *Age of Migration*, 162.

seek overseas professionals. Technical experts and executives get posted by multinational companies. Hebrews provides a parallel in Jesus, who comes to earth with a unique set of qualifications. He is "holy, innocent, unstained, separated from sinners, exalted above the heavens" (Heb 7:26) and "made perfect forever" (Heb 7:28). He "continues forever" (Heb 7:24) and so can "save completely" (Heb 7:25). He is God's Son, the "appointed heir of all things" (Heb 1:2b), and "faithful over God's house as a son" (Heb 3:6). The requisite qualification for OT pilgrims is faith (Heb 11:1–39), the same as for the readers (Heb 4:1–11).

Asian Reality Two: Perseverance

A characteristic of Asians is perseverance. One Hong Kong–based researcher credits the Asian social and cultural context for students' superior performance in math over those in the West.[11] In particular, the Confucian countries of China, Japan, Korea, and Singapore value education and hard work. Doing well in math has less to do with native intellect and is more dependent on determination and sheer effort. Parents push their children to do well and are not satisfied with mediocre results. Asian students are driven and push themselves. This relatively small aspect of the culture can be seen in other areas as well. The virtues of perseverance, personal industry, and not giving up characterize many Asians.

A story entailing unflinching determination centers on Malala Yousafzai, a girls education advocate, and young Asian girls like her who refuse the traditional roles assigned to their gender in order to pursue a vastly different future through education.[12] Of course, not all Asians persevere toward their dreams, but enough of them do to suggest that Asian readers may resonate with Hebrews and its major theme of persevering faith.

Key passages throughout the letter confirm the overarching theme and exhortation of Hebrews to center on persevering faith.[13] Hebrews 10:36–39

11 Linda Yeung, "Asian Students' Superiority at Maths Due to Confucian Focus on Hard Work," *South China Morning Post*, accessed April 29, 2019, https://tinyurl.com/3emv942z.

12 Room to Read, "In Honor of Malala Day: The Power of Perseverance," Room to Read, accessed April 30, 2019, https://www.roomtoread.org/the-latest/in-honor-of-malala-day-the-power-of-perseverance.

13 For a full list, see Gilbert Soo Hoo, "Our Sabbath-Rest in the Lord According to the Psalms," *Helix* (February 7, 2019): 9–10.

presents one of the most sweeping exhortations: "You have need of perseverance in order that, after doing the will of God, you may receive the promise. For yet a little while longer, the one who is coming will come and not delay. And my righteous one should live by faith but, if he should shrink back, my soul would not be pleased with him. But we are not of timidity that leads to destruction but of faith that leads to the preservation of the soul." This exhortation follows immediately after the writer recalling his readers' past joyfulness in enduring reproach and affliction and being victimized (Heb 10:32–34). Then he urges them to continue steadfast in the midst of trials (Heb 10:35–39).

The eschatological "one who is coming will come and not delay" (Heb 10:37) anticipates the return of Christ (Heb 9:28). The idea of eagerly waiting for Christ to return connects Hebrews 9:28 with Hebrews 10:37. Clearly, readers must prepare to weather any challenge until Christ comes—the *terminus ad quem*. Given all the OT examples of perseverance in Hebrews 11, readers must cling to the promises even if death precedes fulfillment.[14] Because of their practice of asceticism (complete fasting, severely restricted diet, mortification of the flesh), Jains may be able to empathize with the call to persevere through trials and afflictions.[15] However, their goals differ from those presented in Hebrews in that they strive to achieve liberation from karma.[16] They also actively seek self-deprivation, whereas the suffering of Christians is not self-inflicted.

Asian Reality Three: Parental Discipline

Parental discipline describes another Asian reality or virtue.[17] Traditionally, discipline rests primarily with the father, who is often seen as stern and

14 See Roger Nicole, "Some Comments on Hebrews 6:4–6 and the Doctrine of the Perseverance of God with the Saints," in *Current Issues in Biblical and Patristic Interpretation: Studies in Honor of Merrill C. Tenney Presented by His Former Students*, ed. Gerald F. Hawthorne (Grand Rapids, MI: Eerdmans, 1975), 355–64.

15 John E. Cort, "Singing the Glory of Asceticism: Devotion of Asceticism in Jainism," *Journal of the American Academy of Religion* 70, no. 4 (2002): 719–42.

16 Cort, 736.

17 Edwin Gembul, "The Difference between an Asian Parent and a Western One," Asian Parent, accessed May 1, 2019, https://sg.theasianparent.com/difference-parenting-styles-asian-western-parents.

distant.[18] His authority is not to be challenged. Children are expected to listen to and align with his expectations and directives. Their behavior reflects on the family, especially before outsiders.

Parental discipline is a high priority across the diversity of Asian culture and religious adherence. Hindu, Buddhist, Muslim, and Christian parents discipline their children to insert their religious values and principles into their parenting.[19] One study identifies the direct link between Chinese parenting styles and the core values of Confucianism and Taoism.[20] Both doctrines reject individuality and self-assertion and promote a balance between the natural, human, and spiritual.[21] The study states, "Taoism emphasizes self-control and interpersonal harmony, whereas Confucianism is concerned with fulfilling social obligations, establishing interrelationships with others, conforming to norms, respecting parents and elders, and achieving family reputation through individual achievement."[22] Hence Asian parents ensure that their core values are passed on to their children through discipline.

Citing Proverbs 3:12, Hebrews 12:6 affirms the legitimacy of our relationship to the Father. Discipline and reproof manifest the Father's love and objective to refine them. Hebrews 12:7bc asserts that truth: "God deals with you as children, for what child does a father not discipline?" A lack of discipline implies illegitimacy (Heb 12:8). The Father disciplines us to instill his core values in us—another Asian reality seen in Hebrews.

---

18 Sham'ah Md-Yunus, "Childcare Practices in Three Asian Countries," *International Journal of Early Childhood* 37, no. 1 (2005): 44. But recent trends show a lessening of authoritarianism; Md-Yunus, 44–45.

19 Hindu families in India nurture the appreciation of prayer, worship, and respect for their elders; Melinda Kedro, "Parenting in the Indian Culture," Hello Motherhood, November 28, 2018, https://www.hellomotherhood.com/parenting-in-the-indian-culture-9889722.html.

20 Y. Xu, J. M. Farver, Z. Zhang, Q. Zeng, L. Yu, and B. Cai, "Mainland Chinese Parenting Styles and Parent-Child Interaction," *International Journal of Behavioral Development* 29, no. 6 (2005): 524–31.

21 Xu et al., 525.

22 Xu et al., 525.

Asian Reality Four: Honor and Shame

This reality of honor and shame, as a major motif applied to Jesus, facilitates the overall message of the letter. As the Son (Heb 1:2), Jesus receives greater honor than the angels (Heb 1:4–14; 2:2–4), Moses (Heb 3:1–6; 8:2, 5), and the Levitical priests (implied in Heb 7:1–19; 8:3–13; 9:6–15). The stature of each foil greatly highlights Jesus's superiority. If they are important and deemed honorable, then Jesus must be even more important and worthy of greater honor.

As bearers of important messages from the Lord (Heb 2:2), the angels' communiqué demands proper respect. They have greater honor than humanity (Heb 2:6–7) and even supersede Jesus in glory temporarily (Heb 2:9). The amount of text devoted to comparing Jesus with them (Heb 1:4–14) demonstrates their lofty position. Thus Jesus is more honorable than angels. Moses occupies a place of reverence in Israel throughout its history. Indeed, Jesus cites Moses as authoritative in matters of the Law (e.g., Matt 8:4; Mark 1:44; 7:10; Luke 24:44; John 5:45–47). Hebrews acknowledges Moses's faithfulness in God's house, likely the people of God, as a servant (Heb 3:5). Jesus also proves faithful but as a Son over God's house (Heb 3:6). Thus Jesus is superior over Moses as a son would be over a servant in honor and inheritance.

Of the three foils, the Levitical priesthood receives the most coverage in serving as a model providing the principles and qualifications to which Jesus conforms as high priest. Our focus, however, centers on Jesus's superiority over the Levitical priests. The first point of comparison implies his moral superiority in that he has never sinned (Heb 4:15; 7:26–28). Second, Jesus belongs to another category of priesthood, the order of Melchizedek (Heb 5:6, 10; 6:20). In his narrative of Melchizedek's encounter with Abraham (Heb 7:1–10), the writer of Hebrews emphasizes the respectful homage Abraham accords to Melchizedek through the gift of a tenth of the spoils (Heb 7:4). As patriarch (Heb 7:4), Abraham possesses great honor and yet acknowledges one greater from whom he receives a blessing (Heb 7:6). Taking advantage of Genesis's omission of Melchizedek's biographical details, the writer proclaims, "He is without father or mother or genealogy, having neither beginning of days nor end of life, but resembling the Son of God he continues a priest forever" (Heb 7:3). Melchizedek showcases two significant characteristics descriptive also of Jesus: eternality and greatness in honor. The basis of his priesthood rests on "the power of an indestructible life" (Heb 7:16). Jesus proves superior to the Levites for two other reasons: God designates him a priest with an oath (Heb 7:20–21), and he guarantees a better covenant (Heb 7:22, 18–19).

Jesus enjoys both ascribed honor (Heb 1:2–3a, 4–13) and acquired honor (Heb 1:3b; 2:9–11, 14–18; 3:1–6; 7:20–28; 9:11–28; 12:2). His eternal throne (Heb 1:8b) implies an eternal rule as king. He has ascribed honor not only because of his position, as Hebrews 1:9b implies, but also because of the righteousness of his rule (Heb 1:8c–9a), suggesting that he also acquired honor. God initiates the honor-and-shame process for Jesus by first ascribing honor to his Son as the heir (Heb 1:2b) who possesses the radiance of God's glory and exact character of his nature (Heb 1:3a, 5–6, 8). Jesus obediently takes the inferior status of a human (Heb 2:6–9a) and suffers the shame of the cross (Heb 12:2d) outside the gate (Heb 13:12). After making purification for sins, he gains great honor when he sits at the right hand of the Majesty on high (Heb 1:3c), functioning as a merciful and faithful high priest (Heb 2:17–18). Jesus's ascribed honor enables him to acquire further honor through suffering (Heb 5:8–10). Thus Jesus attains acquired honor. Hebrews 2:11 explicitly declares Jesus is not ashamed to embrace humanity. He willingly sacrifices his divine prerogatives temporarily to complete his mission, ignoring any shame associated with descending into the world of sinners and being identified with them.

In Hebrews 7:1–10, the writer argues by the principle of transitivity that Melchizedek possesses greater stature and honor than Levi. The line of reasoning proceeds as follows: because Melchizedek was greater than Abraham, and Abraham was greater than Levi as Levi's progenitor, then Melchizedek was greater than Levi. Indeed, the writer infers that Levi paid tithes to Melchizedek through Abraham (Heb 7:9–10). The writer then applies this principle to Jesus, who is appointed a priest forever after the order of Melchizedek (Heb 7:11–17). Jesus's superiority over the Levitical priests is further reinforced. First, the Levitical priesthood failed to secure perfection for anyone, thereby requiring an alternative (Heb 7:11). Second, the former priests could not continue because of short lifespans (Heb 7:23a), whereas Jesus continues forever (Heb 7:23b), signifying an effective ministry (Heb 7:25). Third, in contrast to high priests with moral shortcomings, Jesus as the Son has been made perfect forever (Heb 7:28).

Thus Jesus is superior to all—angels, Moses, and the Levitical priests. He begins with ascribed honor due to being designated the Son of God and then gains acquired honor through being perfected in suffering to become a merciful and faithful high priest seated at the right hand of the Majesty. Ascribed honor initiates the process toward acquired honor. The former is a necessary prerequisite to the latter, and the latter is the climatic consummation of the former. Along a different axis, the author of Hebrews shames his readers in 5:11–6:12 in hopes of motivating them to redress their present failure to appropriate the benefits they have in Christ in view of the dire consequences for failing to do so.[23] The readers have had sufficient time to mature in their faith to become teachers, but they have failed. Hence Hebrews employs two kinds of shame—shame "before the Christian community for being unambitious and immature" and shame "before God for rejecting God's benefits."[24]

Asian Reality Five: Harsh Consequences

Visitors in Southeast Asia[25] should be familiar with the harsh consequences for committing any one of a number of offenses, even if they can get away with it in their home country. One travelogue cautions would-be tourists about offenses that can result in catastrophe: exposing the private parts of one's body, wearing inappropriate or revealing clothing, and getting caught carrying illegal drugs can result in heavy fines, imprisonment, deportation, and even the death penalty.[26] Participating in local politics may be perceived as outside interference with local affairs and can stir resentment on the part of locals whose memories of colonization remain fresh. Again, offenders can expect heavy fines, imprisonment, and deportation. Disrespecting the local royalty or high government officials results in automatic heavy fines and imprisonment.[27]

Ironically, Asian countries may have stiff penalties against rape or other forms of attacks against women but feature abysmal records of convictions

23 Peter S. Perry, "Making Fear Personal: Hebrews 5.11–6.12 and the Argument from Shame," *JSNT* 32, no. 1 (2009): 99–125.

24 Perry, 121.

25 Cambodia, Indonesia, Laos, Malaysia, Philippines, Singapore, Thailand, and Vietnam.

26 Michael Aquino, "Tourists Behaving Badly: What Not to Do in Southeast Asia," accessed May 4, 2019.

27 See Carlton Tan, "Lee Kuan Yew Leaves a Legacy of Authoritarian Pragmatism," *Guardian*, March 23, 2015, https://www.theguardian.com/world/2015/mar/23/lee-kuan-yews-legacy-of-authoritarian-pragmatism-will-serve-singapore-well.

because of the severity of the punishment.[28] This discrepancy appears to uncover the gender bias against women by law enforcement in favor of leniency for the male perpetrators. This Asian reality will be discussed in the next section.

Not surprisingly, then, Asian readers of the Letter to the Hebrews, especially those from Southeast Asia, would find the warnings with the associated threat of severe consequences familiar. Hebrews features five warning passages that ought to be examined together as a single warning appearing five times in the course of the letter.[29] Taking the sin warned against as apostasy, the consequence is eternal condemnation.[30] This would be comparable to the death penalty as implemented in Southeast Asia.

Asian Reality Six: Gender Issues

Hebrews presents a few examples of women of faith. Sarah conceived though she was well beyond the childbearing years (Heb 11:11–12). Rahab took an enormous risk in welcoming the spies (Heb 11:31). Women received back the dead by resurrection (Heb 11:35). The descriptions about exemplary faith fit both men and women (Heb 11:1–2, 6, 13–16, 36–40).

The preponderance of examples in Hebrews 11 is men. The writer names eight men with a brief summary for each. He mentions another six men by name accompanied by a collective summary for them all. Overall, those named with individual summaries break down to eight men and two women. However, two of the named men assume a prominent role in redemptive history—Abraham with seven verses (Heb 11:8–10, 12, 17–19) and Moses with five (Heb 11:24–28)—whereas Sarah and Rahab have only one verse each. The women enjoy comparable coverage to Abel, Enoch, Noah, Isaac, Jacob, and Joseph, each also with a single verse. Indeed, the writer merely mentions Gideon, Barak, Samson, Jephthah, David, Samuel, and unnamed prophets without any individual summary. Based on the amount of text devoted to each character, the two women fare quite well, with only Abraham and Moses exceeding them.

28 Divya Arya, "India Death Penalty: Does It Actually Deter Rape?," BBC, accessed May 5, 2019, https://www.bbc.com/news/world-asia-india-44922084.

29 Scot McKnight cites the five warning passages as Hebrews 2:1–4; 3:7–4:13; 5:11–6:12; 10:19–39; 12:1–29; "The Warning Passages of Hebrews: A Formal Analysis and Theological Conclusions," *TJ* 13 (1992): 22.

30 See Soo Hoo, "Our Sabbath-Rest," 9–11.

Interestingly, the writer stops his summaries after Rahab. Joshua and Caleb, Rahab's contemporaries, are conspicuously absent from the list. Does this mean that the writer regarded Rahab as more noteworthy than them? Understandably, the rest of Hebrews highlights Christ as high priest, Melchizedek as his prototype, and Moses and the Levitical priests as his foils—all male. Does the writer have gender bias? To be fair, we need to acknowledge that he presents all the examples, men and women, as role models for all his readers.

How might gender-sensitive Asians read Hebrews? Culturally, the distance between modern readers in Asia and this letter could vary considerably. In Southeast Asia, where women traditionally have been favorably regarded compared to those in South and East Asia,[31] their reading of Hebrews may not generate the intense feelings of being marginalized as those from other Asian regions would feel. A recent article highlights India's millions of "unwanted" girls.[32] The marked preference for sons rather than daughters has characterized the nation for millennia. How might an Indian woman growing up and living in such a culture read Hebrews? Would she be repulsed by the divine promise of Isaac, the future blessings for Jacob and Esau and Joseph's sons, and the beauty of the infant Moses? Would she feel marginalized by no mention of daughters?

Yet the highlighting of Sarah's faith that empowered her to bear the promised son should provide a much-needed balance. Now, it may seem that motherhood exalts her to occupy a spot on the list. Then she is indistinguishable from the countless number of Asian women who are relegated to the home and motherhood as the only viable career option. However, the writer of Hebrews commends her for her faith, thereby making her the equal of her husband. Both are characterized by the same virtue. She is equal partners with him in receiving the promise and experiencing the initial fulfillment in their son. The concluding epithet of Hebrews 11:16 includes the two of them and others: "But now they desire something better that is something heavenly.

31 Barbara Watson Andaya, "Women in Southeast Asia," Asia Society, accessed May 7, 2019, https://asiasociety.org/education/women-southeast-asia. For a similar sketch of women in China, see Patricia Ebrey, "Women in Traditional China," Asia Society, accessed May 7, 2019, https://asiasociety.org/education/women-traditional-china.

32 Euan McKirdy, "India's Gender Inequality Has Led to Millions of 'Unwanted' Girls," CNN, January 30, 2018, https://edition.cnn.com/2018/01/30/health/india-unwanted-girls-intl/index.html.

Wherefore God is not ashamed to be called their God, for he has prepared a city for them." Ultimately, God highly esteems both Abraham and Sarah and so prepares a heavenly city as their eternal destination.

Pharaoh's daughter hired Moses's mother to raise him until she gave him back to be raised in the Egyptian court (Exod 2:9–10). Within a limited period, his mother must have instilled in Moses an awareness of his true identity with the people of God (Heb 11:24–25), choosing to bear the reproach of Christ (Heb 11:26–27). His mother transferred her faith to Moses, who is commemorated in later Judaism and the Christian Scriptures.

Hebrews portrays Rahab from a position of strength, cunning, and courage. She assumes military significance in that Joshua and the Israelites could not succeed in capturing Jericho without her intervention. The spies collected valuable information on the city. But unless they could brief Joshua, that information would prove useless. Rahab defied her king in protecting them and instructing them in how to escape. If her king discovered her treason, she would have been executed along with her family. But she recognized Israel's God as "God in heaven above and on earth beneath" (Josh 2:11). Here we find Rahab the equal of any man for strategic value and significance in the conquest. An entire nation depended on her exercise of faith to succeed.

Hebrews' coverage of women uplifts them to a status equal with men in demonstrating persevering faith that inspires future generations of readers (Heb 12:1). In this manner, Hebrews proves to be countercultural to the pervasive Asian attitude toward women. Although core Buddhist doctrine appears to exhibit a lack of gender bias, societal attitudes and practices, particularly in predominately Buddhist regions, still favor males over females.[33] Contemporary Muslim attitudes may be influenced by the political-cultural context. For example, in liberal-secular Europe, social and governmental pressure may have a greater impact on women's status than Islamic beliefs alone.[34] But in other parts of the world, Muslim prejudicial attitude and treatment of women remain unmitigated. The same can be said of predominantly Hindu India in spite of the recent rise in scholarship and female researchers on women

33 Chand R. Sirimanne, "Buddhism and Women: The Dhamma Has No Gender," *Journal of International Women's Studies* 18, no. 1 (2016): 273–92.

34 Schirin Amir-Moazami, Christine M. Jacobsen, and Maleiha Malik, "Islam and Gender in Europe: Subjectivities, Politics and Piety," *Feminist Review* 98 (2011): 1–8.

and gender studies related to Hinduism.[35] For regions where Confucianism forges a prevailing influence, the traditional patriarchal practice of society holds sway, although some writers attempt to argue for gender equity based on the teachings of some sacred texts on human nature and virtue.[36]

Asian Reality Seven: Favored Son

Asian readers may readily recognize the obvious preferential treatment of Jesus as the Son in Hebrews in spite of recent trends to the contrary in Asia.[37] It would seem that God himself gave favorable treatment to his Son, inheriting a more excellent name (Heb 1:4), demanding a respectful hearing (Heb 2:1–3), subjecting everything to him (Heb 2:8), appointing him high priest (Heb 5:5–6), exalting him above the heavens (Heb 7:26), and punishing any who reject him (Heb 10:29). But these trappings of being the favored Son came at great personal cost. Of course Jesus enjoyed the privileges of being the favored Son, but at the same time, he carried heavy responsibilities that only he was qualified to fulfill. He had to be made perfect through suffering (Heb 2:10) outside the city gates as he endured reproach (Heb 13:12–13) and the shame associated with the cross (Heb 12:2). Hebrews portrays Jesus as obedient, humble, and submissive to the perfecting process in order to become a merciful and faithful high priest (Heb 2:17–18). Jesus modeled perseverance and joy, despising the shame (Heb 12:2), for believers to emulate (Heb 12:1, 3–17). Rather than being an object of envy or resentment like Asian-favored sons, Jesus is the object of hope and trust, a surety in challenging times. His favored status works toward our blessed advantage.

35 Julia Leslie, "Gender and Religion: Gender and Hinduism," in *Encyclopedia of Religion* (2005), accessed September 12, 2019, https://tinyurl.com/wsms3hfr.

36 Kelly James Clark and Robin Wang, "A Confucian Defense of Gender Equity," *Journal of the American Academy of Religion* 72, no. 2 (2004): 395–422.

37 See, e.g., Tania Branigan, "China's Great Gender Crisis," *Guardian*, November 2, 2011, https://www.theguardian.com/world/2011/nov/02/chinas-great-gender-crisis.

AN ASIAN LETTER

With seven Asian realities emerging from the Letter to the Hebrews, readers may understandably view Hebrews as an Asian letter. Each reality correlates with a major aspect of the letter and not merely an incidental side note.

Pilgrimage or migration affects many Asians, whether directly or indirectly. Countries heavily dependent on foreign labor, like Singapore, feature many local families employing domestic help, and industries like construction and shipyard work are populated with migrant workers primarily from China, India, and Bangladesh. We easily recall these common experiences and bring them to bear as we read about the journeys of Jesus, the OT saints, the wilderness generation, and even we as readers plodding through our own faith journey. There is no sense of permanence where we live and work. The specter of transition hangs over us, sometimes heavily.

The major theme of persevering faith has its modern-day parallel in the perseverance of many Asians. They face a daunting challenge as migrant workers with limited recourse when confronted by employer abuse or enigmatic and unresponsive social support systems, or as women living in a male-dominated culture with very few viable options to pursue their dreams.

As we read of the Father's discipline (Heb 12:5–11), we vividly recall our earthly fathers who may not often verbalize their love for us but who demonstrate it through their discipline and guidance in shaping us to become what we are today. They may have been strict and even emotionally distant, but they laid the foundation for a productive life. Their desire, as our Father's, is that we embrace the family's values and embody them.

As a prominent cultural trait in Asia, honor and shame mirror the life and ministry of our high priest, Jesus Christ. Perhaps here is where Hebrews is most Asian through its central motif of Jesus's ascribed and acquired honor. The Father designates him as the Son with a name more honorable than that of the angels. But as he enters the realm of humanity and endures the reproach of the cross, he progressively experiences more shame, fulfilling the Father's will (Heb 10:5–10). He then ascends to sit at the right hand of the Majesty on high, a position of greatest honor. He begins his journey with ascribed honor and then gains acquired honor through obedience, suffering, and being made perfect to become a faithful and merciful high priest forever.

Hebrews utilizes shame to provide strong motivation both positively and negatively. With Jesus as a compelling example of scorning the shame of the cross, the author exhorts readers to follow in his footsteps even if that should bring shame (Heb 12:2–3). The writer commends their public shame in the past to strengthen their resolve when enduring hardship (Heb 10:32–36). Negatively, he rebukes readers for failing to appropriate God's benefits in order to grow and persevere in the faith (Heb 5:11–6:12). Shame, then, functions to push rather lethargic readers to action, something to which Asians would be sensitive and likely responsive.

We Asians are aware of the harsh consequences of various offenses in different Asian countries, ranging from lengthy prison terms to ultimately the death penalty, so we exercise great care to avoid transgressing any of the published laws of the land. Hence when we encounter the five separate warnings in Hebrews that coalesce into one forceful threat of eternal damnation for apostasy, we take the collective warning seriously. As Asian authorities wield absolute control over their jurisdictions and we learn not to challenge them, likely we will respect the authority the Father possesses over his domain.

Although marginalized in many parts of Asia, women can find refuge in the Letter to the Hebrews. It affirms that they are the equal of any man if they have persevering faith. In fact, in cases of misogyny, women may require greater endurance to not only survive but also overcome. They can be role models and a source of inspiration to both men and women. The promises in Hebrews are equally theirs to claim. Jesus Christ is as much their high priest as he is for men.

The Asian preference for sons appears to find expression and support in Hebrews. But if we understand "preference" to mean designation for a special mission to redeem and help humanity, then perhaps we would not be so quick to accuse the Father of discriminating against daughters in particular and women in general. The Son's mission cost him dearly when he submitted to the shame of the incarnation and then the crucifixion. His ascribed honor positioned him to obtain acquired honor through a life of holiness and sacrifice. In view of these seven Asian realities, then, we may conclude that the author had Asians in mind for his readership, and we Asian readers gratefully receive Hebrews as a personal letter addressed specifically to us.

A SUGGESTED ASIAN HERMENEUTIC

Although the text remains constant, its interpretation needs to offer a relevant message to a new generation of readers, specifically in Asia. Mirroring an important hermeneutic by the writer of Hebrews, where the new supersedes the old,[38] we likewise strive for something new and meaningful that can speak more effectively to Asians today. We are not seeking something new for the sake of being innovative. Rather, we need to adapt to the changing landscape where a significant number of readers come from Asia steeped in Asian culture and faith traditions.

The Asian realities found in Hebrews present a starting point. As a proposal, let me suggest the honor-and-shame motif that is at once so Asian and also so pertinent to the focal point of Hebrews, Jesus Christ our high priest, and us Asian readers. Typically Asians are shame-adversative, so Hebrews, with its positive view and use of shame, may persuade readers to regard shame as something necessary to achieve their spiritual goals. The path to Jesus's acquired honor went through the shame of the cross (Heb 12:2; 13:12), and the writer commends his readers for enduring the public shame of persecution and having their possessions confiscated, which evidences persevering faith (Heb 10:32–36). He exhorts them to bear Jesus's shame outside the camp (Heb 13:13). Then a hermeneutic of shame as the pathway to acquired honor may be the lens through which we read the writer's message.

As modeled by the OT saints, the pathway to acquired honor may require enduring shame—the shame of torture (Heb 11:35); of being mocked and caned, chained, and imprisoned (Heb 11:36); of stoning as if condemned or cursed (Lev 20:27; 24:23; Josh 7:25; Heb 11:37a); and of poverty, destitution, persecution, and mistreatment (Heb 11:37d). Persevering to be faithful to the very end, they were commended (Heb 11:39a). Hence my proposal becomes "A hermeneutic of perseverance in overcoming shame, a form of divine discipline, with the prospect of serious consequences for failure to persevere, as the pilgrimage to acquired honor." In the following discussions, I hope to offer pointers indicating the right direction for more fully developing an Asian hermeneutics.

38 James W. Thompson, "The New Is Better: A Neglected Aspect of the Hermeneutics of Hebrews," *CBQ* 73 (2011): 54761.

Discussion One

The dichotomy of honor and shame does not prepare the Asian reader for Hebrews, which depicts shame not so much as the polar opposite of honor but rather as a prerequisite of honor. One must experience shame in order to acquire honor, as Jesus demonstrated. Without shame, one cannot achieve honor. The key to forbearing shame is faith, as Hebrews 11 records.

Hebrews dismisses the dichotomy so ingrained in Asian culture. But in fact, Hebrews seems to be quite Asian in view of the yin-yang concept in Chinese philosophy.[39] Rather than regarding yin and yang as polar opposites, they complement one another, where each harbors something of the other. Together, they build a composite whole. It is a matter not of "either-or" but of "both-and."[40] Hebrews depicts both honor and shame as one organic whole; each is necessary to the other. This interaction, where one influences the other and vice versa, highlights the principle of reciprocity.[41] The interaction is dynamic. As readers experience shame, they progress to acquired honor. Here we acknowledge the imperfection of the analogy of yin and yang, which can continue ad infinitum, but shame has a terminus ad quem when one finally obtains acquired honor. That point transcends this life within which the yin-yang analogy still holds.

A dynamic interaction exists between text and reader.[42] Readers change from aversion to shame to regarding it as essential, and the text becomes clearer and more relevant. In yin-yang terminology, this interchange strives to achieve balance and harmony.[43]

Discussion Two

Scripture affirms certain aspects of culture to be strengths or virtues. The virtues of perseverance (Heb 10:32, 36; 11:25, 27; 12:1–3, 7) and discipline (Heb 12:5–13) position Asian readers to have the advantage. Because these virtues are integral to their culture, they need only redirect these strengths to facilitate

39 Hyun Chul Paul Kim, "Interpretative Modes of Yin-Yang Dynamics as an Asian Hermeneutics," *Biblical Interpretation* 9, no. 3 (2001): 287–308.

40 Kim, 291–92.

41 Kim, 294–96.

42 Kim, 300.

43 Kim, 299–300.

their pilgrimage to acquired honor. In that sense, they should feel at home reading Hebrews. Perhaps they may recall the admonition of their parents, who sought to instill these traits in them. Indeed, Hebrews 12:5–13 employs the motif of a father exhorting his son to submit to the hardship of discipline based on the example of Jesus himself (Heb 12:2–3), who obediently submitted to his Father (Heb 2:10; 3:2, 6). The corollary virtues of respect for and obedience to the father's authority undergirds the aforementioned virtues. At the same time, independence and going one's own way counter traditional Confucianist ideals.[44] Jesus exemplifies filial piety to the Father and a collective identity with the family of humanity. The context of family alluded to in Hebrews 2:10–12, within which these Asian virtues are preserved and reinforced, exerts a powerful influence in Asian societies and forms a basis for Hebrews. Hence we find alignment of the biblical text with Asian values.

Discussion Three

The yin-yang principle addresses the marginalization of women and the favored son mentality through the pursuit of balance and harmony.[45] Balance requires advocating the equality of women with men and daughters with sons. Hebrews offers such a balanced and harmonious view. It champions the marginalized and levels the playing field between the favored and the unfavored. Faith is the great equalizer—both women and men are equally capable of faith (Hebrews 11), and Jesus as high priest intercedes for both (Heb 2:17–18). The warnings against unbelief apply equally to both genders (Heb 2:1–4; 3:7–4:11; 5:11–6:12; 10:26–39; 12:14–29), and the promises are for both (Heb 4:1; 6:12–20; 9:15; 10:23, 36; 11:11, 39–40). In stating that Jesus identified with humanity and suffered for their sake (Heb 2:10–12), Hebrews portrays the Lord as valuing both men and women equally. He makes no differentiation based on gender. He is high priest to all who are tempted (Heb 2:17–18). Indeed, men and women will inhabit the city of the living God, the heavenly Jerusalem (Heb 12:22). Both genders will find their names inscribed in heaven (Heb 12:23).

44 For a scholarly study, see Mijung Park and Catherine Chesla, "Revisiting Confucianism as a Conceptual Framework for Asian Family Study," *Journal of Family Nursing* 13, no. 3 (2007): 293–311.

45 Kim, "Interpretative Modes," 303.

Discussion Four

Many of us Asian readers are pilgrims journeying in the Diaspora. Diasporic Abraham "made his home in the promised land like a stranger in a foreign land . . . as did Isaac and Jacob" (Heb 11:9). But he "was looking forward to the city with foundations whose architect and builder is God" (Heb 11:10). All the saints with faith's eyes saw the distant fulfillment of the promises, "admitting that they were foreigners and strangers on earth" (Heb 11:13d). "They longed for a country—a heavenly one" (Heb 11:16a). They were destitute and mistreated, wandering about and living in makeshift dwellings (Heb 11:37d–38). They lived in "places" but never "home." However long we live and work in a particular place, we are still foreigners, seen that way by the locals and made to feel that way.[46] Two characteristics describe diasporic people: hybridization and liminality.[47] They are familiar with at least two different cultures, and they can move between the two with relative ease. Abraham was hybridized to the local dialect and customs of the Hittites and so was able to negotiate for a burial site in their land (Gen 23:3–20). Liminality relates to the uncertainty and ambiguity of transition. Foreigners living in a nonnative land experience what one writer calls "in-betweenness."[48]

We diasporic Asians need a diasporic hermeneutics.[49] We are in an earthly diaspora with heaven as our true home. Hybridized, we can effectively navigate within this world, although we are careful not to adopt values that weaken our faith. The liminality of our status of being in the world and not of it can cause uncertainty: "How do I preserve my witness?" We continue to direct our prayers to heaven.[50] Most profoundly, we identify with Jesus the sojourner between heaven and earth, who, in the time of his earthly stay, lived and ministered in the margins (Heb 12:2–3). He was made like us in every aspect, including our diasporic existence, marginality,

46 Kah-Jin Jeffrey Kuan, "My Journey into Diasporic Hermeneutics," *Union Seminary Quarterly Review* 56, nos. 1–2 (2002): 50–54.

47 Kuan, 53.

48 Fumitaka Matsuoka, *Out of Silence: Emerging Themes in Asian American Churches* (Cleveland: United Church, 1995), 54, cited in Kuan, "Diasporic Hermeneutics," 52.

49 Tsaurayi Kudakwashe Mapfeka, *Esther in Diaspora: Toward an Alternative Interpretive Framework* (Leiden: Brill, 2019), 52–94.

50 Daniel L. Smith-Christopher, *A Biblical Theology of Exile* (Minneapolis: Fortress, 2002), 114–15.

and shame (Heb 2:17). He understands our plight and offers substantial assistance (Heb 2:18).

Discussion Five

Another aspect of an Asian hermeneutics is hope for the diasporic, marginalized Asian reader through the paschal mystery.[51] This mystery represents a motif in Hebrews as a past event with continuing benefits—the death and resurrection of Jesus Christ. The power emanating from this event liberates and empowers us to break free from the bondage of marginalization, liminality, and oppression. We seek to address the injustices and prejudices experienced. Emboldened, we visualize a better future and strive to make it happen. The Scriptures facilitate the formation of our identity[52]—objects of God's love, recipients of his grace, and targeted humanity whom Jesus helps (Heb 2:16). Unshackled from forces that strive to silence us (e.g., racism, colonialism, economics), we voice our thoughts, feelings, convictions, and even outrage at the injustices perpetrated against us.

Undergirding our discovery of hope from and identity in the text is reading the text metaphorically.[53] Held in tension with a literal interpretation, a metaphor creates an apparent inconsistency or absurdity between two things hitherto deemed unrelated and, as a result of resemblance, generates new information.[54] The two meanings, the literal and the metaphorical, are not separated levels of significance but one single whole where the primary meaning (literal) serves as the only means to access the secondary meaning (metaphorical). The literal interpretation asks what the text meant for its author and original readers. The metaphorical interpretation answers the question of what the text means today to us Asian readers.

A metaphorical reading calls for three strategies of interpretation.[55] First, interpretation evolves into a performative act where the interpreter imaginatively enters into the realm of the readers. Second, the interpreter brings a

51 Eunjoo Mary Kim, "Hermeneutics and Asian American Preaching," *Semeia* 90–91 (2002): 269–90, 280–81.

52 Kim, 278–79.

53 Kim, 281–83.

54 Paul Ricoeur, *Interpretation Theory: Discourse and the Surplus of Meaning* (Fort Worth: Texas Christian University Press, 1976), 50–53.

55 Kim, "Hermeneutics," 282–83.

combination of interpretive methods to bear on the text. An eclectic ensemble of traditional, modern, and postmodern methodologies would prove more fruitful than employing any one approach. Third, the interpreter relates the readers and their stories with the text and its story. Paraphrasing the text in terms of the readers' situation facilitates them seeing the relevance of the text and experiencing its impact.

Discussion Six

An Asian reality impacting our hermeneutical model is the community in the reading experience.[56] The community dialogues in critiquing presuppositions and interpretations in striving for consensus on how the text speaks. This process characterizes Asian hermeneutics as critical hermeneutics that move the community to a reading more in tune with the concerns of readers collectively. Yet the multiplicity of cultures, religions, and languages descriptive of Asia suggests narrowing the boundaries to those sharing the same sociocultural location and "lifeworld."[57] Then potentially many Asian communities of faith may emerge, with each given a voice to champion a particular hermeneutical approach. When these communities interact with and critique each other, it could result in a blended Asian hermeneutics.[58] But even if that ideal remains unobtainable, among the multitude of Asian voices, each voice is valued and given a hearing, with no voice taken as superior to any other voice.

CONCLUSION

Seven Asian realities emerge from reading Hebrews and form the basis for an Asian hermeneutics. The Chinese philosophy of yin and yang reads the text as the flow between honor and shame. Shame is not something to be not

56 Simon S. M. Kwan, "Asian Critical Hermeneutics amidst the Economic Development of Asia," *Asia Journal of Theology* 13, no. 2 (1999): 354–74.

57 E. S. Fiorenza, "The Church as a Community of Interpretation: Political Theology between Discourse Ethics and Hermeneutical Reconstruction," in *Habermas, Modernity and Public Theology*, ed. D. S. Browning and E. S. Fiorenza (New York: Crossroad, 1992), 68, cited in Kwan, "Asian Critical Hermeneutics," 369.

58 See Chloe Sun, "Recent Research on Asian and Asian American Hermeneutics Related to the Hebrew Bible," *Currents in Biblical Research* 17, no. 3 (2019): 240.

avoided but welcomed as perhaps the only means to obtain acquired honor. We embrace both honor and shame. The yin-yang pursuit of balance and harmony compels us to seek equality between men and women and to rectify the preference of sons over daughters. A yin-yang hermeneutics offers the framework to find women the equal of men in the quest for acquired honor and to explain shame as imbalance and disharmony. Shame is shameful only if one wallows in self-pity, but it becomes a badge of honor if it spurs us in our pilgrimage to acquired honor.

The diasporic aspect of Asian hermeneutics speaks to our identity as sojourners looking to our heavenly home. Earth is only a transitory place. We accept the in-betweenness, never totally comfortable in or accepted by the world, as confirmation that we remain true to our identity and do not compromise our scruples. The centrality of Christ, although he lived in the margins, enables us living in the margins to move to the center in finding our voice to redress what marginalized us in the first place. A metaphorical reading transports us Asian readers from the world of the text and the world behind the text to our world before the text. The text becomes meaningful personally. We empathize with those marginalized and encourage them by declaring, "God is the God of the marginalized. And because he himself was marginalized, he knows how you feel and wants you to know that he cares." Our role as metaphorical interpreters is to offer readings that empathize, encourage, and give hope by demonstrating that the text still speaks to the marginalized today.

FURTHER READING

Allen, D. L. 2010. *Hebrews: An Exegetical and Theological Exposition of Holy Scripture.* NAC 35. Nashville: B&H.

Cockerill, G. L. 2012. *The Epistle to the Hebrews.* NICNT. Grand Rapids, MI: Eerdmans.

deSilva, D. A. 2012. *The Letter to the Hebrews in Social-Scientific Perspective.* Cascade Companions 15. Eugene, OR: Wipf & Stock.

Ellingworth, P. 2015. *The Epistle to the Hebrews.* NIGTC. Grand Rapids, MI: Eerdmans.

Guthrie, G. H. 2002. *Hebrews.* TNTC. Grand Rapids, MI: Eerdmans.

Kim, H. C. P. 2001. "Interpretative Modes of Yin-Yang Dynamics as an Asian Hermeneutics." *Biblical Interpretation* 9, no. 3: 287–308.

Perry, P. S. 2009. "Making Fear Personal: Hebrews 5.11–6.12 and the Argument from Shame." *JSNT* 32, no. 1: 99–125.

Schreiner, T. R. 2015. *Commentary on Hebrews*. Biblical Theology for Christian Proclamation. Nashville: B & H.

Thompson, J. W. 2011. "The New Is Better: A Neglected Aspect of the Hermeneutics of Hebrews." *CBQ* 73:547–561.

NINETEEN

The Letter of James

Daniel K. Eng
Western Seminary
Portland, Oregon, USA

The growing number of resources on the Epistle of James provides readers with ample discussion on its introductory matters and the text itself. Most notably, scholars have questioned the view that James is a haphazard collection of wisdom sayings, and they have examined different themes that repeat through the epistle. In what follows, I will summarize the introductory issues, including authorship, audience, and structure. After that, I will examine the rhetoric of James with a modern Asian audience in mind. I will also explore the themes of James that particularly resonate with Asian cultures and worldviews.

CRITICAL INTRODUCTION OF JAMES

In what follows, we will examine the introductory issues surrounding James: its authorship, audience, date, and occasion. These issues will assist the reader in framing the content of the epistle within its context. Throughout the treatment below, I will explore how these issues intersect with Asian realities.

Authorship

The epistle of James identifies its author as "James, a servant of God and the Lord Jesus Christ" (1:1). While James (Jacob) was a fairly common name, the lack of specification in the epistle suggests that this particular James needed no introduction—he was a well-known James. The NT describes several men called James, with the three most prominent being James the son of Zebedee, one of the Twelve (see Mark 1:19); James the son of Alphaeus, also one of the Twelve (see Mark 3:18); and James "the brother of the Lord" (Gal 1:19), the leader of the church in Jerusalem (Acts 15:13–19). Out of these three, the third is the most likely. The son of Zebedee was martyred rather early (Acts 12:2) in the church's development, making him unlikely to be the author. James the son of Alphaeus, who may be the one called "James the small" (Mark 15:40), is relatively obscure, making it unlikely that he would write an authoritative letter using only his name without other identification.

James the brother of Jesus and the son of Mary and Joseph, also called James the Just, is the most likely candidate for the author of this epistle. The witness of the early church traditions (Origen, Eusebius, Jerome, the Council of Carthage) attributes the epistle to James the Just. Also, the Greek of the epistle has significant similarities to the words attributed to James at the Jerusalem Council (Acts 15:13–21).[1] Besides, as we will see, the Epistle of James contains many echoes of the teachings of Jesus, especially the Sermon on the Mount. For example, James teaches denouncing judgment of one another (see Matthew 19:23–24). The injunction in James 5:12 to let your yes be yes and your no be no appears in Matthew 5:37. There are echoes of the Matthean Beatitudes in particular; James urges his hearers to have joy amid trials (Jas 1:2; see Matthew 5:10–12), communicates a blessing on the poor (Jas 2:5; see Matthew 5:3; Luke 6:20), and has other statements of blessing (Jas 1:12; 1:25; 5:11). James must have known the teachings of his brother well.

The NT indicates that James held great prominence in the early church. At first, he was skeptical about Jesus's identity during his earthly ministry (John 7:5; see Mark 3:21). However, Paul later singles out James as one of the eyewitnesses to the risen Jesus (1 Cor 15:7), suggesting that James became a convert as a result. Along with the other siblings of Jesus and the disciples (Acts 1:14), he was likely in the upper room after Jesus's ascension to await the Holy Spirit in Jerusalem. Paul identifies James as one of the "apostles" (Gal 1:19) and names him first among the "pillars," which also includes Cephas and John (Gal 2:9). Also, James held high authority in the church. He was

1 Scot McKnight, *The Letter of James*, NICNT (Grand Rapids, MI: Eerdmans, 2011), 24–25.

said to have sent out representatives of the church (Gal 2:12). He presides over the Jerusalem Council in Acts 15, making a decision and having the last word after Peter speaks. Later, he receives Paul and his companions on their return to Jerusalem, and they give a report to him about their work among the gentiles (Acts 21:17–26).[2] Thus we observe the influential leadership that James has in early Christianity.

Audience

As the leader of the Jerusalem church, James held considerable authority with early Jewish Christians. The epistle is addressed to the "twelve tribes of the diaspora" (Jas 1:1), or Jews who are outside of Palestine. Because James does not specify the locations of these diaspora Jewish readers, one can reasonably include Jewish Christians who are in Asia as part of James's audience. It is believed that Christianity reached India by the mid-first century. These Jewish Christians probably had an existing relationship with James, likely being some of the ones who fled Jerusalem during persecution (see Acts 8:1; 11:19). The author's familiarity with the LXX (Jas 4:6) and OT figures (Jam 2:21–23, 25; 5:10–11, 17) corroborates the view that the hearers are indeed Jewish. The designation "twelve tribes of the diaspora" indicates that these Jews outside the land identified with hope for the restoration of the nation of Israel. While they are as far as Asia, they feel the stigma of being far away, and they long for the kingdom to return. In fact, Jewish expectations for restoration were so widespread that E. P. Sanders suggests that references to *twelve* would "necessarily mean restoration" of Israel.[3]

Date

The question of the dating of James is intimately linked to the question of its authorship. Some consider the epistle to be pseudepigraphical, dating it as late as the late second century. However, if James the Just is indeed the author of this epistle, it must be dated before his martyrdom in 62 CE. Aside from authorship, there are solid reasons to assign an early date to this epistle. First, the

2 See Richard Bauckham, "James at the Centre," *Journal of the European Pentecostal Theological Association* 14 (1995): 23–33; William C. Varner, *James: A Commentary on the Greek Text* (Lexington, KY: Fontes, 2017), 7–11.

3 See E. P. Sanders, *Jesus and Judaism* (Philadelphia: Fortress, 1985), 98.

reference to a synagogue (2:2) suggests a time earlier than the parting of the ways between Jews and Christians.[4] Second, the relatively primitive theology, especially regarding Christ, suggests an early date.[5] Third, references to church leadership are scant in James, suggesting an early stage of the church.[6] Fourth, there is no hint of any conflict between Jews and gentiles, which is addressed at the Jerusalem Council (traditionally dated around 50 CE) with James playing a significant role. Fifth, while the content in James 2:14–26 regarding justification, faith, and deeds appears to contradict Paul's teaching, especially in Romans and Galatians, further examination of the terms used reveals that James uses the words differently. This discrepancy demonstrates either a misunderstanding or unfamiliarity with Pauline teaching on justification, of which James and Paul would have discussed in person at the time of the Jerusalem Council. Together, these observations suggest that we can date James in the mid- to late forties CE.

Occasion

The circumstances of the epistle are not explicitly stated, but the text offers some clues. The Jewish hearers of James are undergoing trials (see Jas 1:2–4, 12). At least some are being oppressed by the rich, being dragged into court (2:6). The hearers are encouraged to follow the example of the suffering and patience of the prophets who spoke in the name of the Lord (5:10). This encouragement implies that they are suffering from their association with the Lord as well. Also, the text appears to indicate that the hearers' communities had quarrels and discord (4:1–2) as well as unconfessed sins (5:16).

A primary concern for James in his epistle is that his hearers would be judged favorably in the eschaton. The epistle contains a repeated motif of eschatological judgment. First, there are repeated references to eschatological concepts, like a great reversal (1:9–11; 2:5; 4:6; 5:1–3) and a Parousia (5:7–9). Second, the term κρίνω (judge) and its cognates appear twenty times in the epistle, dispersed throughout the text. Also, the judgment inherent in testing

4 Dan G. McCartney, *James*, BECNT (Grand Rapids, MI: Baker Academic, 2009), 15.

5 D. A. Carson and Douglas J. Moo, *An Introduction to the New Testament*, 2nd ed. (Grand Rapids, MI: Zondervan, 2005), 627.

6 Gary M. Burge, Lynn H. Cohick, and Gene L. Green, *The New Testament in Antiquity: A Survey of the New Testament within Its Cultural Context* (Grand Rapids, MI: Zondervan, 2009), 382.

(1:3, 12) and the court-related language (2:9, 11, 21–25; 5:4) point to a constant concern for judgment. In the epistle, God is affirmed as the only one who can judge (4:12), and James urges his hearers to keep judgment in view as they choose their actions (2:12; 4:11–12; 5:7–12). James writes so that his diaspora hearers will act in ways that will lead to favorable judgment.

Structure of James

A discussion of the structure of James begins with chapter 1, which serves as the introductory prologue of the epistle, introducing the topics that will occur in chapters 2–5.

Salutation (1:1)

Joy in perseverance through trials (1:2–4)
- Binary choice: be single-minded to God in asking for wisdom (1:5–8)
- Binary choice: identify with the lowly and not the rich (1:9–11)

Blessedness for the one persevering through trial (1:12)
- Binary choice: choose life, not death, by yielding to temptation (1:13–15)
- Binary choice: stay loyal to the generous God (1:16–18)
- Binary choice: be quick to listen and obey the word (1:19–24)

Blessedness for the one who perseveres in obedience to the law (1:25)

Preview of the body: bridling the tongue and caring for the poor (1:26–27)

Not showing partiality to the rich (2:1–13)

Having a faith that works together with deeds, especially caring for others (2:14–25)

Having singly beneficial use of the tongue (3:1–12)

Having wisdom from above that results in peace (3:13–18)

Being humble and submitting oneself to God (4:1–12)

Apostrophe: rich merchants and oppressive rich who are condemned (4:13–17; 5:1–6)

Being patient for the Parousia (5:7–11)

Final exhortations: avoid oaths, pray for each other, be on the path of truth (5:12–20)

THE FORM AND RHETORIC OF JAMES FROM AN ASIAN PERSPECTIVE

James presents itself as a Greek epistle, with its opening and closing content. Its opening (1:1) contains its author (James), a descriptive phrase ("a servant of God and of the Lord Jesus Christ"), the recipients ("to the twelve tribes of the diaspora"), and a greeting ("Greetings").[7] Its closing content includes elements common to the ending of Greek epistles, including the phrase "above all" (5:12), content about oaths (5:12), and content about prayer (5:13–18).[8] However, James also shares some elements with wisdom literature. Like Proverbs and Sirach, the content of James urges its readers to live righteously in a manner better than they currently are. It often presents wise sayings in aphoristic forms (e.g., 2:13; 3:18). Much like Confucius, a Jina, or a guru, James teaches pithy, timeless truths that are easily memorized. He is concerned with integrity (1:4, 27; 3:9–12) and peace within the community (3:14–4:1; 4:11; 5:9).

While some have applied patterns of progressive logic to James, such attempts have not produced a consensus and may be misguided. James often displays asyndeton, the lack of conjunctions and other connecting words that

7 See Jeffrey A. D. Weima, *Paul the Ancient Letter Writer: An Introduction to Epistolary Analysis* (Grand Rapids, MI: Baker Academic, 2016), 11–50.

8 See Francis Xavier J. Exler, "The Form of the Ancient Greek Letter: A Study in Greek Epistolography" (PhD diss., Catholic University of America, 1923), 113–14, 127–32; Fred O. Francis, "The Form and Function of the Opening and Closing Paragraphs of James and 1 John," *ZNW* 61 (1970): 125.

show a progression of clauses. The content of the epistle often switches topics without warning (see, for example, the sections starting at 2:1, 3:1, and 3:13). Such constructions may seem nonsensical to the Western reader accustomed to unfolding logic. However, James often displays the literary device of catchwords, or the linking together of sections of text based on a common word (such as *lack* between 1:4 and 1:5 or *trial/tempt* between 1:12 and 1:13). The author appears to move from one topic to the next by connecting a concept to the previous section.[9] Eastern readers familiar with this approach to teaching and writing can be comfortable with James's progressions of thought.

JAMES AND THE CULTURES AND WORLDVIEWS OF ASIA

The Epistle of James displays notable points of contact with Asian cultures and worldviews. In what follows, I will examine several ways the content of James speaks to modern Asian contexts. Special attention will be given to both East Asian and South Asian settings.

Perseverance and Devotion

The virtues of industriousness and discipline are celebrated in many Asian cultures, particularly those steeped in Confucian and Shinto values. Confucius's philosophy of a harmonious society includes the affirmation of hard work, loyalty, and dedication. In Confucian cultures, personal sacrifice and devotion are encouraged because of the belief that all of society will function well as a result.[10] Thus, hard work is celebrated; parents instill industriousness in their children in many East Asian cultures.

Industriousness also has a high value in other Asian societies. Hindus often speak of self-restraint through wisdom, seeking liberation from worldly desires. Sikhism promotes honesty and hard work of everyday people. Buddhists promote patience through difficulty by building inner strength. Many

9 See Daniel K. Eng, "The Role of Semitic Catchwords in Interpreting the Epistle of James," *TynBul* 70 (2019): 245–67.

10 See Charles Rarick, "Confucius on Management: Understanding Chinese Cultural Values and Managerial Practices," *Journal of International Management Studies* 2, no. 2 (2008): 22–28.

practice mindfulness to develop inner peace and not react with anger to circumstances.

The value of perseverance in the Epistle of James resonates with such Asian cultures that uphold industriousness and patience. James urges his hearers to rejoice amid trials because such events build their perseverance, which will work to make them perfect and complete (1:2–4). The hearers are encouraged that the ones who persevere through these trials, not abandoning the faith but staying loyal to God, will be rewarded. Indeed, the man who perseveres can look forward to the crown of life (1:12). James points to the prophets, who were patient through their suffering for speaking in God's name (5:10). Also, the figure of Job is upheld as an example of perseverance, as he experienced much suffering but did not curse God. In the end, according to James, the Lord was compassionate and merciful to Job (5:11). Through the promises of future well-being and reward, James exhorts his hearers to persevere in the same way as the OT figures. They are encouraged to be patient (5:7), to not complain (5:9), and to place their hope in God's mercy.

Unlike the Confucian work ethic, the call to perseverance in James does not find its motivation in building the quality of society. In fact, the hearers are urged not to be friends of the world but to align themselves with God (4:4). The reward for their perseverance is found not in this life but in the life to come (see 1:12).

Harmony in the Community

Throughout his epistle, James demonstrates his concern for the well-being of the community, especially its harmony. The many commands in James are primarily lived out within horizontal relationships. In other words, the exhortations of James address how one acts toward one's neighbor. This demonstrates religion that is pure before God (1:27) and faith that saves (2:14). The priority of relational harmony is also prized by many Asians. For example, the principles of Confucianism include the value of social harmony, demonstrated in the philosophy of the five relationships.[11] Hindus affirm the value of the social body acting as one. Jainas, who reject the dogmatism of Buddhism and Hinduism, strive for peace between those who disagree.

11 The five relationships are ruler-subject, father-son, husband-wife, older-younger, and friend-friend.

Those who adhere to the Bahá'í faith seek the well-being of all by promoting the unity of all religions.

Like many Asian philosophies and faiths, James urges his hearers to seek the peace of the community. However, harmonious relationships are not the highest priority in James's epistle. Instead, the commands for the community, such as being slow to anger (1:19), refraining from cursing (3:9–12), or making peace (3:18), are set within one's relationship with God. James states that religion that is pure before God involves caring for the less fortunate. He evaluates whether a particular faith can save by examining how one treats a neighbor (2:14–17). In accordance, he associates disorder, jealousy, and selfishness with what is earthly and demonic (3:14–16). In addition, the anger of humans does not bring out the righteousness of God (1:20). Quarrels in the community reveal that one is engaging with the world (4:1–4). Those who speak or grumble against another can expect to be condemned (4:11; 5:9). Through these commands, James teaches that peace in the community reflects loyalty to God, which results in God's favor.

For the Asian Christians, striving for community harmony may look much like the efforts rooted in Confucianism, Hinduism, Jainism, or the Bahá'í faith. There is an affinity between the commands of James and the values found in Asia. However, it is loyalty to God and his commandments that make up the foundation of the appeals to harmony. This peace and unity will be rewarded in the end, as James states in 1:12 and 5:7.

The Afterlife and Present Suffering

The widespread belief in karma in many Asian societies impacts how one views suffering and trials. Karma, the principle of moral causation, a fundamental belief in many forms of Buddhism, Sikhism, Hinduism, and Jainism, teaches a cause-and-effect relationship between one's present actions and one's state when one is rebirthed in the next life (samsara). As a result, those who believe in karma often attribute suffering to evil deeds done in a former life. Belief in karma functions as motivation for a person to do good deeds, such as generosity and kindness.

The Epistle of James also teaches life after death, but it is not a repeated cycle of rebirth. There is an eternal state that comes after this life, and James explains that there will be an eschatological judgment when the end comes. He teaches of the Parousia, the coming of the Lord (5:7–8). With the Parousia comes the Judge (5:9), who is the only one who can save and destroy (4:12). James exhorts his hearers that if they persevere under trial, they will be approved and will receive the crown of life (1:12). In addition to the crown, there are other descriptions of rewards that are set in the eschaton: a reversal of the fortunes of the lowly (1:9; 4:6, 10), being rich in faith and heirs to the kingdom (2:5), being saved by the Judge (4:12; see 2:14), and a reward of blessing (1:12, 25; 5:11). Thus James teaches that there are afterlife consequences of one's present life.

However, unlike the principle of karma, James teaches that present suffering and trials do not necessarily happen because one previously engaged in wicked deeds. The opening exhortation (1:2–4) contains a theodicy of sorts: the hearers of James are not facing trials because they are being punished for sin. Trials serve as a test of faith (1:3), much like the furnace serves as a test of the genuineness of precious metals. God, in the role of the metal-assayer, is the one to approve the people in their trial (1:12) and determine whether they receive eternal rewards.

Many Asian Christians are suffering for their faith. In many places, they are disowned and ostracized by their families. They often face discrimination from the workplace, get arrested, or have threats made on their lives. The call to follow Jesus involves counting the cost and paying the price. James urges his diaspora Christian readers to view suffering as a test of their faith. He gives the example of the prophets who suffered for speaking in the name of God (5:10). They will be blessed if they persevere in the faith (see 1:2–4, 12; 5:11).

Honor and Shame

The prominence of honor and shame is a notable similarity between the ancient Mediterranean world and modern Asian cultures. In such collectivistic cultures, the group remains the highest priority, with the most immediate group being the family. Honor is a positive social value associated with how one is viewed in the group. Shame is a state that results from failing to meet the group's expectations. Both honor and shame can be ascribed through one's associations, like family lineage, or achieved through actions that build a good or bad reputation. A good reputation is of high value. A Japanese proverb says, "Life is for one generation; a good name is forever." Also, one is expected to put the collective above one's own needs in a collectivistic culture. One's reputation affects the honor of the group, and vice versa.

The priority of the collective in James resonates with those in Asia with a collectivistic rather than individualistic identity. The epistle regularly uses familial language; he refers to his readers as "my brothers" (1:2, 16, 19; 2:1, 5, 14; 3:1, 10, 12; 4:11; 5:7, 9, 10, 12, 19), often adding the qualifier "beloved" (1:16, 19; 2:5), and he refers to God as the Father (1:17, 27; 2:21; 3:9). He exhorts them to make the collective a priority, calling for the care of a needy brother or sister (2:15), peacemaking (3:17), beneficial speech toward one another (3:9; 4:11; 5:9), and prayer for one another (5:14–18).

In a similar fashion as much Asian rhetoric, James uses the dynamics of honor and shame to motivate his hearers. The epistle's exhortations demonstrate the priority of relationships within the collective as well as concern for the group's reputation. James urges them to consider the "honorable name" by which they are called (2:7) and appeals to the esteemed status of Abraham as a "friend of God" (2:23).

Asian readers accustomed to indirect ways of exhortation may be taken aback by the directness of James's words in some places. His sense of urgency is so strong that he resorts to name-calling, calling his interlocutor an "empty person" (2:20) and those quarrelling with one another "adulteresses" (4:4). He labels his readers as "sinners" and "double-minded" (4:8) to motivate them to repent and submit to God. These descriptors should not be taken lightly—the situation is dire. Such direct confrontation is often the last resort in honor-based cultures that prefer more subtler forms of reprimand.

The juxtaposition of the OT exemplars in the latter half of James 2 is especially poignant in an honor-based culture, especially East Asian cultures that display veneration of their ancestors. While discussing the need for one to have faith that works together with deeds, James refers to two figures, Abraham and Rahab. It should not be a surprise to the Jewish readers of James that their celebrated patriarch Abraham was justified and given the honorific title "a friend of God" (2:23–24). However, it is remarkable that Rahab, the Canaanite harlot, is justified as well (2:25). The pairing of the two examples demonstrates that one is justified by God by the same standard, regardless of one's reputation. Even if one does not have ascribed honor, one can be justified before God with faith that saves (2:14).[12]

12 See Robert J. Foster, *The Significance of Exemplars for the Interpretation of the Letter of James*, WUNT 2/376 (Tübingen: Mohr Siebeck, 2014), 59–127.

Loyalty

Cultures steeped in Confucian ethics place a high value on loyalty and duty. Confucius constantly promoted the virtue of trustworthiness and allegiance in one's relationships (e.g., *Analects* 1.8; 2.20; 3.19; 7.24; 9.25; 12.10; 15.6). Such commitment to one's relationship is the foundation of a harmonious society.

The religions of Asia also place a high value on duty and loyalty. For example, the collectivistic cultures in which Islam has thrived consider the duty to society as a great virtue. For Hindus, dharma encompasses concepts like order, seeking of truth, obligation, and ethics, especially in application to the social order. Sikhs often view the present life as an opportunity to express their duty and union with *Akal Purakh*.

Similarly, James promotes the values of allegiance and trustworthiness. However, to James, one's loyalty should be to God alone. James constantly exhorts his hearers to demonstrate allegiance to God. In dualistic language reminiscent of the Deuteronomic choice between life and death, James calls his audience to choose the better of the two paths. It is those who prove themselves loyal to God who will receive a favorable verdict at eschatological judgment (1:12; 2:12–13; 3:1; 4:12; 5:9).

As he uses the language of friendship, James appeals to the practice of reciprocity between parties in the ancient world. Relationships of pledged loyalty were based on an agreement for mutual benefit, not just fondness. As a result, friendship with one party would preclude friendship with an opposing party or individual. James challenges his hearers to choose friendship with God like Abraham did (2:23). They cannot be friends with the world (4:4).[13]

Socioeconomic Disparity

Extreme poverty exists throughout Asia. South and East Asia, in particular, contain a high concentration of the world's poor. Even with global efforts to improve the quality of life for all people, inequality persists. The poor are often marginalized, not having the influence to impact government policies. Social systems are often biased against the less fortunate in Asia, especially

13 See Alicia J. Batten, *Friendship and Benefaction in James*, Emory Studies in Early Christianity 15 (Dorset, UK: Deo, 2010), 9–54, 145–76.

against lower castes, indigenous people, and women. Poor health abounds, including hunger and disease.

A recurring motif in the Epistle of James is socioeconomic disparity. In general, the poor are favored, and the rich are condemned in the epistle. The oppression of the poor is a familiar biblical theme (see, for example, Prov 14:20, 31; 17:5; 19:4, 7; 22:7, 22; Ps 35:10). James continues these themes in his epistle. On one side of the spectrum, James writes about the lowly (1:9), orphans and widows (1:27), those in dirty clothing (2:3), those who are poorly clothed and hungry (2:15), and defrauded laborers (5:4). On the other side, he writes about the rich who are humiliated (1:10–11), the rich who oppress the readers of the epistle and drag them into court (2:6), the arrogant merchants with the means to travel (4:13–16), and the rich who cheat their workers (5:1–6). In what follows, I will examine the dynamics of socioeconomic disparity in James in the context of modern Asian cultures in two areas: the caste system and caring for the poor.

The Caste System and Social Mobility

James 2:1–9 describes a hypothetical scenario that resonates with those who seek upward mobility in a class or caste system. James poses a situation where two men come into the assembly of the readers of the epistle: one dressed in fine clothes and one dressed in filthy clothes. He describes a scenario where they are kind to the rich man, giving him the seat of honor. At the same time, they marginalize the poor man, having him stand or sit at their feet. Such favoritism reflects sycophancy, hoping to gain the favor of the rich man for their benefit. There remains an element of social mobility in this account, as James portrays the hearers showing partiality to the rich to gain favor.

Dalits, those in the lowest caste in modern South Asia, experience the marginalization like the poor man in this passage. They are often discriminated against, shunned from society, and called untouchables. The widespread belief in karma is a significant factor in keeping the Dalits poor and marginalized. Because many believe that a person's social status is tied to the deeds one does in previous lives, those of the lowest caste are considered to have deserved their plight. As a result, Dalits have struggled to be free of the oppression that comes from being born into this caste.

The situation described in James 2:1–6 is similar to Dalits' efforts to gain social standing. Behind the efforts of showing favoritism to the rich is a belief that one can improve one's status. Similarly, Dalits believe that they can improve their social status by converting to Christianity. The Scriptures teach that all are equal in the sight of God, so those of lower caste often think that adhering to Christianity will free them of oppression. As a result, beliefs akin to the prosperity gospel abound in such environments, as people seek temporal and material reasons to convert.

The principle of reciprocity, prevalent in Confucian cultures,[14] is also being leveraged in James's hypothetical scenario. When the subjects show favoritism to the rich man, they hope to procure something in return in the future. This appeal to obligation would resonate with many East Asian readers. For example, the Japanese principle of *giri* (duty, obligation) drives people to give gifts or perform acts of service for others. In turn, the recipients are expected to reciprocate gifts or favors in the future. This social dynamic of reciprocity is affirmed in many Asian cultures.

However, James turns the tables on this attempt at social mobility or creating obligation for future favors from the rich. He condemns this favoritism toward the rich man (2:1, 4). Showing partiality to procure reciprocal benefits is unacceptable to James because of the actions of the rich. The rich are the ones who oppress others (see 5:4), even dragging them into court (2:6).

The implications of James's assertion in 2:1–9 in Asian cultures cannot be minimized. While those in lower castes and the materially poor may desire to have a better life by escaping oppression, James affirms that it is the poor who are ideal candidates to receive eternal reward. In other words, they do not have to escape poverty in the present life to have eternal riches. The poor who love God will receive the blessings described in 2:5. They are not temporal blessings, to the disappointment of those who hope to gain something in this world. Instead, the riches in 2:5 are determined by God and will occur in the eschaton. Thus James urges his readers to align with God, showing favor to those whom God favors. This will result in eternal rewards and not temporal rewards. Dalits can be assured that they are prime candidates for God's favor, and if they love God (2:5), they can look forward to eternal rewards. Also, reciprocity is not abolished but redirected. Showing favor to the poor

14 Virstan B. Y. Choy, "Decision Making and Conflict in the Congregation," in *People on the Way: Asian North Americans Discovering Christ, Culture, and Community*, ed. David Ng (Valley Forge, PA: Judson, 1996), 251.

and aligning with them rather than the rich can express love for God. James promises rewards for those who love God (1:12; 2:5)

Caring for the Poor

With the high concentration of poor people in many Asian countries, different attempts are made to reduce the socioeconomic disparity. Some Asian societies address inequality by having a system of communism, having the absence of social classes and a collective ownership of property. Others address it by encouraging those who have wealth to voluntarily give to the poor. The Bhoodhan Movement, for example, is a land reform effort that aimed to convince wealthy landowners in India to provide land to poor laborers. Confucius taught that generosity benefits society because it encourages others toward humaneness (*Analects* 8.2).[15] Similarly, generosity, or *dāna*, is one of the highest virtues of Hinduism, especially expressed in almsgiving (e.g., *Rig Veda* X.117).

James also teaches his hearers to care for the poor. God's favor on the less fortunate is a consistent biblical theme (e.g., 2 Sam 22:28; Job 34:28; Isa 14:30). Aligning with the rich and dishonoring the poor (Jas 2:6) are condemned by James because the poor themselves are favored by God. They are the ones chosen by God to be rich in faith and to inherit the kingdom (2:5). Note that James does not say that all the poor without distinction are promised this reward; it is the people who love God (2:5). The reward of being "rich in faith" most likely means "rich in the sphere of faith," or according to God's standards.[16] Besides, the poor who love God are promised the kingdom, a favorable future state for the righteous, which is connected to eschatological salvation.[17] James continues a recurring theme in the Scriptures, condemning those who mistreat the poor (e.g., 1 Sam 2:8; Amos 2:7; Isa 3:14–15) and promising reward for those who show kindness to the poor (e.g., Prov 19:17; Matthew 19:21; Mark 10:21; Luke 18:22; 19:8–9). While the poor are indeed materially needy, the term also carries a connotation with dependence on God

15 Confucius, *The Analects of Confucius*, trans. Burton Watson (New York: Columbia University Press, 2007), 54.

16 Peter H. Davids, *The Epistle of James*, NIGTC (Exeter, UK: Paternoster, 1982), 111–12; James Hardy Ropes, *A Critical and Exegetical Commentary on the Epistle of St. James*, ICC (Edinburgh: T&T Clark, 1916), 194.

17 See Douglas J. Moo, *The Letter of James*, PilNTC (Grand Rapids, MI: Eerdmans, 2000), 107.

(e.g., Ps 22:24; 69:32; 101:1). In fact, the designation *poor* is even used in apposition with the people of God (Ps 72:2; Isa 3:15). In sum, the teachings of James align with the consistent biblical witness that demonstrates God's predilection for the poor.

James indicates that caring for the poor is valued by God. Using cultic language, he writes that part of pure and undefiled religion, which is acceptable to God, is caring for orphans and widows (Jam 1:27). He teaches that the kind of faith that saves (2:14) is accompanied by good deeds, with caring for a destitute brother or sister as the example of such acts (2:15). Later, James condemns the wicked, wealthy landowners who cheat their workers using graphic imagery that their flesh will be eaten like metal is corroded (5:3).

The Diaspora: Immigrants and Refugees

The journeys of refugees and immigrants are intimately woven into the fabric of Asia. Many move from their homes in Asia to other places, and others move to Asian locations. They desperately seek to settle in an unfamiliar land. While some have chosen to migrate, many forcibly relocated. In the year 2013, the number of forcibly displaced people worldwide exceeded fifty million,[18] the highest it has been since the Second World War.[19] Immigrants and refugees often face difficulties becoming self-reliant, especially with limited health care and employment opportunities.[20] They are often discriminated against in a new land that previously held much promise. With their experience and the collectivistic nature of their cultures of origin, they often create and join communities with other migrants. These become their primary support networks.

The Christian Diaspora readers of the Epistle of James faced challenges similar to Asian immigrants and refugees. They relocated far from their home, many longing to return. They also faced difficulties because of their ethnicity

18 Lisa Joyce and Pranee Liamputtong, "Acculturation Stress and Social Support for Young Refugees in Regional Areas," *Children and Youth Services Review* 77 (2017): 18.

19 Jennifer Simmelink McCleary, "Applying a Collective Resilience Framework to Refugees' Perceptions of Recovery from Harmful Alcohol Use," *Traumatology, Resilience and Trauma: Expanding Definitions, Uses, and Contexts* 23, no. 1 (2017): 82.

20 Sungkyu Lee, Sunha Choi, Laurel Proulx, and Jennifer Cornwell, "Community Integration of Burmese Refugees in the United States," *Asian American Journal of Psychology* 6, no. 4 (2015): 333.

and their faith (see 1:2; 2:6–7; 5:10). They likely formed Jewish Christian enclaves, receiving support from one another in their new land.

James displays deep concern for these Jewish Christian communities. His commands to his Diaspora readers are to be carried out largely in the context of their communities. They are to meet the needs of their impoverished brothers and sisters (2:15–16), pursue peace within their communities (3:17–18), and refrain from quarrelling with one another (4:1–4). James condemns speaking evil (4:11) and grumbling (5:9) against one another. He calls them to pray for one another, confessing sins and seeking healing for them (5:16). Finally, he urges them to bring back anyone who wanders from the truth (5:19–20). James teaches that one's faith and allegiance to God is demonstrated through how they treats their brothers and sisters. This is how one can demonstrate that they have a faith that saves.

CONCLUSION

James's epistle addresses followers of Christ who are far away from their homeland. As they experience hardship and oppression, the hearers of James are exhorted to persevere in loyalty to God and staying on the way of truth. Through many commands to act righteously in community, James continually reminds them that their actions have eternal consequences. They are encouraged that their patience and endurance through the trials will be rewarded in the end.

There is much in the epistle that appeals to Asian readers. The values of duty, loyalty, and harmony resonate deeply with their cultural ideals. Also, the socioeconomic disparity of the original hearers of James is a significant point of continuity with modern Asian realities. Asian readers would find that much of the epistle is readily applicable, as they consider how their actions bring life to their faith in Christ.

FURTHER READING

Allison, D. C. 2013. *James: A Critical and Exegetical Commentary.* ICC. New York: Bloomsbury T&T Clark.

Blomberg, C. L., and M. J. Kamell. 2008. *James*. ZECNT. Grand Rapids, MI: Zondervan.

Cargal, T. B. 1993. *Restoring the Diaspora: Discursive Structure and Purpose in the Epistle of James*. Atlanta: Society of Biblical Literature.

Chester, A., and R. P. Martin. 1994. *The Theology of the Letters of James, Peter, and Jude*. Cambridge: Cambridge University Press.

Cheung, L. L. 2003. *The Genre, Composition and Hermeneutics of James*. Carlisle, UK: Paternoster.

Cheung, L. L., and A. B. Spurgeon. 2018. *James: A Pastoral and Contextual Commentary*. Asia Bible Commentary. Carlisle, UK: Langham Global Library.

Eng, D. K. 2018. *James: An Honor-Shame Paraphrase*. Edited by Jayson Georges. N.p.: Time Press.

James, A. 2015. "James." In *South Asia Bible Commentary*, edited by Brian Wintle, 1732–1740. Grand Rapids, MI: Zondervan.

McKnight, S. 2011. *The Letter of James*. NICNT. Grand Rapids, MI: Eerdmans.

Mongstad-Kvammen, I. 2013. *Toward a Postcolonial Reading of the Epistle of James: James 2:1–13 in Its Roman Imperial Context*. Leiden: Brill.

Moo, D. J. 2000. *The Letter of James*. PilNTC. Grand Rapids, MI: Eerdmans.

Varner, W. C. 2017. *James: A Commentary on the Greek Text*. Lexington, KY: Fontes.

TWENTY

The Letters of Peter

Layang Seng Ja
Kachin Theological College and Seminary
Kachin State, Myanmar

First and 2 Peter are usually categorized among the Catholic Epistles. The term *Catholic* also indicates that the letters address a wider Christian community, scattered throughout the ancient Mediterranean world.[1] The authors tell their readers how they should deal with the problems they face.[2] First Peter stresses that persecution is part of Christian life, a test, and an opportunity to imitate Christ. First Peter encourages the Petrine community to rejoice in the resurrection of Jesus and guides them to the reassurance and hope this offers to them.[3] Second Peter focuses on the crisis of eschatology caused by the delay of Christ's return and the dangers caused by the appearance of false teachers among his readers.

Our response as Asians to these letters will depend on the situations in which we find ourselves. As Christian minorities, we may feel that we are under similar pressures to those described in 1 Peter. Should we do as the letter says and obey the authorities? Many Asian churches have felt it wise to avoid confrontation,

1 Andrew Chester and Ralph P. Martin, *New Testament Theology: The Theology of the Letters of James, Peter, and Jude* (Cambridge: Cambridge University Press, 1994), 87.

2 E. F. Mason and T. W. Martin, eds., *Reading 1–2 Peter and Jude*, Resources for Biblical Study 77 (Atlanta: SBL, 2014), 51.

3 James D. G. Dunn, *Jesus according to the New Testament* (Grand Rapids, MI: Eerdmans, 2019), 163.

considering that it is essential for their survival. Others feel that such an approach is a sellout. How do we define Christianity, and what are our attitudes toward those who think differently? These are issues that demand reflection.

THE HISTORICAL CONTEXT OF FIRST PETER

Authorship

Peter, one of the best known figures in the early church, is mentioned more than 150 times in the NT.[4] Two of these letters claim to be written by the apostle Peter (1 Pet 1:2; 2 Pet 1:1, 16, 18). For a long time, the claim that the apostle Peter wrote both letters was undisputed. However, Peter was an illiterate fisherman, and even if he might have picked up some Greek, it is unlikely that he would have written such sophisticated Greek and been so familiar with the Greek version of the OT. Some scholars get around these difficulties by claiming he had a secretary who wrote 1 Peter (see 1 Pet 5:12). E. G. Selwyn argued that Silvanus was assisting apostle Peter to write down the epistle (5:12).[5] Is this was so, the wording would be the secretary's, not Peter's. Others have argued that the letter is pseudepigraphical. F. W. Beare, for instance, argued that the background to the letter is the situation described by Pliny the Younger. As governor of Bithynia in 112 CE, Pliny wrote to the emperor Trajan about the empire's policy toward Christians. But 112 CE is long after Peter's death. However, elsewhere Beare contradicts himself by claiming that the letter is a literary fiction, a pseudepigraphical work written toward the end of the first century in the name of the apostle to scattered subapostolic churches in western and central Asia Minor (1 Pet 1:1).[6] Others have argued for an earlier dating, and at times the letter itself seems to be referring to possible persecution (1 Pet 1:3–4:11) and actual persecution (1 Pet 4:12–5:11).[7]

4 Walter A. Elwell and Robert W. Yarbrough, *Encountering the New Testament: A Historical and Theological Survey* (Grand Rapids, MI: Baker Academic, 2013), 344.

5 Peter R. Rodgers, "Book of 1 Peter," in *Dictionary for Theological Interpretation of the Bible*, ed. Kevin J. Vanhoozer (Grand Rapids, MI: Baker, 2005), 1057.

6 Rodgers, 1057.

7 Raymond E. Brown, *An Introduction to the New Testament* (London: Doubleday, 1997), 706–7.

It may well be said that Silvanus (whose name is the Latinized equivalent of Silas) wrote the letter on behalf of Peter.[8] Silvanus was one of the leading men in the Jerusalem church (Acts 15:22, 32) and was a Roman citizen (Acts 16:37–38).[9] He is mentioned as accompanying Paul on the second missionary journey (Acts 15:40) and going with Paul and Timothy in 2 Corinthians 1:19.[10] So Silvanus might have served as secretary or coauthor of 1 Peter.[11] What may matter more is how the Petrine epistles might have brought comfort not only to the first readers but also to succeeding generations, including our own time where churches in Asia face discrimination and persecution by dominant powers.[12] Because Palestine is in Asia and most of the churches at the time were likely in Asia Minor / Asian Turkey, the recipients and the author were Asians.

Date, Genre, and Structure of 1 Peter

If the letter was written by Peter himself, it then probably dates to the early sixties CE. Selwyn, quoting Guthrie, points out that the doctrine and ecclesiastical organization are fairly early and would suit a date not much after 60 CE.[13] If written by Peter's assistant, it may be not later than the eighties.[14] If it was written by someone else within the Petrine tradition, it may be later. First Peter is based on a Christological presentation of Jesus, which is central to the message. The genre of the letter can be considered as a "general letter" or

8 Bart D. Ehrman, *The New Testament: A Historical Introduction to the Early Christian Writings* (Oxford: Oxford University Press, 2000), 400; also see Brown, *Introduction to the New Testament*, 707.

9 Pheme Perkins, *First and Second Peter, James, and Jude*, Interpretation: A Bible Commentary for Teaching and Preaching (Louisville: Westminster John Knox, 1995), 2–3.

10 D. A. Carson, Douglas J. Moo, and Leon Morris, *An Introduction to the New Testament* (Leicester, UK: Apollos, 1993), 433–35.

11 D. A. Hagner, *The New Testament: A Historical and Theological Introduction* (Grand Rapids, MI: Baker, 2012), 690; David L. Bartlett, "The First Letter of Peter: Introduction, Commentary and Reflections," in *The New Interpreter's Bible* (Nashville: Abingdon, 1998), 12:234.

12 Paul J. Achtemeier, Joel B. Green, and Marianne Meye Thompson, *Introducing the New Testament: Its Literature and Theology* (Grand Rapids, MI: Eerdmans, 2001), 519–20.

13 Edward Gordon Selwyn, *The First Epistle of St. Peter: The Greek Text with Introduction, Notes and Essays* (1981; repr., New York: Macmillan, 1946), 56–58.

14 Hagner, *New Testament*, 689.

a "circular letter" to many regions of Asia Minor (1:1).[15] Keener states, "Leaders of the Jerusalem priesthood sent out encyclicals, letters to Diaspora Jewish communities, by means of messengers; Peter's letter is similar to these but on a smaller scale of readership."[16] The structure of 1 Peter can be outlined as follows:

Opening greetings (1:1–2)

Hope and perseverance will lead to life (1:3–12)

Christian life to be built up in Christ (1:13–2:10)
    Being holy (1:13–25)
    Being God's people (2:1–10)

Life in exile (2:11–4:11)
    Living honorably among the gentiles (2:11–17)
    Living honorably in the household (2:18–3:7)
    Being faithful followers while suffering (3:13–4:11)

Encouragement and final greetings (5:1–14).[17]

The epistle follows the conventions of the ancient letters. It begins with the sender saluting the addressees and greeting them with blessings and thanksgiving (1:1–2). The main body contains a series of exhortations explaining their responsibilities as Christians in these trying times (1:13–5:11). The letter ends with the author's motivation for writing, more greetings, and a desire that his readers should give each other the kiss of peace as was expected of those who belong to Christ (5:12–14). In doing so, the writer is urging his audience to see the need for harmony within the congregation.[18]

15 Craig S. Keener, *The IVP Background Commentary: New Testament* (Downers Grove, IL: InterVarsity, 1993), 707.

16 Keener, 707.

17 See Raymond E. Brown, *An Introduction to the New Testament* (Bangalore: Theological Publications in India, 2009), 706.

18 See Donald Guthrie, *NT Introduction*, rev. ed. (Leicester, UK: Apollos, 1990), 800–804.

The writer, then, is offering his readers comfort in a difficult situation. He begins by explaining what a Christian life is. Christians belong not to this world but to the next. In this world, they are "in exile" among gentiles, nonbelievers. They must follow the example of Christ himself and accept their suffering as necessary for achieving glory in the next life.[19]

AN ASIAN READING OF FIRST PETER

Julian Price Love argues that there is no developed Christology in 1 Peter,[20] whereas Michaels points out that 1 Peter's Christology is rich and fully developed.[21] Welton Gaddy holds that the person of Jesus is portrayed as the Suffering Servant who died to redeem people. This suggests not a low but rather a high Christology. The epistle refers to Jesus as the resurrected one who has gone to heaven and is at the right hand of God, with angels, authorities, and powers made subject to him (3:21–22).[22] It is clear that Jesus is at the center of the epistle's exhortations and encouragement (1 Pet 4:4).[23]

Like Asian Christians, 1 Peter employs Christological traditions to support its moral exhortation of the believers who were suffering, ridiculed, and socially harassed on account of their faith.[24] It applies to all Asian Christians who are in such a situation. Christian minorities in countries where the majority are Buddhists, Hindus, and Muslims are under considerable pressure, and like the Christians addressed in 1 Peter, they are often viewed as outsiders. To take one example, Buddha's teachings emphasize, "When a person has right thoughts, his/her thoughts will become increasingly benevolent, harmless, and selfless and filled with love and compassion."[25] First Peter is filled with the

19 Brown, *Introduction to the New Testament*, 706–8.

20 Julian Price Love, "The First Epistle of Peter," *Interpretation* 8 (1954): 71.

21 J. Ramsey Michaels, "Catholic Christologies in the Catholic Epistles," in *Contours of Christology in the New Testament*, ed. Richard N. Longenecker (Grand Rapids, MI: Eerdmans, 2005), 274.

22 Welton Gaddy, "Preaching from 1 Peter," *Review and Expositor* 79, no. 3 (1982): 477.

23 Frank J. Matera, *New Testament Christology* (Louisville: Westminster John Knox, 1999), 174.

24 Matera, 174.

25 K. Sri Dhammananda, *What Buddhists Believe* (Taipei, Taiwan: Corporate Body of the Buddha Educational Foundation, 1993), 81.

flavor of the Myanmar Buddhist context because the author advocates right thought and right action as the cost of being Jesus's followers in a challenging situation.

Identity Crisis: Petrine Community

As in the case of the Petrine community, Christians in Myanmar are in a similar situation. Both are going through an identity crisis, living as they do in societies where they are a minority in both religion and culture. It does appear that Peter's readers did not take part in the official emperor worship, or indeed worship of the gods most people worshipped. By this they excluded themselves from much of the civic life that was bound up with this worship. Myanmar Christians also distinguish themselves from the majority by not taking part in Buddhist worship, which is so much a part of the national identity and is a state religion. Extremist Buddhists, known as the *MaBaTha*, spread hate speech and incite their followers to act violently. MaBaTha is led by prominent Buddhist monks who have the support of the military. They exert more influence on many Myanmar Buddhists than the government itself.[26]

Because national identity is tied to Buddhism and the Bama language and culture, there are many groups who fall outside. Hence there are many conflicts with those with a different identity from the majority—Rakhine, Kachin, Karen, Was, and Shan. Some of these ethnic minorities are Christians, such as Kachin and Chin; some may be both Christian and Buddhist, such as Karen; and many of Rakhine are Muslim. Consequently, the pressure is on these groups to conform to the majority religion and culture. If Christians remain faithful to their identity in Christ, different forms of discrimination and persecution follow as a consequence. Very often, Hindus attack Muslims and Christians in India, Muslims attack Christians in Pakistan, and conservative and nationalistic Buddhists attack minority Christians in Myanmar.

The Petrine Epistles are part of the "Catholic" epistles because they claim to be intended for either a very wide or an undefined audience.[27] For instance, the salutation in 1 Peter 1:1 is "to God's elect strangers of the Diaspora," and

26 *Buddhism and State Power in Myanmar: Asia Report N°290* (Brussels: International Crisis Group, 2017).

27 Michaels, "Catholic Christologies," 268.

2 Peter 1:1 also is "to those who have received a faith as precious as ours."[28] The phrase "exiles in the dispersion" suggests that the addressees were Jewish people, for the Greek term *diaspora* is a standard term for Jews living outside of Palestine. However, the term may be used metaphorically. This is very likely because the epistle claims its author was Peter, who was the first apostle to non-Jews (see Acts 10 and 11). Referring to 1 Peter 4:3–4, Delbert Burket considers that the recipients of 1 Peter were made up of gentile converts who withdrew from participation in the religious and social events of the wider community.[29] Evidently, a relationship existed between the author and his readers because the writer appears familiar with their situation. He exhorts the faith community to remain true to their professed faith and warns against the consequences of apostasy due to their current identity crisis in this threatening situation.

First Peter addresses people suffering under a crisis. Peter writes that they have "to suffer grief in all kinds of trials" (1:6). Later, he writes about their "fiery ordeals" (4:12), probably an allusion to the final judgment. He suggests that much of the abuse is verbal: opponents "speak maliciously against your good behaviour" (3:16), "heap abuse upon you" (4:4), and insult them because of their identity in Christ (4:14).[30] From the second century BCE until well after the time of 1 Peter, Rome feared foreign religions from the east that corrupted family life and plotted secret mayhem. For many who lived within the empire and for the educated elite who governed them, Christianity seemed to fall into this category.[31]

Peter wrote to console Christians living in such circumstances. He has three dominant concerns. First, he does not want his audience to succumb to the pressure society is exerting on them. Society has marginalized Christians, and they know that they can escape marginalization by returning to their previous ways of life (1:14, 18; 4:3). They can do this either by renouncing their faith or by compromising with prevailing religious practices. Second, he wants to be sure that the Christians to whom he writes provide no fodder for pagan

28 Achtemeier, Green, and Thompson, *Introducing the New Testament*, 492.

29 Delbert Burket, *An Introduction to the New Testament and the Origins of Christianity* (Cambridge: Cambridge University Press, 2012), 448.

30 Frank Thielman, *Theology of the New Testament* (Grand Rapids, MI: Zondervan, 2005), 625.

31 Thielman, 653.

slander by unnecessarily violating pagan social mores. They should submit to the various civil authorities (2:13–14) and should not use "their freedom as a cover-up for evil" (2:16, 18; 3:1, 5, 7; 5:5). They should shame their neighbors by their impeccable conduct (2:15; 3:16) and attract them to the worship of God (2:12; 3:1–2). Third, Peter wants to take his readers off the defensive and encourage them to engage in active witness both through their conduct and through reasoned speech to their detractors. They should not become like the rest of the society and thus become invisible. Instead, they should strive to be models of good behavior.[32] In his letter, he both testifies to God's grace and exhorts his readers to remain faithful to their vocation as the people of God, despite the persecution this entails (see 5:12).[33]

Crucified Jesus: A Role Model for Asian Christians

Theologically and practically, Asian Christian communities clearly understand that confessing Jesus means accepting the crucified Jesus as a role model for their conduct. Folktales help us theologize contextually, as C. S. Song rightly points out: "There is something deep in folktales and fairy stories—actually and spiritually deep."[34] The atonement concept is present in Kachin myth. In that myth, someone has to suffer and die. He must be crucified and shed his blood in order to rescue and save life for his community. The hanged man is a sacrifice whose blood liberates others and gives them life. He is also a role model and a source of strength for his community.[35] This makes it easier for the Kachin to grasp the meaning of the gospel and the idea of atonement. It was foreshadowed in their own folklore.

First Peter highlights the role of the hanged Christ as mediator and role model. When faced with unbearable situations, we should try to follow his example. His life, his ministry on earth, and his death show us the way. Those who profess him and are baptized into a new life[36] must live in a manner worthy of the redemption they have received and conduct themselves in

32 Thielman, 653.

33 Thielman, 654.

34 C. S. Song, *Tell Us Our Names: Story Theology from an Asian Perspective* (Maryknoll, NY: Orbis, 1984), iv.

35 Lecture note of Pungga Ja Li, *The Kachin Ideology and Myth* (Laiza: 2015).

36 Robert W. Wall, "Teaching 1 Peter as Scripture," *Word and World* 24 (2004): 373.

accordance with their new status as the people of God.[37] Matera observes that Peter roots "his moral exhortation in a Christology that focuses on the suffering of Christ."[38] Likewise, Roy B. Zuck underlines the significance of Peter's emphasis that Christ needed to suffer and die to accomplish God's will (1:11). Peter himself had vehemently denied this when Christ had foretold his death (Mark 8:31–33).[39] The prophets foretold the suffering of Christ, which he had to endure to demonstrate his present glory. In the same way, Christians will share in Christ's glory if they suffer (1:10–11).

In three passages (1:18–21; 2:21–25; 3:18–22), the writer explains five stages of Christ's spiritual journey: his preexistence, incarnation, suffering and crucifixion, resurrection, and exaltation and glorification. Even before he created the world, God chose Christ to save us. Much later, Christ was revealed through the incarnation for the sake of the sinners. He shed his blood and died as a lamb without blemish. Here the Lamb is not a passive victim (John 1:29) but an active Redeemer who carried our sins (2:24). Jesus the Lamb is sacrificed once for all.[40] Moreover, God accepted the sacrifice by raising Christ from the dead and granting him glory.

Second, in 1 Peter 2:21–25, Peter describes Christ's death as "suffering." He refers to the agony Christ endured before and on the cross. In instructing slaves to obey their masters, the letter presents Christ as an example of innocent but patient suffering. Christians are called to suffer injustice without retaliation, and Peter emphasizes the exemplary significance of Christ's death. Jesus is our substitute, paying the price we should pay for our sins. He did not die for his own guilt but for the sins of others. In doing so, he suffered and submitted himself to God's will and justice. Here Peter quotes the description of the Suffering Servant in Isaiah 53 and shows that Jesus fulfilled that role in his death.[41] 1 Peter 2:24 underlines the transformative power of Christ's work on the cross.

Third, Petrine passages also emphasize the substitutionary nature of Christ's death (3:18–22). He "suffered once for all concerning sins, the just for

37 Matera, *New Testament Christology*, 176.
38 Matera, 176.
39 R. B. Zuck, *New Testament Theology* (Chicago: Moody, 1995), 441.
40 Michaels, "Catholic Christologies," 277.
41 Zuck, *New Testament Theology*, 442.

the unjust." Here the emphasis is on the note of finality: there is no further need for Christ to suffer. What he did once was sufficient to reconcile humanity to God.[42] The passage describes Christ as "righteous" (δίκαιος)—that is, one who stands in a proper relationship with God. The purpose of Christ's suffering is stated as "to lead us to God." Zuck sees this as the portrayal of Christ's mediatory role in opening the way to God.[43] Matera observes this as the soteriological effect of Christ's suffering.[44] Furthermore, Jesus's death and resurrection are explained as "put to death in the flesh" (θανατωθεὶς μὲν σαρκὶ) and "alive in the spirit" (ζῳοποιηθεὶς δὲ πνεύματι; 1 Pet 3:18). Paul Achtemeier, citing Matera, suggests Christ was put to death by humans but raised by God's Spirit.[45] Matera sees this as two different modes of being: the mode of what is purely human and destined for corruption, and the realm of God's Spirit that is incorruptible.[46]

Christ's victory over spirits is also described in 3:19. Peter describes how Christ preached to the spirits in prison. Who are these spirits, and what was the message of Christ's proclamation? According to D. A. deSilva, two principal lines of thought emerge from the history of interpretation.[47] The most probable interpretation of the natural meaning of "spirits" is angelic beings rather than the souls of human beings, for the misbehavior of the angels, mentioned in Genesis 6:1–4, is closely associated with the story of the flood in both Genesis and 1 Enoch. Besides, Enoch is sent to the imprisoned spirits to preach their judgment rather than their salvation (1 Enoch 16:3).[48] Accordingly, Christ's message is understood as the victorious message of his triumph to the doomed spirits. In this point, Peter appears to emphasize that Christ's declaration of victory over the fallen angels would then assure the believers of their victory over the hostile forces and the demonic powers ultimately behind those forces (1 Pet 5:8–9).[49]

42 Matera, *New Testament Christology*, 181.
43 Zuck, *New Testament Theology*, 444.
44 Matera, *New Testament Christology*, 181.
45 Achtemeier, Green, and Thompson, *Introducing the New Testament*, 182.
46 Matera, *New Testament Christology*, 182.
47 David A. deSilva, *An Introduction to the New Testament: Contexts, Methods and Ministry Formation* (Leicester, UK: Apollos, 2004), 854.
48 deSilva, 182.
49 deSilva, 854.

The final event in this passage is Christ's exaltation at God's right hand and the submission of all spiritual powers to him. In raising Christ from the dead, God established him over every spiritual power. Among the images applied to Christ, the most prominent are the spotless and unblemished Lamb (1:19); the living Stone that is elect and precious in God's sight and forms the cornerstone of a spiritual house (2:4–6); the Shepherd and Guardian of our lives (2:25); and the Chief Shepherd (5:4). Among these, the suffering of Christ impresses the most.[50] Therefore, it can be said that the Christology of 1 Peter is a Christology of suffering. Christ's suffering was uniquely redemptive. As Matera rightly points out, by focusing on the suffering of Christ, 1 Peter shows the intimate relationship between Christology and the Christian life. The past suffering of Christ is the present condition of believers, whereas the present glory of Christ is the future glory of those who follow his steps.[51] Christology, then, is at the heart of 1 Peter and a promise of healing to the suffering community. As many Asian Christian communities are facing hostility and persecution, such a promise is pertinent.

Christ-Centered Hope While Suffering

What does it mean for Asian Christians to be true disciples? It means that our hope is centered on Christ. There are certain similarities here with Buddha's teaching about *dukkha* (suffering) and the path to Nirvana. After his enlightenment, Buddha preached his first sermon about the Four Noble Truths—"the truth of suffering, the cause of suffering, the end of suffering and the eightfold path that leads to *nirvana*."[52] To achieve true liberation, Buddha's followers must be tested and pass through suffering. Albeit in a different form, the idea of Christians having to be tried and tested to get to heaven is already familiar in Myanmar culture and indeed elsewhere in Asia where Buddhism is widespread.

First Peter also emphasizes the cost of discipleship while offering Christ-centered hope. The author tells the community they will face critical situations. He frequently uses the words "suffer" (2:19, 20, 21, 23; 3:14, 17, 18; 4:1,

50 Matera, *New Testament Christology*, 184.

51 Matera, 184.

52 M. V. Ram Kumar Ratnam, *Dukkha: Suffering in Early Buddhism* (New Delhi: Discovery, 2003), 45.

15, 19; 5:10) and "suffering" (1:11; 4:13; 5:1, 9). He emphasizes that on the cross, Christ suffered too, setting an example (2:21–23). Christ was rejected by humans but chosen by God as a precious cornerstone in God's spiritual house. Similarly, Christians who are rejected by society must find status, dignity, and identity in Jesus (2:4–10). When Christ returns, those who share this suffering will also share his glory (1:3–13; 3:14; 4:12–14; 5:1). Therefore, Peter urges his audience to rejoice and consider their suffering as a blessing (4:13–14). Furthermore, Peter urges that it is better to suffer for doing what is right than for doing wrong (2:20; 3:17; 4:15–16).[53] Peter urges us to emulate the example of Christ by doing what is right and sharing in Christ's suffering.[54] It is through Christ's suffering and resurrection (1:3) that God in his mercy gives Christians a new birth and a living hope (1:21; 3:5). By standing firm in this hope, we bear witness against the forces of evil (3:15, 22).[55]

Struggling with Christian Ethics: Being Holy

Like the community addressed in 1 Peter, the Asian Christian community is wrestling with Christian morality and ethics while dealing with a critical situation. It is very challenging to live a holy life in a hostile environment. How shall we cope with discrimination and persecution? The societies we live in are fiercely competitive and full of malice and corruption. Politicians and leaders at local and national levels seem interested only in money and power. We are minorities in countries where the dominant religions are Islam, Hinduism, Buddhism, and others. As such, Christians in Myanmar are often regarded as second-class citizens. Our loyalty is questioned. Henary Van Tio, an ethnic Chin Christian, was chosen by Aung San Suu Kyi's government as vice president of Myanmar. He has been constantly opposed by Burmese nationalists. Thousands called for Henary Van Tio's removal from office simply because he was neither Bama nor Buddhist.[56] The majority see us Christians as having

53 Burket, *Introduction*, 478; I. Howard Marshall, Stephen Travis, and Ian Paul, *Exploring the New Testament: A Guide to the Letters and Revelation* (Downers Grove, IL: IVP Academic, 2011), 2:282; Duane F. Watson and Terrance Callan, *First and Second Peter: Paideia Commentary of the New Testament Series* (Grand Rapids, MI: Baker, 2012), 15.

54 Watson and Callan, *First and Second Peter*, 15.

55 Marshall, Travis, and Paul, *Exploring the New Testament*, 2:288.

56 Awng Kyaw Min, "Nationalists Rally against Both Vice Presidents," *Myanmar Times*, April 5, 2016.

betrayed the national identity because we share the religion of our former colonial masters. In our daily lives, we are surrounded by majority religious communities and their pagodas, shrines, way of thinking, conduct, and behavior. The challenge is to maintain our faith in such an environment and live according to Christian ethics. We have the model of Christ to show us the way.

First Peter is addressed to a community facing similar challenges. They too were a minority viewed with suspicion on account of their religion and for failing to conform to social norms. The answer proposed is *imitatio Christi*, the imitation of Christ.[57] Peter exhorts his community to "abstain from sinful desires" (2:11) and "live such good lives among the pagans that, though they accuse you of doing wrong, they may see your good deeds" (2:12). He takes up the fundamental calling of Israel—"You shall be holy, for I am holy" (Lev 11:44–45; 19:2; 20:7, 26)—and makes it a key theme of the letter's appeal to its readers (1 Pet 1:16).[58] In so doing, he hopes that the Christians' good conduct will silence those who speak against them as evildoers (2:15; 3:16). They should be holy in all their conduct (1:15, 17) among the gentiles (2:12) and follow a "household code" (2:18–25; 3:1–6).[59] In other words, they are called to be marked off from the surrounding society by their distinctive lifestyle. To be "sanctified" (1:2, 15–16, 22) involves leaving aside the former way of life and becoming obedient to God (1:2, 14; 4:1–4).[60]

Religious Persecution and Homelessness

First Peter describes a situation where Christians meet hostile criticism and even persecution for their faith. There are many cults, but the key one is worship of the Roman emperor. Nominal acceptance of this is viewed as a pledge of allegiance to the state. Religious freedom is not practiced in many Asian countries, so the religion of the majority becomes a symbol and pillar of the state—for instance, Islam in Malaysia, Buddhism in Myanmar, communism as an ideology in China, and Hinduism in India. Let us take one example. Myanmar is home to more than 135 ethnic groups, the largest of which is the Bama or Burman tribe, which comprises 60 percent of the population and

57 Watson and Callan, *First and Second Peter*, 15.
58 Marshall, Travis, and Paul, *Exploring the New Testament*, 2:282.
59 Burket, *Introduction*, 478.
60 Marshall, Travis, and Paul, *Exploring the New Testament*, 2:282.

is Buddhist. The country is run for the benefit of the Bama majority and for those who share their belief in Buddhism. They oppress other ethnic groups who have different beliefs. They have set up Buddhism as the state religion and are spending a considerable amount of the country's income on building and renovating Buddhist temples and images while neglecting development for the entire population.[61]

Minority Christians continue to live in an intolerable situation under a Burmese military regime and nationalist Buddhist monks. Because of religious and ethnic discrimination, economic stagnation, exploitation, and civil wars have broken out. Many from the ethnic minorities have fled to neighboring countries such as Bangladesh, China, India, Malaysia, and Thailand in search of safety. Thousands of Rohingya have fled because Muslims are considered a threat, and the Burmese government regards them as illegal immigrants despite the fact that Rohingya have lived within the boundaries of present-day Myanmar for a long time.[62]

The parallels with 1 Peter are clear. In the epistle, the writer addresses a situation of cultural dislocation. The commitment to follow Jesus makes the readers "homeless" in their own land. The author writes of the emptiness of the ways they abandoned for their faith and affirms their identity as "a chosen people, a royal priesthood, and a holy nation." Their home is with God. In God's household, we are to use our various gifts to serve and love one another (4:8–11) and stand together in solidarity. While facing persecution from outside, the inner community of Christ must be strengthened by mutual service. In doing so, they may triumph over the trials they face. Christians must conduct themselves "among the Gentiles" (2:12) in good and honorable ways that their persecutors cannot help but notice (2:15, 20; 3:13–17; 4:19).[63]

61 Layang Seng Ja, "The Role of Jesus for the Kachins: Understanding Jesus from the Present Kachin Context," in *Theology under the Bo Tree*, ed. Thomas Cung Bik (Yangon: MIT, 2017), 203–5.

62 Lian Hand Do, "Life as Refugees Was Not a Choice: The Burmese Refugees Plight," *CTC Bulletin* 28, no. 1 (December 2012): 76.

63 Marshall, Travis, and Paul, *Exploring the New Testament*, 2:282.

Passed-On Traditions of Jesus's Teaching

In contrast to the Western world, in Asia, tradition and culture are handed down from generation to generation through a male-dominant hierarchical system. Asian communities are not individually oriented but are group oriented and male centered. The job of handing down norms, values, and stories is vital if the group is to preserve its identity. Although the wisdom of both mother and father is transmitted orally generation after generation, it is a male or father figure to whom society gives prominence. Consequently, the wisdom, knowledge, and contributions of women are ignored and considered insignificant. Asian Christians are often proud to say that their faith and knowledge of Jesus were handed down to them from the missionaries, from forefathers, and from generation to generation. This results in a predominantly male perspective so that in Myanmar and most Asian churches, women are denied leadership roles and are expected to obey male leaders.

In the specific context of the Kachin church community in Myanmar, Kachin Baptist Christian women face double oppression, from inside and outside their community. Buddhist teaching discriminates against women. For them, being born as a woman is the result of bad karma or an indication of a lack of merit in previous lives. In contrast, manhood is thought to be close to god; therefore, women must honor and worship men as they would god. For more than a century, many Kachin patriarchal leaders have taught that women are secondary beings. Kachin Baptist ministers have barred women from exercising ministerial and leadership roles. The Christian tradition, like the Buddhist tradition, has a strong pro-male bias.

Similarly, 1 Peter reflects the pro-male bias of its time and place. Roman and Hellenistic culture gave prominence to the father, the master, and the ruling class. Children had to obey their fathers, slaves their masters, women their husbands, and subjects their rulers—who were always men. It was a man's world. It is in contrast to what we read in the Gospels and Acts. In the Gospels, we see that women played a more important part than was usual at that time, and from Acts we see women playing prominent roles in the early church.

By the time 1 Peter was written, the four Gospels must have been circulating among Christian communities.[64] Even if the writer did not have

64 James D. G. Dunn, *Jesus according to the New Testament* (Grand Rapids, MI: Eerdmans, 2019), 164.

the texts at hand, we may presume that he would have heard the traditions on which they were based. Although Jesus always welcomed women in his ministry, 1 Peter is totally silent about the role of women during Jesus's lifetime in the context of the early Christian community. First Peter appears to suggest that the tradition of Jesus was handed down to the present community in the name of a pro-male disciple of Jesus. We can set up a table with citations on the left from 1 Peter and citations from the Gospels on the right. As we will see, the actual wording of the Gospels is hardly ever echoed, but the sense is. The nearest echoes of the Jesus tradition are as follows:

FIRST PETER	JESUS'S WORDS IN THE GOSPEL TRADITION
Into an inheritance that can never perish, spoil or fade—kept in heaven for you. (1 Pet 1:4)	Make purses for yourselves that do not wear out, an unfailing treasure in heaven, where no thief comes near and no moth destroys. (Luke 12:33)
Therefore prepare your minds for action, discipline yourselves; set all your hope on the grace that Jesus Christ will bring you when he is revealed. (1 Pet 1:13)	Be dressed for action and have your lamps lit . . . so that they may open the door for him as soon as he comes and knocks. (Luke 12:35)
But if you endure when you do right and suffer for it, you have God's approval . . . so that you should follow in his steps, "He committed no sin, and no deceit was found in his mouth." When he was abused, he did not return abuse, when he suffered. (1 Pet 2:18–23)	Love your enemies, do good to those who hate you, bless those who curse you, pray for those who abuse you. . . . Do to others as you would have them do to you. (Luke 6:27–36)
Do not repay evil for evil or abuse for abuse; but, on the contrary, repay with a blessing. It is for this that you were called that you might inherit a blessing. (1 Pet 3:9)	Love your enemies, do good to those who hate you, bless those who curse you, pray for those who abuse you. (Luke 6:27–28)
Discipline yourselves, keep alert. Like a roaring lion your adversary the devil prowls around, looking for someone to devour. Resist him, steadfast in your faith. (1 Pet 5:8–9)	Listen! Satan has demanded to sift all of you like wheat, but I have prayed for you that your own faith may not fail. (Luke 22:31–32)

FIRST PETER *(continued)*	JESUS'S WORDS IN THE GOSPEL TRADITION *(continued)*
Do not lord it over those in your charge, but be examples to the flock. And when the chief shepherd appears, you will win the crown of glory that never fades away. In the same way, you who are younger must accept the authority of the elders. And all of you must clothe yourselves with humility in your dealings with one another for "God opposes the proud, but gives grace to the humble." (1 Pet 5:3–5)	The greatest among you must become like the youngest, and the leader like one who serves. For who is greater, the one who is at the table or the one who serves? Is it not the one at the table? But I am among you as one who serves. (Luke 22:25–30)
Conduct yourselves honourably among the Gentiles, so that, though they malign you as evildoers, they may see your honourable deeds and glorify God when he comes to judge. (1 Pet 2:12)	Let your light shine before others, so that they may see your good works and give glory to your Father in heaven. (Matthew 5:16)
For the Lord's sake accept the authority of every human institution, whether of the emperor as supreme, or of governors. . . . For it is God's will that by doing right you should silence the ignorance of the foolish. As servants of God, live as free people, yet do not use your freedom as a pretext for evil. Honour everyone. Love the family of believers. Fear God. Honour the emperor. (1 Pet 2:13–17)	"From whom do kings of the earth take toll or tribute? From their children or from others?" . . . However, so that we do not give offense to them, go to the sea and cast a hook. . . . Take that and give it to them for you and me. (Matt 17:25–27)
But even if you do suffer for doing what is right, you are blessed. Do not fear what they fear, and do not be intimidated. (1 Pet 3:14)	Blessed are those who are persecuted for righteousness' sake, for theirs is the kingdom of heaven. (Matt 5:10)
But rejoice insofar as you are sharing Christ's sufferings, so that you may also be glad and shout for joy when his glory is revealed. If you are reviled for the name of Christ, you are blessed, because the spirit of glory, which is the Spirit of God, is resting on you. (1 Pet 4:13–14)	Blessed are those who are persecuted for righteousness' sake . . . when people revile you and persecute you and utter all kinds of evil against you falsely on my account. (Matt 5:10–11)

FIRST PETER *(continued)*	JESUS'S WORDS IN THE GOSPEL TRADITION *(continued)*
Although you have not seen him, you love him; and even though you do not see him now, you believe in him and rejoice with an indescribable and glorious joy, for you are receiving the outcome of your faith, the salvation of your souls. (1 Pet 1:8–9)	Have you believed because you have seen me? Blessed are those who have not seen and yet have come to believe. (John 20:29)

AUTHOR, AUDIENCE, GENRE, AND STRUCTURE OF SECOND PETER

The writer of 2 Peter states that he is Simon Peter, "a servant and apostle of Jesus Christ." After Peter became the disciple of Jesus, he was always part of the inner circle of three (Matthew 16:17; 17:1; Mark 5:37; 9:2–8).[65] Simon Peter takes risks; he risks proclaiming Jesus the Messiah, risks stepping out of the boat, and risks following the group who arrested Jesus right into the courtyard of the high priest. Peter is often the spokesperson for the Twelve. It is thus understandable that the writer claimed he was Peter.[66] However, the claim is highly problematic. As we have seen with 1 Peter, how likely is it that a fisherman, who was probably illiterate and whose mother tongue was Aramaic, should be able to write this kind of Greek?[67] With 1 Peter, we can possibly get around this problem by saying Peter used a secretary, Sylvanus, who did know Greek. But it is clear that 2 Peter was not written by the same writer, even if he claims to have written both (2 Pet 3:1).[68] Stylistically, the letter is written in an elaborate, late Hellenistic style that stands in contrast to the more straightforward style of 1 Peter. Theologically, Christ's second coming and the Last

65 Peter H. Davids, *The Letters of 2 Peter and Jude* (Grand Rapids, MI: Eerdmans, 2006), 123.

66 Robert G. Gromacki, *New Testament Survey* (Grand Rapids, MI: Baker, 2005), 359–61.

67 Dale B. Martin, *New Testament History and Literature* (New Haven, CT: Yale University Press, 2012), 368, 371.

68 Mark Allan Powell, *Introducing the New Testament* (Grand Rapids, MI: Baker, 2009), 482.

Judgment are close at hand in 1 Peter, whereas in 2 Peter, some Christians have come to doubt they will ever take place.[69] It is much more likely that the writer was a Hellenized Jew because he was familiar with the Greek version of the Jewish Bible[70] and Hellenistic ethical (2 Pet 1:5–7) and philosophical concepts (2 Pet 3:10).[71]

In terms of audience, 2 Peter and 1 Peter appear to have been written to no specific audience but to readers scattered among a pagan community and facing some challenges due to their new identity in Christ. Possibly, 2 Peter is addressed to a community that had previously received 1 Peter (3:1, 15). Basically, it warns them about those who come with false teaching. These teachers appear to support their lifestyle with a denial of the return of Christ and the Last Judgement. The genre of 2 Peter appears to be a "farewell speech" or "testament" such as one can find in Jewish literature.[72] It is also a warning to the community of Christ to stand steadfast and firm in the faith they received. This genre has three main features in the Jewish and NT examples: first, a speaker announces that he is going to die soon; second, a speaker gives a summary of his ethical and religious instruction; and third, a speaker gives revelation about the future. The same parallel genre is obviously depicted in 2 Peter:[73] first, in 1:12–15, Peter speaks of his imminent death; second, in 1:3–11, Peter gives a summary of his ethical and religious teaching; and third, in 2:1–3 and 3:1–4, he predicts the rise of false teachers. Second Peter uses this genre as a way to defeat doctrinal strife within the community. In more detail, 2 Peter has the following structure.[74]

Greetings (1:1–2)

Additional qualifications to confirm one's calling and election (1:3–11)

Peter's task before departure: Jesus's tradition is passed down (1:12–21)

69 D. Edmond Hiebert, *An Introduction to the NT* (Waynesboro, GA: Gabriel, 2003), 133–44.

70 R. Bauckham, *Jude, 2 Peter*, Word Biblical Commentary 50 (Waco, TX: Word, 1983), 135.

71 Daniel J. Harrington, *Jude and 2 Peter*, Sacra Pagina 15 (Collegeville, MN, Liturgical, 2003), 236.

72 Marshall, Travis, and Paul, *Exploring the New Testament*, 2:297.

73 See Marshall, Travis, and Paul, 2:297.

74 Marshall, Travis, and Paul, 2:297.

The prediction of false teachers and their destruction (2:1–22)

The day of the Lord (3:1–18).[75]

The body of the letter emphasizes that the readers have received the truth directly from God (1:16–21). So when false prophets arrive, God will punish them as he punished the fallen angels. Our duty is to resist and stand by the truth, no matter when Christ will return in judgment. We must be faithful and patient.

We can also see that to some extent, 2 Peter conforms to the conventions of an ancient letter: a greeting section naming the author and recipients with a blessing, the body of the letter with its purpose, and a closing summing up and exhortation. To whom exactly is the author writing? This is left vague. Similarly, with the deathbed genre, he mentions briefly that he is about to die (1:13–15) before moving on. Formally, 2 Peter fits the genres of an epistle and a deathbed testament, without making much of either.

AN ASIAN READING OF 2 PETER

Sheep Stealing by Intruders

The religious confusion described in 2 Peter 2–3 echoes in the Asian Christian community. Globalization has brought various doctrines that challenge the traditional Christianity handed down by our fathers. Preachers claim to be prophets, seers, and true ambassadors of God. Their message is aimed at those who are already Christians rather than to convert non-Christians. In Myanmar, some parachurch leaders and preachers claim that those who are in Christ do not need to ask God for forgiveness and do not need to have a life of prayer because Christ has already taken away their sins. Often these teachers do not have a proper biblical training at a theological institution. They spread confusion and mislead believers within the Christian community. For instance, preacher David Lar, a well-known speaker, has been a threat to many churches in Myanmar for his strong opposition to mainstream denominations.[76] The

75 For more details, see Guthrie, *NT Introduction*, 855–57.

76 Reuters World News, "Myanmar Charges Preacher for Defying Virus Ban on Service," April 15, 2020.

Myanmar council of churches has already stated that he does not belong to any official denomination but is a private preacher.[77] Myanmar Christians constantly encounter various scoffers and false teachers who lead believers astray.

Second Peter also describes his opponents as "scoffers" without elaborating much. However, from the text, one can figure out what problems these teachers present. The first point is the Christological issue (2 Pet 2). They "despise authority" (2:10) and "even deny the Master who bought them" (2:1).[78] They are under Hellenistic influence, most likely the doctrine of Epicureanism, because the epistle says this is "especially true of those who follow the corrupt desire of the flesh."[79] They are thus guilty of gross immorality. "They count it pleasure to revel in the daytime. . . . They have eyes full of adultery, insatiable for sin. . . . Forsaking the right way, they have gone astray. . . . They are experts in greed" (2:13–15). They entice others, promising them a "freedom" that ends in corruption (2:19).[80]

In 2 Peter, Jesus is the Savior through his righteousness. The language is close to that of Paul.[81] In addition, Peter speaks of Jesus as the Lord (1:3–4). Thus the Christology of 2 Peter centers on the revelation of God in Jesus, emphasizing that Jesus gives believers knowledge (1:2, 3, 5, 6, 8) of himself and of God.[82]

Divine Punishment

The second point of dispute with these false teachers is that they scoff at the idea that Jesus will return (2 Pet 3:3–5). Early Christians believed that Jesus would return within a generation. Second Peter seeks to justify Jesus's delay by distinguishing between divine time and human time: with God, "a thousand years are like a single day" (Ps 90:4).[83]

Second Peter uses the gospel tradition of transfiguration to describe the relationship between "our Lord Jesus Christ" (1:16) and "God the Father"

77 See Statement of Myanmar Council of Churches (MCC) on David Lar's preaching, April 17, 2020.

78 Hagner, *New Testament*, 718.

79 Jerome H. Neyrey, *2 Peter, Jude: A New Translation with Introduction and Commentary*, AB 37C (New York: Doubleday, 1993), 122–28.

80 Hagner, *New Testament*, 718.

81 Marshall, Travis, and Paul, *Exploring the New Testament*, 2:675.

82 Michaels, "Catholic Christologies," 280.

83 Burket, *Introduction*, 437.

(1:17). It also uses the tradition to support the prophecy that Jesus will come again in power (Parousia).[84] The false prophets deny the Master who bought his people from condemnation (2:1). Here the intruders preach that Lord Jesus Christ is powerless, and therefore there will be no Parousia or Final Judgment on sin (2–3). Peter warns the scoffers not to mistake the forbearance of the Lord. He gives several examples of God condemning sinners—fallen angels, cast in chains of darkness, the ungodly people drowned in the flood, and Sodom and Gomorrah burned to ashes—while saving the righteous such as Noah and Lot (2:4–7). Judgment is delayed not because the Judge is powerless but because he is merciful, for this gives people an opportunity for repentance and salvation (2:20; 3:7, 8–9, 10, 15). Instead of doubting that it will ever come, we are encouraged to rejoice in the promise of "a new heaven and a new earth where righteousness dwells" (3:13).

There are not just stylistic reasons for thinking 1 and 2 Peter were not written by the same person. A writer may change his approach to fit his audience and topic, but the differences between the two go beyond that. In 1 Peter, the second coming is not something in some unknown future, for judgment "begins with God's household . . . with us" (1 Pet 4:17). A few verses earlier (v. 7), "the end of all things is near." In 2 Peter, the sureness and suddenness of the "Day of the Lord" is stressed, but not its imminence. Likewise, 2 Peter focuses on judgment, whereas 1 Peter focuses on the reward of the righteous. When it comes to evidence to support his arguments, 1 Peter cites the example of the suffering Jesus, whereas 2 Peter refers only to the glorified Jesus (and then mostly as judge). First Peter is almost totally devoid of self-references, whereas 2 Peter contains more than one personal reference. Perhaps this difference is due to 2 Peter purporting to be a deathbed warning.

As a minority, Myanmar Christians suffer, as did the Christians addressed in 2 Peter. The latter were attacked for not adhering to the imperial or any of the local cults. Because of this, their beliefs were mocked. Similarly, nationalist Buddhist monks mock the Christian God as an invisible god and a criminal who was crucified on the cross. They also condemn the God of the OT as a foolish figure who killed many human beings.[85] In short, they

84 Marshall, Travis, and Paul, *Exploring the New Testament*, 2:675.

85 Ashin Ahgadama, *The God Who Killed Human Beings: A Foolish Creator*, Buddha's Glory Series 2 (unpublished manuscript, April 2020).

claim Christianity is inferior to their Buddhist religion. Normally, all Buddhists know that they should try to keep a basic minimum of five precepts each day: "I abstain from killing living beings. I abstain from taking what is not given. I abstain from sexual misconduct. I abstain from saying what is not true. I abstain from taking drinks and drugs that are intoxicating and cause forgetfulness."[86] The form of Buddhism advocated by Bama nationalists breaches all five precepts. By promoting a national identity based on a state religion and a single ethnic identity, it makes enemies of all those of us who do not fit into this model.

According to the report of the Kachin Baptist Convention, the Myanmar military destroyed sixty-six churches and over two hundred villages in Kachin State and Kachin villages in Northern Shan States from 2011 to 2016. Thousands of Kachins have been made homeless, made ill from starvation and disease, turned into orphans, and even killed and maimed.[87] The Kachin faith community longs for liberation and divine judgment over the perpetrators. Just as the community addressed in 2 Peter anticipated divine punishment, the Kachins believe that God's judgment is delayed not because the Judge is powerless but because he is merciful and gives people an opportunity for repentance.

DEFENDER OF EXTERNAL AND INTERNAL ANTAGONISTS

First and 2 Peter address Christians under pressure. The overall theme of 1 and 2 Peter is the cost of discipleship.[88] First Peter calls us to stand firm when faced with external hostility. Second Peter urges us to defend the faith against false prophets within the community. These epistles invite us as true disciples to imitate Christ and follow his example. Suffering and death are part of discipleship (Mark 8:34–38; 1 Pet 4:19). The Petrine epistles tell us that proper response of Christians is to do the will of God rather than follow our own desires (4:1–2). We should emulate Christ's example of good moral conduct by "doing good" no matter the cost (2:12, 15, 20; 3:6, 13, 17; 4:19).

86 Eugenia Kaw, *Buddhism and Education in Burman: Varying Conditions for a Social Ethos in the Path to "Nibbana"* (PhD diss., Princeton University, 2005), 182.

87 Seng Ja, "Role of Jesus," 211.

88 Ehrman, *New Testament*, 407.

Indeed, being a faithful disciple of Christ means following and doing the will of God, especially in situations where one suffers for it (3:17; 4:19). Christian conduct extends to fulfilling Jesus's command to love one's enemies. This understanding is implicit in the letters' emphasis on humility, gentleness, and nonretaliation as the proper response to those who oppress the community (2:12, 15–25; 3:8–17).[89] In the midst of suffering, the Christian community was called not to oppose to those evildoers but to respond with humility and submission.

Discipleship has a cost, as Bonhoeffer pointed out. Asian Christian communities face similar situations to those described in the Petrine letters, and they face similar challenges in Pakistan,[90] India, and China, to mention only a few countries. Asian Christians encounter persecution and hostility from outside the community and division created by false teaching from within the community. Ever since the Thein Sein government in 2010, Myanmar has claimed to be moving toward a democratic system. In fact, the military still exercises control behind the scenes. Aung San Suu Kyi's government has become a living shield for the terrorist acts committed by the Burmese military. The present government and military continue the Burmanization policy. Thus other ethnic minorities and the Kachin Christians[91] live in a country run for the benefit of the Bama majority and for those who share their belief in Buddhism. They oppress other ethnic groups who have different beliefs.[92]

Although 99 percent of the minority ethnic Kachin population are Christians[93] and Christianity is the main religion in Kachin State, the Kachin faith community is oppressed and discriminated against by the Bama people in every aspect of life. Even though the cost of discipleship is high, the resurrection of Christ provides hope for the future and strength for the present. The resurrection itself is both a guarantee of final glory for the faithful and the ground of present Christian joy—even in suffering.[94] In 1 Peter 2:9–10, Peter confers on

89 Watson and Callan, *First and Second Peter*, 16.

90 "Why Are Pakistan's Christians Targeted?," BBC, October 30, 2018, https://masihitv.com/why-are-pakistani-christians-targeted/.

91 The Kachin are Jingpaw, Rawang, Zaiwa, Longwo, and Lachit.

92 Seng Ja, "Role of Jesus," 203–5.

93 Kallie Szczepanski, "Who Are the Kachin People?," ThoughtCo, July 3, 2019, https://www.thoughtco.com/who-are-the-kachin-people-195178.

94 Bartlett, "First Letter of Peter," 254.

his readers a new identity by addressing them in language that the OT applies to Israel (Exod 19:5–6; Isa 43:20–21; Hos 2:23).[95] Such words of reassurance and redefinition will enable "aliens and exiles" to handle their situation and encourage them to stand firm on the new identity they have received in Jesus.

CONCLUSION

Asian Christians face challenges that vary from context to context. Many will find parallels between those faced by the Christians addressed in 1 and 2 Peter. As a minority religious group, many face suspicion and hostility, as the congregations written to in 1 Peter. As a Kachin Christian, I find echoes of my people's situation in both letters and can find inspiration and comfort in both. I am sure many other Asian Christians will do likewise.

The letters also present other challenges. Are we to take the exhortations of 1 Peter literally? Are we always to obey authorities even when we know that they are wrong? Many Christians have taken a quite different standpoint to 1 Peter. First Peter urges us to obey those in authority above us. Others have seen that in some circumstances, we may be obliged to oppose those in authority. This is the case when obedience makes us complicit in evil. As the Nuremburg Trials have made clear, "I was simply obeying orders" is not acceptable as an excuse.[96] I have already mentioned Dietrich Bonhoeffer, who was hanged at KZ Flossenburg on April 9, 1945, for his opposition to the Hitler regime. He took the cost of discipleship seriously.[97] There are several Asian Christians who took similar positions to Bonhoeffer. Toyohiko Kagawa (1868–1960) evangelized Japan's poor, advocated women's suffrage, and apologized to China for the Japanese invasion. He was arrested several times.[98] Tadao Yanaihara (1893–1961), a Quaker, criticized Japan's conquests during the Second World War and was forced to resign from his teaching posts.[99]

95 Marshall, Travis, and Paul, *Exploring the New Testament*, 2:282.

96 Olivia Goldhill, *Nuremberg Neurology* (February 21, 2016).

97 Franklin Sherman, "Dietrich Bonhoeffer: German Theologian," *Encyclopaedia Britannica Online*, accessed April 5, 2020, https://www.britannica.com/biography/Dietrich-Bonhoeffer.

98 Cyrill James Davey, *Kagawa of Japan* (New York: Abingdon, 1961).

99 David Williams, "A Moral Beacon in Japan's Darkest Days," *Japan Times*, December 26, 2000, https://tinyurl.com/573fmf5d.

Likewise, are we to remain passive when the Myanmar army, with the support of the present Aung San Suu Kyi's government, burns villages, tortures and kills men and children, rapes women, and bulldozes to the ground Rohingya villages and the Kachin people? Are we to support the legal system when it imprisons journalists reporting on abuse? Are the victims of trafficking to obey their masters? Are women always to obey their fathers and husbands and never take leading positions within the church? Is not the Jesus of the Gospels a defender of the defenseless, the poor, the oppressed, and the outsiders? And are not we, as his followers, obliged to stand up in their defense no matter what it costs us? We are told to love our enemies, yet the God of 2 Peter is a God of wrath intent on punishing evildoers. When we read the Petrine Epistles today from an Asian point of view, we are surely provoked to ask these questions.

FURTHER READING

Bartlett, D. L. 1998. "The First Letter of Peter: Introduction, Commentary and Reflections." In *The New Interpreter's Bible* 12, edited by Leander Keck, 227–319. Nashville: Abingdon.

Davids, P. H. 2006. *The Letters of 2 Peter and Jude*. Grand Rapids, MI: Eerdmans.

Dunn, J. D. G. 2019. *Jesus according to the New Testament*. Grand Rapids, MI: Eerdmans.

Ehrman, B. D. 2000. *The New Testament: A Historical Introduction to the Early Christian Writings*. Oxford: Oxford University Press.

Harrington, D. J. 2003. *Jude and 2 Peter: Sacra Pagina 15*. Collegeville, MN, Liturgical.

Kaw, E. 2005. *Buddhism and Education in Burman: Varying Conditions for a Social Ethos in the Path to "Nibbana."* PhD diss., Princeton University.

Marshall, I. H. 2004. *New Testament Theology*. Downers Grove, IL: InterVarsity.

Neyrey, J. 1993. *2 Peter, Jude: A New Translation with Introduction and Commentary*. AB 37C. New York: Doubleday.

Pheme, P. 1995. *First and Second Peter, James, and Jude*. Interpretation: A Bible Commentary for Teaching and Preaching. Louisville: Westminster John Knox.

Ram, K. R. M. V. 2003. *Dukkha: Suffering in Early Buddhism*. New Delhi: Discovery.

Seng Ja, L. 2017. "The Role of Jesus for the Kachins: Understanding Jesus from the Present Kachin Context." In *Theology under the Bo Tree: Contextual Theologies in Myanmar*, edited by Thomas Cung Bik, 20–40. Yangon: Myanmar Institute of Theology.

Wall, R. W. 2004. "Teaching 1 Peter as Scripture." *Word and World* 24, no. 4 (Fall): 368–77.

Waston, D. F., and T. Callan. 2012. *First and Second Peter: Paideia Commentary of the New Testament Series*. Grand Rapids, MI: Baker.

TWENTY-ONE

The Letters of John

Sookgoo Shin
Torch Trinity Graduate University
Seoul, Korea

The Letters of John were written during the years when the early church faced various internal and external conflicts, which led to disunity within the body of early Christians. The missionary endeavor was hindered by the disruptive teachings of false teachers. First John has occupied a central place in the history of Asian Christianity due to its heavy emphasis on Christology and ethics. In the case of Christology, 1 John was used repeatedly throughout the Asian church history to refute the heretical claims made against the core beliefs of Orthodox Christianity, especially regarding the identity of Jesus Christ. As for ethics, 1 John has been a source of inspiration and reconciliation by providing the highest form of ethics, which directs readers to the sacrificial love that should be practiced within a believing community.

Though not as widely appreciated as 1 John due to its brevity and their lacking significant doctrinal teachings, 2 and 3 John are not entirely disregarded by the Asian churches. In fact, if you walk into the entrance hall of the world's largest church, located in Seoul, you will see the huge board, which has 3 John 2 written on it: "Beloved, I pray that all may go well with you and that you may be in good health, as it goes well with your soul." Due to being the catchphrase of this megachurch and also its long-standing association with the Prosperity Gospel movement, most Korean Christians would know 3 John 2 by heart. What follows is an attempt to read the letters of John from an Asian perspective.

Authorship

Exploring the issue of authorship for the letters of John is an extraordinarily difficult task because the letters themselves do not offer much concrete evidence so as to pinpoint the author. However, this does not mean that they are void of any meaningful traces that might shed light on the issue of authorship. There is a broad scholarly consensus that these letters are directly related or at least heavily influenced by another NT book, John's Gospel. Any careful reader would easily spot the similarities between 1 John and John's Gospel in terms of its vocabulary, tone, and thought. In fact, a simple count of common words or phrases that appear in both John's Gospel and 1 John shows a remarkable overlap between them compared to any other NT books.[1] Though the Gospel and 1 John may not have had the same recipient, such similarities between them make it very probable that they share the similar conceptual and historical background. For this reason, both John's Gospel and 1 John were generally believed to have been written by John, the disciple of Christ.

The issue of authorship gets more complicated when 2 and 3 John are taken into consideration. Unlike 1 John, the external evidence for 2 and 3 John is not too strong, and the authenticity of these letters was not accepted as widely as 1 John. Scholars are divided on the issue of whether or not the author of 1 John also wrote 2 and 3 John because 1 John remains anonymous, whereas the author of 2 and 3 John specifies himself as the elder. Papias's words in Eusebius's *Ecclesiastical History* shed some light on this matter: "If ever anyone came who had followed the presbyters, I inquired into the words of the presbyters, what Andrew or Peter or Philip or Thomas or James or *John* or Matthew, or any other of the Lord's disciples had said, and what Aristion and the presbyter *John*, the Lord's disciples, were saying" (3.39.4; emphasis mine).

It is not unreasonable that these two Johns may be referring to the same individual for a couple of reasons. First, we need to note that disciples are also called presbyters, most of whom would have been dead by the time of writing as signified by the past tense. Second, John is mentioned again in the second group because he may have been Jesus's only disciple who would have been

1 See A. E. Brooke, *A Critical and Exegetical Commentary on the Johannine Epistles*, ICC (Edinburgh: T&T Clark, 1912), i–xix.

still alive then.[2] In fact, it was not uncommon for Jesus's disciples to be called elders, as seen in 1 Peter 5:1. Though we have limited evidence, there are nonetheless significant similarities between 2 and 3 Johns and 1 John,[3] and if the author of John's Gospel wrote 1 John, it is possible that he would have also written 2 and 3 John due to the overlaps between these writings. However, the fact that 1 John remains anonymous unlike 2 and 3 John should be taken seriously, and we must be modest about what we opt for.[4]

Date

Dating an ancient document is a notoriously challenging task, and the Letters of John are not the exception. One helpful way forward in this regard is to examine whether the letters of John precede or follow the Gospel of John in terms of chronological priority. Though scholars are divided on this particular issue, the priority of John's Gospel has gained more scholarly support for several reasons.[5]

First, all the identified names in the letters of John are Greco-Roman names (Gaius, Diotrephes, Demetrius), which indicates that there were a good number of gentile believers (or at least Hellenized Jews) in John's community. This does not mean that there were no gentile believers in the earlier stage of community portrayed in the Gospel, but the fact that the church leaders would carry non-Jewish names may signify that some time would have elapsed before seeing gentile Christians taking up leadership roles within the community.

Second, the conflict that is found in the Letters of John is not so much with outsiders but rather with insiders. Unlike John's Gospel, where Jesus's followers were being expelled from the synagogue, the Letters of John are more concerned with the heretical teachings coming from former fellow believers. The fact that the Letters of John do not mention any external conflict may show that they were written in a later period, when internal conflict became more dangerous than external attacks.[6]

2 I. Howard Marshall, *The Epistles of John*, NICNT (Grand Rapids, MI: Eerdmans, 1978), 42–46.
3 Raymond Brown, *The Epistles of John*, AB 30 (New York: Doubleday, 1982), 755–56.
4 See Judith Lieu, *I, II, & III John: A Commentary*, TNTL (Louisville: Westminster John Knox, 2008), 6–9.
5 See Brown, *Epistles of John*, 32–35.
6 Brown, 35.

Third, there are many areas of thought in the letters where we see gradual conceptual development from the Gospel. For example, one can easily trace the conceptual development in terms of ethics in 1 John. In John's Gospel, we read of a simple love command, whereas in 1 John, we see far more detailed instructions on how love should be practiced among believers, probably due to new ethical challenges faced by later Christians. Moreover, the warning against the false teachings, especially regarding Christology, may point to the newly arising crisis where later Christians have drifted away from the orthodox teaching due to the influences of multiple heretical movements at that time.

The fact that such false teachings were affecting a number of churches that were under the pastoral leadership of John may affirm that the Letters of John were written at a later time when the ecclesiastical structure was already in place. If our assumption about the priority of the Gospel is correct, we can reasonably place the Letters of John in the last decade of the first century because the Gospel is generally believed to be written sometime between 75 and 85 CE.

Place

Traditionally, it is believed that John spent the latter years of his life in Ephesus (*Against Heresies*, 3.1.1). It is highly probable that he was a respected "elder" among the churches in Asia Minor, and he wrote 1–3 John in Ephesus to remedy the theological and ecclesiastical challenges faced by the churches under his leadership. It would be difficult to imagine that John wrote these letters to the groups of people who were living outside Asia Minor because John had to be physically close enough to his recipients to be able to exert his spiritual influence over them.

Recently, Yarborough made an insightful observation in his commentary that the traces of the seven churches in Revelation can be readily spotted in the Letters of John. Scholars have suggested that there is no concrete historical setting behind John's letters, but Yarborough refuted such a long-standing argument by showing that "there is a known world around the Christian community of John's place and time, attested by sources of some historical reliability."[7] Yarborough's detailed analysis adds weight to the possibility that the Letters of John originated from and were sent to the groups of Christians in Asia Minor.

7 Robert W. Yarbrough, *1–3 John*, BECNT (Grand Rapids, MI: Baker, 2008), 17–21.

Structures of 1, 2, 3 John

Unlike 2 and 3 John, which clearly possess the epistolary structure, the structure of 1 John is not so clear-cut because it has the literary features that are rather hybrid in style and repetitive in content. A quick survey of commentaries will tell us how divided scholars are on the structure of 1 John. Despite its complicated arrangement, I see the two major literary characteristics that largely split 1 John into two parts, the first part being christotheological and the second part being ethical.

First John

- Prologue (1:1–4)
- God is light (1:5–3:10)
    - Walking in light by avoiding sin (1:5–2:2)
    - Abiding in Christ by keeping his commands (2:3–11)
    - New identity and new attitude toward the world (2:12–17)
    - Warning against antichrists (2:18–27)
    - God's children who practice righteousness (2:28–3:10)
- God is love (3:11–5:12)
    - Brotherly love as assurance before God (3:11–24)
    - Discerning the spirits (4:1–6)
    - God's love as the basis of our love and of overcoming the world (4:7–5:4)
    - Testimony that leads to eternal life (5:5–12)
- Conclusion (5:13–21)

Second John

- Personal greetings (vv. 1–3)
- Walking in truth and love (vv. 4–11)
- Closing (v. 12)

Third John

- Personal greetings (vv. 1–2)
- Hospitality to God's workers (vv. 3–8)
- Admonition to Diotrephes (vv. 9–12)
- Closing (vv. 13–15)

The Occasion and Purpose of 1 John

Even a casual reader of 1 John will immediately sense that there is a crisis in a community of which John is part. What caused conflicts among John's readers is not crystal clear, but 1 John 2:19 evidently indicates that some of the members from the community were influenced by heretical teachings and abandoned the truth. The negative impact these secessionists had on John's community must have been immense because John does not hesitate to call them "deceivers" (2 John 7), "liars" (1 John 2:4, 22; 4:20), and even "antichrists" (1 John 2:18, 22; 4:3; 2 John 7).

Though the major thrust of the letters of John is pastoral, it is difficult not to recognize the polemical tone of the letters.[8] In fact, John is at pains to highlight the irreconcilable differences between John's readers and their opponents in terms of their understanding of Jesus's identity and accepted Christian lifestyle. The letters of John are particularly concerned with these aforementioned facets of Christianity because Christology and ethics are the two major pillars that uphold the integrity of Christian faith. As for Christology, the letters speak unforgivingly of those who deny that Jesus is the Christ (1 John 2:22, 23); deny the Son and the Father (1 John 2:23); deny that Jesus has come in the flesh (1 John 4:2; 2 John 7); and deny that Jesus has come from God (1 John 4:3). In contrast, the secessionists also had issues with their lifestyle, and the letters warn them harshly for their misbehavior, which reveals their true identity. These are the people who walk in darkness and lie (1 John 1:6), claim to be without sin (1 John 1:8–10), do not keep the commandments (1 John 2:4), walk in the same way in which they walked (1 John 2:6), hate their brothers (1 John 2:9; 3:15; 4:20), and love the world and things in the world (1 John 2:15).

Then what are the possible causes for this dramatic schism between Johannine Christians and the opponents? Various proposals have been made regarding the sources of these errors among the secessionists. First of all, Gnosticism has been suggested as one of the prominent influences upon the secessionists. Such speculation is not too far-fetched because the Gospel of John was well received and studied among the gnostics due to its dualistic and spiritual language, which was seen as compatible with that of Gnosticism. In

8 Colin G. Kruse, *The Letters of John*, PNTC (Grand Rapids, MI: Eerdmans, 2000), 16.

the Gospel of John, Jesus is portrayed as the preexistent logos (John 1:1–3) who came from heaven to earth to reveal the divine truth or knowledge (John 3:1–15) that sets people free (John 8:32).[9] If the letters of John were derived from the Johannine tradition, which finds its origin in John's Gospel, it is not unlikely that the opponents in John's letters may have been impacted by the gnostic interpretation of the Gospel. The fact that the opponents do not take sin seriously may indicate that they might have adopted the gnostic teaching that salvation entails being saved from ignorance, not sin.

Another possible source would be Docetism, which denies the humanity of Jesus. Doscetism was somewhat related to Gnosticism and views flesh as inherently evil; those who followed docetic teachings denied that Jesus came into the world in flesh. The high emphasis on the humanity of Jesus in the letters of John may point to the fact that some of the Christians within the Johannine community fell victim to the docetic movement or to a teaching of Cerinthus, who, according to Irenaeus (*Against Heresies*, 1.26.1; 3.3.4), advocated that the earthly Jesus was joined to the Christ of the Spirit at baptism and that the fleshly Jesus and the divine Christ must be considered as two distinct entities.[10]

Although Gnosticism and Docetism are the possible root causes for the schism within the Johannine community, other issues such as assimilation to pagan customs among gentile believers or lingering ties with the synagogue among the Jewish Christians could have impacted the Johannine community in a profoundly devastating way. Ephesus was well-known for being the cosmopolitan center of culture and commerce, as well as the home of the cults of Artemis, so it is possible that some gentile Christians may not have detached themselves completely from the practices of pagan worship, claiming that such participation was not sinful.[11] To make things worse, some Jewish Christians may have been somewhat reluctant to fully dissociate themselves from the local synagogue due to social pressure, and thus they ended up denying Jesus as the Messiah and the Son of God. It is also possible that Jewish Christians

9 Mark Allan Powell, *Introducing the New Testament* (Grand Rapids, MI: Baker, 2009), 498.

10 George L. Parsenios, *First, Second, and Third John*, Paideia (Grand Rapids, MI: Baker, 2014), 22.

11 Paul N. Anderson, *From Crisis to Christ: A Contextual Introduction to the New Testament* (Nashville: Abingdon, 2014), 341.

had issues with gentile Christians for not being Jewish enough, and such a conflict between gentile and Jewish Christians may have triggered the latter to leave John's congregation and rejoin their local synagogue.[12] What is at stake in both cases is Christology, which is the bedrock of Christianity.

From an Asian perspective, it is not too surprising to see early Christians having conflicting views on the identity of Jesus Christ. The religious landscape of the Greco-Roman world was not homogeneous, especially in Asia Minor. Various pagan religious beliefs collided with one another, so it would have been challenging for individuals to hold steadfast to one set of beliefs. A similar phenomenon is also found in many Asian countries, where an eclectic mixture of shamanism, Confucianism, Buddhism, and other religious elements have been shaping the minds of native people for thousands of years.

When Christianity was first introduced to these Asian countries, it came into direct confrontation with the core values of local religions previously mentioned. Furthermore, the religious rituals such as ancestor worship and the worship of spirits and idols were strictly discouraged among the converts due to Christian monotheism. Such rejection of local religious practices could result in being abandoned by family and friends and even being persecuted severely until one denied Christian faith.[13] The well-being and prosperity of one's family and even community was believed to be dependent upon their devotion to their local gods; it was not desirable at all to worship a foreign god exclusively.

Whenever there was a disaster that involved a huge loss of human life or property, the townspeople would blame Christians for bringing bad luck to the community by worshipping a foreign god, and such a stigma was directly related to family honor, which must be protected at all costs, especially in a small town where everyone knew one another. Furthermore, such prolonged persecution led to the ghetto mentality and caused Christians to be "distrustful of contact with the broader society."[14] Though the Letters of John do not explicitly mention external persecution to the Christian community (1 John 5:4; John 16:33), the continuous exposure to false teachings would have caused a similar defensive mentality among Johannine Christians.

12 Anderson, 343.

13 James H. Grayson, "The Emplantation of Christianity: Anthropological Examination of the Korean Church," *Transformation* 26 (2009): 166.

14 Grayson, 168.

The Occasion and Purpose of 2 and 3 John

Second John is concerned with the same issue of heresy as found in 1 John. The only difference is that 2 John is written to an individual identified as the "chosen lady." The title "chosen lady" has invited various proposals from scholars as to what the title actually refers to. It was commonly believed that the title refers to one of the female leaders of a Johannine sister church, but nowadays the majority of scholars opt for an interpretation that sees the title as a representation of a Christian community.[15] The fact that John addresses the recipient of 2 John as the "chosen lady" signifies that he is writing to a different group of Christians than 1 John. Furthermore, the fact that John gives a similar piece of warning against the false teaching regarding Christology indicates that false teachers must have been traveling quite extensively to various churches to expand their territory.

Though 2 John is much shorter than 1 John, the tone of its warning against the false teaching in 2 John is much stricter and harsher than 1 John. John warns his readers to reject the false teachers, but he even goes a step further by saying that greeting any of the false teachers is the same as participating in their evil deeds (v. 11). John may have taken such an extreme stance because he had already experienced how cunning and deceiving these false teachers were in his own community (1 John 2:18–19), and he wanted other communities to watch out and block the penetration of false teachers into their communities at all cost.

Third John takes a somewhat different route, and the focus is no longer on heretical teachings but rather on the ecclesiastical conflict.[16] John is writing to an individual named Gaius, and the way John calls Gaius and his community (children; v. 4) shows that this particular community was also under John's supervision. It is not clear from the text exactly what kind of role John played among these neighboring churches, but there is no question that John was in a position where he could influence these churches with his apostolic authority. Unlike Gaius, whom John compliments for his generous support for his fellow itinerant missionaries, John has serious complaints against Diotrephes, who is trying to take away the church from John's leadership through ill means

15 Yarbrough, *1–3 John*, 334.
16 Marshall, *Epistles of John*, 12.

(vv. 9–10), such as threatening people not to welcome the brothers even sent by the elder lest they may be cast out of the church. Third John clearly teaches that ecclesiastical disloyalty is as harmful and dangerous to the well-being of the community as heretical teachings and thus must not be tolerated in any case. It seems the central supervision was still a dominant way of overseeing Christian communities rather than giving full autonomy to an individual local leader, at least within the Johannine circle.

What is often overlooked in the Western interpretation of 3 John is the severity of Diotrephes's action toward the elder, especially from an Asian perspective. What Asian people dread most is to lose face in the public, and one of the worst ways of losing face is to be humiliated by one's underlings. Losing face in such a way is to have one's reputation and authority damaged within a community to which one belongs. The parable of the prodigal son in Luke 15:11–32 is the prime example where the father loses face through his insolent son, who asks for his portion of inheritance while the father is still alive. The father loses face because the son's impetuous action could be taken as the son wishing for his father's untimely death.[17] Such an action would bring contempt not only upon the son himself but also upon his father and even the entire family clan because the son's misbehavior would have been perceived by others as the father's failure to raise his son properly.

In a similar manner, Diotrephes's public defiance against the elder's authority would bring dishonor to the elder because one's reputation or honor exists only when one is recognized in hierarchical social relationships. Furthermore, unfounded allegations against the elder would jeopardize the whole Christian community because the senior spiritual leader's influence over the congregation would be absolute in both the Middle Eastern and Asian contexts. From this Asian perspective, it is easier to see how damaging Diotrephes's behavior is to the harmony and well-being of the community.

Genre

One of the most debated issues of the Letters of John is the genre of 1 John. Unlike 2 and 3 John, which contain the formal epistolary structures, 1 John does not conform well to Greco-Roman epistolary convention. First John does not

17 Kenneth E. Bailey, *The Cross and the Prodigal: Luke 15 through the Eyes of Middle Eastern Peasants* (Downers Grove, IL: InterVarsity, 2005), 42.

contain an opening salutation or greeting, and it also lacks the final greeting or farewell. For that reason, scholars have been wondering whether an epistle is the best literary category to describe the genre of 1 John. Various literary genres have been proposed to identify the most appropriate literary type of 1 John. Is 1 John closer to a general religious tractate, homily, or diatribe? Or is 1 John still qualified to be classified as a letter even though it may not have proper literary features of ancient Greco-Roman letters? As recent research has shown, genre is not confined to fixed patterns but rather possesses literary characteristics that are often flexible and diverse in literary form and feature. Alexander rightly notes that an epistolary genre is "fluid, flexible, and adaptable to a wide variety of situations and subjects."[18]

When 1 John is examined in light of epistolary conventions of East Asia, it is not surprising to find letters that lack certain epistolary markers under certain conditions. In early medieval China, the prescript of a letter was often missing for the sake of brevity or when the author was recognizable to the recipients through means of the handwriting or the envelope. The proem of a letter would also be found missing when admonitory letters were written to younger members of one's family in order to show "the superior authority of the writer, who can take the relationship to the addressee for granted and can thus come straight to the point."[19] Based on such a literary practice, it is possible that 1 John was written to a community or to communities that John was directly part of, and thus he did not see it necessary to include any introductory greeting.[20]

In cases of letters of recommendations and condolence, a proem may also not be included because such letters were "intended for an audience beyond the immediate addressee."[21] As seen above, the research on the Chinese epistolary practice shows that "irregularities are not infrequent"[22] in the letter closing as well. In other words, both Western and Asian scholars note that an epistolary genre is not only fluid but also can take various shapes.

18 Loveday Alexander, "Hellenistic Letter-Forms and the Structure of Philippians," *JSNT* 37 (1989): 90.

19 Antje Richter, *Letters and Epistolary Culture in Early Medieval China* (Seattle: University of Washington Press, 2013), 80.

20 Brown, *Epistles of John*, 654.

21 Richter, *Letters*, 80.

22 Richter, 109.

Though 1 John may not have all the proper literary markers of a letter, it still reads like a letter because he clearly states that he is writing (2:1, 7, 8, 12, 13, 14, 21, 26; 5:13) to a group of people who are called "beloved" (2:7; 3:2, 21; 4:1, 7, 11), and such a title seems to indicate the level of intimacy John enjoyed with those to whom he writes. The recipients are also called "children," and except in Galatians 4:19, this particular title is found only in the Johannine writings (John 13:33; 1 John 2:1, 12, 28; 3:7, 18; 4:4; 5:21). The fact that John is able to call them "children" shows that John likely holds authority over or is a respectful figure to them.

Despite this seemingly solid relationship between John and his "children," the context makes it evident that John had to write these letters to warn them against the false teachings that undermine their faith in the person of Jesus. Furthermore, the issues that 1 John is concerned with are certainly shaped by the specific communal situations, and thus 1 John seems to be written primarily as a circular letter for those churches that were once greatly influenced by the teachings and ministry of John but somehow found themselves being threatened by unorthodox teachings. Therefore, 1 John is best considered a circular letter to a group of churches over which John had direct authority.[23]

Rhetorical Analysis

As seen in the discussion of genre, 1 John also presents serious challenges to the issue of rhetoric. Unlike 2 and 3 John, various rhetorical techniques are complicatedly utilized throughout 1 John, and scholars have proposed numerous solutions in order to delineate the rhetorical elements of 1 John.[24] One of the most distinctive rhetorical features of 1 John is the heavy use of the first-person plural verbs in chapter 1. These verbs seem to indicate the existence of common beliefs that both John and the recipients share, and John urges his recipients to continue to identify themselves with the apostolic beliefs regarding the identity of Jesus and the importance of embodying a righteous lifestyle.

Such an intentional use of the first-person plural verbs is also found in the first chapter of John's Gospel, where the readers are encouraged to side with the experiences of the author (John 1:14, 16). In the case of John's Gospel, a rhetorical aim of using the first-person plural verbs at the beginning is to

23 See Brown, *Epistles of John*, 86–92.
24 See Kruse, *Letters of John*, 29–31.

"encourage his readers to read these narratives carefully for themselves and to become part of the community that has already seen the glory of the *Logos* and received his grace."[25] In contrast, 1 John seems to use the same literary technique to remind the readers of the core beliefs that may have faded away in their community and to warn them not to drift away from the orthodox teachings that they have received from John himself.

Another rhetorically effective way of reading 1 John is to read it in light of epideictic rhetoric, which seeks to persuade people to adopt certain values or virtues that are crucial for the well-being or unity of a community. According to Watson, 1 John carries many rhetorical characteristics that are similar to those of epideictic rhetoric, and he provides a detailed analysis of how 1 John primarily encourages its readers to remain steadfast to a set of beliefs or values that were already known to the community.[26] Epideictic rhetoric is also closely connected to the technique of amplification, which is evident in "the repetitive and emphatic character of 1 John."[27] Though studying 1 John in light of ancient Greco-Roman rhetoric is helpful and necessary for understanding the intention of the author, it often fails to appreciate the corporate or collective nature of its audience. In fact, 1 John was not intended to be read by an individual but rather by a congregation.

What is distinctive about Eastern (Asian) rhetoric is that it focuses on the harmony of a community rather than the persuasion of individuals. The aim of rhetoric in the Asian context is not to steer someone's action based on personal benefits or gains but to maintain the collective unity or communal harmony. To do that, it is highly essential that everyone in the community should respect and abide by the established communal values, rituals, and morals. What, then, is the most powerful driving force that motivates people to honor the communal harmony? As seen previously, Asian people are extremely sensitive about losing face in their own communities, and for that reason, face as "one's image as perceived by others"[28] is the most effective rhetorical strategy.

25 Sookgoo Shin, *Ethics in the Gospel of John*, BIS 168 (Leiden: Brill, 2018), 55.

26 See Duane F. Watson, "Amplification Techniques in 1 John: The Interaction of Rhetorical Style and Invention," *JSNT* 51 (1993): 100–118.

27 Kruse, *Letters of John*, 30.

28 Yong-Kang Wei, "Rhetoric as Collective Ethos: From Classical Chinese Texts to Postmodern Corporate Images" (PhD diss., Iowa State University, 2004), 75.

In other words, rhetoric in the Asian context is never a personal issue but an interpersonal one that is aimed at constructing the ethos of a community.[29]

What is unique about Johannine rhetoric is that both the Gospel and Letters of John effectively employ antithetical or dualistic motifs in a way that persuades the reader to adopt the values and morals of the Johannine community. In John 3:6 Jesus uses a dualistic motif in order to describe what salvation is: "That which is born of the flesh is flesh, and that which is born of the Spirit is spirit."[30] This passage shows that there is an unbridgeable gap between those who believe and those who do not. In a similar manner, 1 John also utilizes many dualistic passages that make a clear distinction between who is in truth and who is not:

1:5. . . . . God is light, and in him is no darkness at all.

2:9 . . . . Whoever says he is in the light and hates his brother is still in darkness.

2:15 . . . . If anyone loves the world, the love of the Father is not in him.

4:2–3 . . . . . . Every spirit that confesses that Jesus Christ has come in the flesh is from God, and every spirit that does not confess Jesus is not from God.[31]

Based on Asian rhetoric, these passages carry not only soteriological significance but also sociological significance. Soteriologically, the rejection of the core Johannine doctrines will put one into spiritual darkness, whereas sociologically, one's infidelity would be considered a threat to the harmony and unity of the community, and such disloyalty will put oneself to shame by being excluded from the community. As argued above, the ultimate purpose of Asian rhetoric is to establish the collective ethos, which values the interpersonal more than the personal. Thus nothing is more essential than abiding by

29 Wei, 78.

30 Parsenios, *First, Second, and Third John*, 17.

31 Parsenios, 17.

the norms or expectations of a community of which one is part, lest one may lose face and credibility within one's own community.

Losing one's place in one's community could be fatal in the Greco-Roman world as much as in Asian contexts because one's identity finds its value and meaning only when one belongs to a community (collective identity). For Asians, the shame and loss of honor within one's community is worse than death, and such honor-shame dynamics may have played an important role in John's community as well. Therefore, the dualistic passages in 1 John have the function of enhancing a collective identity among the readers by showing that one's place in a community is guaranteed only through faithful adherence to the truth, and also by stirring up their sense of honor and shame.

CENTRAL THEMES FROM AN ASIAN PERSPECTIVE

Though many themes can be examined from the Asian perspective, three themes surface predominantly from the letters of John.

Testing the Spirits

In 1 John, the theme of testing the spirits is a major theological thrust that is closely tied to false teachers and antichrists, who are deceiving believers with the false theological and christological teachings (2:18–27). In 1 John 4, John uses a more aggressive tone and urges his readers not to trust but to test the spirits. The spiritual realm is reserved not only for the Spirit of God; it can also be easily intruded by evil spirits (see Eph 6:12). For that reason, the spiritual gifts such as healing, tongues, or prophecy can be manipulated (or even be faked), and thus it can become somewhat dubious and difficult to discern whether these spiritual phenomena come from God or from evil spirits.[32] In fact, it may be possible that some of the false teachers advocated the truthfulness of their teaching based on their ability to perform extraordinary spiritual gifts. Christian communities, however, should not easily believe the words of individuals who may claim to be inspired by a spirit; they must test whether they are genuinely from God. Such a spiritual testing requires more than checking what they can do. It must be based on their actual confession

32 Marshall, *Epistles of John*, 204.

that "the incarnation was not a temporary event but the permanent union of God and man in Jesus Christ."[33]

The commandment of testing the spirits cannot be more relevant in the Asian religious landscape. Whether or not one is a Christian, the existence of spirits is almost never questioned among Asians, who are heavily influenced by the shamanistic tradition. In fact, the first generation of Western missionaries to countries like Korea or Japan often faced a great challenge to explain the identity or the role of the Holy Spirit because local people commonly believed in spirits such as the spirits of the nature, the spirits of the elementals, the spirits of ancestors, and the spirits of the dead. These spirits were often thought to possess the power to bless or curse human beings.

It was not uncommon for Koreans to visit shamans or exorcists when their loved ones got sick or any misfortune struck their home. Suffering victims would invite a shaman to their house to perform a ritual to appease evil spirits because they believed the calamities occurred due to their inadequate devotion to supernatural beings. Thus Western missionaries were often forced to perform exorcism or healing (mostly through the use of medicine) to show that the Spirit of God was more powerful than shamanic spirits. However, the influence of shamanism did not go away even after Christianity became a dominant religion in Korea. There were still many Christians who would go see a fortune teller at the beginning of the year to see how their new year would unfold, and many continued to practice ancestral worship even after conversion. A historian of Korean Christianity wrote eloquently on this point: "New converts often transferred ideas from old belief systems onto Christianity, including the idea that Christianity simply had more powerful magic, with its own talismans and spirits. Evidence of remnant animistic ideas can be found in the hybrid belief that a piece of a Christian leaflet or a copy of the gospel, which had the smell of Western ink and contained the 'Jesus doctrine,' could be a powerful talisman. Such believers put copies of the gospel under the fetishes to cast out their evil influence when they burned the fetishes."[34] After the Korean War, Christianity played a crucial role in the economic, political, and social modernization of Korea and saw a great

33 Marshall, 205.

34 Sung-Deuk Oak, "Healing and Exorcism: Christian Encounters with Shamanism in Early Modern Korea," *Asian Ethnology* 69 (2010): 100.

spiritual revival in the seventies and eighties.[35] The Korean church also witnessed a significant growth in the number of cultic movements. The majority of leaders of the well-known cults were once greatly influenced by shamanism, Buddhism, or a hybrid of both. They also often claimed to have gone through some sort of mystical encounters with divine beings, and they came up with a new set of beliefs that were different from any other existing religions. These cultic leaders had to present their "spiritual enlightenment" in a way that was acceptable to people, and they regarded Christianity as an ideal religion that can accommodate different spiritual experiences or phenomena. Especially with the resurgence of Charismatic and Pentecostal forms of Christianity, mystical and supernatural experiences of these cultic leaders did not seem too abnormal but rather sounded attractive to many Christians. Due to the highly religious nature of Korean society and the influence of shamanism in the lives of Koreans, many cultic movements sprang up under the name of Christianity in a short period of time, and Korean Protestant churches used 1 John as a primary resource to fight against the heretical teachings and warn Christians to test the spirits.

Love

What is unique about 1 John is that despite its heavy emphasis on sound Christology for one's salvation, John offers another additional requirement that must be verified in the lives of believers as to prove the genuineness of their faith in Christ: love. Love in the Letters of John is not an abstract term that is to be analyzed philosophically. It is practically and intimately connected to knowing and abiding in God (2:3–6; 3:23–24; 4:7–8, 12, 16), walking in the light (2:9–11), being God's child (2:29; 3:10; 4:7), eternal life (3:14), confidence at the judgment (4:17–18), and our own love for God (4:20–5:1).[36]

Christology and ethics (love) always intersect in the Letters of John in such a way that one validates another. Such a perspective on love focuses on the importance of community because love becomes concretely evident only when it is practiced in relation to other people. Love must not be reduced to a feeling of affection for other people but must propel believers to actively pursue the

35 Andrew Eungi Kim, "Characteristics of Religious Life in South Korea: A Sociological Survey," *Review of Religious Research* 43 (2002): 301.

36 David Rensberger, *1 John, 2 John, 3 John*, ANTC (Nashville: Abingdon, 1997), 37.

benefits of others by sacrificially loving their brothers and sisters (3:17–18). Furthermore, lacking in love is not just a moral failure but is tantamount to being dead (3:14) and in darkness, where the light of truth is not found (2:9–10).

Such intimate love espoused by 1 John is especially important where the unity and welfare of the church are being threatened by false teachers and the persecution of the world (3:13). Unless the whole community is tightly bound by the love for one another, the members of the community will not able to stand the pressures of the world and will become vulnerable targets for the false teachers. Thus love has the function of primarily protecting believers from the external attacks and also showing the world that Jesus is indeed from God. Then how can believers show such sacrificial love to one another? The source of love for believers does not lie in themselves but can only be drawn from Jesus himself, who has shown the perfect example of sacrificial love (3:16; 4:11, 19). The theme of imitation is as prominent in 1 John (2:6; 3:2–7; 4:17) as in the Gospel of John (13:15, 34; 15:12; 17:16, 18, 21, 22), and "this imitation is not a mechanical conformity but a loving response to the love of God abiding within."[37] It is Jesus's sacrifice on the cross that becomes the basis of love among believers, and it is only through such sacrificial love that the message of the gospel carries its impact and the love of God is perfected in the lives of the believers.

Though love is a universal phenomenon, love as understood and practiced in the East Asian context differs from the love postulated in the Letters of John. The understanding of love among Asians is much colored by the influence of Confucianism, which has been the backbone of the culture and thought of East Asia over the last two millennia. One of the major differences between Confucius's love and Johannine love is that the former finds its origin in the goodness of humanity, whereas the latter finds its origin in the love of God. According to Confucius, "love is a natural and spontaneous feeling that requires cultivation through education."[38] In fact, Confucius believed that human beings possess not only innate knowledge of the good but also the innate ability to be good.[39] For that reason, there is no room for God or any other spirits in

37 Rensberger, 38.

38 Lee Yuen Ting, "Confucius," in *Encyclopedia of Love in World Religions*, ed. Yudit Kornberg Greenberg (Santa Barbara, CA: ABC-CLIO, 2007), 1:135–36.

39 Dong Lui, "A Comparison between the Christian and Confucian Major Doctrines: A Survey," *Canadian Social Science* 3 (2007): 113–14.

Confucianism, but "evil is caused by people's inability to avoid the negative influences of their environment."[40] Thus, love is not something that is God-given for Confucians; it is hard-earned. A Confucian view of love is somewhat in line with that of Greco-Roman world, where people believed that they could develop a genuine love for one another through pursing the study of philosophy.

Love in Confucianism is first and foremost directed to the immediate family, such as parents, siblings, and relatives, but then one must aim to achieve universal love, which must be extended to all people, even to nature and animals.[41] Such universal love was encouraged to promote unity and harmony among the citizens, and Confucius also heavily emphasized the Golden Rule, which commands people not to impose on others what they do not wish for themselves. Despite some obvious similarities, Confucius's failure to acknowledge the need for divine love in loving others and the original sin of humanity makes it difficult to bridge the gap between love advocated by Confucianism and Christianity. Furthermore, many Asians would often find the Christian love inappropriate because it emphasizes love for God more than love for parents (filial piety), which is the highest ideal in Confucianism.

Care for the Marginalized

In line with the previous discussion, heavy emphasis on love in 1 John has been the basis of multiple Asian theologies that were developed as a reaction to the gloomy reality of social and political oppression and discrimination among the marginalized. First John 3:16–18 has played a pivotal role in providing a biblical understanding of how Christian love should be practiced in the real world. In particular, Minjung and Dalit theologies have developed their idea of justice and peace based on this Johannine vision of love. *Minjung* is a term that denotes a group of people who were politically oppressed and economically exploited under the dictatorship during the seventies and eighties in South Korea, and *Dalits* refer to members of the lowest social group in the Hindu caste system. According to these theologies, the oppressed people

40 Lui, 114.

41 Qiyong Guo et al., "The Values of Confucian Benevolence and the Universality of the Confucian Way of Extending Love," *Frontiers of Philosophy in China* 1 (2012): 23, https://tinyurl.com/29dryptd.

are God's particular concern,[42] and they need to be redeemed not only from their sins but also from worldly oppression that is often due to capitalism, racism, casteism, patriarchy, feudalism, and colonization. For these oppressed people to become the subjects of history, the church as a whole must actively pursue the rights of these marginalized people by loving and caring for them with actions (1 John 3:17, 18; 4:20).

Moreover, Christianity portrayed in 1 John is a religion of love that requires its followers to lay down their lives for the sake of others (1 John 3:16). In fact, coming to Jesus according to the Johannine worldview is more than having one's sins forgiven; it is about being shaped into the likeness of Jesus. The profundity of Jesus's love for his people becomes the standard by which one should love others, and 1 John even goes so far to state that hating and oppressing one's brother is as fatal as remaining in darkness (1 John 2:9). Minjung and Dalit theologies have taken the Johannine vision of love to their own cultural and political contexts and come up with powerful but nonviolent resistance against social ills. This is the prime example of how the biblical teaching can impact the wider world by bringing justice to the broken world.

CONCLUSION

The Letters of John have served as the theological frontline in the earlier stage of evangelism in Asia for its pivotal role in providing a theological defense against various heretical movements. Countries like South Korea or China have seen a rapid growth not only of the Protestant Church but also of numerous forms of heresy. Whenever the church encountered threats from cultic movements, 1 John has been one of the first books to turn to for guidance due to its profound teaching on Christology and spiritual discernment.

Similarly, the rapid growth of the economy in many parts of Asia over the last three decades has resulted in the rise of income inequality and materialism, which have been a cause of schism and conflict among Christians. Furthermore, as the Asian churches grew in number and influence, much of

42 Hans Ucko, *The People and the People of God: Minjung and Dalit Theology in Interaction with Jewish-Christian Dialogue*, ES 17 (Münster: LIT, 2002), 3.

what was taught in the letters of John was soon forgotten, and some churches prided themselves in their luxurious church buildings and growing number of members. What becomes clear from the example of these churches is that right teaching does not always lead to right living. Instead, right teaching without the transformation of the Spirit often begets pride and a false sense of satisfaction about one's own spiritual condition. It was once again the Letters of John that played an essential role in a wholesome understanding of Christian spirituality. These letters greatly emphasize a need to be transformed in the likeness of Christ in terms of love and unity.

When the Letters of John are correctly read and interpreted, one cannot help but be stirred to embrace the Christian faith holistically. Being a child of God according to the Letters of John is not just a matter of holding on to a set of beliefs; it is also living out the commands of Jesus, which concretely validate one's standing in the family of God.

FURTHER READING

Anderson, P. N. 2014. *From Crisis to Christ: A Contextual Introduction to the New Testament*. Nashville: Abingdon.

Kruse, C. G. 2000. *The Letter of John*. PNTC. Grand Rapids, MI: Eerdmans.

Lieu, J. 2008. *I, II, & III John: A Commentary*. TNTL. Louisville: Westminster John Knox.

Parsenios, G. L. 2014. *First, Second, and Third John*. Paideia. Grand Rapids, MI: Baker.

Richter, A. 2013. *Letters and Epistolary Culture in Early Medieval China*. Seattle: University of Washington Press.

Shin, S. 2018. *Ethics in the Gospel of John: Discipleship as Moral Progress*. BIS 168. Leiden: Brill.

Ting, L. Y. 2008. "Confucius." In *Encyclopedia of Love in World Religions* 1, edited by Yudit Kornberg Greenberg, 135–136. Santa Barbara, CA: ABC-CLIO.

Ucko, H. 2002. *The People and the People of God: Minjung and Dalit Theology in Interaction with Jewish-Christian Dialogue*. ES 17. Münster: LIT.

Wei, Y.-K. 2004. "Rhetoric as Collective Ethos: From Classical Chinese Texts to Postmodern Corporate Images." PhD diss., Iowa State University.

Yarbrough, R. W. 2008. *1–3 John*. BECNT. Grand Rapids, MI: Baker.

TWENTY-TWO

The Letter of Jude

J. Stanly Jones
Union Biblical Seminary
Pune, India

The Epistle of Jude is one of the shortest books in the NT and often the most neglected because of its brevity and due to its intertextual dependence on the Jewish apocalyptic writings such as 1 Enoch and Assumption of Moses. Another reason for its neglect is its focus on judgment, which could be less appealing to those familiar with prosperity preaching. However, these same factors make this book interesting, particularly in the Asian context. Traditionally, a linear structure has been suggested for this epistle, where the focus was on the issue of the "false teachers" who intruded into the community from outside. This exclusive emphasis on false teachers quite isolated the epistle from the actual ecclesiastical context (i.e., the community of Jude). Despite the amount of space the letter devotes to polemic, Jude is not a direct attack on his opponents; rather, it is a letter of exhortation written for the believing community, who are "called" and "beloved," to encourage their struggle for the faith. This commentary on Jude reads the epistle as a letter of exhortation with focus on both the false teachers and judgment.

PRELIMINARY CONCERNS

The following section examines the introductory concerns with regard to the epistle of Jude, such as its authorship, date, recipients, purpose, and structure; the identity of the opponents; and its canonical concerns.

Authorship

The question of authorship is complex. The letter is attributed to Jude, "a servant of Jesus Christ and brother of James" (v. 1). While some argue for pseudonymous authorship from a later time,[1] others accept genuine authorship from an early time.[2] Arguments against authenticity include the fine quality of the literary Greek employed in the letter, as well as the call "to remember the apostolic predictions" (v. 17), suggesting that the apostolic era is a past event. These features speak against an early dating of the letter and thus question the authorship by Jude, one of Jesus's blood relatives. It is argued that the Greek in the letter seems too polished to come from a first-century Galilean Jew. For instance, Kelly states, "While a Galilean like Jude must have spoken Greek fluently, it is not easy to imagine him handling the language with such art."[3] However, studies have shown that such a fine quality of Greek was common in Palestine, especially in Galilee, during the time of the apostles themselves.[4] According to Schreiner, the influence of Hellenistic culture on Palestine was significant in the first century, and if Jude traveled as a missionary, "he could have acquired greater facility in Greek to foster his ministry."[5] Thus a Jewish missionary would certainly require the competence of Greek vocabulary and the rhetorical skills that are exhibited in the letter to be successful.

1 J. N. D. Kelly, *A Commentary on the Epistles of Peter and Jude* (Grand Rapids, MI: Baker, 1969), 234; Bo Reicke, *The Epistles of James, Peter, and Jude*, Anchor Bible 37 (Garden City, NY: Doubleday, 1964), 191; E. M. Sidebottom, *James, Jude and 2 Peter* (London: Thomas Nelson, 1967), 79.

2 Richard J. Bauckham, *Jude–2 Peter*, Word Biblical Commentary 50 (Dallas: Word, 1983), 15–16; Ruth Anne Reese, *Writing Jude: The Reader, the Text, and the Author in Constructs of Power and Desire* (London: Brill, 2000), 140; John Painter and David A. deSilva, *James and Jude*, Paidea Commentaries on the New Testament (Grand Rapids, MI: Baker Academic, 2012), 179–82.

3 Kelly, *Commentary on the Epistles*, 233.

4 See Painter and deSilva, *James and Jude*, 180.

5 Thomas R. Schreiner, *1 and 2 Peter and Jude*, NAC 37 (Nashville: B&H, 2003), 407.

Another argument for the letter's pseudonymous status is that the letter seems to consider the apostolic age as a past era (v. 17) and appears to be aware of a set form of doctrine (v. 3). However, these arguments have been countered by the fact that Jude is asking his readers to recall not the apostolic era but "the instruction they received at their conversion, from the apostles who founded their church[es]."[6] Thus, it is not the apostles themselves but their "mission" that belongs to the past. Because Jude was evidently not the founder of the church to which he writes, he speaks of the teaching of the founding apostles rather than his own.[7] Similarly, the fixed form of doctrine that critics refer to in verse 3 is not a crystalized set of doctrines as such, but it simply refers to the "gospel message" that was shared to them by the apostles.[8]

For authenticity, it has often been argued that it is difficult to explain the reason for the author adopting a pseudonymous name of a person not so significant in the history of early Christianity. Even if it could be argued that because Jude comes from the Palestinian context in which the family of Jesus was revered, and thus Jude would be a figure of authority, it is strange that the letter does not call Jude by the authoritative title "the brother of Jesus" but only as "brother of James," which easily supports the hypothesis of authenticity rather than pseudonymity.[9] Arguments for authenticity thus include the reference to "the brother of James." Consequently, Jude is identified as a brother of Jesus, though Jude presents himself in the letter as a "servant of Jesus."

Date

Assigning a date to the Epistle of Jude depends on the conclusion as to whether the letter is authentic, its postapostolic character, and the identity of the opponents. Proposals for dating Jude range from 50 to 120 CE. Sidebottom suggests a date between 100 and 120 CE,[10] whereas Kümmel suggests a date during the turn of the second century.[11] Arguments for a later date include the epistle's alleged postapostolic character and the identity of Jude's opponents as

6 Bauckham, *Jude–2 Peter*, 13.
7 Bauckham, 13.
8 Bauckham, 9.
9 Bauckham, 14.
10 Sidebottom, *James, Jude and 2 Peter*, 78.
11 W. G. Kümmel, *Introduction to the NT* (Nashville: Abingdon, 1975), 429.

gnostics. To identify the epistle's postapostolic character, usually three factors are taken into consideration: a fading expectation of Jesus's imminent return, an increased interest in institutionalization of church offices, and the crystallization of the faith into set forms. However, it is observed that none of these features are evident in Jude. The Parousia hope is lively (vv. 1, 14, 21, 24), and the whole argument of the main midrashic section of the letter (vv. 5–19) is based on the expectation that the false teachers are to be judged on the day of Parousia (vv. 14–15). This vigorous hope for the imminent return of Jesus is contrary to early Catholicism, where the church settles down for a long stay in the world.[12]

There is also no evidence of the institutionalization of church offices in Jude (vv. 8, 11, 16), which is an important indication of the postapostolic era. In a context of the false teachers intruding upon the community, Jude does not appeal to the church leaders such as elders or bishops entrusted with special responsibility to suppress the opponents and guard the faith against such heretical deviations. Instead, Jude addressed the whole community, which is responsible for upholding the gospel (v. 3). Jude's response to the threat from the false teachers is quite different from that of the PE, whose emphasis was on ecclesiastical offices.[13]

Also, the argument for classifying Jude as a form of early Catholicism is based on verse 3, understood to refer to a fixed form of doctrine, passed down from the apostles, which serves as a base against heresies. But Bauckham argues that this is a misinterpretation of verse 3, which simply refers to the "gospel" and not to any form of fixed "doctrines." It merely urges its readers to remain faithful to the gospel that they received at their conversion. This is similar to the language Paul used against false teaching even in his earliest letters (Gal 1:6–9; Rom 6:17; 1 Cor 15:1–11; 1 Thess 4:1–2).[14] Thus if Jude is not referring to a fixed form of faith or to an established set of doctrine, labeling Jude as a form of early Catholicism and dating it in the second century is not convincing.

In contrast, because Jude's readers are familiar not only with the OT but also with the Jewish Apocrypha as well, this may be implying that Jude is

12 Painter and deSilva, *James and Jude*, 179.

13 Bauckham, *Jude–2 Peter*, 9.

14 Bauckham, 9.

written quite early, perhaps before the fall of Jerusalem in 70 CE. An earlier date is also advocated by the fact that Jude is being quoted in the *Didache*, which was written before 100 CE, and also by Polycarp (about 150 CE), and the Muratorian Canon (about 175 CE). For an earlier date, Ellis suggests 55–65 CE. Ellis's dating is based on Jude's apprehension of the situation (vv. 3–5) and his reference to James "as though he is still the active leader of the Hebraist mission."[15] J. A. T. Robinson dates the epistle in 60–62 CE,[16] Bauckham proposes a date before 62 CE,[17] and Guthrie gives a date in 65–80 CE.[18] Thus, it seems likely that a date in the sixties is closest.

Recipients

Considering the information in the letter, it is difficult to establish the readers because Jude identifies his readers only theologically—as those who are "called," who are "beloved in God" and "kept safe" for Jesus Christ (v. 1b). From this information, one can deduce that the recipients of this letter were Christians, but it is difficult to ascertain where they lived and who they were. There are two opinions for the location of Jude's audience. While some scholars suggest a setting in Alexandria, Egypt, others suggest Syria or Palestine. Gunther argues that Jude was written for Alexandrian believers. Gunther's argument is particularly dependent upon the notion that Jude was written against a gnostic heresy. According to Gunther, Egypt is the most likely place where such doctrines flourished and where the authority of James and Jude would be esteemed highly among converts from its huge Alexandrian Jewish population.[19] However, according to Schreiner, because evidence for the existence of a Gnostic heresy is lacking in the first-century Egyptian context, the main argument for an Alexandrian destination fails.[20] Kelly argues for a Palestinian context, "for it was there that Jude probably worked and that his and James's names were highly regarded."[21] Along with Kelly, the other

15 E. Earl Ellis, *Prophecy and Hermeneutic in Early Christianity: New Testament Essays* (Eugene, OR: Wipf & Stock, 1978), 236.

16 J. A. T. Robinson, *Redating the New Testament* (Philadelphia: Westminster, 1976), 197–98.

17 Bauckham, *Jude–2 Peter*, 13–14.

18 Donald Guthrie, *New Testament Introduction*, rev. ed. (Leicester, UK: Apollos, 1990), 233.

19 For details, see John J. Gunther, "The Alexandrian Epistle of Jude," *NTS* 30 (1984): 550.

20 Schreiner, *Peter and Jude*, 410.

21 Kelly, *Commentary on the Epistles*, 234.

scholars who argue for a Palestinian context include Richard J. Bauckham, J. D. Charles, and Gene L. Green.[22]

Jude's preference for OT and noncanonical Jewish writings and Jude's recipients being familiar with these texts (v. 5) suggest that the recipients of Jude were Jewish rather than gentile readers. However, it is also possible that Jude is addressing the gentile converts because Jewish antinomianism was not a common phenomenon in first-century context, and the intruders in Jude were clearly immoral in their lifestyle.[23] Thus, it is possible to conclude that the readers were a mixed audience of Greek-speaking Jews and gentiles living somewhere in Palestine or Syria.

Purpose

Jude's purpose is twofold: to expose the false teachers who have infiltrated the church and to encourage the believers to stand firm for the truth in the midst of such false teachings. Jude is thus an exhortation written to a community disturbed by the presence of "ungodly" intruders. These intruders are apparently itinerant teachers or prophets who were common in the early church and whose doctrines and practices varied with the apostolic tradition (vv. 4, 17–19). Appealing to their charismatic authority, these false teachers present themselves as the only truly spiritual people. However, their motivation is identified as financial gain (vv. 11–12, 16), and they seem to have succeeded in gathering a following of their own (vv. 19, 22–23). These false teachers and prophets are further seen as threatening to lead people astray by their moral laxity. Jude's purpose, therefore, is to alert the congregation of the presence of these intruders, condemn their behavior, and exhort the believers to remain faithful in the midst of such dangers (vv. 3–4).[24]

22 Richard J. Bauckham, *Jude and the Relatives of Jesus in the Early Church* (London: Bloomsbury, 2015), 131–33, 177–78; J. D. Charles, "Jude's Use of Pseudepigraphical Source-Material as Part of a Literary Strategy," *NTS* 37 (1991): 130–45; Gene L. Green, *Jude and 2 Peter* (Grand Rapids, MI: Baker Academic, 2008), 12–13.

23 Schreiner, *Peter and Jude*, 410.

24 Rohun Park, "The Letter of Jude," in *A Postcolonial Commentary on the NT Writings*, ed. Fernando F. Segovia and R. S. Sugirtharajah (London: T&T Clark, 2009), 427.

Structure

The letter is structured typically as that of an epistle beginning with a salutation (v. 1), followed by the greeting (v. 2) and occasion (vv. 3–4). In the occasion, the author explains the intention of the change of subject (v. 3), and he justifies the reason for the change of subject as the worrying presence of false teachers (v. 4). The main section of the letter (vv. 5–19) carries the weight of the author's message. Following a well-known pattern of "text and interpretation," this section quotes intertextual references from the OT and other Jewish writings as an authoritative message followed by an interpretative application to the readers' context.[25]

Following the main section, which carries the message of judgment, the letter then goes on to encourage the believers with exhortations (vv. 20–23). This final exhortation ends with the concluding doxology (vv. 24–25), which evidences the author's confidence in his readers that they will remain faithful and receive mercy. Though the central section of the Midrash (vv. 5–19) is the main content of the letter, "the structure of the letter indicates that the Midrash, though important, is important only as necessary background to the appeal (vv. 20–23), which is Jude's main purpose in writing."[26] According to Bauckham, Jude's epistle is an "epistolary sermon" that "could have been delivered as a homily if Jude and his readers had been able to meet."[27] Because of this reason, Jude concludes with a doxology (vv. 24–25) that is appropriate if the letter is read in a congregational worship setting, rather than the usual way of concluding a letter with greetings and travel plans.[28] A brief outline of the letter as just described follows:

Introduction and salutation (vv. 1–2)

Statement of the occasion (vv. 3–4)

Main section: warning against false teachers (vv. 5–19)

25 Andrew Chester and Ralph P. Martin, *The Theology of the Letters of James, Peter, and Jude* (Cambridge: Cambridge University Press, 1994), 67.

26 Bauckham, *Jude–2 Peter*, 4.

27 Bauckham, 3.

28 Painter and deSilva, *James and Jude*, 186.

Exhortation to believers (vv. 20–23)

Concluding doxology (vv. 24–25)

Relationship with Second Peter

With regard to the relationship between Jude and 2 Peter, if one compares Jude 4–18 and 2 Peter 2:1–18; 3:1–3, it is obvious that some kind of literary relationship exists between these two epistles. Until modern criticism it was believed that Jude was dependent on 2 Peter. Modern commentators are in agreement that 2 Peter is dependent on Jude.[29] The most important literary reason for preferring 2 Peter's dependence on Jude, according to Bauckham, is that the structure and wording of Jude 4–18 "has been composed with exquisite care, whereas the corresponding parts of 2 Peter, while by no means carelessly composed, are by comparison more loosely structured."[30] Also, Jude's midrashic structure is entirely absent in 2 Peter. Thus it is more difficult to imagine Jude constructing his elaborate midrash with 2 Peter before him than to consider how the author of 2 Peter could have seen Jude as an useful material for composing his teaching on denunciation of the false teachers.[31]

Jude's Opponents

Though it is difficult to identify the false teachers in Jude's community with any known heretic group in the early church, some have suggested that the false teachers belonged to an early form of Gnosticism. It is noted that according to the early church father Irenaeus, Cain and Korah were heroes to some gnostic groups, and hence Jude is refuting that position by using them as negative examples (v. 11). Similarly, Holloway argues that denigrating angels (v. 8) and denying Jesus (v. 4) may have been characteristic of some gnostics.[32] Other arguments for a gnostic opponent includes a docetic Christology (v. 4), doctrines of the celestial beings that deny the unity of God (vv. 4, 8), and the gnostic division of humans into pneumatics and psychics (v. 19). But according to Bauckham, these teachings, if read into Jude's words, may not be

29 See Sidebottom, *James, Jude and 2 Peter*, 65–69; Bauckham, *Jude–2 Peter*, 141–43.

30 Bauckham, *Jude–2 Peter*, 141.

31 Bauckham, 141.

32 Gary Holloway, *James and Jude* (Joplin, MO: College Press, 1996), 137–38.

sufficient to prove a serious opposition to gnostic teaching. Bauckham argues that what is missing in the letter for a gnostic opposition "is the cosmological dualism of true Gnosticism."[33] Even though the opponents' sense of moral autonomy and spiritual status and their attitude to law resemble the views of many later gnostics, it is difficult to prove that the community's "indulgence in sins of the flesh was linked to a disparagement of the body as material."[34] In the absence of evidence to locate a cosmological dualism, it becomes difficult to identify the opponents in Jude as gnostics.

Arguing against a gnostic background, Bauckham and Guthrie say that everything Jude informs in his letter about the false teachers is related to their antinomianism.[35] They reject moral authority, that of the law of Moses (vv. 8–10) or that of Christ himself (vv. 4, 8). They have misunderstood grace and perverted it into license (v. 4). They believe they are so advanced spiritually, as evidenced by their dreams and visions (v. 8), and that they are no longer subject to God's law. Thinking themselves free from all moral restraint, they conduct themselves unethically (vv. 4, 8, 10, 16, 23), care only for themselves (v. 12), and end up like unreasoning animals (v. 10).[36] These antinomian characters of the opponents make it possible to conclude the false teachers in Jude were antinomians.

Another possibility is that the opponents of Jude are "itinerant charismatics." It is evident that Jude's opponents are not simply members of the church but teachers in the sense of itinerant charismatics (vv. 11–13). They are present at the church's fellowship meals (v. 12), where they impart their knowledge to the community. Like other itinerant teachers in the early church, they are also dependent on the hospitality of the community. Jude accuses them that their ministry is being motivated by greed for the material gain they receive from their followers (vv. 11–12). Their substandard moral teaching helps them please the followers and thus find favor from them (v. 16). Most of these characteristics can be paralleled with other early Christian literature where such itinerant charismatics were frequently a source of trouble in the churches

33 Bauckham, *Jude–2 Peter*, 12.
34 Bauckham, 12.
35 See Bauckham, *Relatives of Jesus*, 162–65.
36 Holloway, *James and Jude*, 138.

(2 Cor 10–11; 1 John 4:1; 2 John 10; *Did.* 11–12).[37] This is also reflected in the Pastoral Epistles and the Epistles of John.[38]

Canonical Context

It is significant that although Jude is a very short letter, it has not been lost and has found its place in the NT canon. Among the early church fathers, the Muratorian Canon refers to the Epistle of Jude as Scripture as early as 175 CE. Similarly, Tertullian (*De cult. Fem.* 1.3) and Clement of Alexandria regarded it as canonical (see Eusebius, *Hist. Eccl.* 6.14.1).[39] Christian leaders from the late second century through the fourth century continued to use Jude because its polemic proved useful in dealing with different heretical movements that arose during this period.[40] However, in later times, Jude came to be doubted by some. In the early Christian community, the Epistle of Jude was placed among the seven NT books whose canonicity has been disputed.[41] The canonicity of the book has often been questioned because of its citation to the Apocrypha, in particular the use of 1 Enoch and Assumption of Moses. However, Schreiner states that the use of pseudepigraphic books is in itself an indirect support of its authenticity, because anyone whose intention is to authenticate their writing as Scripture would be careful and concerned about quoting "unscriptural" apocryphal books.[42]

Jude fell into neglect after the Reformation. Martin Luther considered it to be pseudonymous because according to him, Jude is dependent on and contained in 2 Peter, and hence it is not an apostolic writing. Hence Luther did not include it among the "true, certain chief books of the New Testament."[43] Luther is followed by other Reformers, who made similar estimates and

37 Bauckham, *Jude–2 Peter*, 12.

38 For example, 1 Tim 1:6–7, 19; 4:1, 7; 6:3–5, 20; 2 Tim 1:13; 2:14, 16, 25; 3:1, 13; 4:3–4; Titus 1:10, 16; 3:9; 1 John 2:18, 22, 26; 4:1; 2 John 7; 3 John 9. See Holloway, *James and Jude*, 138.

39 Schreiner, *Peter and Jude*, 408.

40 Painter and deSilva, *James and Jude*, 188.

41 B. M. Metzger, *The Canon of the NT: Its Origin, Development and Significance* (Oxford: Clarendon, 1987), 19.

42 Schreiner, *Peter and Jude*, 408.

43 Kümmel, *Introduction to the NT*, 429.

dismissed the letter as deuterocanonical or apocryphal.[44] Strong prejudices arose in the nineteenth century against Jude as an alleged example of postapostolic "early Catholicism" coming from a later period. In the twentieth century, "prejudice against Jude's intolerance toward diversity of voice and practice has worked against its recovering ground as a canonical voice."[45] Though for most of Christian history the Letter of Jude had been on the sidelines, in recent times it has emerged as a distinctive part of the NT, particularly with its emphasis on apocalyptic teaching and intertextual reading, as well as its polemic against the false teachers.

MAJOR THEMES

The Letter of Jude displays certain important themes that are significant in the context of Asian cultures and worldviews. The following are some of these themes from Jude that are relevant in the Asian context.

Religious and Cultural Assimilation

The examples Jude cites are drawn from Palestinian Jewish Scriptural tradition, so it is possible to assume that the intruders against whom Jude is warning must be encouraging some sort of religious and cultural assimilation to the dominant Greco-Roman culture. It was important for Jude's readers to cope with the Christian faith in the context of their social and cultural assimilation with the Greco-Roman culture and the sociopolitical situation in which they were placed. In such a context, "by reminding his readers of disobedient angels and Israelites from the past who engaged in dangerous intercourse with unbelieving gentiles, Jude may be seen as urging his readers to remain within a Jewish-Christian definition of life and faith."[46] Jude argues that faithfulness to Christ and the gospel must always take precedence to any other worldly allegiance (vv. 17–19). This is particularly relevant in today's context, where there exist many competing influences, such as materialism, liberalism, factionalism, and more competing for the

44 For details, see Metzger, *Canon of the NT*, 244.
45 Painter and deSilva, *James and Jude*, 188.
46 Park, "Letter of Jude," 428.

believer's loyalty. Jude is arguing against a temptation to assimilate Christian faith with the political and social standards of the day.

However, the world has become more interconnected and "smaller" due to globalization. Along with interconnectedness, globalization also "intensifies cultural identities and thus induces ethnification."[47] In such a context, a renewed awareness of one's own reality should go alongside a sense of global interconnectedness. It requires the church to be local and regional and at the same time assimilate "in the body of Christ worldwide,"[48] without compromising the tenets of faith. Christians in Asia live in a multicultural and multireligious context, where they are still a minority in the midst of other religious traditions such as Hinduism, Buddhism, and Islam. In such a context, there is a danger of taking the path of either absolute exclusivism or unconditional inclusivism.

Appeal for Unity

Jude encourages his readers to rejoice over what they all have in common in Christ—that is, the "common faith" (v. 3). When false teaching intervenes with essential doctrine, what is common must be fought for. In such a context, believers must unite together in identifying and combating false teaching. Jude's appeal to unity (v. 19) and a common faith (v. 3) in the context of "sound doctrine" implies that the church has to promote unity and love as part of its "sound doctrine."

The church in Asia, though a minority, is divided among different factions such as the Catholics, Protestants, Charismatics, and other religious groups competing with one another in doctrinal basis. Aggressive attempts of propagating one's own doctrine over others, without respecting other strands of faith traditions, often lead to violence and rivalry. In such a context, a divided church in Asia cannot withstand the organized attacks from those opposed to the church. Particularly in India and its neighboring countries, churches and believers are being attacked, and Christians are threatened with social boycott to force them to abandon their faith. In such a context, where Christians are a minority, the need to work together as Christians is important to resist the attack from within and outside. Christians need to be united in the common faith, and such ecumenical unity is essential for the church in Asia to reach greater heights.

47 Timoteo D. Gener, "Christologies in Asia: Trends and Reflections," *JAET* 17, no. 2 (2013): 21.
48 Gener, 21.

A False Dichotomy between the Secular and the Religious

The false teachers in Jude's community are characterized by the fact that they are ungodly in their character, and they teach that grace allows Christians to sin as they please (v. 4). While Jude's opponents use the tactic of antinomianism to "detach accepted moral stands from the will of God," Jude sees their "contempt for the commandments as presumptuousness in relation to God himself, rooted in resistance to his will."[49] Probably the false teachers believed that as people of the spirit, they will be spared from judgment irrespective of their immoral behavior. Hence along with rejection of moral authority, they indulge in immorality, including sexual misconduct (vv. 6–8, 10), deliberately flouting standards of Jewish-Christian morality. It seems that the false teachers have self-claimed prophetic authority on the basis of revelations they received in a state of religious ecstasy, which Jude refers to as "dreaming" (v. 8). This religious experience prompted them to encourage their followers to reject moral restrictions that, in their understanding, apply to ordinary people but not to the "spiritual" person.[50]

The relation that Jude maintains between spirituality and morality is impressive. For Jude, spirituality is not abstract; it is an integral part of Christian life. This moral appeal has relevance to the context where spirituality is viewed as alien to moral conduct. Any proper spirituality must be related to one's behavior and conduct. Western influence on Asian spirituality normally keeps a passive attitude on the issue of morality, whereas Asian spirituality transcends the dichotomy between spirituality and morality. For instance, in *Asian Millenarianism*, H. B. Rhee refers to a religious tradition known in parts of Vietnam as Buu Son Ky Huong and describes its evolution into the Hoa Hao sect, a quasi-Buddhist tradition. In Hoa Hao ideology, the religious dimension cannot be separated from the secular. It believes that religious values have implications at the secular level, and religious solutions are usually proposed to address social and political issues. This ideology of Hoa Hao evolved as an antidote to a widely felt concern about the secularization of politics and the absence of moral sanctions from new economic relationships in Vietnam.[51]

49 Bauckham, *Jude–2 Peter*, 11.

50 Painter and deSilva, *James and Jude*, 184; Bauckham, *Jude–2 Peter*, 11.

51 Hong Beom Rhee, *Asian Millenarianism: An Interdisciplinary Study of the Taiping and Tonghak Rebellions in a Global Context* (New York: Cambria, 2007), 75.

Another Asian philosophical tradition that emphasizes a harmony between spirituality and morality is Confucianism. Confucianism transcends the dichotomy between religion and humanism, considering the way of life itself as a manifestation of the sacred. One of the doctrines of Confucianism is the harmony and unity between the secular and the sacred.[52] The Confucian way of life embodies self, community, nature, and heaven in an ethic of care and responsibility, which is the Confucian idea of humanity.[53]

In the contemporary world, a sharp decline in ethical emphasis among churches and other religious organizations and a significant rise in secularism have made the tie between morality and religion somewhat vague. In such a context, living a moral life should be considered as identical with spirituality. Being moral allows us to live honestly and purely in a world filled with corruption, injustice, inequality, and the suffering of the poor and the oppressed. The church cannot remain aloof toward these ethical issues if it needs to remain truly spiritual.

The Lordship of Christ

Apart from the opening address and greeting of this letter, where Jude refers to Jesus as simply "Jesus Christ" (v. 1), once he moves into the main content of the letter, Jude always combines "Jesus Christ" with "our Lord" (vv. 4, 17, 21, 25). This title "Lord" suggests Jesus's explicit authority. The first reference to Jesus's lordship occurs in the polemic against false teachers (v. 4), which takes an emphatic form: "our only Master" (*monon despotēn*) and "Lord" (*kurios*). *Despotēs* (Master) was a common designation for the master of the household, who exercised authority over one's family and slaves. The term was also used for state rulers, who exercised unlimited power over their subjects. The Roman emperor himself was referred to as the "supreme father of the empire." Similarly, the title *kurios* was also commonly used to refer to the Roman emperors. In such a context, the authority of Jesus as Master and Lord becomes the ground for Jude's polemic.[54] This stress on lordship reflects a clear antiempire

52 Xinzhong Yao, *An Introduction to Confucianism* (Cambridge: Cambridge University Press, 2000), 45.

53 Zhao Dunhua, *Dialogues of Philosophies, Religions and Civilizations in the Era of Globalization* (Washington, DC: Peking University, 2007), 14.

54 Park, "Letter of Jude," 430.

rhetoric that acknowledges Jesus over the caesar, who deserves the believers' total loyalty.

However, this lordship ideology has been interpreted by colonial and patriarchal powers to suit their own agendas. For instance, apart from using the lordship image to justify political and economic domination, this lordship ideology of colonial powers had also impacted and domesticated the vibrant precolonial Asian women's self-understanding of power in the community. The image of "lord" has been used against Asian women, perpetuating their submissive and oppressed status in society and the church. The Asian woman's man is her lord and master in the sense that she has to obey the father before marriage, the husband in marriage, and the son in widowhood.[55] In the context where master and lord were understood in relation to the ruler of the household and of the state, who exercised power over their subjects, the lordship of Christ means that Jesus's "Lordship is exact opposite of patriarchal Lordship."[56] Chung H. Kyung states, "Jesus' lordship says no to patriarchal domination, freeing Asian women from false authority and empowering them to obey only God and not men."[57] She further says, "The liberative dimension of the Lord image of Jesus frees Asian women from the false authority of the world over them and empowers them to claim true authority which springs from life-giving experiences."[58] While patriarchal and colonial understanding of lordship means oppression and domination, the lordship of Christ means the power that liberates people. Thus the titles *kurios* and *despotēs* transformed their meaning radically when used to name the lordship of Jesus Christ.[59]

Apocalyptic Teaching: Prediction of God's Judgment on the Wicked

In the main section of the letter, Jude provides a variety of examples from Palestinian Jewish Scriptural tradition: the disobedience of Israelites during the exodus (v. 5); the displacement of the angels (v. 6); the destruction of Sodom and Gomorrah (v. 7); the battle between the archangel Michael and

55 Chung Hyun Kyung, "Who Is Jesus for Asian Women?," in *Liberation Theology: An Introduction Reader*, ed. Curt Cadorette et al. (Eugene, OR: Wipf & Stock, 1992), 128.

56 Kyung, 129.

57 Kyung, 129.

58 Kyung, 128.

59 Kyung, 129.

the devil (vv. 9–10); the erroneous ways of Cain, Balaam, and Korah (v. 11); and the prophecy of Enoch concerning God's punishment (vv. 14–16). These examples from Israel's salvation history recall the fate of the disobedient and rebellious ones who were punished because of their apostasy as they rebelled against God's authority and teachings. These judgments from history become a typological example of Jude's own opponents and their followers.

By citing these intertextual examples, Jude seeks to make his readers aware of the opponents and their destiny. Jude's examples involve not only sin but also judgment. God's acts in the history of Israel is a warning that point forward to God's act against the false teachers and their adherents. According to Jude, "believers need to see such acts of God as a type of prophecy regarding the judgement to be rendered on those who pretend to surpass Jesus' lordship."[60] This message of judgment is relevant today, where "churches are prone to sentimentality, suffer from moral breakdown, and too often fail to pronounce a definitive word of judgment because of an inadequate definition of love."[61] In such a context, Jude's teaching reminds one that heretic teaching and immoral living will have dismal consequences.

This prediction of God's judgment against the ungodly has parallels in Asian religious traditions, including Buddhism. According to the Buddhist understanding of judgment, the individual's destiny is determined by karma, the effect of one's deeds. There is no single judgment day in most Buddhist sects, and the goal of judgment mostly implies another opportunity for a person to escape suffering and attain Nirvana.[62] This is similar to what Jude is intending to convey in his letter. The doxology (vv. 24–25) with which Jude concludes his letter following the examples of doom from history and a call to persevere is in fact an assurance for the believers that those using this opportunity to rectify their ways depending on God's grace will be saved from the doomsday. Thus Jude's intention of apocalyptic teaching is not to frighten the believers but to encourage them to resist evil and escape judgment.

60 Park, "Letter of Jude," 432.

61 Schreiner, *Peter and Jude*, 403.

62 Dinitia Smith, "Apocalyptic Meditations: Every Faith Has a View," *New York Times*, April 3, 1999, https://www.nytimes.com/1999/04/03/arts/apocalyptic-meditations-every-faith-has-a-view.html.

In the words of Thomas Robbins and Susan Palmer, "An apocalypse is not simply an end. It is also and more importantly a beginning, an uncovering, an illumination unveiled precisely at the very moment of the greatest darkness and danger."[63] This Greek concept of the apocalypse (*apo*, reversal; *kalyptein*, to cover) has basically the same meaning as the Korean term *Kaebyok*, which means "the opening or the beginning of the world." *Kaebyok* was a cosmic chronology that claimed a new era was beginning. In the West, cosmic changes typically signaled a conclusion, but in Asian spirituality such as *Kaebyok*, it signaled a beginning of new hope, the process of transformation of the world from the old destiny to the new destiny, emphasizing the beginning of the world more than the ending of the world.[64]

According to non-Asian apocalyptic tradition, God will bring judgment in the final days, but according to the Asian religious apocalyptic traditions such as Hinduism, Buddhism, and Zoroastrianism, the law of nature (karma) itself will bring about the final days.[65] Karma, the principle of moral causation, teaches a cause-and-effect relationship between one's present actions and afterlife. The belief in karma functions as motivation for a person to resist evil and do good deeds. In Hinduism, there are several cycles of time, and there are several doomsdays (*pralaya*) that are usually preceded by a period of moral decay. Hinduism has no single day of judgment in the Christian sense, but by contrast, judgment is pronounced at the end of an individual life.[66] These apocalyptic traditions ensure that errant teaching and dissolute living will have dire consequences, and they also encourage their followers to resist evil and escape judgment.

Exhortation: Have Mercy

One main purpose of Jude is the call to mercy. Most often one is left with the impression that Jude is nothing more than a sharp critique of opponents in the church. Yet the letter ends on a triple call to merciful action to those who are stumbling and are in danger of falling under God's judgment. In the words of

63 Thomas Robbins and Susan J. Palmer, eds., *Millennium Messiahs, and Mayhem* (New York: Routledge, 1997), 65.

64 Rhee, *Asian Millenarianism*, 81.

65 Rhee, 211.

66 Smith, "Apocalyptic Meditations."

Keating, Jude is a powerful example of "mercy triumphing over judgment."[67] There are three groups of people Jude is referring to in his concluding exhortation: first, "have mercy on some, who are wavering" (v. 22); second, "save others by snatching them out of the fire" (v. 23a); and third, "have mercy on still others with fear" (v. 23b). These groups include the believers who are questioning their position in salvation experience, are probably influenced negatively by the false teachers, and thus practice immorality. Instead of only rebuking such people, one also needs to show mercy. According to Painter and deSilva, along with warning and judgment, "it is important not to lose sight of Jude's proclamation of the love of God throughout his brief letter. Those who follow the apostles' teaching and use God's grace to pursue holiness rather than self-indulgence are 'beloved' (vv. 1, 3, 5, 17, 20), urged to keep themselves in God's love (v. 21), and assured of God's commitment to keep them so that they will encounter God without fear or cause for rejection (v. 24)."[68] Thus while Jude is concerned about warning and judgment, he never fails to encourage his readers to show mercy to fellow believers and even to their opponents. By emphasizing God's love and grace along with warning and judgment, Jude bears the full witness of God's character. Even the judgment comes only because of resistance to mercy. God's judgment in no way vindicates the use of violence toward others, nor does it free believers from the responsibility to live in ways that privilege mercy and salvation over judgment and violence.[69]

The idea of nonviolence as an ethical principle is shared by many of the Asian religious traditions. Mahavira, the propagator of Jainism, proclaimed *ahimsa* as one of the five supreme ethical principles. In Dhammapada, a Buddhist sacred text, it is stated, "He who lives a life of self-restraint rooted in *ahimsa* attains to the state of immortality." According to the Vedic culture, "By controlling sensual desires . . . and observance of *ahimsa*, a *sanyasi* attains *moksha*." In Mahabharata, one of the greatest Indian epics, it is said, "*Ahimsa* is in itself a complete religion and *himsa* [violence] is a great sin."[70] Mahatma

67 Daniel Keating, *First and Second Peter, Jude* (Grand Rapids, MI: Baker Academic, 2011), 194.

68 Painter and deSilva, *James and Jude*, 217.

69 Richard B. Hays, *The Moral Vision of the New Testament: Community, Cross, New Creation* (San Francisco: HarperOne, 1996), 336.

70 See Sohan Lal Jain Gandhi, "The Jain Principle of Ahimsa and Ecology," jainsamaj.org, accessed April 10, 2020, https://www.jainsamaj.org/content.php?url=Jain_Principle_of_Ahimsa_and.

Gandhi was among the first to convert the idea of nonviolence into the language of civil movements. Gandhi's legacy of *ahimsa* has created a deep impact on the world. He demonstrated the immense power of *ahimsa* by using it as an effective weapon against colonial intruders.

The accepted Christian practice toward erring fellow beings is to point out their immorality and warn them in a spirit of Christian love. Jude combines warning, judgment, and mercy as the response to the false teachers and their followers or potential followers in the community as a genuine Christian response toward one's enemies.

Hermeneutical: Use of Intertextual Reading in Asian Context

Jude uses several quotes and allusions from the OT and other Jewish Scriptures, including noncanonical traditions, to establish his argument against false teachers (vv. 5–16). Jude uses these texts because his readers were familiar with these Jewish Scriptures. The references to Cain, Balaam, Korah, and the citation of Assumption of Moses and 1 Enoch are not merely to the OT and apocryphal texts as such but also to the haggadic traditions about these figures that had grown around these texts in the first century. The introduction to these teachings—"Now I desire to remind you, though you are fully informed" (v. 5)—indicates that the content of the teaching was part of the parenthetic tradition that was familiar to these churches during the time which Jude wrote. This reminds us that along with traditional religious scripture, texts common and familiar to the readers need to be used in our interpretations.

Intertextual reading helps in identifying various relationships between one text and another, as well as the influence of one text upon another text. An intertextual reading brings to the text a preunderstanding informed by Asia's rich religious and cultural tradition, so as to discover in it resonances missed by the Western exegetes.[71] Kwok Pui-lan notes, "Asian Christians are heirs to both the biblical story and to our own story as Asian people, and we are concerned to bring the two in dialogue with one another."[72] Resources for a contextual reading

71 George Soares-Prabhu, "The Historical Critical Method: Reflections on Its Relevance for the Study of the Gospels in India Today," in *Theologizing in India*, ed. M. Amaladoss, T. K. John, and G. Gispert-Sauch (Bangalore: Theological Publications in India, 1981), 343.

72 Kwok Pui-lan, "Discovering the Bible in the Nonbiblical World," in *Voices from the Margin: Interpreting the Bible in the Third World*, ed. R. S. Sugirtharajah (Maryknoll, NY: Orbis, 1991), 304.

of the Bible are to be found both in the biblical studies and in the resources of ordinary indigenous poor and marginalized communities.[73] Innumerable indigenous legends, stories, poems, and songs that are part of the varied and rich cultural heritage of Asia still remain largely unexplored. Intertextual reading can also be of much help for better understanding and appreciation of the scriptures of other religious traditions. It could act as a catalyst in fostering communal harmony in the context of increasing communal tensions and disharmony.[74]

The challenge of the Church is to work with the "others," cooperating with secular and religious organizations, whose understanding of mission is different from the church's. In the present context, where scant regard is given to other faith traditions, intertextual and interreligious reading helps acknowledge the integrity of people of other faiths.[75] In the words of Sugirtharajah, "In a multifaith context, the lesson is to be less arrogant of one's faith and learn, listen, and draw new lessons from one another's spiritual troves."[76] In a context of cultural and religious plurality, a sense of superiority of one's culture and religion leads to discrimination and oppression of the other, whereas appreciation and willingness to learn from others lead to harmony and peaceful coexistence.

Honor and Shame

Honor and shame is one of the prominent similarities between the first-century Mediterranean world and contemporary Asian cultures. In a collectivistic culture such as that of the Mediterranean world and Asia, the community remains the highest priority. In such a cultural context, honor becomes the basis of one's reputation, of one's social standing. According to Malina, "Honor is the value of a person in his or her own eyes plus that person's value in the eyes of his or her social group. Honor is a claim to worth along with the social acknowledgement of worth."[77]

73 See Joseph Patmury, ed., *Doing Theology with the Poetic Traditions of India: Focus on Dalit and Tribal Poems* (Bangalore: PTCA/SATHRI, 1996).

74 See George M. Soares-Prabhu, "Two Mission Commands: An Interpretation of Matthew 28:16–20 in the Light of a Buddhist Text," in *Voices from the Margin. Interpreting the Bible in the Third World*, ed. R. S. Sugirtharajah (Maryknoll, NY: Orbis, 2006), 338.

75 R. S. Sugirtharajah, "The Syrophoenician Woman," *Expository Times* 98, no. 1 (1986): 13.

76 Sugirtharajah, 15.

77 B. J. Malina, *The New Testament World: Insights from Cultural Anthropology* (Atlanta: Westminster John Knox, 2001), 30.

In his commentary on Jude and 2 Peter, Andrew M. Mbuvi compares Jude's community with the small groups that were part of the Greco-Roman culture that met regularly for social and religious purposes. Apart from gathering for shared meals and fellowships, these groups also acted as social networks for members (see v. 12). Members were expected to value the group's honor by following certain ethical responsibilities, and failing to adhere to such ethical codes led to the person shaming the group. Placing the letter of Jude in the world of Greco-Roman associations highlights the group dynamics reflected in the letter.[78] Jude exhibits this group's honor in calling his readers beloved (vv. 1, 17, 20), referring to God as the Father (v. 1), exhorting the members to have mercy on other members (vv. 22–23), requesting to pray in the Holy Spirit (v. 20), identifying the intruders and their followers as those who bring shame to the group (v. 4), and so on.

In a context of the false teachers intruding the community, Jude does not appeal to individual leaders to suppress the opponents and guard the faith against such heretical deviations. Instead, Jude address the whole community, who is responsible for upholding the gospel (v. 3). Also referring to 1 Enoch 1:9 in verses 14–15, Jude says that God comes "to execute judgment on all, and to convict everyone of all the deeds of ungodliness," which refers to the entire congregation and not exclusively the false teachers.[79] John J. Pilch, in a comparative study between the contemporary nonagrarian society and the agrarian society that was the background of the NT, concludes that in the first-century Mediterranean society reflected in NT writings, human activity was centered on collateral (including family, neighbors, and patron/client) and lineal (hierarchically or vertically oriented) relationships.[80]

For Jude, when false teachers intrude and spread heresies, the community's honor is at stake. Honor is restored when the community members identify the false teachers and resist their heretic teachings. Those who fail to live up to the ethical principles of the community are deemed inappropriate for such communities because they bring shame instead of honor. Jude uses the dynamics

78 Andrew M. Mbuvi, *Jude and 2 Peter*, New Covenant Commentary Series (Eugene, OR: Wipf & Stock, 2015).

79 Painter and deSilva, *James and Jude*, 215–16.

80 See John J. Pilch, *Healing in the New Testament: Insights from Medical and Mediterranean Anthropology* (Minneapolis: Fortress, 2000), 4.

of honor and shame to motivate his readers. The exhortations in the epistle demonstrate a concern for the reputation of the group.

Social Identity

Jude identifies himself as the "slave" of Jesus Christ (v. 1). Undoubtedly, *slave* is used here metaphorically to express the type of commitment Jude perceives himself as having toward Jesus Christ. Even though slaves did not enjoy a good social standing in society, it was not uncommon for masters to use slaves as their spokespersons. Such occasions provided the slave with conferred authority by playing the role of the master's ambassador. Jude is thus aware that as a slave of Jesus Christ, he enjoys certain honor while at the same time exhibiting humility. Also, by claiming to be the brother of James, who had a significant repute within the larger Christian community in Jerusalem, Jude manages to stake a claim of authority, besides exhibiting humility.[81]

According to Andrew Mbuvi, Jude's restructuring of his identity in relation to the person of Jesus provides a useful lesson: "Jude, while he could have chosen to use the bloodline (brother of Jesus) to construct his identity, instead chooses to identify himself as a slave of Jesus (a theological construction). Jude prioritizes his theological identity over what perhaps others would have preferred, the bloodline that would have given him more claim to authority as a sibling of the Lord. Instead, by not only downplaying the use of biological identity as his primary one, and instead using a theological identity that also embraces a deep humility."[82] Thus it seems like what was an insignificant part in Jude's writing in terms of his identity has an important lesson for the church today. True Christian identity should incorporate and exhibit authority along with humility.

In the Indian context, culturizing and ethnicizing of the caste system over the centuries has made caste the core symbol of community and a defining feature of Indian social structure. Just like *doulos* (slave), the concept of Dalit has negative connotations and has been used to denigrate the socially deprived.[83] The exploitation and discrimination of the Dalits, and their protest and revolt as the response to such exploitation, have initiated the process of

81 Mbuvi, *Jude and 2 Peter*, 26–27.
82 Mbuvi, 30.
83 Mbuvi, 28.

self-assertion and consciousness among the Dalits, providing a new identity for them. This new identity strengthens their resolve to fight discrimination and determine the path of liberation.

For instance, Dalits in India adopt their own unique cultural identity to resist dominant Hinduism culture. One such cultural pillar is drum beating, which remains at the heart of the Dalit social world. Beating a drum is a symbol of resistance to the social and ritual boundaries of caste. Dalits who were often associated with pollution were used by upper-caste Hindus to play drum (*parai*) for the funeral of the upper castes, thus associating the drum with pollution and death. However, Dalit Christians use this as part of liturgy in the church, thus reversing its association with degradation by transforming the psyche of the Dalits with a sense of healing pride in their culture.[84]

Further, the close identification of Christianity in Asia with colonization and the church's consequent lack of rootedness in Asian cultures are major concerns for the church's mission today. In such a context, the biggest challenge for the church in Asia is to rediscover the identity of Asian Christianity and its mission. This is all the more significant because by and large, Christianity's origin is rooted in Asia. Though over the decades Asian churches have tried to establish their own identities, such as replacing westernized liturgy and music with indigenous ones, in the context of ecclesiastical traditions and interpretations, they are very much influenced by the historical colonial past. To be a witness in Asia's multireligious context, the church has to integrate itself in its local, cultural, and indigenous roots. Exclusion and rejection of one's own cultural context can be devastating to the growth of the church in an Asian context.

CONCLUSION

The Epistle of Jude is one of the smallest books in the NT, but it is unique in its use of the Apocrypha and in its approach to ecclesiastical doctrines. Rejected by many through the course of Church history, this epistle has found its canonical place partly because of its polemic against false teachers and

84 Z. C. Sherinian, *Tamil Folk Music: As Dalit Liberation Theology* (Bloomington: Indiana University Press, 2014), 119.

heretics. Jude's warning and exhortations are valid not only for the church of the first century but also in our postmodern Asian context as well. Jude's emphasis on the lordship of Christ, ethical morality, and social identity as well as his condemnation on false teachings convey a powerful message for the contemporary Asian church. In a context of increasing religious tension and hostilities, the church is in danger of taking the path of either absolute exclusivism or unconditional inclusion. While accepting different expressions of faith, it is essential to recognize the lordship of Christ as the core of Christian faith. The challenge of the church is to incorporate these teachings and work with the "others," cooperating with secular and religious organizations whose understanding of mission is different from the church's. Jude's use of intertextual method in achieving this objective is perhaps an encouragement to Asian churches to use local resources in our interpretations and, in the process, restore the identity of Asian Christianity.

FURTHER READING

Gener, T. D. 2013. "Christologies in Asia: Trends and Reflections." *Journal of Asian Evangelical Theology* 17, no. 2: 17–40.

Green, G. L. 2008. *Jude and 2 Peter*. Grand Rapids, MI: Baker Academic.

Keating, D. 2011. *First and Second Peter, Jude*. Grand Rapids, MI: Baker Academic.

Kelly, J. N. D. 1969. *A Commentary on the Epistles of Peter and Jude*. Grand Rapids, MI: Baker.

Mbuvi, A. M. 2015. *Jude and 2 Peter*. New Covenant Commentary Series. Eugene, OR: Wipf & Stock.

Painter, J., and D. A. deSilva. 2012. *James and Jude*. Paidea Commentaries on the New Testament. Grand Rapids, MI: Baker Academic.

Park, R. 2009. "The Letter of Jude." In *A Postcolonial Commentary on the NT Writings*, 424–435, edited by Fernando F. Segovia and R. S. Sugirtharajah. London: T&T Clark.

Reese, R. A. 2000. *Writing Jude: The Reader, the Text, and the Author in Constructs of Power and Desire*. London: Brill.

Reicke, B. 1964. *The Epistles of James, Peter, and Jude*. Anchor Bible 37. Garden City, NY: Doubleday.

Schreiner, T. R. 2003. *1 and 2 Peter and Jude*. New American Commentary 37. Nashville: B&H.

Sherinian, Z. C. 2014. *Tamil Folk Music: As Dalit Liberation Theology*. Bloomington: Indiana University Press.

Soares-Prabhu, G. M. 2006. "Two Mission Commands: An Interpretation of Matthew 28:16–20 in the Light of a Buddhist Text." In *Voices from the Margin. Interpreting the Bible in the Third World*, edited by R. S. Sugirtharajah, 331–46. New York: Orbis.

TWENTY-THREE

The Book of Revelation

Biju Chacko
New Theological College
Dehradun, India

Undoubtedly, the book of Revelation has stirred many debates among Christians throughout the centuries. Shillington avers that "perhaps the book of Revelation is best understood when it is put to Music."[1] There is surely a poetical force, though it has a disturbing plot.[2] It is an anti-imperial postcolonial narrative, with a grotesque critique of empire and hegemonies of all times and forms.[3] Though the book of Revelation played a pivotal role in the formation of church dogma on eschatology, it is more dramatic than it is dogmatic, more musical than prosaic, more visionary than programmatic.[4] These dramatic, musical, and visionary textures mean it belongs more to Asian cultures than any others.

Its high-pitched tone and seemingly reclusive framework underscored the fears and anxieties of the early Christian community (Asian Christian communities). Its generic character refuses to yield a single and simple interpretation.

1 V. George Shillington, *The New Testament in Context* (New York: T&T Clark, 2008), 275.

2 Christopher A. Frilingos, *Spectacles of Empire: Monsters, Martyrs and the Book of Revelation* (Philadelphia: University of Pennsylvania Press, 2004), 1.

3 See Bas Wielenga, *Revelation to John: Turning into Songs of Moses and the Lamb* (New Delhi: ISPCK, 2009), xv. There are authors who see this as an imperial narrative. For example, see Robert M. Royalty Jr., *The Streets of Heaven: The Ideology of Wealth in the Apocalypse of John* (Macon, GA: Mercer University Press, 1998), 246.

4 Shillington, *New Testament in Context*, 276.

With its highly symbolic articulation and theological textures, the author calls for a firm stand in the light of the coming of the new heaven and the new earth, the advent of the Lord's judgment and salvation. The attempt here is to see this literature through Asian eyes. Since the generic features are significant in understanding any literature, it is important to locate this book in the context of apocalyptic literature.

APOCALYPTIC LITERATURE

Apocalyptic ideas definitely played a pivotal role in Judaism as well as in Christianity. The famous statement of Ernst Käsemann, "Apocalyptic was the mother of all Christian theology,"[5] though a bit overstated, exemplifies this. Yet this literature received only random attention in the beginning as observed by Koch.[6] Apocalyptic literature is a kind of resistant literature that has its own form, content, and function. But such resistant literature was not limited to Judaism and Christianity.[7] The apocalyptic literature is a reflection of the resilience of ostracized communities in their given context.

The word *apocalyptic* is derived from the Greek word Ἀποκάλυψις, which means revelation or disclosure of things. Scholars frequently used terms like *apocalyptic*, *apocalypticism*, and *apocalypse*.[8] *Apocalyptic* is often referred to as a movement, and *apocalypticism* is a social ideology that propels any apocalyptic movement.[9] Apocalyptic literature is the product of such movements. Thus recent scholarship considers apocalypse as a particular literary genre. J. J. Collins identifies two types of apocalypses—namely, historical apocalypses, in which revelation is most often conveyed in symbolic visions and presents an overview of history culminating in a crisis, and apocalypses involving otherworldly journeys, which are mystical in orientation.[10] Russell avers that

5 E. Käsemann, "The Beginnings of Christian Theology," *Journal for Theology and the Church* 6 (1969): 40.

6 Klaus Koch, *The Rediscovery of Apocalyptic* (London: SCM, 1972).

7 See C. I. David Joy, *Karthru Kahalam Dhvanikkumbol* [When the trumpet of the Lord will sound] (Tiruvalla: Theological Literature Council, 2016), 12.

8 J. J. Collins, *The Apocalyptic Imagination* (New York: Crossroad, 1987), 1.

9 Collins, 2.

10 See J. J. Collins, "Introduction: Towards a Morphology of a Genre," *Semeia 14* (1979): 21–59.

apocalyptic literature is "esoteric in character, literary in form, symbolic in language and pseudonymous in authorship."[11]

REVELATION AS AN APOCALYPTIC BOOK: THE GENRE OF THE BOOK

The first work that is introduced as an *apokalypsis* is Revelation.[12] At first impression, Revelation resembles a letter to be read by an audience (1:3–4; 22:18). The main body of the book resembles a homily. Apocalyptic literature is often considered as an offshoot of biblical prophecy (1:3; 22:7, 10).[13] Therefore, Revelation has its moorings in the prophetic tradition and identifies itself as a prophecy. Luke Timothy Johnson points out three distinguishing aspects by which Revelation breaks the mold of the ordinary apocalypse and becomes unique: the creative and artistic style; the resemblance of Jewish Merkabah mysticism, especially in the heavenly hall scenes with its hymns and liturgy; and above all, its portrayal of Christ by an author who is well-known to readers (not pseudonymous) and describes his own experience of the risen Lord.[14] Scholars have argued for the hybridity of this literature.[15] Such hybridity is seen in the confluence of epistolary framework and identification as a prophecy, yet the book begins with a specification as apocalypse. Therefore, it should be treated above all as a Christian apocalypse.

11 D. S. Russell, *The Message and Method of Jewish Apocalyptic* (Philadelphia: Westminster, 1964), 106.

12 Collins, *Apocalyptic Imagination*, 3.

13 D. S. Russell, *Between the Testaments* (London: SCM, 1960), 93; see P. D. Hanson, *The Dawn of Apocalyptic* (Philadelphia: Fortress, 1975), 402–13.

14 L. T. Johnson, *The Writings of the New Testament: An Interpretation* (Bangalore: Theological Publications in India, 1986), 577–78.

15 Ben Witherington, *Revelation: The New Cambridge Bible Commentary* (Cambridge: Cambridge University Press, 2003), 32–33; Elizabeth Schüssler Fiorenza, *The Book of Revelation: Justice and Judgment*, 2nd ed. (Minneapolis: Fortress, 1998), 149.

Authorship

The author introduces himself in the book as John, the servant of Jesus Christ (1:1, see 1:4, 9; 22:8), and later as a prophet (22:9). The writer takes it for granted that the readers will know him without giving further details. He is well informed about the audience and their spiritual condition (2:2–5, 13, 19, 21; 3:10). It seems that though he is writing in Greek, John's first language was Hebrew. According to early Christian testimony, the author was John the apostle.[16] But many scholars questioned this traditional view for the following reasons. First, the author does not appeal to his apostolic authority, and not even once does the author state he was an eyewitness of Jesus's ministry.[17] Second, if one accepts that John the apostle is the authority behind the Fourth Gospel, then it would be impossible to regard him as the author of Revelation because there are major differences between them in language, style, content, and theology.[18] At the same time, there are sufficient common themes between them to suggest some kind of relationship between them.[19]

Some commentators have sought to identify the author with prominent figures who bore the name John, including John the presbyter, John Mark, and even John the Baptist.[20] What can be said with certainty is that the author was a Jewish Christian prophet whose name was John and who was well versed in the apocalyptic traditions of his time.[21] He stands in the category of the Hebrew prophets. There is a possibility that this author might have hailed from some part of Asia Minor or had been living in some part of Asia Minor for quite some time. Even if one may argue that the Gospel and Revelation are from two authors, it seems they belonged to the same theological school in Asia Minor.

16 See D. A. Carson and Douglas Moo, *An Introduction to the New Testament*, 2nd ed. (Grand Rapids, MI: Zondervan, 2005), 700–702.

17 Raymond E. Brown, *An Introduction to the New Testament* (Bangalore: Theological Publications in India, 2009), 802–3.

18 See S. E. Porter, "The Language of the Apocalypse in Recent Discussion," *New Testament Studies* 35 (1989): 582–603. See also Witherington, *Revelation*, 2.

19 See Witherington, *Revelation*, 3.

20 J. M. Ford, *Revelation: A New Translation with Introduction and Commentary*, Anchor Bible (New York; Doubleday, 1975), 28–30.

21 See Witherington, *Revelation*, 2.

Date

There are at least three important views regarding the date of writing. A number of commentators share the view that Revelation was written toward the end of the first century, around 95 CE. There are others who think that the content of the book is more related to the time of Nero, a turbulent time that led to the Roman-Jewish war; if so, the book might have been written a little earlier, around 68 CE.[22] The third proposal is during the reign of Vespasian, between 75 and 79 CE.[23] However, the internal evidences seem to support a date toward the end of the first century CE. Many scholars argued that the situation of the churches reflected in Revelation 2–3 favors a later date.[24] Revelation seems to have been written during the period of persecution, a period of intense tension between the church and the state. The exile of the author to the island of Patmos (1:9); the murder of Antipas, a member of the church at Pergamum (2:13); and the depiction of the Roman emperor as a beast who makes war on the saints are indications of such tensions. Witherington argues that "the Christological references that counterbalance Christ against the lordship of the Emperor best suit a post-Neronian period of NT history."[25] In short, the cumulative evidences suggest a date toward the end of the first century CE.

The Sociopolitical Context and the Readers

John states clearly at the outset itself that he was in the Island of Patmos,[26] and there he received the commission of the risen Lord to write to the seven churches in Asia Minor (1:9–11). John's vision is set in a "ritual time," that is, on the Lord's Day. Revelation was written during the time of social conflict between Rome and Christians. In heightening the conflict, the imperial cult and its magnitudes played a key role. Osborne asserts that any conclusive view

22 C. Rowland, *Open Heaven: A Study of Apocalyptic in Judaism and Early Christianity* (London: SPCK, 1982), 403–13.

23 See G. R. Osborne, *Revelation: Baker Exegetical Commentary on the New Testament* (Grand Rapids, MI: Baker Academics, 2002), 6–9.

24 Tacitus, *Annales*, 14:27.

25 See Witherington, *Revelation*, 5.

26 See Leonard L. Thompson, "Ordinary Lives: John and His First Readers," in *Reading the Book of Revelation: A Resource for Students*, ed. David L. Barr (Atlanta: SBL, 2003), 26.

on social setting will be determined by one's outlook regarding the imperial cult and the extent of persecution.[27] Witherington contends that there is good evidence that Christians did go through severe persecution, and especially during and after Domitian's time, Christians were under significant social pressure to conform to the imperial cult.[28]

Imperial cult was one of the prominent features of first century CE Roman world, which acted as a social link that connected all people.[29] Participation in the imperial cult became the mark of their loyalty to the empire, whereas, for Christians, it violated their loyalty to Christ.[30] As a result, many of the cities in Asia Minor competed in building temples for the emperor and paying homage to him. In addition to this, there were also tensions between Judaism and Christianity and even among Christian communities with regard to the degree of accommodation.[31] It would be difficult to deduce any particular social situation from the visions, precisely because it is in "nesting-mythic language."[32] These congregations addressed in the early chapters are on the cities.[33] The readers of the book of Revelation largely hailed from the lower socioeconomic strata.

27 Osborne, *Revelation*, 10; see Witherington, *Revelation*, 6–10.

28 Witherington, *Revelation*, 6–10. Witherington cites the works of T. B. Slater and S. R. F. Price to support his views. See T. B. Slater, "On the Social Setting of the Revelation," *NTS* 44 (1998): 238. See S. R. F. Price, *Rituals and Power: The Roman Imperial Cult in Asia Minor* (Cambridge: Cambridge University Press, 1984), 123–26, 197–98. In contrast, Thomson states that Christians did live well under Domitian's rule and that persecutions were local in nature. See Leonard L. Thompson, *The Book of Revelation: Apocalypse and Empire* (New York: Oxford University Press, 1990), 6–8. For A. Y. Collins, the main problem was economic exploitation and cultural imperialism of Rome. See A. Y. Collins, "Apocalypse and Politics," *The Looking Glass: Essays in Celebration of a Precursor: For Robert W. Funk*, Forum 8, no. 3–4 (1992): 297–312. Kraybill also feels that the issue is not persecution but compromise. See J. N. Kraybill, *Imperial Cult and Commerce in John's Apocalypse*, JSNT Suppl Series 132 (Sheffield: SAP, 1996), 16–18.

29 See Eduard Lohse, *The New Testament Environment*, trans. John E. Steely (Nashville: Abingdon, 1971), 216.

30 Helmut Koester, *Introduction to the New Testament: History, Culture and Religion of the Hellenistic Age* (Philadelphia: Fortress, 1982), 1:371.

31 See Craig R. Koester, *Revelation: A New Translation with Introduction and Commentary*, The Anchor Yale Bible (New Haven, CT: Yale University Press, 2014), 85.

32 Leonard L. Thompson, *The Book of Revelation: Apocalypse and Empire* (New York: Oxford University Press, 1990), 6.

33 Witherington, *Revelation*, 7.

The readers might have faced actual social crises like local harassment, ridicule, discrimination, and oppression for their religious beliefs.[34] They suffered martyrdom (Rev 2:13), and were upset with heretical teachings. By noting the combination of various terms like prophet/prophesy, servant, witness/testimony, and holy ones occurring in the book, Johnson suggests that it is a community of saints carrying out their prophetic office by bearing witness to Jesus, and thus it is a prophetic community.[35] Like the prophets in the OT, they were speaking truth to power (see Rev 19:10). Christian communities in Asia, as people living in a polyglotic and multireligious context, share similarities with the readers of Revelation. They also face socioreligious excommunication in their own land for their faith convictions and confessions. Therefore, Revelation is a favorite book in the Asian context because it provides a theology of hope and resistance. The community of Revelation shares a lot of similarities with the Bhakti movement in India.[36] In the devotional literature, *bhakti* is used to describe the unquestionable faith and absolute devotion to God. It was a socioreligious resistant movement that emerged among the lower socioeconomic group in a highly caste-ridden Indian society. It resisted the evils of Hinduism and the onslaught of the religion of the ruling Muslim and other religious groups.[37] Therefore, this community was tossed between the social evils of the caste system and the onslaught of the imperial religion, just as the community of Revelation was tossed between Jewish cultural nationalists and the religion of the Roman Empire.

The Purpose of the Book of Revelation

What could have been the purpose of the author of Revelation in carefully formulating such an account? The answer to this question is intricately related to the methods of interpretations applied to this book.[38] Right from the beginning,

34 Slater, "Social Setting," 241. See Witherington, *Revelation*, 8.

35 Johnson, *Writings of the New Testament*, 582–83.

36 The Sanskrit root for *bhakti* (*bhaja),* means "to utter" but has the sense of "adoration or to love with honor."

37 See "Bhakti Movement: Causes, Hindu Society and Features," History Discussion, accessed May 15, 2020, https://www.historydiscussion.net/history-of-india/bhakti-movement-causes-hindu-society-and-features/3166.

38 See A. Wainwright, *Mysterious Apocalypse: Interpreting the Book of Revelation* (Nashville: Abingdon, 1993).

there have been conflicts over the material interpretation (things will happen materially) and mystical-symbolical interpretation (imagining that the events related are referring to spiritual realities) that continue even today.[39] The Western fathers often questioned the canonicity of this book. Church fathers like Papias, Melito of Sardis, Justin Martyr, Irenaeus, and others have seen this book as a blueprint of the future. In the symbolic reading, Revelation was not predicting the future; rather, it was representing images of struggle between good and evil in the world.[40] Biblical studies keeping a European framework at the center envisioned an interpretation in which all that is good in the book represents Europe, and evil represents other geographical regions.[41]

Historically, there are at least four different types of interpretations: allegorical, preteristic, historical, and futuristic. All four approaches have some value because the book has certainly allegorical elements, spiritual insights, historical events, and prophetical features. It was written to churches facing daunting consequences due to their testimony about Jesus Christ and their positioning as the followers of the Lord Jesus Christ, so in an imperial-hegemonic context, the purpose of offering practical comfort cannot be easily dismissed. In addition to this, there could be several other purposes: it is written to provide the reader a better understanding of what their faith in Christ would do for them, to provide a constant reminder to Christians that Christ would return at any time, and therefore to challenge them to being faithful just as Christ remained faithful. The intention to provide a counterrhetoric to imperial ideologies also should not be taken lightly.

The Structure and Outline of the Book

Though the structure of the book is very complex, the author has integrated various parts of his work into a literary whole. There are many who see a structural division according to Revelation 1:19, in which the phrase "what you have seen" refers to the vision in chapter 1, "what is now" indicates the letters to seven churches in chapters 2–3, and "what will soon take place" covers

39 David L. Barr, "Introduction, Reading Revelation Today: Consensus and Innovations," in *Reading the Book of Revelation: A Resource for Students*, ed. David L. Barr (Atlanta: SBL, 2003), 2.

40 Barr, 2.

41 David Joy, *Karthru Kahalam Dhvanikkumbol*, 16.

the rest. One of the ways to divide text is to look at the repeated phrases like "what must come to pass" (1:1, 19; 4:1; 22:6) or the expression "in the Spirit" (1:10; 4:2; 17:3; 21:10).[42] The material in between is the visionary experience. Similarly, the repeated phrase *en pneumati* (in Spirit) beginning at 1:10 with three major transitions at 4:2; 17:3, and 21:10, associated with the verb *laleo* (speak), indicates that it is structurally significant.[43]

Thus, 1:9–18 is the description of John's vision of the glorious appearance of Christ, and chapters 2–3 describe Christ's seven messages to the *ekklesia.* Similarly, in 4:1–2, John is taken up again to heaven and envisions the heavenly throne room (chs. 4–5) and develops the sequence of judgments until the end of chapter 16. The next occurrences of *en pneumati* in 17:3 and 21:10 bring a parallel between the opening of new visions in 17:1–3 and 21:9–10 and the conclusion of these visions in 19:9b–10 and 22:6–9, respectively.[44] There are others who see this book as a seven-act play, in which each act has seven scenes (Fiorenza),[45] and some argue for a chiastic structure (Lund).[46] More often the three series of seven in chapters 6–16 are used as the basis of structure. However, Bauckham's arguments and divisions seem rational in proving the literary seam and unity. He avers that the major divisions of the book, in addition to the prologue and epilogue, are as follows: first, the inaugural vision of Christ, including seven messages to the churches (1:9–3:22); second, the inaugural vision of heaven (4–5), leading to the sequence of judgment (6–16); third, Babylon the harlot (17:1–19:10); fourth, the transition from Babylon to New Jerusalem (19:11–21:8); fifth, the New Jerusalem the bride (21:9–22:9).[47] The following outline proposed is based on this pattern:

The prologue (1:1–8)

The inaugural vision and the message to the seven churches (1:9–3:22)

42 Carson and Moo, *Introduction to the New Testament*, 697.

43 Richard Bauckham, *The Climax of Prophecy: Studies on the Book of Revelation* (Edinburgh: T&T Clark, 1993), 3.

44 Bauckham, 4.

45 Fiorenza, *The Book of Revelation: Justice and Judgment* (Philadelphia: Fortress, 1985), 174–77.

46 N. W. Lund, *Studies in the Book of Revelation* (Chicago: Covenant, 1955), 34–35.

47 Bauckham, *Climax of Prophecy*, 6.

The vision of heaven and the heavenly court room (4:1–5:14)

The sequence of judgment (6:1–16:21)

The final judgment of Babylon (17:1–18:24)

The Hallelujah chorus and the end of the evil at Parousia (19:1–21)

The thousand-year reign and the white throne judgment (20:1–11)

The new heaven and new earth (21:1–22:5)

The epilogue (22:6–21)

READING THE BOOK OF REVELATION FROM AN ASIAN PERSPECTIVE

Revelation introduces itself as the "Revelation of Jesus Christ" (1:1). There is a chain of revelation established from the beginning that forms the interconnectedness between God, heaven, earth, and the intermediaries. The Island of Patmos is the locale where John received this revelation. Patmos was not just a barren, rocky, and lonely place but a populated place that had a temple of Artemis and gymnasia.[48] John is drawing the readers to his visionary experiences so the words "the readers hear" are not John's but through him the words of God, Christ, and the Spirit. Thereby, the hearers are brought into relation with otherworldly realities.[49] In John's visions, heaven and earth come together, affecting each other and, at the end, ultimately transforming into new heaven and new earth.[50] The collectivistic worldview and the cultural value of interdependence in Asia makes Revelation very much at home in Asia.

48 Koester, *Revelation*, 239–42. See David A. deSilva, *An Introduction to the New Testament: Contexts, Methods and Ministry Formation*, 2nd ed. (Downers Grove, IL: IVP Academic, 2018), 796.

49 deSilva, *Introduction to the New Testament*, 806.

50 See Bas Weilenga, *Revelation* (New Delhi: ISPCK, 2009), xxiii.

The Message to the Seven Churches

David deSilva, in his book *Seeing Things in John's Way*, has brilliantly argued for the need of taking seriously the milieu of the seven churches in Asia Minor.[51] The audience of Revelation suffered alienation and social pressures and was constantly allured by Roman power and its promise of prosperity and peace. In addition to the conflict with the Romans and other Jewish sects, these churches also faced several internal problems. There were prophets who preached social accommodation and compromise and definitely had a large following, as in the church of Thyatira. John confronts the readers with his message of imminent visitation of God and his Messiah (1:4, 8). The immediacy of God's visitation is emphasized repeatedly (3:11; 14:6–7; 16:15; 22:7, 12). John's message is grounded in his vision of the risen Lord. This religious visionary experience was in the fellowship of the Spirit on the Lord's Day. Such a fellowship disrupts the distance and connects John with the world of God and with the community, as he received the commission to write to them (1:11, 19).[52] In Asian contexts, such interconnections are visible expressions of community life, in which the world of God is interwoven with the cosmos.

In his first visionary experience, John sees the seven golden lampstands, which represent the seven churches (1:20), and in the center of that he sees one like the Son of Man. John's description of the Son of Man is definitely drawn from Daniel and Ezekiel (see Ezek 1:26; Dan 7:13). The image at the center of the lampstands holding seven stars in the right hand (1:16) echoes astrological beliefs.[53] Astrological beliefs, in which the lives of people are intrinsically connected with the stars of the planet, are a common trait in most Asian countries. The author counters such astrological beliefs by affirming their faith in the risen Lord—that is, it is not the stars or planets that determine what happens; it is Christ, who is *pantocrator*, the one who is the creator of the planets and stars. Just as the Roman emperors, who wielded untold powers and ranked as "lord and god," gave edicts to their subjects, Jesus the *pantocrator* gives edicts to the seven churches.[54]

51 See David A. deSilva, *Seeing Things John's Way: The Rhetoric of the Book of Revelation* (Louisville: Westminster John Knox, 2009).

52 Weilenga, *Revelation*, 8.

53 See Bruce J. Malina, *On the Genre and Message of Revelation: Star Visions and Sky Journeys* (Peabody, MA: Hendrickson, 1995).

54 Malina, 254–55.

John unravels "what is" there and then, regarding the situation of these churches in Asia Minor. Each letter begins with a formula "I know" and ends with a call to hear "what the Spirit says."[55] Each letter is addressed to the "angels" of the churches. This is like the concept of "guardian angels" in many of the Asian villages, where each village is under the guardianship of a local deity.[56] John may be alluding to such a widespread belief that nations have their heavenly counterparts and the earthly struggles are reflected in the heavens (Rev 12:7; see Dan 10:13). Wielenga asserts that these angels can be seen as the heavenly representatives of the people of those cities who at the same time confront and replace the traditional guardians.[57] Looking through such a countercultural lens, it is an assurance to the cities in Asia Minor, or for cities and villages anywhere, that their cries and struggles are represented in heaven.

Though the specific historical, economic, sociopolitical, and religiocultural characteristics of these cities are echoed, these churches are asked to set their focus on a forthcoming event: Christ's coming with the clouds (1:7). They are asked to resist the temptation to compromise and accommodate the imperial programs. In the light of the impending crisis—that is, the second death (2:10–11)—they are asked to turn their attention from everyday challenges to the ultimate crisis.[58] The ecclesia is asked to prepare itself to encounter Christ not only in the future but also as one walking in their midst now. While waiting for his coming, the church is called to engage in witnessing with an uncompromising allegiance to Christ, even if that leads to death. Modeling after Jesus, the faithful witness, they also need to speak truth to power.

There were other churches in Asia Minor, but these seven churches are addressed, and seven is a symbolic number of fullness.[59] Thus, the seven churches in Asia Minor represent the whole church, specifically the representation of the Asian church. Persecution is a reality for many of the Asian churches. There is allurement of the imperial promises of economic prosperity to those who bow down before the empire, and that conflicts with the prophets

55 Wielenga, *Revelation*, 14.
56 Malina, *Genre and Message of Revelation*, 255.
57 See Wielenga, *Revelation*, 14–15.
58 deSilva, *Introduction to the New Testament*, 812.
59 Weilenga, *Revelation*, 13.

of compromise, who dilute the truth and remain silent without speaking truth to power. Poverty, malnourishment, homelessness, and the socioeconomic disparities cannot be glossed over.

These struggles against the powers of evil and death are an unavoidable thing in the Asian context, as it is everywhere. Just as the Ephesian church is counseled that they need to come back to the "first love," churches in Asia need to turn to this first love expression. Hence sharing is an important cultural value in Asia; the message is to turn to such cultural expressions. According to Weilenga, the lukewarm indifference to fellow creatures, like the Laodicean church, is the sort of spirituality that leads to the destruction of the creation.[60] Persecution of the minority communities is an issue to be addressed in the Asian context. But the churches are called to speak truth to power, even if that leads to martyrdom. There are societal pressures to accommodate with the policies of the empire, but the church is called to resist such temptations and remain as faithful witness.

Worship and Liturgy in Revelation: Revelation as an Honor Discourse

The central question in Revelation is, Who is worthy of honor and worship? In answering this, John keeps the very throne of God as the center of visionary experience (chs. 4–5) and displays through his discourse "the consequences of both giving God the honour that is exclusively God's due and violating God's honour, by bestowing it to others."[61] Though bestowing honor to the emperor or any others may bring temporary advantages, it will ultimately result in disgrace and shame. Honor and shame were important cultural values of Mediterranean (Asian) society. DeSilva, therefore, rightly calls this book an "honour discourse."[62]

Revelation shows, rather than tells, its audience how to offer prayer and worship.[63] In loudly proclaiming the lordship of God and God's Messiah, the ruler of the earth (1:5; 11:15), it portrays numerous scenes of liturgy and

60 Weilenga, 32.

61 deSilva, *Introduction to the New Testament*, 813.

62 See David A. deSilva, "Honour Discourse and Rhetorical Strategy of the Apocalypse of John," *JSNT* 71 (1998): 80–87.

63 Wes Howard-Brook and Anthony Gwyther, *Unveiling the Empire: Reading Revelation Then and Now* (Maryknoll, NY: Orbis, 1999), 197; also see David Peterson, *Engaging with God: A Biblical Theology of Worship* (Downers Grove, IL: IVP Academic, 1992), 261.

worship. The seven scenes of worship (4:2–11; 5:1–14; 7:9–17; 11:15–18; 14:1–5; 15:2–4; 19:1–8), with powerful images of loud and dramatic liturgy, serve several vital functions.[64] In these worship scenes, there is an echo of themes from Psalms 95–100, a collection of songs celebrating the victory and enthronement of the divine warrior in heaven over all gods of the earth.[65] In Revelation's portrayal of heavenly worship, the worthiness of God is based on his being the Creator (4:2–11), and the worthiness of the Lamb (5:1–14) is based on the act of redemption, the sacrificial death of Jesus Christ. The Lamb purchased back for God a holy people from every tribe and language and nation, making them a community of priests and a kingdom for God (5:9–10). This new act of creating a hybrid community certainly demands a passionate response of gratitude. These worship scenes hush and spoof the liturgy of both the imperial cult and mystery cults in Roman Asia.

Most of the descriptions in these scenes, though echoing OT themes, reflect a lot of similarities with the imperial cult.[66] The portrayal of worship also reflects Mediterranean cultural values such as the patron-client system. A specific practice known from the Roman world in John's time was the morning salutation.[67] The acts of honor given to God are not simply a morning routine but a ceaseless celebration of God's power magnanimously poured out on those who acknowledge his reign. The sung words of praise are accompanied by a highly charged ritual act: the elders' prostration and casting of their crowns before the throne. In antiquity, a common sign of vassalage was the taking of the diadem (symbol of royalty) by the conquered ruler and the placing of that diadem at the feet of the conqueror. The performance of the elders should be understood as an imitation of such an act of subordination.

Worship is shown to be primarily a political act: one worships whomever or whatever one affirms as possessing true power to affect people's lives, the central currency of politics in all ages. The proclamation of Yahweh as "our

64 Howard-Brook and Gwyther list five such reasons. See Howard-Brook and Gwyther, *Unveiling the Empire*, 197.

65 Howard-Brook and Gwyther, 197.

66 David E. Aune, *Revelation 1–5*, vol. 52A, *Word Biblical Commentary* (Dallas: Word, 1997), 293.

67 This is a practice in which clients would gather around the door of the patron's house in vocal acclamation, prepared to follow the patron on his morning rounds and applaud his speeches and other public acts.

Lord and God" and the ritual act of casting of crowns is in direct opposition to the emperor and expresses another aspect of God's power: either one falls down voluntarily in worship before the holy one, or one falls in destructive ruin in refusing to participate in such worship.[68] Once one knows that there is a God and that God stands against empire, one must choose whether one falls down in joyous worship or in stubborn resistance to that God.[69]

These worship scenes are filled with singing new songs, a practice long associated with the biblical liturgical passages describing the celebration of a divine act of liberation (Ps 40:2–4; 96; 98; 144:9–11; 149; Isa 42:9–10; see Jonah 2; Acts 16:25–27). The divine acts of liberation, as deSilva avers, refer to various deeds like creation, redemption, bestowal of dignity, formation of multicultural community, reconciliation, truth, justice, and holiness.[70] These scenes do not gloss over the resistance and rebellion against God's due honor. There are rival centers of worship, false religion, and bogus spirituality to which many are attracted (see 9:20–21). Such worship definitely invites divine judgment. John remaps the whole cosmos and presents the heavenly throne room, heavenly beings, myriads of angels, and uncountable number of a multicultural community as singing new songs so the hybrid Christian community may persevere in their commitment and generate solidarity within the ecclesia.

Revelation's liturgy, songs, worship, and rituals are joyously familiar in song-filled congregational services of Asian Pentecostal and Charismatic churches. Such song-filled worship atmosphere and chanting of liturgies are common elements in most Asian cultures and religions. In India, music is seen as a way of reaching god, and many gods and goddesses are themselves seen holding musical instruments. Sacred music and chanting of Sanskrit mantras are part of the Hindu worship and religious experience. Sound (*sabda*) is understood as *Nada Brahma* (god), and Vedic sacrifices are filled with such chanting and music, which have symbolic rituals just as we see in Revelation. The Bhakti tradition is filled with *bhajans* and *Kirtans* as part of their liturgies and devotional songs. The Bhakti movement was a countercultural movement that emerged in the context of socioreligious evils and thus

68 See Brian W. John, *The Emperor Domitian* (New York: Routledge, 1992), 108–9.

69 Howard-Brook and Gwyther, *Unveiling the Empire*, 207.

70 deSilva, *Introduction to the New Testament*, 814.

took a stand against hegemonies. Similarly, the worship scenes and liturgies in Revelation calls the Christian communities in Roman Asia, and everywhere, to take a stand against the empire and celebrate the reign of the only just and true God.[71]

The Portrayal of Christ and the Singable Christology in Revelation

The phrase "Revelation of Jesus Christ" at the very beginning and the glorious vision of the risen Lord are reminders that Christology is at the heart of John's apocalypse. Therefore, John's reflection on Christ is a key to understanding the work as a whole.[72] The repeated occurrence of the titles "Lord" (twenty-three times, interchangeably used with God and Christ) and "lamb" (twenty-eight times) indicate the importance of the lordship of Jesus and his sacrificial death. From the beginning, Revelation picks up a lot of OT images and names applied to Yahweh and applies them to Christ.[73] The use of the same self-designation for both God and Christ suggests that John identifies Christ as God's divine agent.[74] This book does not depict Jesus as a second god but includes him in the eternal being of the one God. In presenting Jesus as the *Kyrios*, John is countering the imperial claims to universal lordship. The title "Alpha and Omega" is used interchangeably for God and Jesus (see 1:8, 17–18, 22:13). John portrays Christ's sovereignty and presents him as the Lord of all ages.[75]

The title that dominates the second part of the book is Lamb.[76] Revelation 5:5 states Christ as the "Lion from the tribe of Judah, the Root of David," a strong militaristic image of the Davidic Messiah (see Gen 49:9–12). But this image soon gives way to the slaughtered lamb (5:6). The term *esphagmenon* (to slay) echoes a sacrificial imagery. Jesus is depicted as the Passover Lamb who offers himself as a sacrifice. This imagery, following the imagery of a lion, is to convey the theme that the new conquest is achieved not through imperial

71 Howard-Brook and Gwyther, *Unveiling the Empire*, 221.

72 Witherington, *Revelation*, 27.

73 Witherington, 28.

74 See M. M. Thompson, "John, Gospel of," in *DJG*, ed. Joel B. Green and Scott McKnight (Downers Grove, IL: InterVarsity, 1992), 368–83.

75 G. R. Beasley-Murray, *The Book of Revelation* (Eugene, OR: Wipf & Stock, 1981), 59.

76 Donald Guthrie, "Christology in the Book of Revelation," in *Jesus of Nazareth: Lord and Christ*, ed. Joel B. Green et al. (Grand Rapids, MI: Eerdmans, 1994), 398.

means of violence but through the sacrificial death. This act is again described as ransoming people for God by his blood (5:9). The idea of ransoming echoes God's liberative act of his people from the slavery of Egypt (see Deut 7:8; Exod 12:12, 23). John combines this with the Suffering Servant who is portrayed as a sacrificial lamb (Isa 53). This ransoming act effectively redeemed people from every tribe, tongue, and nation (5:9–10), creating a multicultural community, like many Asian communities.

This lamb in Revelation is further described as one with "seven horns and seven eyes" (5:6; see 1 Enoch 90:9–12). In the apocalyptic traditions, the word *horn* refers to power and authority, and the eyes indicate the all-seeing aspect of the lamb (Zech 4:10).[77] Aune comments that the imagery of the lamb in Revelation has two primary motifs: as a ruler/leader and as a sacrificial metaphor.[78] The lamb that is described as "standing" (5:6) is a reference to his resurrection. This expression transforms the Jewish imagery of a slain lamb, which is now glorified and powerful as it is standing by the throne of God.[79] This is a unique interpretation of the author.

Revelation lays emphasis on Jesus as the faithful witness (*martus*). Jesus's witness reaches its zenith in his death and the violence inflicted on him by the Romans in collusion with the Jewish cultural nationalists. It is through this martyrdom that Jesus conquered the world and redeemed people. This aspect of Christology runs through the whole book, and thus it invites the readers to be faithful martyrs even if it leads one to death. *Ahimsa* (nonviolence) and *satyagraha* (insistence on truth) as passive political resistance against the imperial domination are great teachings from Asian religions and Indian reformers such as Mahatma Gandhi. It is speaking truth to power and countering them through insistence on truth and nonviolent resistance. Jesus's martyrdom and the ongoing struggles of the church in the Roman imperial context should be interpreted as modes of nonviolent resistance. Thus the Christology of Revelation is a martyr Christology.

The Christology in Revelation is also a singable Christology. Hymns and songs were essential modes of faith expressions in the context of worship and liturgy in the Jewish and Greco-Roman society. The first-century

77 Osborne, *Revelation*, 257.

78 Aune, *Revelation 1–5*, 52A:352.

79 See Witherington, *Revelation*, 30.

context displays a world of religiosity wherein songs and hymns were sung in praise of gods and goddesses.[80] The early church also followed this method and communicated their theological convictions through hymns and songs. No wonder that John, while presenting his understanding of Christ to the first century audience, described it using hymns. This new song explained the author's convictions about Christ: the person and work of Jesus Christ. The expression *new* is in the sense of distinctiveness, superiority, and nature. These songs are sung by a community, in which the whole cosmos is involved. This singable Christology is a clarion call for the readers to sing out their faith expression. The singable forms of faith expression are one of the salient features of Asian communities. Many traditional societies in Asia, with their folk songs, sing out their history, struggles, and faith convictions. These are also songs of resistance and hope. This community is a kind of bhakti movement in Asian and Indian terms, as they considered themselves the bride of Christ for their groom.[81] The bhakti is visible in their devotion to the deity and often expressed in singable forms. Out of such bhakti, they burst out into songs, expressing their convictions and confessions. It is this bhakti that enables them to witness and stand against all odds.

Images of God in the Book of Revelation

Only in two places in Revelation does God himself speak: at the beginning of John's account of the vision (1:8) and also at the end (21:5–8). God himself declared that he is "the Alpha and the Omega," which represents the first and the last letters of Greek alphabet. This is a variation of the phrase "I am the beginning and the end." This designation stems from Deutero-Isaiah, and it occurs three times (41:4; 44:6; 48:12). In their exilic context, these divine self-designations form part of the polemics to assert Yahweh's sovereignty over the gods of Babylon. To those who doubted the very existence of Yahweh in the exile, the prophet reminds them that Yahweh alone is responsible for the creation of the earth and deliverance in the past and in the future. In this context,

80 R. P. Martin, "Hymns, Hymn Fragments, Songs, Spiritual Songs," in *Dictionary of Paul and His Letters*, ed. Gerald F. Hawthorne, Ralph P. Martin, and Daniel G. Reid (Downers Grove, IL: InterVarsity, 1993), 419–23.

81 See A. J. Appasamy, *Christianity as Bhaktimarga: A Study of Johannine Doctrine of Love* (Madras: CLS, 1930).

God declares that "I am the first" (I am your creator) and "I am the last" (I am your deliverer). Richard Bauckham has noted, "God precedes all things, as their creator, and he will bring all things to eschatological fulfilment. He is the origin and goal of all history. He has the first word, in creation, and the last word, in new creation."[82] In the Greek philosophical tradition, this phrase is an indication of eternity of the supreme God, which is taken over by the Jewish writers, like Josephus and Philo. So John was using a phrase that was in current usage referring to the eternity of God.

This self-designation of God is followed by two other epithets: the one who is and who was and who is to come, and the Almighty. The designation "one who is and who was and who is to come" occurs five times in this book with slight variations (Rev 1:4; 1:8; 4:8; 11:17 and 16:5). In the OT, the name Yahweh is interpreted only once (Exod 3:14), where this name is associated with the verb *hayah* (to be): "I am who I am." This can denote even the eternal existence. Thus later Jewish interpreters sought to link this name in Exodus 3:14 with God's eternal existence, indicating the past, present, and future tenses.[83] Such formulae with three tenses of existence were used for Greek gods or the supreme god of philosophy.[84]

The God of the present, past, and future is several times called the *pantokrator* (Almighty), which is used seven times in this book (1:8; 4:8; 11:17; 15:3; 16:7; 19:6; 21:22). This Greek word, translating the Hebrew term *Zebaoth* (the Lord of hosts), literally means "the ruler of all."[85] In the OT, this term indicates Yahweh's unrivaled power over all things.[86] This term indicates that nothing human can undo or overthrow God or God's purposes because he controls everything.[87] Seven times God is described as sitting upon his throne (4:9; 5:1, 7, 13; 6:16; 7:15; 21:5), and this central symbol stands for God's sovereignty. There is an echo of the texts like Isaiah 6, Ezekiel 1, and the description of Ancient of Days sitting on the throne in Daniel 7. This is oppositional

82 Richard Bauckham, *Theology of the Book of Revelation* (Cambridge: Cambridge University Press, 1993), 27.

83 See Bauckham, 28–29.

84 David E. Aune, *Prophecy in Early Christianity and in the Ancient Mediterranean World* (Grand Rapids, MI: Eerdmans, 1983), 280–81.

85 Weilenga, *Revelation*, 7.

86 Bauckham, *Book of Revelation*, 30.

87 Wielenga, *Revelation*, 7.

symbolism against the pretenders on earth who present themselves as god and as sitting on the throne.

Revelation depicts God's activity as the Creator (4:11) and also as the Judge, illustrating God's role as the Alpha and the Omega. God is described as the Judge of the world and evil powers because God alone is holy (15:4; 16:5), true (6:10), and righteous in judgment (15:3; 16:7). There are three series of judgments in Revelation: the seven seal openings (6:1–17; 8:1, 3–5), the seven trumpets (8:2, 6–21; 11:14–19), and the seven bowls (15:5–16:21). The powers of evil that destroy this creation are the beast, the dragon, and the empire (Babylon/Rome). Because God is faithful to his creation, God will destroy these powers. Asian religiocultural traditions are filled with rich materials, especially in their variety of religious scriptures, which express God as eternal, timeless in nature, Creator, and one who is faithful to his creation. For example, in Hinduism, God is *Sanatana* (eternal), and he is the *adi* (beginning) and the *antya* (end). God is timeless, and in him the past, the present, and the future coexist. Hinduism talks about the incarnations of god to judge and annihilate those who destroy the creation and thus save the creation.

Feminine Images

Some of the most memorable symbols in Revelation focus on female figures, all of which are aligned either with God or with Satan. It is interesting to look into how these feminine figures are portrayed in Revelation.

Jezebel (2:20–23)

Jezebel is the only historical female character in Revelation, and it is evident that the author is seeking to silence her. This could be a symbolic name, and the author's intention is to associate this rival prophetess with the Israelite queen who worshipped Baal and opposed Elijah (1 Kings 16:31; 19:1–3).[88] Selvidge calls it a "malicious myth" that conjures up images of a despised queen who sought to challenge Yahweh.[89] The accusation is that she is claiming divine right from the Son of God (2:18) and is "teaching and beguiling

88 See Tina Pippin, *Apocalyptic Bodies: The Biblical End of the World in Text and Image* (London: Routledge, 1999), 32–42.

89 Marla J. Selvidge, "Powerful and Powerless Women in the Apocalypse," *Neotestamentica* 26 (1992): 159.

my servants to practice fornication and eat food offered to idols." The verbs "to beguile" and "to deceive" are frequently used by John to describe the evil activity of the dragon (12:9), the beast (13:14), Babylon (18:23), and Satan (20:8). Fornication in this respect probably represents idolatry rather than sexual immorality (see Hos 2:1–13; Exod 34:16; Isa 57:7–13).

The first of Jezebel's idolatry was described as her many whoredoms and sorceries (2 Kings 9:22). It seems Jezebel permitted eating food offered to idols and allowed participation in Greco-Roman religious festivals. This theological stance would definitely bring political and economic advantages to Christians living in trading cities of Asia Minor. This is regarded by John as an unnecessary compromise, characterizing such activity as adultery (2:22–23). Selvidge comments that John's polemics should be interpreted as implying that Jezebel was a successful person, one who used her prophetic talents and teachings to persuade people to follow her religious beliefs.[90] She may be an itinerant preacher who was having great influence in Christian communities of Asia Minor.[91] It is better to take this name as a cryptic name for a movement under the leadership of a prophetess.

The Woman Clothed with the Sun (12:1–6, 13–17)

The vision in chapter 12, which describes the conflict between a dragon and a woman clothed with the sun, is difficult to interpret. The dragon is diabolically powerful (12:3–4) and is poised to devour—literally eat (*kataphage*)—the woman's newborn child. But God snatches the male child to heaven. The woman is given eagle's wings to flee to the wilderness (12:13–17). The dragon chases her and tries to drown her, but she is saved by the earth, which swallows the water. But in the future, the dragon will make war with the woman's offspring (12:17). It is evident that John combines images from the Hebrew Scriptures with ancient mythical images about the birth of gods and divine battles with monsters of chaos.[92] Duff argues that the unnamed woman in chapter 12 and Babylon, the harlot in chapter 17, are the female archetypes

90 Selvidge, 159.

91 See B. Varghese, *Velipadu Pusthaka Vyakhyanam*, Interpretation of the Book of Revelation (Thiruvalla: Rhema, 2007), 66.

92 For a detailed treatment, see A. Y. Collins, *The Combat Myth in the Book of Revelation* (Missoula: Scholars, 1976), 101–56.

in Revelation.[93] All other female characters are portrayed in such a way that they side with either of these two.[94]

With regard to the interpretation of this female figure, there are several proposals. Later Christian exegetes identified her with Mary when pairing the story with the fleeing of Jesus's family to Egypt (Matt 2). The rescuing of the child probably alludes to the resurrection or exaltation of Jesus. Some claim that it represents Eve, and the dragon is called the ancient serpent (Rev 12:9, 17; Gen 3:15). The third interpretation is to identify this woman with the church. But it is difficult to interpret the church as the mother of the Messiah. A more probable suggestion is to regard this woman as the messianic community, the church in continuity with Israel. Thus many interpret this woman as representing the true people of Israel, who gave birth to the Messiah and the church (see Isa 66:7–13). In addition to this, there is exodus imagery behind this portrayal. Israel was also threatened by water, and the eagle's wings are reminiscent of Exodus 19:4. Thus a combination of the third and fourth views seems to be the most likely one.[95]

144,000 Followers of the Lamb (14:1–5)

In Revelation 14:1–5, which belongs to the second cycle of visions (12:1–22:5), John sees the 144,000 followers of the Lamb, who had his name and his Father's name on their foreheads (14:1). This symbolic number is already mentioned in 7:1–8 as an assembly consisting of twelve thousand persons from each of the twelve tribes of Israel.[96] These figures stand in stark contrast with the counterimage of those who worship the beast, bearing the mark of the beast (13:16). These followers are a particular group of the community of God who would rather die than worship the beast or receive its mark (see 7:4–17; 14:1; 20:4). This group is described as *amomoi* (unblemished), a technical term that denotes the absence of defects on the sacrificial animal, and thus the imagery of the sacrifice is evident at the backdrop of their portrayal. But

93 Paul B. Duff, *Who Rides the Beast: Prophetic Rivalry and the Rhetoric of Crisis in the Churches of Apocalypse* (New York: Oxford University Press, 2001), 85.

94 Duff, 86–87.

95 See Elizabeth Schüssler Fiorenza, *Revelation: Vision of a Just World* (Minneapolis: Fortress, 1991), 81.

96 See David Joy, *Karthru Kahalam Dhvanikkumbol*, 195–96.

John adds a symbolic expression in stating that these figures have not defiled themselves with women but have kept themselves as virgins (*parthenoi*). This needs to be read along with the holy war traditions in the Hebrew Bible (see Deut 23:9–14; Josh 3:5; 7:13; 1 Sam 21:5). But the adjectival term *virgins* here implies that they go beyond the standard of purity required for holy war. This symbolic expression, then, is a counterimage in the context of many immoral factors that were prevalent in the Roman-ruled Asia Minor.[97] This is a metaphorical expression referring to the people of God, both male and female. This is not a reference to celibacy but to those who refuse idolatry associated with the imperial cult.[98]

The Whore of Babylon (14:8; 16:19; 17:1–19:5)

The image of Babylon is first introduced in Revelation 14:8, where the city is portrayed as a woman who is able to seduce nations with the wine of her wrath of fornication, indicating seductive sexuality as an image of idolatry. Babylon is presented as adorned in luxurious attire, and her name is worn on the forehead: "Babylon, the great, mother of whores and earth's abominations" (17:5). Feminist readers pointed a patriarchal bias in this metaphor of harlot. But John follows the footsteps of the prophets who used this metaphor in their critique of idolatry as prostitution.[99] There is also an echo of the image of goddess Roma on ancient coins as seated on Rome's seven hills and the Tiber River running below.[100] The readers of this book in Asia Minor were confronted with a lot of visual impressions of imperial Rome, so this image amounts to one of the counterimages in Revelation.[101] In doing this, John is turning the glorious portrayal of a goddess into a Roman prostitute to convince his readers of the true character of Rome. The mysterious name, Babylon the great (16:19; 17:5; 18:2, 10, 21), was a symbolic designation to Rome. Thus in the Jewish and early Christian literature of this period, Rome was understood as the contemporary counterpart of Babylon (see *Sibylline Oracle* 5:143, 159).

97 Robert H. Mounce, *The Book of Revelation* (Grand Rapids, MI: Eerdmans, 1977), 264.
98 Fiorenza, *Revelation*, 88.
99 Wielenga, *Revelation*, 112.
100 Osborne, *Revelation*, 437.
101 Bauckham, *Book of Revelation*, 17.

John portrays Rome as a harlot in order to condemn its idolatry. The destruction of Babylon described in 17:16–18, where she is subjected to death, is interpreted by some people as an image of rape, fire, and cannibalism.[102] Interestingly, it is said that this will be done by the beast. There are three major charges against the city of Rome: idolatry and sorcery (18:23), violence, and excessive wealth and extravagance (18:3–9). Thus it is a severe critique on Rome and its exploitative methods in amassing wealth.

The New Jerusalem (19:7; 21:1–22:5; 22:17)

The city of New Jerusalem is a symbolic city and a counterimage of Babylon (Rome). Bauckham avers that the readers of this book lived, both geographically and symbolically, between Rome and Jerusalem.[103] This New Jerusalem is coming down from heaven and is described as a woman and a city, the bride and wife of the Lamb (19:7; 21:2, 9). New Jerusalem stands in contrast with evil Babylon and symbolizes splendor and universal dominion.[104] This alternative portrayal is needed to help the readers to dissociate themselves from the corrupting influence of Babylon. Bauckham argues that Jerusalem can be considered as the place, people, and presence of God.[105] According to the Jewish tradition, the New Jerusalem was to be kept in heaven until the last days (see 2 Esdras 7:26; 8:52; 9:38–10:60). The New Jerusalem is the renewed world of God.

There are feminist scholars who would argue that the positive message of Revelation is portrayed through negative feminine images.[106] Therefore, many draw attention to the apparent ambivalence in John's use of the imagery, particularly his virgin/harlot and good/evil dichotomy. Some feminists regard this as dangerous and disturbing because the author characterizes women as either wholly good or wholly bad, which reflects a culture that emphasizes male control over female sexuality. According to Selvidge, negative feminine images in Revelation project vivacious and intelligent women

102 See Stephen D. Moore, *Untold Tales in the Book of Revelation: Sex and Gender, Empire and Ecology* (Atlanta: SBL, 2014), 126–54.

103 Bauckham, *Book of Revelation*, 126.

104 Bauckham, 128.

105 Bauckham, 132.

106 See Susan R. Garrett, "Revelation," in *The Women's Bible Commentary*, ed. C. A. Newsom and Sharon H. Ringe (London: Westminster John Knox, 1992), 377–82.

who control congregations (Jezebel) and even empires (Babylon), whereas positive images are beautifully dressed women who have no control over themselves.[107] But it should be noted that such polarization of women into categories is a prominent feature of texts produced in patriarchal society. At the same time, the positive feminine images as the counterimages of the empire should not be overlooked. Fiorenza comments that John uses these feminine images to symbolize the present murderous reality of the imperial world as well as the life-nurturing reality of the renewed world of God, and it should not be misconstrued as actual behavior of individual women.[108]

The portrayal of women in Revelation resembles the representation of women in Asian religious scriptures in many ways. In Hinduism, women are presented as *Sakti*, the most powerful and the empowering force, the essence of the universe. Their position is venerated as goddess on the one hand and limited and controlled by the patriarchal system (an obedient daughter, housewife, and mother) on the other hand. Existing along with positive portrayals of women, there are also misogynist renderings of women as snares and temptresses.

Images of Evil

The author also develops images of evil and offers a heavenly perspective on the Roman Empire and unmasks its identity. Bauckham argues, "Revelation portrays the Roman Empire as a system of violent oppression founded on conquest, maintained by violence and oppression."[109] There are two major symbols of empire (Rome) in Revelation: the beast (ch. 13) and the harlot Babylon (chs. 17–18). The beast represents the military and political power (and the violence) of Roman emperors, and the harlot Babylon is the symbol of economic exploitation. There is a close connection between the beast and the harlot, as depicted by the vision of the harlot riding on the beast (17:3). This is an indication that the power of Rome is derived from and is promoted by the conquests and successes of the political and military powers of the emperors.

One of the distinctive features of Revelation 13 and 17 is the image of the sea monster, or the beast that will come from the sea. The vision of two beasts

107 Selvidge, "Powerful and Powerless Women," 158.
108 Fiorenza, *Revelation*, 95–96.
109 Bauckham, *Book of Revelation*, 35.

(ch. 13) is influenced by traditions in the book of Daniel concerning the vision of four beasts coming out of the sea (Dan 7:2–8), and particularly the fourth beast, who is said to have seven horns (7:7). The sea beast in Revelation 13 contains features of all four beasts, but John combines this with the symbolical image of Leviathan, the seven-headed serpent who rises from the sea and represents the forces of evil (see Isa 27:1). For the author, this beast represents Rome, the culmination and incarnation of all evil powers.[110] The beast derives its power from the dragon (13:2). The book of Revelation portrays evil in the trinitarian form, an imitation of God in trinity: the dragon (the ancient serpent), the false prophet (see 16:13; 19:20), and the antichrist.[111] This beast possesses seven heads, and the identity of the head with the mortal wound (13:3) is debated. The head with a mortal wound is later identified with the beast itself (v. 12), thus suggesting that the beast signifies the Roman Empire in general and one emperor in particular.[112]

Such identification would definitely draw our attention toward the legends developed concerning the emperor Nero. Among the Jews and Christians, Nero was considered a murderous tyrant.[113] At the same time, a number of his subjects, particularly those in the eastern provinces of the empire (e.g., Parthia), showed great respect toward Nero. The reference to being "wounded by the sword" (13:14) reminds the reader that Nero committed suicide by thrusting a sword into his own throat (68 CE).[114] Numerous false Neros also appeared from about a year after his death, and thus the legend developed that Nero would return from the east.[115] In Revelation, this would make the parody of Jesus's death and resurrection (13:3–4).

Thus the beast, personified in the emperor, is portrayed as the antichrist. One of the distinctive features of the antichrist was that he would claim to be God (13:1, 5). The statement that there are blasphemous names on the seven

110 See Varghese, *Velipadu Pusthaka Vyakhyanam*, 110; see also Charles C. Ryrie, *Revelation* (Chicago: Moody, 1968), 82–83.

111 Varghese, *Velipadu Pusthaka Vyakhyanam*, 111; Bauckham, *Book of Revelation*, 23–25.

112 See David Joy, *Karthru Kahalam Dhvanikkumbol*, 192.

113 See John Pollini, "Burning Rome, Burning Christians," in *A Cambridge Companion to the Age of Nero*, ed. Shadi Bartsch, Kirk Freudenburg, and Cedric Littlewood (Cambridge: Cambridge University Press, 2017), 213–36.

114 History Collection (website), accessed February 7, 2020, https://historycollection.co/.

115 Collins, *Combat Myth*, 176–83.

heads of the beast could be understood as an allusion to the titles of divinity attributed to the Roman emperor such as "lord, saviour, son of god, our lord and god."[116] A number of Rome's subjects responded positively to these claims (13:3–4). The second beast, coming from the earth (13:11–18), who is known as the false prophet (16:13; 19:20), promotes this imperial cult by setting up an image of the beast, giving it the status of a divine being and thus promoting its worship.

The author employs numerology in giving the identity of the beast and declares the need for wisdom. The mysterious number 666 has been a subject of considerable debate among NT scholars.[117] The use of the word *psephizo* (to calculate or count up) is an indication that the process of *gematria* is involved in this identification.[118] In addition to this, the natural way to understand the phrase *arithmos gar anthropou estin* (for it is the number of a man) is that the number relates to the name of some human individual.[119] One of the most popular interpretations is to consider it as standing for Neron Kaisar (using Hebrew characters).[120] It is certain that this is the portrayal of evil and its personification, which is intricately connected with empire and its supporters through emperors.

However, this image needs to be read along with the image of the beast in Revelation 17. The two must be identified with one another: both possess seven heads and ten horns, both carry blasphemous names, and in both cases, one of the heads is identified with the beast himself. The beast and its heads become interchangeable, for the empire's authority is personified in its emperor. In 17:10, the beast's seven heads are cryptically identified as the seven kings, out of which five have fallen, one is, and the other has not yet come. The beast that was and is not is himself the eighth and is one of the seven (17:9–11). Here there is a clear reference to the city of Rome, which is built on seven hills, and also its rulers.[121] There is a strong critique of the

116 Osborne, *Revelation*, 491.

117 There are many who interpret the beast as the Roman Empire, like Charles, Mounce, A. Y. Collins, G. K. Beale, Richard Bauckham, and others. This is because the beast in Daniel stands for world empires, whereas it is interpreted as a person by Johnson, Chilton, Krodel, and others.

118 Collins, *Combat Myth*, 174.

119 R. H. Charles, *Revelation of St. John* (London: T&T Clark, 1970), 364–65.

120 Osborne, *Revelation*, 519–20.

121 Simon J. Kistenmaker, *Exposition of the Book of Revelation* (Grand Rapids, MI: Baker, 2001), 472; see Osborne, *Revelation*, 617–20.

empire as demonic or satanic through such symbols. It is interesting to note that the beast is portrayed as a parody of Christ who opposes God and God's people but will ultimately be destroyed and will not prevail over the sovereignty of God and his plans.

There are numerous passages in Revelation that suggest the presentation of the beast has deliberately been patterned on the presentation of Christ.[122] These parallels or similarities are regarded as parodies (for example, consider these passages: 13:1=5:6; 13:2/4=2:28/3:21; 13:3=1:18/2:8; 17:8/11=1:7/2:5/3:11/22:7/12; 17:8=1:4/8/4:8; 13:4=5:8/14). Because Revelation is concerned with the conflict between the Christian church and contemporary society as represented by Rome, this portrayal is to expose the true character of the empire. The crucial point, as Weilenga has rightly noted, is to expose the reality of evil, and such a discerning is the first step to break away from them.[123] However, the author offers consolation by exposing the ultimate destruction of the beast (15:2). Roman rule can never truly compete with the eternal rule of God and Christ. In the Asian context, Hinduism (Buddhism and Jainism) does not have the concept of demons (Greek mythology) or the devil (Christian concept). Rather, it has the concept of karma, which is not evil as such. At the same time, the conflict between *sura* (devas, the benevolent gods) and *asura* (the malevolent gods) became a dominant thought. *Asura* can refer to human or divine leaders. In this sense, the conflict is between the forces of good and evil.

God's New World: The Hope of the Despairing World

Revelation ends with a vision of God's new heaven and new earth (21:1–22:21). This new world order is described in 21:1–8. This could be called the "manifesto of Christ's second coming."[124] After describing the unholy trinity (beast, false prophet, and the devil/dragon) being thrown into the lake of fire, the author presents the new heaven and the new earth. This new world is prepared for God's people, who are symbolically presented as the New Jerusalem, which is the saved community of Christ all over the world.[125] The present

122 See Moore, *Untold Tales*, 13–37.

123 Wielenga, *Revelation*, xxxiv.

124 David Joy, *Karthru Kahalam Dhvanikkumbol*, 204.

125 David Joy, 204–5.

world order has become a world built upon lies, hypocrisy, murder, glorification of violence, poverty, tears, and economic disparities and exploitation. No wonder that the author passionately longs for a new world. More than the idea of heaven (though it is not completely avoided) in this vision, the idea of New Jerusalem and a new Eden on the renewed earth comes to the fore.[126] In the new world that God creates, the dichotomy of heaven and earth is disrupted (20:11; 21:1); the new heaven and new earth become one.[127]

This new world would be inherited by the overcomers (21:7–8). This world is created for the community of God, a multicultural hybrid community. God will be at home in this new world. God, who began history, will lead it to its consummation at the *eschaton*. Before the new order can be inaugurated, the old order has to be destroyed. That is why the sea as the symbol of evil is not there in the new order (21:1). It is this hope amid despair that empowers the church to resist the empire and be strengthened in its faith. In the Asian context, the *Ramarajya* concept advocated by Mahatma Gandhi looks for a new world, which is not simply a replacement of native in place of the foreign (British Empire) but a world of justice and equality.

CONCLUSION

Revelation was written to communities in Asia Minor that were a group of beleaguered religious neophytes and persecuted minorities in the Roman Empire. Therefore, as an apocalyptic literature, it is the good news for such people in situations of severe oppression. This book deals with the sociopolitical problems of these communities, encouraging them to stand firm amid imperial atrocities, economic exploitation, and religious syncretism. It unmasks the realities of the empire through its symbolic language. This book invites the reader to see the new heaven and new earth, the new world order, that God is shaping for his people. The prophetic critique of this book should not be limited to John's Babylon. Just as the early Christians found it difficult to avoid worshipping the beast, the communities in an Asian context also have temptations from other forms of worshipping the beast, the demonic

126 Osborne, *Revelation*, 730.
127 Osborne, 730.

forces of death, by idolizing state and its apparatus or by deification of caste and religious communities. At the center of the book is the vision of God the sovereign who turns the wheels of the history. Every other reality should be viewed from this symbolic world that John creates for his readers. The new world that God shapes is for those who conquer. The paradigm for conquering is the slain Lamb. Revelation portrays a multicultural community from every tribe, tongue, and nation following the slain Lamb, singing a new song, and it is in praise of the Lamb who was slain. This community looks like an Asian community with its multicultural varieties.

FURTHER READING

Aune, D. E. 1997. *Revelation 1–5*. Vol. 52A of *Word Biblical Commentary*, edited by David Allan Howard, Glenn W. Barker, and Ralph P. Martin. Dallas: Word.

Beasley-Murray, G. R. 1981. *The Book of Revelation*. Eugene, OR: Wipf & Stock.

Collins, A. Y. 1976. *The Combat Myth in the Book of Revelation*. Missoula, MT: Scholars.

Collins, J. J. 1987. *The Apocalyptic Imagination: An Introduction to the Jewish Matrix of Christianity*. New York: Crossroad.

deSilva, D. A. 2009. *Seeing Things John's Way: The Rhetoric of the Book of Revelation*. Louisville: Westminster John Knox.

Fiorenza, E. S. 1998. *The Book of Revelation: Justice and Judgment*. 2nd ed. Minneapolis: Fortress.

Johnson, L. T. 1986. *The Writings of the New Testament: An Interpretation*. Bangalore: Theological Publications in India.

Joy, D. 2016. *Karthru Kahalam Dhvanikkumbol* [When the trumpet of the Lord will sound]. Tiruvalla: Theological Literature Council.

Kraybill, J. N. 1996. *Imperial Cult and Commerce in John's Apocalypse*. JSNT Suppl. Series 132. Sheffield, UK: SAP.

Morris, L. 1987. *The Revelation of St. John*. Rev. ed. TNTC. Grand Rapids, MI: Eerdmans.

Mounce, R. H. 1977. *The Book of Revelation*. Grand Rapids, MI: Eerdmans.

Osborne, G. R. 2002. *Revelation: Baker Exegetical Commentary on the New Testament*. Grand Rapids, MI: Baker Academics.

Wainwright, A. 1993. *Mysterious Apocalypse: Interpreting the Book of Revelation.* Nashville: Abingdon.

Wielenga, B. 2009. *Revelation to John: Turning into Songs of Moses and the Lamb.* New Delhi: ISPCK.

Witherington, B. 2003. *Revelation: The New Cambridge Bible Commentary.* Cambridge: Cambridge University Press.

Index